# Lecture Notes in Artificial Intelligence     8245

Subseries of Lecture Notes in Computer Science

T0242189

# Lecture Notes in Artificial Intelligence 8215

## Subseries of Lecture Notes in Computer Science

### LNAI Series Editors

Randy Goebel
*University of Alberta, Edmonton, Canada*
Yuzuru Tanaka
*Hokkaido University, Sapporo, Japan*
Wolfgang Wahlster
*DFKI and Saarland University, Saarbrücken, Germany*

### LNAI Founding Series Editor

Joerg Siekmann
*DFKI and Saarland University, Saarbrücken, Germany*

Massimo Cossentino
Amal El Fallah Seghrouchni
Michael Winikoff (Eds.)

# Engineering Multi-Agent Systems

First International Workshop, EMAS 2013
St. Paul, MN, USA, May 6-7, 2013
Revised Selected Papers

 Springer

Volume Editors

Massimo Cossentino
ICAR/CNR
Viale delle Scienze, ed.11
90128 Palermo, Italy
E-mail: cossentino@pa.icar.cnr.it

Amal El Fallah Seghrouchni
University Pierre and Marie Curie, LIP6
4, Place Jussieu
75252 Paris Cedex 0, France
E-mail: amal.elfallah@lip6.fr

Michael Winikoff
University of Otago
P.O. Box 56
Dunedin 9054, New Zealand
E-mail: michael.winikoff@otago.ac.nz

ISSN 0302-9743                               e-ISSN 1611-3349
ISBN 978-3-642-45342-7                       e-ISBN 978-3-642-45343-4
DOI 10.1007/978-3-642-45343-4
Springer Heidelberg New York Dordrecht London

Library of Congress Control Number: 2013955252

CR Subject Classification (1998): I.2.11, I.2, D.2, D.1, F.3

LNCS Sublibrary: SL 7 – Artificial Intelligence

*Typesetting:* Camera-ready by author, data conversion by Scientific Publishing Services, Chennai, India

Printed on acid-free paper

Springer is part of Springer Science+Business Media (www.springer.com)

# Preface

This volume contains the papers presented at EMAS 2013: the First International Workshop on Engineering Multi-Agent Systems held during May 5–6, 2013, in Saint Paul, Minnesota.

Although much progress has been made, the design, implementation, and deployment of multi-agent systems still poses many challenges. Some of these concern design and software engineering aspects, for example, how to effectively design agents and their interactions? Other challenges concern implementation, for instance, how to effectively implement multi-agent coordination or organizations? Further challenges concern use of logic-based techniques for verification of agent systems.

It is increasingly apparent that there are benefits in considering design and implementation challenges together. For example, design artifacts can be used to support and assist with debugging and testing. Another example is the development of agent-oriented programming languages that result in programs that are more readily verifiable. A final example is the use of declarative techniques that span design and implementation. This unveils a tight interlacement among the different research issues in multi-agent systems engineering.

This naturally resulted in a workshop that brought together the previously separate topics (but overlapping communities) that focus on software engineering aspects (AOSE), programming aspects (ProMAS), and the application of declarative techniques to design, programming, and verification (DALT).

Furthermore, a natural complement to *research* papers on engineering multi-agent systems is *application* papers that describe developed applications and lessons learned as well as the engineering challenges identified in building and deploying the applications.

The EMAS workshop thus explicitly pursued three goals:

1. To progress and further develop the understanding of how to engineer multi-agent systems.
2. To bring together the communities that are concerned with different aspects of engineering multi-agent systems, and by doing so, allow for better interchange of ideas between the communities, thus exploiting the synergies discussed above.
3. To provide a venue where people who have developed applications could articulate the lessons learned and engineering challenges identified in building and deploying their applications, and have these lessons influence further research in the field.

The call for papers explicitly addressed application papers and research papers that were concerned with any aspect of the engineering of multi-agent systems, specifically including any topics that would fall within the scope of one or more of the three parent workshops:

- Agent-Oriented Software Engineering (AOSE)
- Declarative Agent Languages and Technologies (DALT)
- Programming Multi-Agent Systems (ProMAS)

EMAS 2013 received 31 submissions (one was withdrawn before being reviewed). Each paper was reviewed by three reviewers, and we accepted 19 papers, including two application papers. The papers were presented at the workshop, and then revised and extended for these post-proceedings. The revised and extended post-proceeding versions were reviewed by one of the original reviewers. Of the 19 papers presented at EMAS 2013, 14 appear in revised and extended form in these post-proceedings. One of the papers presented at the workshop (by Gerard et al.) is, by the authors' request, not included in the proceedings in full form, but as an extended abstract, and can be found in the front matter of this volume.

In addition to the papers that were presented at EMAS, these post-proceedings also include a paper contributed by the workshop's invited speaker, Associate Professor Luciano Baresi, and his colleagues.

Additionally, following the tradition of previous ProMAS editions, these post-proceedings also include material from the agent competition (`http://multiagentcontest.org/`), organized by Tobias Ahlbrecht, Jürgen Dix, Michael Köster, and Federico Schlesinger (all from Clausthal University of Technology) in September 2013. After an overview of the contest by the organizers, there are five papers from this year's participants. This part of the proceedings concludes with another paper that compiles the answers of all the teams to 50 questions stated by the organizers. These questions concern almost all engineering aspects of multi-agent systems and help to compare and put into perspective the different approaches selected by the five teams.

The EMAS 2013 chairs would like to acknowledge the great review work done by members of the Program Committee. Reviews were in general detailed (and, we hope, useful to the authors), and there was a very high degree of consensus amongst the reviewers.

October 2013

Massimo Cossentino
Amal El Fallah Seghrouchni
Michael Winikoff

# Organization

## Steering Committee

EMAS is overseen by a (merged) Steering Committee from the three "parent" workshops (original Steering Committee indicated below).

| | |
|---|---|
| Matteo Baldoni | DALT, Italy |
| Rafael Bordini | ProMAS, Brazil |
| Mehdi Dastani | ProMAS, The Netherlands |
| Jürgen Dix | ProMAS, Germany |
| Amal El Fallah Seghrouchni | ProMAS, France |
| Paolo Giorgini | AOSE, Italy |
| Jörg P. Müller | AOSE, Germany |
| M. Birna Van Riemsdijk | DALT, The Netherlands |
| Tran Cao Son | DALT, USA |
| Gerhard Weiss | AOSE, The Netherlands |
| Danny Weyns | AOSE, Sweden |
| Michael Winikoff | DALT and AOSE, New Zealand |

## EMAS 2013 Workshop Chairs

| | |
|---|---|
| Massimo Cossentino | National Research Council of Italy, Italy |
| Amal El Fallah Seghrouchni | LIP6 - Pierre and Marie Curie University, France |
| Michael Winikoff | University of Otago, New Zealand |

## Program Committee

| | |
|---|---|
| Natasha Alechina | University of Nottingham, UK |
| Matteo Baldoni | Università degli Studi di Torino, Italy |
| Cristina Baroglio | Università degli Studi di Torino, Italy |
| Jeremy Baxter | QinetiQ, UK |
| Olivier Boissier | ENS Mines Saint-Etienne, France |
| Rafael Bordini | Pontifical Catholic University of Rio Grande do Sul, Brazil |
| Lars Braubach | University of Hamburg, Germany |
| Rem Collier | University College Dublin, Ireland |
| Mehdi Dastani | Utrecht University, The Netherlands |
| Scott Deloach | Kansas State University, USA |
| Louise Dennis | University of Liverpool, UK |

# Composing Commitment Protocols
## (Extended Abstract)

Scott N. Gerard[1], Pankaj R. Telang[2], Anup K. Kalia[2], and Munindar P. Singh[2]

[1] IBM, Research Triangle Park, Durham, NC 27709, USA
sgerard@us.ibm.com
[2] Department of Computer Science, NC State University, Raleigh, NC 27695, USA
ptelang@gmail.com, {akkalia,singh}@ncsu.edu

**Keywords:** Commitments, Agent communication, Verification of multiagent systems, Communication protocols, Model checking.

We consider *(commitment) protocols* specified formally in terms of their roles, their messages, and the meanings of their messages (expressed as commitments). Although protocols offer significant benefits over traditional approaches, protocols are not fully viable for the following reasons. One, specifying in one shot an adequate protocol for a complex scenario is nontrivial. Two, implementing agents who can play roles in such a comprehensive protocol is difficult because the differing details of the protocols complicate reusing parts of agent implementations.

In an important advance over previous work, we show how to *compose* complex protocols from existing constituent protocols, thereby facilitating reuse. We address two role-specific aspects of composition: (1) *role requirements*, capturing the benefits a role receives from the composite protocol; and (2) *role accountability*, capturing the commitments a role makes to other roles—to promote their joint enactments of the composite protocol. Our approach yields benefits in business requirements elicitation (natural abstraction); enactment (flexibility); and compliance and validation (ascribing accountability for each requirement to a specific role).

Our approach, *Positron*, extends our previous Proton work [3]. Positron (a) provides a formal language in which to express composite protocols based on existing constituent protocols; (b) recursively expands nested constituent protocols; (c) introduces *composite protocol diagrams* (CPDs) as a graphical notation, conveying important features of the composite protocol to business and technical stakeholders; (d) introduces *role requirements* and *role accountabilities*; (e) incorporates a methodology for composing commitment protocols; and (f) implements a decision procedure and mechanical verification of protocols with respect to role requirements, role accountabilities, and enactments, compiling formulas to CTL temporal logic, and employing MCMAS [4], a leading model checker, to verify if the composite protocol satisfies those formulas.

To demonstrate the broad applicability of Positron, our methodology successfully creates composite protocols for scenarios from three different business domains: AGFIL, automobile insurance claims processing [2]; Quote To Cash, an important business process for manufacturing supply chains [5]; and ASPE, a healthcare process for breast cancer diagnosis [1]. Positron successfully verifies all role and enactment requirements.

Positron gains an advantage over traditional approaches by focusing on high-level business relationships realized as constituent protocols, and by focusing on commitments rather than control flow. Because role accountabilities are stated as commitments, if a requirement fails, we can trace the failure back to a specific role. CPDs summarize relevant details about a composite protocol and we expect they will prove valuable, because they bring together both technical and business descriptions of protocols, helping bridge the Business-IT Divide [6].

# References

1. ASPE. The importance of radiology and pathology communication in the diagnosis and staging of cancer: Mammography as a case study (November 2010), Office of the Assistant Secretary for Planning and Evaluation, U.S. Department of Health and Human Services, http://aspe.hhs.gov/sp/reports/2010/PathRad/index.shtml
2. Browne, S., Kellett, M.: Insurance (motor damage claims) scenario. Document D1.a, CrossFlow Consortium (1999)
3. Gerard, S.N., Singh, M.P.: Formalizing and verifying protocol refinements. ACM Transactions on Intelligent Systems and Technology, TIST (2013)
4. Lomuscio, A., Qu, H., Raimondi, F.: Mcmas: A model checker for the verification of multi-agent systems. In: Bouajjani, A., Maler, O. (eds.) CAV 2009. LNCS, vol. 5643, pp. 682–688. Springer, Heidelberg (2009)
5. Oracle. Automating the Quote-to-Cash process (June 2009), http://www.oracle.com/us/industries/045546.pdf
6. Smith, H., Fingar, P.: Business Process Management: The Third Wave. Megan-Kiffer Press, Tampa (2002)

# Table of Contents

# SeSaMe: Towards a Semantic Self Adaptive Middleware for Smart Spaces*

Luciano Baresi, Sam Guinea, and Adnan Shahzada

Politecnico di Milano
Dipartimento di Elettronica, Informazione e Bioingegneria
Piazza L. da Vinci, 32 - 20133 Milano, Italy
{baresi,guinea,shahzada}@elet.polimi.it

**Abstract.** Smart spaces are inherently complex and dynamic systems, where diverse devices, sensors, actuators and computational elements need to interact with one another. A middleware infrastructure can provide suitable abstractions that simplify the task, and allow designers to ignore the details of the underlying elements. Unfortunately, however, existing middleware solutions do not generalize well to different kinds of spaces, since they often fail to address the scalability and dynamism of such spaces.

In this paper we propose SeSaMe, a semantic and self-adaptive middleware infrastructure for highly dynamic and massive smart spaces. SeSaMe establishes a "backbone" to let components connect to the system without any prior knowledge of its topology. It is capable of maintaining the system's overall reliability, even when multiple components leave or fail unexpectedly, and of coping with message congestion, by dynamically altering the system's topology. SeSaMe also provides a simple declarative language for defining how one wants the system to evolve over time, and semantic technologies for harmonizing the interaction of different kinds of components. The main new features of SeSaMe are exemplified on two example smart spaces with significantly different characteristics.

## 1 Introduction

The pervasive use of information and communication technologies is transforming the environments in which we live into *smart* spaces. A smart space is thus *"a physical world that is richly and invisibly interwoven with sensors, actuators, displays and computational elements, embedded seamlessly in the everyday objects of our lives, and connected through a network."* [24]. The resulting system is a live entity where users interact with the environment through dedicated applications that are hosted, for example, on their mobile terminals. The space can act

---

* This research was partially funded by the European Commission, Programme IDEAS-ERC, Project 227977 SMScom. Adnan Shahzada is supported by the Joint Open Lab "S-Cube", sponsored by Telecom Italia S.p.A. - Innovation division, Milan, Italy.

M. Cossentino et al. (Eds.): EMAS 2013, LNAI 8245, pp. 1–18, 2013.
© Springer-Verlag Berlin Heidelberg 2013

as a problem solver, in particular moments, help users live better and healthier lives, foster sustainable behaviors, or help accomplish tasks more efficiently.

The term *smart space* can refer to radically different situations. Houses and offices are usually characterized by a small (limited) number of users, low dynamism, and scarce turnover. In contrast, subway stations, malls, museums, and exhibition centers must serve a high (or even huge) number of users that form big, dynamic communities. In both cases, the ecosystem of interconnected devices must provide its services seamlessly, and all users should be treated equally.

Such live and dynamic systems come with severe requirements in terms of device integration, scalability, flexibility, and reliability. A proper identification of the actual requirements, and a careful design of the foreseen solution, must be fostered by a *smart* middleware infrastructure. This infrastructure must provide a robust and reliable backbone to integrate the different devices, while hiding their peculiarities, offer well-defined abstractions and interfaces for the development of user-oriented applications, and supply efficient solutions to coordinate and organize the large number of interacting entities. The middleware must also help the system self-configure and self-adjust its behavior according to different needs: for example, continuous care must be paid to load balancing and congestion control.

This paper paves the ground to SeSaMe, our proposal of a SEmantic, Self-Adaptive MiddlewarE infrastructure for highly dynamic and massive smart spaces. SeSaMe borrows its roots from A-3 [11], a middleware developed by the first two authors. A-3 is a self-organizing distributed middleware for designing and implementing distributed systems that are inherently dynamic in nature, and large in scale and volume. It presents a group-based solution for coordinating distributed components (from now on "nodes") that might need to join or leave the system unexpectedly. An A-3 group clusters nodes with "similar" characteristics. These groups can be exploited in various ways to cluster devices, and/or users, so that they can act as single coordinated entities. For each group, A-3 chooses a *supervisor* node that is in charge of coordinating the group's elements, and of communicating with other existing groups (i.e., with other supervisors). Since each node can play different roles in the system, a node can participate in different groups at the same time. A-3 also offers basic self-organizing primitives that can be used to specify how groups can be re-organized at runtime.

SeSaMe extends A-3 in several directions. It will offer a set of new abstractions and interfaces that ease the creation of user-oriented applications. In particular, it will provide means for components to connect to the system with no prior knowledge of its topology, and it provides means to ensure reliability and avoid message congestion in the wake of high component churn rates. At run-time, the idea is to separate the behavior of the middleware from its configuration. For this we define a special-purpose language for defining how groups should be formed with respect to the different nodes' characteristics, how they can be split or merged, and how nodes should be replicated to improve reliability.

SeSaMe also tackles the problem of harmonizing device heterogeneity in a smart space. SeSaMe will provide a semantic layer, based on RDF (Resource

Description Framework) to ease the integration of diverse devices, but also to facilitate the communication with users that "speak" particular languages. This has an impact both on basic group setup, and on how a group transitions from one configuration to the next, since we must absolutely avoid losing significant information. The same kinds of problems apply when we want to move certain nodes from one smart space to another, and/or compose independent smart spaces after the user moves or changes his/her preferences.

We are also working on self-adaptive and self-healing capabilities, to both optimize the behavior of the system, and to be able to cope with unforeseen situations and faults. All these features go in the direction of a more robust and stable system that can offer its services in "any" situation.

These new features are exemplified on two examples: a smart office and an exhibition center. The first represents a simple, static smart space with a limited number of users, while the second embeds the characteristics of a fully dynamic and massive space.

The rest of the paper is organized as follows. Section 2 presents the two example smart spaces. Section 3 provides a brief summary of the key characteristics of A-3, while Section 4 introduces the requirements behind SeSaMe and the new features we are working on. Section 5 surveys the state of the art in the field, and Section 6 concludes the paper.

## 2   Smart Spaces

Smart spaces can vary in terms of complexity, dynamism, scale, mobility, and type of services offered to their users. This is why we present two different smart spaces that have quite different characteristics; the reader should consider them as representatives of two different families of systems. We will use them throughout the paper to exemplify the features provided by SeSaMe.

In a typical smart *office* most of the devices are static, and mobility is only on the user's part. The idea is to leverage the automation facilities provided by the building. Each room is equipped with lights, air conditioning, heating, and shutters; and provides appropriate light, temperature, and smoke sensors. Some rooms also have printers. Each person entering the space has a badge, and dedicated sensors detect his/her presence in a room.

The first scenario is about adjusting the light in various rooms according to user activities and overall energy consumption. If there are no users in a room, all the lights should be turned off; while if one or more users enter the office, the lights should be switched on accordingly. Moreover, if the amount of ambient light goes above a given threshold, more lights should not be turned on, in order to save energy. Similarly, the light and shutters should also be adjusted based on the intensity of light, and on the activities being pursued. For example, lights can be dimmed, and shutters can be closed, during a presentation.

The second scenario deals with the efficient use of heating and air conditioning to avoid waisting energy. The temperature should be managed according to the preferences of the actual users in a room, but it should also be distributed uniformly among the various rooms. The thermostat in each room must adopt a compromise between a purely local policy and a building-wide solution, to avoid waisting energy with useless and dangerous spikes.

Finally, the system must also take into account the smart management of available printers. The system offers a single "virtual" printer. This means that every time someone wants to print something, s/he is told which physical printer will actually serve the request. This allows people to use the closest printer currently available, and to avoid printers that are out of order or congested.

In contrast, a typical *exhibition center* must manage thousands of visitors each day. Usually, there are multiple areas and stands for different companies and products. Visitors have different interests, most of them are usually only interested in some specific areas of an exhibition, and sometimes they are unable to find where they want to go.

To help visitors with their visit, we assume everyone is provided with an RFID tag for localization, and a smartphone/tablet that can run an application they can use to register, declare their interests, get navigational help, and discover new and different opportunities.

This technology-assisted navigation helps visitors save time, and provides them with a more useful experience. Moreover, it can also help the organizers manage the crowd by properly distributing the different groups of people, and avoiding tedious queues. The exhibition also provides big displays to help people find the right directions (the use of mobile devices is not always convenient). These screens can detect the presence of people in their surrounding, and can provide useful information such as directions, advertisements, and further information on when and how to leave the area.

The same smart infrastructure can also be used to coordinate people in the case of an emergency. It can help evacuate people in a well coordinated manner by providing information about the safest and nearest exits, and by telling people to use all the emergency exits uniformly.

## 3  A-3 in a Nutshell

A-3 is a middleware for the design and implementation of distributed systems that comprise very large numbers of components. In particular, it allows system designers to develop highly scalable systems, that can also cope with components (or nodes) that enter and/or leave the system with extremely high churn rates.

A-3 is entirely based around the notion of "group". The group is an abstraction that allows us to cluster nodes that have similar qualities, needs, or goals. As a result, we obtain an entity that is intrinsically less dynamic, and easier to manage, than a single node.

Each A-3 group is made up of a *supervisor* node, which can be selected either statically or dynamically, and of multiple *follower* nodes. The supervisor and its followers use a special connector to communicate, as shown in Figure 1. The connector supports asynchronous messaging with virtual synchrony, but limits communication in the following way: followers can only send messages to their supervisor, while a supervisor can target a selected follower, or broadcast a message to all the nodes in its group. The idea is that a follower will send messages to its supervisor to inform it about its behavior, while a supervisor will send messages to it followers to inform them about any new coordination directives.

A group provides an abstraction for reasoning about the coordination and management of a single set of nodes. It does not, however, allow us to coordinate or manage the entire system. To enable global coordination, A-3 allows group to be "composed". Group composition is achieved by allowing a node to belong to more than one group at a time, and by allowing it to play different roles in different groups (e.g., a node can be a supervisor in group A and a follower in group B). This way designers can construct different kinds of organizational structures, depending on the application's coordination needs. Figure 2 shows some of the possible organizational structures (e.g., hierarchical, circular, flat). These structures allow groups to share "local" knowledge, and, through appropriate compositional design, reach a "global" understanding and coordination of the entire system. In the figure, black circles represent supervisors, white circles represent followers, and circles that are half black and half white are components that play both the supervisor and the follower role, in different groups.

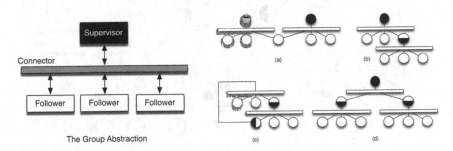

**Fig. 1.** Group Abstraction     **Fig. 2.** Group Compositions

In A-3, group participants are also always kept up-to-date with regards to what nodes are entering or leaving the group's virtual boundaries. On the one hand, this information can be used by the supervisor to manage the group more intelligently. For example, a supervisor can decide to split the group into smaller sub-groups, to avoid congestion; or it can decide to merge groups that are too small into larger ones, to ensure that the topology does not become too susceptible to high node churn rates. On the the other hand, this information can also be used by followers to react to supervisor failures. For example, A-3 allows supervisors to store coordination data directly to their groups; this is achieved by replicating the data across the group's own nodes. This way, when a supervisor fails, the followers can initiate a distributed leader-election algorithm, and the new supervisor can recover the stored data and reprise any ongoing coordination activities.

## 4   SeSaMe

SeSaMe is a distributed middleware for smart spaces that borrows some basic concepts from A-3, while adding new features that specifically target the peculiar needs of smart spaces. To this end, SeSaMe proposes a better separation of concerns between the sensing/actuating infrastructure and the components in charge of its efficient, autonomic management. Sensors, actuators, displays and computational elements define the *Components Layer*, while special-purpose components *Smart Space Managers* (SSM) define the *Management Layer*. At both levels, components are still divided into supervisors and followers, grouped together according to common needs and goals, and groups are composed properly. The two layers impose that each lower-level group be (indirectly) managed by an upper level node. This means that each supervisor of a group of components is connected, as a follower, to an SSM. This way it can receive updates from the management layer as to how it should coordinate its group. The SSMs can also be connected among themselves to share information, which can then be used to better manage the groups.

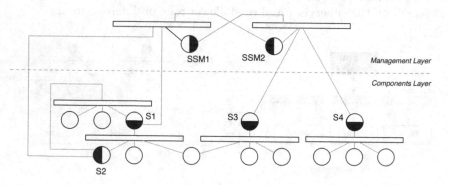

**Fig. 3.** Example configuration of a Smart Space

Figure 3 shows an example of a SeSaMe topology. As we can see, the components layer comprises 4 groups —supervised by nodes $S1$, $S2$, $S3$, and $S4$, respectively— that are composed to satisfy their reciprocal needs. The management layer is made up of two SSMs: $SSM1$ and $SSM2$. Each is configured to be a supervisor of the other, thus ensuring a two-way information exchange between them.

The two layers come from the idea of distinguishing between (more) stable, static components, which provide the "backbone" of the system, and the dynamic ones that correspond to the different devices (users) that enter and leave the system. If the physical infrastructure allows for the identification of stable peers, the management layer is also in charge of the reliability of the whole systems: clearly situations like *first-responder* solutions cannot count on these reliable backbone and dedicated solutions must be put in place. However we consider this last case to be future work, and, therefore, out of the scope of this paper.

The management layer becomes responsible for different management tasks. The first consists in managing new node connections. Every time a new node connects to the system, the SSMs collaborate to find the most appropriate component group in which to include it, depending on its needs, goals, and capabilities. The second consists in managing node disconnections, to ensure the overall system reliability. In practice, the SSMs can collaborate to modify the system's topology accordingly. The third consists in managing congestion, to ensure that messaging is always achieved efficiently throughout the system.

Figure 4 presents the high-level architecture of SeSaMe and introduces two further novel contributions. The first is a new declarative language that one can use to explain what groups should be present in the system (*Config rules*), how they should be composed, and how they should evolve over time. The second is an ontology-based semantic layer that allows different kinds of sensors, actuators, and computational elements to become part of the system and interact seamlessly.

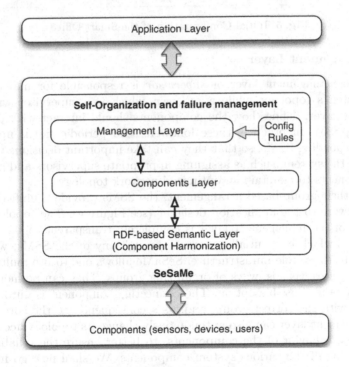

**Fig. 4.** The SeSaMe Architecture

Before we provide more details regarding SeSaMe's novel contributions, we provide the initial setups of the components layers of our smart office and exhibition center scenarios. In the office scenario we have groups that depend on component types (e.g., lights, air conditioners, shutters and heaters), and we have groups that depend on the desired functionality (e.g., temperature management, light adjustments, spatial adjustments, etc.). As shown in Figure 5, some of the devices actually participate in more than one group at a time (e.g., the shutters belong to both the light and temperature adjustment groups). Similarly, in the exhibition center scenario, people (their devices) are grouped based on their interests and on their location, and can belong to more than one group at a time.

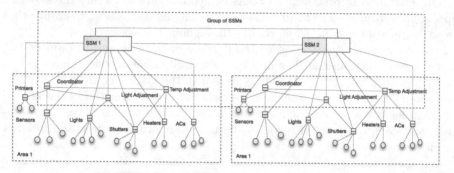

**Fig. 5.** Initial Configuration of the Smart Office

### 4.1  Management Layer

Within the management layer, a *supervisor* is responsible for managing the overall system's topology, while a *follower*, which is a supervisor within the components layer, defines how the components should interact with their corresponding SSM. In practice, these followers send periodic status updates to their corresponding SSMs, so that they can take important decisions regarding changes in the system, such as assigning appropriate supervisors and groups to new components to maintain an optimized network topology.

Due to their group-based arrangement, the SSMs provide a unified view of the middleware to the application designer (see Figure 4). The topological organization of the management layer is completely transparent to the system's components, which can initially connect through any of the SSMs, which act as proxies to the whole infrastructure. SeSaMe allows one to use multiple governing structures, that is, ways of organizing groups. They can be hierarchical, flat, or any other possible option. The connecting component is automatically associated with the correct group, and, as a consequence, to the correct SSM. The management layer can also autonomously change its topology according to the dynamic behavior of the components, to better ensure the reliability and load balancing of the various system components. We shall now go into more detail as to how the management layer helps the smart space system cope with *dynamism and self-configuration*, *reliability*, and *congestion management*.

**Dynamism and Self Configuration.** The management layer deals with dynamism by supporting the automated formation of new groups. A new component can connect to any existing group, or create a new one. This means that SeSaMe automatically identifies the right group supervisor (*follower* at management level) and links the new component to it. If the component can play different roles, that is, it can belong to different groups, the management layer will decide its group memberships according to all its roles. Note that group formation is handled by maintaining shared lists of the existing groups and supervisors within the management layer.

SeSaMe takes many different aspects into account when selecting what group a component should join. Let us first consider the case in which the new component can only play a single supervisor role. When it connects, the selected SSM searches for the corresponding group in the shared group list. If such a group does not exist, it creates a new group with that component as the supervisor, asks the component to activate its (management) follower role, and updates the lists of shared groups and supervisors. If, on the other hand, one or more acceptable groups already exist, the management layer will decide, based on the system's desired configuration (see Section 4.2), how to add the component to the already existing groups. Based on performance and resource utilization, the management layer will select the group with less followers, and less message exchanges.

If the new component can play multiple supervisor and follower roles, the management layer enacts the above procedures for each and every one of the component's roles. This implies that the component will become part of all the groups that it can be part of, at that particular time. If a component can play both the supervisor and the follower role in a specific group, the management layer will decide its role based on the system's overall needs. The component will become a supervisor if any of the existing groups are congested. Otherwise, the new component will become a follower.

In the exhibition center scenario, whenever a user connects to the system (space), the user's interests are matched to the various existing groups, and s/he is assigned to a group (or to a set of groups) accordingly. This happens if this does not affect the balance and efficiency of the network. For example, if a user can be part of both the "Technology" and the "Sports" groups, and the group for technology oriented stands is congested, the management layer will start by adding the user to the sports group. If the new component happens to become a supervisor in that group, then it will also start executing the (management) follower role.

**Reliability.** SeSaMe is capable of automatically managing situations in which components leave the system unexpectedly. If the node leaving the system is a follower, the SSM in charge of it decides whether this should cause any groups to merge or re-organize to satisfy the desired system configuration.

If the component leaving the system is a supervisor, SeSaMe has three possibilities. In the first, it communicates the event to its followers, so that they can reconnect to the system by interacting with any of the SSMs in the management layer. In the second, one of the orphaned followers is called to substitute the failing supervisor. Orphaned components start by simply reconnecting to the management layer. The first component to reconnect, that can also play the supervisor role, gets promoted to supervisor status. From there on, the SSMs collaborate to progressively send all the orphaned components to this new group.

In the third, the SSM that was responsible for the failing supervisor takes its place. The SSMs in the management layer then collaborate to send all the reconnecting orphans to that SSM, which will hold on to them until a new supervisor becomes available.

For example, in our office scenario, we can use these techniques to tackle printer failures by providing a "virtual" printer. If a device attempts to use a failed printer, the SSM replacing that printer can take care of the printing jobs by collaborating with other SSMs to find a substitute printer. This ensures that the service is provided reliably. Similarly, if a display in the exhibition scenario fails, the SSMs can collaborate to connect users to other displays in the vicinity.

Moreover, the ability of a component to be part of multiple groups at a time raises the problem that it may receive conflicting directives from the different supervisors. For example, it might be the case that the light adjustment group may prefer a shutter to be opened whereas the temperature adjustment group wants it to be closed. SeSaMe fosters the idea that a well designed system would not have to face these situations. However, the interactions among the different groups, and the system-specific composition of the commands issued by the different supervisors provide a further way to manage them. The last option is that the internal logic of each single component can always specify how to deal with these spurious, conflicting cases. This means that either the groups are composed in such a way that the commands issued by the temperature supervisors can filter those issued by the light managers. Otherwise, the shutter itself can be programmed to decide that the commands received from a temperature supervisor override the commands received from the other supervisors.

**Congestion Management.** As previously stated, the SSMs are continuously updated by the components' supervisors so that they can take decisions regarding the system's topology. These updates include the number of messages that the components' supervisors have received and sent in a given time, the size of the group they are supervising, and the number of groups they are a member of. The SSMs process this information and act according to the desired system configuration. For instance, if an SSM finds out that the size of a given group of components has exceeded the maximum size limit or that the number of messages that are sent or received by the supervisor in a given time has been higher than the specified threshold, it will split that group by finding another appropriate supervisor and will distribute the components among the two groups. In case no other group of that type is available, the SSM will try to select a component of the original group that can take the role of supervisor and will then split the components by changing the role of that component from follower to supervisor within the components layer. Note that the new supervisor will also act as a follower of the SSM and the management layer will then be updated of the status of this new group. Similarly, if the SSM finds out that a group is too small or it only exchanged few messages in a given amount of time, it tries to find another similar group and merges the two together.

In the exhibition scenario, the system will guide a group of users to their desired destinations, but if the system finds out that a group (of people) is exceeding the set highest limit, it can split the group into multiple sub-groups, and guide them to the locations in a way that avoids message, and people congestion. For example, it can route different sub-groups differently within the exhibitions' premise. If an emergency situation ever arises, the same techniques can be used to route people to different exits, avoiding, once again, message and people congestion.

## 4.2   Declarative Configuration of the Management Layer

One of SeSaMe's main novel contributions is that it allows one to declaratively express his/her desiderata for the system's topology. All the decisions taken at the management layer are made according to this specification. The language can express component group types, their initial topology, and various thresholds for group merging and splitting. We call these thresholds the self-organizing parameters (SOPs). Our simple declarative language has the following syntax:

```
<configuration> =:> <groups definition> ; <initial topology>; <parameters>
<groups definition> =:> Groups ; <groups>
<groups> =:> <group> | <group>; <groups>
<group> =:> <group Info> | <group Info>; <parameters>
<group Info> =:> GroupDescription GroupSupervisorRole GroupFollowerRole
<initial topology> =:> Topology ; <topology>
<topology> =:> <initial group> | <topology>
<initial group> =:> GroupId <group> ; <components>
<components> =:> <component> | <components>
<component> =:> componentId ; <role>
<role> =:> Supervisor | Follower
<parameters> =:> Parameters ; <parameter definition>
<parameter definition> =:> <group size>; <max no. of messages>;
   <update frequency>;
<min no. of messages>;
<group size> =:> groupSize <size>
<max no. of messages> =:> maxNoMsgs <no. of msgs>
<update frequency> =:> updateFrequency <frequency in milliseconds>
<min no. of messages> =:>  minNoMsgs <no. of msgs>
```

Each group is defined by a group description, its corresponding supervisor and follower roles, and its SOP values. If no SOP values are defined for a particular group, SeSaMe uses a default set of SOP values. The SOPs include the maximum group size, the status update frequency, and the maximum and minimum number of messages per time unit accepted by the group's supervisor. The maximum group size limits the number of components that can be accepted within a group; if a group exceeds this limit, either it is split into new subgroups, or some of its components are re-assigned to another group with the same characteristics. The maximum and minimum number of messages determine the acceptable communication load for a group's supervisor. The group will split if the communication load exceeds the higher threshold to avoid congestion; two groups will merge, if possible, when one or both of them go below their thresholds.

We now provide an example of how our language can be used to define the initial topology and evolution rules of our smart office scenario (please refer to Figure 5).

```
Groups
LightSensorsGroup    LightSensorSupervisor    LightSensorFollower
TempSensorsGroup     TempSensorSupervisor     TempSensorFollower
LightsGroup          SupervisorLight          FollowerLight
ShuttersGroup        SupervisorShutter        FollowerShutter
ACsGroup             SupervisorAC             FollowerAC
LightAdjustment      LightingSupervisor       LightingFollower
TempAdjustment       TempSupervisor           TempFollower


Topology
Group1    LightSensorsGroup    LightSensorSupervisor    LightSensorFollower
LightSensor     Supervisor
LightSensor2    Follower
LightSensor3    Follower


Group2    LightsGroup    LightSensorSupervisor    LightSensorFollower
Light1          Supervisor
Light2          Follower
Light3          Follower
Light4          Follower


Group3    TempSensorsGroup    TempSensorSupervisor    TempSensorFollower
TempSensor1     Supervisor
TempSensor2     Follower
TempSensor3     Follower


Group4    ShuttersGroup    SupervisorShutter    FollowerShutter
Shutter1        Supervisor
Shutter2        Follower
Shutter3        Follower
Shutter4        Follower


Group5    LightAdjustment    LightingSupervisor    LightingFollower
LightingSV      Supervisor
Light1          Follower
Shutter1        Follower


Parameters
groupSize 15
maxNoMsgs 200
updateFrequency 2
maxNoMsgs 20
```

## 4.3  Harmonizing Heterogeneous Components

Interaction and information exchange among large numbers of heterogeneous devices is a major issue while developing applications for smart spaces. Our middleware provides a semantic layer for enabling diverse devices to communicate and exchange information with each other. The devices will use a set of common semantic models, based on Resource Description Framework (RDF), to enable easy linking of cross-domain data. In practice, we define both the components and their messages in terms of RDF-based semantic ontologies, so that SeSaMe can integrate and organize the devices. All components have access to a common repository that stores the data in a format supported by RDF.

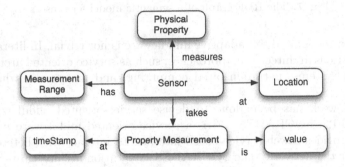

**Fig. 6.** The Sensor Ontology

In our smart office example, each room has its own set of sensors; they feed information into the system using a specified model, and, thanks to that model, all the other components can interpret their values. Figure 6 shows a simple example ontology model for the sensors. Each sensor is defined by its location, the physical property it measures, the range within which its values can be output, the actual reading, and a timestamp. An example of how this sensor ontology can be used to represent information in RDF is shown in Figure 7. The RDF graph shows the property measurements of two sensors $S1$ and $S2$, located in *Room*01 and *Room*02, respectively. Both these sensors measure temperatures; $S1$ can sense temperatures between $-100$ and $100$ degrees, whereas $S2$ can measure temperatures between $-50$ and $100$ degrees. The graph also shows one measurement for each sensor (i.e., the value and its timestamp). Thanks to this model the sensors can "speak" the same language, and the system can digest the information they generate. Similarly, the semantic model is also used to define roles for various components, so that the SSMs can associate the components with relevant groups by matching relevant ontological information.

## 5  Related Work

Many researchers [19,1] have investigated and developed middleware solutions for smart spaces. Due to the inherent complexity of these spaces, the task of

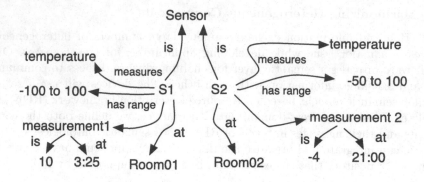

**Fig. 7.** The RDF graph of a semantic model for sensors

developing a robust and self-adaptive middleware is not trivial. In literature, we find that various architectural approaches, such as service oriented architecture, multi-agent systems, nature-inspired computing, and many others have been employed.

A lot of work has been done to devise service-oriented middleware solutions [22,26,12]. SOCRADES [3] is a service oriented middleware infrastructure that provides a web-service-based interface to interact with heterogeneous devices over the network. The SOCRADES integration architecture (SIA) [21] features a sophisticated event-driven messaging system that enables applications to consume data on specific events, from devices whose functionality is abstracted as web services. It does not, however, support contextual information, and it does not show how the system will scale and organize itself in dynamic environments. Reyes and Wong also propose a service-oriented middleware [20] for integrating various sensors and actuating devices within a smart home setting. It exposes different devices as services that can be used by the application designer to build various applications. The proposed architecture is very restrictive and domain specific, and does not generalize well to various kinds of smart spaces. RUNES [9] offers a publish-subscribe middleware solution with dynamic reconfiguration capabilities, and targets sensor networks and embedded systems. It has good device coordination mechanisms, but it does not optimize the network's behavior, for example by delegating more tasks to devices with more resources. The problem with most of these systems is that they are usually static and operate without knowledge of their environments, and they are unable to adapt themselves to evolving needs and requirements [25]. Therefore, it is generally difficult to deploy these systems in the real-time dynamic and large scale systems we are interested in as they lack the self-organization and self-adaptive capabilities.

Multi-agent systems is another paradigm that has been used intensively in attempt to build middleware infrastructures of highly dynamic, autonomous and mobile smart spaces. ASPECS [8] is a comprehensive agent-oriented software process for engineering complex systems. It is based on a holonic organizational meta-model, and provides a step-by-step modeling guide and tools for all the development phases, from requirements gathering to implementation.

ASPECS is similar to our approach, in a sense that holons of agents also compose to create new holons, but it focuses on systems with hierarchical configurations. We, on the other hand, advocate that the self-adaptive organization of components is more flexible, since it can support linear, circular, hierarchical configurations, and more. Similarly, SETH [16] is also an agent-based hierarchical architecture for smart spaces. The architecture can be deployed in layers, which allows one to create complex smart environments by means of inheritance and aggregation relationships. Every smart space in SETH is represented by a Smart Space Agent Platform (SSAP) that hosts all other smart space and system level agents.Though it provides the hierarchical and location-based aggregation of different spaces and groups of devices, it does not provide any self-configuration abilities and does not offer any reliability in case of component failures. Rubén et. al propose a multi-agent architecture [10] that considers sensors in a space as devices used by the controller agents residing in an upper layer. It is built upon INGENIAS [14], a Model Driven Engineering methodology for the development of multi-agent systems. Agents are organized according to roles related to aspects such as component management, communication, and data processing. Such an organization ensures the separation of concerns for different components, and it decouples data management from network dynamics. This system targets scalability and uses roles and groups to address non-functional requirements, but is mostly focused towards wireless sensor networks. EasyMeeting [7] extends Vigil [15] by adding context-aware support for assisting speakers and audiences during presentation meetings and it exploits the Cobra [6] architecture for context management. The issues that are yet to be addressed with the proposed architecture are the scalability of knowledge sharing in distributed and dynamic environments, and performance analysis in the presence of large scale networks. In general, multi-agent systems exhibit autonomic, self-configuration and self-adaptation characteristics, but they do not guarantee the reliable integration and provision of devices and services in a smart space. Unlike traditional distributed systems where fault tolerant techniques are often employed at low level and usually they are part of the infrastructure, in multi-agent systems we need to implement these decision making policies at a more abstract level of design and this involves planning and cooperation of agents that are autonomous in their behavior and hence can lead to uncertain states in case agents fail to understand their role at either activity or organization level.

ASCENS [25] describes a systematic approach to engineer ensembles, that is, software systems with large amounts of heterogeneous devices operating in open and non-deterministic environments, and in which there are complex interactions among nodes, humans, or other systems. The proposed approach is focused on the fact that these systems should be reliable and should be able to adapt themselves according to the changing environment and unforeseen situations. It provides tools and languages for requirements modeling, service composition and adaptation. The project is still active and they are developing self-awareness and self-adaptation capabilities for the current model.

There is another research dimension for self-adaptive middleware for smart spaces that puts forward the idea of using nature-inspired computing [4,23,2,13]. Most of these solutions are inspired by ecological systems, bio-chemical processes, and social networks. Miorandi et al. [18] outline some of the work done with project BIONETS. Nature is inherently capable of handling problems such as scale, heterogeneity, dynamism, and high complexity, and sustaining equilibrium and balance without a central controlling authority. The paper describes some of the nature-inspired computing paradigms such as chemical computing, artificial chemistry, evolutionary games and artificial embryogenesis. The SAPERE model [4,5] promotes self-adaptivity by means of spatially-situated and chemically-inspired interactions between services and devices. It models a pervasive service environment as a spatial substrate that makes use of natural laws. [27,23] argue that in the next few years there will be a very high density of sensors and other smart mobile devices, and that the conventional service-oriented architecture will not be able to support such dynamic and large-scale systems. These nature-inspired architectures are very interesting theoretically, but there is no infrastructure that provides all the functional and non-functional requirements of a smart space. Instead of trying to evolve ambitious ecosystems of heterogeneous devices and computational elements, we are working on incorporating some of these nature-inspired algorithms to enhance the self-adaptive and self-healing capabilities of SeSaMe. We believe this approach to be more realistic and practical.

## 6    Conclusions and Future Work

This paper outlines SeSaMe, a semantic and self-adaptive middleware for large, dynamic smart spaces. SeSaMe extends the capabilities of A-3 by providing a distributed management layer, on top of the existing group-based coordination model, which takes care of autonomic organizational decisions. The management layer supports automated group formation, group self-configuration and self-healing, and congestion management. We provide a declarative language that one can use to define rules as to how SeSaMe should coordinate the evolution of the topology of the system. SeSaMe also addresses the issue of managing communication between heterogeneous components by providing a semantic layer, based on RDF, that simplifies the integration of different kinds of devices. We also presented two example smart spaces, with different functional and non-functional requirements, and explained how our proposed middleware can support various kinds of applications in different domains and situations.

As for future work, we intend to incorporate nature and bio-inspired computing techniques, to enhance the self-organization and self-adaptation capabilities of our middleware. For example, swarm intelligence follows the principle of having decentralized, coordinated, and self-organizing agents working autonomously for a greater goal. It resembles our approach, in the sense that we also believe that every system component should act autonomously, according to its role in the system, and to the components with which it is grouped. We are also interested in studying means to aggregate multiple smart spaces, and build smart digital cities in which we have many smart spaces interacting and sharing knowledge and services.

# References

1. Atzori, L., Iera, A., Morabito, G.: The Internet of Things: A survey. Computer Networks 54(15), 2787–2805 (2010)
2. Babaoglu, O., Canright, G., Deutsch, A., Caro, G.A., Ducatelle, F., Gambardella, L.M., Ganguly, N., Jelasity, M., Montemanni, R., Montresor, A., Urnes, T.: Design Patterns from Biology for Distributed Computing. ACM Transactions on Autonomous and Adaptive Systems 1(1), 26–66 (2006)
3. Cannata, A., Gerosa, M., Taisch, M.: Socrades: A Framework for Developing Intelligent Systems in Manufacturing. In: Proceedings of IEEE International Conference on Industrial Engineering and Engineering Management, pp. 1904–1908 (2008)
4. Castelli, G., Mamei, M., Rosi, A., Zambonelli, F.: Pervasive Middleware Goes Social: The SAPERE Approach. In: Proceeding of 5th IEEE Conference on Self-Adaptive and Self-Organizing Systems, Workshops, pp. 9–14 (2011)
5. Castelli, G., Mamei, M., Zambonelli, F.: The Changing Role of Pervasive Middleware: From Discovery and Orchestration to Recommendation and Planning. In: Proceedings of 9th IEEE International Conference on Pervasive Computing and Communications, Workshops, pp. 214–219 (2011)
6. Chen, H.: An Intelligent Broker Architecture for Pervasive Context-Aware Systems. PhD thesis, University of Maryland, Baltimore County (December 2004)
7. Chen, H., Finin, T., Joshi, A., Kagal, L., Perich, F., Chakraborty, D.: Intelligent Agents Meet the Semantic Web in Smart Spaces. IEEE Internet Computing 8(6), 69–79 (2004)
8. Cossentino, M., Gaud, N., Hilaire, V., Galland, S., Koukam, A.: Aspecs: An Agent-oriented Software Process for Engineering Complex Systems. Autonomous Agents and Multi-Agent Systems 20(2), 260–304 (2010)
9. Costa, P., Coulson, G., Gold, R., Lad, M., Mascolo, C., Mottola, L., Picco, G.P., Sivaharan, T., Weerasinghe, N., Zachariadis, S.: The RUNES Middleware for Networked Embedded Systems and Its Application in a Disaster Management Scenario. In: Proceedings of the Fifth IEEE International Conference on Pervasive Computing and Communications, pp. 69–78 (2007)
10. Fuentes-Fernandez, R., Guijarro, M., Pajares, G.: A Multi-Agent System Architecture for Sensor Networks. Sensors 9(12), 10244–10269 (2009)
11. Guinea, S., Saeedi, P.: Coordination of Distributed Systems through Self-Organizing Group Topologies. In: Proceedings of the 7th International Symposium on Software Engineering for Adaptive and Self-Managing Systems, pp. 63–72 (2012)
12. Gurgen, L., Roncancio, C., Labbé, C., Bottaro, A., Olive, V.: Streamware: A Service-oriented Middleware for Heterogeneous Sensor Data Management. In: Proceedings of the 5th International Conference on Pervasive Services, pp. 121–130 (2008)
13. Herold, S., Klus, H., Niebuhr, D., Rausch, A.: Engineering of IT Ecosystems: Design of Ultra-Large-Scale Software-Intensive Systems. In: Proceedings of the 2nd International Workshop on Ultra-large-scale Software-Intensive Systems, pp. 49–52 (2008)

14. Juan, P., Jorge, J.G., Rubén, F.: The INGENIAS Methodology and Tools. In: Agent-Oriented Methodologies, pp. 236–276. Idea Group Publishing (2005)
15. Kagal, L., Undercoffer, J., Perich, F., Joshi, A., Finin, T., Yesha, Y.: Vigil: Providing Trust for Enhanced Security in Pervasive Systems, NTIS Technical Report (2002)
16. Marsa-Maestre, I., Lopez-Carmona, M., Velasco, J., Paricio, A.: Mobile Devices for Personal Smart Spaces. In: Proceedings of the 21st International Conference on Advanced Information Networking and Applications Workshops, vol. 2, pp. 623–628 (2007)
17. Marsa-Maestre, I., Lopez-Carmona, M.A., Velasco, J.R.: A Hierarchical, Agent-based Service-oriented Architecture for Smart Environments. Service Oriented Computing and Applications 2(4), 167–185 (2008)
18. Miorandi, D., Carreras, I., Altman, E., Yamamoto, L., Chlamtac, I.: Bio-Inspired Approaches for Autonomic Pervasive Computing Systems. In: Liò, P., Yoneki, E., Crowcroft, J., Verma, D.C. (eds.) BIOWIRE 2007. LNCS, vol. 5151, pp. 217–228. Springer, Heidelberg (2008)
19. Raychoudhury, V., Cao, J., Kumar, M., Zhang, D.: Middleware for Pervasive Computing: A Survey. Pervasive Mobile Computing 9(2), 177–200 (2013)
20. Reyes Alamo, J., Wong, J.: Service-oriented Middleware for Smart Home Applications. In: Proceedings of IEEE Wireless Hive Networks Conference, pp. 1–4 (2008)
21. Spiess, P., Karnouskos, S., Guinard, D., Savio, D., Baecker, O., Souza, L., Trifa, V.: SoA-based Integration of the Internet of Things in Enterprise Services. In: Proceedings of the IEEE International Conference on Web Services, pp. 968–975 (2009)
22. Teixeira, T., Hachem, S., Issarny, V., Georgantas, N.: Service Oriented Middleware for the Internet of Things: A Perspective. In: Abramowicz, W., Llorente, I.M., Surridge, M., Zisman, A., Vayssière, J. (eds.) ServiceWave 2011. LNCS, vol. 6994, pp. 220–229. Springer, Heidelberg (2011)
23. Villalba, C., Rosi, A., Viroli, M., Zambonelli, F.: Nature-Inspired Spatial Metaphors for Pervasive Service Ecosystems. In: Proceedings of the 2nd IEEE International Conference on Self-Adaptive and Self-Organizing Systems, Workshops, pp. 332–337 (2008)
24. Weiser, M., Gold, R., Brown, J.S.: The Origins of Ubiquitous Computing Research at PARC in the Late 1980s. IBM System Journal 38(4), 693–696 (1999)
25. Wirsing, M., Hölzl, M., Tribastone, M., Zambonelli, F.: ASCENS: Engineering Autonomic Service-Component Ensembles. In: Beckert, B., Bonsangue, M.M. (eds.) FMCO 2011. LNCS, vol. 7542, pp. 1–24. Springer, Heidelberg (2012)
26. Yuebin, B., Haixing, J., Qingmian, H., Jun, H., Depei, Q.: Midcase: A Service-oriented Middleware Enabling Context-awareness for Smart Environment. In: Proceedings of International Conference on Multimedia and Ubiquitous Engineering, pp. 946–951 (2007)
27. Zambonelli, F., Viroli, M.: From Service-Oriented Architectures to Nature-Inspired Pervasive Service Ecosystems. In: Proceedings of the 11th National Workshop from Objects to Agents (2010)

# Propagating AUML Protocols
# to Detailed Design

Yoosef Abushark* and John Thangarajah

School of Computer Science and IT, RMIT University, Melbourne, Australia
{yoosef.abushark,john.thangarajah}@rmit.edu.au

**Abstract.** The interaction between agents is a key aspect of multi-agent systems. AUML sequence diagrams are commonly used to specify these interactions between agents in terms of *interaction protocols*. Whilst most of the popular agent oriented software engineering methodologies such as Prometheus, Tropos, O-MaSE, INGENIAS and GAIA support AUML protocol specifications in the design, the supportive tools do not provide any mechanisms for ensuring that the detailed design, and consequently the implementations, faithfully follow these protocols. In this paper, we show how AUML protocol specifications in the Prometheus methodology can be *automatically* propagated to the detailed design of the methodology by creating appropriate artefacts. The approach is general to all design methodologies that follow the BDI model of agents. We empirically show that the manual translation of protocols to the detailed design even for a simple AUML protocol can be a tedious and error-prone task for even relatively experienced users. The evaluation shows that our automated approach address these issues to a large extent.

**Keywords:** AOSE Methodology, Multi-agent system, Inter-Agent Interaction Protocols.

## 1 Introduction

Intelligent Agent Systems are gaining popularity for building complex applications such as Unmanned Aerial Vehicles [20] and Electronic trading agents [22]. Features such as autonomy, proactivity, flexibility, robustness and social ability, are what makes these multi-agent systems (MAS) suitable for developing applications that operate in highly dynamic environments. However, these very features also makes developing and testing multi-agent systems a difficult and challenging task.

A number of architectures have been proposed to developing MAS, in particular, the popular Belief-Desire-Intention (BDI) agent architecture [21] where agents are developed using mental attitudes of beliefs, goals, plans, events, and so on. A number of agent oriented software engineering (AOSE) methodologies have been proposed for designing and implementing systems based on the

---

* Aknowledges King Abdulaziz University for scholarship.

M. Cossentino et al. (Eds.): EMAS 2013, LNAI 8245, pp. 19–37, 2013.

BDI model of agency. Amongst them, Prometheus [17], Tropos[3], O-MaSE [7,6], INGENIAS [18] and GAIA[25,12] are some of the most commonly used.

In multi-agent systems inter-agent interaction plays a significant role. For example, in an agent-based trading system, the buyer and seller agents need to communicate with each other in order to complete a sale transaction. The above agent design methodologies allow the designers to capture these interactions in the form of *interaction protocols*. A common representation of interaction protocols, in the context of AOSE, is AUML (Agent Unified Modelling Language) sequence diagrams [15], as adopted by the above mentioned design methodologies. An AUML sequence diagram captures all the possible legal exchange of messages between agents including the temporal aspects.

Although most of the AOSE methodologies consider agent interaction protocols an essential part of the methodology, they provide little (if any) support for ensuring that the interaction protocols are faithfully translated from specification to the detailed design artefacts. It is up to the designer to ensure that the protocols are indeed followed by the system, which can be a tedious and error-prone task that often result in a mismatch between the specification and implementation.

In this paper we present an approach to address the above. In most of the AOSE methodologies, the *detailed design* (the lowest level) is the closest to implementation and often can be auto-generated to skeleton code. In this work, we provide a mechanism for automatically creating these detailed design structures from the AUML protocol specification. We base our approach on the Prometheus methodology. For example, in the Prometheus methodology the development of protocols occurs in the 'Architectural Design' phase, but they do not get mapped fully to the detailed design phase of each agent which will be eventually translated to skeleton code in the JACK agent language [23].

In the following section, we briefly describe the AUML protocol specification and how it relates to the current AOSE methodologies. We then describe some of our propagation mechanisms in Section 3 including the factors that influence the algorithms. We then evaluate our approach in Section 4 and show that even for a simple protocol, relatively experienced users take a considerable amount of time to manually translate protocols to implementation and also produce a number of errors in terms of not adhering to the protocol specification. Our approach overcomes these drawbacks and provides a significant time saving as well as a more reliable system with respect to protocols.

## 2   Background

AUML sequence diagrams are a popular way of representing protocols and has been adopted by many AOSE methodologies. There are however other approaches such as the Finite State Machine approach used in the work on Electronic Institutions [1].

In this section we briefly describe the AUML protocol notation and the current support for protocol development in some of the most common AOSE methodologies; Tropos, O-MaSE, INGENIAS, GAIA and Prometheus.

## 2.1   AUML Protocol Specification

AUML is an extension of the standard Unified Modelling Language (UML) used
in the object-oriented paradigm [15]. The purpose of AUML is to generate artefacts that support the development environment throughout the development
lifecycle. Even though the AUML notation supports the entire development life-
cycle, in this work we are only concerned with the AUML notation for modelling
agent interaction protocols. More specifically, the AUML sequence diagrams.

AUML sequence diagrams [13], also called a Protocol Diagrams [2], is one of
the dynamic AUML models that shows the flow of messages between agents and
the order of those messages. Agents that implement the protocol must be able to
send and receive the messages in the order specified. AUML sequence diagrams
are similar to UML sequence diagrams that are used in the Object-Oriented
paradigm. However, instead of having instances of objects as the main entities
of the diagram, agents (or agent roles) are the main entities [16].

In addition to message flow, AUML sequence diagrams also allow *constructs*
and *guards* to be specified. Constructs control the execution flow of messages
specified and guards specify when a particular sequence of messages is valid (or
not). The AUML sequence diagram has eight different constructs, as follows:

- ALT (alternative): can have multiple regions, with only one region that is
  executed based on the region's guard (the condition that must be true for the
  region to be executed). It is possible that none of the Alternative's regions
  get executed. To overcome such a situation, the 'else option' needs to be
  forced [13].
- OPT (option): is a single region that may or may not occur based on the
  guard of the construct.
- LOOP: indicates the repetition of a sequence of messages for a fixed number
  of iterations based on a number or a logical condition.
- BREAK: shows that the communication has been interrupted and termi-
  nated.
- STOP: indicates the end of the agent's lifeline.
- PAR (parallel): allows the communication to be made in parallel.
- REF (reference): enables the designer to include another sub-protocol within
  the modelled protocol by referring to the name of that sub-protocol.
- Continues [goto / label]: is used to control the execution of the sequence of
  a protocol through two directives: 'goto' and 'label'. The designer can make
  the sequence jump to a specific point within the protocol.

AUML sequence diagrams can be constructed in two ways; using either graphical
or textual notations [24]. Figure 1 shows a simple AUML sequence diagram in
both its graphical and textual notations. The figure illustrates the interaction
between two player agents in a gold mining game. 'Player:A' agent asks 'Player:B'
agent whether it has gold or not. The 'Player:B' agent may reply with either
'Yes' or 'No', based on the 'Carrying Gold' boolean predicate. Thus, the reply
is embedded in an 'ALT' construct.

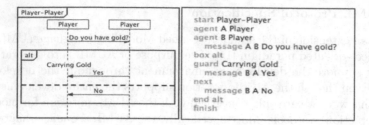

**Fig. 1.** AUML Sequence Diagram & Textual Notation

Whilst the graphical notation is an intuitive form to visualize the protocol, the textual notation is a structured way of constructing the protocol that is fast, easy to write and edit. In order to textually construct an AUML interaction protocol the written AUML textual notations must be well structured according to the rules specified in [24]. The Prometheus Design Tool (PDT) which supports the Prometheus design methodology allows the users to specify protocols using the textual notation and generates the visual diagram from it. We use the structured textual notation for implementing our protocol propagation techniques outlined in Section 3.

## 2.2 AOSE Methodologies and Protocols

In AOSE, there has been little research into ensuring the faithful implementation of protocol specifications. We consider here five of the most commonly used AOSE methodologies: Tropos, O-MaSE, INGENIAS, GAIA and Prometheus. Despite the fact that these methodologies do offer development environments through their supported tools, none of them adequately support the propagation of the interaction protocols to lower design levels. We explore each of them below:

***Tropos Methodology***: In Tropos, the interaction protocols are specified in AUML as a part of the capability modelling activity in the detailed design phase. The Tropos methodology has many tools to support the methodology [14] and help with generating the design artefacts. One of these is the TAOM4e tool [7]. This tool has a code generation feature that takes a detailed design and provides skeleton code in the JADE agent language [14].

The UML2JADE code generator, which is part of TAOM4e, is used to generate JADE agent code with respect to the agent interaction diagrams. The JADE agent code is generated through the transformation from the interaction diagrams meta-model to the JADE meta-model that leads to the creation of a XMI (XML Metadata Interchange) file that helps to produce the capability files [19]. This meta-model propagation is limited to propagating the messages exchanged between the agents within the protocol but does not enforce the ordering specified in the protocols which is the key contribution of the work we present. Given that no ordering is enforced, the AUML constructs are also not considered in the propagation.

Further, the limited transformation is done directly from the AUML specification to code, rather than to the lower design levels, which precludes the designer from being able to modify and control the protocol elements at a design level. For example, a plan that sends a particular message in a protocol may perform other tasks that need to be modelled at the design level.

**O-MaSE Methodology**: O-MaSE consists of three design phases: requirements, analysis and design. Protocol development occurs in the design stage which has seven tasks[9]: model agent classes, model protocols, model plans, model policies, model capabilities, model actions and model services. O-MaSE uses AUML sequence diagrams for modelling the interaction protocols between agents[6].

The O-MaSE methodology offers a development environment for developing agent-based systems through agentTool III (a$T^3$) [14]. a$T^3$ provides a complete code generation facility that produces an implementation skeleton code of the intended agent-based system according to the detailed models of that system[14]. However, it does not support the propagation of the modelled protocols to these detailed models [8].

**INGENIAS Methodology**: The INGENIAS methodology considers agent systems from five viewpoints: organisation, agent, goals/tasks, interactions and environment [18]. The designers are provided a set of concepts and relationships to describe each viewpoint in terms of design elements. These viewpoints represent the meta-models of the intended system. The definition of interaction protocols in this methodology is part of the interaction viewpoint designing process. Even though the methodology has its own notations (Grasia) for modelling protocols, it accepts AUML sequence diagrams to model the interactions [18].

The INGENIAS Development Kit (IDK) is an integrated development environment that supports the methodology's development life-cycle [10]. The tool provides code generation capability that transforms the system's meta-models into implementation code that targets the JADE platform [18]. Thus, the tool does not support the diagrammatic propagation of the design elements. Since the code generator can only identify the Grasia notations [11] and the IDK does not support the transformation of the AUML notations to Grasia, the propagation of AUML protocols is not supported in INGENIAS.

**GAIA Methodology**: The GAIA methodology enables agent designers to analyse and design an agent-based system through two main phases: the analysis and design phases[25]. In the analysis phase, the designers elicit all the possible entities of the intended system by using abstract concepts from the requirement statements. One of these entities is the roles that are needed in the system and the interaction between them[25]. Thus, two models result from the analysis phase: roles, which are later mapped to agents, and interaction models that capture the communication between agents in the system. In the design phase, the models derived from the analysis phases get detailed to a lower level of abstraction[25]. Three models are generated as the design phase's output as follows: the agent model, the service model and the acquaintance model that

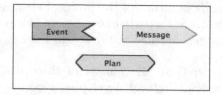

**Fig. 2.** PDT V 0.4 Notations Legend

defines the communication links between agents. Even though GAIA uses its own notations for modelling interaction protocols, the integration of AUML within the methodology has been recommended [4].

The GAIA for Eclipse designing tool (GAIA4E) aids the agent designers in documenting the activities of the methodology in terms of design artefacts [5]. The GAIA4E tool does not support the propagation of the created models, including the interaction models, in the earlier phases to the later phases of the methodology.

***Prometheus Methodology:*** The Prometheus methodology consists of three phases: the system specification phase, the architectural design phase and the detailed design phase [17].

In the system specification phase, a translation of the problem that the intended system needs to solve is done based on the user requirements. Briefly, the requirements are taken as an input and the initial picture of the system is drawn by defining the goals and the basic functionalities of the system. In this phase, the external entities (actors), system inputs (percepts) and system outputs (actions) of the intended system are defined. The primary output from this phase comprises two parts: system goals and scenarios.

The architectural design phase concerns the internal architecture of the system. Based on the system goals and scenarios from the previous phase, the roles and agent types of the system are determined. The system overview diagram captures the agents of the system, for each agent the events it handles and actions it generates, and the interaction protocols between those agents that communicate. Interaction protocols are modelled using AUML sequence diagrams.

In the detailed design phase, each agent type identified in the architectural design phase is designed in detail to fulfill its responsibilities according to the system overview diagram. Each agent has its own agent overview diagram where the agent is designed and detailed in terms of events, plans and belief sets.

The Prometheus Design Tool (PDT)[1] [16] is a graphical tool that supports each phase of the methodology and provides designers with many features, such as visual editing, type safety, information propagation, report generation, cross-checking, and so on [16]. The code generation feature transforms the detailed design to skeleton code in the JACK agent language [23].

In PDT, protocols are specified using the AUML textual notation and AUML diagrams are generated by the tool. PDT currently supports the propagation of

---

[1] The PDT version used in this paper is 0.4 (refer to Figure2 for the design notions).

**Fig. 3.** Single Message Propagation

the agent and message entities in a protocol to lower level design diagrams. The propagation of the protocol trigger, the sequence flow and protocol constructs are however not supported. The onus is on the designer to manually map these elements to the detailed design phase which will then be translated to code. In this paper, we present an approach for propagating complete AUML protocol specifications to the detailed design phase of the Prometheus methodology.

## 3   Propagation Mechanism

We now describe the mechanisms for propagating protocols from the AUML specification to the detailed design in the Prometheus methodology. Although, we chose Prometheus as the target methodology the approach is applicable to any approach that follows the general BDI model. In our approach we consider: (i) protocols that contain the ALT and OPT constructs only (including those with multiple such constructs), as they are two of the most commonly used protocol constructs; and (ii) simple AUML protocols without such constructs. We do not consider nested constructs at this stage which we leave as future work.

We begin by describing the factors that influence the propagation mechanisms and then describe the propagation mechanism by illustrating some examples.

### 3.1   The Factors

The automated protocol propagation task is to create the necessary design artefacts, that is, events and plans in the respective agent overview diagrams such that the sequence of message flow specified in the protocol (including constructs if any) is adhered to. The detailed design is then translated to code. There are three factors that influence the protocol propagation to the detailed design:

– protocol participants.
– protocol trigger.
– protocol sequence flow.

**Protocol Participants:** The messages in a protocol are between two participants (internal agents or actors that are external to the system) and there can be many participants in a single protocol.

Where a participant is denoted as an agent in the AUML textual notation (see Figure 1 for an example) an 'Agent' entity is created in the System Overview diagram, if it does not already exist. The details of each agent, that is, the

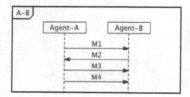

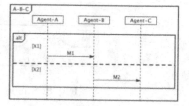

**Fig. 4.** AUML Protocol With No Constructs

**Fig. 5.** Protocol triggered by multiple agents

messages that it receives and sends, the data that it accesses and so on are detailed in the individual agent's Agent Overview diagram.

In a protocol an agent can play two roles: *Sender* or *Receiver* for a particular message. The sender agent needs to be able to send the message and the receiver agent needs to be able to receive and handle (act upon) the received message. The message therefore needs to be propagated into both the agents together with a plan in the sender agent that sends the message and a plan in the receiver agent to handle the message. For example, Figure 3 shows the propagation of a single message from one agent to another.

**Protocol Trigger:** The *protocol trigger* is the event (possibly external) that triggers the posting of the first message of the protocol, thus initiating the execution of the protocol. It is important to factor this into the protocol propagation. It is often the case that the protocol trigger is captured by the agent that sends the first message of the protocol. However, in some cases it may be captured by more than one agent.

For example, in Figure 4 the first message ('M1') is sent by 'Agent-A', hence, the protocol trigger would be captured only by 'Agent-A'. However, the first message of the protocol in Figure 5 might be 'M1' from 'Agent-A' or 'M2' from 'Agent-B' depending on the construct's guards. Hence, both agents need to capture the protocol's trigger with the guards propagated to the respective plans as *context conditions*[2] that handles the trigger of each agent.

**Protocol Sequence Flow:** The sequence flow of an interaction protocol is the execution order of the communication between the participants. Thus, the propagation of the interaction protocols must ensure this sequence flow. When there are multiple messages, there are 3 distinct cases that influence the propagation mechanism: (1) Multiple messages sent in sequence from one agent, (2) Participants exchange messages and (3) Protocol contains constructs (ALT/OPT).

*1. Multiple messages sent in sequence from one agent*
The first case is where an agent sends multiple messages to other agents continuously, for example, 'M3' and 'M4' in Figure 4. The significant point here is to

---

[2] Context conditions are logical conditions that determine the applicability of plans, much like pre-conditions in traditional planning systems.

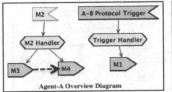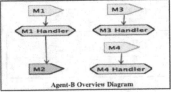

**Fig. 6.** Agent Overview diagrams for the protocol in Figure 3

ensure that 'Agent-A' posts these messages in the same order specified, in other words, 'Agent-A' must not post 'M4' before posting 'M3'.

Currently in the Prometheus methodology (and PDT) there is no mechanism for specifying such an ordering, hence we introduce a new notation, a dashed-arrow, between the messages indicating the order of posting. For example, see Figure 6 which illustrates the propagation for the protocol in Figure 4. In 'Agent-A' overview diagram, 'M3' is posted prior to 'M4'.

Note that, even if the messages were posted by different plans, we show the ordering of messages via dashed-arrows between messages rather than between the plans, as the protocol only specifies ordering of messages, not plans. Further, ordering the plans is too strict, unnecessary and possibly undesirable as the plans may contain steps other than the posting of the message and are often executed concurrently.

### 2. Participants exchange messages

The second situation is when the protocol participants exchange messages between each other. For example, see the order of messages 'M1', 'M2' and 'M3' in Figure 4. In this case, it is important to ensure that 'Agent-A' sends 'M3' after receiving 'M2' and that 'Agent-B' sends 'M2' after receiving 'M1'.

We enforce this ordering when messages are exchanged by having the plan that handles the incoming message post the outgoing message. For example, for the protocol in Figure 4, 'Agent-A' will have 'M1' posted by the protocol trigger handler plan as it is the first message of the protocol, and 'M3', 'M4' posted by the 'M2 Handler' plan. Similarly 'Agent-B' has a plan that handles 'M1' and posts 'M2', ensuring that ordering (see Figure 6).

### 3. Protocol contains a construct

The third situation arises when an interaction protocol contains a construct. In addition to enforcing the control specified in the construct (which we describe in the next subsection), having messages before and/or after a construct also affects the propagation mechanisms.

*Before:* If there are messages before the construct, then the last message before the construct is treated as the trigger for the construct which is created as an internal event. To illustrate this consider the protocol in Figure 7, which shows the protocol and the propagated 'Agent-A Overview Diagram'. The plan that posts the message 'M1' will also post an internal event 'ALT trigger' to trigger

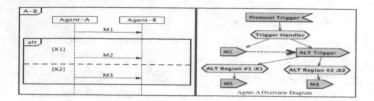

**Fig. 7.** Message before a construct

the ALT construct. This internal event is handled by two plans with the guards of the ALT construct posting 'M2' and 'M3' respectively.

*After:* In the cases where there are messages after a construct, the propagation mechanism needs to consider the fact that the construct in some instances may not occur. For example, in the protocol specified in Figure 8, if the guards 'X1' and 'X2' both evaluate to false, the ALT construct will not execute and the message flow should continue on past the construct.

Considering the direction of the first and last message of a construct's regions, the occurrence of messages before and after a construct and the direction of those messages, provides many combinations of unique cases to be considered when propagating protocols (though, some of the cases are uncommon and unlikely to appear in practice).

In developing the propagation techniques we discovered nineteen unique cases for a protocol with just an ALT construct, and twelve unique cases for the OPT construct. Due to spatial reasons we do not attempt to describe all these cases nor the full details of the algorithms in this paper. However, in order to illustrate the propagation algorithms we step through a particular example with an ALT construct in the next section. We also highlight a situation where designer intervention is necessary. For a full list of all the different cases including cases where a protocol contains multiple constructs we refer the reader to a detailed appendix which we have placed online (anonymously) at `http://tinyurl.com/propagation-cases`. Similarly, the algorithms in the form of pseudo-code can be found at `http://tinyurl.com/propagation-algorithms`.

## 3.2   ALT Construct Example

The ALT construct consists of at least two regions, each with its own execution condition (region guard). Only one of the construct's regions will be executed (possibly none). A region may have more than a single message within it, in which case the guard is applicable to the first message of the region. In this particular example, we consider the protocol shown in Figure 8 where the ALT construct is at the start of the protocol and there is a message that follows it. The complete Agent Overview diagrams generated by our propagation mechanism is shown in Figure 9.

The protocol propagation must consider the propagation factors discussed earlier: protocol participants, protocol trigger and protocol sequence flow.

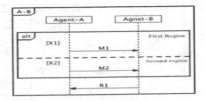

**Fig. 8.** AUML Protocol (ALT Example)

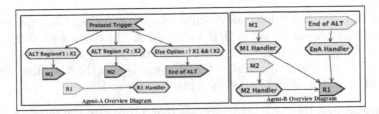

**Fig. 9.** Agent Overview Diagrams (ALT Example)

**The protocol participants** are propagated by creating 'Agent-A' and 'Agent-B' in the System Overview diagram.

**The protocol trigger** in this case triggers the ALT construct as it is at the start of the protocol. Given that the first message of both the regions in the ALT construct is sent from 'Agent-A', the trigger is propagated to the 'Agent-A Overview Diagram' as follows:

- A 'Protocol Trigger' event is created.
- Three plans are created to handle the trigger event: 'ALT Region#1' plan, 'ALT Region#2' plan and 'Else Option' plan. The first two plans are given as context conditions the guards of the respective ALT regions. The last plan is created to handle the case where neither of the ALT regions execute, hence the context condition is the negation of the conjunction of the two guards (that is, !(X1&&X2)).

**The sequence flow** is then considered. First the ALT construct is dealt with as follows:

- First, plans for dealing with the two regions of the ALT construct and a plan to handle the case when the construct does not get executed needs to be created. However, these were already created when propagating the protocol trigger.
- Each region contains just one message, each sent from 'Agent-A' to 'Agent-B'. Thus, messages 'M1' and 'M2' are added to the 'Agent-A Overview Diagram' and attached to the corresponding ALT region plans as messages posted. These messages are also added to the 'Agent-B Overview Diagram' as incoming messages and plans 'M1-Handler' and 'M2-Handler' are created to handle them.

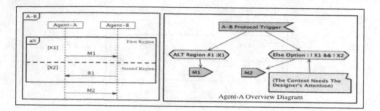

**Fig. 10.** Illustration of the Special Case

- If the ALT construct does not execute (else-option) then the sequence flow is such that 'Agent-B' sends 'R1' to 'Agent-A'. In order for this to occur, 'Agent-A' needs to notify 'Agent-B' that the ALT construct has ended. Hence, we add an event 'End of ALT' that is sent by the 'Else Option' plan in 'Agent-A' and handled by a plan in 'Agent-B'.

Having propagated the ALT construct, we then propagate the message 'R1' to 'Agent-B' as sent by all three plans that signifies the end of the ALT construct and to 'Agent-A' as an incoming message handled by plan 'R1-Handler'.

**A Special Case:** In the situation where the messages of the ALT regions are not sent in the same direction, for example as in Figure 10, forcing the else-option as done above presents the following challenge. The plan that enforces the else-option in 'Agent-A' for example, will have as the context the negation of both the guards. The guard 'X2' however, may be local to 'Agent-B' as the relevant message is sent from that agent. The designer therefore, needs to take this into consideration and ensure that the else-option plans do have access to the necessary guard conditions. To address this issue, the propagation algorithms create a *note*[3] attached to the else-option plan that face this issue, as shown in Figure 10.

## 4 Evaluation

In this section, we perform a simple evaluation to validate that:

- manually propagating protocols from specification to detailed design and subsequently code can be a time-costly and error-prone task; and
- our automated propagation mechanisms significantly reduces these costs.

We do this by creating a simple system with a basic protocol specification and have it propagated to the detailed design and code in two ways: (i) by using the proposed automated approach and (ii) by using two human participants that are relatively experienced in using Prometheus and the JACK agent language. The first participant was a recent graduate who had studied agent programming and

---

[3] A design artefact in PDT that allows the designer to attach comments to any entity in the design.

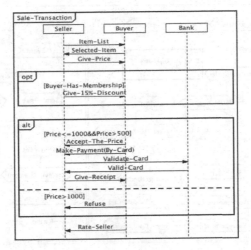

**Fig. 11.** Sale Transaction AUML Diagram

design, and had worked on projects across a year using PDT and JACK. The $2^{nd}$ participant had 2.5+ years experience as a software developer using PDT and JACK. We then compare the relative costs and examine the correctness of the different solutions.

## 4.1 Experimental Setup

We developed a prototype 'eTrading-System' as a multi-agent system with three agents; 'Seller Agent', 'Buyer Agent' and 'Bank Agent'. We specified one interaction protocol, *'Sale Transaction'* where the agents communicate with each other as shown in Figure 11. The system was designed in PDT up until the System Overview diagram. The task was then to complete the Agent Overview diagrams, auto-generate code, and complete the implementation. Completing the system code from the auto-generated code involves implementing:

- the context conditions of the plan[4].
- the body of the plan which posts the relevant messages.
- the protocol trigger that initiates the protocol.

The participants were given these instructions. Participants also tested and debugged their systems and finished when they were confident that their systems followed the protocol specification.

---

[4] If the context condition was specified in the design it would be propagated as a comment into the plan.

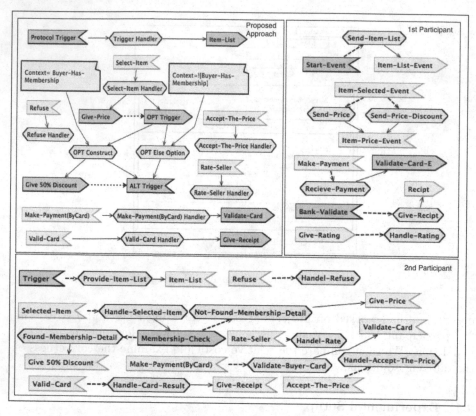

**Fig. 12.** Seller Overview Diagrams

In order to determine whether the automated approach does save development time, we observed the participants and recorded the following timing information:

- *Propagation time*: time taken for propagating the protocol to the detailed design phase (first draft).
- *Implementation time*: time taken for completing the code including the plans' contexts, plan bodies and protocol trigger.
- *Debugging time*: time taken for testing and debugging the completed system. This testing includes executing suitable test cases and when errors are found, fixing the agent's detailed design by adding and removing entities (events and plans). By *error* we mean, when the protocol is not followed. We also record here the number of iterations between code and design.

The implementation and execution of the systems were done locally on a client machine, without any external entities, such as servers. After all three systems ( the three versions of 'eTrading-System' that were developed by the two human participants and the proposed automated approach) were completed, we augmented the plans and agent code with log statements to keep track of the activity of the system.

**Table 1.** Time costs

| — | Automated | 1st | 2nd |
|---|---|---|---|
| **Propagation Time** | Instantaneous | 75 minutes | 50 minutes |
| **Implementation Time** | 30 minutes | 64 minutes | 80 minutes |
| **Testing & Debugging Time** | 25 minutes with 0 iteration | 130 minutes with 5 iterations | 120 minutes with 3 iteration |
| **Total Time** | 55 minutes | 296 minutes | 250 minutes |

**Table 2.** Number of errors in the systems

| Approach Used | Automated | 1st | 2nd |
|---|---|---|---|
| # Errors | 0 | 18 | 6 |

## 4.2  Results

Due to spatial reasons we do not attempt to show and analyze the detailed design of the agents produced in each of the three systems, however, in Figure 12 we present the Agent Overview digram of the 'Seller' agent as detailed in the three systems.

Table 1 shows the time-cost for developing the 3 systems. As evident from the results, even for the relatively simple protocol with just two constructs, there is a significant saving in development time when the automated propagation is used (over three hours of savings for even an experienced agent program developer like the $2^{nd}$ participant). For a system that contains a number of protocols, including more complex protocols than our test system, the time savings would indeed be much greater.

The marked difference is in the 'Propagation Time' and 'Debugging Time'. The propagation time is instantaneous using the automated approach, whilst the manual propagation by the human participants took over an hour for each.

The debugging time when using the automated approach is for testing the system. As the tests did not result in any errors, there were no iterations between code and design. This was not the case for the manual propagation by the test participants.

Note that, neither of the propagation time nor the number of iterations between code and design for debugging will increase as the number of protocols increase when using the automated approach[5]. However, they will increase (on average linearly) with the number of protocols when manually propagating.

We see that there is also a significant saving (more than 50%) in 'Implementation Time' when using the automated approach. This is due to the fact that the protocol trigger and context conditions of plans are propagated to the detailed design from the protocol specification. The overhead for the test participants was to figure these aspects out.

---

[5] There may be exceptional situations where protocol specific debugging is required.

### 4.3   Error Analysis

To test whether the implemented systems did indeed follow the protocol specification, we ran each system with 6 different test cases that represent the 6
different sequence flows[6] as specified by the protocol. By following the activity
logs and cross-checking with the protocol specification we determined if there
were any errors in the test execution and recorded these errors. We considered
the following as errors in the interaction:

- if any message that is expected to be sent is not sent.
- if any message that is expected to be sent once gets sent many times.
- if any message sent is not handled.

Table 2 shows the total number of errors detected in testing the three systems.
As shown, the system that followed the automated propagation mechanisms produced no errors, which validates the correctness of the propagation algorithms
for the protocol specified. The systems developed by the test participants however, produced 18 and 6 errors, respectively. As with the time-costs we would
expect these errors to increase with an increase in the number of protocols and
their complexity.

**Cause of errors:** The first participant made errors in handling the sequence
flow between the OPT and ALT construct and also did not implement some of
the messages in the protocol as messages.

His implementation was such that after the 'Give-Price' message is sent, the
ALT is always triggered. The ALT is also triggered after the OPT gets executed,
thus executing the ALT construct twice (resulting in 6 errors). In our proposed
approach, we avoid this issue by creating an event that triggers the OPT and
ALT constructs appropriately (similar to what is described in Section 3.2).

There were also two messages ('Accept-The-Price' and 'Refuse') that were not
implemented as messages in the system, instead they were embedded as business
logic in plans (resulting in 12 errors).

The more experienced second participant also made a few mistakes. His implementation resulted in the message before the OPT ('Give-Price') and the OPT
construct being exclusive. This meant that only one of them ever got executed,
even though, both should be executed in the case where the guard of the OPT
is true. In our proposed approach the plan that posts the 'Give-Price' message
also posts a trigger for the OPT construct which is handled by a plan that gets
executed only if the guard of the OPT is true.

We note also that there were several mismatches between the design and the
code for both participants.

## 5   Conclusion

Interaction between agents is a central aspect of multi-agent systems. AUML
sequence diagrams are a popular means for specifying these interactions and

---

[6] There are 3 guards that result in 6 different combinations.

is the adopted model in current AOSE methodologies. The lack of support for propagating these protocols to more detailed design level of these methodologies, means that the onus is on the designers to ensure that the protocols are faithfully implemented. In this paper, we showed empirically that this manual propagation of protocols is a time consuming and error-prone task even for a relatively experienced agent system programmer.

To overcome the above, in this paper we proposed an approach for automating the process of propagating the protocol specifications to the detailed design levels in the Prometheus methodology. We identified the factors that influence the propagation, the different cases that the mechanism needs to consider and the algorithms that performs the automated propagation. This approach can be extended to other AOSE methodologies that follow the BDI model of agency.

The evaluation that we conducted showed that by automating this process, the development time is significantly reduced and the resulting system is more reliable than the manual process. Whilst the evaluation was not comprehensive in terms of the number of participants and variation of protocol specifications, it provided a good indication of the kind of benefits that our automated approach provides and the difficulty of the manual propagation. We note that, one of the participants was an experienced programmer and hence envisage novice programmers to encounter much more difficulty. Further, the test system contained a single protocol, with just two constructs. It is fair to assume that a larger system with many more protocols, some, more complex, will see a greatly increased benefit in adopting such an automated approach.

In this work, we only considered two of the AUML protocol constructs in our propagation mechanisms. As future work, we will extend this to all the constructs and also consider nested protocol structures. In addition, we will find ways to overcome the 'Special Case' in section 3.2 . Currently, we do not check for the correctness of the protocol specification before we perform the propagation. Hence, errors in specification will result in errors in the detailed design and subsequently the implementation.

We are investigating mechanisms by which we can check the validity of the protocol specification. specifically, in the case where the system has multiple protocols, as conflicting specifications amongst protocols may occur. In our approach, we did not consider timeouts, which are important for some systems, we will investigate how timeouts may be handled. Further, as future work we will investigate the issue of scalability and performance of our approach which we do not address in this work.

## References

1. Arcos, J., Esteva, M., Noriega, P., Rodríguez-Aguilar, J., Sierra, C.: An integrated development environment for electronic institutions. In: Software Agent-Based Applications, Platforms and Development Kits, pp. 121–142 (2005)
2. Bergenti, F., Poggi, A.: Exploiting UML in the design of multi-agent systems. In: Omicini, A., Tolksdorf, R., Zambonelli, F. (eds.) ESAW 2000. LNCS (LNAI), vol. 1972, pp. 106–113. Springer, Heidelberg (2000)

3. Bresciani, P., Perini, A., Giorgini, P., Giunchiglia, F., Mylopoulos, J.: Tropos: An agent oriented software development methodology. Autonomous Agents and Multi-Agent Saytems 8(3), 203–236 (2004)

4. Cernuzzi, L., Zambonelli, F.: Experiencing AUML in the GAIA methodology. In: Proceedings of the 6th ICEIS, pp. 283–288. Citeseer (2004)

5. Cernuzzi, L., Zambonelli, F.: GAIA4e: A tool supporting the design of mas using gaia. In: ICEIS (4), pp. 82–88 (2009)

6. DeLoach, S., Oyenan, W., Garcia-Ojeda, J., Valenzuela, J.: O-MaSE: A customizable approach to developing multiagent development processes (2007)

7. DeLoach, S., Padgham, L., Perini, A., Susi, A.: Using three AOSE toolkits to develop a sample design. International Journal of Agent-Oriented Software Engineering 3(4), 416–476 (2009)

8. Garcia-Ojeda, J., DeLoach, S., et al.: agentTool III: from process definition to code generation. In: Proceedings of the 8th International Conference on Autonomous Agents and Multi-Agent Saytems, vol. 2, pp. 1393–1394. International Foundation for Autonomous Agents and Multi-Agent Saytems (2009)

9. Garcia-Ojeda, J.C., DeLoach, S.A., Robby, Oyenan, W.H., Valenzuela, J.: O-maSE: A customizable approach to developing multiagent development processes. In: Luck, M., Padgham, L. (eds.) Agent-Oriented Software Engineering VIII. LNCS, vol. 4951, pp. 1–15. Springer, Heidelberg (2008)

10. Gomez-Sanz, J., Fuentes, R., Pavón, J., García-Magariño, I.: INGENIAS development kit: a visual multi-agent system development environment. In: Proceedings of the 7th International Joint Conference on Autonomous Agents and Multi-Agent Saytems: Demo Papers, pp. 1675–1676. International Foundation for Autonomous Agents and Multi-Agent Saytems (2008)

11. Gómez-Sanz, J.J., Pavón, J.: Implementing multi-agent systems organizations with INGENIAS. In: Bordini, R.H., Dastani, M., Dix, J., El Fallah Seghrouchni, A. (eds.) PROMAS 2005. LNCS (LNAI), vol. 3862, pp. 236–251. Springer, Heidelberg (2006)

12. Gorodetsky, V., Karsaev, O., Samoylov, V., Konushy, V.: Support for analysis, design, and implementation stages with MASDK. In: Luck, M., Gomez-Sanz, J.J. (eds.) AOSE 2008. LNCS, vol. 5386, pp. 272–287. Springer, Heidelberg (2009)

13. Huget, M.-P., Odell, J.: Representing agent interaction protocols with agent UML. In: Odell, J.J., Giorgini, P., Müller, J.P. (eds.) AOSE 2004. LNCS, vol. 3382, pp. 16–30. Springer, Heidelberg (2005)

14. Morandini, M., Nguyen, D.C., Perini, A., Siena, A., Susi, A.: Tool-supported development with tropos: The conference management system case study. In: Luck, M., Padgham, L. (eds.) AOSE 2007. LNCS, vol. 4951, pp. 182–196. Springer, Heidelberg (2008)

15. Odell, J.J., Van Dyke Parunak, H., Bauer, B.: Representing agent interaction protocols in UML. In: Ciancarini, P., Wooldridge, M.J. (eds.) AOSE 2000. LNCS, vol. 1957, pp. 121–140. Springer, Heidelberg (2001)

16. Padgham, L., Thangarajah, J., Winikoff, M.: Prometheus design tool. In: Proceedings of the 23rd AAAI Conference on AI, pp. 1882–1883 (2008)

17. Padgham, L., Winikoff, M.: Developing intelligent agent systems: a practical guide, vol. 1. Wiley (2004)

18. Pavón, J., Gómez-Sanz, J.J.: Agent oriented software engineering with INGENIAS. In: Mařík, V., Müller, J.P., Pěchouček, M. (eds.) CEEMAS 2003. LNCS (LNAI), vol. 2691, pp. 394–403. Springer, Heidelberg (2003)

19. Penserini, L., Perini, A., Susi, A., Mylopoulos, J.: From stakeholder intentions to software agent implementations. In: Martinez, F.H., Pohl, K. (eds.) CAiSE 2006. LNCS, vol. 4001, pp. 465–479. Springer, Heidelberg (2006)
20. Pěchouček, M., Mařík, V.: Industrial deployment of multi-agent technologies: Review and selectedcase studies. Journal of Autonomous Agents and Multi-Agent Systems 17, 397–431 (2008)
21. Rao, A., Georgeff, M., et al.: BDI agents: From theory to practice. In: Proceedings of the First International Conference on Multi-Agent Systems (95), San Francisco, pp. 312–319 (1995)
22. Wellman, M.P., Greenwald, A., Stone, P.: Autonomous Bidding Agents: Strategies and Lessons from the Trading Agent Competition. MIT Press (2007)
23. Winikoff, M.: JACK intelligent agents: An industrial strength platform. In: Multi-Agent Programming, pp. 175–193 (2005)
24. Winikoff, M.: Towards making agent UML practical: a textual notation and a tool. In: Fifth International Conference on Quality Software, pp. 401–406 (2005)
25. Wooldridge, M., Jennings, N., Kinny, D.: The GAIA methodology for agent oriented analysis and design. Autonomous Agents and Multi-Agent Saytems 3(3), 285–312 (2000)

# 2COMM: A Commitment-Based MAS Architecture

Matteo Baldoni, Cristina Baroglio, and Federico Capuzzimati

Università degli Studi di Torino — Dipartimento di Informatica
c.so Svizzera 185, I-10149 Torino (Italy)
{matteo.baldoni,cristina.baroglio,federico.capuzzimati}@unito.it

**Abstract.** Social expectations and social dependencies are a key characteristic of interaction, which should be explicitly accounted for by the agent platform, supporting the coordination of the involved autonomous peers. To this aim, it is necessary to provide a normative characterization of coordination and give a social meaning to the agents' actions. We focus on one of the best-known agent platforms, Jade, and show that it is possible to account for the social layer of interaction by exploiting commitment-based protocols, by modifying the Jade Methodology so as to include the new features in a seamless way, and by relying on the notion of artifact, along the direction outlined in the Mercurio proposal.

**Keywords:** Commitment-based Interaction Protocols, Agents & Artifacts Model, JADE, JADE Methodology, Agent-Oriented Software Engineering.

## 1 Introduction and Motivation

Interaction creates *social expectations* and *dependencies* in the involved partners [38,18,34,23]. These should be explicitly accounted for by the *agent platform* to allow the coordination of autonomous entities. In order to create social expectations on the agents' behavior, it is necessary to introduce a *normative* characterization of coordination and give a social meaning to their actions. An agent that understands such a specification and that publicly accepts it (i.e. that declares it will behave according to it) allows reasoning about its behavior [21]. This is the key to the development of open environment systems, made of autonomous and heterogeneous components. By not supplying such abstractions, current platforms do not supply agents the means for *observing* or *reasoning* about such meanings of interaction, and do not supply the designers the means to explicitly *express* and *characterize* them when developing an interaction model.

One prominent example is JADE [10,11], which is a well-established development environment for multi-agent systems, FIPA-compliant and actually used for industrial applications, and which notoriously does not provide of a social and observational semantics. One of the aims of the Mercurio framework [4,3] is to fill this gap by introducing in JADE the means for exploiting *commitments* and *commitment-based protocols*, which are well-known for featuring the social

M. Cossentino et al. (Eds.): EMAS 2013, LNAI 8245, pp. 38–57, 2013.

and observational semantics [34,35,41], JADE lacks of. Our starting point for introducing commitment-based protocols inside JADE is the JADE Methodology [30]. This methodology is particularly interesting because it is intrinsically agent-oriented and it is not the adaptation of an object-oriented methodology, and it combines a top-down approach with a bottom-up one, possibly allowing the integration with legacy, non agent-based systems. It concerns two of the four main phases of the standard software development cycle: the *analysis phase* and the *design phase*.

Following [4], we rely on a form of indirect communication among agents that envisages the use of *artifacts*: commitment-based communication artifacts implement interaction protocols as well as monitoring functionalities for the verification that the on-going interaction respects the protocol, for detecting violations and violators, and so forth. Artifacts, therefore, encode the social layer of the multi-agent system: as a programmable communication channel an artifact contains what in the terminology of commitment protocols is called "the social state", and captures it as an interaction session among the parties. Artifacts also supply agents the social actions that are necessary to the interaction – that is, actions that allow agents to enter into and to comply with commitments – together with their social meaning and, as a consequence, they capture the coordination rules of the protocol. The reification of commitment protocols allows agents to act on them, e.g. to examine them (for instance, to decide whether to play one of the foreseen roles), use them (which entails that they explicitly accept the corresponding regulation), negotiate their construction, specialize them, and compose them. The advantage of relying on indirect communication is that it allows more variegated ways of interacting, not hindering message exchange when necessary.

In this paper we show that our proposal can be integrated *seamlessly* within the JADE Methodology, simply by substituting the selection of JADE FIPA protocols with the selection/construction of appropriate communication artifacts. We also use the methodology to show the differences between these two alternatives with the help of an example from a financial setting.

Section 2 reports the relevant background, necessary to understand the proposal. Section 3 is the core of the paper, containing the original proposal. Section 4 applies the concepts to an illustrative example, from a financial setting. A discussion also involving related works ends the paper.

## 2   Background

We briefly report the technical, methodological and theoretical background required for our work. We use the proposal in [4] as a high-level reference architecture. In this work, the authors outline the basic ideas for an interaction-oriented agent framework, grounding the social semantics of interaction on commitments, and proposing the A&A (Agents and Artifacts) Metamodel as a means to obtain a form of indirect, observable communication. Let us, then, explain the fundamental bricks to build our architecture, whose overview is reported in Figure 1.

*JADE framework.* JADE is a popular and industry adopted agent framework. It offers to developers a Java middleware 100% FIPA-compliant (Foundation for Intelligent Physical Agents, [1]) plus a set of command-line and graphical tools, supporting development and debugging/testing activities. Its robustness and well-proven reliability makes JADE a preferred choice in developing MAS. It is currently used in many research and industrial projects jointly with its most popular and promising extension, WADE [17]. A JADE-based system is composed of one or more *containers*, each grouping a set of agents in a logical *node* and representing a single JADE runtime. The overall set of containers is called a *platform*, and can spread across various physical hosts. The resulting architecture hides the underlying layer, allowing support for different low-level frameworks (JEE, JSE, JME, etc.). The platform reference container is called *main container*, and represents the entry point to the system. JADE provides communication and infrastructure services, allowing agents, deployed in different containers, to discover and interact with each other, in a transparent way from the developer's logical point of view.

*Commitment Protocols.* Agents share a social state that contains commitments and other literals that are relevant to their interaction. A *commitment* $C(x, y, r, p)$ denotes a contractual relationship between a debtor $x$ and a creditor $y$: $x$ commits to $y$ to bring about the consequent condition $p$ when the antecedent condition $r$ holds. A commitment, when active, functions as a directed obligation from a debtor to a creditor. However, unlike a traditional obligation, a commitment may be manipulated, e.g., delegated, assigned, or released [37]. Importantly, commitments have a regulative value: the social expectation is that agents respect the commitments which involve them and, in particular, the debtor is considered responsible of realizing the consequent condition. Thus, the agents' behavior is affected by the commitments that are present in the social state. A *commitment protocol* usually consists of a set of actions, whose semantics is shared (and agreed upon) by all of the interacting agents [41,40,20]. The semantics of the social actions is given in terms of operations which modify the social state by, e.g., adding a new commitment, releasing another agent from some commitment, satisfying a commitment, see [41].

*CArtAgO.* CArtAgO is a framework based on the A&A model. It extends the agent programming paradigm with the first-class entity of *artifact*: a resource that an agent can use, and that models working environments ([32]). In order to properly model a MAS, CArtAgO proposes to explicitly model the environment where pro-active agents live, work, act and communicate. It provides a way to define and organize *workspaces*, logical groups of artifacts, that can be joined by agents at runtime and where agents can create, use, share and compose artifacts to support individual and collective, cooperative or antagonistic activities. The environment is itself programmable as a dynamic first class abstraction, it is an active part of a MAS, encapsulating services and functionalities. The A&A model decouples the notion of agent from the notion of environment. The overall engineering of the MAS results more flexible, easy to understand, modular and reusable. CArtAgO provides an API to program *artifacts* that agents can use, regardless of the agent programming language or the agent framework used. This is possible by means of the *agent body* metaphor: CArtAgO provides a native agent entity, which allows using the framework as a complete MAS platform as well as it allows mapping the agents of some platform onto the CArtAgO agents, which, in this way, becomes a kind of "proxy" in the artifacts workspace. The developed agent is the mind, that uses the CArtAgO agent as a body, interacting with artifacts and sensing the environment. An agent interacts with an artifact by means of public *operations*. An operation can be equipped with a *guard*: a condition that must hold so that the operation will produce its effects. It is not an execution condition: when the guard does not hold the action is performed anyhow but without consequences.

## 3   Reifying Commitment Protocols with Artifacts

Artifacts naturally lend themselves to provide a suitable means for realizing mediated communication channels among agents. To this aim, it is necessary to encode inside the communication artifacts a normative characterization to the actions it offers to agents and that allow them to interact. We propose to interpret commitment protocols as environments, within which agents interact. The public interface of artifacts allows agents to examine the encoded interaction protocol. As a consequence, the act of using an artifact can be interpreted as a declaration of acceptance of the coordination rules. This will generate social expectations about the agent's behavior and agrees with the characterization of norms in [21]. Moreover, the fact that the behavior of agents on artifacts is observable and that interactions only occur through artifacts, agrees with the view that regulations can only concern observable behavior [22]. The resulting programmable environment provides a flexible communication channel that is suitable for realizing open systems. Notice that the use of a programming environment does not mean that the social state will necessarily be centralized: an artifact can be composed by a distributed network of artifacts.

Figure 1 sketches the way in which we propose to use CArtAgO so as to account also for social commitments inside JADE. We named this first realization of the Mercurio architecture *2COMM* (standing for "Communication & Commitment"). 2COMM realizes mediated interaction by means of communication artifacts, which, in our proposal, replace the JADE-based FIPA protocols and which reify commitment-based protocols [4]. At the bottom level, the JADE framework supplies standard agent services: message passing, distributed containers, naming and yellow pages services, agent mobility. When needed, an agent can *enact* a certain protocol role, thus using a communication artifact by CArtAgO. This provides a set of operations by means of which agents participate in a mediated interaction session. Each artifact (protocol enactment) maintains a *social state*, that is, a collection of *social facts* and *commitments* involving the roles of the corresponding protocol, following Yolum and Singh's commitment protocol model [40].

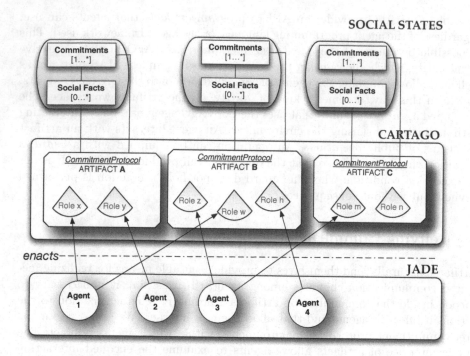

**Fig. 1.** A sketch of 2COMM

## 3.1  Communication Artifact

We follow the ontological model for organizational roles proposed in [13,14], which is characterized by three aspects: (1) *Foundation*: a role must always be associated with an institution it belongs to and with its player; (2) *Definitional dependence*: the definition of the role must be given inside the definition of the institution it belongs to; (3) *Institutional empowerment*: the actions defined for the role in the definition of the institution have access to the state of the institution and of the other roles, thus, they are called *powers*; instead, the actions that a player must offer for playing a role are called *requirements*.

Communication artifacts realize a kind of mediated interaction that is guided by commitment-based protocols. Figure 2 shows the UML schema of the super-type of communication artifacts implementing specific interaction protocols (e.g., Contract Net, Net Bill, Brokering): the *CommitmentCommunicationArtifact*. We call an instance of an artifact of type CommitmentCommunicationArtifact an *interaction session*. It represents an on-going protocol interaction, with a specific social state that is observable by the interacting agents, that play the protocol roles. The CommitmentCommunicationArtifact presents an observable property, *enactedRoles*, that is the collection of the roles of the protocol (definitional dependence [13,14]). Actions have a social effect only when they are executed by the

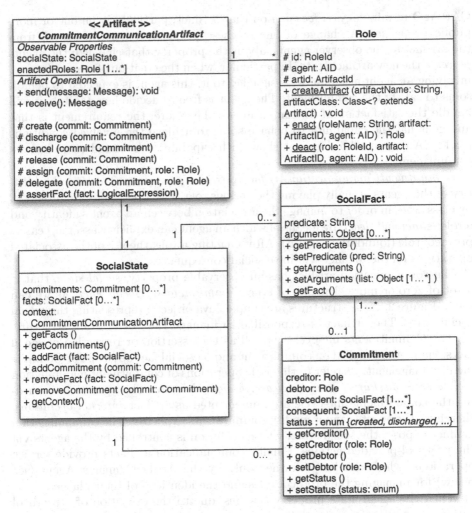

**Fig. 2.** The UML Class diagram for the core of 2COMM

role they are assigned to, but actions are not defined at this super level, rather they are provided by the instantiations of the CommitmentCommunicationArtifact, i.e. by artifacts implementing specific protocols. Each protocol action is implemented as a public *operation*, which is associated to a role by means of an *operation guard* (institutional empowerment [13,14]): the guard checks who is performing the operation; if the agent is not the one playing the right role, the action simply has no effect, otherwise, the fact that the action was executed is registered in the social state together with its meaning. An action can have some additional guards, implementing *context preconditions*: this condition specifies the context in which it makes sense that the action produces the described social effect. An artifact can be monitored by an observer agent, that, following the

CArtAgO terminology, is *focusing* on that artifact, particularly on one or more public properties. A change of one of these properties causes a *signal*, from the artifact to the observer agents, about the property that changed: the agents *perceive* the new artifact state. In particular, when the creation of a commitment, involving an agent as a debtor, is signaled to it, this agent is expected to behave so as to satisfy the commitment. The agent is free to decide how (and if) it will handle the satisfaction of its commitments. Therefore, the requirement is that an agent has the capability to behave so as to achieve the involved conditions [13,14]. An agent who does not show such capabilities is bound to violate its commitments.

*CommitmentCommunicationArtifact* provides a property, tracking the identity of the agents actually playing the various role. Two operations are provided, by class *Role*, in order to manage the association between an agent's identity and a role: *enact* and *deact*, by means of which an agent can explicitly assume/cease a protocol role (foundation [13,14]). After enacting a role, the use of the associated operations on the artifact will have social consequences.

The communication artifact has an observable property, *social state*, that is a set of zero or more elements of type *Commitment* or *Social Fact*. As we can see in Figure 2, these structures are simple Java objects, representing the actual social state. The artifact is responsible to manage the Social State structure, i.e. the Commitments life-cycle, as well as the assertion or retraction of social facts, via methods called on commitment and on social fact objects. For Commitment management, we refer to the basic operations of commitment manipulation [40]: *create, discharge, cancel, release, assign, delegate*. The operations regarding the commitments life-cycle are implemented as artifact *internal operations*, therefore, the agents cannot modify commitments explicitly. The communication artifact exposes the social state, whose evolution is controlled by the agents via the protocol-provided actions. Finally, communication artifacts provide service operations, which can be performed only by the ArtifactManager Agent (see below) for managing the protocol roles and the identities of their players.

When the social state property changes, due to the execution of a protocol action (an artifact operation) on the communication artifact, all of the agents using the artifact will be notified, allowing them to react (or not) to the evolution of the interaction. This mechanism is a core part of the CArtAgO framework.

The *ArtifactManager Agent* plays the role of a Yellow Pages Agent for communication artifacts, or, in other terms, of an artifact broker. It has a crucial role: it is a "communication channel" broker, gathering requests for both focused or broadcasting calls for interaction. As such, it provides a collection of utility services. It supplies information about the interaction protocols (e.g. it provides the XML describing a given protocol, it allows a search for a protocol, a list of active communication channels, a list of interacting agents); it answers to requests about the status of an existing interaction session; it notifies the subscriber agents a particular session availability, and so on. Its main purpose is to prepare the communication artifact among the interacting agents, and to supply it to the requesting agents. It can also enable other interested agents to monitor, audit, or, more generally, observe the social state evolution. The communications between the ArtifactManager Agent and the requesting agents is realized via FIPA-ACL messages: when a requester sends a request ACL message to the ArtifactManager Agent, specifying the protocol and the role it wants to enact, the latter will do the following steps:

1. Check if the requested protocol is available;
2. Check if the requested role is foreseen by the protocol;
3. Create/retrieve a communication artifact of the requested type;
4. Set the requested artifact role field to the agent identifier (AID) of the requester;
5. Respond to the requester with the artifact's reference;
6. Possibly inform other interested agents of the availability of the communication artifact.

The initialization procedure is modeled as a simple FIPA Request Interaction Protocol, where the content of messages consists of the communication artifact request parameters. After this phase, the agent can use the *enact* operation to start playing the requested role. The use of an agent does not necessarily imply a centralization of the yellow pages: agents may directly create communication artifacts; yellow pages can be federated.

## 3.2  Using Mediated Communication at Runtime

In the following, we show a scenario in which a communication artifact is used, to better explain how to leverage the communication artifacts and the Artifact-Manager Agent. We adopt the well-known FIPA Contract Net Protocol (CNP), modeling it as a commitment-based protocol and implementing a corresponding artifact. The scenario is depicted in Figure 3.

The JADE infrastructure is extended with the ArtifactManager Agent, that provides a Yellow Pages service for communication artifacts. It can respond to ACL Messages, that encode requests of a new Communication Atifact, either with a *Failure* message or an *Agree* message. In the latter case, it will either prepare a new instance of the requested communication artifact, or it will return an already existing artifact. For instance, suppose that agent *A1* has to assign a task, and agents *A2* and *A3* have the capability of performing it. Suppose that *A2* and *A3* already registered to the ArtifactManager Agent (*ArA* for brevity), and that this has already instantiated a Contract Net Protocol communication artifact (*CNPCA* for brevity). At this time, the (partial) state of *CNPCA* is:

- **Initiator:** null
- **Participants:** {A2.*AID*, A3.*AID*}

where *AID* is the JADE Agent Identifier. *A1*, then, asks *ArA* for a *CNPCA*, following the procedure described before, without specifying a particular participant. *ArA* matches this request with the already prepared *CNPCA*: the match

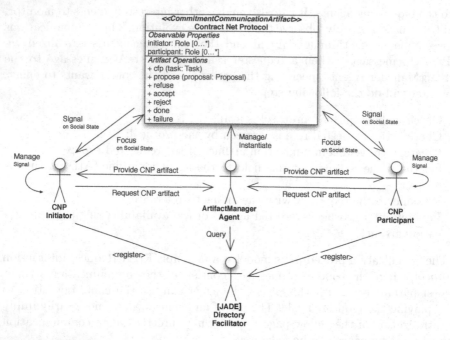

**Fig. 3.** Possible interactions between the main elements of our proposal, in a CNP example

is successful, inasmuch the Initiator role is not played by any agent. So, *ArA* stores *A1.AID* in the *Initiator* property of *CNPCA*, and returns its reference to *A1*. Following the CArtAgO terminology, agents *A1, A2* and *A3 focus on* the *SocialState* property of *CNPCA* immediately after having its reference. This means that any change to the social state will be signaled to the three agents, who can take decisions accordingly. The agents interact with one another via operations on *CNPCA*, and observe the social state evolution in order to reason about which actions to take.

An agent can stop playing a protocol role at anytime by executing the *deact* operation. The artifact unregisters its AID from the AID-role mapping list. On the other hand, an agent may enact a partially executed role within an interaction session. What about commitments in such cases? In this work we focused only on the communicational and interaction-related aspects of playing protocol roles: sanctions or other action concerning the institutional (or organizational) levels are not accounted for yet. Simply, since responsibilities are associated to roles, deacting a role yields that the resigning agent will not need anymore to fulfill them, while a substituting agent needs to accept the current commitments of the role it is assuming [40]. A reference model to include, in the future, also institutional aspects could be the JaCaMo proposal [15].

## 3.3  Using Mediated Communication at Design Time

We assume that MAS designers know a collection of communication artifacts, each representing a commitment-based protocol. Each protocol is enriched with an XML-based description of it, a *Protocol Manual*, available both at design- and at run-time. It is an add-on to the CArtAgO artifact manual, with orthogonal scopes and purposes. It can be used by MAS and agent designers as a guideline for understanding whether an agent is suitable for a protocol role as well as for understanding whether a protocol role suits the purposes of an agent. From a methodological point of view, the designer needs the Protocol Manual to know the social consequences of the actions supplied by an artifact, in terms of social facts and commitments, so he/she can design agent behaviors accordingly. Then, depending on the implemented behavior, the agent will decide how to use information about the social state evolution, how to fulfill commitments, which social action (i.e. a public artifact operation) to execute and when. Ideally, the designer should equip the agent with the behaviors that are necessary to bring about the conditions of the commitments it will possibly take. This protocol-centric design, jointly with the commitment nature of protocols, avoids a critical facet of JADE protocols. Here, a pattern of interaction is projected on a set of JADE behaviors, one for each role, thus making a global view of the protocol and its maintenance difficult, and binding the very interaction to ad-hoc behaviors. Consequently, the risk of conflicting behaviors, not devised at design time, increases. This way, the designer can leverage a library of programmable communication artifacts, focusing on the internal agent behavior without being concerned about ad-hoc shaped communication behaviors.

## 4  JADE Methodology Revised

The JADE Methodology is a JADE founded agent-oriented software engineering methodology. It proposes a fully agent-based approach, instead of adapting Object-Oriented techniques (like MASE [39], Adelfe [12] or MESSAGE [16]). It concerns the *analysis* and the *design* phases of the software development life cycle. The methodology considers agents as "pieces of autonomous code, able to communicate with each other" [30], thus following a weak notion of agency; it does not account for mentalistic/humanistic agents properties.

In the analysis phase, the first step is the identification of *use cases*, i.e. functional requirements of the overall system, which are captured as standard Use-cases UML Diagrams (Figure 4). Starting from this, the designer can point out an initial set of agent types: an agent type for each user/device and for each resource. The agent paradigm foresees that even external devices and software/hardware resources (e.g. legacy systems, databases, external data sources) are represented with an agent. The designer, then, identifies *responsibilities*, i.e. the activities provided by system each agent is responsible for; and *acquaintances*, that is relationships between agents aimed at fulfilling some responsibility. The results are a *Responsibility table* and an *Agent diagram* (Figure 5) with initial acquaintances. No distinction is made between acquaintances and

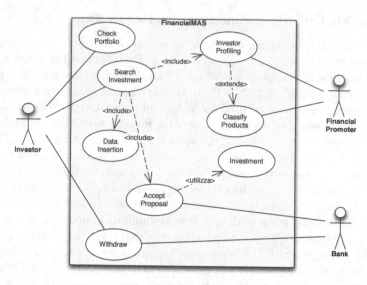

**Fig. 4.** The FinancialMAS Use Cases

responsibilities: in fact, the mentioned table will contain both. The analysis is completed by executing activities related to agents/acquaintances refinement, to define discover services and to add management/deployment information. The design phase starts with the *interaction specification* step, where an interaction table is produced. It refers to the responsibility table in order to define interactions between JADE agents, specifying the interacting agents, the protocol and protocol role (e.g. Initiator or Responder), the reference responsibility, and a triggering condition.

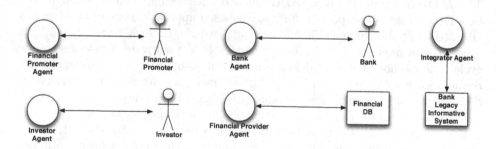

**Fig. 5.** The FinancialMAS Agent Type Diagram

It is suggested to use, when possible, standard JADE protocol behaviors, that must be added to an agent's behavior set to implement the corresponding protocol role. The subsequent steps focus on the specification of agent interactions with users and resources; the definition of a yellow page services, using the JADE Directory Facilitator; the implementation of agent behaviors, starting

**Table 1.** Responsibility Table for FinancialMAS

| Agent Type | No. | Responsibility |
|---|---|---|
| Investor agent (IA) | 1 | Let investor search for investments proposals |
| | 2 | Assist investor in setting search parameters and data |
| | 3 | Support the individuation of the investor's risk profile |
| | 4 | Support in proposal acceptance |
| | 5 | Withdraw from an investment contract |
| Financial Promoter agent (FP) | 1 | Respond to investment searches |
| | 2 | Assist financial promoter in risk-classifying financial products |
| | 3 | Determine the investor's profile |
| | 4 | Support individuation of the investor's risk profile |
| Bank agent (BA) | 1 | Support bank in investment contract subscription |
| | 2 | Assist bank in investment conclusion |
| Financial Provider agent (FV) | 1 | Provide financial and aggregate news information |
| Integration agent (IntA) | 1 | Serve and support integration with legacy bank informative systems |

**Table 2.** Interaction Table for FinancialMAS: who interacts with whom, to fulfill which duty, by using which protocol

| Interaction | R.ty | Interaction Protocol | Role | With | When |
|---|---|---|---|---|---|
| **Investor Agent** | | | | | |
| Search Investment | 1 | CNP | Initiator | FP | Investor searches an investment |
| Profiling | 3 | Query | Participant | FP | Investor chose a Financial Promoter |
| Proposal Acceptance | 4 | Query | Participant | BA | Investor chose a financial product |
| Withdraw | 5 | Request | Initiator | BA | After Investor accepted a proposal |
| **Financial Promoter Agent** | | | | | |
| Respond to Search | 1 | CNP | Participant | IA | Investor searches an investment |
| Profiling | 3 | Query | Initiator | IA | Investor chose a Financial Promoter |
| Fin. Prod. Classif. | 2 | Query | Initiator | FV | FP starts fin. prod. classif. |
| **Bank Agent** | | | | | |
| Proposal Acceptance | 1 | Query | Initiator | IA | Investor chose a financial product |
| Withdraw | 3 | Request | Participant | IA | After Investor accepted a proposal |
| **Financial Provider Agent** | | | | | |
| Fin. Prod. Classif. | 1 | Query | Participant | FP | FP starts fin. prod. classif. |

from JADE protocol behaviors related to responsibilities. A last effort is the definition of a shared, system-wide ontology.

We show how it is possible to integrate, within the JADE Methodology [30], an account of commitment-based protocols with the help of a real-world scenario, we call *FinancialMAS*. For brevity, we show only the fundamental steps needed to draft the system and to highlight the benefits of reifying commitment-based protocols by means of artifacts, and thus based on mediated interaction. By applying the steps of the methodology, we obtained an initial design prototype for FinancialMAS, concerning an initial set of agents and the so called *responsibility table* (Table 1). In the terminology of the JADE Methodology, *responsibilities* amount to functional duties, agents are responsible for, from an overall MAS point of view. To handle them, agents possibly need to *interact* with one another. The result of this analysis is an *Interaction table* (Table 2). At this point, instead of realizing protocols via distributed JADE behaviors, we implement them via *commitment-based communication artifacts.* We assume to have already designed artifacts for common interaction protocols, like the Contract Net Protocol, the Query Protocol, and the Request Protocol. The resulting model is depicted in Figure 6. For the sake of comparison, in Figure 7 we zoomed into the one of the commitment artifacts, the *Contract Net Protocol* artifact, reported as a UML diagram, while in Figure 8 we highlight the very same protocol, implemented via pure JADE behaviors.

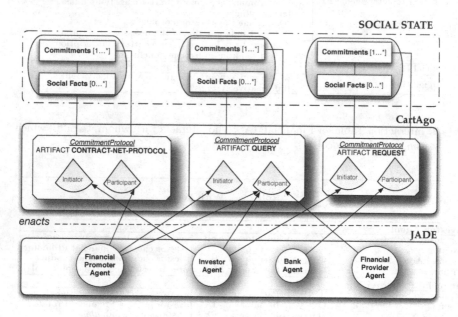

**Fig. 6.** FinancialMAS Commitment-based Interaction Architecture

2COMM proposes a clear notion of *Role* that an agent must enact to participate in an interaction session, so the designer must only implement the behaviors for fulfilling the commitments caused by the execution of a protocol *actions*. We refer to the following description of CNP based on commitment protocols (this is just an example, alternatives and variants can be found in papers like [42,24]):

*cfp* **means** create($C(i, p, propose, accept \lor reject)$)
*accept* **means** *none*
*reject* **means** release($C(p, i, accept, done \lor failure)$)
*propose* **means** create($C(p, i, accept, done \lor failure)$)
*refuse* **means** release($C(i, p, propose, accept \lor reject)$)
*done* **means** *none*
*failure* **means** *none*

In the case of CNP, two roles are foreseen, *Initiator* ($i$) and *Participant* ($p$). Playing a role gives an agent *powers*, in terms of social state modification (i.e. the state of the interaction session) as a consequence of its actions, and the

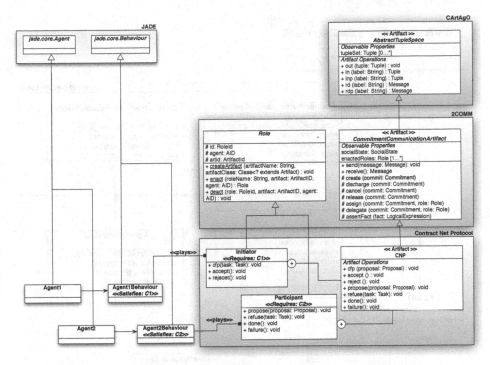

**Fig. 7.** The UML diagram for the 2COMM implementation of CNP

agent designer can use them if, when and how he/she wants. For instance, for what concerns the update of the social state, when an agent playing the role Initiator executes the artifact action *cfp*, the social state is modified by creating the commitment *C(i, p, propose, accept ∨ reject)*. On the one hand, this change binds *i* to either accept or reject a proposal, if one is received; the agent is free to decide not only which course of action to take but also how to realize acceptance or rejection. On the other hand, this change is signaled to the agent playing the role Participant, who will handle it in some manner (depending on its behaviors) and decide whether sending a proposal. Instead, when a *accept* is executed the raised event automatically discharges a commitment created by a *cfp*.

This approach is illustrated in Figure 7. We modeled CNP as a Commitment Communication Artifact. Roles are *inner classes* within the artifacts, allowing JADE agents to use them. The protocol consists of a set of *social actions*, each of which has both an impact on the social state of the interaction and on the communication between agents. Actions are attributed to roles. For instance, action *cfp* is attributed to the role *Initiator*. For what concerns communication, the execution of a social action amounts to sending the content to be communicated through the tuple space provided by CArtAgO. This result is obtained by exploiting the method *send* of the CommitmentCommunicationArtifact. Commitments are handled as an instance of the class SocialState which is part of the CommitmentCommunicationArtifact. For example, consider the social

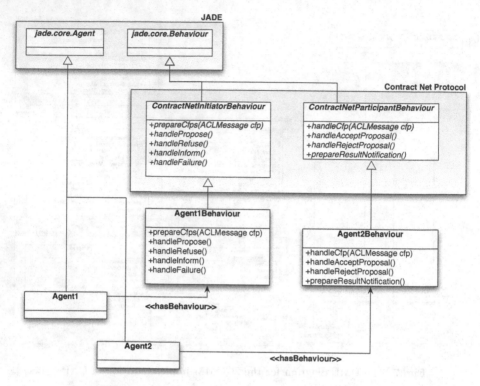

**Fig. 8.** UML diagram for the JADE implementation of CNP

action *cfp*, whose execution creates a commitment. This result is achieved through the execution of the following artifact operation:

```
@OPERATION
public void cfp(Task task, Role initiator, Role participant) {
    Message cfp = new Message();
    // setting of cfp parameters
    send(cfp);
    create(new Commitment(initiator, participant, new Fact(''propose''),
            new CompositeExpression(LogicalOperatorType.OR,
                    new Fact(''accept''), new Fact(''reject''))));
}
```

The first part of the operation manages the communication level, while the latter manages the creation of the commitment. The action *cfp* attributed to the role Initiator merely calls the described artifact operation.

An agent that will to play as a certain role can inspect the commitments that are required by the role itself, which are the commitments it will possibly be involved in as a debtor. In order to be able to satisfy them, the agent needs to have appropriate behaviors, otherwise its role execution is bound to fail. Notice that the agent is autonomous in selecting which social actions to execute and when as well as how to behave in order to satisfy its commitments.

Looking at Figure 8, the reader can perceive a major drawback of the original JADE approach: being part of an interaction protocol entails the adoption of an entire behavior, that must be added to the set of the internal agent behaviors. The resulting agent design breaks the autonomy of the agent, since the agent has an additional behavior for each role of each interaction it takes part to, increasing the possibility of conflicts between behaviors, and increasing the overall agent design complexity. In fact, being such behaviors FSMBehaviors, they implement Finite State Machines, i.e. they rigidly prescribe the sequences of actions that the agent is allowed to execute without any flexibility. Thus, it is not possible to intervene on the logic by which actions are sequentialized but only to realize the methods that the predefined behavior requires to redefine, which roughly correspond to decision points. Furthermore, this approach hinders the observability of the interaction, unless the designer adds specific sniffing or audit agents to log every message passed. In performance-critical applications, having more agents and producing a message overhead can produce undesirable scenarios.

# 5   Related Works, Discussion and Future Work

2COMM is a first step towards the implementation of the Mercurio architecture, proposed in [3,4]. It realizes a programmable communication channel by means of artifacts, which is interaction-centric, exploits the social meaning of interaction supplied by commitment protocols, and enables the development of monitoring functionalities. The realization of roles is inspired by [8,9]. The use of commitments gives a normative value to the encoded protocol, while the act of using a communication artifact amounts to the explicit acceptance, by the agent, of the rules of the protocol. This makes the current proposal very different from [7], whose aim was the introduction of the notion of role, as in [8,9], inside JADE. The proposal conjugates the flexibility and the openness that are typical of MAS with the need of modularity and compositionality that are typical of design and development methodologies. The realization of commitment protocols as artifacts is an advancement of research on commitment-based approaches, w.r.t. approaches like [19], where commitment management resides in a middleware which, in turn, relies on a message-exchange communication infrastructure. Even though the function of the middleware recalls that of our artifacts, artifacts are, by their nature, distributed (and not centralized), they can be the result of the composition of other artifacts, can be manipulated and customized by the agents themselves. Moreover, the adoption of tuple spaces allows more variegated forms of communication where communication actions are not limited to utterances.

We believe that a commitment approach brings relevant advantages in terms of design and modeling flexibility, modularity and traceability. The resulting artifact explicitly provides a notion of *Role* that is decoupled from the interacting agent, instead of cabling it into an agent behavior (as in the JADE Methodology) or of composing different atomic roles to build an agent type (as in the GAIA Methodology [43]). Both approaches break into inner agent definitions, hindering the agent autonomy and the openness of the system. The artifact entity supplies a natural way for logging and audit purposes, leveraging the concept of social state (and its evolution). In a pure agent environment (like JADE), a similar result is obtained via a massive use of either message-sniffing agents and/or auditing agents, with a consequent overhead of the number of messages that are passed. This is, for example, the case of the proposal in [29]. By being an observable property, the social state provides the agent society a clear vision of who is responsible of what, in which protocol interaction, and when an agent acted so as to fulfill its commitments.

2COMM focuses on the interaction protocol layer, leaving aside issues concerning the society of agents in which the interaction takes place. Thus, it does not, for instance, tackle how to deal with violations of commitments. In order to properly handle these aspects it would be interesting to combine its use with proposals from the area of e-institutions. Concerning this field 2COMM would provide an improvement in that it would introduce the possibility to account for indirect forms of communication. As [25] witness, there is an emerging need of defining a more abstract notion of action, which is not limited to direct speech acts, whose use is not always natural. Along this direction, it is relevant to mention the OCeAN meta-model for artificial institutions [26], which encompasses a notion of commitment, and for which a possible architecture is discussed in [31]. For what concerns organizations, instead, there are some attempts to integrate them with artifacts, e.g. ORA4MAS [27] and JaCaMo http://jacamo.sourceforge.net, which also accounts for BDI agents. Following the A&A perspective, artifacts are concrete bricks used to structure the agents' world: part of which is the organizational infrastructure, part amounts to artifacts introduced by specific MAS applications, including entities/services belonging to the external environment. In [27] the organizational infrastructure is based on $Moise^+$, which allows both for the enforcement and the regimentation of the rules of the organization. This is done by defining a set of conditions to be achieved and the roles that are permitted or obliged to perform them. The limit of this approach is that it cannot capture contexts in which regulations are, more generally, norms because norms cannot be restricted to achievement goals. Recently, the use of a communication infrastructure based on artifacts has been proposed to define, in an explicit and clear way, interaction in JaCaMo [33]. Nevertheless, the proposal does not supply a normative account of communication.

Finally, we think that our proposal can give significant contributions in industrial applicative contexts, for the realization of business processes and, in particular, of human-oriented workflows, whose nature is intrinsically social and where the notion of commitment plays a fundamental role [28]. In [36], the authors present LoST, a commitment-based model for the definition of declarative protocols, which is based on local history vectors of sent/received messages, associated to each of the interacting agents. LoST enables the representation and monitoring of (business) protocols when it is necessary to transfer local knowledge about occurring interactions between the agents. It works as an adapter for message transfer between agents. 2COMM, instead, provides agents an environment by which they communicate and, if this is requested, they can perform actions which do not amount to utterances but still entail social effects.

As a future work, we devise an extension of 2COMM for tackling a more expressive protocol language, with support for temporal constraints, see also [2]. This goal can easily be achieved by defining new artifact types that provide developers the appropriate protocol language primitives, such as those offered by 2CL [6][5].

**Acknowledgments.** The authors would like to thank the reviewers for their comments and the participants to the EMAS 2013 workshop for the discussions.

# References

1. FIPA specifications, http://www.fipa.org
2. Baldoni, M., Baroglio, C.: Some Thoughts about Commitment Protocols. In: Baldoni, M., Dennis, L., Mascardi, V., Vasconcelos, W. (eds.) DALT 2012. LNCS, vol. 7784, pp. 190–196. Springer, Heidelberg (2013)
3. Baldoni, M., Baroglio, C., Bergenti, F., Marengo, E., Mascardi, V., Patti, V., Ricci, A., Santi, A.: An interaction-oriented agent framework for open environments. In: Pirrone, R., Sorbello, F. (eds.) AI*IA 2011. LNCS, vol. 6934, pp. 68–79. Springer, Heidelberg (2011)
4. Baldoni, M., Baroglio, C., Marengo, E., Patti, V., Ricci, A.: Back to the future: An interaction-oriented framework for social computing. In: First Int. Workshop on Req. Eng. for Social Computing, RESC, pp. 2–5. IEEE (2011)
5. Baldoni, M., Baroglio, C., Capuzzimati, F., Marengo, E., Patti, V.: A generalized commitment machine for 2CL protocols and its implementation. In: Baldoni, M., Dennis, L., Mascardi, V., Vasconcelos, W. (eds.) DALT 2012. LNCS, vol. 7784, pp. 96–115. Springer, Heidelberg (2013)
6. Baldoni, M., Baroglio, C., Marengo, E., Patti, V., Capuzzimati, F.: Engineering commitment-based business protocols with 2CL methodology. J. of Autonomous Agents and Multi-Agent Systems (to appear, August 2013)
7. Baldoni, M., Boella, G., Genovese, V., Mugnaini, A., Grenna, R., van der Torre, L.: A Middleware for Modeling Organizations and Roles in Jade. In: Braubach, L., Briot, J.-P., Thangarajah, J. (eds.) ProMAS 2009. LNCS, vol. 5919, pp. 100–117. Springer, Heidelberg (2010)
8. Baldoni, M., Boella, G., van der Torre, L.W.N.: Bridging agent theory and object orientation: Agent-like communication among objects. In: Bordini, R.H., Dastani, M., Dix, J., El Fallah Seghrouchni, A. (eds.) PROMAS 2006. LNCS (LNAI), vol. 4411, pp. 149–164. Springer, Heidelberg (2007)
9. Baldoni, M., Boella, G., van der Torre, L.: Interaction between Objects in power-java. Journal of Object Technology 6(2) (2007)
10. Bellifemine, F., Poggi, A.: JADE A FIPA-compliant agent framework. In: Proceedings of PAAM (1999)
11. Bellifemine, F., Poggi, A., Rimassa, G.: Developing multi-agent systems with a FIPA-compliant agent framework. Software-Practice and Experience, 103–128 (July 1999, 2001)
12. Bernon, C., Gleizes, M.P., Peyruqueou, S., Picard, G.: Adelfe: A methodology for adaptive multi-agent systems engineering. In: Petta, P., Tolksdorf, R., Zambonelli, F. (eds.) ESAW 2002. LNCS (LNAI), vol. 2577, pp. 156–169. Springer, Heidelberg (2003)

13. Boella, G., van der Torre, L.W.N.: An agent oriented ontology of social reality. In: Procs. of Formal Ontologies in Information Systems (FOIS). IOS Press (2004)
14. Boella, G., van der Torre, L.W.N.: The ontological properties of social roles in multi-agent systems: definitional dependence, powers and roles playing roles. Artificial Intelligence and Law 15(3), 201–221 (2007)
15. Boissier, O., Bordini, R.H., Hbner, J., Ricci, A., Santi, A.: Multi-agent oriented programming with jacamo. Science of Computer Programming (2011)
16. Caire, G., Coulier, W., Garijo, F.J., Gomez, J., Pavón, J., Leal, F., Chainho, P., Kearney, P.E., Stark, J., Evans, R., Massonet, P.: Agent Oriented Analysis Using Message/UML. In: Wooldridge, M.J., Weiß, G., Ciancarini, P. (eds.) AOSE 2001. LNCS, vol. 2222, pp. 119–135. Springer, Heidelberg (2002)
17. Caire, G., Gotta, D., Banzi, M.: Wade: a software platform to develop mission critical applications exploiting agents and workflows. In: AAMAS (Industry Track), pp. 29–36. IFAAMAS (2008)
18. Castelfranchi, C.: Principles of Individual Social Action. In: Contemporary Action Theory: Social Action, vol. 2, pp. 163–192. Kluwer, Dordrecht (1997)
19. Chopra, A.K., Singh, M.P.: An Architecture for Multiagent Systems: An Approach Based on Commitments. In: Proc. of ProMAS (2009)
20. Chopra, A.K.: Commitment Alignment: Semantics, Patterns, and Decision Procedures for Distributed Computing. PhD thesis, North Carolina State University, Raleigh, NC (2009)
21. Conte, R., Castelfranchi, C., Dignum, F.: Autonomous Norm Acceptance. In: Papadimitriou, C., Singh, M.P., Müller, J.P. (eds.) ATAL 1998. LNCS (LNAI), vol. 1555, pp. 99–112. Springer, Heidelberg (1999)
22. Dastani, M., Grossi, D., Meyer, J.-J.C., Tinnemeier, N.: Normative multi-agent programs and their logics. In: Meyer, J.-J.C., Broersen, J. (eds.) KRAMAS 2008. LNCS, vol. 5605, pp. 16–31. Springer, Heidelberg (2009)
23. Dietz, J.L.G.: Understanding and Modeling Business Processes with DEMO. In: Akoka, J., Bouzeghoub, M., Comyn-Wattiau, I., Métais, E. (eds.) ER 1999. LNCS, vol. 1728, pp. 188–202. Springer, Heidelberg (1999)
24. El-Menshawy, M., Bentahar, J., Dssouli, R.: Symbolic model checking commitment protocols using reduction. In: Omicini, A., Sardina, S., Vasconcelos, W. (eds.) DALT 2010. LNCS, vol. 6619, pp. 185–203. Springer, Heidelberg (2011)
25. Fornara, N., Viganò, F., Colombetti, M.: Agent communication and artificial institutions. Autonomous Agents and Multi-Agent Systems 14(2), 121–142 (2007)
26. Fornara, N., Viganò, F., Verdicchio, M., Colombetti, M.: Artificial institutions: a model of institutional reality for open multiagent systems. Artif. Intell. Law 16(1), 89–105 (2008)
27. Hubner, J.F., Boissier, O., Kitio, R., Ricci, A.: Instrumenting multi-agent organisations with organisational artifacts and agents: "Giving the organisational power back to the agents". Autonomous Agents and Multi-Agent Systems 20 (2009)
28. Medina-Mora, R., Winograd, T., Flores, R., Flores, F.: The action workflow approach to workflow management technology. Inf. Soc. 9(4), 391–404 (1993)
29. Nguyen, M.T., Fuhrer, P., Pasquier-Rocha, J.: Enhancing e-health information systems with agent technology. Int. J. Telemedicine Appl. 2009, 1:1–1:13 (2009)
30. Nikraz, M., Caire, G., Bahri, P.A.: A Methodology for the Analysis and Design of Multi-Agent Systems using JADE (May 2006)
31. Okouya, D., Fornara, N., Colombetti, M.: An infrastructure for the design and development of open interaction systems. In: Cossentino, M., El Fallah Seghrouchni, A., Winikoff, M. (eds.) EMAS 2013. LNCS (LNAI), vol. 8245, pp. 217–236. Springer, Heidelberg (2013)

32. Ricci, A., Piunti, M., Viroli, M.: Environment programming in multi-agent systems: an artifact-based perspective. Autonomous Agents and Multi-Agent Systems 23(2), 158–192 (2011)
33. Rodrigues, T.F., da Rocha Costa, A.C., Dimuro, G.P.: A Communication Infrastructure Based on Artifacts for the JaCaMo Platform. In: Cossentino, M., El Fallah Seghrouchni, A., Winikoff, M. (eds.) EMAS 2013. LNCS (LNAI), vol. 8245, Springer, Heidelberg (2013)
34. Singh, M.P.: An Ontology for Commitments in Multiagent Systems. Artif. Intell. Law 7(1), 97–113 (1999)
35. Singh, M.P.: A social semantics for agent communication languages. In: Dignum, F.P.M., Greaves, M. (eds.) Issues in Agent Communication. LNCS, vol. 1916, pp. 31–45. Springer, Heidelberg (2000)
36. Singh, M.P.: LoST: Local Transfer - An Architectural Style for the Distributed Enactment of Business Protocols. In: Proc. of the 9th Internactional Conference on Web Services, pp. 57–64. IEEE Computer Society (2011)
37. Telang, P.R., Singh, M.P.: Specifying and Verifying Cross-Organizational Business Models: An Agent-Oriented Approach. IEEE Transactions on Services Computing, 1–14 (2011)
38. Winograd, T., Flores, F.: Understanding computers and cognition - a new foundation for design. Addison-Wesley (1987)
39. Wood, M.F., DeLoach, S.A.: An overview of the multiagent systems engineering methodology. In: Ciancarini, P., Wooldridge, M.J. (eds.) AOSE 2000. LNCS, vol. 1957, pp. 207–221. Springer, Heidelberg (2001)
40. Yolum, P., Singh, M.P.: Designing and executing protocols using the event calculus. In: Proc. of the 5th Int. Conf. on Autonomous Agents, AGENTS 2001, pp. 27–28 (2001)
41. Yolum, P., Singh, M.P.: Commitment Machines. In: Meyer, J.-J.C., Tambe, M. (eds.) ATAL 2001. LNCS (LNAI), vol. 2333, pp. 235–247. Springer, Heidelberg (2002)
42. Yolum, P.: Design time analysis of multiagent protocols. Data Knowledge Engineering 63(1), 137–154 (2007)
43. Zambonelli, F., Jennings, N.R., Wooldridge, M.: Developing multiagent systems: The gaia methodology. ACM Trans. Softw. Eng. Methodol. 12(3), 317–370 (2003)

# Benchmarking Communication
# in Actor- and Agent-Based Languages

Rafael C. Cardoso[1], Jomi F. Hübner[2], and Rafael H. Bordini[1]

[1] FACIN–PUCRS
Porto Alegre - RS, Brazil
rafael.caue@acad.pucrs.br
r.bordini@pucrs.br

[2] DAS–UFSC
Florianópolis - SC, Brazil
jomi@das.ufsc.br

**Abstract.** This paper presents the results of communication benchmarks comparing an agent-oriented programming language and two actor-oriented programming languages. It is based on an existing benchmark for programming languages and two variations on that benchmark. We selected Erlang and Akka (using the Scala interface) to represent actor languages, and Jason as the agent language representative. We also present those three scenarios and the respective results in regards to time, core usage, and memory. Even though BDI engines typically used for agent languages provide sophisticated programming abstractions that require significant platform overhead to facilitate the development of complex agents, our initial results show that Jason has reasonable performance for this type of benchmark, where actor-based languages were expected to do significantly better than agent languages.

**Keywords:** benchmarking, agents, actors, Jason, Erlang, Akka, Scala.

## 1 Introduction

Jason is one of the best-known platforms for the development of multi-agent systems based on agent-oriented programming. Various authors have included Jason in their comparisons and analyses of agent programming languages. For example, Jason was included in a qualitative comparison of features available in Erlang, Jason, and Java [21]; in a universal criteria catalog for agent development artifacts [11]; in a quantitative analysis of 2APL, GOAL, and Jason regarding their similarity and the time it takes for them to reach specific states [7]; a performance evaluation of Jason when used for distributed crowd simulations [17]; an approach to query caching and a performance analysis of its usage in Jason, 2APL, and GOAL [3]; and finally an implementation of Jason in Erlang and a benchmark for evaluating its performance [16]. In those cases where performance was considered, Jason typically showed excellent results.

M. Cossentino et al. (Eds.): EMAS 2013, LNAI 8245, pp. 58–77, 2013.

However, there is no quantitative analysis — to the best of our knowledge — of how well agent languages can do compared actor languages. Because the actor approach is by design lighter than agents and because actor languages have been improved over a much longer period than modern agent programming languages, comparing performance on traditional programming language benchmarks is a much harder challenge for Jason than those it previously faced, and this is precisely what we do in this paper.

Our motivation for this recent line of work came from the idea of doing some benchmarking experiments in order to investigate whether some variations of usual benchmarking scenarios, taking into consideration features of agent programming, would allow us to conclude whether certain scenarios could be more appropriate for actors rather than agents and vice-versa, both in terms of naturalness of the paradigm for developing the applications and in terms of actual performance for the natural solutions in both paradigms. Even if it turns out that we cannot immediately find a scenario that is intrinsically more appropriate for agents, we could still use the outcome of our work to point out some flaws or deficiencies in current agent-based languages, and learn something from the longer experience with actor-based languages, thus making it possible to improve performance for agent-based languages in the future.

We started by taking an Erlang program for a token passing problem available in the Computer Language Benchmarks Game website (`http://shootout.alioth.debian.org/`) and we wrote a Jason and Akka version for it. We then changed that benchmark to a different scenario where the only difference is that a number of tokens were being passed simultaneously, and all three programs were changed accordingly. While Jason had the worst performance in regards to elapsed time, it matched closely the performance of Akka, at least for our current experiments. Erlang showed the best performance in all cases, which was expected as it is known to have an efficient virtual machine and used in industrial applications. Finally, for the third scenario, we added a notion of token types in order to assess the reactivity of each language[1].

The results reported in this paper were obtained from runs on a dedicated computer with six physical cores (no hyperthreading). We also show the results for the same scenarios but limiting the number of cores to three, with the purpose of analysing the difference that it makes to run the same experiment on increasing numbers of cores. The experiments presented in this paper are not supposed to stress-test the languages but rather to compare them in normal day-to-day usage measuring the performance, scalability, and reactivity of the communication aspect of the languages. Because this comparison cannot be done directly, as the actor model is by design lighter than the agent model and each language has a different runtime environment, we make use of scale factors to compare the languages.

---

[1] The code for all scenarios/languages used in this paper is available at
`https://github.com/rafaelcaue/`
`Actor-Agent-based-benchmark-for-communication.`

We also considered including JACK [12] as a second agent language representative, but we decided not to do all of the experiments with JACK because of two main reasons: first, unlike the other selected languages, JACK is commercial software; and second, the results for JACK in the first two scenarios showed that it seems not to take advantage of multiple cores, so it cannot be compared to the other three languages used for these experiments. A summary of the results for those experiments can be found at the end of Sections 4.1 and 4.2.

In summary, this paper aims to present results about the performance of agent-based languages, particularly Jason, against actor-based languages, using variations of a well-known benchmark for communication in programming languages. It also aims to instigate the agent programming community to further benchmark various aspects of agent-oriented programming languages.

In a previous short version of this paper [13], the Scala Actors library for actor programming was used, but at the time of writing this paper it is no longer the default actor library in Scala 2.10 and it will be deprecated in Scala 2.11. Therefore, in our experiments we replaced Scala Actors with the new default library for Scala actor programming, Akka. Although they are similar, both being Scala libraries, Akka implements an actor *system* [31] whereas Scala Actors does not.

The remainder of this paper is organised as follows. The next section provides a brief summary of related work. Section 3 gives an introduction to the three programming languages we compare in this paper. Section 4 shows the description of each scenario used in the experiments as well as all the results obtained. Section 5 includes an analysis of the results, and we conclude the paper in Section 6.

## 2    Related Work

In this section we will show several benchmarks and evaluations about actor and agent programming languages found in the literature, but to the best of our knowledge there is none that focus on benchmarking both the actor and agent models together.

A strictly qualitative analysis of multi-agent system development kits can be found in [8], where they assign weights to criteria in five categories: sociality, advanced attitudes, software engineering, implementation, and technical issues. Each development kit is ranked based on that criteria with values 100, 50, and 0 that correspond to the level of support as a percentage. The overall results indicated that the development kits with the best values were, in descending order: AgentBuilder, JACK, AgentSheets, and OpenCybele. That study did not include any quantitative analysis.

A more varied study is that in [28], focusing on criteria such as Java support, performance evaluation, development support, and performance on message passing. The benchmark is on the message transport system: a sender formulates a message and sends it to a receiver, recording the starting time, and when the receiver gets the message he sends it back to the sender. This process is repeated up to 4000 messages and the sender records the time at the end. The benchmarked toolkits were Jade, Zeus, and JACK, and this benchmark was run on a computer with a single core and 256 MB of RAM, which is what was commonly available at the time that study was conducted, but does not take advantage of the concurrency that the agent model is capable of.

An extensive performance evaluation of agent communication is available in [2]. It tries to provide some explanations for weaknesses found during the experiments in three multi-agent platforms: Jade, Madkit, and AgentScape. The results concluded that all three multi-agent platforms performed poorly and with low scalability. As in the studies above, the computer used to run the experiments had a single core, thus not taking proper advantage of concurrency and multi-core processors that are now common.

In [22], several actor-oriented programming languages are benchmarked, using the threadring and the chameneos-redux benchmarks from the Computer Language Benchmarks Game website, as well as a simple implementation of the fibonacci sequence. There is also a qualitative analysis of the actor properties that are present in each of those language that uses the Java Virtual Machine (JVM); those languages are: SALSA, Scala Actors, Kilim, Actor Architecture, JavAct, ActorFoundry, and Jetlang. Erlang does not use JVM, but was included in the benchmarks as it was the most widely used Actor language at the time. Kilim and Erlang displayed the best performance overall, but Kilim only provides basic message passing support. For those experiments, a dual core processor was used.

Finally, in [27], an agent-oriented programming language called simpAL is introduced, aiming to integrate autonomous and reactive behaviour; the authors claim that this is a problem not easily achievable with object-oriented and actor-oriented languages. The results of a brief benchmark where an agent reacts to a message by incrementing a counter and printing a message are presented, comparing simpAL with Jason, Erlang, and ActorFoundry. As in the study above, a dual core processor was used.

Some of the studies mentioned here were conducted with much older versions of the languages used in our experiments, and computer hardware has changed significantly since then, in particular for multi-core technology that has become commonplace.

## 3  Agent and Actor Programming Languages

In this section, we briefly discuss the main aspects of the three programming languages that we chose for this comparison work. We only present some of the fundamentals of each language, which can help understand the scenarios implemented in the experiments. However, we assume some familiarity of the reader with the actor and agent paradigms and, of course, prior knowledge of those three programming languages (as well as functional programming and Java) would be helpful.

Actor-oriented programming languages are based on the actor model [1], with an actor being a lightweight process that does not share state with other actors and communicates by asynchronous message passing through mailboxes. Agent-oriented programming languages are based on the agent model [30], which is an extension of the actor model. While both agents and actors are lightweight processes and reactive, agents are more complex entities, typically capable of "practical reasoning" (i.e., logic-based reasoning about the best action to take) [9,10].

## 3.1   Jason

Jason is a platform for the development of multi-agent systems that is based on an agent-oriented programming language. The logic-based BDI-inspired language AgentSpeak, initially conceived by Rao [26], was later extended in a series of publications by Bordini, Hübner, and colleagues, so as to make it suitable as a practical agent programming language. These extensions led to the variant of AgentSpeak that is made available in Jason [10]. Jason is implemented in Java, thus its programs run on a JVM, which also allows support for user-defined "internal actions" that are programmed in Java and run internally within an agent rather than changing the environment, as normal actions do.

In Jason, an agent is an entity composed of a set of *beliefs*, representing agent's current state and knowledge about the environment in which it is situated, a set of *goals*, which correspond to tasks the agent has to perform/achieve, a set of *intentions*, which are tasks the agent is committed to achieve, and a set of *plans* which are courses of *actions* triggered by *events*.

Events can be related to changes in either the agent's belief base or its goals. The agent reacts to the events creating new intentions, provided there is an applicable plan for that event. Therefore, each intention represents a particular "focus of attention" for the various tasks currently being done by the agent: they all compete for the agent's choice of intention to be further executed in a given execution step. Last, we must mention the "pool of threads" functionality of Jason, declared by using (pool, $x$) next to the infrastructure of choice. Enabling a pool of thread means that rather than creating a thread for each agent, Jason creates only a fixed number of threads that agents compete for (unless they have nothing to do). In our experiments, we chose the size of the thread pool to be the number of cores used in each experiment, in order to increase performance on multi-core processors ($x$ was either 3, 6, or 12 depending on the experiment).

## 3.2   Erlang

Erlang [5], acronym for Ericsson Language (where it was developed), is a functional language with dynamic typing. Erlang is supported by an extensive library collection know as OTP, originally an acronym for Open Telecom Platform (before 2000 when Erlang became open source). The Erlang Run-Time System (ERTS) application is responsible for low-level operations, including the Erlang virtual machine called Bodgan's Erlang Abstract Machine (BEAM) [4].

Concurrent programming is the focus of Erlang, using processes (the concurrency model usually referred by Erlang users is the process model, but it corresponds directly to the actor model) that are as much lightweight as possible. It even has its own scheduler in the virtual machine, so a process in Erlang has nothing to do with heavyweight operating system processes.

Communication between processes is based on message passing, with each process having its own mailbox that is used to store the messages. Messages can be sent asynchronously and if a message matching the pattern is found in the queue, it is processed and its variables instantiated before the expressions in the body are evaluated. Functions are also defined by pattern matching and expressions as usual in functional languages. For further details, we refer the interested reader to [23,14].

### 3.3   Akka

Akka can be used either with Scala or directly with Java. In this paper we chose to use the Akka library for Scala as it provides a syntax that is similar to other common actor programming languages. Scala is considered a multi-paradigm language, as it combines features of object-oriented and functional programming languages. It differs from Erlang on its type system, as Scala is a statically typed language, and intended as a general purpose programming language. The name Scala comes from "scalable language", as it was designed to help the development of systems where scalability is an issue. Scala programs run on a JVM, so it has direct integration with Java, allowing the use of existing Java code within Scala systems [24].

This facilitates extensibility of the language, and resulted in the creation of many libraries, such as Scala Actors (currently to be deprecated) and Akka: two libraries that provides concurrent programming based on actors for Scala programming. An actor can communicate asynchronously with another by exchanging messages through the actor's mailbox; an actor then generates an appropriate response for each message it receives [18].

It is important to note that the actors used in the experiments reported in this paper are event-based actors, not thread-based actors. In Scala Actors the expression we used in the control loop for an event-based actor is `react`, while for thread-based actors the expression would be `receive` [19]. In Akka, this option is part of the `MessageDispatcher`, a mechanism responsible for optimally dividing CPU resources among tasks. The default event-based dispatcher is *fork-join-executor*, while the thread-based dispatcher is *thread-pool-executor*. Although Scala has many other interesting concepts, only the basics that suffice for some understanding the scenarios in Section 4 are covered here. For a more in-depth reading of Scala, we refer the reader to [29] and, more specifically for Akka, [31].

## 4   The Benchmarking Experiments

The Computer Language Benchmarks Game (http://shootout.alioth.
debian.org/) provides performance evaluation for approximately twenty four
languages on various benchmark problems. Although they evaluate the performance on computers with multiple cores, the tasks and most of the languages
are not appropriate for concurrent programming. A python script is available
on their website that does repeated measurements of CPU time, elapsed time,
resident memory usage, and CPU load for each core. It does so for various programs written in different programming languages, the script then summarises
those measurements on a sheet for easy viewing.

Each program is run as a child-process of a Python script using Popen. The
script is fully customisable and it is easy to add new languages, so we were able
to adapt it to our experiments. For the experiments described below, we chose
to take three measurements with the script: CPU load for each core, elapsed
time, and resident memory. The script measures the percentage load of a core
through the GTop library, on Unix systems, taking the CPU-idle and CPU-total
values before forking the child-process and after it exits, where the percentage
represents the time that a core was not-idle; elapsed time uses time.time()
to get the time before forking and after exiting; and resident memory is measured by sampling GLIBTOP_PROC_MEM_RESIDENT for the program every
0.2 seconds.

The scenarios described in the next sections focus on the message passing
aspect of communication, testing the support for asynchronous message passing, concurrency and reactivity of each language; features that are essential for
actor- and agent-based languages alike. To run the experiments, we used an
Intel®Xeon®Six-Core E5645 CPU @ 2.40GHz (6 physical, 12 logical cores with
HyperThreadring) machine with 12B of DDR3 1333 MHz RAM, 1TB hard disk
drive, running the operating system Ubuntu 12.10 64 bits; the versions of the
languages used were Jason 1.3.9, Erlang R16B01 erts 5.10.2, Scala 2.10.2, and
Akka 2.1.4; the additional software used was Java OpenJDK 64-Bit Server VM,
Java 1.7.0_21, and Python 2.7.3.

### 4.1   Scenario 1

The first scenario is a simple case of passing one token $N$ times through a ring of
"workers" (i.e., agents, processes, or actors, depending on the language). Each
program for this scenario should:

- create 500 linked workers (named 1 to 500);
- worker 500 should be linked to worker 1, forming an unbroken ring;
- pass a token to worker 1;
- each worker passes the token to its neighbouring worker;
- the program halts when the token has been passed (between any two workers)
  $N$ times.

As an additional memory experiment, we also varied the number of workers. We measured time and core load for this variation, but omitted them in this paper since they did not show anything different from the other experiments. The Erlang code for this scenario is that available at (http://shootout.alioth. debian.org/), except that we removed unnecessary print statements, and changed the number of workers to 500, simply because it represents an intermediate value between the number of tokens used later in Scenario 2 and the number of workers needed for the memory experiments.

We ran experiments for Scenario 1 with six different configurations for $N$, measuring elapsed time, core load, and memory: $N = 500$; $N = 5,000$; $N = 50,000$; $N = 500,000$; $N = 5,000,000$; and $N = 50,000,000$. And again with three different configurations of number of workers $(W)$, this time with $N$ fixed at 5 million, for memory measurements: $W = 50$; $W = 500$; and $W = 5,000$.

**Table 1.** Elapsed time in seconds – Scenario 1, varying $N$

| 6 cores | 500 | 5k | 50k | 500k | 5m | 50m |
|---|---|---|---|---|---|---|
| Jason | 0.818 | 1.33 | 1.99 | 5.393 | 37.973 | 360.07 |
| Erlang | 0.137 | 0.139 | 0.163 | 0.382 | 2.537 | 21.63 |
| Akka | 1.139 | 1.688 | 2.256 | 4.799 | 29.038 | 278.934 |
| **3 cores** | **500** | **5k** | **50k** | **500k** | **5m** | **50m** |
| Jason | 0.911 | 1.355 | 2.036 | 5.954 | 42.891 | 410.622 |
| Erlang | 0.12 | 0.124 | 0.144 | 0.345 | 2.338 | 22.602 |
| Akka | 1.089 | 1.65 | 2.095 | 3.895 | 20.062 | 183.994 |

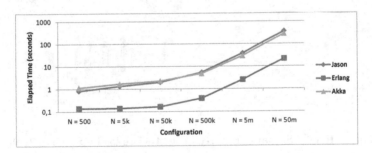

**Fig. 1.** Elapsed time – Scenario 1

The results for the first benchmark (Scenario 1), using the Python "bencher" script, can be seen in the following graphs[2]. All the numbers shown are based on the results collected through 5 repeated measurements of each program with each of the six configurations; in particular, the numbers shown represent the turn with lowest (best) value of elapsed time among the 5 different runs. Figure 1 presents the measurements of elapsed running time in seconds based on the

---

[2] All the graphs presented in this paper are in logarithmic scale, given that $N$ grows exponentially.

values in Table 1. Figure 2 shows the CPU load measurements for each of the six cores, for the three languages we are comparing. To improve readability we present core loads only for the three highest values of $N$. Jason used on average 39% of each core in all three configurations; Erlang used mostly one core, 72% for $N = 500k$, 95% for $N = 5m$ and 99% for $N = 50m$; Akka used on average 61% of each core for the first configuration, 79% for the second, and 82% for the last configuration. We show the memory results in Figure 5.

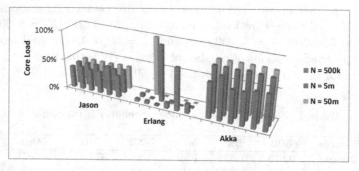

**Fig. 2.** Core load – Scenario 1

We also show the results for the same configurations running with only three cores; see Figures 3 and 4. In regards to CPU load using three cores, Jason used on average 67% of each core; Erlang again used mostly only one core, 69% for the first configuration and 100% for the last two; Akka averaged 78% for the first configuration and 97% for the last two. Memory use is presented in Figure 6.

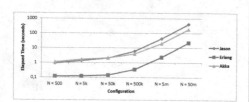
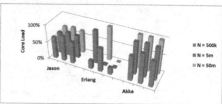

**Fig. 3.** Elapsed time – Scenario 1, three cores      **Fig. 4.** Core load – Scenario 1, three cores

For the sake of readability we present the results for the extra memory experiments (Figure 13), where we vary the number of workers, in Section 4.2 next to the memory experiments for Scenario 2. The numbers used represent the average resident memory used in megabytes collected through 5 repeated measurements.

As reported in Section 1, we also considered using JACK for the experiments, as in this first scenario it had 9.72 seconds for the measurement of elapsed time with $N = 500,000$, which was only 4.3 seconds slower than Jason. JACK used, on average, 28% of each core in this experiment, and a surprising 1035 MB of resident memory.

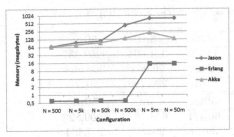  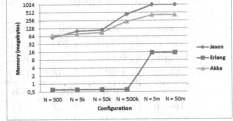

**Fig. 5.** Memory – Scenario 1    **Fig. 6.** Memory – Scenario 1, three cores

## 4.2  Scenario 2

This scenario is a minor variation of Scenario 1, where we added more tokens and allowed them to be passed concurrently. So rather than passing only one token, in Scenario 2 at the start of a run 50 tokens are distributed around the ring using the following equation:

$$I * (W/T)$$

where $I$ is the number of the current token to be sent, $W$ is the total number of workers, and $T$ is the total number of tokens. Each of these 50 tokens have to be passed $N$ times, and because neither agents nor actors share state, an extra agent or actor is needed for counting the tokens that have finished: this is necessary because in order for the Python bencher script to carry on running all the experiments it needs the programs to halt, which can only happen when all 50 tokens have been passed $N$ times each.

The results for the second benchmark are shown in the following graphs; as before, we pick the run with the lowest elapsed time. Figure 7 shows the measurements of elapsed running time in seconds based on the values in Table 2. Figure 8 shows the measurements for the six cores, for each of the languages: Jason averaged 96% in all three configurations; Erlang averaged 83% for $N = 500k$, 85% for $N = 5m$ and 91% for $N = 50m$; and Akka averaged 93% for the first, 95% for the second, and 96% for the last configuration. In Figure 11, we show the resident memory used in megabytes, collected through 5 repeated measurements. We show the results for three cores in Figures 9, 10, and 12. In regards to CPU load using three cores only, the three languages averaged 98%. Finally, we vary $W$ as shown in Figure 14 for the memory experiments.

Although JACK had average results in Scenario 1, it could not effectively handle the concurrency in Scenario 2, taking 228.476 seconds for the measurement of elapsed time for $N = 500,000$, which was far off from the results of any of the other three languages. JACK used, on average, 43% of each core in this experiment, and 1242 MB of resident memory, which is also much higher than any of the other languages for this configuration. This disparity between the results for the two scenarios was an important factor in JACK not being included in the rest of the experiments.

**Table 2.** Elapsed time in seconds – Scenario 2, varying $N$

| 6 cores | 500 | 5k | 50k | 500k | 5m | 50m |
|---|---|---|---|---|---|---|
| Jason | 1.315 | 1.769 | 4.761 | 32.575 | 321.694 | 3269.337 |
| Erlang | 0.141 | 0.165 | 0.421 | 2.89 | 26.964 | 260.868 |
| Akka | 1.522 | 2.048 | 3.956 | 23.613 | 220.796 | 2291.755 |
| **3 cores** | **500** | **5k** | **50k** | **500k** | **5m** | **50m** |
| Jason | 1.684 | 2.417 | 7.944 | 60.471 | 604.162 | 6009.822 |
| Erlang | 0.128 | 0.158 | 0.424 | 3.074 | 29.534 | 295.334 |
| Akka | 1.758 | 2.255 | 4.595 | 25.906 | 243.17 | 2370.131 |

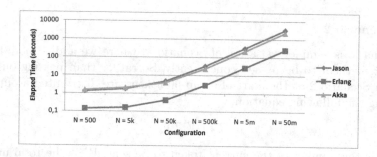

**Fig. 7.** Elapsed time – Scenario 2

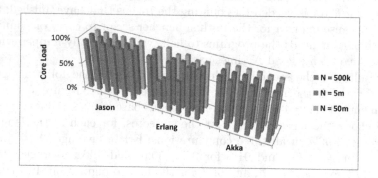

**Fig. 8.** Core load – Scenario 2

## 4.3   Scenario 3

As a follow up to Scenario 2, this time $N$ is fixed at 500 and a new type of token was introduced in the ring; we call it "token type 1". The 50 previous tokens from Scenario 2 are now referred to as "token type 2" and they work exactly the same way as in the previous scenario. We created 1,000 type 1 tokens, two per worker, to simulate the "mundane tasks" that the workers would normally be doing while waiting for the "special" type 2 tokens to arrive. When a worker acquires a token type 1 it starts a loop simulating a computing load (we used an empty loop of 1000 iterations), and when it finishes that work load on the type 1 token,

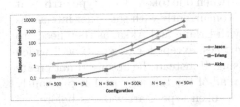

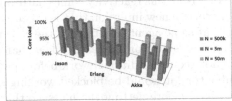

**Fig. 9.** Elapsed time – Scenario 2, three cores

**Fig. 10.** Core load – Scenario 2, three cores

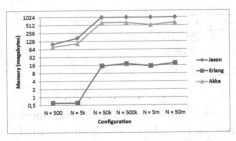

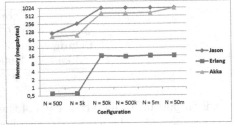

**Fig. 11.** Memory – Scenario 2

**Fig. 12.** Memory – Scenario 2, three cores

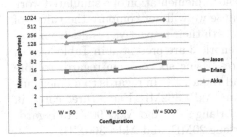

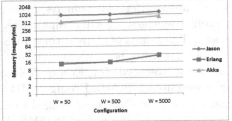

**Fig. 13.** Memory – Scenario 1, varying $W$

**Fig. 14.** Memory – Scenario 2, varying $W$

it passes that token on to the next worker in the ring, but the token counter is not decreased so that tokens of type 1 never stop moving around the ring. On the other hand, if a worker acquired a token type 2, as soon as it realises it, the worker would pass that token directly to the next worker in the ring. A run of Scenario 3 ends when all 50 tokens type 2 have been passed 500 times each.

These modifications were introduced mainly to evaluate the reaction time when receiving a token type 2 while still busy with the tokens of type 1 (i.e., to assess the reactivity to communication for each platform), so we decided to take the fastest configuration of Scenario 2, $N = 500$, which could then be compared with the new results obtained for Scenario 3.

In Jason, this reactivity comes naturally: when one token of any type arrives, it generates a new intention that is executed concurrently with the other intentions of that same agent. That is not the case with Erlang and Akka, as they need[3] to create a "subactor" for each token that arrives, except for tokens type 2 which do not require additional work before passing. If instead the actor did not create subactors, it would be blocked working on all of the tokens type 1 it previously received before getting the message that a token type 2 arrived. As before, we pick the run with the lowest elapsed time from 5 separate runs.

**Table 3.** Elapsed time in seconds – Scenario 3

|        | 6 cores | 3 cores |
|--------|---------|---------|
| Jason  | 13.925  | 23.776  |
| Erlang | 0.501   | 0.808   |
| Akka   | 3.906   | 5.110   |

It is important to note that each of the three languages used a different mechanism to simulate the work load of tokens type 1. In Jason the loop was made through plan recursion, in Erlang through tail recursive functions, and in Akka with a simple *for* loop in Java. Because a worker will always be working on at least one token type 1, these variations of the implementation of a simulated work load do not interfere with our results because we will not compare the values of different languages, we will compare them with their respective results from Scenario 2. The results of elapsed time for Scenario 3 are presented in Table 3, with $N = 500$ for using both six and three cores. Using six cores, in regards to core load, Jason averaged 90%, Erlang 77%, and Akka 79%. In regards to memory usage, Jason used 1790MB, Erlang 21MB, and Akka 362MB. Using three cores, in regards to core load, Jason averaged 95%, Erlang 91%, and Akka 90%. In regards to memory usage, Jason used 1843MB, Erlang 20MB, and Akka 360MB.

## 5   Analysis of the Results

The elapsed time graphs for Scenario 1 (Figure 1) and Scenario 2 (Figure 7) show Jason and Akka close to each other, while Erlang remains distant as the fastest language. In both cases, Jason actually managed to be faster than Akka in the first configurations, even if by a low margin. When limiting the number of cores to three, Scenario 1 is improved for Akka as its elapsed time lowers considerably with each configuration. This can be explained by the time spent switching threads to cores, but not so for Erlang that was already using mostly only one core when it had six available, and Jason that had a lower CPU load (average 39%) than Akka (average 82%) in the last configuration. Because this scenario is not concurrent, Erlang's behaviour is the optimal one, as using mostly one

---

[3] Of course this is not the only way to implement such reactivity in the actor languages, but it would be the most "natural" and easiest to program in that paradigm.

core allows it to maintain its performance when the number of available cores changes. The results for three cores in Scenario 2 indicate a major decline in performance for Jason, which makes sense since Scenario 2 requires concurrency and having fewer processors should increase the elapsed time, although that is not exactly the case with Erlang and Akka as their performance only drops by a small margin.

Such performance becomes clearer when observing the scale factors in Table 4 for Scenarios 1 and 2. Scale factors represent the proportional increase in time when scaling up the experiment configurations such as number of token passes, and denotes the degradation of performance. For example, Jason's scale factor 9.482 (six cores) from 5m to 50m in Scenario 1 is calculated by dividing its elapsed time in 50m, 360.07 seconds, by its elapsed time in 5m, 37.973. These variations between configurations, i.e. changes in the number of token passes, represent an increase in the amount of message passing that characterise the communication aspect analysed in this paper. We selected only the three highest values for $N$ due to the fact that the other configurations only showed small variations between them.

The scale factors for Scenario 1 show Erlang as the language with the lowest increase in scale factors: 1.86 (i.e. the scale factor from configuration 5m to 50m, 8.526, minus the scale factor from 500k to 5m, 6.641) compared to 2.44 for Jason and 3.56 for Akka. Those differences change when limiting the number of cores to three, as Jason becomes the one with the lowest increase in scale factor: its difference between scale factors is 2.37, followed by 2.89 for Erlang and 4.02 for Akka. A low difference value between scale factors is desirable as it represents good scalability between scenario configurations, which in this case is represented by an increase in the number of messages that have to be passed as the number of token passes increases. When looking at the results for Scenario 2, with six cores, Jason takes the lead with a difference factor of 0.29 compared to 0.35 for Erlang and 1.03 for Akka. Those difference factors get even smaller when using only three cores, which suggests that in concurrency-based scenarios such as this, the languages allow better scaling with lower numbers of cores, even though the elapsed time of each program is faster with more cores.

The scale factors for Scenario 3 are presented in Table 6; for example, Akka scale factor of 2.566 (six cores) is calculated by taking the elapsed time of 3.906 in Scenario 3 and dividing it by the elapsed time of 1.522 for the similar configuration of Scenario 2, where $N = 500$. This particular scale factor represents the reactivity that was possible for each language in Scenario 3 when compared to its non-reactive counterpart, and shows Akka as the most reactive language, followed by Erlang and then Jason. However, note that Jason did not require any extra programming effort in order to obtain the reactive behaviour.

Regardless of whether the scenario is concurrent or not, Jason manages to match closely the performance of the actor languages, and even surpasses them in some cases. The scale factors in Table 5 represent the performance degradation of moving from a scenario with only 1 token (non-concurrent) to a scenario with 50 tokens (concurrent). For example, the scale factor for Jason with $N = 500k$ using six cores means that its elapsed time in Scenario 1, multiplied by 6.04, results in its elapsed time of Scenario 2 for the same configuration. Using six cores, Jason also displays a smaller variation between configurations when compared to the other two languages, but when using only three cores we can observe a substantial increase in the scale factors of the three languages, suggesting the importance of using as many cores as possible, which is even more evident in the case of Jason and Akka.

**Table 4.** Scale factors for Scenario 1 and 2

| 6 Cores | Scenario 1 | | Scenario 2 | |
|---------|------------|------------|------------|------------|
|         | 500k to 5m | 5m to 50m  | 500k to 5m | 5m to 50m  |
| Jason   | 7.041      | 9.482      | 9.875      | 10.163     |
| Erlang  | 6.641      | 8.526      | 9.33       | 9.675      |
| Akka    | 6.051      | 9.606      | 9.351      | 10.379     |
| **3 Cores** | **500k to 5m** | **5m to 50m** | **500k to 5m** | **5m to 50m** |
| Jason   | 7.203      | 9.574      | 9.891      | 9.947      |
| Erlang  | 6.777      | 9.667      | 9.608      | 10         |
| Akka    | 5.151      | 9.171      | 9.387      | 9.747      |

**Table 5.** Scale factors between Scenarios 1 and 2

| 6 Cores | 500k   | 5m     | 50m    |
|---------|--------|--------|--------|
| Jason   | 6.04   | 8.472  | 9.08   |
| Erlang  | 7.565  | 10.522 | 12.06  |
| Akka    | 4.92   | 7.604  | 8.216  |
| **3 Cores** | **500k** | **5m** | **50m** |
| Jason   | 10.156 | 14.086 | 14.636 |
| Erlang  | 8.91   | 12.632 | 13.067 |
| Akka    | 6.651  | 12.121 | 12.882 |

**Table 6.** Scale factors for Scenario 3

|        | 6 cores | 3 cores |
|--------|---------|---------|
| Jason  | 10.589  | 14.119  |
| Erlang | 3.553   | 6.313   |
| Akka   | 2.566   | 2.907   |

The results in Figure 2 show that Jason and Akka have an even distribution of core load, while Erlang uses for the most part only one core. We should consider that Scenario 1 does not require concurrency, so it is acceptable that mostly one core is used. The same behaviour holds when we use only three cores, except that the load of each core gets higher for Jason and Akka, as they now have less cores available to use.

Moving to the CPU-load graph for Scenario 2 (Figure 8), we can see that Erlang starts to use all the six cores evenly as the number of token passes increases, with both Erlang and Jason having higher core load than in Scenario 1, while Akka maintained its high usage of each core. Using three cores in this case pushed the core load higher, especially for $N = 500k$ and $N = 5m$, which were the cases that Erlang was not using to the maximum all the cores. As the the number of token passes increased, the core load also increased for both Erlang and Akka, but remained constant for Jason in both scenarios with six and three cores.

Memory in Scenario 1 (Figure 5) was constant during the initial variations of $N$, but had a quick increase in the heavier configurations. For Scenario 2 (Figure 11), such increase happened in an earlier configuration, remaining constant after that, possibly due to garbage collecting in the JVM for Jason and Akka, and BEAM for Erlang. Because we were only varying the number of token passes ($N$) — that is, the programs were only running for a longer period of time with each configuration — it makes sense for the languages to present this pattern of having a single episode of sharp memory increase and then maintaining it constant. In Scenario 3, however, Jason used a lot more memory than the other languages, which is to be expected when compared to Erlang as it has its own virtual machine, but Akka is also based on Java and runs on a JVM just as Jason does. This is possibly due to the fact that in Jason the empty loop of Scenario 3 is implemented as plan recursion, which means that each goal generates an intention that would be executed along with the intentions of the tokens type 2 and which is formed by a stack of plans that grows with each recursion, differently from the actor languages that would simply create a subactor for the loop when needed.

When we consider the memory experiments varying $W$, all three languages had the expected increase in used memory with the increase in the number of workers. Jason has the highest memory usage of the three languages, which was predictable since each agent has a more complex internal structure than an actor. In Scenario 2, however, where we also have an increase in the number of tokens passed and they can be passed concurrently, Jason surprisingly starts to follow closely the performance of Akka. As both languages are implemented in Java, this suggests that the garbage collector and the JVM play an even bigger role in memory management as the previous experiments already suggested.

The experiments presented in the previous section were made with hyperthreading disabled, i.e. only physical cores were used. As an additional experiment, we also ran all the experiments with hyperthreading on, which means that there were a total of 12 logical cores available in the machine with 6 physical cores. The elapsed time results for Scenario 1 and 2 are presented in Figures 15 and 16, respectively, based on the values in Table 7. The results for Scenario 1 shows the same as the previous experiments: Jason and Akka present a drop in performance, as having more cores in a non-concurrent scenario can be detrimental to their performance; Erlang maintains its performance as it mostly uses one core. The main advantage of hyperthreading, however, is to improve performance for threaded applications, so it would be a fair assumption to say that with the concurrency of Scenario 2 the results were expected to be improved. It did improve by a small margin for Jason and Erlang, but presented a major decrease in performance for Akka, even though Akka had the highest core load usage of the languages. We do not present the rest of the results for the hyperthreading experiments as they had similar results as the experiments with six cores in regards to core load and memory usage.

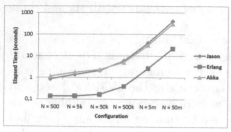 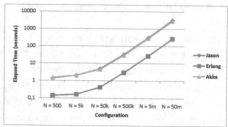

**Fig. 15.** Elapsed time – Scenario 1, 12 cores

**Fig. 16.** Elapsed time – Scenario 2, 12 cores

**Table 7.** Elapsed time in seconds – Scenarios 1 and 2, 12 cores

| Scenario 1 | 500 | 5k | 50k | 500k | 5m | 50m |
|---|---|---|---|---|---|---|
| Jason | 0.856 | 1.374 | 2.105 | 5.787 | 38.983 | 401.122 |
| Erlang | 0.14 | 0.141 | 0.168 | 0.393 | 2.637 | 21.812 |
| Akka | 1.151 | 1.727 | 2.313 | 5.032 | 31.166 | 303.815 |
| Scenario 2 | 500 | 5k | 50k | 500k | 5m | 50m |
| Jason | 1.384 | 2.04 | 4.875 | 33.201 | 305.213 | 3258.409 |
| Erlang | 0.141 | 0.167 | 0.425 | 2.966 | 26.871 | 269.051 |
| Akka | 1.508 | 2.002 | 4.561 | 29.417 | 282.356 | 2827.483 |

Having its own virtual machine and runtime environment execution certainly helps Erlang to achieve the performance presented in this paper, although we cannot say to what extent this may affect its overall performance. Clearly there are advantages in using Java and the JVM for Jason and Akka, but this places a limit on the performance that they can achieve, especially in regards to memory and core load management.

On a more qualitative note, it is interesting to observe the code size of the solutions. In all scenarios, Jason uses significantly fewer lines of code compared to Erlang and Akka, and – although this is subjective – the programs seem more intuitive, simpler, and readable. The interested readers can see all programs used for the three languages at https://github.com/rafaelcaue/Actor-Agent-based-benchmark-for-communication.

## 6    Conclusion

In this paper, we presented an analysis of the results from experiments on three different communication scenarios. Scenario 1, where a token is passed sequentially, Scenario 2 where multiple tokens are passed concurrently, and Scenario 3, where reactivity is needed for tokens type 2 to be passed faster. Where scaling between configurations were considered, Erlang did better in almost all cases, with Jason close to it, followed by Akka. Erlang stood distant as the one with significantly better performance than the other two languages at both elapsed time and memory used for these scenarios. Jason, as a representative from a "heavier" paradigm, did not disappoint, following closely on both aspects, scalability and performance, and even surpassing the two actor languages in some aspects, showing that agent-oriented programming languages can perform surprisingly close to its predecessors as far as communication is concerned. For Erlang and Akka, at least in our current experiments, its more efficient to have a processor with a higher clock speed than with more cores, while Jason takes more advantage of having extra cores instead of the higher clock speed.

Future work includes running the experiments reported here on machines with a higher number of cores, and analyzing other issues such as fairness. Furthermore, we intend to benchmark also other agent and actor programming languages, including 2APL [15], GOAL [20], and Jadex [25] in the agent language representatives, and ActorFoundry [6] in the actor languages. To complement the work on benchmarking, we also aim to consider the fundamentals of programming languages for a more qualitative comparison of the languages.

There has been very little research on benchmarking for agent programming languages, so we expect to report various other results in the near future, and we also expect to see similar efforts by other research groups, covering the great variety of agent programming languages. In order to support such efforts, we have developed a website — http://www.inf.pucrs.br/maop.benchmarking/ — to serve as a repository of benchmarks specifically designed for comparison of the existing agent programming languages. Benchmarking programming languages can sometimes lead to performance improvements, and is an important step towards mainstreaming of the agent model.

**Acknowledgments.** We are grateful for the support given by CAPES and by CNPq (grant numbers 306301/2012-1 and 308095/2012-0).

# References

1. Agha, G.: Actors: a model of concurrent computation in distributed systems. MIT Press, Cambridge (1986)
2. Alberola, J.M., Such, J.M., Garcia-Fornes, A., Espinosa, A., Botti, V.: A performance evaluation of three multiagent platforms. Artif. Intell. Rev. 34(2), 145–176 (2010)
3. Alechina, N., Behrens, T., Hindriks, K., Logan, B.: Query Caching in Agent Programming Languages. In: Proceedings of ProMAS-2012, Held with AAMAS 2012, Valencia, Spain, pp. 117–131 (June 2012)
4. Armstrong, J.: Programming Erlang: Software for a Concurrent World. Pragmatic Bookshelf (2007)
5. Armstrong, J.: Erlang. Commun. ACM 53(9), 68–75 (2010)
6. Astley, M.: The Actor Foundry: A Java-based Actor Programming Environment. Open Systems Laboratory, University of Illinois at Urbana-Champaign (1998)
7. Behrens, T.M., Hindriks, K., Hübner, J., Dastani, M.: Putting APL Platforms to the Test: Agent Similarity and Execution Performance. Technical Report IfI-10-09, Clausthal University of Technology (2010)

8. Bitting, E., Carter, J., Ghorbani, A.A.: Multiagent System Development Kits: An Evaluation. In: Proceedings of the 1st Annual Conference on Communication Networks and Services Research (CNSR 2003), CNSR Project, pp. 80–92 (2003)

9. Bordini, R.H., Dastani, M., Dix, J., El Fallah Seghrouchni, A. (eds.): Multi-Agent Programming: Languages, Tools and Applications. Springer (2009)

10. Bordini, R.H., Hübner, J.F., Wooldridge, M.: Programming Multi-agent Systems in AgentSpeak Using *Jason*. Wiley Series in Agent Technology. John Wiley & Sons (2007)

11. Braubach, L., Pokahr, A., Lamersdorf, W.: A Universal Criteria Catalog for Evaluation of Heterogeneous Agent Development Artifacts. In: Jung, B., Michel, F., Ricci, A., Petta, P. (eds.) From Agent Theory to Agent Implementation (AT2AI-6), pp. 19–28 (2008)

12. Busetta, P., Ronnquist, R., Hodgson, A., Lucas, A.: JACK Intelligent Agents - Components for Intelligent Agents in Java AgentLink News (2) (1999)

13. Cardoso, R.C., Hübner, J.F., Bordini, R.H.: Benchmarking Communication in Agent- and Actor-Based Languages (Extended Abstract). In: Proceedings of the AAMAS 2013, Saint Paul, Minnesota, USA, pp. 1267–1268 (2013)

14. Cesarini, F., Thompson, S.: ERLANG Programming, 1st edn. O'Reilly Media, Inc. (2009)

15. Dastani, M.: 2APL: a practical agent programming language. Autonomous Agents and Multi-Agent Systems 16(3), 214–248 (2008)

16. Díaz, Á.F., Earle, C.B., Fredlund, L.-Å.: eJason: An Implementation of Jason in Erlang. In: Dastani, M., Hübner, J.F., Logan, B. (eds.) ProMAS 2012. LNCS, vol. 7837, pp. 1–16. Springer, Heidelberg (2013)

17. Fernández, V., Grimaldo, F., Lozano, M., Orduña, J.M.: Evaluating Jason for Distributed Crowd Simulations. In: Filipe, J., Fred, A.L.N., Sharp, B. (eds.) ICAART (2), pp. 206–211. INSTICC Press (2010)

18. Haller, P., Odersky, M.: Event-based programming without inversion of control. In: Lightfoot, D.E., Ren, X.-M. (eds.) JMLC 2006. LNCS, vol. 4228, pp. 4–22. Springer, Heidelberg (2006)

19. Haller, P., Odersky, M.: Scala Actors: Unifying thread-based and event-based programming. Theor. Comput. Sci. 410(2-3), 202–220 (2009)

20. Hindriks, K.V., de Boer, F.S., van der Hoek, W., Meyer, J.-J.C.: Agent Programming with Declarative Goals. In: Castelfranchi, C., Lespérance, Y. (eds.) ATAL 2000. LNCS (LNAI), vol. 1986, pp. 228–243. Springer, Heidelberg (2001)

21. Jordan, H., Botterweck, G., Huget, M.-P., Collier, R.: A feature model of actor, agent, and object programming languages. In: Proceedings of AGERE 2011, pp. 147–158. ACM, New York (2011)

22. Karmani, R.K., Shali, A., Agha, G.: Actor frameworks for the JVM platform: a comparative analysis. In: Proceedings of the 7th International Conference on Principles and Practice of Programming in Java, PPPJ 2009, pp. 11–20. ACM, New York (2009)

23. Logan, M., Merritt, E., Carlsson, R.: Erlang and OTP in Action. Manning (November 2010)

24. Odersky, M., et al.: An Overview of the Scala Programming Language. Technical Report IC/2004/64, EPFL Lausanne, Switzerland (2004)

25. Pokahr, A., Braubach, L., Lamersdorf, W.: Jadex: Implementing a bdi-infrastructure for jade agents. EXP - in search of innovation (Special Issue on JADE) 3(3), 76–85 (2003)

26. Rao, A.S.: AgentSpeak(L): BDI Agents Speak Out in a Logical Computable Language. In: Perram, J., Van de Velde, W. (eds.) MAAMAW 1996. LNCS, vol. 1038, pp. 42–55. Springer, Heidelberg (1996)
27. Ricci, A., Santi, A.: Programming abstractions for integrating autonomous and reactive behaviors: an agent-oriented approach. In: Proceedings of AGERE! 2012, pp. 83–94. ACM, New York (2012)
28. Shakshuki, E., Jun, Y.: Multi-agent Development Toolkits: An Evaluation. In: Orchard, B., Yang, C., Ali, M. (eds.) IEA/AIE 2004. LNCS (LNAI), vol. 3029, pp. 209–218. Springer, Heidelberg (2004)
29. Suereth, J.: Scal. In: Depth. Manning Publications Co. (2012)
30. Wooldridge, M., Jennings, N.R.: Intelligent Agents: Theory and Practice. Knowledge Engineering Review 10, 115–152 (1995)
31. Wyatt, D.: Akka Concurrency. Artima Incorporation, USA (2013)

# Applying an O-MaSE Compliant Process to Develop a Holonic Multiagent System for the Evaluation of Intelligent Power Distribution Systems

Denise Case and Scott DeLoach

Department of Computing and Information Sciences
Kansas State University,
234 Nichols Hall, Manhattan, Kansas, USA
{dmcase,sdeloach}@ksu.edu

**Abstract.** This paper describes the application of an Organization-based Multiagent System Engineering (O-MaSE) compliant process to the development of a holonic multiagent system (MAS) for testing control algorithms for an intelligent power distribution system. The paper describes the Adaptive O-MaSE (AO-MaSE) process, which provides architects and developers a structured approach for testing and iteratively adding functionality in complex, adaptive systems. The paper describes the holonic MAS architecture for the intelligent power distribution system, the challenges encountered while developing the holonic architecture, the lessons learned during the project, and demonstrates how the application of the process enhanced project development.

**Keywords:** Agent-oriented software engineering, holonic multi-agent systems, adaptive systems, smart infrastructure, intelligent power distribution systems.

## 1    Introduction

Multiagent systems (MAS) are getting significant attention for Power Distribution Systems (PDS) and there is a growing interest in the application of holonic multiagent systems (HMAS) to PDS [22]. HMAS are adaptive, communicative, and autonomous – traits they receive from their MAS heritage – and their hierarchical, recursive structure is a natural fit for PDS systems. Holonic comes from the Greek word holon, a union formed from holos meaning whole and on meaning parts [19]. Thus, holons are parts that are also wholes. In an HMAS, the holon indicates an agent *participating* in one organization that also represents an entire organization itself. The overall organization of nested holonic organization agents is called a holarchy [8]. This hierarchical composition mechanism defines a powerful framework for distributing intelligence and finding local solutions in a recursive manner.

The primary goal of the Intelligent Power Distribution System (IPDS) project at Kansas State University is to demonstrate an HMAS architecture capable of adaptively controlling future PDS that are expected to include a large number of renewable power generators, energy storage devices, and advanced metering and control devices.

M. Cossentino et al. (Eds.): EMAS 2013, LNAI 8245, pp. 78–96, 2013.

Specifically, we are considering PDS with a high penetration (between 25% and 75%) of home-based PV systems. The HMAS architecture will also be used to support new analytical algorithms aimed at limiting the impact of information delay, quality and flow on the PDS. The purpose of this paper is to present the O-MaSE compliant software engineering process that we used while developing our prototype HMAS architecture for the IPDS project.


## 2    Background

Power distribution is estimated to account for approximately 40% of the capital investment in power systems worldwide, roughly comparable to the amount invested in generation, and about twice that invested in transmission assets [22]. PDS automation has lagged the advances in generation, due in part to the distributed nature and the massive number of components that make up the system. Power distribution begins with the primary circuit leaving a substation. It includes a distribution network of 3-phase feeder lines that branch into single-phase lateral lines and a variety of supporting equipment. Lateral lines distribute power through shared transformers that ultimately feed a set of electricity consumers, such as individual homes. Traditionally, control of the system, like the energy, has flowed from the central power source outward and downward toward the end consumer.

However, the increasing presence of renewable, distributed energy resources creates a bidirectional flow of power in the system. Rather than solely consuming power, home owners are installing increasing numbers of rooftop photovoltaic (PV) systems that generate power from solar radiation. The PV electricity generated during peak hours of the day can be greater than what is consumed by the associated home and creates an opportunity for homeowners to sell excess power into the grid. Distributed energy suppliers introduce a need for enhanced information flows, including online auctioning of power between growing numbers of market participants. At the same time, distributed energy sources are subject to intermittency. Wind fluctuation and passing clouds can introduce rapid variation in the amount of power flowing into the system. Rapid change in generation creates significant challenges for maintaining voltages within desired ranges. However, coordinated volt/var control can help provide consistent voltage to consumers while reducing rapid cycling of equipment, improving efficiency, and reducing the overall cost of power generation.

Centralized control is supported by load tap changers (LTC) near the substation that have a limited number of setting changes per day (more rapid cycling is expensive and shortens the equipment life). Distributed control can be supported by the addition of smart inverters that moderate a PV system's reactive power to offset generation changes and by line capacitors employed in various places along the grid.

Distributed control equipment coupled with centralized, large impact devices like the LTCs create an excellent opportunity for distributed intelligent systems that can adapt reactively and proactively to offer substantial benefits. In addition, distributed intelligent systems can help the increasingly connected remote nodes that are both electricity producers and consumers (*prosumers*) work together when disconnected from the grid. During this *islanded mode* participants can work together to provide electricity to critical loads, even though the lack of a stable power source (i.e., power from the grid) creates additional challenges for power supply and quality.

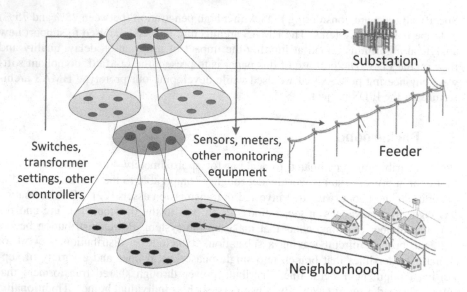

**Fig. 1.** Application of Holonic MAS in a Power Distribution System

The mapping of our prototype HMAS architecture to a physical distribution system is shown in Fig. 1. The left side of Fig. 1 illustrates the HMAS holarchy of adaptive agent organizations and the right side illustrates the physical system. The lowest level of the holarchy shows peer agents representing single homes acting within a local organization at the neighborhood level (assumed to be represented by the pole transformer serving that set of homes). Each neighborhood organization is represented by a corresponding neighborhood organization agent in the higher lateral-level organization. Nested organizations reflect the physical system from the originating substation down to individual consumer homes. The holarchy, like the physical network, recursively aggregates the systems and organizations to provide an integrated model of the system and provides a framework that allows the IPDS be able to learn and support adaptive, distributed control.

# 3     Related Work

## 3.1     Smart Infrastructure Optimization with Agents

Smart infrastructure optimization involves some of the most complex and critical systems in modern society [22]. Agent technology offers a way to manage the inherent complexity of such systems. Agents can be used to represent simple variables in a computer program as well as complex, distributed, intelligent objects involving potentially infinite numbers of states, decisions, and actions and reactions [23]. When modeling power systems, we are especially interested in agent traits such as autonomy, heterogeneity, adaptivity, social ability, communicability, flexibility, and concurrence [26]. Agents implement goal-based behavior and IPDS agents must demonstrate the ability to support the objectives of their respective owners while also acting cooperatively to achieve common objectives, such as maintaining critical loads and system efficiency.

Current research projects include a variety of studies involving the application of MAS to power systems, with active research projects focusing on power auctioning, negotiating, volt/var control, distributed communications, and other focus areas [3, 13, 18, 20, 23, 24, 25]. Recent research has also applied HMAS to PDS [2, 15, 17], sometimes in concert with specific agent-oriented software engineering methodologies. Power flow, quality, and control lends itself to distributed, recursive optimization where possible. Some local optimization can be distributed and may not result in propagation throughout the hierarchy, while the system as a whole may be impacted by larger, more centralized control options such as load tap changes. Using a flexible, holonic architecture will allow us to evaluate a variety of control algorithms and strategies.

### 3.2    Agent-Oriented Software Engineering Methodologies

For the IPDS project, we needed a reactive, proactive, model-driven, proven MAS framework with a supporting formal process methodology. Several agent-oriented engineering methodologies are available for developing complex, adaptive systems and the methodologies include the metamodels and process flows that provide the structure necessary to engineer MAS. Methodologies that have been successfully employed include ADELFE, ASPECS, INGENIAS, O-MaSE, PASSI, Prometheus, SODA, and Tropos [8]. Some methodologies, such as ASPECS and ANEMONA support holonic concepts [1, 7, 11] and O-MaSE enables hierarchical decomposition via organizational agents. We selected O-MaSE and the associated Organization-based Agent Architecture (OBAA) for our foundations because of the unique tools and process flexibility provided. Together with the agentTool3 integrated development environment, they offer a flexible, extensible system to support reactive control as well as predictive capabilities and proactive control.

## 4    Foundations

### 4.1    O-MaSE Process Framework

O-MaSE is an organization-based, role-centered process framework that consists of three main components: a metamodel, method fragments, and guidelines [10]. The metamodel describes system components as shown in Fig. 2. Method fragments define engineering roles, their activities, and the resulting work products, such as the goal models, role models, and plan diagrams that define the system. Each aspect of O-MaSE is supported by agentTool3 modeling tools, which support method creation and maintenance, model creation and verification, and code generation and maintenance.

Linnenberg et al. used the O-MaSE methodology and agentTool3 to develop DEMAPOS (DEcentralized MArket Based POwer Control System) [19] for power trading and we have followed the DEMAPOS convention of combining entities capable of producing and/or consuming electricity into the notion of prosumer agents.

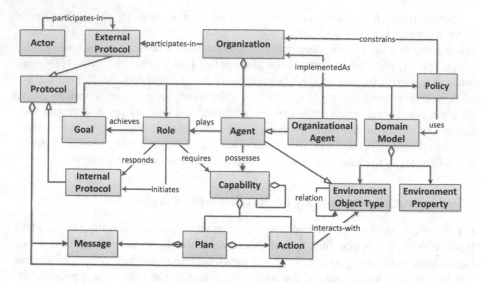

**Fig. 2.** The O-MaSE Metamodel (multiplicities not shown)

## 4.2 Holonic Multiagent Architectures

Holonic multiagent architectures introduce additional elements to MAS. Cossentino et al. describe the multilevel interplay between local organizations [7] where an agent participating locally in an organization may represent the entire lower-level organization while also participating as an agent in a higher-level organization. A holonic organization agent may play different roles in different organizations simultaneously as shown in Fig. 4. Participation in multiple organizations is not unique to holonic agents; rather it is the recursive representation of progressively distributed agent organizations that made the holonic approach desirable for evaluating IPDS.

We evaluated a variety of existing systems to provide core MAS functionality and selected the Organization-based Agent Architecture (OBAA) as our foundation. OBAA has been employed in a variety of adaptive systems [21]. OBAA agents include a shared control component enabling basic communication capabilities within the local organization coupled with an embedded knowledge representation of the organization in which the agent operates. In OBAA, each control component coordinates with the team and maintains a complete copy of the local organization knowledge. Each OBAA agent also has a domain-specific execution component that manages roles and capabilities as shown in Fig. 3.

The primary objective of the generic OBAA architecture is to offer a general framework of classes from which domain-specific adaptive systems can be built. The OBAA framework is built on the Organization Model for Complex, Adaptive Systems, OMACS [10], and includes an executable goal model, GMODS [9]. The control component parts provide the functionality for agents to get initialized, register with an acting supervisor and, once the registration process is complete, to begin executing their assigned tasks. An initial agent registration process was defined to get the system running; it will be enhanced to incorporate leader election as the project continues.

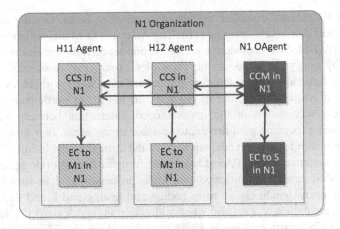

**Fig. 3.** Each participating OBAA agent includes a control component and a domain-specific execution component to enable participation in the organization

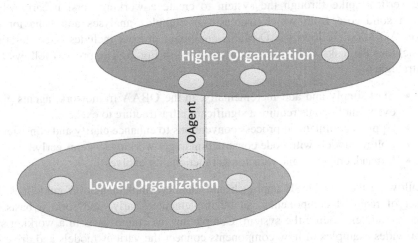

**Fig. 4.** A holonic organization agent (OAgent) serves as the master agent in its lower-level organization (blue) and a peer agent in a higher-level organization (purple)

## 5  AO-MaSE: An O-MaSE Compliant Process

O-MaSE provides a foundation supporting tailored software engineering implementations. A compliant process must meet the following requirements: (1) no new constraints may be placed on existing entities and relationships in the O-MaSE metamodel, (2) the method guideline pre-conditions must not become stronger or post-conditions made weaker, and (3) no existing metamodel entities, tasks, work products, or method-roles may be eliminated [9].

MAS and HMAS are complex models of complex systems. Getting started with such frameworks can be challenging [16]. The Adaptive O-MaSE software engineering process (AO-MaSE) provides a set of recommendations for dealing with that complexity by applying some of the principles commonly associated with agile processes [4]. Several of these agile principles are associated with MAS in general and include an ability to respond to changes, an ability to participate in ongoing collaboration, a recognition of the importance of interaction between autonomous participants, and a focus on goal-driven, executable components. In a similar way, the AO-MaSE approach focuses on adaptability and the structured evolution of a working system. Other systems such as PASSI have gone further to incorporate agile processes [5]. Agile PASSI research confirmed that agile processes tend to spend less time on design and correspondingly more in coding and testing and found that a quicker move to implementation was helpful when addressing high-risk areas [5]. In addition, research at the University of Vigo in Spain has adapted the INGENIAS methodology to follow the agile process SCRUM with promising results [12].

In AO-MaSE, the architect begins by creating a fully executable but limited scope vertical spike through the system to create a working version early which offers a solid core from which increasingly complex analyses and behavior can evolve. AO-MaSE follows the O-MaSE compliant process includes three iterations that includes the tasks and work products shown in Fig. 5. The process follows four key strategies:

- Start simply and add incrementally; in the OBAA framework, agents given even simple goals require a significant infrastructure to execute.
- Apply recommended process conventions to enhance clarity and consistency.
- Follow models with code construction to get working systems early.
- Expand, enhance, and refactor as functionality evolves.

By following the AO-MaSE approach and detailed implementation guidelines, the full set of required components can be implemented early, and form a basis for expanding and enhancing the system. Completing the connections in a working system provides examples of how components connect the various models and drive the behavior of the system. For example, event triggers on the goal model may appear as transitions in the plan diagrams and domain objects may appear in method parameters in plan states and associated capabilities. A working version that connects the parts provides a concrete example for software engineers and developers that have little experience in agent-oriented engineering. The method construction guidelines provide the ability for a team of software engineers and subject matter experts to work collaboratively to select key elements for implementation and to develop associated work products including requirements specifications, goal models, organization models, domain models, role models, role plans, plan states, capabilities, protocols, policies, and code.

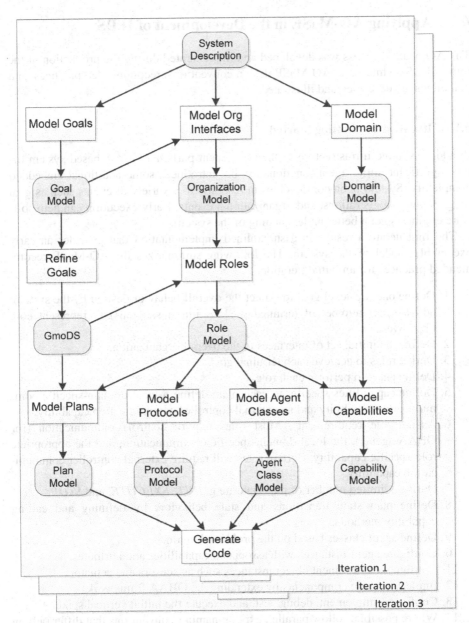

**Fig. 5.** AO-MaSE Iterative Process (tasks are shown as rectangles, work products are shown as rounded rectangles)

# 6    Applying AO-MaSE in the Development of IPDS

The AO-MaSE process was developed and implemented during the production of the initial IPDS architecture. AO-MaSE design conventions, recommended practices, and guidelines are described and illustrated.

## 6.1    Iteration 1 – Getting Started

In addition to the infrastructure of the component parts, an OBAA-based system offers significant initial agent functionality, but introduces some additional embedded complexity. System behavior develops in response to a variety of events such as goal triggers, agent registrations, and organizational events. Early execution can help software engineers get a better understanding of the system.

The first iteration results in a streamlined implementation that provides an early executable model of the system. The following summarizes the AO-MaSE recommended practices for an initial iteration.

1. Define one top-level goal to reflect the overall behavior desired by the system; add a small number of terminal goals (without subgoals) to represent core objectives.
2. Define the initial set of interfaces to the overall organization.
3. Define roles to achieve each terminal goal.
4. Define plans to perform each role.
5. Define capabilities specific to each plan; define a local domain-specific communication capability and an external controller communication capability.
6. Assign role requirements. Most roles require control communication (for OBAA agents), the local domain-specific communication, and the appropriate role-specific capability. Certain roles will require external controller communication capability.
7. Define a limited number of plan states, e.g. *INIT*, *EXECUTE*, and *STOP*.
8. Define plan state transitions and state behaviors by defining and calling capability methods.
9. Define agent classes based on the problem domain.
10. Configure agent instances with associated capabilities and attributes.
11. Configure environment object instances such as sensors and actuators.
12. Implement code components by extending the OBAA framework.
13. Configure, implement, debug, test, and execute the initial vertical spike.
14. Where possible, follow parallel, explicit naming conventions that differ only in type (as shown in the IPDS models).

The project began with the specification of requirements. From the set of requirements for the initial phase of the project we selected an initial focus that allowed us to test core functionality – the distribution and management of goals within a local organization.

Since achieving each goal requires substantial infrastructure, we started with a small set of core objectives. The top goal of each recursive organization is Support IPDS, as shown in It will guide agent organizations while connected to the grid and while running in islanded mode.

The organization model was developed to define the boundaries and interfaces for the system. Each IPDS would seek an external controller that would both receive requests and send requests/guidelines down to the system, enabling centralized control and communications from the primary energy supplier. Inputs were provided to characterize the organization's goals. The goal model was drafted and then refined to show the supervisor triggering a manage instance goal for each participant. The domain model began to reflect the objects in the environment and included a smart meter object and a PV system, along with equipment attributes and unique identifiers.

Following the guidelines, we created a role for each terminal goal, a plan for each role, and gave each plan three initial states: (1) *INIT* for performing actions that will only need to be done once, (2) a role-specific state that captures the main work of the role, and (3) a *STOP* state consisting of behaviors to be executed when finishing the plan. The recommended capabilities were defined. As plan states were developed in the plan diagrams, we were specifying the methods required of each capability. Parallel naming conventions for goals, roles, plans, and role-specific default capabilities aided clarity and were used to employ additional code automation. Agent classes did not parallel the goal or plan names. Instead, they reflected the physical installation or focus of the agent type. We began with a Neighborhood Agent class, expected to run on or near a transformer serving 2-6 homes, and a Prosumer agent class, expected to be installed on or near a home-based smart meter.

As the OMACS components developed, they were implemented in the OBAA-based IPDS framework. Agent and Environment configuration files were used to instantiate specific agents and objects for a variety of test cases.

The OBAA framework can be employed immediately if one control component master is declared for any local organization. We began with one supervisor neighborhood agent (the control component master) and two prosumer agents (both control component slaves) to test the ability of the system to solve adapt to changing local conditions. Some key models from Iteration 1 are shown in Fig. 6. The models illustrate the parallel naming conventions between goals, roles, and plans, and although only a small subset of the models created are included, helps illustrate the infrastructure support underlying an agent-based adaptive system.

## 6.2    Iteration 2 – Filling in the Framework

With a working simulation provided during Iteration 1, the focus in Iteration 2 shifted to adding functionality to address a variety of potential challenges. We began working with the new holonic organization agents and the development focused on enhancing the plan states and capability method calls. Additional capability classes were added, providing additional differentiation and room for expanded functionality. Capabilities were implemented with simple algorithms that served to define the expected interfaces that would be required to support more complex optimization algorithms that were being developed in parallel research projects.

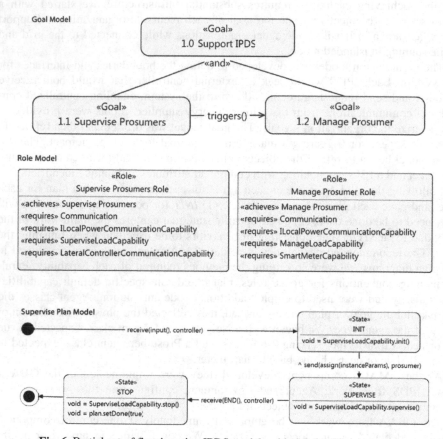

**Fig. 6.** Partial set of first-iteration IPDS models with AO-MaSE conventions

The goal model was enhanced to include parameterized goals with the external controller providing combined guidelines for the organization. Additional triggers were added to the refined goal model. The supervise goal, which had been distributing combined goals among participants during the INIT state, was enhanced to adapt participant goals during the SUPERVISE state in response to each participant's simulated history.

Organization guidelines were grouped into objects with defined purposes, making the system easier to expand as requirements were added. Three types of guidelines were given to each organization: combined load guidelines, combined power quality guidelines, and evaluation guidelines that reflected desired feedback intervals and forecast horizons. As a holarchy, the combined organization guidelines could be adapted in response to temporal conditions just as local participant guidelines were adapted. Plan states continued to evolve to reflect more complex logic and additional actions and events were added to define the transitions between states. Objects and attributes were added to the domain model as more external devices were defined.

Capabilities grew in functionality as plan state logic developed. Capability methods were enhanced to include simulation interfaces and smart meter sensor capabilities began obtaining simulated device data from MatLab®. As capabilities became more complex, they were refactored into smaller, more specific capabilities that in turn began to grow in functionality. An IPDS Builder component was added to support the reliable generation of test cases.

## 6.3    Iteration 3 – Extending Functionality

The third iteration focused on extending the refined goal model; introducing forecasting goals and adding supporting agent types. Although goal changes represent a relatively major change to the IPDS design, by following the guidelines and recommended process and code policies, we were able to add new features more easily. Additional goals brought additional triggering events and goal parameters. The expanding goal models and role models are shown in Fig. 7.

As communications are added to plan diagrams, they include the specification of the performative, the type of message content, and the role of the agent with which the communication takes place. Message classes and their associated message content classes were implemented for each communication capability.

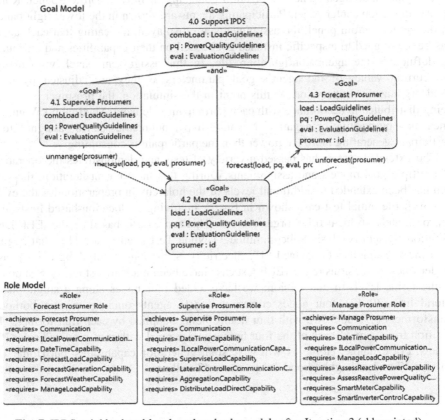

**Fig. 7.** IPDS neighborhood-level goal and role models after Iteration 3 (abbreviated)

As an IPDS organization starts up, agents participating in the organization register with the control component master. The specification goal tree gets instantiated and activates the top level goal along with any non-triggered, non-preceded leaf goals. For example, as the goal plan for the Supervise Prosumers goal is executed, the Supervise Prosumers Plan INIT state triggers an instance of the Manage Prosumer goal for each participant. As each home agent gets assigned to a Manage Prosumer Role, it first enters the Manage Prosumer Plan INIT state, and then triggers a new instance of an associated Forecast Prosumer goal.

The home agent then transitions to the Manage Prosumer MANAGE state and begins sensing consumption and generation readings, which it reports back to the Supervisor, alerting the Supervisor if it detects an out-of-bounds condition. The supervisor optimizes combined local guidelines within the organization, adapting participant goals to maximize compliance. If guidelines cannot be met within the local organization, the supervisor will raise a request to the external controller who will, in turn, attempt to address the request from within the controller agent's local organization, recursively raising requests up the holarchy until a solution is available.

Fig. 8 shows a view into a running IPDS system. There is one debug window for each organization agent. The organization goals appear in each top left panel. Roles appear in the top center panel. Participating agents are shown in the lower right panel. In the center bottom panel, the assignments are displayed, indicating that each agent has been assigned to a specific instance goal based on their capabilities and attributes as defined in the agent configuration file. In this assignment panel, we can see the current values of the agent's goal parameters as they are adjusted by their local organization supervisor. At this point in the simulation, the prosumer goals are being distributed in accordance with each participant's demand. Maximum kW guidelines may be positive or negative. Negative upper boundaries can be assigned to a participant generating more PV power than the participant is consuming.

The extended system has passed a variety of tests and demonstrates the operation of multiple goal models and assignments. During this most recent iteration, the system has been extended to additional levels of the holarchy in preparation for the evaluation of the initial test case shown in Fig. 9, involving 62 location-based hosts and approximately 46 local IPDS organizations. This test case is based on the IEEE Distribution System Analysis Subcommittee 37-Node Test Feeder case [14] that begins with the substation node labeled "1". Electricity is distributed out along the 3-phase feeder lines. Extensions to the IEEE test case have been made to test the system down to the home level. In our version, we have added four nodes along a single-phase lateral line (39–42), four nodes corresponding to agents running on neighborhood transformers (43,48,53,58), with four homes being supplied by each transformer. In our first trials, one of each of the four homes is equipped with roof-mounted solar PV panels. For example, Home 44 will have solar generation capabilities, but Home 45, 46, and 47 under Neighborhood Transformer 43 will not.

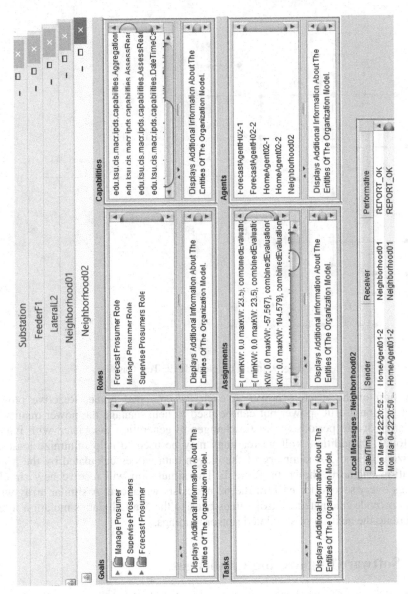

**Fig. 8.** Simple IPDS Holarchy (Substation, Feeder, Laterals, Neighborhoods)

Each number on the test case diagram corresponds to a physical location or node that could host IPDS agents. These locations may have sensors and/or actuators depending on the physical configuration being simulated. Generally, we assume that real power (P) and reactive power (Q) consumption (load) values are available by phase at each of the nodes. In addition, homes equipped with PV may have sensor readings available for the real power generated. Actuators or controllable equipment range from a single load tap changer at the top of the distribution network, down through capacitors on the three-phase feeders to smart inverters, which allow for some

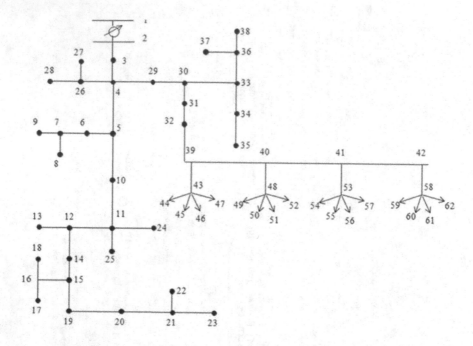

**Fig. 9.** Initial 62-Node IEEE Test Case

moderation of the reactive power at each PV-equipped home. Reactive power is typically "non-useful" power but can be used to help manage the power quality characteristics during periods of drastic changes in generation associated with intermittent clouds. In addition, voltage readings may be used to help minimize losses and optimize efficiency. A summary of the eleven data values calculated by the MatLab simulation engine is shown in Table 1. The simulation will receive new simulated readings every second for each of the 62 nodes shown above. A similar array will be used to provide calculated control values back to the MatLab data simulation in order to calculate the next set of simulated sensor readings.

# 7    Software Engineering Challenges

Architecting complex, adaptive systems can be challenging. Employing existing components can facilitate design, but a true understanding of the interrelationships between framework components may take a while to develop. Designing a new organization-based HMAS for IPDS required developing a detailed understanding of the O-MaSE metamodel, the OBAA framework, and GMoDS, and understanding the connections between the various elements, how they were related to code structures and most importantly, how they drive behavior during execution. Initial attempts took longer than expected. The AO-MaSE process was developed as a way to illustrate the system design in a concrete manner. Standards have allowed greater automation and agentTool3 has been updated. The process of debugging configuration files resulted

**Table 1.** Simulated Second-by-Second Data Values (calculated in MatLab)

| Abbrev | Description | Phase | Type | Value |
|---|---|---|---|---|
| PA | Column 1 - Phase A - P (load) | A | Load | P |
| QA | Column 2 - Phase A - Q (load) | A | Load | Q |
| PB | Column 3 - Phase B - P (load) | B | Load | P |
| QB | Column 4 - Phase B - Q (load) | B | Load | Q |
| PC | Column 5 - Phase C - P (load) | C | Load | P |
| QC | Column 6 - Phase C - Q (load) | C | Load | Q |
| PG | Column 7 - P (generation) | - | Gen | P |
| QG | Column 8 - Q (generation) | - | Gen | Q |
| VA | Column 9 - Voltage Phase A | A | Load | Voltage |
| VB | Column 10 - Voltage Phase B | B | Load | Voltage |
| VC | Column 11 - Voltage Phase C | C | Load | Voltage |

in the creation of IPDS builder factories that were used to generate additional test cases. Strict naming and documentation requirements improve clarity and consistency. Although the number of classes required is substantial, the focus of each is such that enhancements have been proceeding in parallel. The IPDS simulation must be able to evaluate control strategies that are not yet defined and the ability to quickly respond to new requirements and system enhancements will continue to be crucial. Additional automated testing offers support for evolutionary refactoring as the system functionality expands and initial experiments with new specification and testing frameworks appears promising.

## 8    Results

The project resulted in the development of a standard, repeatable process for implementing IPDS simulations. The AO-MaSE process and the model-driven tools provide a complete path through the design, specification, implementation, and execution of a MAS. The process was used to test implementation of the required goals, roles, capabilities, and plans required for the initial IEEE test cases developed by the electrical engineering simulation team. The AO-MaSE process was employed during the development of a new type of organization that will allow the additional implementation of self-management capabilities for agents participating in multiple organizations. The process and tools provided a path that has allowed implementation of new iterations of end-to-end functionality within days. A comparison of O-MaSE compliant systems, some of which were developed using the AO-MaSE guidelines and some of which were not, is shown in Table 2.

**Table 2.** Implementation of O-MaSE-compliant MAS with and without AO-MaSE

| Feature | AO-MaSE initial iterations | O-MaSE final implementation |
|---------|---------------------------|----------------------------|
| Goal – role correspondence. | Direct 1-1 correspondence facilitates initial modeling and subsequent debugging. | No correspondence required; multiple roles may achieve a goal. |
| Roles – plan correspondence. | Direct 1-1 correspondence facilitates initial modeling and subsequent debugging. | No correspondence required. |
| Plans and plan state consistency. | Plans initially implemented using automated INIT-EXECUTE-STOP template. | Plans created and refined independently as flexible finite state models. |
| Post-fix object type naming standards. | Consistent application of post-fix object type names (e.g. SmartMeter*Capability*, ManagePower*Goal*) improves code readability and maintainability. | Post-fix object type names not required. Less code clarity and increased need for commenting or familiarity for implementation and debugging. |
| Clearly-defined design process. | Yes. Application of process framework and agentTool3 modeling tools clearly described. | Yes. Application of process framework and agentTool3 modeling tools clearly described. |
| Clearly-defined implementation process. | Yes. Well-defined and structured implementation process and guidelines provided. | Flexible process for implementation; few direct guidelines. |

## 9    Conclusions

This paper describes the iterative design and construction of an architecture prototype for an intelligent power distribution system with the AO-MaSE process. It describes a recommended software engineering process employing specific design conventions that begin simply and focus on moving sooner from initial concepts to code construction while creating an evolving, iterative framework suited to the development of complex, adaptive, intelligent, autonomic systems.

The effort includes policy recommendations and detailed guidelines that produce a vertical slice of a complex system earlier in the process, forming a working core that enables early feedback into the behavior of a complex, recursive HMAS. Architectures that do not perform as expected can be abandoned sooner and alternate versions can be tested. The process is compliant with the proven O-MaSE process framework and enables the full functionality needed for complex control systems yet offers a structured path towards implementation that addresses several challenges encountered when developing MAS. Specific recommendations are included with examples taken from the initial IPDS implementation.

## 10    Future Work

Our initial iterations have allowed us to test several critical issues early. The next phase will involve an initial assessment of potential self-organizing abilities, grid-based leader election algorithms, implementation of voltage/var control strategies during periods of renewable intermittency, initial critical power supply strategies, and reconnection approaches after islanded operation. A real-time visualization of PDS operation will be created and agent negotiation and support capabilities will be tested between complementary lateral power lines in our 62-node test case and additional extended test cases. The AO-MaSE process will continue to be employed and refined to support a more adaptive implementation of evolving functionality. Additional implementation of agile-recommended testing strategies may be included as well, based on some of the interesting work being done with SADAAM, test agents, and test-driven development in agile agent-oriented software engineering [6].

## References

1. Argente, E., Julian, V., Botti, V.: MAS modeling based on organizations. In: Luck, M., Gomez-Sanz, J.J. (eds.) AOSE 2008. LNCS, vol. 5386, pp. 16–30. Springer, Heidelberg (2009)
2. Asano, H.: Holonic Energy Systems: Coevolution of Distributed Energy Resources and Existing Network Energy. In: International Symposium on Distributed Energy Systems and Micro Grids, The University of Tokyo, December 7-8 (2005)
3. Baxevanos, I.S., Labridis, D.P.: Implementing multiagent systems technology for power distribution network control and protection management. IEEE Transactions on Power Delivery 22(1), 433–443 (2007)
4. Beck, K., Beedle, M., Van Bennekum, A., Cockburn, A., Cunningham, W., Fowler, M., Thomas, D.: Manifesto for agile software development. The Agile Alliance, 2002-04 (2001)
5. Chella, A., Cossentino, M., Sabatucci, L., Seidita, V.: Agile PASSI: An agile process for designing agents. International Journal of Computer Systems Science & Engineering 21(2), 133–144 (2006)
6. Clynch, N., Collier, R.: Sadaam: Software agent development-an agile methodology. In: Proceedings of the Workshop of Languages, Methodologies, and Development Tools for Multi-agent Systems (LADS 2007), Durham, UK (2007)
7. Cossentino, M., Gaud, N., Hilaire, V., Galland, S., Koukam, A.: ASPECS: an agent-oriented software process for engineering complex systems. J. of Auton. Agents and Multiagent Syst. 20, 260–304 (2009)
8. Cossentino, M., Gleizes, M.-P., Molesini, A., Omicini, A.: Processes Engineering and AOSE. In: Gleizes, M.-P., Gomez-Sanz, J.J. (eds.) AOSE 2009. LNCS, vol. 6038, pp. 191–212. Springer, Heidelberg (2011)
9. Cossentino, M., Gaud, N., Galland, S., Hilaire, V., Koukam, A.: A holonic metamodel for agent-oriented analysis and design. In: Mařík, V., Vyatkin, V., Colombo, A.W. (eds.) HoloMAS 2007. LNCS (LNAI), vol. 4659, pp. 237–246. Springer, Heidelberg (2007)
10. DeLoach, S.A., Garcia-Ojeda, J.C.: O-MaSE: A customisable approach to designing and building complex, adaptive multi-agent systems. International Journal of Agent-Oriented Software Engineering 4(3), 244–280 (2010)

11. Gaud, N., Galland, S., Hilaire, V., Koukam, A.: An organisational platform for holonic and multiagent systems. In: Hindriks, K.V., Pokahr, A., Sardina, S. (eds.) ProMAS 2008. LNCS, vol. 5442, pp. 104–119. Springer, Heidelberg (2009)
12. Gómez-Rodríguez, A.M., González-Moreno, J.C.: Comparing agile processes for agent oriented software engineering. In: Ali Babar, M., Vierimaa, M., Oivo, M. (eds.) PROFES 2010. LNCS, vol. 6156, pp. 206–219. Springer, Heidelberg (2010)
13. Huang, K., Cartes, D.A., Srivastava, S.K.: A multiagent-based algorithm for ring-structured shipboard power system reconfiguration. IEEE Transactions on Systems, Man, and Cybernetics, Part C: Applications and Reviews 37(5), 1016–1021 (2007)
14. IEEE Power and Energy Society: Distribution Test Feeders, http://ewh.ieee.org/soc/pes/dsacom/testfeeders/
15. Ionita, S.: Multi Agent Holonic Based Architecture for Communication and Learning about Power Demand in Residential Areas, Machine Learning and Applications. In: 2009 Fourth International Conference on Machine Learning and Applications, pp. 644–649 (2009)
16. Jennings, N.R.: On agent-based software engineering. Artificial intelligence 117(2), 277–296 (2000)
17. Jiang, Z.: Agent-based power sharing scheme for active hybrid power sources. Journal of Power Sources 177(1), 231–238 (2008)
18. Kim, H.M., Kinoshita, T.: Multiagent system for Microgrid operation based on power market environment. In: 31st International Telecommunications Energy Conference (INTELEC), pp. 1–5. IEEE (2009)
19. Linnenberg, T., Wior, I., Schreiber, S., Fay, A.: A market-based multi-agent-system for decentralized power and grid control. In: 2011 IEEE 16th Conference on Emerging Technologies & Factory Automation (ETFA), September 5-9, pp. 1–8 (2011)
20. Malekpour, A.R., Pahwa, A.: Reactive power and voltage control in distribution systems with photovoltaic generation. In: North American Power Symposium (NAPS), pp. 1–6 (September 2012)
21. Oyenan, W.H., DeLoach, S.A.: Towards a systematic approach for designing autonomic systems. Web Intelligence and Agent Systems 8(1), 79–97 (2010)
22. Pahwa, A., DeLoach, S.A., Das, S., Natarajan, B., Ou, X., Andresen, D., Schulz, N., Singh, G.: Holonic multi-agent control of power distribution systems of the future. In: CIGRE Grid of the FutureSymposium (2012)
23. Vishwanathan, V., McCalley, J., Honavar, V.: A multiagent system infrastructure and negotiation framework for electric power systems. In: 2001 IEEE Porto Power Tech Proceedings, vol. 1, p. 6. IEEE (2001)
24. Zabet, I., Montazeri, M.: Decentralized control and management systems for power industry via multiagent systems technology. In: 2010 4th International Power Engineering and Optimization Conference (PEOCO), pp. 549–556 (2010)
25. Zhong, Z., McCalley, J.D., Vishwanathan, V., Honavar, V.: Multiagent system solutions for distributed computing, communications, and data integration needs in the power industry. Power Engineering Society General Meeting 1, 45–49 (2004)
26. Zhou, Z., Chan, W.K.V., Chow, J.H.: Agent-based simulation of electricity markets: a survey of tools. Artificial Intelligence Review 28(4), 305–342 (2007)

# Embedding Agents in Business Processes Using Enterprise Integration Patterns

Stephen Cranefield and Surangika Ranathunga

Department of Information Science, University of Otago, Dunedin, New Zealand
{scranefield,surangika}@infoscience.otago.ac.nz

**Abstract.** This paper addresses the issue of integrating agents with a variety of external resources and services, as found in enterprise computing environments. We propose an approach for interfacing agents and existing message routing and mediation engines based on the *message endpoint* pattern from the enterprise integration patterns of Hohpe and Woolf. A design for agent percept, action and message endpoints is presented, and an architecture for connecting the Jason agent platform to the Apache Camel enterprise integration framework using these types of endpoint is described. The approach is illustrated by means of a business process use case, and a number of Camel routes are presented. These demonstrate the benefits of interfacing agents to external services via a specialised message routing tool that supports enterprise integration patterns.

## 1 Introduction

This research is based on the premise that agents could play a valuable role in enhancing business processes with adaptive and goal-directed behaviour. However, most research in this direction tends to be revolutionary in approach (e.g. commitment-based models of business processes [12]), and there is little current uptake of agent technology in enterprise computing. While there could be great benefits for implementing business processes using multi-agent systems, in this paper we focus on the shorter-term goal of facilitating the inclusion of agents as *components* of business processes, within standard enterprise computing environments. This goal raises a number of challenges:

1. Modern enterprise computing environments comprise a diverse range of middleware and server technologies. How can we support agent programmers in interacting with this diversity of external systems?
2. Industry experience with enterprise application integration (EAI) has shown the benefits of separating service coordination and application logic. How can we achieve this separation when integrating agents with external enterprise services?
3. Agent programmers are a scarce resource. How can we facilitate mainstream EAI programmers to encode the logic for coordinating agents with external services, leaving the agent programmers to focus on core agent concerns (e.g. goals and plans)?

The current solutions for integrating agents with external computing infrastructure are: (a) to access these resources and services directly from agent code (if using a conventional programming language), (b) to implement user-defined agent actions or an

M. Cossentino et al. (Eds.): EMAS 2013, LNAI 8245, pp. 97–116, 2013.

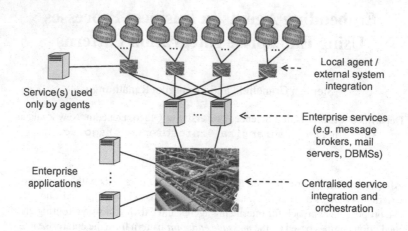

**Fig. 1.** The proposed MAS integration model[1]

environment model to encapsulate these interactions, (c) to provide custom support in an agent platform for specific types of external service, or (d) to provide a generic interface for calling external resources and services, either using a platform-specific API [11] or by encapsulating them as agents [5], artifacts [10] or active components [8]. However, none of these approaches are a good solution when agents need to be integrated with a range of technologies. They either require agent developers to learn a variety of APIs, or they assume that agent platform developers or their users will provide wrapper templates for a significant number of commonly used technologies.

Motivated by the above challenges, this paper proposes an alternative approach: the use of a direct bridge between agents and the mainstream industry technology for enterprise application integration: message routing and mediation engines, and in particular, those that support the *enterprise integration patterns* (EIP) of Hohpe and Woolf [6]. Our integration approach is illustrated in Figure 1. In this figure, each "pipes" graphic represents a messaging-based service coordination tool, such as an enterprise service bus [4]. The larger one represents an organisation's existing message-based infrastructure for managing business processes by coordinating information passing between applications and services. We propose that agents can be embedded into this infrastructure by integrating them with their own local message-routing and mediation engines, such as the lightweight Java-based Apache Camel enterprise integration framework [7]. This integration is based on the EIP *message endpoint* pattern, and in this paper we present the design of endpoints that can translate agent action executions and messages to EIP messages, and from EIP messages to agent percepts and messages.

We describe an implemented architecture for connecting the Jason agent platform [3] to Camel using these "agent endpoints". The approach is illustrated by means of a business process use case, which we address by integrating Jason agents with a database management system, a mail server, a message broker and the Apache ZooKeeper coordi-

---

[1] Pipes photo by Hervé Cozanet, source: http://commons.wikimedia.org/wiki/File:Piping_system_on_a_chemical_tanker.jpg (CC BY-SA 3.0)

nation server. A number of Camel routes handling aspects of this use case are presented to demonstrate the benefits of interfacing agents to external services via a specialised message routing tool that supports enterprise integration patterns.

## 2  Enterprise Integration Patterns

Enterprise computing environments typically comprise hundreds and possibly thousands of applications [6]. These may use a variety of communication protocols and interface technologies due to departmental autonomy (e.g. to acquire "best of breed" applications for specific business problems), incremental and opportunistic growth, mergers, etc. To preserve loose coupling between the diverse applications involved in the automation of business processes, and thus facilitate maintenance and extensibility, the use of middleware products based on asynchronous message-passing has emerged as the mainstream approach for *enterprise application integration*. In this approach, applications interact by sending and receiving structured messages to and from named queues or publish-subscribe 'topics' managed by (possibly federated) *message brokers*. Message routing and transformation rules can be executed by the message broker or by specialised message routing and mediation engines, thus providing a single location for the specification of business processes. The concept of the *enterprise service bus* extends this idea further by integrating message brokers with middleware for deploying and interacting with various type of service, such as web services [4].

Hohpe and Woolf [6] have identified 65 "enterprise integration patterns" (EIPs) for solving basic problems that commonly arise in messaging-based enterprise application integration, such as the *scatter-gather* pattern: "How do you maintain the overall message flow when a message needs to be sent to multiple recipients, each of which may send a reply?" A number of middleware tools have direct support for these patterns, including Apache Camel.

## 3  Apache Camel

Camel is an open source Java framework for executing message routing and mediation rules that are defined using domain-specific languages (DSLs) based on Java and Scala, or by using XML configuration files. In the work reported in this paper we have used the Java DSL.

Camel is based on the EIP concepts of *routes* and *endpoints*. A Camel application comprises a set of *route definitions* that are executed by the Camel engine. Each route receives messages from a *consumer endpoint*, performs a sequence of processing steps on each message, such as filtering and transforming messages, and then either sends the processed messages to one or more *producer endpoints* or sends it back as a response to the consumer endpoint. Endpoints can be "direct" links to other routes in the application (i.e. messages leaving one route may flow directly into another route) or they may represent connections to external resources and services. For example, a *mail* endpoint may be used as a consumer to receive messages representing unread mail in a specified account on a mail server, or as a producer that sends mail to a server. Camel has more than 130 *components* defined to provide a variety of endpoint types. These enable sending and/or receiving messages to and from external resources such as files, databases, message brokers, generic web services, specific Amazon and Google services, RSS and Atom feeds, and Twitter. To enable this diversity of endpoint types, Camel's concept of a message is very general: a message has headers (a map from names to Java objects), a body (which can be any Java object) and optional attachments.

The code below defines two simple Camel routes. These use the agent component described in this paper to enable "local" agents (those running within the same process as the Camel routes) to communicate with remote agents via a message broker.

```
from("agent:message")
.setHeader("CamelJmsDestinationName",
           simple("$headers.receiver.split(\"_\")[0]"))
.to("jms:dummy")


from("jms:"+containerId).to("agent:message");
```

These routes are defined using Camel's Java DSL. This is a Java API for constructing routes via a sequence of method calls. The `from` method creates a consumer endpoint and the `to` method creates a producer endpoint. Endpoints are specified using uniform resource identifiers (URIs), with the first part of the URI (the scheme) identifying the type of the endpoint. Other parts of the URI provide additional details, and the various endpoint types provided by Camel make use of URI parameters to provide configuration details for the instantiation of the endpoint. The routes shown above use two types of endpoint: our agent message endpoints described in Section 5.2, and standard Camel JMS endpoints for sending and receiving messages from a message broker using the Java Message Service.

The first route definition above creates an endpoint that receives all messages sent by local agents. For each agent message received, this endpoint copies the message content into the body of a new Camel message, and records the other message details using Camel message headers named `sender`, `receiver` and `illoc_force` (these correspond directly to Jason message properties).

Our architecture allows multiple distributed instances of Camel, each with their own set of local agents running within an *agent container*, so all agents are created with names of the form `containerId__localName`. The second and third lines of the first route above use Camel's "Simple" expression language to extract the first part of the name, which identifies the agent container that the message recipient is attached to, and stores this as the value of a specific header predefined by the JMS component. When the message is processed by the JMS producer endpoint, this header is used to override the queue or topic name that appears as a mandatory component of a JMS endpoint URI (hence the "dummy" message queue name at the end of the first route above). This illustrates two aspects of the use of message headers in Camel: they are commonly used within routes to store information needed later in the route, and they can affect the handling of messages by endpoints.

The second route definition above creates a JMS endpoint that receives messages from a message broker (the address of the broker is provided to Camel's JMS component on initialisation). The endpoint listens to a specific queue, which is named after the unique identifier for the local agent container (note that there may be agent containers associated with other Camel instances running elsewhere on the network or in other processes). The JMS consumer endpoint copies the body and the message headers from the received JMS messages to create Camel message objects. The route specifies that these messages flow from the JMS consumer endpoint directly to an agent message producer endpoint. This endpoint generates agent messages corresponding to the Camel messages and delivers them to the appropriate agents. The agent producer endpoint does the reverse of the Camel-to-agent message mapping described above.

Note that Camel routes can be significantly more complicated than those shown above, as later examples in this paper will demonstrate. In particular, the Java DSL includes methods for conditional branching, exception-handling and for starting, stopping, suspending and resuming routes. In addition, an important feature of Camel is the provision of methods that can be used singly or in combination to implement enterprise integration patterns such as splitting and aggregating messages, or to "enrich" messages with content obtained by making synchronous calls to other services via endpoints.

## 4   The Jason BDI Agent Platform

Jason [3] is an open source Java-based development platform for BDI agents written using an extension of the AgentSpeak programming language. A Jason agent consists of a set of *beliefs* (which may include Prolog-like Horn clauses for inferring beliefs from other beliefs) and a set of *plans*. Here we give a brief overview of Jason's plan structure, syntax and execution cycle, to help readers understand the agent code appearing in the discussion of our use case scenario (Listing 2). Jason plans have the following form, where each element is a Prolog-like term:

```
Event : Condition <- BodyFormula1 ; ... ; BodyFormulaN.
```

Event is the event that triggers the plan, provided that the (optional) Condition (a query on beliefs) currently holds. Various types of events are supported, but most commonly a plan is triggered by the addition of a belief to the belief base (indicated by a '+' prefix) or the creation of a new goal (indicated by a '+!' prefix). The body formulas can be queries on the belief base (if prefixed by '?'), the creation of new goals (indicated by a '!' prefix), or the execution of an *action*. A '.' prefix on an action indicates that it is part of Jason's library of "internal actions". These implement useful predicates (such as list membership), allow agents to send *messages* to each other, and provide operations that alter the state of the agent's *BDI execution engine*.

Steps in the BDI execution cycle include getting *percepts* from the *environment* (an instantiation of a class that the programmer must provide), storing any new percepts as beliefs, and executing the body of plans in response to events. In each cycle, only one body formula is executed, so a plan can take multiple cycles to execute. When a plan creates a new goal, this goal must be successfully achieved by another plan execution before the original plan can continue executing.

By default, a Jason agent automatically includes plans that respond to the arrival of messages. In particular, a "tell" message results in its content being added as a new belief, and an "achieve" message causes its content to be adopted as a new goal.

# 5   A Jason/Camel Bridge

In this section we briefly describe the architecture of our Jason/Camel bridge and discuss how we map between the conceptual models of agents and Camel. In particular, we describe the design and interpretation of *agent* endpoints for Camel (and other EIP-based message routing middleware).

## 5.1   Application Architecture

Our Jason/Camel bridge[2] consists of an "agent component" for Camel and an application template that integrates the Jason BDI interpreter with a Camel context. The agent component for Camel is a factory for creating both consumer and producer *agent* endpoints.

Our integration architecture extends the structure of a standard Camel application by adding an agent container. On initialisation, this container locates all Jason agent source (.asl) files in a given directory[3] and, for each agent, instantiates our extension of the `SimpleJasonAgent` class[4]. This class allows the Jason BDI interpreter to be used without any of the existing Jason "infrastructures" for agent communication. It is responsible for providing the BDI interpreter with methods to call to get percepts, to perform actions, and to send and check for messages. We chose this as the most lightweight approach for embedding Jason agents into business processes via Camel.

Our `SimpleJasonAgent` class maintains concurrently accessible queues for percepts of two types (*transient* and *persistent*—see Section 5.2) and for incoming messages. Messages and percepts on these queues are read when the BDI interpreter calls the agent's methods for getting percepts and messages. The agent container writes messages and percepts to the queues for the relevant agents after receiving them from `agent:message` and `agent:percept` endpoints that appear in Camel routes. An endpoint for producing percepts chooses whether percepts are transient or persistent based on the endpoint URI parameters and/or the headers of the Camel message being processed. Transient percepts are cleared after an agent has perceived them, whereas persistent ones will be repeatedly perceived (but may be overwritten by other percepts with the same functor—see the discussion of the `updateMode` URI parameter and message header in Section 5.2).

On construction, each agent is passed a list of agent consumer endpoints, and these are used to deliver messages and actions—the endpoints are responsible for selecting which of these match their configuration parameters. The resulting Camel messages are processed using Camel's `InOnly` message exchange pattern (implementing a one-way message flow), unless specified otherwise by a route or an endpoint URI.

Inter-agent messaging via a message broker, as implemented by the routes shown earlier in Section 3, requires the existence of a separate message queue for each agent

---

[2] `http://github.com/scranefield/camel-agent`

[3] This simple approach could be replaced in the future by the use of OSGi "bundles" to package and deploy Camel contexts together with their associated agents.

[4] `http://jason.sourceforge.net/faq/`
`faq.html#SECTION00057000000000000000`

container. To enable this functionality, our application class has a optional configuration parameter specifying that an Apache ZooKeeper[5] server should be used to dynamically obtain a unique identifier for the container.

A ZooKeeper server maintains a set of named nodes, arranged in a tree structure, to which system configuration information can be read and written by clients. The nodes are kept in memory to enable high performance, but transaction logs and persistent snapshots are also used to provide reliability. The data can be replicated across a cluster of ZooKeeper servers. Nodes can be persistent or *ephemeral*—a node of the latter type is automatically deleted if the client session that created it is no longer maintaining a "heartbeat". Nodes can also be *sequential*. These have a unique number appended to the specified node name, based on a counter associated with the parent node. A client can place a *watch* for changes to the data recorded in a node, the existence of a node, or the set of children of a node. Together, these features can be used to implement a range of distributed coordination mechanisms, such as distributed queues, barriers and locks, maintaining lists of active group members, and electing group leaders.

Our application class obtains the agent container identifier by requesting the creation of a ZooKeeper ephemeral sequence node with the path `containers/container` and receives in response the name of the created node with a sequence number appended.

ZooKeeper servers can also be accessed from within Camel routes, via ZooKeeper endpoints. This functionality is illustrated in the business process use case presented in Section 6.

## 5.2   Agent Endpoint Design

We support two types of agent *consumer* endpoints: *action* and *message* endpoints. Endpoints of these types are configured by their URI parameters to receive selected action invocation and message sending events from the connected agents. The endpoints translate these events to Camel messages to be processed by routes. The details of the agent messages and actions are encoded in the headers and body of the Camel message, as shown in Table 1. For example, the content of an agent message is placed in the body of the Camel message, and the `illoc_force` (illocutionary force), `sender`, `receiver`, `msg_id` and `annotations` properties of the agent message are stored on the Camel message using headers with these names.

A route definition creates these types of endpoints by calling the `from` method with an argument that is a string of the form `"agent:message?options"` or `"agent:action?options"`. The options are specified using the standard URI query parameter syntax `?opt1=v1&opt2=v2....` Camel messages are only generated by these endpoints if the selection criteria specified by the optional parameters are satisfied. The parameters recognised by these endpoint types are shown in Table 1 and explained below.

We also support two types of agent *producer* endpoints, which generate *messages* and *percepts*, respectively, for the local agents. These messages and percepts are created from Camel messages that reach the endpoints via Camel routes, and their content is

---

[5] `http://zookeeper.apache.org/`

**Table 1.** Agent endpoint types

### Consumer endpoints

| Endpoint type | Optional parameters | Camel headers set | Camel body contains |
|---|---|---|---|
| `agent:message` | `illoc_force,` `sender, receiver,` `annotations,` `match, replace` | `illoc_force,` `sender, receiver,` `annotations,` `msg_id` | The message content (as a string) |
| `agent:action` | `actor,` `annotations,` `match, replace,` `resultHeaderMap` | `actor,` `annotations,` `actionName,` `params` | The action term (as a string) |

### Producer endpoints

| Endpoint type | Optional parameters | Camel headers used | Camel body expected to be |
|---|---|---|---|
| `agent:message` | `illoc_force,` `sender, receiver,` `annotations` | `illoc_force,` `sender, receiver,` `annotations` | The message content (as a string) |
| `agent:percept` | `receiver,` `annotations,` `persistent,` `updateMode` | `receiver,` `annotations,` `persistent,` `updateMode` | The percept (as a string) |

taken from the body and headers of those Camel messages and the endpoint URI parameters. As shown in Table 1, the URI parameters supported for the producer endpoints are mirrored by the headers that the endpoints check. This is because these message headers can be used to override the URI parameters when converting a Camel message to an agent message or percept. This allows Camel routes to dynamically control the delivery and construction of agent messages and percepts.

The URI endpoint parameters and Camel message headers are used as agent message and action selectors (for consumer endpoints) or to specify generated percepts or agent messages (for producer endpoints). Below, we provide some additional details for some of the parameter and header options.

**receiver:** We interpret the value "`all`" for this URI parameter and message header as meaning that only broadcast messages should be selected by a message consumer endpoint or that the message should be sent to all local agents from a message or percept producer endpoint. This is the default value for a producer. No agent can have this name because the agent container identifier is prepended to the names of all agents on creation. The `receiver` value can also be a comma-separated list of recipients when provided to a message or percept producer endpoint.

**annotations:** Jason supports the attachment of a list of *annotation* terms to a literal. An `annotations` URI parameter or header can be specified for controlling the selection of messages or actions by a consumer endpoint or to trigger the generation of annotations by a producer endpoint. The values are specified as a comma-separated list of strings (for the parameter) or as a Java list of strings (when using a header).

**match and replace:** These are used on consumer endpoints. A match parameter specifies a regular expression, and a Camel message is only generated if this matches the incoming message or action (in string format). The Java regular expression syntax is used, and pairs of parentheses may be used to specify 'groups' in the pattern. The values corresponding to these groups in the matched string are recorded and used when processing a replace parameter (if present). A replace parameter specifies a string to be used as the body of the generated Camel message. This can contain group variables (in the form $n$), and these are replaced with the values that were recorded during matching.

**resultHeaderMap:** An action consumer endpoint supports both synchronous and asynchronous actions. An asynchronous action corresponds to a Jason *external* action (which cannot contain variables), and the endpoint always returns the result true to the agent that performed the action. In order to allow the handling of agent actions with variables that are instantiated during execution, we implemented a Java class that provides a new Jason *internal* action: camelagent.syncAction (see Listing 2). This takes an action term as an argument, sends this to an action consumer endpoint that is configured to receive that action, waits for Camel to finish processing it, and then uses the response message from Camel to ground the arguments of the action term[6]. An action endpoint processing this type of action must have a resultHeaderMap endpoint parameter. Its value should be a comma-separated list of *header-name* : *argument-index* pairs. When a Camel message completes the route, for each of these pairs, the value of the header with name *header-name* is unified with the argument of the action term at index *argument-index*.

**persistent and updateMode:** As described in Section 5.1, percepts delivered to agents by a percept producer endpoint can be transient (the default) or persistent. The choice is controlled by the persistent URI parameters or a message header with that name. In addition, persistent percepts with the same functor and arity but different argument values can either *accumulate* in an agent's persistent percepts list (the default), or each new percept of that form can *replace* previous ones. The latter case is useful for percepts that represent the state of an external resource. This can also apply to transient beliefs to prevent multiple percepts with the same functor and arity being queued up between consecutive perceptions by an agent. A value of "replace" for an updateMode URI parameter or a Camel message header with that name can be used to specify the percept replacement behaviour.

Figure 2 illustrates the four combinations that are possible for these two parameter settings, along with some example uses for each case. 1) A norm violation event might be encoded as a transient accumulating percept if the agent needs to perceive all violations that occurred since it last polled for percepts. 2) In contrast, a sensor reading might be treated as a transient percept that replaces any previous readings since the agent's last perception if the agent is only interested in receiving the most recent sensor reading. In these two cases we have assumed that the events are not being modelled as part of the persistent state of the environment—an agent must choose to record the violation events and sensor readings as self-authored beliefs ("mental notes") if it wishes

---

[6] For this to be possible, the Camel route processing the action invocation must be configured to use Camel's InOut "message exchange pattern" (see Listing 1).

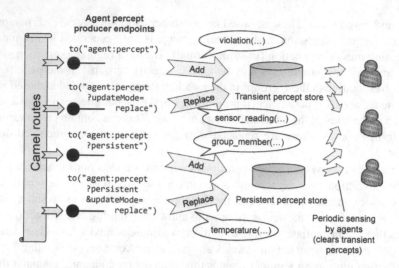

**Fig. 2.** Persistence and update mode options for percept producer endpoints

to remember them. The final two cases are for percepts that are modelled as part of the environment's state, rather than events. 3) The structure of an organisation, including information about the membership of groups, might be modelled as state that is directly perceivable by agents as percepts. As multiple group memberships will exist, new percepts of this type should accumulate rather than replace old ones[7]. 4) The final case is for percepts representing persistent state that should not accumulate between agent perceptions. For example, an agent might expect to directly perceive the temperature, but only need the current value.

# 6   A Business Process Use Case

In this section we illustrate the use of the Jason/Camel bridge by describing a hypothetical business process in which agents could play a valuable role by performing flexible rule-driven decision making. This use case addresses the problem of achieving more targeted information flow within an organisation and reducing the overuse of the CC header in email messages[8]. Our solution, shown in Figure 3, assumes the existence of a specific "to.share" email account. Users with information they think may be of interest to others can mail it to this account. These messages are monitored by a set of agents, with each agent responsible for considering the interests and needs of a subset of users. The sets of users assigned to the agents form a partition of the complete user base. The

---

[7] In this case it will also be necessary to remove percepts relating to group memberships that no longer hold. In future work we will add a `delete` percept update mode and a more refined version of the `replace` update mode that specifies which arguments of the percept should match when selecting old percepts to replace.

[8] Our approach could equally well be used to allow agents to monitor other communication channels, e.g. Camel supports Twitter endpoints.

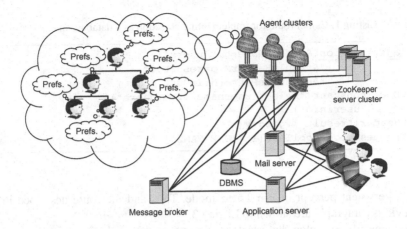

**Fig. 3.** Architecture of our use case

agents base their decision on knowledge of the roles of users and the organisational structure (stored in a database), as well as specific rules that may optionally be provided by users to encode their preferences for receiving information. We assume that these rules are created using a graphical web interface that provides end users with an abstraction layer on top of Jason's Prolog-like rule syntax. Once the agents have determined which users might be interested in an email message, the message is forwarded to those users' mail accounts via SMTP.

Our system design for implementing this business process involves coordinated use of agents, a mail server, a database management system, a message broker and ZooKeeper, with the coordination performed by Camel routes. The key routes are as follows[9].

1. On start-up, each agent calls `camelagent.syncAction` to perform synchronous actions to retrieve (respectively) the current list of users and a set of Jason rules defining predicates related to the organisation structure ontology that is used in later stages of agent processing. These actions are mapped to database queries by Camel routes configured to use Camel's `InOut` message exchange pattern, this allowing a result to be returned and the arguments of the actions instantiated. The agents then record this information as beliefs. The route that implements the `get_users(Users)` action is shown in Listing 1.
2. On start-up, each agent also performs a `register` action. A route maps this to the creation of an ephemeral sequential node in ZooKeeper (under the node `/agents`).
3. A route is watching the children of the ZooKeeper node `/agents`. Whenever there is a change (due to Camel contexts and their associated agent containers starting and stopping), the route sends an updated list of active agents to its local agents

---

[9] Note that the two example routes presented earlier in Section 3 are not used because agents in this application do not send messages to each other. Instead the distributed instances of Camel act as mediators, using agent messaging to request their local agents to evaluate the relevance of each new email message to their allocated users.

**Listing 1.** Camel route for implementing an action as a database query

```
from("agent:action?&actionName=get_users" +
              "&resultHeaderMap=result:0" +
              "&exchangePattern=InOut"        )
  .setBody(constant("select username from users"))
  .to("jdbc:userinfo")
  .setHeader("result").groovy(
     "request.body.collect{it['USERNAME']}");
```

as a persistent percept in `replace` mode. This, and the route described in the previous paragraph, are shown in Listing 3.

4. The agents have a plan that reacts to changes in their beliefs about the currently registered and running agents. When a change occurs, they each run an algorithm (common to all agents) to divide the list of users amongst them, based on their own position in the list of agents. They maintain a belief recording the users they are responsible for, and then invoke a synchronous action to obtain from the database the rules provided by those users (or default rules provided by the organisation) for evaluating the relevance of email messages to them. These rules are asserted into the belief base.

5. Whenever there is a change to the information in the database, a notification of the change is sent to a specific publish-subscribe topic on a message broker (a topic is needed rather than a queue to allow *all* running Camel contexts to receive the message). A route monitors this topic for changes to different database tables, and notifies the local agents using transient percepts. The route also suspends the email polling route (see below) for a period of time to give agents a chance to respond to these percepts by reloading the information from the database.

6. A set of routes polls the "to.share" email account for new mail using a mail consumer endpoint, and then uses the scatter-gather pattern to send a message to all local agents asking them to evaluate which of their assigned users the message is relevant for, waits for the replies until a given timeout, and then aggregates the lists of recommended users. The email message is then sent via an SMTP endpoint to this list of users. These routes are illustrated graphically in Figure 4 and shown in Listing 4.

This design illustrates an important feature of our approach to integrating agents with Camel: Camel can act as both the environment for agents (i.e. it can be a source of percepts and can execute agent actions) and as a communicating agent itself (i.e. it can send and receive messages). In the latter case Camel routes can initiate requests to agents and process their responses, as in the use of the scatter-gather pattern in this example. Alternatively, as shown in Section 3, Camel can act as message-routing middleware to interconnect agents, e.g. using a message broker. We believe this flexibility is a strength of our endpoint-based integration approach, and the choice of which types of agent endpoint (percept, action or message) to use for any given application is application-dependent. In our solution design above, we have opted to treat ZooKeeper

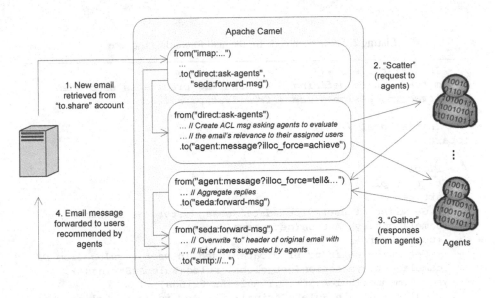

**Fig. 4.** Mail forwarding based on recommendations from agents and the scatter-gather patttern

and the database as part of the agent environmènt, so agents interact with these components using actions and percepts. In contrast, the routes that handle the scatter-gather pattern are treated as a pseudo-agent that communicates via agent messaging.

We have implemented the core functionality of our solution design, excluding the interaction with users to create email-evaluation rules (we assume these already exist in the database) and the integration with a message broker to receive and handle notifications that information in the database has changed. The Jason code (common to all agents) can be seen in Listing 2. As the coordination logic is factored out and encoded in the Camel routes, the agent code is significantly simpler than would be needed without the use of our Jason/Camel bridge. Most of the agent behaviour is to react to percepts sent from Camel by performing actions (e.g. to fetch an updated list of users). In response to the goal to evaluate a message, the agent must call the users' rules, record the users recommended by these rules in a list, and send this in a message to Camel. The coordination of the scatter-gather process is handled by Camel routes, using Camel's high-level support for the aggregation of messages.

Listings 1, 3 and 4 show the routes for three aspects of the system's functionality. We underline the beginnings of the agent endpoint URIs to highlight where the integration with agents occurs. Listing 1 shows how the execution of an agent action invocation with a free variable can be implemented by a Camel route with the `InOut` message exchange pattern (specified using the standard Camel URI parameter `exchangePattern`). The route sends an SQL query to a pre-configured database connection, the returned result is converted to an AgentSpeak list of strings using a Groovy expression, and then the `result` header is used to store the result. The consumer endpoint URI has a `resultHeaderMap` parameter specifying that the endpoint should unify the value of the `result` header with the argument of the action literal at index 0.

**Listing 2.** Jason agent code for the mail forwarding use case

```
1  /** Initial beliefs **/
2  // Omitted: rules defining list-handling predicates used when
3  // extracting assigned users from list of all users
4
5  /** Initial goal **/
6  !start.
7
8  /** Plans **/
9  /* Start-up plan */
10 +!start <-
11     // Get list of users from database and store as a belief
12     camelagent.syncAction(get_users(Users));
13     +users(Users);
14     // Get rules defining predicates used in user's rules from DB
15     camelagent.syncAction(get_global_rules(RulesAsStrings));
16     for (.member(RuleAsString, RulesAsStrings)) {
17        rules.add_rule(RuleAsString);   // Add rules to belief base
18     };
19     register. // Register self with ZooKeeper - see Listing 3
20
21 /* Handle changes to registered agents detected by ZooKeeper */
22 +registered_agents(L) : .my_name(Me) & not .member(Me, L) <-
23     .abolish(my_users(_)).
24
25 +registered_agents(L): .my_name(Me) & index(Me, L, I) <-
26     // Omitted: code to select agent's assigned users (MyUsers)
27     -+my_users(MyUsers);
28     // Get rules defining 'role' and 'relevant' predicates from DB
29     camelagent.syncAction(get_rules(MyUsers, RulesAsStrings));
30     // Update belief base with new rules (replacing old ones)
31     .abolish(role(_,_,_));
32     .abolish(relevant(_,_,_,_));
33     for (.member(RuleAsString, RulesAsStrings)) {
34        rules.add_rule(RuleAsString);
35     }.
36
37 /* Find relevant users for an email message. This goal is
38    generated by an 'achieve' message sent from a Camel route. */
39 +!check_relevance(ID, From, Subject, Body) <-
40     ?my_users(Users);
41     .findall(User, (.member(User, Users) &
42                     relevant(User, From, Subject, Body)),
43             RelevantUsers);
44     .println("Relevant users: ", RelevantUsers);
45     if (RelevantUsers \== []) {
46        .send(router, tell, relevant(ID, RelevantUsers))
47     }.
```

**Listing 3.** Camel routes for tracking active agents via ZooKeeper

```
1    // Implement registration by creating a new ZooKeeper sequence
2    // node with the agent name as its content
3    from("agent:action?actionName=register")
4      // Process only one register action from each agent
5      .idempotentConsumer(
6        header("actor"),
7        MemoryIdempotentRepository.memoryIdempotentRepository(100)
8      ).eager(true)
9      .setBody(header("actor")) // Put actor name in message body
10     .to("zookeeper://" + zkserver + "/agents/agent" +
11          "?create=true&createMode=EPHEMERAL_SEQUENTIAL");
12
13   //Watch agents node in ZooKeeper for changes to list of children
14   from("zookeeper://" + zkserver + "/agents" +
15          "?listChildren=true&repeat=true")
16     .setHeader("numChildren", simple("${body.size}"))
17     .split(body()) // Split agent node list into separate messages
18     .process(new Processor() {
19       public void process(Exchange exchange) throws Exception {
20         // Map the ZooKeeper node name for an agent to the agent
21         // name by getting the content of the ZooKeeper node
22         ConsumerTemplate consumer = camel.createConsumerTemplate();
23         String agentName =
24           consumer.receiveBody("zookeeper://"+zkserver+"/agents/"
25                                 + exchange.getIn().getBody(),
26                                 String.class);
27         exchange.getIn().setBody(agentName);
28       }})
29     // Aggregate mapped names into a single message containing a
30     // list of names. All messages will have the same headers - any
31     // will do as the message correlation id
32     .aggregate(header("numChildren"),
33               new ArrayListAggregationStrategy()
34     ).completionSize(header("numChildren"))
35     .setBody(simple("registered_agents(${bodyAs(String)})"))
36     .to("agent:percept?persistent=true&updateMode=replace");
```

**Listing 4.** Camel routes for forwarding email based on agent recommendations

```
1  // Poll for email messages
2  from("imaps://mail.bigcorp.com?username=to.share"
3       +"&password="+mailPassword+"&delete=true&copyTo=processed")
4    .setHeader("id", simple("\"${id}\""))
5    .removeHeader("to")
6    .to("seda:forward-message", "direct:ask-agents");
7
8  // Request agents to evaluate message on behalf of their
9  // allocated users
10 from("direct:ask-agents")
11   .convertBodyTo(String.class)
12   .setBody(
13     simple("check_relevance(" +
14            "${header.id}, " +
15            "\"${headerAs('from',SanitisedString)}\", " +
16            "\"${headerAs('subject',SanitisedString)}\", " +
17            "\"${bodyAs(SanitisedString)}\")"))
18   .setHeader("receiver", constant("all"))
19   .setHeader("sender", constant("router"))
20   .to("agent:message?illoc_force=achieve");
21
22 // Receive responses from agents and aggregate them to get a
23 // single lists of relevant users
24 from("agent:message?illoc_force=tell" +
25                 "&receiver=router" +
26                 "&match=relevant\\((.*),(.*)\\)" +
27                 "&replace=$1:$2")
28   .setHeader("id", simple("${body.split(\":\")[0]}"))
29   .setBody(simple("${body.split(\":\")[2]}"))
30   .aggregate(header("id"),
31           new SetUnionAggregationStrategy()
32   ).completionTimeout(2000)
33   .setHeader("to").groovy("request.getBody(String)[1..-2]")
34   .to("seda:forward-message");
35
36 // Aggregate original mail message with message summarising
37 // interested users in "to" header, and send it
38 from("seda:forward-message")
39   .aggregate(header("id"),
40           new CombineBodyAndHeaderAggregationStrategy("to")
41   ).completionSize(2)
42   .setHeader("from", constant("to.share@bigcorp.com"))
43   .to("smtp://to.share@mail.bigcorp.com?password="+mailPassword);
```

Listing 3 illustrates how Camel provides a convenient way to use ZooKeeper to monitor the active members of a distributed group of agents, and to map this information to agent percepts. The first route (lines 3–11) implements the agent `register` action by creating an ephemeral sequential node (see Section 5.1) in a ZooKeeper server to represent the agent and storing its name in that node. Camel's support for the *idempotent receiver* enterprise integration pattern provides a simple way to filter out duplicate registration requests from agents. The second route (lines 14–36) is triggered by changes to the set of ZooKeeper sequence nodes representing agents. On each change, it receives a message listing the current sequence nodes. The *splitter* pattern is used (line 17) to obtain a separate message for each node, and each of these triggers a query to ZooKeeper to get the agent name stored at that node (lines 22–27). Finally (lines 32–34), the *aggregator* pattern is used to combine the names into a list stored in the body of a single message, and that is sent to the local agents as the argument of a percept (lines 35–36). For brevity we have omitted some more verbose code that is needed to temporarily suspend the receipt of email while agents react to changes in the list of registered agents (and therefore the allocation of users to agents).

In the first route in Listing 4, the *to.share* mail account is polled for new mail (lines 2–3). A Camel message representing each new mail message is generated and the Camel message exchange identifier is written to a message header for latter use in correlating the agent responses with this Camel message (line 4). The message is then forwarded to two other routes (line 6). One is started asynchronously (via a "seda" endpoint, which queues incoming messages) and the other synchronously (via a "direct" endpoint). The second route (lines 10–20) sends an *achieve* request to the local agents, asking them to consider whether the mail is relevant to any of their allocated users. The third route (lines 24–34) handles messages sent by agents in response to this goal, which contain lists of potentially interested users. The *aggregator* pattern (lines 30–32) is used to produce, for each email message, a single message containing a combined list of users to forward it to. This is sent to the final route (lines 38–43), which also has (in a queue) the Camel message containing the email message that is waiting to be forwarded. This route uses the *aggregator* pattern again to combine the email message and the list of users to send the message to (stored in the `to` header). Finally, an SMTP endpoint is used to send the mail to these users.

## 7 Related Work

One of the oldest approaches to integrating agents with other technologies is the use of *wrappers* or *transducers* that make the functionality of all the tools to be interconnected available through agent communication [5]. The overall system coordination can then be treated as a pure multi-agent system coordination problem. However, this approach has not gained traction in industry and we do not see it as a viable approach for integrating agents into enterprise computing environments.

A pragmatic but low-level approach for integrating agents with external systems is to call them directly from the agent program. If an agent platform is a framework for using a mainstream programming language for agent development (e.g. JADE[10]), then

---

[10] http://jade.tilab.com/

it is possible for agents to use whatever protocols and client libraries are supported in that language to invoke external services directly from within agents or to monitor for external events. An interpreter for a specialised agent programming language may allow user-defined code in the underlying implementation language to implement functionality called by the agent program. For example, new "internal actions" for Jason can be developed in Java, and these can use any Java communication libraries for external interaction. An agent's environment abstraction is another potential location for user customisation. For example, a Jason developer can implement an environment class that acts as a facade for external interaction, e.g. to connect agents to a virtual world [9].

The integration of agents with web services has been an important topic over the last decade, and some agent platforms provide specific support for this. For example, the online documentation for the JADE platform includes tutorials on calling web services from JADE and exposing agent services as web services, and the Jack WebBots [1] framework allows web applications to be built using agents.

More generally, it would be possible for the developers of an agent platform (or its community) to provide support for connecting agents to a range of external resource and service types. For example, the IMPACT agent platform [11] includes a module that provides a uniform interface for connecting agents to external services, with support for a small number of service types already implemented.

The A&A (Agents and Artifacts) meta-model extends the concept of an agent environment to include *artifacts*. These represent resources and tools with observable properties and specific operations that agents can invoke. These can be used to provide services internal to an MAS, or as an interface to external services, such as web services [10]. However, it is unlikely that the developer and user community for any agent-specific technology, whether a specific platform like IMPACT or a more general approach such as A&A, could rival the scale and diversity provided by a more mainstream integration technology such as Camel, which supports more than 130 endpoint types. Also, for the case of A&A, an agent developer would need to learn multiple APIs (for each artifact type) when integrating agents with different types of external service. This is not the case in our approach (see Section 8).

The *active components* paradigm is a combination of a component model with agent concepts [8]. Active components can communicate via method calls or asynchronous messages and may be hierarchically composed of subcomponents. They run within a management infrastructure that controls non-functional properties such as persistence and replication. They may have internal architectures of different types, and this heterogeneity, combined with a uniform external interface model, facilitates the interoperation of different types of system that are encapsulated as active components. As with artifacts, the success of this approach for large-scale integration rests on the availability of active components encapsulating a wide range of service types.

Behrens et al. [2] present a proposal for an environment interface standard (EIS) for connecting agent platforms to arbitrary environments, based on an analysis of the environment interfaces offered by existing agent platforms and a set of desirable design principles. This work could pave the way for portability of environments between agent platforms. However, this is orthogonal to our integration approach, which is based on using configuration of endpoints rather than an API to interface agents with external components. While Camel could be interfaced with agents via the EIS (or encapsulated within an active component or artifact), all this would achieve is to allow Camel to be used from agents that are not programmed in Java. The interface would need to reproduce the Camel API for defining and executing routes, and an agent endpoint design such as the one presented in Section 5.2 would still be needed. However, the proposed EIS includes the use of an standard "interface intermediate language" to represent actions, percepts and events. This could be used in our endpoint design to ensure that Camel routes using our agent endpoints could connect to multiple agent platforms.

# 8   Conclusion

In this paper we have proposed a novel approach, based on accepted enterprise integration patterns, for integrating agents with external resources and services using capabilities of existing enterprise integration technology. By using a mainstream technology we can benefit from the competitive market for robust integration tools (or the larger user base for open source software), and can have access to a much larger range of pre-built components for connecting to different resource and service types. This is evidenced by Camel's large number of available endpoint types.

We presented the design of an interface between agents and the Camel integration framework in terms of the "endpoint" enterprise integration pattern. This can serve as a pattern for interconnecting agents with any type of message-based middleware.

In our approach, the logic for integrating agents with external systems makes use of the expressive Camel DSL, with its high-level support for common message-processing patterns, and the configuration options for Camel's many endpoint types. The latter represents a trade-off: configuring an endpoint by URI parameters and message headers is unlikely to provide the full capabilities of an API for interacting with that type of external system, but it provides the most commonly used functionality and the configuration options can be learned with much less effort than an API. However, there will still be applications that need a more traditional API-based approach for accessing external systems from agents.

We described an implemented architecture for this approach and illustrated its practical use in a hypothetical (but, we think, plausible) business process use case. The Camel routes we presented demonstrate the benefits of using a specialist coordination tool such as Camel for handling the coordination of distributed agents and services, leaving the agent code to provide only the high level adaptive business logic. This division of responsibilities also enables a division of implementation effort: the coordination logic can be developed by business process architects using a programming paradigm that directly supports common enterprise integration patterns, and less development time is needed from (currently scarce) agent programmers. An agent programmer using our framework does not need to learn any APIs for client libraries or protocols—the agent code can be based entirely on the traditional agent concepts of messages, actions and plans. The developer of the message-routing logic does not need to know much about agents except the basic concepts encoded in the agent endpoint design (*message*, *illocutionary force*, *action*, *percept*, etc.) and the syntax of the agent messages to be sent from and received by the message routes.

Currently, in our architecture Camel replaces the agent environment and the message-passing middleware. This is not essential to our approach. The architecture could be extended to include a traditional agent environment as well as a Camel engine that executes routes containing agent endpoints. In this hybrid approach, agents would receive percepts from both the environment and Camel, and any actions not handled by a Camel route would be executed in the environment.

# References

1. Agent Oriented Software: JACK Intelligent Agents WebBot manual (2011), http://www.aosgrp.com/documentation/jack/WebBot_Manual_WEB/
2. Behrens, T.M., Hindriks, K.V., Dix, J.: Towards an environment interface standard for agent platforms. Annals of Mathematics and Artificial Intelligence 61, 261–295 (2011)
3. Bordini, R.H., Hübner, J.F., Wooldridge, M.: Programming Multi-Agent Systems in Agent-Speak using Jason. Wiley (2007)
4. Chappell, D.: Enterprise Service Bus: Theory in Practice. O'Reilly (2004)
5. Genesereth, M.R., Ketchpel, S.P.: Software agents. Communications of the ACM 37(7), 48–53 (1994)
6. Hohpe, G., Woolf, B.: Enterprise Integration Patterns: Designing, Building, and Deploying Messaging Solutions. Addison-Wesley (2004)
7. Ibsen, C., Anstey, J.: Camel in Action. Manning (2010)
8. Pokahr, A., Braubach, L., Jander, K.: Unifying agent and component concepts. In: Dix, J., Witteveen, C. (eds.) MATES 2010. LNCS, vol. 6251, pp. 100–112. Springer, Heidelberg (2010)
9. Ranathunga, S., Cranefield, S., Purvis, M.: Interfacing a cognitive agent platform with Second Life. In: Beer, M., Brom, C., Dignum, F., Soo, V.-W. (eds.) AEGS 2011. LNCS (LNAI), vol. 7471, pp. 1–21. Springer, Heidelberg (2012)
10. Ricci, A., Piunti, M., Viroli, M.: Environment programming in multi-agent systems: an artifact-based perspective. Autonomous Agents and Multi-Agent Systems 23(2), 158–192 (2011)
11. Rogers, T.J., Ross, R., Subrahmanian, V.: IMPACT: A system for building agent applications. Journal of Intelligent Information Systems 14, 95–113 (2000)
12. Telang, P.R., Singh, M.P.: Comma: A commitment-based business modeling methodology and its empirical evaluation. In: Proceedings of the 11th International Conference on Autonomous Agents and Multiagent Systems, pp. 1073–1080. IFAAMAS (2012)

# Belief Caching in 2APL

Mehdi Dastani[1] and Marc van Zee[2]

[1] Department of Information and Computing Science,
Utrecht University, The Netherlands
m.m.dastani@uu.nl

[2] Department of Individual and Collective Reasoning,
University of Luxembourg, Luxembourg
marc.vanzee@uni.lu

**Abstract.** The BDI-oriented multi-agent programming language 2APL allows the implementation of an agent's beliefs in terms of logical facts and rules. An agent's beliefs represent information about its surrounding environment including other agents. Repeated querying of the beliefs by the 2APL interpreter causes unnecessary overhead resulting in poor run-time performance of the interpreter. We propose an extension to 2APL to reduce the number of such queries by using belief caching. We show that our proposal implements belief caching and extends an existing caching proposal. Moreover, we provide formal proofs establishing that our extension does not affect the execution behavior of 2APL. Benchmarking results indicate that belief caching leads to significant improvements.

## 1 Introduction

The multi-agent programming language 2APL[1] supports the implementation of individual agents that can perform high-level reasoning and deliberation about their information (i.e., beliefs) and objectives (i.e., goals to achieve) in order to decide what actions to perform [4]. Beliefs and goals in 2APL are declarative; Beliefs are represented by a set of Horn clauses and goals are represented by conjunctions of first-order atoms. While this allows the development of flexible and declarative agent programs, repeated inferencing triggered by queries to the beliefs can result in poor performance. When developing multi-agent systems for time critical applications, performance issues are often a key concern, potentially adversely impacting the adoption of BDI-based agent programming languages and platforms as an implementation technology [1]. For example, if agent programming languages want to provide better support for implementing autonomous robots, one of the requirements is real-time reactivity to events, which is currently lacking [10].

We present an inference method based on caching within the 2APL interpreter that reduces the number of belief queries. Our motivation for this approach is based on the observation that belief queries are responsible for most of the deliberation time within a 2APL deliberation cycle and that most belief queries

---

[1] For more information, see: http://apapl.sourceforge.net/

M. Cossentino et al. (Eds.): EMAS 2013, LNAI 8245, pp. 117–136, 2013.
© Springer-Verlag Berlin Heidelberg 2013

are redundant because they are being performed repeatedly while relevant parts of the belief base do not change such that the result of such queries remains the same. Using the notion of caching is therefore likely to be an optimization. We implement belief caching in the 2APL interpreter by performing a belief query only if the belief base has been updated in a way that is relevant to this query. We exploit the fact that both belief queries and belief updates are static in 2APL programs, which makes it possible to determine what belief update will change what belief query at compile-time. In order to do this, we define the notion of *relevance* for belief queries by making use of *query dependency sets* in the belief base.

Recently, it is shown [1] that it is theoretically possible to improve the run-time execution of BDI-based agent programs using belief caching. However, this proposal focuses purely on the optimization of belief queries within one so-called *update cycle*, which consists of a *query phase* and an *update phase*. Our approach specializes this idea to an update cycle *for each individual query* that may cover multiple deliberation cycles. We show that the update cycle of [1] is contained in our proposal and that our proposal is more fine-grained leading to an increased number of queries answered by the cached beliefs.

The idea of using query dependencies to optimize the performance of logic programs, or theorem proving in general, is not new. For instance, this idea is applied to Datalog program [6] where the problem of detecting independence of queries from updates is reduced to the equivalence problem, i.e., proving that the program before the update is equivalent to the program after the update. In particular, the notion of *query reachability* that is used in [6] is similar to our notion of *query relevance*, although our approach is based on Prolog as the inference engine, which is considerably more expressive than Datalog (e.g., more complex terms, no constraints on negation).

Another related work is [7,8] where the notion of *relevance reasoning* is used to reason with the relevant parts of a knowledge base. They discuss the problem of deriving irrelevant facts for a Horn-rule knowledge base using a tool called the *query tree*. This query tree is the used in two ways: 1) to determine which facts are relevant to a query and 2) to guide the inference engine by determining in which sequence the rules should be applied. The main difference between this idea and our approach is that [7] and [8] consider a single query for a set of Horn clauses and asks what are the irrelevant parts. We extend this by iteratively caching queries and only executing them when the relevant part of the knowledge base has been changed.

A well-known form of caching that is used in the logic programming community is called *tabled logic programming*[2], which uses memorization to optimize performance and prevent non-termination by avoiding infinite and redundant paths of computation. The central data structure is a table in which encountered subgoals and corresponding solutions are stored. One can see our approach as applying tabling on a "meta-level", storing the results of substitutions in the

---

[2] See http://www.cs.cmu.edu/~twelf/guide-1-4/twelf_5.html for more information.

2APL interpreter, and not in the inference engine as done in logic programming. We do not change the working of the inference engine, but we reduce the number of calls to this engine by caching queries.

We have implemented our belief caching approach into the latest version of 2APL.[3] Additionally, we have implemented a generative benchmarking tool, which allows the reader to test the working of belief caching easily. The manual for the benchmarking tool can be found in the 2APL manual.

The structure of this paper is as follows. In Section 2, we introduce 2APL together with the parts that are relevant to our analysis. In Section 3, we introduce our belief caching approach, compare it with the abstract performance model as proposed in [1], and show how our approach can be seen as an extension to this work. In Section 4 we will give a formal characterization of our proposal and show that it does not affect the execution behaviour of 2APL. Finally, we provide implementation details and benchmarking results in Section 5.

## 2    2APL - A Practical Agent Programming Language

The programming language 2APL is developed to implement multi-agent systems [4]. In 2APL, individual agents are programmed in terms of beliefs, goals, actions, plans, events, and three types of practical reasoning rules. The beliefs and goals of 2APL agents are implemented in a declarative way, while plans are implemented in an imperative style. The declarative part of the programming language supports the implementation of an agent's reasoning task and the update of its mental state. The imperative part of the programming language facilitates the implementation of plans, control flow, and mechanisms such as procedure calls, recursion, and interfacing with legacy codes. 2APL agents can perform different types of actions such as belief and goal update actions, belief and goal test actions (belief and goal queries), external actions (including sense actions) and communication actions. The practical reasoning rules can be applied to generate plans. The first type of rules is designed to generate plans for achieving goals (so-called Planning Goal rules, or PG rules), the second to process external events, messages and abstract actions (so-called Procedure Call rules, or PC rules), and the third to process internal events for repairing failed plans (so-called Plan Repair rules, or PR rules). Each practical reasoning rule has a belief query that specifies the belief state in which the rule can be applied.

2APL agents are autonomous in the sense that they continuously *deliberate* on their mental states (beliefs, goals and plans) in order to decide which plans to select and execute. This deliberation mechanism, which is an integral part of the 2APL interpreter, iterates over a reasoning cycle, depicted in Figure 1. The reasoning cycle starts by applying applicable PG rules of an agent program in order to generate *plans* to achieve the agent's goals. The reasoning cycle continues by executing the generated plans. Then, the received internal and external events and messages are processed by applying PC and PR rules.

---

[3] The sources of the latest 2APL version can be downloaded from
http://www.apapl.sourceforge.net/

We would like to emphasize that the application of all practical reasoning rules as well as the execution of belief test actions require queries to the belief base. The fact that the application of practical reasoning rules is the core activity of each reasoning cycle implies that the belief query actions constitute the most frequent operations in the reasoning cycle. Therefore, any significant reduction in the number of belief queries is expected to improve the performance of the 2APL interpreter. Moreover, repeated queries occur often in 2APL [1]. This means that belief queries not only occur often, but it will also be possible to perform caching over the repeated queries.

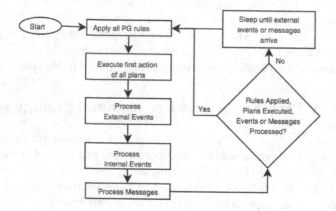

**Fig. 1.** The 2APL deliberation cycle

## 2.1 Belief Queries

Belief queries can occur at two places in a 2APL program: as *guards* in the practical reasoning rules and as *belief test actions* in a plan. We will discuss each of them separately. In what follows, we denote a belief query with $\beta$ and substitutions with $\tau$.

**Practical Reasoning Rules.** As mentioned, 2APL programs may involve three kinds of practical reasoning rules, each of which contains a belief query. The three types of practical reasoning rules share the same syntax. A *practical reasoning rule* in 2APL has the form $H \leftarrow \beta \mid \pi$ where $H$ is the head of the rule, $\beta$ is the guard of the rule representing a belief query, and $\pi$ is the body of the rule representing a plan. The representation of $H$ is different for each rule type. In case of the PG rule, $H$ is a goal expression represented by a conjunction of positive first-order atoms. For a PC rule, $H$ is either a message, an event or an abstract action represented by a first-order atom. Finally, in case of a PR rule, $H$ is a plan whose execution has failed and is represented by a sequence of actions containing variables. The belief query $\beta$ may contain conjunctions and disjunctions of first-order literals. A successful query of this guard results in a substitution that can be applied to instantiate variables that occur in the body of the rule. Finally, $\pi$ is the plan that will be added to the plan base if the rule is applied. The complete description of 2APL constructs can be found in [4].

```
beliefs:
  dist(50).
  new_speed(X) :- X is int(random(10)).

  fuel(1000).
  enough_fuel(X)  :- fuel(Y), X =< Y.

beliefupdates:
  { dist(X) and fuel(F) } Forward(Y)  { not dist(X), not fuel(F), dist(X - Y), fuel(F - Y) }
  { dist(X) and fuel(F) } Backward(Y) { not dist(X), not fuel(F), dist(X + Y), fuel(F - Y) }

goals:
  driveForward(5).

pgrules:
  driveForward(Speed) <- enough_fuel(Speed) and dist(D) | {
    Forward(Speed);
    if B(D <= 0 and new_speed(NewSpeed)) {
      dropgoal(driveForward(Speed));
      adopta(driveBackward(NewSpeed));
    }
  }

  driveBackward(Speed) <- enough_fuel(Speed) and dist(D) | {
    Backward(Speed);
    if B(D >= 100 and new_speed(NewSpeed)) {
      dropgoal(driveBackward(Speed));
      adopta(driveForward(NewSpeed));
    }
  }
```

**Fig. 2.** Driver: Example 2APL program

An example of a 2APL program is depicted in Figure 2. This program consists of a single agent that will repeatedly move towards and away from a target until it runs out of fuel. The distance X of the agent from the target is represented by the belief fact dist(X). Initially, the agent is halfway from the target (the distance is 50) and will start moving forward with a speed of 5 (represented by the goal driveForward(5)). This will select the first PG rule, which is applied with the substitution [Speed/5] resulting from the unification of the head with the goal base, and the substitution [D/50] resulting from the unification of the belief query in the guard of the rule with the belief base. This rule is repeatedly applied until the agent reaches the target (D <= 0). Then the goal driveForward(5) will be replaced with the goal driveBackward(NewSpeed), where NewSpeed is a random integer between 0 and 10. This will activate the second PG rule, which does exactly the opposite as the first PG rule. This process will repeat until the agent runs out of fuel (i.e. enough_fuel(Speed) can no longer be entailed from the belief base).

As this example might suggest, practical reasoning rules are applied in 2APL in the following way. First the head is instantiated, resulting in a substitution, which we will denote by $\tau_1$. In case of our example, applying the first PG rule with the head driveForward(Speed) results in substitution $\tau_1 = $ [Speed/5]. Subsequently, the substitution $\tau_1$ is applied to the guard of the rule, creating a new belief query, which in case of our example is enough_fuel(5) and distance(D). Note that the application of $\tau_1$ to the guard of a rule does not necessarily instantiate all variables involved in the guard (in case of our example variable D) such that querying the guard to which $\tau_1$ is applied can result in a new substitution, which we will denote by $\tau_2$. Finally, we would like to emphasize that if there are multiple substitutions for a query possible, then the first substitution is returned. In the case of our example, the new substitution is $\tau_2 = $ [D/50].

**Belief Test Action.** A belief test action occurs in a plan and checks whether the agent has certain beliefs. A belief test action is an expression of the form B($\phi$), where $\phi$ is a belief query represented by a conjunction or disjunction of first-order literals. The execution of a belief test action is basically a belief query to the belief base that can generate a substitution. Since a belief test action occurs in a plan, it may be preceded by some other actions that share variables. This means that some of the variables of a belief test action may already have value instantiation through earlier computed substitutions, which we denote by $\tau_1$ (e.g., substitution resulted from the guard of the practical reasoning rule whose application has generated the plan, or from earlier actions in the same plan). Similar to practical reasoning rules, we first apply the earlier computed substitution $\tau_1$ to the query of the belief test action and then use the new query to check the belief base. The new query will result in a new substitution which we denote by $\tau_2$.

In the case of our example, the belief test action B(D <= 0 and new_speed (NewSpeed)) contains the variable D that is instantiated when the PG rule is applied. This means that $\tau_1$ will contain a substitution for D. It also contains the variable NewSpeed that is not instantiated before the belief query is performed, which means that it will be instantiated by the belief query. Therefore, $\tau_2$ will contain a substitution for NewSpeed.

## 2.2   Belief Updates

2APL contains two different types of belief update actions. The first type of belief update action requires a belief update specification. Each belief update specification is characterized by a triple consisting of the action name represented as a first-order atom starting with a capitalized letter, a precondition represented by a set of first-order literals, and a post-condition that is also represented by a set of first-order literals. One of the belief updates of the example in Figure 2 is:

```
{ dist(X) and fuel(F) } Forward(Y) { not dist(X), not fuel(F), dist(X - Y), fuel(F - Y) }
```

This triple specifies that any belief update action that unifies with this action name (e.g. Forward(5)) can be executed when the pre-condition can be derived from the belief base (when dist(X) and fuel(F) can be derived from the belief base for some substitution of the variables X and F, for instance distance(50) and fuel(1000)). The execution of the belief update action ensures that the post-condition is derivable from the belief base (e.g. not dist(50) and not fuel(1000) and dist(45) and fuel(995) is derivable from the belief base after the execution of Forward(5)). Note that the action call Forward(5) will instantiate the variable Y and that variable Y in the post-condition is instantiated with the same value.

The second type of belief update action does not require a belief update specification and consists of a first-order atom preceded by either the plus (+) or the minus (−) operator. An update action with the plus operator adds the atom to the agent's belief base while an update action with the minus operator will remove the atom from the agent's belief base. For example, the plan "-dist(50); +dist(45);" will remove the fact dist(50) from the belief base and add the fact dist(45) to it. Note that the syntax of simple update actions is the same as the syntax of belief updates in Jason [2].

# 3   Extending 2APL with Belief Caching

In the previous section, we observed that repeated belief queries demand a substantial amount of processing time of each deliberation cycle and we analyzed belief queries and belief updates in 2APL in order to infer when the result of a belief query will not change and caching can be applied. The answer of a belief query remains unchanged if the following three conditions are satisfied: 1) the part of the belief base that is relevant for the query is not changed, 2) in the case of a practical reasoning rule where the head and the guard share variables, the unification of the head provides a substitution that assigns the same values as the cached values to the shared variables, and 3) in the case of a belief test action that shares variables with some actions that precede it, the substitution originating from the preceding actions assigns the same value as the cached values to the shared variables. As long as these conditions are fulfilled for a belief query $\beta$, repeated querying of $\beta$ returns the same substitutions for its involved variables, such that the query can be cached until one of the conditions is no longer met.

We will illustrate these conditions using the example in Figure 2. Consider the belief query in the guard of the first PG rule (enough_fuel(Speed) and dist(D)). The first condition states that the relevant part of the belief base should not be changed for this belief query. This will ensure that two identical belief queries provide the same result. If one of the belief updates Forward(Y) or Backward(Y) is successfully executed, it will update the value of dist(X) in the belief base and thus possibly change the result of the query in the guard of the rule, because this guard contains dist(D). Therefore, the query will have to be performed again and caching does not apply. The second condition states that the substitution of the variables that occur both in head and the guard of the rule should remain unchanged. This means that the substitution of the variable Speed in the rule head should be the same as the previous query, which will ensure that the new belief query in the rule guard enough_fuel(Speed) and dist(D) is the same as previous query. The third condition does not apply.

We consider now the belief query action B(D <= 0 and new_speed(NewSpeed)). The first condition states again that the belief base should not change in a relevant way. Since no belief update action can update the value of the predicate new_speed in the belief base, the result of this query cannot be affected by a belief update action. This means that the first condition is always fulfilled. The second condition does not apply. The third condition states that the variables shared with earlier actions (in this case the instantiation of D) should have the same instantiated value as in the previous execution of the query. In our case this means that the earlier substitution resulted from the execution of the belief query enough_fuel(Speed) and dist(D) should contain the same value instantiation for the variable D as in the current substitution for D.

In order to verify whether the first condition holds it is necessary to determine which facts are relevant to belief queries. For this, we calculate the *dependency sets* for all belief queries in a program. The dependency set of a belief query contains all the atoms that can possibly affect the result of the query. Moreover, we calculate the relevant queries for a belief update action as follows: If the post-condition of a belief update action contains an atom that is in the dependency set of a belief query, this query will be added to the list of *relevant queries* for this belief update action. We build our idea of belief caching based on the relevant queries of the update actions. In particular, when the belief update action is invoked, a *changed* flag will be set in its relevant queries. Thus, if the belief base has changed in a relevant way for a belief query, the *changed* flag will be TRUE for this query.

Note that it is possible to calculate the dependency sets of the queries and relevant queries for the belief update actions at compile-time because belief update actions and belief queries are static in 2APL, i.e., no new atoms will be added to the belief base at run-time. This means that this extension will be practically costless in terms of run-time performance. The extension we propose is two-fold. Firstly, the belief queries are extended with a cache to store previous substitutions, a *changed* flag and a decision mechanism to apply caching. Secondly, the definition of a belief update is extended such that it is possible to determine the relevant queries for each belief update. We will explain each extension in more detail in the next two sections.

## 3.1   Extended Belief Queries

Recall from Section 2.1 that both types of belief queries (guards of practical reasoning rules and belief test actions) involve two substitutions $\tau_1$ and $\tau_2$. $\tau_1$ is the substitution that contains all variables that have been instantiated before the belief query, while $\tau_2$ is the substitution that contains all variables resulting from executing the query to the belief base.

To distinguish between belief queries that contain variables which are already instantiated, i.e. belief queries that contain variables that occur in $\tau_1$, and those that do not, we introduce the flag *shared* for each belief query $\beta$ and use $\beta.shared$ to refer to this flag. This flag is set (i.e., it has the value TRUE) when the code fragment before the query and the query itself *share* variables. In the case that the query occurs in the guard of a practical reasoning rule, this code fragment is the head of the practical reasoning rule. In the case that the query occurs in a belief query action, the code fragment is the actions that precedes the belief query action.

**Definition 1 (Shared belief query).** *Let $H \leftarrow \beta \mid \pi$ be a practical reasoning rule and $Var(X)$ is the set of variables that occur in expression $X$. The flag* shared *of the belief query $\beta$ is set iff $H$ and $\beta$ share variables, i.e.:*

$$Var(H) \cap Var(\beta) \neq \emptyset \implies \beta.shared = \text{TRUE},$$

*Moreover, let $\pi$ (the body of the practical reasoning rule) be a plan of the form $\pi';B(\beta);\pi''$. Then, the flag* shared *of the belief query $\beta$ is set iff $\pi'$ and $\beta$ share variables, i.e.:*

$$Var(\pi') \cap Var(\beta) \neq \emptyset \implies \beta.shared = \text{TRUE},$$

For example, in Figure 2 the belief queries in both PG rules are shared because the variable Speed occurs both in the rule head and rule guard. Similarly, the belief query actions in both rules are shared because the variable D occurs both in the rule guard and the belief query action.

In order to perform caching, both substitutions $\tau_1$ and $\tau_2$ are stored for each query $\beta$ so that they can be re-used for the next query of $\beta$. Therefore we introduce for each query $\beta$ the substitutions $\tau_1$ and $\tau_2$. We cache these substitutions related to query $\beta$ and denote them by $\beta.\tau_1$ and $\beta.\tau_2$. We would like to emphasize that it may also be possible to store a history of substitutions $\tau_1$ and $\tau_2$ in order to reduce even more queries. This is particularly effective for when $\tau_1$ and $\tau_2$ share variables and $\tau_1$ changes, and the belief base does not change. Next, we introduce for each belief query $\beta$ the flag *changed* that will be set whenever the belief base has been updated in relevant way, which means that caching does not apply and the query $\beta$ should be executed with respect to the belief base. The flag *changed* associated with the belief query $\beta$ is denoted by $\beta.changed$. This flag is set by belief update actions, which we will discuss in the next section. For now we simply assume that this flag always has the correct value.

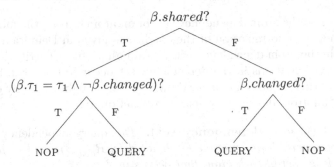

**Fig. 3.** The belief query caching mechanism

Using these variables it is possible to define a decision mechanism that implements belief caching for the belief queries (Figure 3). If the relevant part of the belief base has been changed for the query $\beta$ (i.e., $\beta.changed$ is TRUE), the belief

---

[3] When a leaf contains NOP, this means that no operation is performed.

query will always be executed. If query $\beta$ is shared and the cached substitution $\beta.\tau_1$ is different from the current substitution $\tau_1$, the belief query $\beta$ is executed as well. The reason for this is that the cached substitution $\beta.\tau_1$ applied to $\beta$ will result in a different query than applying the new substitution $\tau_1$ (which is different from $\beta.\tau_1$) to $\beta$. After executing each belief query $\beta$, the corresponding flag $\beta.changed$ is set to FALSE.

## 3.2  Extended Belief Updates

In this section we will define precisely how the caching flag $\beta.changed$ is set for the belief queries. Recall from Section 2 that the only way in which the belief base can be updated is by belief updates. We will make use of *dependency sets* for queries, which we will now introduce. These dependency sets are defined for the belief base of 2APL, which is a general logic program.

**Definition 2 (Atom dependency [9]).** *An atom $a$ depends on an atom $b$ in a logic program $P$ iff (i) there exists a clause $C$ in $P$ such that $a$ is the head of $C$ and $b$ occurs in the body of $C$, or (ii) there exists a clause $C$ in $P$ such that $a$ is the head of $C$ and there is an atom $c$ in the body of $C$ that depends on $b$.*

Note that the second condition of Definition 2 is recursive, meaning that an atom $a$ can depend on an atom $b$ via any number of clauses $C_1, C_2, ..., C_n$, given that $a$ occurs in the head of $C_1$, the head of each clause $C_i$ occurs in the body of the previous clause $C_{i-1}$ (given that $i > 1$) and $b$ occurs in the body of $C_n$.

Let $\pi(P)$ be the set of atoms occurring in the general logic program $P$. The atom dependencies in $P$ is a binary relation $R_{dpd} \subseteq \pi(P) \times \pi(P)$.

**Definition 3 (Dependency set [9]).** *The dependency set for an atom $a$ in a logic program $P$, denoted by $R^*_{dpd}(a)$, contains all atoms $b$ that $a$ depends on.*

We can calculate the atom dependency set for an atom $a$ using the following two steps, which are a reformulation of the conditions given in Definition 2: 1) Add the atom $a$ in the atom dependency set, 2) Add all atoms occurring in the body of clauses in which atoms in the dependency set occur in the head. Step (2) is repeated until this set does no longer grow. We can straightforwardly extend the definition of an atom dependency set for a belief query.

**Definition 4 (Query dependency set).** *The query dependency set for a query $\beta$ to a general logic program $P$, denoted by $R^*_{dpd}(\beta)$, is the union of the atom dependency set of each atom that occurs in $\beta$.*

$$R^*_{dpd}(\beta) = \bigcup_{a \in \beta} R^*_{dpd}(a).$$

Suppose a query $\beta$ is executed at deliberation cycles $C_1$ and $C_2$ and that the previous substitution $\beta.\tau_1$ is equal to the current substitution $\tau_1$. The only way in which the result of this query can change is if the substitution in $C_2$ of a variable $X$ that occurs in an atom in the dependency set of $\beta$ is different from the substitution of $X$ in $C_1$. So, if an atom that occurs in the post-condition of a belief update is a member of the query dependency set of a belief query, then that belief update action can affect the substitution of such a variable $X$.

Consider for instance the belief query enough_fuel(Speed) and dist(D) that occurs in the guard of the first PG rule in the example program in Figure 2. According to Definition 4, the query dependency set for a query $\beta$ is the union of the atom dependency set of each atom that occurs in this query. In this case, this is the union of the atom dependency sets of the atoms enough_fuel and dist. This is calculuated using the belief base:

```
dist(50).
new_speed(X)  :- X is int(random(10)).
fuel(1000).
enough_fuel(X)   :- fuel(Y), X =< Y.
```

We calculate the atom dependency set using the algorithm that we stated directly after Definition 3. First add enough_fuel to the set. Then add all atoms occurring in the body of rules in which enough_fuel occurs in the head. This means that fuel is added to the set, because the last rule in the logic program fulfills this condition. The atom dependency set is now {enough_fuel, fuel}. After this step, adding atoms that occur in the body of rules in which enough_fuel or fuel occur in the head does not increase the size of the set, which means that the atom dependency set is complete. Because the atom dist does not occur in any clause where there are atoms in the body, the atom dependency set of this atom is simply {dist}. This means that the query dependency set of enough_fuel(Speed) and dist(D) is {enough_fuel, fuel, dist}.

Now, if an atom that occurs in the post-condition of a belief update is a member of this set as well, it can affect the result of this query. Recall that the belief updates of Figure 2 are:

```
{ dist(X) and fuel(F) } Forward(Y)  { not dist(X), not fuel(F), dist(X - Y), fuel(F - Y) }
{ dist(X) and fuel(F) } Backward(Y) { not dist(X), not fuel(F), dist(X + Y), fuel(F - Y) }
```

Since both belief updates contain the atom dist and the atom fuel and both these atoms occur in the query dependency set of the belief query enough_fuel(Speed) and dist(D), both belief updates are *relevant* for this query. We make the concept of belief query relevance more clear in the following definition.

**Definition 5 (Belief query relevance).** *A belief update $\alpha$ is relevant for a belief query $\beta$ if there exists an atom a that occurs both in the postcondition of $\alpha$ and in the dependency set of $\beta$.*

All relevant queries for a belief update are put in a set and activated whenever the belief update action is executed by setting the *changed* flag of these queries to TRUE.

**Definition 6 (Extended belief update).** *We add to each belief update $\alpha$ a set relevantQueries containing belief queries and execute the algorithm depicted* *in Algorithm 1 at compile-time. We also add for each belief update the algorithm depicted in Algorithm 2 that is executed when the belief update action is executed. Call the resulting belief update an* extended belief update.

---

**Algorithm 1.** Collect relevant queries for each belief update action

1: **procedure** collectRelevantQueries()
2: **for all** beliefupdate $\alpha$ **do**
3:     **for all** query $\beta$ **do**
4:         **if** $\exists p : p \in R^*_{dpd}(\beta) \wedge p \in postcondition(\alpha)$ **then**
5:             $\alpha.relevantQueries.put(\beta)$
6:         **end if**
7:     **end for**
8: **end for**
9: **end procedure**

---

**Algorithm 2.** Reset caching for relevant queries for each belief update action

1: **procedure** setRelevantQueries $(\alpha)$
2: **for** query $\beta$ in $\alpha.relevantQueries$ **do**
3:     $\beta.changed \leftarrow$ TRUE
4: **end for**
5: **end procedure**

---

### 3.3   Abstract Performance Model

The abstract performance model for logic-based agent programming languages, as proposed in [1], can be used in order to measure the effect of belief caching. According to this model, the three steps in the deliberation cycle of a 2APL agent can be mapped onto two kinds of knowledge representation functionality: the *query phase* and the *update phase*. Together, they constitute an *update cycle* (Figure 4). The query phase is a phase in which one or more belief queries are performed, and in which no belief updates take place. As soon as a single belief update occurs, the model switches to the update phase. It will remain in the update phase until a single belief query takes place. The belief caching mechanism proposed in [1], which we will call the *original caching mechanism*, is to cache the queries *within one query phase* by making use of a hash table that contains all queries that have been performed in this query phase. This will ensure that the belief base has not been changed, simply because no belief update has occurred. The complete cache is cleared as soon as the model switches to the update phase, i.e. a single belief update takes place.

Our implementation is more fine-grained, though, since it refines the general update cycle of [1] to an update cycle *for each individual belief query*. This means that each single belief query goes through the update cycle of Figure 4. Therefore the number of update cycles for individual queries are independent,

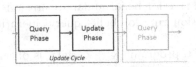

**Fig. 4.** The abstract performance model [1]

while in the case of [1] a single belief update will reset the cache of *all* queries. This means that our proposal will lead to more belief caching in the case that the update cycles of the individual belief queries are not identical, a situation which frequently occurs.

## 4    Formal Characterization

The execution of a 2APL program, which is based on the 2APL deliberation cycle [4], results in a sequence of program states. We consider the execution of a 2APL program as a sequence of states $C_0 \xrightarrow{x_1} C_1 \xrightarrow{x_2} C_2 \xrightarrow{x_3} \ldots$, where $C_i$ denotes the configuration of an agent after the $i$-th execution step, and $x_i$ is a (meta-) operation such as a belief query or a belief update (see [4] for other 2APL operations). We use the definition of an agent's state from the original 2APL operational semantics (see [4], Definition 1).

**Definition 7.** *(Individual agent configuration) The configuration of an individual 2APL agent is defined as $C = \langle \iota, \sigma, \gamma, \Pi, \theta, \xi \rangle$ where $\iota$ is a string representing the agent's identifier, $\sigma$ is the belief base, $\gamma$ is the goal base, $\Pi$ is the agent's plan base, $\theta$ is a ground substitution, and $\xi$ is the agent's event base.*

For this paper, we are only interested in the changes of the belief base and the substitutions that are resulted from querying the belief base during the program execution. We denote the belief base and the substitution base of an individual agent configuration $C$ with $C^\sigma$ and $C^\theta$, respectively. Moreover, we use $query(\sigma, \beta)$ to denote the belief query (meta-) operation which performs the query $\beta$ on the belief base $\sigma$ and results in a substitution $\tau_\beta$. In the following, we use $\tau_\beta = query(\sigma, \beta)$ to denote that $\tau_\beta$ is the substitution resulting from querying $\beta$ from belief base $\sigma$ . In the context of this paper, the relevant 2APL transitions are related to belief query and belief update operations.

**Definition 8.** *(State transition) Let $C_i$ be the an individual 2APL agent configuration, and let $C_i^\sigma$ and $C_i^\theta$ be the belief base and the substitution base, respectively. Let $\alpha$ be an update operation, $\beta$ be a query operation, $C_i^\sigma \cdot \alpha$ be the belief base $C_i^\sigma$ updated with action $\alpha$, and $\theta \cdot query(C_i^\sigma, \beta)$ be the substitution base $\theta$ updated with the substitution resulted from querying $\beta$ on belief base $C_i^\sigma$. The following two 2APL transition rules define the effects of belief query and belief update operations.*

*1. $C_i \xrightarrow{\alpha} C_{i+1}$, where $C_{i+1}^\sigma = C_i^\sigma \cdot \alpha$ and $C_{i+1}^\theta = C_i^\theta$*

*2. $C_i \xrightarrow{\beta} C_{i+1}$, where $C_{i+1}^\sigma = C_i^\sigma$ and $C_{i+1}^\theta = C_i^\theta \cdot query(C_i^\sigma, \beta)$*

Note that the transition rule for belief update operations modifies only the belief base and the transition rule for belief query operations modifies only the substitutions.

The execution of 2APL programs with caching is obtained by modifying the standard 2APL program states, to include the cache and the changed flags of the queries, and 2APL transitions related to update and query of the belief base. In the following, we use $Queries(P) = \{\beta_1, \ldots, \beta_n\}$ to denote the set of all queries occurring in the 2APL program $P$ and $\beta.changed = V$ to indicate that the value of the changed flag of query $\beta$ is $V \in \{\top, \bot\}$. Using this information and the notions introduced in Section 3, we can now define the 2APL configuration states extended with caching.

**Definition 9.** *(Extended agent configuration) The configuration of an extended 2APL agent is defined as* $\mathbb{C} = \langle \iota, \sigma, \gamma, \Pi, \theta, \xi, \mathcal{F}, \mathcal{H} \rangle$ *where* $\iota, \sigma, \gamma, \Pi, \theta$ *and* $\xi$ *are the same as in Definition 7, and* $\mathcal{F} = \{\beta.changed = V \mid \beta \in Queries(P)\}$ *and* $\mathcal{H} = \{\tau_{\beta_1}, \ldots, \tau_{\beta_k} \mid \beta_i \in Queries(P)\}$ *are sets storing the values of the query flags and the substitutions of the cached queries, respectively.*

We will write $\mathbb{C}^{\mathcal{F}}$ and $\mathbb{C}^{\mathcal{H}}$ to denote the set of caching flags and the set of cached queries, respectively. Based on the definition of an extended agent configuration, the relevant transitions for 2APL with caching are defined as follows.

**Definition 10.** *Let* $\mathbb{C}_i$ *be a state of 2APL program with caching,* $\mathbb{C}_i^{\mathcal{H}} \cdot \tau_\beta$ *be the cache* $\mathbb{C}_i^{\mathcal{H}}$ *updated with the substitution* $\tau_\beta$*, and* $\mathbb{C}_i^{\mathcal{F}} \cdot F$ *be a set of query flag values* $\mathbb{C}_i^{\mathcal{F}}$ *updated with new values for some of the query flags* $F$ *where* $F \subseteq \{\beta.changed \mid \beta \in Queries(P)\}$*. For 2APL with caching, the following two transition rules replace the belief query and belief update transition rules of standard 2APL, as presented in Definition 8.*

*1.* $\mathbb{C}_i \xrightarrow{\alpha} \mathbb{C}_{i+1}$*, where* $\mathbb{C}_{i+1}^{\sigma} = \mathbb{C}_i^{\sigma} \cdot \alpha$ *,* $\mathbb{C}_{i+1}^{\theta} = \mathbb{C}_i^{\theta}$*, and*
$$\mathbb{C}_{i+1}^{\mathcal{F}} = \mathbb{C}_i^{\mathcal{F}} \cdot \{\beta.changed = \top \mid \beta \in \alpha.relevantQueries\}$$
*2.* $\mathbb{C}_i \xrightarrow{\beta} \mathbb{C}_{i+1}$*, where* $\mathbb{C}_{i+1}^{\sigma} = \mathbb{C}_i^{\sigma}$ *and*

$$
\begin{cases}
\begin{aligned}
\tau_\beta &= query(\mathbb{C}_i^{\sigma}, \beta) \,, & \text{if } \beta.changed = \top \\
\mathbb{C}_{i+1}^{\theta} &= \mathbb{C}_i^{\theta} \cdot \tau_\beta \,, & \\
\mathbb{C}_{i+1}^{\mathcal{H}} &= \mathbb{C}_i^{\mathcal{H}} \cdot \tau_\beta \,, & \\
\mathbb{C}_{i+1}^{\mathcal{F}} &= \mathbb{C}_i^{\mathcal{F}} \cdot \{\beta.changed = \bot\} &
\end{aligned} \\[2ex]
\mathbb{C}_{i+1}^{\theta} = \mathbb{C}_i^{\theta} \cdot \tau_\beta \,, \ \tau_\beta \in \mathcal{H} \qquad\qquad \text{if } \beta.changed = \bot
\end{cases}
$$

The first transition defines the effect of a belief update operation, which besides updating the belief base, sets the *changed* flags of all relevant queries to true, meaning that they are all excluded from caching in the next execution step.

The second transition defines the effect of a belief query operation, conditioned on the value of the *changed* flag of this query. In particular, if this flag is set to true, i.e., when a part of the belief base that is relevant to the query has changed such that the query should be executed again, the query $\beta$ is executed against the belief base, the substitution is stored in the cached queries base, and the *changed* flags of all relevant queries are set to true. If the *changed* flag associated with the query is false (i.e., if the part of the belief base that is relevant to the query has not changed since the last query), then the query can be answered by using the cached value of the query. Initially, the *changed* flags of the set of all belief queries that occur in a 2APL program is set to true.

**Definition 11.** *(Initial Configuration) The initial configuration of an extended 2APL agent is defined as a tuple* $\mathbb{C}_0 = \langle \iota, \sigma_0, \gamma_0, \Pi_0, \theta_0, \xi_0, \mathcal{F}_0, \mathcal{H}_0 \rangle$, *where* $C_0 = \langle \iota, \sigma_0, \gamma_0, \Pi_0, \theta_0, \xi_0 \rangle$ *is the initial configuration of a standard 2APL agent (see Definition 7). The* changed *flag of all belief queries that occur in the 2APL program are initially set to true, i.e.* $\forall \beta \in \mathbb{C}_0^{\mathcal{F}} : \beta.changed = \top$. *The set of cached queries is initially empty, i.e.* $\mathbb{C}_0^{\mathcal{H}} = \varnothing$.

The standard 2APL execution, performed by the 2APL interpreter, is modified by replacing the belief update and belief query transition rules with the modified transition rules as presented in Definition 10. We assume that all other transitions have the same effect on the belief base and substitution base of the program states, i.e., if $\langle \iota, \sigma, \gamma, \Pi, \theta, \xi \rangle \xrightarrow{x} \langle \iota', \sigma', \gamma', \Pi', \theta', \xi' \rangle$ is a transition in an execution of 2APL without caching and $x$ is any operation different from a belief query and a belief update, then $\langle \iota, \sigma, \gamma, \Pi, \theta, \xi, \mathcal{F}, \mathcal{H} \rangle \xrightarrow{x} \langle \iota', \sigma', \gamma', \Pi', \theta', \xi', \mathcal{F}, \mathcal{H} \rangle$ is the transition in the corresponding execution of 2APL with caching.

In order to show that the execution behaviour of 2APL programs do not change under the caching modifications, we need to prove that replacing the standard transition rules for belief update and belief query operations, as presented in Definition 8, with the new transition rules, as presented in Definition 10, does not change the sequence of program states with respect to the belief base and the substitution base. In order to do this, we need to define when a program state without caching is equivalent to a program state with caching.

**Definition 12.** *Let* $C$ *be a state of a 2APL program without caching and* $\mathbb{C}$ *be a state of a 2APL program with caching. We say that* $C$ *is equivalent with* $\mathbb{C}$ *with respect to the belief base and the substitution base, denoted as* $C \sim \mathbb{C}$, *iff* $C = \langle \iota, \sigma, \gamma, \Pi, \theta, \xi \rangle$ *and* $\mathbb{C} = \langle \iota, \sigma, \gamma, \Pi, \theta, \xi, \mathcal{F}, \mathcal{H} \rangle$.

Note that a standard 2APL program state is equivalent with a 2APL program state extended with cache if all state components, except the set of changed flag values and the cache, are identical.

**Theorem 1.** *Let* $C_0 \xrightarrow{x_1} C_1 \xrightarrow{x_2} C_2 \xrightarrow{x_3} \ldots$ *be the execution of a 2APL program without caching and* $\mathbb{C}_0 \xrightarrow{x_1} \mathbb{C}_1 \xrightarrow{x_2} \mathbb{C}_2 \xrightarrow{x_3} \ldots$ *be the execution of the same 2APL program with caching. We have* $\forall i \geq 0 : C_i \sim \mathbb{C}_i$.

*Proof.* We provide the sketches of a proof which is based on induction.

– (Base step:) $C_0 \sim \mathbb{C}_0$. Follows directly from Definition 11.
– (Induction step:) Suppose $C_i \sim \mathbb{C}_i$, then we prove that $C_{i+1} \sim \mathbb{C}_{i+1}$ for $i > 0$. We first note that all transitions of 2APL executions with caching are the same as the corresponding transitions of 2APL without caching, except transitions for belief update and belief queries operations. This means that if $C_i \sim \mathbb{C}_i$, $C_i \xrightarrow{x} C_{i+1}$ is a 2APL execution transition without caching, $x$ is an operation different than belief update or belief query, and $\mathbb{C}_i \xrightarrow{x} \mathbb{C}_{i+1}$, then $C_{i+1} \sim \mathbb{C}_{i+1}$. What remains is to show is that this equivalence holds for transitions of belief update and belief query operations as well. For belief update operation we need to show that if $C_i \sim \mathbb{C}_i$, $C_i \xrightarrow{\alpha} C_{i+1}$, and $\mathbb{C}_i \xrightarrow{\alpha} \mathbb{C}_{i+1}$, then $C_{i+1} \sim \mathbb{C}_{i+1}$. This means that we have to show that $C_{i+1}^\sigma = \mathbb{C}_{i+1}^\sigma$ and $C_{i+1}^\theta = \mathbb{C}_{i+1}^\theta$ (Definition 12). From Definition 8 and 10 we can immediately conclude that a belief update in 2APL without caching has exactly the same effect on its belief base $C^\sigma$ and the substitution base $C^\theta$ as 2APL with caching on its belief base $\mathbb{C}^\sigma$ and substitution base $\mathbb{C}^\theta$. Thus, $C_{i+1} \sim \mathbb{C}_{i+1}$ in the case that the transition is a belief update.

For the belief query operation we need to show that if $C_i \sim \mathbb{C}_i$, $C_i \xrightarrow{\beta} C_{i+1}$ and $\mathbb{C}_i \xrightarrow{\beta} \mathbb{C}_{i+1}$, then $C_{i+1} \sim \mathbb{C}_{i+1}$. First, we observe that a belief query $\beta$ has no effect on the belief bases of both 2APL with caching and 2APL without caching, that is, $C_i^\sigma = C_{i+1}^\sigma$ and $\mathbb{C}_i^\sigma = \mathbb{C}_{i+1}^\sigma$. Since we assumed $C_i \sim \mathbb{C}_i$ we obtain $C_{i+1} \sim \mathbb{C}_{i+1}$. For the substitution base, we consider two cases: $\beta.changed = \top$ and $\beta.changed = \bot$. In the first case, both the substitution bases are updated with the query $\beta$ on the belief base, that is, $C_{i+1}^\theta = C_i^\theta \cdot query(C_i^\sigma, \beta)$ and $\mathbb{C}_{i+1}^\theta = \mathbb{C}_i^\theta \cdot query(\mathbb{C}_i^\sigma, \beta)$, which means that we have $C_{i+1} \sim \mathbb{C}_{i+1}$.

In the second case where $\beta.changed = \bot$, the transition without caching updates the substitution base $C^\theta$ with $query(C^\sigma, \beta)$ while the transition with caching updates the substitution base by the cached substitution $\tau_\beta \in \mathbb{C}^\mathcal{H}$. We thus need to show that $query(C^\sigma, \beta) = \tau_\beta$. Consider the last transition in the 2APL program execution with caching that was based on a belief query operation and through which the *changed* flag of query $\beta$ is set to false. Let this transition be $\mathbb{C}_k \xrightarrow{\beta} \mathbb{C}_{k+1}$ and its corresponding transition without caching be $C_k \xrightarrow{\beta} C_{k+1}$ for $k < i$. Note that in program state $k+1$ it holds that $query(C^\sigma, \beta) = \tau_\beta$ and that $\tau_\beta$ is stored in $\mathbb{C}^\mathcal{H}$. Because there have been no belief base updates relevant for the belief query $\beta$ between program states $k+1$ and $i$ (otherwise the *changed* flag of $\beta$ would have been true, see Definition 5 on query relevance), we can conclude that $query(C^\sigma, \beta)$ provides one and the same substitution in all program states $C$ between $C_{k+1}$ and $C_i$ and thus also in all program states $\mathbb{C}$ between $\mathbb{C}_{k+1}$ and $\mathbb{C}_i$. Note also that $\tau_\beta$ is not modified between program states $\mathbb{C}_{k+1}$ and $\mathbb{C}_i$, because we assumed that the transition from state $k$ to state $k+1$ was the last transition in which the *changed* flag of query $\beta$ was set to false. This implies that $query(C^\sigma, \beta)$ in program state $C_i$ is the same as $\tau_\beta$ in program state $\mathbb{C}_i$ and thus $\mathbb{C}^\theta \cdot query(C^\sigma, \beta) = \mathbb{C}^\theta \cdot \tau_\beta$ such that $C_{i+1} \sim \mathbb{C}_{i+1}$.    □

# 5    Experimentation

We have analyzed the working of belief caching using a benchmarking tool that was developed for this work. We have tested belief caching for three increasingly realistic programs.[4]

## 5.1    Experimental Setup

The first program (`driver`) has been developed to demonstrate the working of belief caching specifically. The code of this program is almost identical to Figure 2, except that the body of the Prolog rule `enough_fuel` has been replaced by a computationally heavy calculation involving integers. The second program (`storage`) has been written for this task as well but is more realistic. It consists of a multi-agent system with 10 different agents that each can store items in a storage list. Agents will attempt to keep their items stock constant while they receive items from the environment. The last program (`marketplace`) is an existing and more sophisticated version of a multi-agent system in which agents have items that they can sell, and have items that they want to buy. Agents can bid for items they desire and sell an item when a bid of another agent meets their demands.

We have compared the results between 2APL with and without belief caching. We use "2APL" to refer to 2APL with no belief caching, and "2APL*" to refer to 2APL with belief caching. All experiments have been performed on a 2.4GHz Intel Core i5, 6 GB 667 MHz DDR3, running Windows 7 and Java 1.6. When showing the benchmarking results, we use $d$ to denote the number of deliberation steps, $Q_b$ for belief queries, $U_b$ for belief updates. $C_{PG}$ for PG rule calls, $C_{PC}$ for PC rules calls, $C_{PR}$ for PR rule calls, and $B$ for the run-time of the program, which we will also refer to as the benchmarking time.

## 5.2    Results

**Driver Program.** We plot the number of deliberation steps per second for a benchmarking time of 50 seconds (Figure 5a). The average value of 2APL lies around 450 deliberation steps per second, and the one of 2APL* around 6500, which is around fifteen times as much.[5]

The only rules that are being used in the `driver` program are PG rules. Therefore, it is of interest to see whether the PG rules are being processed faster because of belief caching. When we plot these values (Figure 5b), we see that 2APL* processes PG rules much faster than 2APL. Where 2APL has an average value of around 7.5 ms per call, the average of 2APL* is around 0.5 ms, which more than 14 times faster.

---

[4] The sources for the used programs can be downloaded from
http://www.marcvanzee.nl/2apl/2apl_beliefcaching_examples.rar

[5] The noise in the results is mainly due to the fact that Java has no automatic garbage collection, which means that this will be done whenever Java judges it appropriate, independent from the benchmark points.

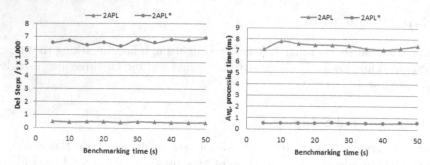

(a) Deliberation steps per second.    (b) Average processing time of a PG rule.

**Fig. 5.** (Driver) Results for $B=50$s

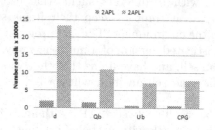

**Fig. 6.** (Driver) Total number of calls for all operations (B=240s)

The reason why PG rules are being processed much faster in 2APL* is because less time is spent on performing belief queries. For completeness, the graph showing the total number of calls in 50 seconds for all relevant operations is depicted in Figure 6, which shows that indeed the number of calls have increased drastically for 2APL*.

**Storage Program.** Figure 7a shows the number of calls for the relevant operations at a benchmark time of 50 seconds. As we can see, the number of deliberation steps has improved with a factor of about 4 for 2APL*, which is significant. The number of belief queries has remained more or less constant, but since much more deliberation steps have been executed, the number of belief queries per deliberation step has decreased a lot. This is shown more clearly in Figure 7b, where we see that the belief queries take up much less processing time in the case of 2APL*.

**Marketplace.** The last program that we have tested contains much simpler belief queries. The question that we would like to answer is whether such a program could also be improved using belief caching. As we see in Figure 8a, the number of deliberation steps increases slightly when using 2APL*, while the number of belief queries decreases with half. This makes sense, because while we save many belief queries, there is not much increase in run-time because the queries are very simple and not time-consuming. This becomes more clear in

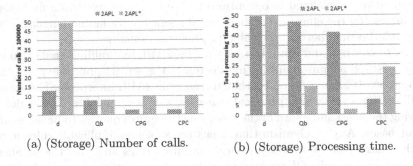

(a) (Storage) Number of calls.          (b) (Storage) Processing time.

**Fig. 7.** (Storage) Benchmarking results for B=200s

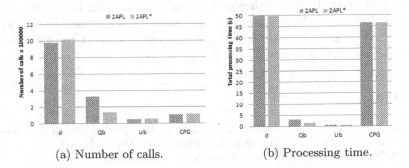

(a) Number of calls.          (b) Processing time.

**Fig. 8.** (Marketplace) Benchmarking results for B=50s

Figure 8b, where the processing time of the different operations is shown. As we can see, the operation time of the belief queries is very small and this does not affect the efficiency of the program greatly.

## 6   Conclusion

We have implemented belief caching into 2APL and showed that it extends the abstract performance model of [1]. Instead of single-cycle caching, our implementation keeps track of an update cycle for each individual belief query. We have implemented belief caching into the latest version of 2APL. The benchmarking results show that belief caching can optimize a 2APL program significantly, because it is an effective way to reduce the number of belief queries. To what extent this decrease will contribute to an increase in deliberation speed depends on the complexity of the belief queries. Our contribution is that the implementation will never lead to a worse performance, because the dependencies between the belief updates and the belief queries can be calculated at compile-time. Logic-based agent programming language are based on a combination of imperative programming with logic-based knowledge bases. Because this approach is relatively new, there has not been much research dedicated towards the optimization of the communication between these two formalisms. Our approach has shown that it can be very beneficial to optimize this. We therefore see it as a first step towards increasing the efficiency of logic-based agent programming languages so that they will become better applicable to practical domains.

We plan to continue our optimization work on 2APL by building goal caching mechanism as well as a mechanism that decreases the set of applicable practical reasoning rules. It should be noted that the current 2APL interpreter checks at each deliberation cycle which practical reasoning rule is applicable. This is done by checking the head and guard of the rules which requires queries to belief, goal, and event bases. Any mechanism that keeps track of non-applicable rules may reduce the number of applicable practical reasoning rules and thus the number of time consuming queries. We believe that our caching mechanism is not limited to 2APL. It can be implemented into logic-based agent programming languages such as Jason [2], GOAL [5], or other multi-agent programming languages that combine logic-based knowledge bases with imperative programming (see [3] for an overview), as long as the set of plan rules do not change at run-time. We leave this issue for further research.

# References

1. Alechina, N., Behrens, T., Hindriks, K.V., Logan, B.: Query Caching in Agent Programming Languages. In: Dastani, M., Hübner, J.F., Logan, B. (eds.) ProMAS 2012. LNCS, vol. 7837, pp. 123–137. Springer, Heidelberg (2013)
2. Bordini, R., Wooldridge, M., Hübner, J.: Programming Multi-Agent Systems in AgentSpeak using Jason (Wiley Series in Agent Technology). John Wiley & Sons (2007) ISBN 0470029005
3. Bordini, R., Dastani, M., Dix, J., Seghrouchni, A.E.F. (eds.): Multi-Agent Programming: Languages, Tools and Applications. Springer (2009)
4. Dastani, M.: 2APL: a practical agent programming language. In: Autonomous Agents and Multi-Agent Systems, pp. 214–248 (2008)
5. Hindriks, K.: Programming Rational Agents in GOAL. In: Multi-Agent Programming: Languages and Tools and Applications (see [3]), pp. 119–157 (2009)
6. Levy, A.Y., Sagiv, Y.: Queries Independent of Updates. In: Proceedings of the 19th International Conference on Very Large Data Bases, pp. 24–27 (1993)
7. Levy, A.: Creating Abstractions Using Relevance Reasoning. In: Proceedings of the Twelfth National Conference on Artificial Intelligence, pp. 588–594 (1994)
8. Levy, A.Y., Fikes, R.E., Sagiv, Y.: Speeding Up Inferences Using Relevance Reasoning: A Formalism and Algorithms. Journal of Artificial Intelligence, 97–1 (1997)
9. DeRaedt, L.: Interactive theory revision: an inductive logic programming approach. Academic Press Ltd. (1992) ISBN 0-12-210730-6
10. Ziafati, P., Dastani, M., Meyer, J.-J., van der Torre, L.: Agent Programming Languages Requirements for Programming Autonomous Robots. In: Dastani, M., Hübner, J.F., Logan, B. (eds.) ProMAS 2012. LNCS, vol. 7837, pp. 35–53. Springer, Heidelberg (2013)

# Deciding between Conflicting Influences

Andreas Schmidt Jensen

Department of Applied Mathematics and Computer Science,
Technical University of Denmark, Kongens Lyngby, Denmark
`ascje@dtu.dk`

**Abstract.** This paper investigates an approach of decision making internally in an agent where a decision is based on preference and expectation. The approach uses a logic for qualitative decision theory proposed by Boutilier to express such notions. To make readily use of this we describe a simple method for generating preference and expectation models that respect certain rules provided by the agents, and we briefly discuss how to integrate the approach into an existing agent programming language.

## 1 Introduction

Agents taking part in a multi-agent system are usually seen as intelligent entities that autonomously are able to bring about (from their own perspectives) desirable states. The designer is in a fixed setting with a controlled number of agents and globally desirable states often able to implement the agents such that their own desirable states coincide with the globally desirable states. In open societies, agents often come from different sources and their desires cannot as such be assumed to match the global desires. A suggestion is to impose an organization on the agents, which can influence the actions of the agent toward the desires of the organization.

When agents are constrained by an organization, their own goals may conflict with those of the organization and they need in such cases to be able to decide which of the conflicting goals to pursue. In some of the previous work toward resolving such conflicts, desires and obligations are ordered a priori, so that an agent either prefers desires over obligations or obligations over desires. This results in agents that are always selfish (considering own goals more important than organizational goals) or always social (vice versa). We argue in this paper that such distinction can be too hard; even a selfish agent could in some cases benefit from preferring certain obligations to its desires. We consider an approach on how to resolve such (and other) conflicts, based on work in the area of qualitative decision theory by Boutilier [4], where the expected consequences of bringing about a state are considered. We show that this result in agents that are not always either social or selfish, but instead are able to decide based on the consequences of bringing about a state.

Our focus is on a general approach toward deciding between different kinds of influences, with the aim to show that although agents are subject to influences

M. Cossentino et al. (Eds.): EMAS 2013, LNAI 8245, pp. 137–155, 2013.
© Springer-Verlag Berlin Heidelberg 2013

from different entities, they are able to make decisions based on the current situation, their preferences and the expected consequence of bringing about a state. We do not focus explicitly on the choice between an agent's desires and the obligations from an organization, but emphasize that the approach is useful in this situation and other situations as well.

To make the approach readily useful we furthermore describe a simple method for generating models for preference and expectation based on basic rules, such as "I prefer to drive to work when it rains", specified by the agents.

The paper is organized as follows: In section 2, we discuss the issues that arise when an agent has to make a decision between conflicting influences. In section 3, we present a new approach on how to solve such conflicts without having to put the agents into the categories "selfish" or "social". We present a method for generating models that conform to the agent's preferences in section 4. In section 5, we discuss a case in which agents have conflicting influences and show that our method enables them to make a decision using their own preference and the expected consequence of bringing about each state. We briefly discuss how to implement the system and integrate it in an existing agent programming language in section 6. Finally, we conclude our work and discuss future research directions in section 7.

## 2    Conflicting Influences

Agents entering an environment will be subject to influences from multiple sources: their own desires, requests from other agents, and obligations from an organization. In the well-known BDI model, an agent's desires become intentions, when the agent commits to bringing about these desires. One could argue that if an agent wants to accept requests from other agents, or if it wants to adhere to the obligations of an organization, these influences are merely desires as well, i.e. the agent simply desires to do so. The incentives for doing so are however not clear, since there should be different reasons for committing to actual desires and to requests or obligations "disguised" as desires. For example, if an agent has a desire to move a box from $A$ to $B$, it typically *wants* to do so. However if the agent wants to pay a bill before its due date, this "desire" has more likely arisen from the fact that the agent does not want to pay a fine, rather than being an actual desire to pay the bill. In such a situation, the desire may actually be an obligation or a request to pay the bill, which means that the agent should reason differently since the actual desire is to avoid paying a fine.

Furthermore, consider an agent that receives an undesirable request from an agent that it desires to help. It may choose to commit to the task even though the task itself is not desirable, because the desire to help the other agent is stronger than the desire not to perform the task (the consequence of *not* helping the other agent might be a bad reputation). Similarly, if an agent is obligated to perform certain tasks for an organization, it should not only be able to consider whether the task is desirable, but also weigh this against the penalty for violating the obligation.

We call something that the agent might choose to intend to do a "decision influence" rather than a desire since it, as argued above, may stem from many different sources rather than being merely desires. The agent naturally has to consider its desires since it would be irrational to ignore them, but the consequence of not reasoning about e.g. obligations might be intolerable so these influence the agent as well. This also means that the agent is not supposed to be reasoning explicitly about whether it should commit to bringing about an arbitrary obligation or desires; they are merely considered influences, and the agent is not concerned with the different types of influences: only the fact that they affect the decision process matters. Several approaches are proposed on how to let agents choose between specific types of influences (typically obligations and desires) [2,5,6,7,8], so we briefly discuss how our approach differs.

In [5] conflicts between beliefs, obligations, intentions and desires are discussed with a focus on a distinction between *internal* conflicts, e.g. contradictory beliefs, conflicting obligations and *external* conflicts, such as a desire which is in conflict with an obligation. The solution proposed, the BOID architecture, imposes a strict ordering between beliefs, obligations, intentions and desires, such that the order of derivation determines the agent's attitude. Thus different agent types emerge; an agent deriving desires before beliefs is a wishful-thinking agent, while an agent deriving obligations before desires is social.

We believe this ordering is too strong; if an agent is social, it will always choose obligations over desires, and vice versa for selfish agents. This might not always be appropriate. For instance, a selfish agent might desire not to go to work, but if the consequence of not fulfilling the obligation of going to work is severe (i.e. getting fired), even a selfish agent should consider this consequence before deciding not to go to work.

Dignum *et al.* suggests that *"both norms and obligations should be explicitly used as influences on an agent's behavior"* [7]. They represent obligations (and norms) using Prohairetic Deontic Logic [10], a preference-based dyadic deontic logic which allows for contrary-to-duty obligations (obligations holding in a sub-ideal context). Furthermore, they propose a modified BDI-interpreter in which selected events are augmented with potential deontic events, which, put simply, are obligations and norms that may become applicable when choosing a plan. For instance, if agent $a$ has an obligation to perform a task for agent $b$, and $a$ does not intend to do so he ought to inform $b$ about this. The modified interpreter generates a number of options depending on these potential events and chooses a relevant plan based on the agent's attitude.

In [8] it is argued that the preference orderings induced by desires, obligations and norms should be combined into a single ordering. It is noted that a common way to do so is to allow that a single preference ordering determine the aggregate ordering, such that the agent might always put obligations over norms and norms over desires, similarly to the BOID architecture. Another approach is also discussed in which the orderings are mapped into a common scale, such that very desirable situations could outweigh the cost of violating certain obligations. Such ordering should be quite dynamic since, for example, obligations toward a trusted agent should become less important if that agent becomes less trustworthy. Simple rules are presented to deal with few alternatives, but it is noted that the situation is more complex if an agent has to choose between three or more alternatives and none of the three orderings agree on a preferred alternative. A simple rule which orders the alternatives in a fixed order results in a very simple-minded agent and it is suggested that the consequences of different situations is considered, however this is not investigated further.

Different types of role enactments are identified in [6] and they describe an approach for verification of consistency of agent goals and role goals. They work with agents and roles in which goals are prioritized using an ordering and investigate what is required to make agents and roles are compatible. This leads to role enacting agents that can prioritize own goals and role goals in a combined ordering, thus not necessarily making agents explicitly selfish or social. They define different enactment types, such as selfish enactment in which the agent includes both own goals and role goals, but gives priority to own goals, and social enactment in which priority is given to the rule goals.

## 2.1   Consequence-Based Decisions

Performing an action will in many cases result in one or more side effects that may or may not be desirable for the agent performing the action. These side effects are part of the consequences of performing the action, and the agent can reason using more information by considering these consequences, thus enabling it to make better decisions. This suggests that in order to reason about bringing about a certain state, the agent should consider what consequences are expected when bringing about that state.

We therefore suggest that the agent should reason about the expected *consequences* of choosing to commit to a decision influence and furthermore that this reasoning should be based on both *preference* and *tolerance*. We use preference for influences and tolerance for expected consequences of influences, and the reason for using tolerance instead of preference in the case of consequences is that the agent should not need to desire the consequences of bringing about a state. Since the consequences are merely side effects, they need not be desired in the same way as the influences are. If a consequence is preferable, then clearly it is also tolerable but the opposite need not be the case (the agent might tolerate going to work even though *prefers* to stay at home). We define a situation as being tolerated when the opposite is not preferred (e.g., working is tolerated if staying at home is not preferred over working). Using the influences, we can build two sets to base a decision on: the set of most preferred influences, *Pref*, and the set of influences with the most tolerable expected consequences, *Tol*. We can identify different strategies for how to make a decision based on these sets, such as considering one set before the other or by using a combination of the sets:

$$Pref \; > \; Tol \qquad\qquad (1)$$

$$Pref \; < \; Tol \qquad\qquad (2)$$

$$Pref \; \cup \; Tol \qquad\qquad (3)$$

$$Pref \; \cap \; Tol \qquad\qquad (4)$$

We can let preferences take precedence (1) such that if a single influence is most preferred (in *Pref*) it is chosen, and only in case of multiple most preferred influences will tolerance be taken into account, or we can let tolerance take precedence (2), which gives the opposite situation. However, this means that only in some cases are both preference and tolerance taken into account, so an agent could choose to commit to something it prefers which leads to an intolerable situations that could have been avoided if both sets were taken into account. We could take the collective influences (3), but then the agent would have to choose between things it prefer and things it tolerate even though the former may be intolerable and the latter could be unwanted. Instead we could let the decision be the influences that are *both* preferred and tolerated (4), thus ensuring that the decision is preferred by the agent and that the consequences can be tolerated. In certain situations, these sets may not coincide, and we argue then that the safest decision is to choose something tolerated, since then even though the influence might not be *most* preferred, at least it will not lead to an intolerable state. Our approach makes use of the last strategy, i.e. taking the intersection of the sets, since it incorporates both measures in all situations, while not resulting in intolerable preferred states.

Note that our approach does not incorporate an explicit notion of organizations; the focus is on many different kinds of influences including the obligations toward an organization. As a result, we model consequences as expectations from the environment, that is, which possible world is the most expected, which is the second most and so on. This means that if the consequences of the violation of an obligation (i.e. sanctions) are specified in an organizational model, these consequences are in our approach modeled such that worlds in which the violation has occurred *and* a sanction has been imposed are more expected than the worlds where the violation has occurred without the agent being sanctioned. This will be evident in the example in section 5 where all expected consequences are incorporated into the same model.

## 3    Modeling Influence and Consequence

We base our work on the Logic for Qualitative Decision Theory (QDT) by Boutilier [4]. We briefly describe the semantics of QDT and define a few new abbreviations to be used in the decision-making.

The basic idea behind the QDT model is as follows. An agent has the ultimate desire of achieving the goals to which it is committed. This can be modeled by a possible worlds-model in which the agent has achieved its goal when it is in a world where those goals hold. The most preferred world in an ideal setting is the world in which the agent has achieved all of its goals. However, such world is often unreachable since the agent could have contradicting goals, other agents could prevent the agent from achieving all of its goals, an organization could impose obligations, which contradict the agent's goals, etc. By ordering the worlds in a preference relation, it is possible to choose the most preferred world(s) in a sub-ideal situation.

In order to decide between influences the consequence of bringing about a state should be taken into account. If the consequence of pursuing a personal desire is to be fired from your workplace, it might not be reasonable to do so even though the desire was more preferred than the obligations from work. We briefly describe QDT below before moving on to modeling the expected consequence of bringing about a state.

A QDT model is of the form:

$$M = \langle W, \leq_P, \leq_N, \pi \rangle,$$

where $W$ is the non-empty set of worlds, $\leq_P$ is the transitive, connected preference ordering[1], $\leq_N$ is the transitive, connected normality ordering, and $\pi$ is the valuation function. The normality ordering is used to model how likely each world is, e.g. it is normally cold when it is snowing, and the preference ordering is used to model an agent's preferences.

The semantics are as follows:

$$M, w \models p \iff p \in \pi(w)$$
$$M, w \models \neg\varphi \iff M, w \not\models \varphi$$
$$M, w \models \varphi \wedge \psi \iff M, w \models \varphi \wedge M, w \models \psi$$
$$M, w \models \Box_P \varphi \iff \forall v \in W, v \leq_P w, M, v \models \varphi$$
$$M, w \models \overleftharpoon{\Box}_P \varphi \iff \forall v \in W, w <_P v, M, v \models \varphi$$
$$M, w \models \Box_N \varphi \iff \forall v \in W, v \leq_N w, M, v \models \varphi$$
$$M, w \models \overleftharpoon{\Box}_N \varphi \iff \forall v \in W, w <_N v, M, v \models \varphi$$

We can define the other operators $(\vee, \rightarrow, \Diamond, \overleftharpoon{\Diamond})$ as usual. Finally, we can talk about a formula being true in all worlds or some worlds: $\overleftrightarrow{\Box}_P \varphi \equiv \Box_P \varphi \wedge \overleftharpoon{\Box}_P \varphi$ and $\overleftrightarrow{\Diamond}_P \varphi \equiv \Diamond_P \varphi \vee \overleftharpoon{\Diamond}_P \varphi$, respectively (similarly for normality). The following abbreviations are defined [4]:

(1)  $I(\psi \mid \varphi) \equiv \overleftrightarrow{\Box}_P \neg\varphi \vee \overleftrightarrow{\Diamond}_P(\varphi \wedge \Box_P(\varphi \rightarrow \psi))$     (Conditional preference)

(2)  $\varphi \leq_P \psi \equiv \overleftrightarrow{\Box}_P(\psi \rightarrow \Diamond_P \varphi)$     (Relative preference)

(3)  $T(\psi \mid \varphi) \equiv \neg I(\neg\psi \mid \varphi)$     (Conditional tolerance)

(4)  $\varphi \Rightarrow \psi \equiv \overleftrightarrow{\Box}_N \neg\varphi \vee \overleftrightarrow{\Diamond}_N(\varphi \wedge \Box_N(\varphi \rightarrow \psi))$     (Normative conditional)

The abbreviations state that (1) $\psi$ is ideally true if $\varphi$ is true, (2) $\varphi$ is at least as preferred as $\psi$, (3) $\psi$ is tolerable given $\varphi$ and (4) that $\psi$ normally is the case when $\varphi$ is.

---

[1] We adopt the notion by Boutilier and others that we prefer minimal models, so $v \leq_P w$ denotes that $v$ is at least as preferred as $w$.

In order to make decisions as motivated above, we define the following abbreviations, which allow us to specify different kinds of relative preference, and relative tolerance.

$$\varphi \not\leq_P \psi \equiv \neg(\varphi \leq_P \psi) \qquad\qquad \text{(Not as preferred)}$$

$$\varphi \approx_P \psi \equiv (\varphi \leq_P \psi \wedge \psi \leq_P \varphi)$$
$$\vee \, (\varphi \not\leq_P \psi \wedge \psi \not\leq_P \varphi) \qquad \text{(Equally preferred)}$$

$$\varphi \leq_{T(\gamma)} \psi \equiv (T(\varphi \mid \gamma) \wedge \neg T(\psi \mid \gamma)) \vee$$
$$((T(\varphi \mid \gamma) \leftrightarrow T(\psi \mid \gamma)) \wedge$$
$$(\varphi \leq_P \psi \vee \varphi \approx_P \psi)) \qquad \text{(Relative tolerance)}$$

Relative tolerance is defined as $\varphi$ being at least as tolerable as $\psi$ w.r.t $\gamma$ when either $\varphi$ is tolerable given $\gamma$ and $\psi$ is not, or both $\varphi$ and $\psi$ are tolerable given $\gamma$ (or both are not), and $\varphi$ is at least as preferred as $\psi$, or they are equally preferable. This means that even if neither is tolerable, they are still comparable.

## 3.1  Making a Decision

We now show how QDT can be used to decide between conflicting influences. We define a model for an agent's decision making as follows:

$$\mathcal{M}_C = \langle M, F, C, B \rangle,$$

where $M$ is a QDT-model as defined above, $F$ is the set of influences, $C$ is the set of controllable propositions[2], and $B$ is the agent's belief base.

The set of potential consequences $C'$ is defined such that if $\varphi \in C$ then $\varphi, \neg\varphi \in C'$. That is, if $\varphi$ is controllable, then one of $\varphi, \neg\varphi$ may be a consequence of bringing about some state.

In order for a potential consequence to be an actual (expected) consequence of $\varphi$, it has to follow from the most normal worlds where $\varphi$ holds. That is, we add $\varphi$ to the belief base $B$, and the potential consequences that follow from the expanded belief base are then the expected consequences. Assuming that $\varphi$ and $B$ are consistent, we add $\varphi$ to $B$ using the *expansion* operator, $+$, of the AGM theory [1], where $B + \varphi$ means adding $\varphi$ to a copy of $B$ and closing the resulting set under logical consequence. We work with a copy of the belief base since the reasoning concerns what happens *if* the literal is added.

If, however, $\varphi$ and $B$ are not consistent, we can use the AGM *revision* operator, $\dot{+}$, which behaves like $+$, but if $\varphi$ and $B$ are not consistent, $B$ is minimally modified to make it consistent with $\varphi$, before adding $\varphi$.

As shown in [3], AGM belief revision can be efficiently implemented in rational agents, making it suitable for our approach. We can now formally define the expected consequence of bringing about a state.

---

[2] A controllable proposition is, roughly, a proposition that the agent is able to influence, directly or indirectly, by an action. E.g., *snow* is not controllable and cannot be a consequence of an action, whereas *work* is.

**Definition 1 (Expected consequences).** *Given an agent's belief base $B$, the set of potential consequences $C'$ and a literal $\varphi$. The expected consequences of bringing about $\varphi$, denoted $EC(\varphi)$, is given by:*

$$EC(\varphi) = \bigwedge C_\varphi \text{ for all } C_\varphi \in \{C_\varphi \mid (B \dotplus \varphi \Rightarrow C_\varphi) \text{ where } C_\varphi \in C'\}$$

*i.e. the conjunction of all literals $C_\varphi$ that are normally consequences of the current belief base $B$ expanded with $\varphi$, such that $B$ remains consistent. If there are no expected consequences, then $EC(\varphi) = \top$.*

Consider a normality ordering in which we have that

$$a \wedge x \Rightarrow b, \qquad a \wedge \neg x \Rightarrow c, \quad d \wedge \neg x \Rightarrow e,$$

and belief base $B = \{x\}$. Then we have that $EC(a) = b$ and $EC(d) = \top$. If $B = \{\neg x\}$, then $EC(a) = c$ and $EC(d) = e$.

**Definition 2 (Most preferred influences).** *Given an agent's set of influences $F$, the most preferred influences then are defined as the set Pref:*

$$Pref = \{\varphi \mid \varphi \in F \wedge \forall \psi \in F \ (\psi \neq \varphi \to \varphi \leq_P \psi)\}$$

**Definition 3 (Most tolerable consequences).** *Given an agent's set of influences $F$, the most preferred influences then are defined as the set Tol:*

$$Tol = \{\varphi \mid \varphi \in F \wedge \forall \psi \in F \ (\psi \neq \varphi \to EC(\varphi) \leq_{T(\varphi \vee \psi)} EC(\psi))\}$$

An agent can make a decision by selecting the most preferred influences having the most tolerable consequences from the set of potentially conflicting influences, $F,$.

**Definition 4 (Decision).** *Given a the set of influences $F$ and the expected consequences $EC(\varphi)$ for all $\varphi \in F$, we can get the set of best influences (the decision) the agent should choose from, Dec, as follows:*

$$Dec = \begin{cases} Tol & \text{if } Tol \cap Pref = \emptyset \\ Tol \cap Pref & \text{otherwise} \end{cases}$$

Given a model $\mathcal{M}_C$, an agent can then choose an arbitrary literal from $Dec$, since all of these will be preferred and have tolerable consequences (or at least have tolerable consequences).

If there are no expected consequences of bringing about a certain proposition, i.e. if $EC(\varphi) = \top$, then $\varphi$ is considered tolerable since we do not expect any consequences. Therefore comparing the relative tolerance for all other consequences, $\psi$, is reduced to comparing $\top \leq_{T(C)} \psi$ and $\psi \leq_{T(C)} \top$. Note that $T(\top \mid \psi)$ is true iff $\psi$ is true in any world[3]. Furthermore, $\top \leq_P \psi$ is always true, and $\psi \leq_P \top$ is true iff $\psi$ is true in all worlds. Thus, it is possible to make a decision even if some influences have no known consequences.

---

[3] Since $T(\top \mid \psi) \equiv \overset{\leftrightarrow}{\diamond}_P \psi \wedge \overset{\leftrightarrow}{\Box}_P(\neg \psi \vee \diamond_P(\psi \wedge \top))$.

In the following, we show that an agent given a model, $\mathcal{M}_C$ can always make a decision.

**Lemma 1.** *Given expressions $\varphi$, $\psi$, and $\gamma$, the following relation holds for relative tolerance:*

$$\neg(\varphi \leq_{T(\gamma)} \psi) \rightarrow (\psi \leq_{T(\gamma)} \varphi)$$

*Proof.* We assume $\neg(\varphi \leq_{T(\gamma)} \psi)$ and prove that $(\psi \leq_{T(\gamma)} \varphi)$. Based on the assumption and the definition of relative tolerance, the following formulas hold:

$$\neg(T(\varphi \mid \gamma) \wedge \neg T(\psi \mid \gamma)) \tag{5}$$

$$\neg((T(\varphi \mid \gamma) \leftrightarrow T(\psi \mid \gamma)) \wedge (\varphi \leq_P \psi \vee \varphi \approx_P \psi)) \tag{6}$$

1. Given (5), we have that either $T(\varphi \mid \gamma) \leftrightarrow T(\psi \mid \gamma)$ or $\neg T(\varphi \mid \gamma) \wedge T(\psi \mid \gamma)$ holds. In the latter case we have that $\psi \leq_{T(\gamma)} \varphi$ by the definition of relative tolerance. Otherwise they are equally tolerable and we have to consider the second case.

2. Given (6), either $\neg(T(\varphi \mid \gamma) \leftrightarrow T(\psi \mid \gamma))$ or $\neg(\varphi \leq_P \psi \vee \varphi \approx_P \psi)$. If the former is the case, then one is tolerated and the other is not. Because of (5), we have that $\neg T(\varphi \mid \gamma) \wedge T(\psi \mid \gamma)$ and therefore $\psi \leq_{T(\gamma)} \varphi$. If the latter is the case then we have that $\neg(\varphi \leq_P \psi) \wedge \neg(\varphi \approx_P \psi)$. In that case we have that $\psi <_P \varphi$ and therefore $\psi \leq_{T(\gamma)} \varphi$. □

**Proposition 1.** *Given a non-empty set of influences $F$ and the expected consequence $EC(\varphi)$ for each $\varphi \in F$, the set of best influences, Dec, is always non-empty.*

*Proof.* If $|F| = 1$ then $Dec = F = Tol = Pref$, since there are no $\psi \neq \varphi$ in $F$. If $|F| > 1$ then we consider each case.

− If $Tol \cap Pref = \emptyset$ then $Dec = Tol$ and we have to show that $Tol \neq \emptyset$. If $Tol = \emptyset$ then there is no $\psi$ such that $EC(\varphi)$ is relatively more tolerated than $EC(\psi)$. Since $|F| > 1$ there is at least one $\psi \neq \varphi$, and by lemma 1 we then have that $EC(\psi)$ is relatively more tolerated than $EC(\varphi)$. Thus $\psi \in Tol$ and $Tol \neq \emptyset$.
− If $Tol \cap Pref \neq \emptyset$ then, since $Dec = Tol \cap Pref$, $Dec$ cannot be empty. □

Proposition 1 shows that the decision procedure will always produce a non-empty result, meaning that we can use the procedure even in situations where there is no conflict between influences.

## 4  Generating Models

The preferences of an agent are usually not described as a model shown above, but will rather be expressions such as "I prefer that it does not rain" or "When it

**Algorithm 1.** Atom retrieval

---

**function** RETRIEVE_ATOMS($F, \mathcal{R}$)
    $At \leftarrow$ POSITIVE($F$)
    $checked \leftarrow \emptyset$
    **for all** $\varphi \in At \setminus checked$ **do**
        $At \leftarrow At \cup$ ATOMS_RULE($\varphi, \mathcal{R}$)
        $checked \leftarrow checked \cup \{\varphi\}$
    **return** $At$

---

rains, I want to stay inside". In order to utilize such preferences in the decision procedure above, a transformation is required. In the following, we present a method, which will generate a QDT-model that respects non-contradictory rules specified by the agent.

Each agent specifies a set of rules of the form $(\varphi, \psi)$, where $\varphi$ and $\psi$ are standard propositional formulas. A rule, $(\varphi, \psi)$, should be read as "if $\varphi$ then normally/preferably $\psi$". Using the notion of possible worlds, we understand a rule as follows. Worlds $w$, in which $w \models \varphi \wedge \psi$, are favored over worlds $w'$, where $w' \models \varphi \wedge \neg\psi$. Thus, a rule is roughly interpreted as the conditionals for preference and normality. In the following, we propose a method for generating preference and normality orderings that respect such rules by utilizing this interpretation. The generic definition of the conditional operators from the previous section is:

$$\text{if } \varphi \text{ then } \psi \equiv \overset{\leftrightarrow}{\square}\neg\varphi \vee \overset{\leftrightarrow}{\lozenge}(\varphi \wedge \square(\varphi \rightarrow \psi)).$$

From this definition, it is clear that there are two ways to ensure that a rule $(\varphi, \psi)$ is respected. Either (a) $\varphi$ is never true or (b) in the most favored world(s) where $\varphi$ is true, $\psi$ is also true. Option (a) is achieved easily; we simply remove all worlds where $\varphi$ is true. However, the agent does probably not intend this, since the rules are most likely specified such that favored situations are actually also possible situations. We therefore require that the method does not remove any worlds from $W$. The method should ensure that after the application of a rule we have $M \models (\varphi, \psi)$. Another natural requirement is that previously applied rules still hold after application of a new rule. If this is not possible, we say that the new rule contradicts previously applied rule, and therefore discard the new rule.

The aim is to generate a model respecting the rules, such that the agent can make a decision based on the model. Given the modal nature of QDT, the generation is based on the notion of possible worlds, $W$, so the first step is to generate $W$. Instead of generating a general model in which all rules are applicable, we create sub-models for different parts of the world. For example, an agent's preference concerning work might not be relevant for decisions in a different context, such as a family party. Furthermore, certain situations are not deemed possible, such as leaving work early and not going to work at all. $W$ is generated using the agent's current influences $F$ to decide which atoms

---

**Algorithm 2.** Rule application

---

$\quad$ **function** APPLY$((\varphi, \psi), W, \leq)$
$\qquad max \leftarrow max(\leq)$
$\qquad$ **for all** $w \in W$ **do**
$\qquad\quad$ **if** $w \models \varphi \wedge \neg\psi$ **then** $W_c \leftarrow w$
$\qquad\quad$ **if** $(w \models \varphi \wedge \psi)$ and $\neg\exists w'(w' \in W \wedge (w', w) \in lock)$ **then**
$\qquad\qquad o(w) = max + 1$
$\qquad\qquad W_s \leftarrow w$
$\qquad$ **if** $W_s = \emptyset$ **then return** $\bot$
$\qquad$ **for all** $w \in W_s, w' \in W_c$ **do** $lock(w, w')$
$\qquad$ **return** $\top$

---

are relevant for making a decision in the context of $F$ and any impossible worlds
are removed. Algorithm 1 retrieves the relevant atoms from $F$ and the set of
rules. POSITIVE$(S)$ is the set of all literals in $S$ with all negative literals made
positive, such that if $\neg\varphi \in S$ then $\varphi \in$ POSITIVE$(S)$. ATOMS_RULE$(\varphi, \mathcal{R})$ returns
a set of all atoms that appear in rules $r \in \mathcal{R}$ where $\varphi$ also appears (e.g. if
$\mathcal{R} = \{(\varphi, \psi_1), (\varphi, \psi_2)\}$ then ATOMS_RULE$(\varphi, \mathcal{R}) = \{\varphi, \psi_1, \psi_2\}$.

Given the set of relevant atoms, $At$, the set of possible worlds contains
a world for each set in $2^{At}$, where each set either contains the atom or its
negation. For instance, given $At = \{a, b\}$, the initial model will be $2^{At} =
\{\{a, b\}, \{\neg a, b\}, \{a, \neg b\}, \{\neg a, \neg b\}\}$. Impossible worlds are specified as simple for-
mulas, e.g. $\neg a \wedge b$. A world that entails such an expression is removed from $W$,
which is then set of possible worlds given $F$.

An ordering, $\leq$, is the result of a mapping from a world to a natural number,
the $o$-value, denoted $o : W \rightarrow \mathcal{N}$, such that worlds with higher numbers are
more favored. Worlds can have the same $o$-value if they are equally favored. The
maximum $o$-value of an ordering $\leq$ is denoted $max(\leq)$.

We propose using a *locking* mechanism in which the ordering between two
worlds can be locked, such that if $lock(w_1, w_2)$ then it must always be the
case that $w_1 < w_2$. We can use this to e.g. lock the ordering between worlds
$w_1 = \{\varphi, \psi\}$ and $w_2 = \{\varphi, \neg\psi\}$ if a rule $(\varphi, \psi)$ is applied by creating a lock,
$lock(w_1, w_2)$, such that $w_1$ is always favored over $w_2$. Then if a rule $(\varphi, \neg\psi)$ is
applied, the ordering cannot be changed so that $w_2$ is favored over $w_1$ because
it would result in the previously applied rule no longer being respected (since $\psi$
would not be entailed by the most favored world where $\varphi$ holds).

Rules are applied using the function APPLY : $(\mathcal{R}, \leq) \rightarrow \{\top, \bot\}$ (algorithm
2). Applying a rule $(\varphi, \psi)$ is done by finding all worlds in which both $\varphi$ and $\psi$
holds (the sought worlds) and all worlds in which $\varphi$ and $\neg\psi$ holds (the contradictory worlds). The sought worlds are given an $o$-value of $max(\leq) + 1$ and all
contradictory worlds are locked in relative position to the sought worlds.

A rule $(\varphi, \psi)$ cannot be applied if there is no world $w$ in which $w \models \varphi \wedge \psi$ or for all such worlds a lock, $lock(w', w)$, exists for some $w'$.

**Proposition 2.** *Given an initial ordering $\leq$ and a set of rules $\mathcal{R} = \{r_1, \ldots, r_n\}$ where each $r_i$ is of the form $(\varphi_i, \psi_i)$, the result of successfully applying rules $r_1$ to $r_i$, $0 < i \leq n$ is an ordering which respects rules $\{r_1, \ldots, r_i\}$.*

*Proof.* When $i = 1$ no previous rules have been applied, so we only have to show that the model respects rule $r_1$ after successful application. We have $o(w) = 1$ for all worlds $w$. Applying $r_1$ can only fail if no worlds entail $\varphi_1 \wedge \psi_1$ or all entailing worlds are locked. Since $lock = \emptyset$ initially, only the former can be the case. But then the rule would describe an impossible world and cannot be applied. Otherwise, after applying $r_1$, it is entailed by the model, since for all worlds $w$ where $w \models \varphi_1 \wedge \psi_1$ we have $o(w) = 2$ and the $o$-value of all other worlds is unchanged. Thus the worlds entailing $r_1$ are most preferred so the rule itself is entailed by the model.

When $i > 1$ we assume that all rules up to and including $r_{i-1}$ have been applied successfully. We therefore have

$$M \models (\varphi_1, \psi_1) \wedge \cdots \wedge (\varphi_{i-1}, \psi_{i-1}).$$

Let $l_i = \{(w, w') \mid w \models \varphi_i \wedge \psi_i \text{ and } w' \models \varphi_i \wedge \neg\psi_i\}$ be the set of locks between worlds with contradictory consequents of a rule $(\varphi_i, \psi_i)$. Before applying $r_i$ the set $lock$ contains

$$lock = l_1 \cup \cdots \cup l_{i-1}$$

Rule $r_i$ can then be applied if there is at least one world $w$ in which $w \models r_i$ and where $w$ is not the second entry of a pair in $lock$ (i.e. there is a world entailing $r_i$ which is not locked by another world). If there is no such world then either the rule describes an impossible world and should be rejected, or a previously applied rule contradicts it, which also means it should be rejected. Otherwise the rule will be successfully applied resulting in a model entailing all rules up to and including $r_i$:

$$M \models (\varphi_1, \psi_1) \wedge \cdots \wedge (\varphi_i, \psi_i),$$

and a new $lock$ set: $lock' = lock \cup l_i$. Assuming that the rule is successfully applied we know that for all $w$ in which $w \models r_i$ we have $o(w) = max(\leq) + 1$. Clearly $r_i$ is then entailed by the model. We then have to show that all rules up to $r_i$ are still entailed as well.

Consider rule $r_j$ where $0 < j < i$. Rule $r_j$ was entailed by the model before applying $r_i$. Therefore there are worlds $w_j$ where $w_j \models \varphi_j \wedge \psi_j$ and no lock of it exists, and $w'_j$ where $w'_j \models \varphi_j \wedge \neg\psi_j$, and for all such worlds we have that $o(w_j) > o(w'_j)$ and $(w_j, w'_j) \in lock$. Thus all worlds contradicting $r_j$ are locked relative to those entailing it. If $w'_j \in W_s$ for some $w'_j$ then some of the sought worlds are locked by $r_j$, but since $W_s$ only contains unlocked worlds, this cannot be the case. Therefore no worlds $w'_j$ will be given a higher $o$-value than any $w_j$ world. Furthermore, since $w'_j$ contains all the worlds that could invalidate $r_j$, clearly $r_j$ is still entailed after applying $r_i$.                                                    □

---

**Algorithm 3.** Model generation

  **function** GENERATE$(F, \mathcal{P}, \mathcal{R})$
    $At \leftarrow$ RETRIEVE_ATOMS$(F, \mathcal{R})$
    $W \leftarrow$ INIT$(At, \mathcal{P})$
    $\leq\; \leftarrow o(W)$
    $\mathcal{R}' \leftarrow$ SORT$(\mathcal{R})$
    **for all** $(\varphi, \psi) \in \mathcal{R}'$ **do**
      APPLY$((\varphi, \psi), W, \leq)$
    **return** $\leq$

---

Even though we can successfully apply a set of rules, the function can be further optimized to maximize the number of successful applications of rules. Note that the use of a locking mechanism decreases the number of worlds that can be moved around every time a rule is successfully applied. Therefore, by minimizing the number of worlds being locked in each iteration, we maximize the number of rules that can be applied. The function $s : \mathcal{R} \to \mathcal{N}$ gives each rule a score, where rules with many propositions and operators receive higher scores than rules with few.

$$s((\top, \psi)) = s(\psi) - 1$$
$$s((\varphi, \psi)) = s(\varphi) + s(\psi)$$
$$s(\varphi \wedge \psi) = s(\varphi) + s(\psi) + 1$$
$$s(\varphi \vee \psi) = s(\varphi) + s(\psi) + 1$$
$$s(\neg \varphi) \quad = s(\varphi) + 1$$
$$s(\top) \quad\quad = 0$$
$$s(p) \quad\quad = 1$$

By applying the highest valued rules (the most specialized) first, we ensure that as few worlds as possible are locked. Notice that that rules where the antecedent is $\top$ will be penalized, since they are very general, whereas $\top$ in the consequent is ignored.

The algorithm GENERATE : $(F, \mathcal{P}, \mathcal{R}) \to\; \leq$ then works as follows (algorithm 3). Retrieve relevant atoms and generate an initial model of possible worlds. Sort rules descending according to their $s$-value using SORT$(\mathcal{R})$. Each rule in $\mathcal{R}$ is then applied using APPLY$((\varphi, \psi), \leq)$. Finally, the algorithm returns the ordering $\leq$, which respects all successfully applied rules.

## 4.1  Application of Equally General Rules

The need for constraining the order of rule application touches upon a shortcoming of the model generation; rule application may fail, if previously applied rules have locked the matching worlds. In many cases this is actually a good thing, since it does not make sense to first apply a rule $r_1 = (\varphi, \psi)$ and then later $r_2 = (\varphi, \neg\psi)$. $r_1$ and $r_2$ are clearly contradictory rules, and both should not be applied at once, since we cannot both expect $\psi$ and $\neg\psi$ when $\varphi$ is true. However, if two rules receive the same score they will be applied in a non-deterministic order which could lead to a situation where applying the rules in one order results in one model, and applying in another order results in a different model. It might even be the case that we can apply both rules using one ordering, while another ordering rejects one of the rules.

Consider rules $\mathcal{R} = \{(\top, A), (\top, B)\}$ and possible worlds $W = 2^{\{A,B\}}$. The rules have equal score and they will therefore be applied in a non-deterministic order. If $(\top, A)$ is applied first the ordering will be $AB < A\overline{B} < \{\overline{A}B, \overline{AB}\}$, whereas the ordering will be $AB < \overline{A}B < \{A\overline{B}, \overline{AB}\}$ if $(\top, B)$ is applied first. The rules satisfy the model in both cases; in the most preferred world(s) both $A$ and $B$ hold, but the ordering of less preferred world differs. We argue that even though this is the case, it is clear that as long as the rules have been successfully applied they are satisfied by the model, which means that the model can be used by the agent to reason about its influences by taking its preferences into account. In situations where certain orderings might reject a rule while other orderings would not, it is evident that the latter ordering is favored[4]. If this is the case, the agent might simply monitor the rule application, and if the algorithm rejects a rule given a certain ordering, the agent can attempt to apply the equally general rules in a different order. However, if all orderings result in rejection of one of the rules, this indicates that some of the rules contradict each other, suggesting that not all the rules can be consistently applied to the model.

## 5    Case Study

In this section, we apply the model to a simple scenario. We consider a situation in which agents are normally expected to go to work, but during snowy weather, they are not expected to go to work. The agent Alice prefers that it does not snow, but when it snows, she wants to stay at home. We have the following rules for expectations of the environment and preferences of the agent:

$$\mathcal{R}_{Env} = \{(\top, work), (snow, \neg work)\}$$
$$\mathcal{R}_{Alice} = \{(\top, \neg snow), (snow, \neg work)\}.$$

The environment expectation rules represent the expectations that originate from different sources such as an organization or other agents.

In the following we let $S$ abbreviate *snow* and $W$ *work*. We denote negation using an overline, e.g. $\overline{S}$ when it is not snowing and we write conjunctions by writing literals next to each other, e.g. $SW$ when it is snowing and the agent is working. From the rules above it is clear that $At = \{W, S\}$. The orderings $\leq_P$ and $\leq_N$ are then generated using the algorithms described above. Figure 1 shows how Alice's preference ordering is generated using her rules.

To make the situation more interesting we add the possibility of *being fired* ($F$) and of *leaving early* ($E$):

$$\mathcal{R}_{Alice} = \{(\top, \overline{S}), (S, \overline{W}), (\top, \overline{F}), (W, E)\}.$$

---

[4] After all, the aim is to apply as many of the rules as possible.

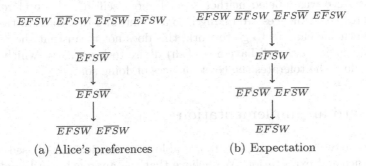

$$(S, \overline{W})$$

$$SW \; \overline{SW} \; SW \; \overline{SW} \qquad \Longrightarrow$$

$$SW \; \overline{SW} \; \overline{SW}$$

$$lock \searrow \downarrow$$

$$SW$$

$$(\top, \overline{S}) \qquad \Longrightarrow$$

$$SW$$

$$lock \uparrow\downarrow \; lock$$

$$\overline{SW}$$

$$lock \uparrow\downarrow$$

$$\overline{SW} \; \overline{SW}$$

**Fig. 1.** Generation of Alice's preferences. Note that some of the locks have been omitted for clarity, e.g. the lock between $\overline{SW}$ and $SW$.

$$\overline{EFSW} \; \overline{EF}SW \; \overline{EFSW} \; E\overline{FSW}$$

$$\downarrow$$

$$\overline{EFS}W$$

$$\downarrow$$

$$E\overline{FS}W$$

$$\downarrow$$

$$\overline{EF}S\overline{W} \; E\overline{F}SW$$

(a) Alice's preferences

$$\overline{EFSW} \; EFSW \; \overline{EF}SW \; E\overline{F}SW$$

$$\downarrow$$

$$E\overline{FS}W$$

$$\downarrow$$

$$\overline{EF}S\overline{W} \; E\overline{FS}W$$

$$\downarrow$$

$$\overline{EFS}W$$

(b) Expectation

**Fig. 2.** The preference and normality orderings generated using the rules and prohibitions specified by the environment and Alice

Thus, she does not want to be fired, and in situations where she chooses to go to work, she prefers to leave early. The rules of the environment are updated to conform to this change; if it snows, one can stay home without being fired but this is not the case when it does not snow.

$$\mathcal{R}_{Env} = \{(\top, W), (S, \overline{FW}), (\overline{SW}, F), (\top, \overline{E}), (W, \overline{F})\}.$$

Furthermore, agents are not expected to leave early and will normally not be fired if they work.

Certain worlds are not possible given the new rules; an agent will not be working if it is fired, and if it is not working, it will not leave early. This is represented by the set of prohibitions: $\mathcal{P} = \{FW, E\overline{W}\}$. Thus, the set of possible worlds $W$ is reduced to those worlds where none of the prohibitions above are entailed. The preference and normality orderings resulting from these rules are shown in figure 2(a) and 2(b).

Alice is now able to decide between her influences using the generated model. Say Alice has a desire to stay at home, but an obligation toward her employer to go to work, i.e. the set of influences is $F = \{W, \overline{W}\}$. We then consider two cases: one where it snows and one where it does not.

a) We have that $B = \{S\}$ so all worlds in which it does not snow are ignored. This leaves us with four possible worlds, where Alice's most preferred world is $\overline{EF}S\overline{W}$, thus $Pref = \{\overline{W}\}$. The expected consequence of both going to work and not going to work is not to be fired, which means that each is equally tolerable, thus $Tol = \{W, \overline{W}\}$. The decision is then the intersection: $Dec = \{\overline{W}\}$.

b) We have that $B = \{\overline{S}\}$, giving four possible worlds. In this case Alice's most preferred worlds are $\overline{EFSW}$ and $\overline{EFSW}$, thus $Pref = \{W, \overline{W}\}$. From the expectations we see that $EC(W) = \overline{EFS}$ and $EC(\overline{W}) = \overline{EFS}$. Since not being fired is more tolerable than being fired, $Tol = \{W\}$, and the decision is then $Dec = \{W\}$.

Note that Alice was labeled neither "social" nor "selfish". Her preference and the expected consequences are taking into account, and this leads to the results above. When she chooses to go to work, this does not mean that she is strictly social. She might very well have a (selfish) desire to leave early, which she can choose to do if she tolerates the consequences of doing so.

# 6    Toward an Implementation

The case study showed that agents are able to make decisions based on rules of preference and expectation. We believe that the approach can be integrated in existing agent systems to let agents make decisions based on their own preferences and the external expectations. We are currently investigating how the procedure can be integrated into the GOAL agent programming language [9]. While this is work in progress, we briefly discuss the work that has been done and some of the implications such integration has.

In GOAL, the choice of committing to different goals and performing actions is relatively simple; a program consists of a list of rules that are either evaluated in linear or random order. This means that either the preference ordering is specified a priori, or it is not specified at all. We believe that by integrating the agents' rules of preference and the expectations into the GOAL system, the agents will be able to make decisions based on preferences in different situations thus providing a different kind of processing order of GOAL rules. This requires that the system is able to understand a specification of preferences and expectations.

We have taken the first steps toward an implementation by implementing a prototype of the system in Prolog[5]. The reason for choosing Prolog is that (1) it makes the implementation of the QDT models quite simple and (2) it allows us to integrate the system directly into the GOAL agent's knowledge base. The set of rules is specified as a list of pairs, `[(Phi,Psi),...]`; prohibitions as simple formulas; and a lock as a pair of lists, such that `(L1,L2)` represents that for all worlds $w_1$ in `L1` and $w_2$ in `L2` is it the case that $w_1 < w_2$.

The basic operators $(\wedge, \neg, \square)$ are implemented straightforwardly; $\wedge$ and $\neg$ are evaluated in the current world and $\square$ in all more preferred (or expected) worlds.

---

[5] The Prolog code that follows has been slightly simplified to be more easily comprehended.

Each abbreviation is then defined, e.g. the conditional preference operator is defined as follows:

```
eval(I(ψ | φ), Ws, W, TV) :-
    eval(⊟_P¬φ ∨ ⧄_P(φ ∧ □_P(φ → ψ))), Ws, W, TV).
```

where Ws is the set of all worlds and W is the current world. eval succeeds if TV can be unified with the truth-value of the formula.

The application of a rule is done using two findall-queries: one to build the set $W_c$ and one for $W_s$.

```
apply_rule(Ws, Ord, (φ,ψ), Lock, W_c, W_s) :-
    findall(W, (member(W,Ws), eval(φ ∧ ¬ψ, Ws, W, t)), W_c),
    findall(W, (member(W,Ws), \+ (member((_,Locked), Lock),
    member(W, Locked)), eval(φ ∧ ψ, Ws, W, t)), W_s).
```

where Ws is the set of all worlds, Ord is the current ordering, $(\varphi, \psi)$ is the rule being applied, Lock is the set of locks, and W_c and W_s are $W_c$ and $W_s$, respectively. The first query succeeds if W_c can be unified with all worlds $w$ in which $w \models \varphi \land \neg\psi$. The second query succeeds if W_s can be unified with all worlds $w$ where $w \models \varphi \land \psi$ *and* $w$ is not locked. A rule is successfully applied when W_s \= [], i.e. $W_s \neq \emptyset$. The ordering can be changed by incrementing the $o$-value for each $w \in W_s$, and the lock is updated to include the pair of lists (W_s, W_c).

Agents make a decision using the sets *Pref* and *Tol*, which are built by following their definitions closely. For example, the set *Pref* is built as follows:

```
pref([],_,_,[]).
pref([φ|FTail], F, Ws, Pref) :-
    checkpref(φ, F, Ws), !, Pref=[φ|Tail],
    pref(FTail, F, Ws, Tail).
pref([_|FTail], F, Ws, Pref) :- pref(FTail, F, Ws, Pref).
```

where F is the set of all influences, Ws is the set of all worlds, and checkpref(Phi, F, Ws) succeeds if $\varphi \leq_P \psi$ for all $\psi \in F$. Pref is then unified with all $\varphi \in F$ that are most preferred. A similar predicate is defined for *Tol*. The final set, *Dec*, is the intersection of *Pref* and *Tol*, or just *Tol* if the intersection is empty, and a decision can then be made using the following Prolog query (here making a decision based on the case study above):

```
?- decision([¬s], P, N, Dec).
Dec = [w].
```

where P and N are the generated preference and normality orderings, and Dec corresponds to *Dec*.

The decision procedure can be used as-is within GOAL, meaning that GOAL agents are able use the decision procedure. However, this also means that the decision of which influence to commit to needs to be implemented directly in the agent's program, which suggests that the programmer will have to understand the mechanisms of the procedure. A more ideal solution would be to integrate the procedure within GOAL, e.g. allowing for another GOAL rule evaluation order (which would then choose a rule matching an influence in *Dec*), requiring only that the programmer to specifies each agent's preferences and the expectations from the environment. This is however out of scope for this paper and is left for future research.

# 7   Conclusion

We have argued that conflicts are prone to arise when agents interact in open societies and enact roles in an organization, since their own desires may be in conflict with obligations toward other agents or the obligations of the role(s) they are enacting. We have discussed why obligations along with desires should be considered influences on the agent's behavior rather than being seen as desires being imposed onto the agent by other entities. Since influences do not necessarily represent states the agent wants to achieve, they should only be pursued if the agent can tolerate their consequences.

Our approach to decide which influences to commit to, which is based on qualitative decision theory, is an attempt to let the agent reason about the influences without taking into account that one influence is a desire, and another is an obligation, since such bias can result in labeling the agent "selfish" or "social" in advance. The approach works by including the consequence of bringing about a state in the reasoning, thus letting the agent consider its preferences, without choosing something that results in an intolerable state. We have argued that this indeed lets the agents reach a decision without strictly preferring certain types of influences to others.

To make the procedure readily available we furthermore have developed a simple method that can generate models to be used in the reasoning process by the use of expressions describing the agent's preferences. By use of a simple locking mechanism, the method generates models, which respect non-contradictory rules specified by the agent such that it is possible to make a decision among a set of influences. The simple nature of the method also allows us to generate the models on the fly, so that if the agent's preferences change during execution a new model can be generated. Since the method works by generating all possible states of relevant sub-models, it may prove to be inefficient in cases that are more complex. Even though we only consider sub-models, it would be natural to investigate how to optimize this. Furthermore, since rules of equal generality are applied non-deterministically, different models may emerge, though they satisfy the same sets of rules; although our goal was to create models satisfying rules, we believe a deterministic procedure is desirable and it could be an interesting direction for future work.

Another direction for further research would be to investigate how to integrate the prototype into the GOAL agent programming language. While we have already built a working prototype of the system in Prolog, much more work needs to be done to successfully integrate it into a full-fledged programming language such as GOAL.

Finally, the non-propositional case should be investigated such that reasoning about the agent's preferences can be done in cases that are more complex. For instance, it should be possible for the agent to prefer being at home, *at(home)*, compared to other places such as work, while still being able to express that being at a café is more preferred than being at home.

**Acknowledgement.** The author would like to thank the reviewers for their useful comments and the attendants at the EMAS workshop for the interesting discussion.

# References

1. Alchourrón, C.E., Gärdenfors, P., Makinson, D.: On the logic of theory change: Partial meet contraction and revision functions. The Journal of Symbolic Logic 50(2), 510–530 (1985)
2. Alechina, N., Dastani, M., Logan, B.: Programming Norm-Aware Agents. In: Proceedings of the 11th International Conference on Autonomous Agents and Multi-agent Systems, AAMAS 2012, vol. 2, pp. 1057–1064. International Foundation for Autonomous Agents and Multiagent Systems, Richland (2012)
3. Alechina, N., Jago, M., Logan, B.: Resource-bounded belief revision and contraction. In: Baldoni, M., Endriss, U., Omicini, A., Torroni, P. (eds.) DALT 2005. LNCS (LNAI), vol. 3904, pp. 141–154. Springer, Heidelberg (2006)
4. Boutilier, C.: Toward a Logic for Qualitative Decision Theory. In: Proceedings of the KR 1994, pp. 75–86. Morgan Kaufmann (1994)
5. Broersen, J., Dastani, M., Hulstijn, J., Huang, Z., Torre, L.v.d.: The BOID Architecture – Conflicts Between Beliefs, Obligations, Intentions and Desires. In: Proceedings of the Fifth International Conference on Autonomous Agents, pp. 9–16. ACM Press (2001)
6. Dastani, M., Dignum, V., Dignum, F.: Role-assignment in open agent societies. In: Proceedings of the Second International Joint Conference on Autonomous Agents and Multiagent Systems, AAMAS 2003, pp. 489–496. ACM, New York (2003)
7. Dignum, F., Morley, D., Sonenberg, E.A., Cavedon, L.: Towards Socially Sophisticated BDI Agents. In: Proceedings of the Fourth International Conference on MultiAgent Systems (ICMAS 2000), pp. 111–118. IEEE Computer Society, Washington, DC (2000)
8. Dignum, F., Kinny, D., Sonenberg, L.: From Desires, Obligations and Norms to Goals. Cognitive Science Quarterly 2 (2002)
9. Hindriks, K.V.: Programming Rational Agents in GOAL. Multi-Agent Programming: Languages, Tools and Applications 2, 119–157 (2009)
10. van der Torre, L., Tan, Y.H.: Contrary-to-duty reasoning with preference-based dyadic obligations. Annals of Mathematics and Artificial Intelligence 27(1-4), 49–78 (1999)

# A Multi-agent Approach to Professional Software Engineering

Marco Lützenberger, Tobias Küster, Thomas Konnerth, Alexander Thiele,
Nils Masuch, Axel Heßler, Jan Keiser, Michael Burkhardt, Silvan Kaiser,
Jakob Tonn, Michael Kaisers, and Sahin Albayrak

Technische Universität Berlin, DAI-Labor
firstname.lastname@dai-labor.de

**Abstract.** The community of agent researchers and engineers has produced a number of interesting and mature results. However, agent technology is still not widely adopted by industrial software developers or
software companies—possibly because existing frameworks are infused
with academic premises that rarely apply to industrial settings. In this
paper, we analyse the requirements of current industry-driven software
projects and show how we are able to cope with these requirements in
the Java Intelligent Agent Componentware agent framework, JIAC V.
We argue that the lack of industry-grade requirements and features in
other agent frameworks is one of the reasons for the slow acceptance
of agent technology in the software industry. The JIAC V framework
tries to bridge that gap—not as a final solution, but as a stepping stone
towards industrial acceptance.

**Keywords:** Agent Framework, MAS Development, Industrial Adoption.

## 1 Introduction

The concept of Agent Oriented Software Engineering, or AOSE, dates back as
far as 1997, when Michael Wooldridge published his seminal article [40] and
established an entirely new branch of research. Fifteen years later, we face nu-
merous theories, methodologies, tools and frameworks, each supporting the development of agent-based software applications in the one or the other aspect.
Yet, despite intensifying research on AOSE, it is far from being audacious to say
that the agent community has as yet failed to convince the industry to adopt
their ideas [1]. The problem of agent-technology to gain foothold in industrial
processes has been discussed vigorously [29,33,38,39] and some reasons for this
problem were already identified. These reasons include poor awareness of industrial needs, disconnection from conventional software engineering, immature
technology, and a focus on research issues that are not necessarily required by
industry [39].

The Java Intelligent Agent Componentware (JIAC) was developed under the
premise to narrow the discrepancy between research and industry. In this paper,
we present the fifth incarnation of our agent framework, namely JIAC V [17].

M. Cossentino et al. (Eds.): EMAS 2013, LNAI 8245, pp. 156–175, 2013.

We are well aware that, after fifteen years of research, the enthusiasm for 'yet another agent framework' can only be moderate. Yet, JIAC does not fall into this category. We argue that—as opposed to well known and established agent frameworks—JIAC was neither explicitly developed as a research framework (cf. Jason [5]), nor streamlined towards the requirements of individual industrial stakeholders (cf. JADE [3]). JIAC was developed under the premise to cover a wide spectrum of requirements and to further the industrial adoption process. The development was focused on the objective to provide a robust communication infrastructure, even beyond the borders of homogeneous computer networks. The modular assembly of JIAC agents allows for multi-agent system (MAS) solutions that are tailored to the application context. JIAC currently offers modules for migration, rule interpretation, persistence, scripting languages, load measurement, OSGi-integration and human-agent communication, to name but a few.

We do not consider JIAC to be an ultimate solution, but rather a step towards industrial acceptance. We argue that, so far, state-of-the-art frameworks were not able to convince the industry of the elegance of the agent paradigm and alternative approaches are strongly required should AOSE ever gain foothold in industrial processes.

We begin this paper with a brief description of different projects in which JIAC was used and respectively mention features that were required for a successful appliance (Section 2). Based on this analysis, we examine the capabilities of well established agent frameworks to deal with the previously collected requirements (Section 3). We use this analysis to substantiate our thesis, that certain features are not sufficiently covered in state-of-the-art approaches. We proceed by presenting the JIAC framework in more detail (Section 4), including a description of standard features, the most relevant extension as well as development tools. Subsequently, we describe selected appliances of JIAC in more detail and respectively underline the technical integration of required framework features (Section 5). Finally, we discuss the role of JIAC within the pool of well established agent frameworks and the agent community and wrap up with a conclusion (Section 6).

## 2    The Case of the JIAC V Framework

In this section we compile a list of requirements that were derived from application projects which we concluded over the last couple of years. Following Weyns at al. [39], there are many reasons that hamper industrial adoption of multi-agent technology. These reasons include poor awareness of industrial needs, disconnection from conventional software engineering, immature technology and a focus on research issues that are not necessarily required by industry [39].

To avoid these pitfalls we used industry-funded projects to develop and extend JIAC and discussed our intentions with our industry partners. In the following we give a short description of the projects in which JIAC V was used and extended towards the requirements of the project and the project partners.

We also emphasise the different domains in which the framework was used and conclude this section by explaining the requirements that arose from these very applications and guided the development of JIAC V.

## 2.1 Project Summaries

The goal of the *Service Centric Home* (**SerCHo**) project was the development of an open service platform that increases life quality at home. The platform was intended to support the quick and easy delivery of new context sensitive services into the home environment and the provisioning of a consistent user interface for these services. In this project we extended JIAC's capabilities to deal with the service metaphor. As such, we have focused on developing a service engineering methodology and tool suite as well as a service delivery platform to simplify service development, deployment and maintenance [15].

The focus of the *Multi Access – Modular Services*, or **MAMS+** project was to allow non-technical persons to fast and easily create, deploy and manage services, according to the users' needs. We have developed a service delivery platform based on our multi-agent framework [35]. The platform integrates modern technologies like IMS/SIP, allows for service composition and features service matching, load-balancing and self-healing mechanisms, to name but a few.

Within the project *Gesteuertes Laden V2.0* (**GL V2.0**, Managed Charging V2.0) [37] the goal was to develop a decentralised intelligent energy management system that uses electric vehicle's batteries as mobile energy storages. The purpose of the developed planning algorithms was to stabilise the energy grid and to maximise the amount of renewable energy within the electric vehicles (EVs) in dependence to forecasts of available wind energy.

To maintain a good standard of living for senior citizens, new technologies have been developed within the **SmartSenior** project. Our work included sensor-based situation -detection, -reaction, -notification and remote management [34]. During a field study the solutions have been successfully installed and tested in the home environments of more than thirty elderly participants.

The project *Energy Efficiency Controlling in the Automotive Industry*, or **EnEffCo**, aims at the implementation of a modular software system [22] to simulate operational modes of plant sections with relevant energy consumption. The software serves as a tool for decision makers in manufacturing, to whom it offers the identification and evaluation of strategies and tactics for establishing cost- and energy-efficient production schedules.

*Intelligent Solutions for Protecting Interdependent Critical Infrastructures* (**ILIas**) is a project aimed towards developing intelligent solutions for protecting critical infrastructures that provide electricity and telecommunication services to the general public [21]. These solutions need to be scalable and reconcile the need for fast automated reaction with manual supervision for highly critical decisions. Software solutions and protection mechanism efficiencies in large-scale networks are evaluated using simulated disaster scenarios. The simulation models are supplemented by a hardware test laboratory where exemplary interdependent energy and telecommunication infrastructures are set up.

The on-going project **BeMobility 2.0** investigates the integration of electric vehicles (EVs) into urban transport and energy networks. In addition to the development of concepts that will combine different mobility services (e.g., vehicles, public transportation, etc.), an energy management system [11] for a Micro Smart Grid is being developed, in which a variety of system components, such as EVs, charging infrastructure, and energy sources, are taken into account.

The aim of the *Connected Living* project is to provide a system for integrating and managing 'smart devices' in future home environments: **CL-OS**. Besides providing a layer of abstraction for controlling devices by diverse vendors, another goal is to supply an infrastructure for developing, publishing and deploying agents or coalition of agents to the users' home environments to help future home user to achieve its goals.

The objective of the project *Extensible Architecture and Service Infrastructure for Cloud-aware Software*, or **EASI Clouds**, is to provide a comprehensive and easy-to-use cloud computing infrastructure with support for cloud interoperability and federation. The infrastructure includes advanced SLA (Service Level Agreement) management for all service layers, facilities for capacity planning, heterogeneous provisioning as well as accounting and billing.

The Multi-Agent Programming Contest is an annual competition that started in 2005 [2]. The contest is an attempt to stimulate research in the field of programming multi-agent system. Our team has been participating since 2007. We use it as a platform to teach students in the field of agent based design and implementation using the JIAC V agent framework.

## 2.2   Requirements Derived from the Projects

During the process of domain analysis and system design of those projects, several requirements have been identified and hence fulfilled in JIAC V. While many of them are typical for industrial or business software frameworks, it is our believe that a multi-agent framework does not have to stand behind.

In many projects the results had to be tested during field trials or user rollouts. Applications had to be running for months without problems. Therefore, *stability and robustness* are key issues for a good user experience. A certain level of robustness was important, especially in dynamic environments, e.g., *deploying and undeploying* new services or agents should not affect other parts of the application. The same holds true in a distributed context, e.g., when new nodes join or leave a system or agents *migrate* between them. The framework has to be able to handle a potentially *large number of agents and agent nodes* without a decrease in performance, a requirement especially affecting communication infrastructure and the distributed service directory. Several projects dealt with service delivery and management of services, resulting in various requirements like *support for service life-cycle, management interfaces, runtime deployment* and *third-party service integration*. Additional requirements related to management and adaptive behaviour are *monitoring and introspection*. It has to be possible to retrieve status information from all framework components in a standardised way. Certain functionalities were required in multiple projects so that *component reuse* became necessary. Additionally, the framework needed to *be extensible* in order to be able to integrate future requirements.

Industrial adoption of agent technology was already discussed in a couple of surveys. These surveys conclude that technical maturity and coherence [39], connections to regular software engineering techniques [38], a comprehensive tool support [33] as well as robustness, feasibility and flexibility [29] are indispensably required for industrial adoption of multi-agent technology. We identified similar requirements and developed JIAC to counter well known problems of industrial adoption and to demonstrate that an agent framework is able to meet industrial requirements.

We proceed this work by emphasising conflicts between the capabilities of other agent frameworks and the above-mentioned requirements for industrial acceptance.

## 3   State of the Art

When we compare the requirements of our projects and those for a successful adoption of agent technology to existing agent frameworks, the results are twofold. On the one hand, platforms like Jason [4] or 3APL [14] have been created on a very strong theoretical background. They feature elaborate implementations of cognitive concepts that are important for the agent research agenda as a whole. On the other hand, even though there have been approaches to extend these frameworks—e.g., JASDL [20] for Jason—they were never intended to be used in an industrial context but geared towards research.

It is difficult to use these frameworks when implementing real world applications that are supposed to run for days, or even weeks. Consider the Gesteuertes Laden V2.0 project as an example for such application (see Section 2 for a summary and also Section 5.1 for more details). In this project, we were supposed to deploy autonomous decision-making software on the hardware of an electric vehicle. At worse, a system crash may have disabled the charging functionality of the vehicle—a non-tolerable situation, especially for the driver. Once a driver has picked a vehicle, it is difficult to access its software and to reboot or update malfunctioning agents. As such, we had to ensure a reliable operation. Academic agent frameworks, however, were not developed under the objective to ensure a reliable operation throughout days or weeks. To be clear about this, it is not our intention to overly criticise the above mentioned frameworks but to emphasise that those frameworks can not be used for the implementation of applications where system crashes cause non-tolerable situations for (test-)users.

More pragmatic approaches such as JADE [3] or the JACK [8] framework are more focused on the engineering and development aspects of applications. The JADE framework in particular has a long list of extensions and additions, such as the Web Service Integration Gateway [12], AgentOWL [24], WADE [9] or the MASE framework [31]. On a point by point basis these extensions seem to fulfil many of our requirements. Nevertheless, we still think it is difficult to use these frameworks for our purpose as most extensions have been developed independently from each other. Using them within the same software project will be tedious if not impossible. In order to convince software developers of the agent paradigm a comprehensive programming framework is required. One can not expect them to collect required extensions before any implementation can be done. Especially the JADE framework with all of its extensions lacks the coherence and unity that we would expect from a modern software framework.

A current agent architecture that tries to bridge the gap between agent technology and the software industry is the Jadex framework [32]. The developers of Jadex have taken a number of approaches to improve Jadex in ways that make it more compatible with industry standards [6]. For instance, cloud concepts were integrated [7], an active component architecture was realised [6] and it is possible to define workflows by means of BPMN (business process modeling notation) [6].

However, while we appreciate the approach to adapt the framework to industry needs, we find that a number of design decisions do not comply with the requirements for our projects. The decision to base the framework on the active component model—with agents as the internal architecture of the components—reverses the control architecture from our point of view. We regard agents as the surrounding structure and expect them to have capabilities that enable communication and interaction. Furthermore, the integration of ontologies and workflows into Jadex is insufficient for us. In Jadex, ontologies are transformed into ADF belief JavaBeans. This procedure decouples them from the actual ontologies on the web—as envisioned by OWL—and thus we consider it a proprietary approach. Workflows on the other hand should be one way to describe capabilities of an agent, not an agent type of their own. As a result, we found the Jadex model to be too different from our vision of software agents, and thus could not model our systems in the way we envision modern agent oriented technologies.

For the above reasons, existing agent frameworks either do not fulfil our requirements for practical applications, or their models are too different from our modelling approach for agent oriented applications. In the following we describe the JIAC framework, which represents our approach to an agent architecture that fulfils our needs.

## 4   The JIAC V Framework

JIAC V is a Java-based multi-agent development framework and runtime environment [27] that has been both developed and deployed in a number of application projects. Based on the requirements of those projects (see Section 2) particular emphasis has been placed on the following aspects:

- robustness, scalability, modularity and extensibility
- adoption of a service-oriented view and integration of third-party services, e.g., provided as web services and/or OSGi bundles
- dynamically adding and removing services, agents, and nodes at runtime
- extensive tool support, both at design time (modelling and development) and at runtime (management and monitoring)

In the following, we describe how these requirements were satisfied in JIAC.

### 4.1   Core Mechanisms of JIAC Agents

One of the core aspects of JIAC is the integration of agents with the Service Oriented Architecture paradigm (SOA) [16]. Using a powerful discovery and messaging infrastructure, JIAC agents can be distributed transparently, even beyond network boundaries. An agent-platform comprises one or more 'agent nodes' which are physically distributed and provide the runtime environment for JIAC agents (see Figure 1). New agents, services, as well as further agent nodes can be deployed at runtime. Agents can interact with each other by means of service invocation, by sending messages to individual agents or multicast-channels, and by complex interaction protocols. Each individual agent's knowledge is stored in a tuple-space based memory. Finally, JIAC agents can be remotely monitored and controlled at runtime via the Java Management Extension Standard (JMX).

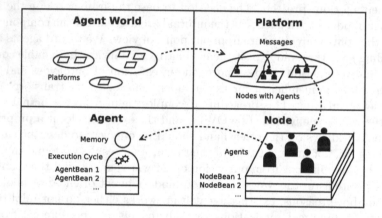

**Fig. 1.** Structural elements of a JIAC V multi-agent system

Each agent contains a number of default components, such as an execution-cycle, a local memory and the communication adaptors. The agents' behaviours and capabilities are implemented in a number of so-called *AgentBeans*, which are controlled by the agent's life cycle. Each AgentBean may:

- implement a number of *life-cycle* methods, which are executed when the agent changes its life-cycle state, such as *initialized*, or *started*,
- implement an *execute*-method, which is called automatically at regular intervals once the agent is running (i.e., cyclic behaviour),
- attach *observers* to the agent's memory, being called for instance each time the agent receives a message or its world model is updated, and
- provide *action* methods, or services, which are exposed to the directory and can be invoked either from within the agent or by other agents.

Using these four mechanisms, it is possible to define all of the agents' capabilities and behaviours [18]. Furthermore, the structure of each agent contains a number of standard components, such as an execution-cycle, a local memory and the communication adaptors. The entire multi-agent system, i.e., which agent has which agent beans and how those agents are distributed to agent nodes, is then set up using one or more Spring[1] configuration files.

## 4.2  Default and Extension Components

JIAC agents contain a number of individual AgentBeans that are implemented as described above as well as a set of standard AgentBeans that constitute the basic capabilities of an agent. One such AgentBean each JIAC agent is equipped with by default is the *Communication Bean*. First, this component manages the inter-agent service communication; second, it allows the agents to exchange messages with other agents or groups of agents on the network, addressing individual agents or multi-casting to message channels. The messages are not restricted to FIPA messages but can have any data as payload.

Complementary to the AgentBeans, there are *NodeBeans*, adding functionality to the node as a whole. Each agent node is equipped with a *Directory Node-Bean*, listing the actions of the different agents, and a *Message Broker NodeBean*, being the counterpart to the agent's communication bean and allowing them to transparently send messages from node to node using ActiveMQ.[2]

Other commonly used AgentBeans and NodeBeans can be added to a multiagent system by appending the respective bean to the agent's configuration. For the composition of services, JIAC includes an *Interpreter* AgentBean for the execution of the high-level service-oriented scripting language *JADL++* [17]. Reactive behaviour of agents can be enabled with a *Drools*[3] rule engine that can be synchronised with the agents' memory.

Extensions to the capabilities of nodes and agents include a *Migration* Node-Bean, that enables strong agent migration between agent nodes, a *Persistence* NodeBean that saves the node configuration and allows for restarting the node later on, and NodeBeans for *Load Measurement* and *Load Balancing* that provide cross-node load information and distribute agents over nodes at start- and runtime. In order to support application development, JIAC also provides generic functionalities such as AgentBeans for *User Management, Human Agent Interfaces*, a *Webserver* NodeBean running an embedded Jetty-server, and a *Web Service Gateway* AgentBean that exposes JIAC actions as web services and vice versa. Last but not least, the *OSGi Gateway* allows JIAC nodes to be executed within an OSGi framework and to access other OSGi services.

## 4.3  Development Methods and Tools

Since JIAC is a Java-based agent framework, the bulk of the development work can be done using conventional Java development tools, such as Eclipse and

---

[1] Spring: http://www.springsource.org/

[2] ActiveMQ: http://activemq.apache.org/

[3] JBoss Drools: http://www.jboss.org/drools/

Maven, as well as supportive tools like XML editors. Still, to improve the efficiency in application development, some additional tools are provided, all of which can be integrated directly into the Eclipse IDE.

A *JIAC Project Wizard* helps with creating new JIAC projects by generating a uniform project structure, including a configured Maven pom.xml file, listing the required dependencies, and a starter class for running the new JIAC application. Further, several Eclipse views provide information about nodes currently running on the network and the agents and services they contain, as well as the possibility to start and to interact with newly created agents and services.

JIAC agents can also be modelled using two high-level graphical editors: The *Visual Service Design Tool (VSDT)* and the *Agent World Editor (AWE)*. Using the VSDT, both the workflows of individual agents as well as their interactions can be modelled as a series of BPMN diagrams [30]. Based on those diagrams, executable JIAC AgentBeans or JADL++ services can be generated [23]. The AWE can be used to create visual representations of an entire multi-agent-system and its components, showing the different agents and agent nodes in a distributed system and the individual services and AgentBeans they provide. From these visual models, the tool can generate the corresponding Spring configuration files as well as JIAC AgentBean stubs [26].

Finally, the running multi-agent system can be monitored and manipulated using the *ASGARD* agent runtime monitor [36], providing a three-dimensional view of all agents running in the local network.

An overview of JIAC's core features and extensions, how they map to the requirements derived from the projects, and how they are used within those projects can be seen in Table 1.

# 5   Applications and Lessons Learned

Many features and components shown in the last section were developed as a consequence of project requirement analyses. The resulting modular structure of the JIAC system enables developers to tailor selected functionalities. In the following, we present industry projects from different domains—namely energy, electric mobility and health—and put emphasis on system engineering aspects.

## 5.1   Planning Electric Vehicle Charging Intervals

*Description:* The goal of Gesteuertes Laden V2.0 [37] was to use electric vehicles as mobile and distributed energy storages in order to utilise wind energy and to stabilise energy grids. As the driver's inherent needs for mobility are always the main objective to fulfil, a mechanism was needed that supports the users in planning charging- and feeding intervals without limiting their flexibility. Our solution was implemented as a live system including real EVs (three Mini-E vehicles provided by the project partner BMW) and charging stations.

**Table 1.** Project Requirements and use of JIAC V features in projects (bold: featured project, see Section 5). The letters next to the features indicate the several requirements the feature contributes to.

| | | SerCHo | MAMS+ | GL 2.0 | Smart Senior | EnEffCo | ILIas | BeMobility 2.0 | CL-OS | EASI Clouds |
|---|---|---|---|---|---|---|---|---|---|---|
| **Requirements** | Robustness, Stability · R | X | X | X | X | X | X | X | X | X |
| | Hot Deployment · D | X | X | - | X | X | X | - | X | X |
| | Agent Migration · A | - | - | - | - | - | X | - | - | X |
| | Scalability · S | X | - | X | - | X | X | - | - | X |
| | Service Life Cycle Mngmt. · L | X | X | - | X | - | - | - | X | - |
| | Third-party API integration · T | X | X | X | X | - | - | - | - | - |
| | Introspection, Monitoring · I | - | - | X | X | X | X | - | - | X |
| | Modularity, Reusability · M | X | X | X | X | X | X | X | X | X |
| **JIAC Core** | Distribution · R AS M | X | X | X | X | X | X | X | - | X |
| | Node Deployment · D S | - | X | X | - | X | - | - | - | X |
| | Services, SOA · LT M | X | X | X | X | - | X | X | X | X |
| | Message-based Comm. · R S | X | - | - | X | X | X | X | - | X |
| | Service Deployment · D L | - | X | - | X | - | X | - | X | - |
| | Agent Deployment · DAS | - | X | - | - | - | - | - | X | X |
| | Management & Monitoring · R I | - | X | X | X | X | X | X | X | X |
| **JIAC Plugins** | Webserver · T M | - | X | - | X | - | - | - | X | - |
| | Interpreter · D L M | - | X | - | X | - | X | - | - | - |
| | Rule Engine · D T M | X | - | - | X | - | X | - | X | - |
| | Migration · DAS | - | X | - | - | - | - | - | - | - |
| | Persistence · R L | - | X | - | X | - | - | - | X | X |
| | Load Balancing · RDASL | - | X | - | - | - | - | - | - | X |
| | Webservice Gateway · T | X | X | X | - | - | - | X | - | - |
| | OSGi Gateway · T M | X | - | - | X | - | - | - | - | X |
| | Human Agent Interface · I | - | X | X | - | X | - | X | - | - |
| | User Management · S | - | X | - | - | - | - | - | X | X |

*Implementation:* In the project, a distributed mobility and energy management system was designed in which each of the involved actors—such as driver, vehicle manufacturer, energy provider, charging station, and grid operator—is represented by a software agent [19]. The system is able to create user-centric day schedules containing journeys, charging and discharging events [28] and takes into account actor-dependent preferences and constraints, such as the driver's appointments, wind forecasts, the EV, available charging stations, and energy grid constraints.

The developed system contains eight software agents in the back-end and three agents within each of the EVs (see Figure 2). More than 100 services are

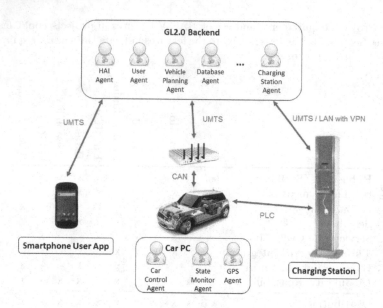

**Fig. 2.** GL V2.0 System Architecture

running simultaneously, offering different tasks, ranging from simple information services to complex planning algorithms. For each user and each electric vehicle an additional agent representation is running in the back-end, taking the main responsibility for developing user and vehicle schedules.

The data exchange between EV and back-end agents is based on unreliable telecommunication networks (e.g., UMTS), therefore failover mechanisms ensure a reconnection after network stabilisation. The coordination of charging and feeding events is processed by the EV agents interacting with the charging stations via power line communication. Third party services such as wind forecasts and charging station status information were embedded into JIAC via the Web Service Gateway. Furthermore, a generic MySQL database agent has been developed. As the user interaction plays an important role, a smartphone application has been developed. The integration into JIAC was done with the Human Agent Interface.

*Lessons Learned:* The system was evaluated within a three-week field test [25]. During this time, the need for a maintainability component, which notifies the developers about the services' availability, became apparent and was subsequently developed and installed. Furthermore, the field test revealed, that the service advertisement messages that propose or refresh the existence of services in each of the local service directories aggregated to a significant amount of traffic. The communication exceeded the bandwidth of the UMTS connection that was used between the CarPC Nodes and Backend Nodes, thus, we decided to increase the service advertisement interval. Given that we already encountered performance issues when dealing with three electric vehicles, we also tried to assess the performance of large-scale distributed systems comprising thousands of electric vehicles. In this case the adaption of the advertisement message rate might not be sufficient, since an extremely high interval would be necessary which in turn would have the drawback that the disappearance of a service would be recognised rather late. Two other possibilities were therefore discussed. On the one hand the concept of the service advertisement messages could be changed. In this case messages are only sent once a new node appears or disappears. However, this approach bears risks in unreliable communication infrastructures, thus we selected the second option, namely a more sophisticated group communication concept. Instead of using one group per node we relaxed this strict assumption and allow nodes to join multiple groups, but not to forward advertisement messages between those. According to our project scenario, the CarPC Nodes now only share a group with those nodes they are really interacting with. The advertisement messages of all other nodes are not being sent via the UMTS connection, which results in a considerably more effective communication.

## 5.2   Multi-agent Systems for an Ageing Society

*Description:* An ageing society causes high costs for health care and services that can be addressed by modern IT. Also, elderly people can regain a higher level of quality of life when using such IT, since dedicated health care will only be required on few occasions. Such a system has been developed in the SmartSenior project, where the focus was set to covering most aspects of daily needs while keeping the system usable. It uses sensors, processors and effectors in order to detect situations at home for performing appropriate (re-)actions [34]. The system has been installed and tested during a field study in 32 apartments.

*Implementation:* In each apartment, two JIAC nodes containing several agents were running. Both nodes have been wrapped as OSGi-Bundles and installed in an OSGi-execution environment (Knopflerfish 3.1). Each agent was designed to perform a specific task, and the interaction among these agents resolved into a global system behaviour. Besides JIAC's communication and service invocation infrastructure, the system also makes use of the rule engine abstraction and service interpreter agents. While it is beyond the scope of this work to explain each agent in detail, an example will demonstrate the interaction and the features of the JIAC framework that have been used.

The main task of the system is to detect and react to specific situations, i.e., sets of specific sensor values in a certain time frame. The sensor values are aggregated and enriched with additional semantic data by a Sensor Agent. This information is then sent to both, a Database Agent, storing the values in a local MySQL database, and the Detection Agent, using the Drools rule engine to detect different situations in the sensor data. Those specific situations are then sent to the Reaction Agent, triggering the appropriate reaction in the form of a service, using the JADL++ interpreter. Finally, a number of different agents provide means for, e.g., displaying a histogram of sensor values to the user, sending out notifications, or integrating with other OSGi services.

The mapping between situations and reactions is modelled in BPMN [30] using the Visual Service Design Tool (see Section 4.3). The processes, which usually include a trigger for situations and a set of services to be executed, are transformed to JADL++ scripts [16] and deployed to the runtime using the distributed service directory and JIAC's JMX interface.

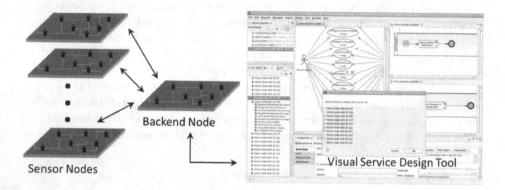

**Fig. 3.** SmartSenior global architecture and deployment chain

In order to be able to remotely deploy (and delete) reaction scripts, each sensor node connects to the back-end node (see Figure 3). The connection needs to be static but fail-safe, therefore it is configured to reconnect every time a disconnect occurs. The back-end node functions as a gateway and provides services to retrieve all registered sensor nodes or to deploy and undeploy reaction-scripts to a specific sensor node. The VSDT connects to the back-end, and via several Eclipse views a user can choose which services are to be deployed or undeployed into which apartment.

*Lessons Learned:* During the eight weeks of the field study, the system was running stable in 32 apartments with no significant errors. Just once, a problem with already processed messages building up in the message queues required a restart of the system after the bug was being fixed. Apart from that, there were no further incidents and the entire system ran smoothly for the entire time.

## 5.3   Distributed Optimisation of Production Schedules

*Description:* The current rise in renewable energy production makes it necessary to either store large amounts of energy in between periods of high energy production, or to adapt energy consumption to energy production. This can be helped by day-ahead energy markets such as the European Energy Exchange AG (EEX), where prices for short-term energy procurement vary according to demand and supply. This provides an incentive to the industry to adapt their production schedules to the energy production that is reflected in the price predictions, e.g., by shifting energy-intense production activities to times with low energy prices, or by filling storage areas with intermediate products when prices are low, to feed on them when energy is more expensive. The aim of the EnEffCo project was to provide a system for optimising production schedules in this regard.

*Implementation:* We developed an optimisation framework that takes as an input a production process model and an energy price curve and produces the optimal production schedule for that setup [22]. For modelling the various production activities and their dependencies, a very simple model is used: Similar to Petri nets, it consists primarily of activities (the individual production steps), and resources (the parts and products consumed and created by those activities). Using this simple model, a wide range of processes can be specified and optimised, from manufacturing processes to charging schedules for electric vehicles [11].

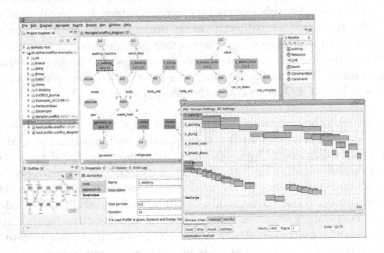

**Fig. 4.** EnEffCo Process Model Editor and Optimisation GUI

Once the process has been modelled, it is sent to the actual optimisation framework (Figure 4). After creating an initial, naive production schedule, evolutionary algorithms are used for mutating and recombining those schedules, by randomly inserting, moving and removing activities, until a satisfactory result (w.r.t. overall energy consumption, energy price, etc.) is reached.

While the actual optimisation algorithm does not make use of the JIAC framework, it is used for transparently distributing and connecting the several components of the system. First, using a simple interaction protocol [22], client agents can distribute their optimisation jobs to any number of optimisation server agents. This way, several 'populations' can be optimised in parallel, improving the chances to find an optimal schedule without increasing the running time of the optimisation. Second, each of the other components of the EnEffCo system, such as the process model editor, a Web frontend, or a database holding energy consumption data for different activities, are connected to each other using JIAC agents.

*Lessons Learned:* While the original plan was to have one agent for each production step, and/or for each (intermediate) product, and to have those agents negotiate when to produce what product, we soon came to the conclusion that it would be much more pragmatic and practical to implement the performance-critical optimisation algorithm in a traditional way and to use agent only at a much higher level, for distributing and integrating the several components. This way, the communication overhead could be reduced drastically.

## 5.4    Managing Cascading Failures in the Power Grid

*Description:* The main motivation behind the ILIas project is that modern infrastructures are interdependent, such as power and telecommunication (TC) grids. In case of failures, this can create cascading effects in several or all of the involved infrastructures. The objective of the project is to research and create intelligent and scalable management systems that provide prediction and reaction to cascading failure effects, so that actions to stabilise the managed infrastructure can be taken. An example for this is the reaction to power outages and the consequent failure of TC networks in the affected areas.

*Implementation:* The approach chosen in ILIas is an agent-based decentralised smart grid management system [10] that observes and controls the grid. Each smart grid entity is managed by a separate management agent that tries to maintain a best-as-possible state for its controlled entity and interacts with neighbouring entities' management agents to provide a balance between its own entities' requirements and overall goals such as (sub-)network stability. As real-world power and TC networks contain very large numbers of entities, scalability was highly important requirement. Using a decentralised management system fulfils the requirements of a scalable and flexible system, as processing load can be distributed over a large number of systems. In addition to that, decentralisation also provides a degree of overall stability, as single points of failure are avoided.

Prediction of grid behaviour is supplied by a simulation of power and TC networks. The management agents are able to interact with both physical as well as simulated smart grid entities, which allows for easy testing of even large scale systems. This agent-based simulation is implemented using the NeSSi$^2$ simulation framework [13] and is able to work both, offline, simulating a predefined scenario, as well as online, by using the current grid state as a starting point to calculate predictions. The human-machine interface is provided by a visual monitoring application (Figure 5) that visualises the smart grid topology.

*Lessons Learned:* As JIAC was already a very mature framework when the ILIas project started, the requirements of the project's objectives did not influence the development of JIAC significantly. Instead the system specification phase revealed that the features offered by JIAC were matching the requirements in

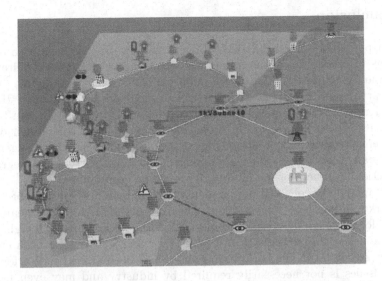

**Fig. 5.** Smart grid live monitoring in ILIas (image detail)

ILIas quite good. For the p2p based approach in ILIas, the most helpful characteristics of the JIAC V Framework were the highly variable communication mechanisms, as well as the general agent based models used. The former were able to automatically adopt to changes in the infrastructure, e.g., when handling failure scenarios, the latter allowed very easy and quickly reconfigurable mappings of a given grid topology into a running management system. The resulting system proved to be very reliable in regard to overall system stability. The agent based models were also important for the required scalability of the system, as they provided the possibility to balance system load by distributing the agents over physically separated systems without any changes in the agent implementations.

During the development of the ILIas solution, two weak points in JIAC that require improvement were found. One of them was found in the lack of supported database services. Occasionally larger amounts of data had to be handled, which required database integration in the application development. As there was no generic solution for this provided by JIAC, an application-specific solution had to be implemented for the project. This functionality could be handled by the framework in the future.

The other field of improvement was the underlying communication infrastructure. While it provided the required flexibility and stability for most of the project's objectives, one weakness was identified in the behaviour with unstable connections, especially in scenarios where a connection would break away for a short time. An improvement for this could consists of better connection failure handling and improved reconnection times, to ensure basic functionality of the agents even without communication as well as minimising times of disconnection.

# 6  Conclusion

In this paper we presented the JIAC V agent framework. The basic idea behind JIAC was to provide an agent framework which meets industrial requirements and is able to facilitate the industrial adoption of the agent paradigm.

We started with a brief description of industrial projects in which JIAC is used and respectively emphasised features that were required for the technical realisation of each project. In doing so, we compiled a comprehensive list of requirements that includes: robustness, stability, hot deployment, agent migration, scalability, service life cycle management, third-party API integration, introspection and monitoring, modularity as well as reusability.

We compared the collected requirements to the capabilities of state-of-the-art framework solutions and thus motivated the necessity of JIAC. To be clear about this, we do not deem JIAC to be superior to other frameworks, though, some (well established) frameworks (e.g., Jason [4] or 3APL [14]) have been created on a very strong academic background and it has been argued that a focus on research issues is not necessarily required by industry and may even hamper industrial adoption [39]. Other frameworks that were geared towards industrial projects (e.g., the JADE framework [3]) were extended without an overarching concept and thus lack the coherence and unity that we would expect from a modern software framework, though, technical maturity and coherence were also identified as important factors on the way to industrial technology adoption [39].

After comparing the collected requirements to the capabilities of state-of-the-art framework solutions, we presented JIAC V in more detail, describing the architecture of JIAC multi-agent systems as well as the modular assembly of JIAC agents. Furthermore, we mentioned basic and extending capabilities of JIAC agents and nodes. Based on this description, we elaborated on selected projects, namely *GL 2.0*, *SmartSenior*, *EnEffCo*, and *ILIas* and emphasised the respective technical integration of required framework features.

As mentioned at the beginning, we certainly recognise that there are many agent frameworks available—each one with a focus on particular multi-agent system characteristics. Yet, as of today, the agent community was not able to convince industrial players to adopt their ideas. As opposed to comparable frameworks, JIAC was never intended to include the cutting edge of agent research but to constitute a robust, reliable, homogeneous and well-documented foundation for the development of agent-based software applications.

It was also our intention to equip JIAC with features that are generally required for extensive industrial appliances. Today, the JIAC framework provides a set of well-evaluated and useful capabilities. Common requirements, such as distribution or access to SOA-compliant services, were integrated as core functionalities. Other, less broadly used features, were developed as optional modules.

We do not consider JIAC to be an ultimate solution for the discrepancy between agent research and the applying industry. Yet, given the fact that JIAC was originally streamlined towards industrial projects and also towards ease of use, it is our opinion that JIAC has the potential to provide new incentives for industrial stakeholders and users who are not all too familiar with the agent paradigm to consider agent technology.

# References

1. Balke, T., Hirsch, B., Lützenberger, M.: Assessing agent applications — r&D vs. R&d. In: Ganzha, M., Jain, L.C. (eds.) Multiagent Systems and Applications — Volume 1: Practice and Experience. Intelligent Systems Reference Library, vol. 45, pp. 1–20. Springer, Heidelberg (2013)
2. Behrens, T., Köster, M., Schlesinger, F., Dix, J., Hübner, J.F.: The multi-agent programming contest 2011: A résumé. In: Dennis, L., Boissier, O., Bordini, R.H. (eds.) ProMAS 2011. LNCS, vol. 7217, pp. 155–172. Springer, Heidelberg (2012)
3. Bellifemine, F., Poggi, A., Rimassa, G.: JADE — A FIPA-compliant agent framework. Internal technical report, CSELT (1999), Part of this report has been also published in Proceedings of PAAM 1999, London, pp. 97–108 (April 1999)
4. Bordini, R.H., Hübner, J.F., et al.: Jason: A Java Based AgentSpeak Interpreter Used with SACI for Multi-Agent Distribution over the Net (February 2007), http://jason.sourceforge.net/Jason.pdf (last visited on March 15, 2013)
5. Bordini, R.H., Hübner, J.F., Wooldridge, M.: Programming Multi-agent Systems in AgentSpeak Using Jason. Wiley Series in Agent Technology. Wiley-Blackwell (October 2007)
6. Braubach, L., Pokahr, A.: Addressing challenges of distributed systems using active components. In: Brazier, F.M.T., Nieuwenhuis, K., Pavlin, G., Warnier, M., Badica, C. (eds.) Intelligent Distributed Computing V. SCI, vol. 382, pp. 141–151. Springer, Heidelberg (2011)
7. Braubach, L., Pokahr, A.: Conceptual integration of agents with WSDL and rEST-ful web services. In: Dastani, M., Hübner, J.F., Logan, B. (eds.) ProMAS 2012. LNCS, vol. 7837, pp. 17–34. Springer, Heidelberg (2013)
8. Busetta, P., Rönnquist, R., Hodgson, A., Lucas, A.: JACK — Components for intelligent agents in java. Tech. rep., Agent Oriented Software Pty, Ltd. (1999)
9. Caire, G., Gotta, D., Banzi, M.: WADE: A software platform to develop mission critical applications exploiting agents and workflows. In: Padgham, L., Parkes, D.C., Müller, J., Parsons, S. (eds.) Proceedings of the 7th International Conference on Autonomous Agents and Multiagent Systems (AAMAS 2008), Estoril, Portugal, pp. 29–36. IFAAMAS (2008)
10. Chinnow, J., Tonn, J., Bsufka, K., Konnerth, T., Albayrak, S.: A tool set for the evaluation of security and reliability in smart grids. In: Cuellar, J. (ed.) Smart-GridSec 2012. LNCS, vol. 7823, pp. 45–57. Springer, Heidelberg (2013)
11. Freund, D., Raab, A.F., Küster, T., Albayrak, S., Strunz, K.: Agent-based integration of an electric car sharing fleet into a smart distribution feeder. In: 3rd IEEE PES International Conference and Exhibition on Innovative Smart Grid Technologies (ISGT Europe), Berlin, Germany, pp. 1–8. IEEE (October 2012)
12. Greenwood, D., Buhler, P., Reitbauer, A.: Web service discovery and composition using the web service integration gateway. In: Proceedings of the 2005 IEEE International Conference on e-Technology, e-Commerce and e-Service (EEE 2005), Hong Kong, China, pp. 789–790. IEEE (2005)

13. Grunewald, D., Lützenberger, M., Chinnow, J., Bye, R., Bsufka, K., Albayrak, S.: Agent-based network security simulation (demonstration). In: Tumer, K., Yolum, P., Sonenberg, L., Stone, P. (eds.) Proceedings of the 10th International Joint Conference on Autonomous Agents and Multiagent Systems, Taipei, Taiwan, Taipei, Taiwan, pp. 1325–1326 (Mai 2011)

14. Hindriks, K.V., Boer, F.S.D., der Hoek, W.V., Meyer, J.J.: Agent programming in 3APL. Autonomous Agents and Multi-Agent Systems 2(4), 357–401 (1999)

15. Hirsch, B., Konnerth, T., Hessler, A., Albayrak, S.: A serviceware framework for designing ambient services. In: Mana, A., Lotz, V. (eds.) Developing Ambient Intelligence (AmID 2006), pp. 124–136. Springer France (2006)

16. Hirsch, B., Konnerth, T., Burkhardt, M., Albayrak, S.: Programming service oriented agents. In: Calisti, M., Dignum, F.P., Kowalczyk, R., Leymann, F., Unland, R. (eds.) Service-Oriented Architecture and (Multi-)Agent Systems Technology. Dagstuhl Seminar Proceedings, vol. 10021, Schloss Dagstuhl - Leibniz-Zentrum für Informatik, Germany (2010)

17. Hirsch, B., Konnerth, T., Heßler, A.: Merging agents and services — The JIAC agent platform. In: Bordini, R.H., Dastani, M., Dix, J., Seghrouchni, A.E.F. (eds.) Multi-Agent Programming: Languages, Tools and Applications, pp. 159–185. Multiagent Systems, Artificial Societies, and Simulated Organizations, Springer (2009)

18. JIAC Development Team: JIAC — Java Intelligent Agent Componentware, Version 5.1.3. DAI-Labor, TU Berlin (October 2012), http://www.jiac.de

19. Keiser, J., Lützenberger, M., Masuch, N.: Agents cut emissions – On how a multi-agent system contributes to a more sustainable energy consumption. Procedia Computer Science 10, 866–873 (2012)

20. Klapiscak, T., Bordini, R.H.: JASDL: A practical programming approach combining agent and semantic web technologies. In: Baldoni, M., Son, T.C., van Riemsdijk, M.B., Winikoff, M. (eds.) DALT 2008. LNCS (LNAI), vol. 5397, pp. 91–110. Springer, Heidelberg (2009)

21. Konnerth, T., Chinnow, J., Kaiser, S., Grunewald, D., Bsufka, K., Albayrak, S.: Integration of simulations and MAS for smart grid management systems. In: Proceedings of the 3rd International Workshop on Agent Technologies for Energy Systems (ATES 2012), Valencia, Spain, pp. 51–58 (2012)

22. Küster, T., Lützenberger, M., Freund, D., Albayrak, S.: Distributed evolutionary optimisation for electricity price responsive manufacturing using multi-agent system technology. Int. Journal on Advances in Intelligent Systems 7(1&2) (2013)

23. Küster, T., Lützenberger, M., Heßler, A., Hirsch, B.: Integrating process modelling into multi-agent system engineering. Multiagent and Grid Systems 8(1), 105–124 (2012)

24. Laclavik, M., Babik, M., Balogh, Z., Hluchy, L.: AgentOWL: Semantic knowledge model and agent architecture. Computing and Informatics 25, 419–437 (2006)

25. Lützenberger, M., Keiser, J., Masuch, N., Albayrak, S.: Agent based assistance for electric vehicles an evaluation. In: Huang, R., Ghorbani, A.A., Pasi, G., Yamaguchi, T., Yen, N.Y., Jin, B. (eds.) AMT 2012. LNCS, vol. 7669, pp. 145–154. Springer, Heidelberg (2012)

26. Lützenberger, M., Küster, T., Heßler, A., Hirsch, B.: Unifying JIAC agent development with AWE. In: Braubach, L., van der Hoek, W., Petta, P., Pokahr, A. (eds.) MATES 2009. LNCS, vol. 5774, pp. 220–225. Springer, Heidelberg (2009)

27. Lützenberger, M., Küster, T., Konnerth, T., Thiele, A., Masuch, N., Heßler, A., Keiser, J., Burkhardt, M., Kaiser, S., Albayrak, S.: JIAC V — A MAS framework for industrial applications (extended abstract). In: Ito, T., Jonker, C., Gini, M., Shehory, O. (eds.) Proceedings of the 12th International Conference on Autonomous Agents and Multiagent Systems, Saint Paul, MN, USA (to appear, 2013)

28. Masuch, N., Keiser, J., Lützenberger, M., Albayrak, S.: Wind power-aware vehicle-to-grid algorithms for sustainable ev energy management systems. In: Proceedings of the IEEE International Electric Vehicle Conference, Greenville, SC, USA, pp. 1–7. IEEE (March 2012)

29. Mařík, V., McFarlane, D.: Industrial adoption of agent-based technologies. IEEE Intelligent Systems 20(1), 27–35 (2005)

30. Object Management Group: Business process modeling notation (BPMN) version 1.2. Specification formal/2009-01-03, Object Management Group (January 2009)

31. Poggi, A., Tomaiuolo, M., Turci, P.: An agent-based service oriented architecture. In: Baldoni, M., Boccalatte, A., Paoli, F.D., Martelli, M., Mascardi, V. (eds.) WOA 2007: Dagli Oggetti agli Agenti. 8th AI*IA/TABOO Joint Workshop 'From Objects to Agents': Agents and Industry: Technological Applications of Software Agents, Genova, Italy, September 24-25, pp. 157–165. Seneca Edizioni Torino (2007)

32. Pokahr, A., Braubach, L., Jander, K.: Unifying agent and component concepts. In: Dix, J., Witteveen, C. (eds.) MATES 2010. LNCS, vol. 6251, pp. 100–112. Springer, Heidelberg (2010)

33. Pěchouček, M., Mařík, V.: Industrial deployment of multi-agent technologies: review and selected case studies. Autonomous Agents and Multi-Agent Systems 17(3), 397–431 (2008)

34. Raddatz, K., Schmidt, A.-D., Thiele, A., Chinnow, J., Grunewald, D., Albayrak, S.: Sensor-basierte Erkennung und Reaktion im häuslichen Umfeld. In: Proceedings of 5th German AAL Congress 2012, Berlin, Germany. VDE Verlag (2012)

35. Thiele, A., Kaiser, S., Konnerth, T., Hirsch, B.: MAMS service framework. In: Kowalczyk, R., Vo, Q.B., Maamar, Z., Huhns, M. (eds.) SOCASE 2009. LNCS, vol. 5907, pp. 126–142. Springer, Heidelberg (2009)

36. Tonn, J., Kaiser, S.: ASGARD – A graphical monitoring tool for distributed agent infrastructures. In: Demazeau, Y., Dignum, F., Corchado, J.M., Pérez, J.B. (eds.) Advances in PAAMS. AISC, vol. 70, pp. 163–173. Springer, Heidelberg (2010)

37. Vattenfall, BMW, TU Berlin, TU Chemnitz, TU Ilmenau: Increasing the effectiveness and efficiency of the applications wind-to-vehicle (W2V) and vehicle-to-grid (V2G) including charging infrastructure (Managed Charging V2.0). Technische Universitätsbibliothek Hannover (TIB) (2011)

38. Weyns, D., Helleboogh, A., Holvoet, T.: How to get multi-agent systems accepted in industry? International Journal of Agent-Oriented Software Engineering (IJAOSE) 3(4), 383–390 (2009)

39. Weyns, D., Van, H., Parunak, D., Shehory, O.: The future of software engineering and multi-agent systems. Special Issue on Future of Software Engineering and Multi-Agent Systems, International Journal of Agent-Oriented Software Engineering, IJAOSE (2008)

40. Wooldridge, M.: Agent-based software engineering. IEE Proceedings — Software 144(1), 26–37 (1997)

# Alternatives to Threshold-Based Desire Selection in Bayesian BDI Agents

Bernardo Luz[1], Felipe Meneguzzi[2], and Rosa Vicari[1]

[1] Informatics Institute, Federal University of Rio Grande do Sul
Av. Bento Gonçalves, 9500 – Porto Alegre, Brazil
{bernardo.luz,rosa}@inf.ufrgs.br
[2] School of Computer Science, Pontifical Catholic University of Rio Grande do Sul
Av. Ipiranga, 6681 – Porto Alegre, Brazil
felipe.meneguzzi@pucrs.br

**Abstract.** Bayesian BDI agents employ bayesian networks to represent uncertain knowledge within an agent's beliefs. Although such models allow a richer belief representation, current models of bayesian BDI agents employ a rather limited strategy for desire selection, namely one based on threshold values on belief probability. Consequently, such an approach precludes an agent from selecting desires conditioned on beliefs with probabilities below a certain threshold, even if those desires could be achieved if they had been selected. To address this limitation, we develop three alternative approaches to desire selection under uncertainty. We show how these approaches allow an agent to sometimes select desires whose belief conditions have very low probabilities and discuss experimental scenarios.

## 1 Introduction

Due to its computable representation of practical reasoning and its folk psychological abstraction to autonomous reasoning, the beliefs, desires and intentions (BDI) model has been extensively studied within the autonomous agents community. Most traditional implementations of BDI agents include a logic-based belief base representing the knowledge an agent has about the world, and plan library that can be selected by an agent when it adopts certain desires. Once a course of action is selected by an agent for execution, it becomes part of an agent's intention to which an agent commits to execute.

Beliefs are traditionally represented by a closed set of ground atomic literals, each of which is associated with a truth value, and consequently does not normally represent uncertainty. Nevertheless, there exist logical formalisms to represent uncertainty regarding an agent's beliefs. Bayesian networks [9] are a popular way of representing uncertain information probabilistically, where parts of it are conditioned on others (e.g., cause and consequence relationships, diseases and symptoms). They are directed acyclic graphs (DAGs), whose nodes

M. Cossentino et al. (Eds.): EMAS 2013, LNAI 8245, pp. 176–195, 2013.

represent event variables associated with two or more possible states, and each state has an explicit occurrence probability.

Given the lack of support for uncertainty in the BDI agent model and the representational power of bayesian networks, there has been work focused on extending the BDI agent model to reason with uncertainty using bayesian networks [4]. This type of agent model no longer relies solely on ground literals to represent an agent's belief base, but rather on a bayesian network.

Traditional BDI agents select desires (or plans with implicit desires) based on a binary condition on the literals of the belief base, under the assumption that this condition is minimal for the desire's viability. The underlying idea is that, if the context condition is not true, then a desire and its associated plans have no chance of being successful. However, even if the context condition is true, a desire might be impossible and an intention associated with it might fail. Similarly, bayesian BDI agents are susceptible to selecting desires that cannot be satisfied in the current world state. Previous approaches to bayesian BDI reasoning [4] have relied on performing desire selection validation by applying a threshold on the probability being evaluated (e.g., that of the desire itself), so that if a certain logical query is less probable than the threshold, then the desire does not meet the minimal requirement to being successful. However, in a probabilistic world, context conditions are less crisply defined. In response, we have developed three alternative desire selection strategies that relax the requirement on the probability threshold for the context condition, and analyze situations where these strategies might be advantageous.

This paper is organized as follows: Section 2.1 presents BDI agents, Section 2.2 presents bayesian networks, Section 2.3 presents bayesian BDI agents, Section 3 presents bayesian BDI reasoning, Section 3.1 presents a threshold-based desire selection process, Section 4 presents alternative approaches to bayesian BDI desire selection, Section 4.1 presents Probability Ranking desire selection, Section 4.2 presents Biased Lottery desire selection, Section 4.3 presents Multi-Desire Biased Random Selection, Section 5 presents an example, and Section 6 presents our final considerations.

## 2    Background

In this section, we review previous efforts upon which our work is based. We start by briefly explaining the BDI model, then proceed to introducing the basics of bayesian networks and finally we enumerate existing work on bayesian BDI agents.

### 2.1    BDI Agents

Autonomous agents are often defined as encapsulated computer systems *situated* in an environment and capable of *flexible* autonomous action in this environment in order to achieve certain goals [5]. The agent must adapt itself to a dynamic environment, while seeking to fulfill its goals. In order to provide a stronger computational grounding for this notion of agent, many architectures have been proposed, among which, one of the most widely studied is the one centered around the mental attitudes of beliefs, desires and intentions (or BDI) [2]. This architecture was originally proposed as a philosophical model of human *practical reasoning*, that is, reasoning aimed at deciding how to act in the world towards achieving one's goals.

Beliefs contain a representation, internal to the agent, of environment elements considered relevant for the agent's reasoning. The state of an agent's beliefs may contain either less information than the current state of the environment (e.g., because of limited sensing ability), or more (e.g., if the agent does additional information processing on its sensing). Desires represent objectives that the agent would like to achieve (i.e., they can be considered an agent's *motivation* [11]). Intentions are those desires that the agent has committed itself to achieving, as well as the steps towards achieving these desires. Agents resist abandoning their intentions, and, should a plan fail, it is often the case that they choose to re-plan.

A BDI agent selects desires through a process that considers the current viability and the absence of conflict with existing intentions. Desires often have preconditioning beliefs that indicate whether or not they should be selected by the agent, as a matter of logical evaluation [8].

## 2.2 Bayesian Networks

Traditional first-order logic approaches to knowledge representation are insufficient to represent certain domains where there is uncertainty in the validity of statements over time [6, 12]. Examples of reasons for this limitation are the high cost of exhaustively representing all possible combinations of truth values using logic rules (laziness), the lack of a complete theory of the domain in question (theoretical ignorance), and the potential impossibility or inviability of performing all necessary tests to ascertain complete truth for certain statements (practical ignorance).

The fact remains that people commonly reason with incomplete knowledge and make decisions based on assumptions over unknown facts. This knowledge comprises what is *known* to be true, what is *not known* and *estimates* based on relationships between elements of the world. (author?) [9] devised a formalism to represent partial knowledge based on the causal relationships between elements in the world, using probability theory to represent how knowledge about one element in the world influences the certainty about others related to it. Here, relationships between elements are represented in a network, and probabilities between related elements are calculated using *Bayes' Rule*, with the resulting formalism being called a *Bayesian Network*. A bayesian network is a type of *causal network* that allows the specification of knowledge where parts of it are conditioned on others, supporting the update of probabilities when new information (i.e., *evidence*) is obtained.

Given two events $A$ and $B$, if we know the probability of $A$ given $B$ and the probability of $B$, we can calculate the probability of seeing both $A$ and $B$, as shown in Equation 1, which represents the *fundamental rule* for probability calculus. It can also be conditioned on another event $C$, as shown in Equation 2.[1]

$$P(A|B)P(B) = P(A \cap B). \tag{1}$$

$$P(A|B \cap C)P(B|C) = P(A \cap B|C). \tag{2}$$

Equation 3 is the key equation behind bayesian networks: *Bayes' Rule*. Bayes' Rule makes it possible to update beliefs about an event $A$, provided that we get information about another event $B$. Thus, $P(A)$ is usually called the *prior probability* of $A$, whereas $P(A|B)$ is called the *posterior probability* of $A$ given $B$. There is also a *general version* of Bayes' Rule, in a context $C$ – exhibited as Equation 4.

$$P(A|B) = \frac{P(B|A)P(A)}{P(B)}. \tag{3}$$

$$P(A|B, C) = \frac{P(B|A, C)P(A|C)}{P(B|C)}. \tag{4}$$

There may be evidence that a given variable is in a certain state. When this happens, it is said that such a variable is *instantiated*. This kind of evidence is called *hard evidence*. Conversely, if a statement about a variable state is made based on dependencies rather than explicit knowledge, it is said that there is *soft evidence* about that variable.

The *d-separation* property tells us if two variables are independent of each other in the current state of the bayesian network. There are three types of connection in the topology of a bayesian network: serial, diverging and converging. Each connection type accounts for a specific reasoning as to whether variables are *d-separated* or *d-connected* (what we call variables that are not d-separated)[2]. In a serial connection, if we have no hard evidence about a variable, evidence about its parent/child passes through it, affecting our beliefs about it and about its uninstantiated child/parent. In a diverging connection, if we have no hard evidence concerning the parent, evidence about one of its children affects our beliefs about the other – uninstantiated – children. In a converging connection, if we have no hard evidence about the child or one of its descendants, evidence about a parent does not influence our beliefs about the other(s).

## 2.3  Bayesian BDI Agents

Although traditional implementations of BDI agents use a logic-based approach to model the world, these approaches fail to account for the uncertainty inherently associated with the real world. In order to address this shortcoming, work has been carried out to switch from a purely logical view of the agent's beliefs

---

[1] The equations in Section 2.2 have been extracted from [6].
[2] "d" is for "directed graph".

based on traditional logic to a bayesian network, integrating it into the reasoning process of BDI agents. Fagundes et al. [4] have created an ontology-based BDI agent in which the belief base is replaced by a bayesian network and the desire selection process relies on probability thresholds to adopt new desires. Kieling and Vicari [7] integrate a bayesian network into an implementation of the Jason [1] AgentSpeak(L) [11] interpreter. Finally, Carrera and Iglesias [3] focus on the process of updating beliefs within a bayesian BDI agent.

## 3    Bayesian BDI Reasoning

In this section, we develop a reasoning cycle that should be general enough that it could be used to describe the reasoning performed by previous work on bayesian BDI agents [3, 4, 7]. Later, we describe a desire selection process that is built around a threshold evaluation, as in [4], within such a reasoning cycle.

In this paper, we consider the belief base to correspond to an entire bayesian network whereby the causal relations between beliefs are explicitly represented. Moreover, given current evidence, we also explicitly represent the probability that a certain variable is in a particular state. Each event variable has $n$ possible states, each with an associated probability, that either is readily available from a *conditional probability table* if the state of all the parent variables is known (i.e., there is hard evidence on each of them) or has to be calculated.

Desires in the bayesian BDI agent model refer to specific event variable states in the bayesian network, and each desire has a preconditioning belief, indicating when that desire can be adopted by the agent. Our choice of belief-preconditioned desire representation follows the tradition of many implemented BDI systems (e.g., [8, 11]). We present two types of desire for bayesian BDI agents: *strong* and *weak*. Strong desires are desires on which there must be *hard evidence* so that they can be considered fulfilled. There may not be any doubt, however small, on whether or not a strong desire has been satisfied. Weak desires are those that are not necessarily expected to be confirmed via hard evidence, but are expected to be believed to be sufficiently likely to be true, i.e., to reach a certain minimum probability value. These may be viewed as desires that accept *soft evidence* as sufficient in order to be considered satisfied. Strong desires may be viewed as a special case of what would otherwise be weak desires, where, given each desire $d$, $P(d) = 1$.

Similarly to traditional BDI agents, intentions are desires to the fulfillment of which the agent has committed itself. The agent will seek a plan – a sequence of actions – that is applicable to the current situation: any plan that is aimed at satisfying at least one of the intentions and whose preconditions are not conclusively denied (i.e., preconditions that are not contradictory to hard evidence) is valid.

Algorithm 1 outlines a generic reasoning cycle for a bayesian BDI agent reasoning within an uncertain environment. First, the agent updates its belief base (i.e., the probabilities in the bayesian network), according to the latest perceptions from the environment (Line 2). Second, the agent evaluates if each desire has been satisfied, removing it from the list of desires if so (Line 3). The agent

---

**Algorithm 1.** Reasoning Cycle for Bayesian BDI Agents

---

1: **procedure** GENERIC BDI REASONING CYCLE
2:    update beliefs based on percept
3:    evaluate desire satisfaction and remove fulfilled desires
4:    evaluate and possibly choose desires
5:    seek plans that might satisfy the chosen desires
6:    for each chosen desire, if an applicable plan has been found, create an intention and associate it with the desire and the plan, which is therefore adopted
7:    if a plan was not found, mark the desire as unsatisfiable at this time
8:    if adopted plan failed, either seek another plan or remove the intention (subject to commitment policy)
9:    if adopted plan succeeded, remove the intention
10: **end procedure**

---

then proceeds to evaluate its possible desires (Line 4), and if a desire has been selected, the agent must commit to it by adopting an intention. Once it has committed it seeks plans capable of satisfying it (Line 5) and then executes the plans in an attempt to achieve the goal (Line 6). For each chosen desire for which no way of attempting to fulfill it has been found, mark it as "unsatisfiable at this time" and refrain from creating an intention for it in the current cycle (Line 7). If there is an adopted plan and it fails, then the agent may either seek an alternate plan or give up on the corresponding intention altogether (Line 8). This is subject to a *commitment policy* that may take into account whether this happened before to the desire associated with this intention, to intentions in general (there could conceivably be some kind of overall environment issue behind the failures), the rate at which alternate plans have proven effective, the computational cost for obtaining such plans – perhaps compared to the cost of desire selection, etc.. Successful plan executions cause their associated intentions to be removed (Line 9).

Since Bayesian BDI agents' beliefs are extended with probabilistic data, it is no longer sufficient to perform the logical evaluation for each desire's preconditions to determine those that are eligible for intention creation. Just as there are degrees of probability in the beliefs, selecting a desire is now a decision made with varying degrees of confidence, which implies that preconditions are no longer strictly about *validity* of selection, but also about *confidence* in a selection that is made under uncertainty. The only case where it is a matter of validity is when there is hard evidence *against* the desire's precondition (i.e., evidence of a different state of the event variable).

Moser et al. [4] performs reasoning using a threshold-based evaluation: if the probability being evaluated is equal to or greater than the threshold value, the associated event variable state is considered valid; in that work, the existence of a belief is dependent on this validation. Such reasoning involves checking if the probability associated with the applicability of the desire satisfies the threshold; if so, the desire may be selected; otherwise, the agent simulates hard evidence on all combinations of the preconditioning event variable states – one state per variable – to determine which such state combinations would, if supported by hard evidence, allow for a threshold-satisfying probability of the event variable state corresponding to the desire itself, if any. New desires are then created from these states, connected to the original desire through causality.

Desires preconditioned on beliefs holding a probability that is exactly equal to zero, i.e., as a result of hard evidence on a state other than the one referred to by the belief in question, but associated with the same event variable, must not be selected. It is important to point out that once an intention has been dropped (i.e., not fulfilled), the desire is added back to the list of desires; without this, failed desires would be lost. Although this is not shown in any of the selection algorithms in this paper, as it is not a part of desire selection itself, it is an underlying assumption of the reasoning cycle.

### 3.1 Threshold-Based Desire Selection

In this section we describe a desire selection process that is threshold-based, which is a key characteristic in previous work [4], in terms of our reasoning cycle. This process is summarized in the pseudocode of Algorithm 2, representing a threshold-based desire selection algorithm in the context of a Bayesian BDI agent. It takes as parameters the numeric threshold value and the list of available *desires* (Line 1). The algorithm traverses the list of desires (Line 2) and, for each one, evaluates whether the probability of its associated precondition is greater than, or equal to the threshold (Line 3). If so, the desire in question is removed from the list of desires (Line 4) and returned (Line 5), thereby refraining from continuing to traverse the list, the implication being that this algorithm only selects one desire. If the entire list of desires is traversed and no desire has been selected (Line 7), the algorithm returns *null* (Line 8), denoting that no new desire is pursued by the agent.

---

**Algorithm 2.** threshold-based selection

1: **function** THRESHOLDBASEDSELECTION(*threshold*, *desires*)
2:     **for each** *desire* such that *desire* ∈ *desires* **do**
3:         **if** *desire.preCondition.probability* ≥ *threshold* **then**
4:             *desires.remove(desire)*
5:             **return** *desire*
6:         **end if**
7:     **end for**
8:     **return** *null*
9: **end function**

---

## 4   Alternatives for Bayesian BDI Desire Selection

The threshold-based desire selection algorithm shown in Section 3 avoids selecting desires whose belief preconditions do not meet a minimal degree of probabilistic

support. As such, it constitutes a relatively simplistic mechanism for desire selection in a probabilistic section, and suffers from two key limitations. On the one
hand, as the selection threshold approaches one, the agent becomes extremely conservative, and may not select any desire and remain idle for long periods of time.

On the other hand, if the threshold approaches zero, the agent becomes less
strict in ensuring the viability of the desires it chooses to pursue. Importantly,
depending on the order in which the desires are checked, the agent might select
desires that are less likely than others.

Moser et al. [4] work with the notion of incompatible desires in Bayesian BDI
agents, which is beyond the scope of this work. These incompatible desires are
sorted by probability and the one with the highest probability is selected. The
selection process for multiple desires that are not considered incompatible is not
a concern in their work; there, competition is not assumed to be a part of the desire selection process. For the algorithms presented in this paper, we assume that
there is a process that filters desires conflicting with existing intentions. Moreover, we assume competition among desires during selection, unless otherwise
specified.

In order to address the limitations of threshold-based selection, we propose
a number of alternative desire selection mechanisms that ensure a finer control
over an agent's choice of desires while taking into consideration the probabilistic
nature of an environment. These approaches eliminate idleness and ensure that
more likely desires are selected more often. In the algorithms developed in this
section, similarly to the desire selection algorithm shown in Section 3, we assume
that once an intention is dropped the desire is added back to the list of desires.

## 4.1  Probability Ranking

This approach involves sorting the desire list in decreasing order of precondition
probability, resulting in a ranking from highest to lowest probability precondition, and picking up the desire backed by the belief most likely to be true. The
pseudocode in Algorithm 3 illustrates the Probability Ranking desire selection
algorithm. Its only parameter is a list of *desires* (Line 1). If there are any desires
(Line 2) the algorithm sorts them by precondition probability (*rankedDesires*,
Line 3), selects the first desire (Line 4), removes it from the list (Line 5) and,
if the probability of that desire's precondition is greater than 0 (Line 6) – to
prevent a desire associated with a contradicted precondition from being selected
– returns that desire (Line 7). Otherwise, the algorithm returns *null* (Line 10).

## 4.2  Biased Lottery

Selecting desires by ranking them over their precondition probability as we show
in Section 4.1 helps ensure that an agent is never idle. However, it is still possible that certain desires will never be selected, even if they were possible but
were weakly supported by the agent's beliefs. Situations where this is detrimental to the agent occur when the agent has not obtained enough evidence about
the environment, or has obtained the wrong evidence. In order to address that

---

**Algorithm 3.** Probability Ranking Selection

---

```
 1: function PROBABILITYRANKINGSELECTION(desires)
 2:     if desires.length > 0 then
 3:         rankedDesires := desires ordered by precondition probability
 4:         desire := rankedDesires.first()
 5:         desires.remove(desire)
 6:         if desire.preCondition.probability > 0 then
 7:             return desire
 8:         end if
 9:     end if
10:     return null
11: end function
```

---

limitation, we now develop a technique that randomly picks desires using their precondition probability to weight this selection. The idea is to randomly generate a number and use it to determine which desire to choose, according to a probability distribution reflecting the probabilities of the desires' preconditions.

In order to generate this probability distribution over the desires, we generate a series of numeric intervals within the $[0, 1]$ range assigning, for each belief, an interval proportional to the probability of their belief precondition. The probabilities, thus, serve as weights that create bias in what would otherwise constitute a purely random selection; it is a nondeterministic desire selection that is subject to bias from the precondition probability. This desire selection method neither disregards desires backed by beliefs holding very low probabilities, nor is designed to embrace them more often than common sense would permit – than such probabilities would suggest. We formalize this selection mechanism in the pseudocode of Algorithm 4, which uses the function described in Algorithm 5 to generate the selection probability intervals. Algorithm 4 takes as input the list of desires (Line 1) and generates a random numeric value (Line 2) and a list of numeric values (Line 3) that correspond to the upper limits (boundaries) for the numeric intervals used in desire selection; Function *GenerateIntervals* (Line 3) is detailed in Algorithm 5. The algorithm proceeds to traverse the list of upper interval limits (Lines 4–10); it uses the randomly generated number to select a desire (Lines 5 and 6), which is then removed from the list of desires and returned (Lines 7 and 8). If the entire list of upper interval limits is traversed and the random value has not been found to belong to any of the intervals (Line 10), the algorithm returns *null* (Line 11).

Algorithm 5 takes as input a list of *desires* (Line 1) and starts by creating a list to store the upper numeric interval limits that will be calculated (*intervals*, Line 2). Provided that there are elements in the input list, the algorithm proceeds to create a list that will contain the *probabilities* of the desires' preconditions (Lines 3 and 4). It also defines a variable *sum* that will be used to store the sum of all such probabilities, initializing it to 0 (Line 5). It then traverses the desire list (Lines 6–9) storing the probabilities of the desires' preconditions

---

**Algorithm 4.** Biased Lottery

---

1: **function** BIASEDLOTTERY(*desires*)
2:     *randomValue* := *random number* $\in [0, 1]$
3:     *intervals* := GENERATEINTERVALS(*desires*)
4:     **for** $i = 0$ **to** *intervals.length* **do**
5:         **if** *randomValue* < *intervals*[*i*] **then**
6:             *desire* := *desires*[*i*]
7:             *desires.remove*(*desire*)
8:             **return** *desire*
9:         **end if**
10:     **end for**
11:     **return** *null*
12: **end function**

---

in the corresponding positions of *probabilities* and accumulating the probability of all desire preconditions in the *sum* variable (Lines 7 and 8). If the sum is greater than 1 (Line 10), it normalizes the *probabilities* and uses these values as interval sizes while generating numeric intervals (Lines 12–14). If not (Line 15), it generates numeric intervals using the *probabilities* as interval sizes (Lines 17–19). Lines 11 and 13 are the normalized equivalents of Lines 16 and 18, calculating and ultimately assigning upper interval limits to the positions in *intervals*.

We do not perform normalization when the sum of the precondition probabilities is less than 1.0, as this would inflate selection probabilities for desires preconditioned on insignificant events. For example, a single desire preconditioned on a belief with 0.0001 probability would be treated as though its probability were 1.0. Note that the numeric intervals for the desires are forced not to intersect with one another, since the one randomly generated number (per selection cycle) is expected to select, at most, one desire-associated numeric interval. Although this algorithm now allows an agent to sometimes pick desires that would not normally be selected, it is still limited to the choice of a single desire.

## 4.3  Multi-desire Biased Random Selection

of each other (e.g., full parallelism is possible), allowing multiple desires to be selected simultaneously. This approach to desire selection removes competition among desires, so long as they do not conflict. It considers non-conflicting desires independently of each other, and allows for the selection of multiple desires at once. We consider a conflict to exist between two desires if they refer to the same event variable, but to different states – all states in the state space of an event variable are mutually exclusive.

If a given desire being evaluated conflicts with a desire that is already designated to be selected at the end of the current selection process, we consider it ineligible for selection. Otherwise, it gets a chance: given a desire $D_i$ preconditioned on a belief holding a probability $P_i$, we say that $D_i$ is assigned a numeric

---

**Algorithm 5.** Biased Lottery – Desire Intervals

1: **function** BIASEDLOTTERY:GENERATEINTERVALS(*desires*)
2:     *intervals*[*desires.length*]
3:     **if** *desires.length* > 0 **then**
4:       *probabilities*[*desires.length*]
5:       *sum* := 0
6:       **for** $i := 0$ **to** *desires.length* **do**
7:         *probabilities*[$i$] := *desires*[$i$].*preCondition.probability*
8:         *sum* := *sum* + *probabilities*[$i$]
9:       **end for**
10:      **if** *sum* > 1 **then**
11:        *intervals*[0] := $\frac{probabilities[0]}{sum}$
12:        **for** $i := 1$ **to** *intervals.length* **do**
13:          *intervals*[$i$] := *intervals*[$i-1$] + $\frac{probabilities[i]}{sum}$
14:        **end for**
15:      **else**
16:        *intervals*[0] := *probabilities*[0]
17:        **for** $i := 1$ **to** *intervals.length* **do**
18:          *intervals*[$i$] := *intervals*[$i-1$] + *probabilities*[$i$]
19:        **end for**
20:      **end if**
21:     **end if**
22:     **return** *intervals*
23: **end function**

---

interval $I_i = [0, P_i]$. For every such desire $D_i$, if a randomly generated numeric value $N_i$ in interval $[0, 1]$ belongs to interval $I_i$, the desire is added to the set of desires to be selected at the end of this selection cycle. Optionally, we may order the desire list in ascending order of precondition probability, prior to the execution of the algorithm, to let a desire supported by a lower precondition have its chance unhindered by potentially conflicting desires that stand a better chance of being selected. If the difference in precondition probabilities of conflicting desires isn't big, however, this may be considered an unwelcome bias, as it could artificially make a supposedly less likely-to-be-selected desire get selected more often than conflicting desire(s) in practice. Another option would be a pure shuffle.

The pseudocode of Algorithm 6 formalizes our proposed approach for Multi-Desire Biased Random Selection. It takes as input the list of *desires* (Line 1), and creates a list that will be used to store any number of desires that may be selected (*selectedDesires*, Line 2). This selection takes place by traversing the list of desires (Lines 3–11), and, if they don't conflict with any of the desires already added to *selectedDesires* (Line 4), randomly picking desires based on their precondition probability (Lines 5–8).

---

**Algorithm 6.** Multi-Desire Biased Random Selection

---

1: **procedure** MULTIDESIREBIASEDRANDOMSELECTION(*desires*)
2:     *selectedDesires* := {}
3:     **for each** *desire* ∈ *desires* **do**
4:         **if** *desire* does not conflict with any element in *selectedDesires* **then**
5:             *randomValue* := *random number* ∈ [0, 1]
6:             **if** *randomValue* ≤ *desire.preCondition.probability* **then**
7:                 *selectedDesires.add*(*desire*)
8:                 *desires.remove*(*desire*)
9:             **end if**
10:        **end if**
11:    **end for**
12:    **return** *selectedDesires*
13: **end procedure**

---

## 5   Example

### 5.1   Description

In order to illustrate the effects of each desire selection strategy described in Section 4, we now introduce a working example to show how an agent would react to situations using our proposed algorithms. Our example scenario consists of a watchman agent that is tasked with guarding an installation and reporting anything out of the ordinary. The presence of suspicious people nearby increases its estimate of a security breach. There is an alarm in the installation, that is effective under normal circumstances. However, there are reports of occasional electrical malfunctions in the installation, which may cause the alarm to ring for no reason or not to ring when it is expected to. Moreover, the watchman becomes interested in seeking evidence that there is not an electrical malfunction if it knows that there are suspicious people nearby. If an electrical malfunction is detected, the watchman must report this. The surrounding area is known for intense traffic, and accidents are more common than in most other areas, resulting in noise that is almost always perceived by the agent. However, noise might be caused by trespassers, though that is not very likely. If the watchman finds out that an accident has occurred, this must be reported as well (e.g., so others keep this in mind if they hear noise). In order to patrol the installation, the watchman periodically chooses between the default and an alternate route, and it becomes more inclined to patrol the alternate route as its belief that a security breach is either imminent or already taking place increases, and conversely, the watchman is more inclined to patrol the default route when everything looks calm. The watchman is also expected to keep an eye open for electrical malfunctions and accidents.

Regarding the relationships among the event variables in the network, we note that: *i*) Evidence of the presence of suspicious people nearby increases the probability of a security breach; *ii*) Evidence of the alarm activating increases

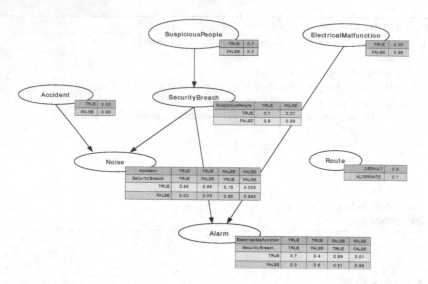

**Fig. 1.** The *Watchman* agent's beliefs

the probability of a security breach occurring, as well as the probability of there being suspicious people nearby. This is still true if there is also evidence of an electrical malfunction, but the probability increase for both event variable states is smaller. If there is evidence that there is no electrical malfunction (e.g., a notification about maintenance very recently performed), the probability increase is the greatest of the three cases; *iii)* evidence of noise increases the probability of a security breach. However, this increase is almost nullified upon evidence of an accident, as this network tells us that an accident is a much more probable cause of noise than a security breach, and the impact of a security breach on the probability of noise if we already know of an accident is small; and *iv)* An increase on the probability of a security breach (e.g., through evidence of suspicious people and noise) increases the probability of the alarm activating, even if there is an electrical malfunction, though then the probability increase is smaller.

The bayesian belief base of the watchman encoding the domain knowledge described in the scenario is represented in Figure 1. Do note that we do not associate the *Route* variable with a belief about the environment state, but rather we associate it with an internal belief associated with the agent's currently chosen route. It is not a part of the reasoning surrounding the probability of a security breach or any of the other event variables, and this is the reason we left it disconnected from all the other network nodes.

This watchman agent has two mutually exclusive strong desires that are periodically renewed:[3] *Route.default(SecurityBreach.false)* and *Route.alternate(SecurityBreach.true)*. That is, the agent desires to patrol the default route if

---

[3] We denote desires in the form `<desire>(<preconditioning belief>)`, where both elements are described as `<event variable>.<state>`.

it believes that there has not been a security breach, and the alternate one otherwise. It also has the strong desire $ElectricalMalfunction.false(SuspiciousPeople.true)$, i.e., the desire to believe (in other words, to find out) that there is no electrical malfunction at the moment, conditioned on the presence of suspicious people nearby, as well as the strong desire $Accident.true(Noise.true)$, i.e., the desire to discover that there has been an accident, if noise has been heard.

Note that evidence on event variables $ElectricalMalfunction$ and $Accident$ alone does not affect the state probabilities of event variable $SecurityBreach$. Only if evidence on $Alarm$ is obtained does evidence on $ElectricalMalfunction$ impact event variable $SecurityBreach$ (e.g., from $P(SecurityBreach|$ $ElectricalMalfunction = false) = P(SecurityBreach) = (0.073, 0.927)^4$ to $P(SecurityBreach|Alarm = true, ElectricalMalfunction = false) = (0.8863,$ $0.1137))$, just as only if evidence on $Noise$ is obtained does evidence on $Accident$ impact $SecurityBreach$ (e.g., from $P(SecurityBreach|Accident = false) =$ $(0.073, 0.927)$ to $P(SecurityBreach|Noise = true, Accident = false) = (0.7026,$ $0.2974))$. Both are cases of converging connections, from $ElectricalMalfunction$ and $SecurityBreach$ to $Alarm$, and from $Accident$ and $SecurityBreach$ to $Noise$, respectively. Additionally, if the state probabilities of event variable $SecurityBreach$ are updated, as in the cases just described, so are those of $SuspiciousPeople$, if the latter is also uninstantiated.

## 5.2  Desire Selection

We now briefly present the result of using each of the four algorithms while working with an initial scenario – where what happens during the execution of each algorithm is not carried over to the next – where there is no hard evidence of any event. Since there is no hard evidence yet, $P(SuspiciousPeople) = (0.7, 0.3)$, and consequently $P(SecurityBreach) = (0.073, 0.927)$; also, $P(Noise) = ($ $0.0624, 0.9376)$. Desire $Route.default$ is preconditioned on a belief that $Security$-$Breach$ is false, which has a 0.927 probability; desire $Route.alternate$ is preconditioned on a belief that $SecurityBreach$ is true, which holds a 0.073 probability; desire $ElectricalMalfunction.false$ is preconditioned on a belief that $SuspiciousPeople$ is true, which holds a 0.7 probability; and desire $Accident.true$ is preconditioned on a belief that $Noise$ is true, which holds a 0.0624 probability.

First, let us consider threshold-based desire selection, with a threshold of 0.75. This means that only $Route.default(SecurityBreach.false)$ is an eligible desire for selection, since $P(SecurityBreach = false) = 0.927$. In a scenario where there is hard evidence of noise (i.e., $P(Noise = true) = 1$), the probability of suspicious people nearby is increased: $P(SuspiciousPeople = true|Noise =$ $true) = 0.7422$. However, desire $ElectricalMalfunction.false(SuspiciousPeople.true)$ still fails to satisfy our threshold even so $(0.7422 < 0.75)$. A lower threshold would work in this case, but a precondition's probability might always be smaller than the threshold, if evidence able to increase its probability enough

---

[4] The probabilities of the event variable states – $true$ and $false$, in this case.

is never obtained – this exemplifies how there may be desires that *are never* selected using this criterion. One might suggest simply lowering the threshold to an extremely low value, but without other criteria we would then simply have a desire selection process that is indifferent to the various probabilities presented.

If we use Probability Ranking desire selection, we get the following ranking:

1. *Route.default(SecurityBreach.false)*: 0.927
2. *ElectricalMalfunction.false(SuspiciousPeople.true)*: 0.7
3. *Route.alternate(SecurityBreach.true)*: 0.073
4. *Accident.true(Noise.true)*: 0.0624

The agent will desire to patrol the default route, then to establish that there is no electrical malfunction, then to patrol the alternate route, and finally to verify if there has been an accident, in this order, unless a belief update (e.g., evidence that *SecurityBreach = true*) causes the ranking to be modified. Note that although the preconditioning probabilities serve as a criterion for sorting the desires, the probability values by themselves have no impact on how often the desires may be selected, so *Accident.true(Noise.true)* will be promptly selected in the absence of higher-ranked desires regardless of the fact that its precondition holds a low probability.

If we use Biased Lottery, we get the following list of numeric intervals for the desires (the order is irrelevant):

– *Route.default(SecurityBreach.false)*: [0.0, 0.526)
– *Route.alternate(SecurityBreach.true)*: [0.526, 0.5674)
– *ElectricalMalfunction.false(SuspiciousPeople.true)*: [0.5674, 0.9646)
– *Accident.true(Noise.true)*: [0.9646, 1.0]

The sum of the desires' precondition probabilities is greater than 1, so these values are normalized in the [0, 1] interval and used to generate the intervals. Following the algorithm, a numeric value in the [0, 1] interval is generated, and whichever interval it belongs to determines which desire is selected – if there were not a normalization, it could also tell us that no desire should be selected, by not belonging to any of the intervals. In this example, desire *Route.default(SecurityBreach.false)* has a 0.526 probability of being selected, desire *Route.alternate(SecurityBreach.true)* has a 0.0414 probability of being selected, desire *ElectricalMalfunction.false(SuspiciousPeople.true)* has a 0.3972 probability of being selected, and desire *Accident.true(Noise.true)* has a 0.0354 probability of being selected, each one competing with the others. So, if the randomly generated number is 0.3 (and thus within the first interval), the agent performs a patrol through the default route, or if the random number is 0.55, the patrol is through the alternate route.

If we use Multi-Desire Biased Random Selection, we get the following list of numeric intervals for the desires (in any order):

– *Route.default(SecurityBreach.false)*: [0.0, 0.927]
– *Route.alternate(SecurityBreach.true)*: [0.0, 0.073]

  – $ElectricalMalfunction.false(SuspiciousPeople.true)$: $[0.0, 0.7]$
  – $Accident.true(Noise.true)$: $[0.0, 0.0624]$

For each of the four desires a numeric value in the $[0, 1]$ interval is generated, and if the numeric value belongs to the corresponding desire's numeric interval, the desire is selected. In this example, desires $Route.default(SecurityBreach.false)$, $Route.alternate(SecurityBreach.true)$, $ElectricalMalfunction.false(SuspiciousPeople.true)$ and $Accident.true(Noise.true)$ have, respectively, 0.927, 0.073, 0.7 and 0.0624 probabilities of being selected when given the chance (i.e., when a random number is generated and checked against the interval designated to the desire). The selection of desires $ElectricalMalfunction.false(SuspiciousPeople.true)$ and $Accident.true(Noise.true)$ is fully independent of the others, while desires $Route.default(SecurityBreach.false)$ and $Route.alternate(SecurityBreach.true)$ conflict with each other, and, in cases where one of them is selected, this prevents the other from getting its chance.

As a subsequent step, we describe initial experiments using the *Watchman* agent to gather data and analyze behavior obtained with the use of the presented desire selection algorithms.

## 5.3   Experimentation

In order to further illustrate agent behavior while using the various presented desire selection algorithms, we implement limited experiments[5].

For our experiments, we create an environment corresponding to the installation, responsible for generating events and providing information on their occurrence to inquiring watchmen (agents). All agents in the experiments are mapped to the same environment, and are thus faced with the same installation events, despite the nondeterministic nature of the latter.

In each cycle, the installation computes the occurrence of a security breach, an electrical malfunction and an accident, each with their own probabilities, which are only visible to the environment. These probabilities do not have an obligation to reflect the probabilities found in the watchman's beliefs, as the latter are but estimates. Nevertheless, conceptually speaking, we assume that, ordinarily, an agent's beliefs have at least *some* have merit to them, and therefore represent information relating to the environment with *some* reliability. Our experiments are limited in that the environment resets the agents every cycle, and these select desires and execute the applicable plans all in one of their own cycles. These plans may or may not be successful in fulfilling the corresponding desires.

The default route, which is the route associated with the belief that there is not a security breach, has a much lower chance of letting the watchman encounter one, but it is also significantly shorter, and the watchman usually chooses to patrol it, under normal circumstances. The alternate route is the opposite: on it,

---

[5] In the Java programming language, using jSMILE, the SMILE [10] library wrapper for Java – SMILE is a library for reasoning in graphical probabilistic models, such as bayesian networks. Our experiment implementation is available at
http://www.inf.ufrgs.br/~bmluz/.

the watchman has a greater chance of detecting a security breach, but its length makes it so that a patrol without detecting a security breach is considered undesirable. Aside from detecting security breaches, the watchman must also beware of electrical malfunctions and accidents, making the appropriate investigations. The data presents the desire selections and their implications, specially in terms of detection counts and distance patrolled per security breach.

Our experiments run over 10000 cycles, with the installation having a 0.005 probability of a security breach along the default route, a 0.1 probability of a security breach along the alternate route, a 0.05 probability of an electrical malfunction and a 0.05 probability of an accident. Also, the assigned lengths for the default and alternate routes are 10 and 30, respectively. We present data from Experiments (i) and (ii) in Tables 1 and 2, where the columns refer to, from left to right: the number of patrols on the default route ($Pat(D)\#$), the number of security breaches detected along the default route ($SecBr(D)\#$), the number of patrols on the alternate route ($Pat(A)\#$), the number of security breaches detected along the alternate route ($SecBr(A)\#$), the average distance patrolled per security breach detected ($Dist{:}SecBr$), the number of electrical malfunction investigations ($Inv(ElMa)\#$), the number of electrical malfunction detections ($ElMa\#$), the number of accident investigations ($Inv(Acc)\#$), and the number of accident detections ($Acc\#$). Electrical malfunction and accident investigations refer to the times when the corresponding desires have been selected and are pursued. The rows refer to: an agent that uses threshold-based selection ($THR$), an agent that uses ProbabilityRanking ($PRK$), the average of five agents that use Biased Lottery ($BLO$) and the average of five agents that use Multi-Desire Biased Random Selection ($MDR$). We use multiple agents for Biased Lottery and Multi-Desire Biased Random Selection due to the variation that results from their nondeterminism.

– *Experiment (i)*: the environment does not provide evidence other than what is necessary for desire satisfaction evaluation – i.e., evidence on event variables *Route*, *ElectricalMalfunction* and *Alarm*, when the events in question do occur and the agent specifically asks about them (when executing a corresponding plan – this invariably means attempting to obtain evidence, in our experiments). In total, there are 54 security breaches along the default route, 1045 security breaches along the alternate route, 504 electrical malfunctions and 491 accidents. Agent THR puts all its efforts into patrolling the default route, ignoring all the other desires, meaning that it does not ever investigate electrical malfunctions or accidents; also, it presents a comparatively poor distance-to-security-breach ratio. Agent PRK does the same, because each cycle the situation in the environment is renewed (all possible events are computed again) – meaning that any updates to the agents in previous cycles become obsolete and the agents are reset. Agent BLO divides its efforts among the desires following a probability distribution that roughly resembles the sizes of the intervals generated using the desires' precondition probabilities (see Section 5.2) – an "ideal" run (one without nondeterministic variations) would have 5260 patrols along the default route (0.526 selection probability), 414 patrols along the alternate route (0.0414 selection probability), 3972 electrical malfunction investigations (0.3972 selection probability) and 354 accident investigations (0.0354 selection probability). Agent MDR covers the possible desires following a probability distribution where only the patrols actually compete with each other (as a result of conflict; we order the list of desires in ascending order of precondition probability), i.e., this watchman does not refrain from investigating electrical malfunctions and accidents because of the patrols, and other than this the precondition probabilities serve as references for the selection rates. Agents BLO and MDR present better (i.e., smaller) distance-per-security-breach ratios than THR and PRK.

**Table 1.** Data gathered in Experiment (i)

|       | Pat(D)# | SecBr(D)# | Pat(A)# | SecBr(A)# | Dist:SecBr | Inv(ElMa)# | ElMa# | Inv(Acc)# | Acc# |
|-------|---------|-----------|---------|-----------|------------|------------|-------|-----------|------|
| THR   | 10000   | 54        | 0       | 0         | 1851.8519  | 0          | 0     | 0         | 0    |
| PRK   | 10000   | 54        | 0       | 0         | 1851.8519  | 0          | 0     | 0         | 0    |
| BLO   | 5274    | 32        | 422     | 42        | 883.7838   | 3956       | 205   | 348       | 15   |
| MDR   | 8606    | 47        | 702     | 68        | 931.4783   | 7009       | 351   | 630       | 29   |

– *Experiment (ii)*: the environment always provides evidence of *Alarm = true* to the agents, in addition to the cases expected in Experiment (i). In total, there are 49 security breaches along the default route, 991 security breaches along the alternate route, 488 electrical malfunctions and 547 accidents. Agent THR puts all its efforts into investigating electrical malfunctions, doing nothing else. Agent PRK does the same. Agent BLO divides its efforts among the desires now giving less attention to the default route, more attention to the alternate route, less attention to investigating electrical malfunctions and more attention to investigating accidents – an ideal run would have 1364 patrols along the default route (0.1364 selection probability), 3552 patrols along the alternate route (0.3552) selection probability, 4333 electrical malfunction investigations (0.4333 selection probability) and 751 accident investigations (0.0751 selection probability). Agent MDR displays the same changes in behavior from Experiment (i) as agent BLO in terms of desire selection rates, except that only the patrols compete with each other.

**Table 2.** Data gathered in Experiment (ii) – *Alarm = true*

|       | Pat(D)# | SecBr(D)# | Pat(A)# | SecBr(A)# | Dist:SecBr | Inv(ElMa)# | ElMa# | Inv(Acc)# | Acc# |
|-------|---------|-----------|---------|-----------|------------|------------|-------|-----------|------|
| THR   | 0       | 0         | 0       | 0         | -          | 10000      | 488   | 0         | 0    |
| PRK   | 0       | 0         | 0       | 0         | -          | 10000      | 488   | 0         | 0    |
| BLO   | 1369    | 7         | 3538    | 348       | 337.5493   | 4316       | 205   | 777       | 43   |
| MDR   | 2736    | 14        | 5238    | 512       | 350.7605   | 8813       | 432   | 1550      | 85   |

Threshold-based selection is better suited to clinging to desires that are supported by high probabilities at the moment than the other algorithms, since they are more prone to being "distracted" by other desires. Since in our experiments the agent is reset every cycle, Probability Ranking yields the same practical results as threshold-based selection (there is always a desire selected by the latter), instead of giving a chance to desires supported by low probabilities – this would allow for particularly strong cases of said distraction. We can see that Biased Lottery and Multi-Desire Biased Random Selection make the agent spread its efforts among the desires, so they are more varied, less predictable and more inclusive. Neither of these blindly cling to certain desires, and this can be a strength or a weakness depending on the context. Multi-Desire Biased Random Selection is the only algorithm here that usually selects more than one desire per cycle, and in our experiments the agent in question immediately proceeds to deal with them all in the same cycle, taking a more aggressive approach. If resources were taken into account, however, this could be considered inappropriate.

# 6    Conclusions

From a conservative standpoint, one may argue that threshold-based selection is sensible as it is, as resources will not be used *without justification*. However, we believe that ignoring desires that are *probabilistically irrelevant* in desire selection is not necessarily a rational choice, since it precludes an agent from exploring an environment. In response, we have developed three desire selection strategies that try to overcome this limitation.

In Probability Ranking selection, desires that would be ignored by threshold-based selection do get a chance, though only after the ones that would be accepted by it. However, it might be undesirable to select a desire preconditioned on a belief holding a very low probability just because there is no better alternative.

In Biased Lottery, we rely on nondeterminism to consider all desires while ensuring that desires backed by beliefs holding high probabilities should be selected more often than those backed by beliefs holding low probabilities, in proportion to their probabilities. Ideally, the probability of selecting each desire would be the same as the one associated with its precondition. However, in the cases where the total sum of desire probabilities is greater than 1, the competition between the desires in question proportionally reduces the individual probabilities of selection for each desire.

In Multi-Desire Biased Random Selection, we also rely on nondeterminism for the same reason. A key difference is that the number of desires possibly selected is not limited to one, and non-conflicting desires are considered independently of one another.

The nondeterministic nature of Biased Lottery and Multi-Desire Biased Random Selection makes it so that the watchman agent's behavior may not be precisely anticipated by a third party (e.g., another agent) intent on exploiting it. Such an exploitation could involve forging an accident to drive away suspicion arising from a noise heard by the watchman, for instance. Hiring an employee to plant false evidence of an electrical malfunction would also impact the watchman's beliefs, as a second, albeit more roundabout method of attempting to manipulate the watchman. This is an agent trait that we now describe as *unpredictable proactiveness*: agent behavior at a specific point in time cannot be *completely* determined by analyzing its beliefs, and is thus resistant to exploitation. Finally, our future work aims to evaluate the algorithms developed in different scenarios, considering de-selection of desires, and to investigate joint uses of Biased Lottery and Multi-Desire Biased Random Selection while considering desire incompatibilities.

# References

[1] Bordini, R.H., Hübner, J.F., Wooldridge, M.: Programming Multi-Agent Systems in AgentSpeak Using Jason. John Wiley & Sons, Ltd. (2007)

[2] Bratman, M., Israel, D.J., Pollack, M.E.: Plans and resource-bounded practical reasoning. Computational Intelligence 4, 349–355 (1988)

[3] Carrera, Á., Iglesias, C.A.: B2DI A Bayesian BDI Agent Model with Causal Belief Updating based on MSBN. In: Proceedings of the 4th International Conference on Agents and Artificial Intelligence (ICAART 2012), pp. 343–346. SciTePress (2012)

[4] Fagundes, M.S., Vicari, R.M., Coelho, H.: Deliberation process in a BDI model with bayesian networks. In: Ghose, A., Governatori, G., Sadananda, R. (eds.) PRIMA 2007. LNCS, vol. 5044, pp. 207–218. Springer, Heidelberg (2009)

[5] Jennings, N.R.: On agent-based software engineering. Artificial Intelligence 117, 277–296 (2000)

[6] Jensen, F.V., Nielsen, T.D.: Bayesian Networks and Decision Graphs, 2nd edn. Springer (2007)

[7] Kieling, G., Vicari, R.M.: Insertion of probabilistic knowledge into BDI agents construction modeled in Bayesian Networks. In: International Conference on Complex, Intelligent, and Software Intensive Systems (CISIS 2011), vol. 1, pp. 115–122. Conference Publishing Services (CPS), Seoul, California (2011)

[8] Móra, M.C., Lopes, J.G., Viccari, R.M., Coelho, H.: BDI models and systems: Reducing the gap. In: Papadimitriou, C., Singh, M.P., Müller, J.P. (eds.) ATAL 1998. LNCS (LNAI), vol. 1555, pp. 11–27. Springer, Heidelberg (1999)

[9] Pearl, J.: Probabilistic Reasoning in Intelligent Systems: Networks of Plausible Inference. Morgan-Kaufmann, San Mateo (1988)

[10] Decision Systems Laboratory - University of Pittsburgh: Genie & smile (May 2012), http://genie.sis.pitt.edu/

[11] Rao, A.S.: AgentSpeak(L): BDI agents speak out in a logical computable language. In: Van de Velde, W., Perram, J.W. (eds.) MAAMAW 1996. LNCS, vol. 1038, pp. 42–55. Springer, Heidelberg (1996)

[12] Russel, S.J., Norvig, P.: Artificial Intelligence: A Modern Approach. Prentice Hall, New Jersey (1994)

# Engineering Pervasive Multiagent Systems in SAPERE

Ambra Molesini[1], Andrea Omicini[1], Mirko Viroli[1], and Franco Zambonelli[2]

[1] Dipartimento di Informatica–Scienza e Ingegneria (DISI)
ALMA MATER STUDIORUM–Università di Bologna, Italy
{ambra.molesini,andrea.omicini,mirko.viroli}@unibo.it
[2] Dipartimento di Scienze e Metodi dell'Ingegneria (DISMI)
Università degli Studi di Modena e Reggio Emilia, Italy
franco.zambonelli@unimore.it

**Abstract** Given the growth of agent-based models and technologies in the last decade, nowadays the applicability of agent-oriented techniques to the engineering of complex systems such as pervasive computing ones critically depends on the availability and effectiveness of agent-oriented *methodologies*. Accordingly, in this paper we take SAPERE pervasive service ecosystems as a reference, and introduce a novel agent-oriented approach aimed at engineering SAPERE systems as multi-agent systems.

## 1  Introduction

The ICT landscape has dramatically changed with the advent of mobile and pervasive computing technologies. The dense spread in our everyday environment of sensor networks, RFID tags, along with the mass diffusion of always-on-line smart phones and mobile social networking, is contributing to shape an integrated infrastructure that can be used for the provisioning of innovative general-purpose digital services [1,2]. In particular, such infrastructure will be used to ubiquitously access services improving interaction with the surrounding physical world as well as the social activities therein. Users will be expectedly able to deploy customised services, making the overall infrastructure as open as the Web currently is [3].

According to the above trends, a great deal of research activity in pervasive computing and service systems has been recently devoted to solve problems associated to the design and development of effective pervasive service systems. They include: supporting self-configuration and context-aware spontaneous composition; enforcing context-awareness and self-adaptability; and ensuring that service frameworks can be highly-adaptive and very long-lasting [4]. Unfortunately, most of the solutions so far are proposed in terms of "add-ons" to be integrated in existing frameworks [5,6,7]. The result is often an increased complexity of current frameworks and, in the end, a lack of clean and usable methodological approaches to the engineering of complex pervasive services systems.

Against this background, here we elaborate on the SAPERE novel approach to the engineering of complex pervasive service system [8]. SAPERE (short for

M. Cossentino et al. (Eds.): EMAS 2013, LNAI 8245, pp. 196–214, 2013.

"Self-Aware PERvasive service Ecosystems") tackles the problem of engineering distributed pervasive service systems by a foundational re-thinking of distributed systems, i.e., grounding on a nature-inspired [9,10], and specifically bio-chemically inspired approach, to effectively support context-awareness, spontaneous service composition, and self-adaptivity. Specifically, SAPERE attacks the program of engineering adaptive pervasive service systems by:

– Modelling and architecting a pervasive infrastructure as a non-layered spatial substrate, hosting the execution of an ecosystem of distributed software agents, each associated to the various individual components of the infrastructure—e.g., devices, sensors, or software services.
– Exploiting the spatial substrate as a sort of shared coordination medium [11] for the agents of the ecosystem. Such a substrate embeds the basic coordination laws (*eco-laws*), which have a bio-chemical inspiration (i.e., agents manifest their activities by data-items acting as sort of chemical molecules that interact by bonding with each other and diffusing across space).
– Making the overall ecosystem behaviour be driven by the spontaneous dynamics resulting from applying the eco-laws, leading to the unplanned, i.e., self-organising, composition of distributed components, and inherently supporting dynamic context-aware and self-adaptive behaviour.

The SAPERE approach makes it easy to develop adaptive pervasive, due to both its rather intuitive programming model and its clean accompanying software engineering methodology.

Accordingly, the remainder of this paper is organised as follows. Section 2 motivates the SAPERE approach and sketches its overall agent-based architecture. Section 3 overviews and exemplifies the underlying programming model along with its coordination model based on eco-laws. Section 4 presents the methodology defined to support the design and development of complex pervasive service systems as multi-agent systems (MAS) based on the SAPERE approach. Section 5 discusses some related work, then Section 6 concludes the paper.

# 2   MAS for Pervasive Service Ecosystems in SAPERE

SAPERE targets emerging pervasive computing scenarios based on agent-based abstractions. This calls for specific requirements for SAPERE systems (Subsection 2.1), and also leads to a specific agent-oriented meta-model (Subsection 2.2).

## 2.1   Basic Requirements

The first key requirement is *situatedness* in the physical and social environment. In SAPERE pervasive systems, each agent represents individuals, software, and data tightly linked to a given space-time situation, which should affect the overall system only based on some notion of locality that can take into account physical issues (such as the position in an articulated environment) or social ones (such as who triggered some activity, and which are his/her social profile and relationships). Accordingly, the underlying meta-model should make sure that agents can access to (and influence) only a limited portion of the overall environment.

The second key requirement is *self-adaptivity*. The overall MAS should exhibit the inner ability to intercept relevant distributed situations, even those not explicitly considered at design-time, and accordingly react with no global supervision to achieve the overall system goals—both implicit and explicit ones. This should be achieved by spontaneous re-distribution and re-shaping of the overall system information and activities.

Finally, since emergent pervasive computing scenarios are based on the opportunistic encounter of devices, humans, data, and activities, with no prior knowledge of each other, a high degree of *openness* is required, which should reflect in the use of semantic-based and fully-decoupled interaction mechanisms.

## 2.2  The SAPERE Meta-model

Once the main requirements for SAPERE systems are introduced, the main abstractions of the SAPERE meta-model can be defined, which tailors multi-agent systems (MAS) for pervasive computing scenarios.

**Agents** — *Agents* are the main abstraction in the SAPERE model. As the *loci* encapsulating autonomy and control, agents are the natural means to model sensors and actuators of pervasive computing system, as well as software services (i.e., web services, situation recognisers, local monitors), and the software managing handheld devices carried by humans.

**LSA** — Because of the need of coordinating different kinds of entities in an open way and without global supervision, a cornerstone of the SAPERE approach is that agents manifest their existence in the MAS by a *uniform representation* called a *Live Semantic Annotation* (LSA). An LSA exposes every information about the agent (state, interface, goal, knowledge) that is pertinent for the system: it is *live* since it should continuously reflect changes in the agent state; it is *semantic* since it should be implicitly or explicitly connected to the context in which such information is produced, interpreted and manipulated; and it has the form of an *annotation*, i.e., a structured piece of information resembling a resource description—as in RDF.

**LSA-space** — Manifestation of LSAs is supported by the so-called *LSA-space*, acting as the true *fabric* of all interactions. There, LSAs are injected by agents, float, and evolve, ultimately reifying all the required information about system activities and processes. The LSA-space is distributed among all devices of the pervasive computing system: the portion of the LSA-space that represents a single locality of the environment is called *local LSA-space*.

**LSA bonding** — In order to make any agent act in a meaningful way with respect to the context in which it is situated, special mechanisms are needed to control the sphere of influence of each agent. To this end, LSAs can include *bonds* (i.e., references) to other LSAs in the same context. Only via a bond to another LSA an agent can read its information, inspect the state/interface of another agent, and act accordingly.

**Eco-laws** — Because of adaptivity, while agents enact their *individual* behaviour by observing their context and updating their LSAs, *global* behaviour (i.e., global coordination in the MAS) is enacted by rules manipulating the LSA-space, called *eco-laws*. Eco-laws can perform deletion/update/movement/re-bonding actions applied to a small set of LSAs in the same locality—similarly to how chemical laws affect molecules.

Thus, agents inject LSAs in the space, which by proper diffusion and aggregation eco-laws establish *fields data structures* [12,13,14] of LSAs, which cover subparts of the network and carry information about the originating LSAs (and agent) and its position in the network. Any agent interested in reading such information will then autonomously manifest this fact in its LSA, which by proper bonding eco-laws will then bond to the local LSA of the field. After all the required information has been read, the agent can affect the field originator by injecting itself an LSA, which spreads back, reach the originator's side, and is read through the same bonding mechanism.

# 3    Programming SAPERE Systems: API and Examples

In this section we overview how SAPERE applications can be programmed, by introducing some of the API of the SAPERE middleware and exemplifying its usage. While the whole articulation of SAPERE programming cannot be fully described here, we intend at least to give readers a clue, and also enable them to better understand the overall SAPERE development methodology.

As for any distributed environment, the execution of SAPERE applications is supported by a middleware infrastructure [15]. The infrastructure is lightweight, and enable a SAPERE node to be installed in tablets and smartphones. From the operational point of view, all SAPERE nodes are at the same level since the middleware code they run could support the same services, and provides the same set of functions—i.e., hosting the LSA space and the eco-laws engine.

From the viewpoint of the individual agents constituting the basic execution unit, middleware provides them with an API for advertising themselves via LSAs, and to support LSA continuous updating. In addition, API enables agents to detect local events, such as the change of some LSAs, or, the enactment of some eco-laws on available LSAs. Eco-laws are built as a set of rules embedded in SAPERE nodes, each hosting a local LSA-space. For each node, the same eco-laws apply to rule the dynamics of both local LSAs (in the form of bonding, aggregation, and decay), and non-locally-situated LSAs (via the spreading eco-law that can propagate LSAs through distributed nodes).

From the viewpoint of the underlying network infrastructure, the middleware transparently absorbs dynamic changes at the arrival/dismissing of supporting devices, without affecting the individual perception of the spatial environment.

## 3.1    The SAPERE API

In the SAPERE model, each agent executing on a node takes care of *(i)* initialising at least one LSA, and possibly more, *(ii)* injecting them on the local LSA

```
AgentNoiseSensor {
    init() {
        float nl = sample();
        injectLSA( [sensor-type = noise; accuracy = 0.1; noise-level = nl] );
    }
    run() {
        while(true) {
            sleep (100);
            float nl = sample();
            updateLSA(noise-level = nl);
}   }   }
```

**Fig. 1.** Pseudo-code of a noise sensor

space, and *(iii)* keeping the values of such LSAs updated to reflect its current situation. Each agent can modify only its own LSAs, and eventually read the LSAs to which has been linked to by a proper bonding eco-law. Moreover, LSAs can be manipulated by eco-laws, as explained in the following sections.

The SAPERE middleware provides agents with the following API:

- injectLSA(lsa) is used by agents to inject an LSA into the tuple space. Each agents must inject at least one LSA at initialisation to exist within the SAPERE ecosystem.
- updateLSA(field, new-value) makes agents atomically update some fields of an LSA to keep it alive. The idea is that specific threads inside agents are launched to ensure that the values of LSAs to be kept alive are promptly updated.
- A set of onEcoLawEvent(lsa) methods makes it possible for an agent to sense and handle whatever events occur on its LSAs. For example, the onBond(lsa) method allows the event represented by the LSA to be bond with another LSA matching the former.

As a first example, Figure 1 reports the (pseudo-)code of an agent that acts as a noise sensor, injecting an LSA with noise level, and periodically updating it.

## 3.2   Matching and Bonding

More generally, LSAs are built as descriptive tuples made by a number of fields in the form of "name-value" properties, and possibly organised in a hierarchical way: the value of a property can be a SubDescription—a set of "name-value" properties, again. By building over tuple-based models [11], the values in a LSA can be either *actual* – yet possibly dynamic and changing over time (which makes LSAs live), or *formal*, that is, not tied to any actual value unless bond to one and representing a dangling connection (typically represented with a "?").

Pattern matching between LSAs – which is at the basis of the triggering of eco-laws – happens when all the properties of a description match, i.e., when for each property whose names correspond (i.e., are semantically equivalent) the associated values match. As in classical tuple-based approaches, a formal

```
Agent AccessNoiseInformation {
    init() {
        injectLSA(sensor-type = noise; noise-level = "?");
    }
    onBond(LSA b) {
        float nl = b.noise-level();
        print("current level of noise = "+ nl);
}    }
```

**Fig. 2.** An agent that inject an LSA matching with that of the noise sensor and enables it to access the corresponding noise-level information

value matches with any corresponding actual value [11]. For instance, the LSA of the noise sensor in Figure 1 can match the following (sensor-type = noise; noise-level = ?), expressing a request for acquiring the current noise level. The properties in the first LSA (e.g., accuracy) are not taken into account by the matching function which considers only inclusive match. The basic reaction of the LSA-space in the presence of two matching LSAs is to bond them.

Bonding upon match is the primary form of interaction among co-located agents in SAPERE—i.e., within the same LSA-space. In particular, bonding can be used to locally discover and access information, as well as to get in touch with and access local services—all of which with a single and unique adaptive mechanism. Basically, the *bonding* eco-law implements a sort of a virtual link between LSAs, whenever two LSAs (or some SubDescriptions within) match, by connecting the respective formal and actual values in a sort of bidirectional and symmetric link: the two agents holding bond LSAs can read each other's LSAs, thus enabling exchange of information.

Thus, once a formal value of an LSA matches with an actual value in an LSA it is bound to, the corresponding agent can access the actual values associated with the formal ones. For instance, the AccessNoiseInformation agent in Figure 2 injects an LSA matching that of Figure 1, thus enabling AgentNoiseSensor in Figure 1 to access the corresponding noise level information.

Bonding is automatically triggered upon match—that is, the middleware looks for possible bonding upon any relevant change to the LSAs. Analogously, debonding takes place automatically whenever matching conditions no longer hold due to some changes to the actual "live" values of some LSAs.

### 3.3 From Bonding to Service Composition

The above example shows how to program SAPERE agents and, depending on the LSAs injected by such agents, how bonding takes place along with exchange of information. However, it is also possible to express a formal field with the syntax "!", to represent a field that is formal unless the other "?" field has been bond. This makes it possible for an LSA to express parameterised services, where

"?" represents the parameter of the service, and "!"field represents the answer that it is able to provide once it has been filled with the parameters.

It should be noted that the bonding eco-law mechanism can be used to enable two agents to spontaneously get in touch with each other and exchange information with a single operation—and, in the case of "!", automatically composing two components and have the first one automatically invoking the services of the second one. That is, unlike traditional discovery of data and services, bonding makes it possible to compose services without distinguishing between the roles of the involved agents, and subsuming the traditionally-separated phases of discovery and invocation.

## 3.4   Aggregation, Decay, and Spreading

The additional eco-laws of *aggregation*, *spreading*, and *decay* can be triggered by agents simply by injecting LSAs with specific properties.

The *aggregation* eco-law means to aggregate LSAs together so as to compute summaries of the current system context. An agent can inject an LSA with an *aggregate* and *type* properties. The *aggregate* property identifies a function to base the aggregation upon. The *type* property identifies which LSAs to aggregate. In particular, it identifies a numerical property of LSAs to be aggregated. In the current implementation, the aggregation eco-law is capable of performing most common order and duplicate insensitive (ODI) aggregation functions [16,17].

The *decay* eco-law enables the vanishing of components from the SAPERE environment: it applies to all LSAs that specify a decay property to update the remaining time to live according to the specific decay function, or actually removing LSAs that, based on their decay property, are expired. For instance, [sensor-type = noise; noise-level = 10; DECAY=1000], makes LSAs be automatically deleted after a second.

The *spreading* eco-law – unlike the two above that act on a single LSA space – enable non-local interactions, and specifically provides a mechanism to send information to remote LSA spaces, and make it possible to distribute information and results across LSA spaces. One of the primary usages of the spreading eco-law is to enable searches for components that are not available locally, and vice versa to enable the remote advertisement of services. For an LSA to be subject to the spread eco-law, it has to include a diffusion field, whose value (along with additional parameters) defines the specific type of propagation.

## 3.5   Towards Self-organisation Patterns

The eco-laws described above represent a necessary and complete to effectively support self-organising, nature-inspired interactions. In fact, by shaping LSAs so as to properly trigger eco-laws in a combined way, it is possible to realise a variety of self-adaptive and self-organising patterns.

For example, aggregation applied to the multiple copies of diffused LSAs can reduce the number of redundant LSAs so as to form a distributed *gradient* structure, also known as *computational force fields* [18]. As detailed in [19,12,13], many different classes of self-organised motion coordination schemes, self-assembly, and distributed navigation can be expressed in terms of gradients. By bringing also the decay eco-law into play, it is possible to build pheromone-based distributed data structures. Further examples can be found in [14].

## 4   Engineering SAPERE Systems: The Methodology

According to Osterweil [20] "software processes are software too": so, in order to build the SAPERE methodology, we follow a path that corresponds to the design of a software system. Thus, we first define the set of the SAPERE *methodology requirements* (Subsection 4.1); then we design the SAPERE *methodology process* (Subsection 4.2).

### 4.1   Requirements for the SAPERE Methodology

The first, obvious requirement is that the SAPERE methodology should support the design and development of SAPERE pervasive service ecosystems according to the above-mentioned meta-model (Subsection 2.2). From the analysis of the state-of-the-art in the Software Engineering area [21] the following methodology requirements can be pointed out:

- Due to the nature of the application domain, the more appealing process model is seemingly the *iterative model*, allowing engineers to iterate the different phases in order to obtain the best design.
- The SAPERE process should be organised in five main phases (*Requirements Analysis, Analysis, Architectural Design, Detailed Design*, and *Implementation*) in order to maintain the coherence with the general structure of standard design methodologies. This would make it easier understanding the methodology also for non-domain experts.
- The first two phases (Requirements Analysis, Analysis) should be very similar to the traditional analysis phases. On the one hand, this should make the adoption of the methodology easier to non-domain expert; on the other hand, it is generally understood that the analysis phase investigates the so called "problem domain", and the "problem" is not directly related to the technologies adopted for resolving it.
- The methodology should provide *specific activities* supporting the designer in the choice of architectural patterns and self-* mechanisms, in order to address the modelling of coordination and services. Coordination should be considered as an emergent property, so that a specific self-organising pattern could be chosen in order to obtain the required coordination goal.
- Since SAPERE deals with the investigation of self-aware pervasive ecosystems, the SAPERE methodology should deal with specific activities of simulation and validation in the Architectural Design phase. In particular, simulation should take inspiration from the existing related works such as [22,23], where a suite of activities such as "Exact Verification", "Simulation", and "Tuning" are already defined in a method fragment. However, the

SAPERE methodology should not adopt the proposed fragment *as is*, but should instead provide a specific version of the aforementioned activities— namely, "Exact Prediction", "Approximate Prediction", "Simulation", and "Tuning". Also, the methodology should provide specific activities for "Validation" and "Quantitative Measures" (respectively, in the Detailed Design and in the Implementation phases) which could provide engineers with effective data and information about the behaviour of the running system.

- From the meta-model point of view, taking inspiration from the work done in the AOSE field [21], the methodology meta-model should be created according to the *transformational structure* – i.e., each phase/domain should feature *its own set of abstractions* as in Model-Driven Engineering – for the sake of clarity, and to make it easier to move from one phase to another.
- The meta-model abstractions belonging to the Requirements Analysis and Analysis phases should come both from traditional problem analysis and from some AOSE methodologies where environment abstractions and environment topology are first-class abstractions. This allows the environment to be taken into account since the first phases of the process.
- The meta-model abstractions belonging to Architectural Design and Detailed Design should be created *ex-novo* drawing from the SAPERE meta-model described in Section 2. In particular, the work done in [8] about the chemical metaphor is very useful for the identification of the design abstractions.

### 4.2   The SAPERE Process

The SAPERE methodology is illustrated according to the IEEE-FIPA Standard Design Process Documentation Template (DPDT) [24], developed as an internationally-recognised standard in order to facilitate the understanding of the methodology, as well as the comparison with others. For the sake of brevity, in the following we outline just the main features of the SAPERE methodology.

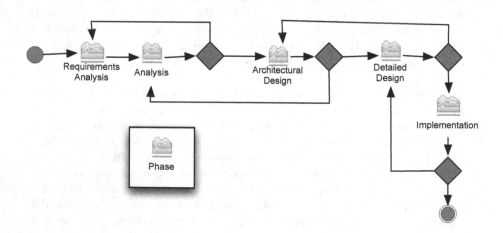

**Fig. 3.** The SAPERE methodology lifecycle

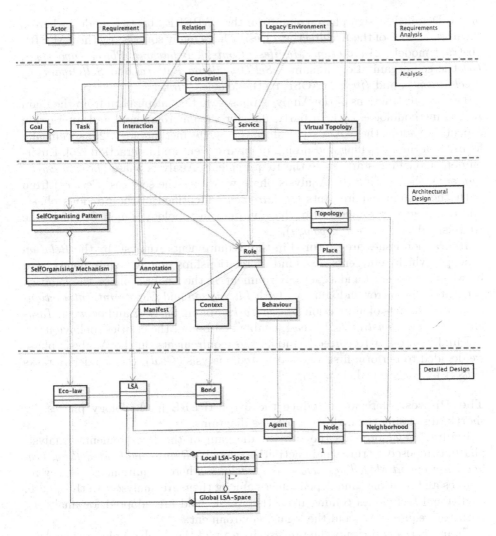

**Fig. 4.** The SAPERE methodology meta-model

**The Lifecycle.** The SAPERE methodology lifecycle is an iterative process composed by five main phases: Requirements Analysis, Analysis, Architectural Design, Detailed Design, and Implementation (Figure 3).

**The Meta-model.** The meta-model of the SAPERE methodology is reported in Figure 4. On the one hand, it complies with the transformational structure (see Subsection 4.1); on the other hand, it is organised in four different domains reflecting the first four methodology phases. Regarding the Implementation phase, a specific meta-model is not required here since the design abstractions have to be mapped onto the SAPERE middleware abstractions. Here we only report the ideas that inspired the meta-model construction. In particular, the abstractions of the Detailed Design phase come from the SAPERE abstract model, whereas the abstractions of the Architectural Design have many sources: *(i)* the SAPERE abstract model – *Annotation, Manifest, Context, Behaviour, Place, Topology* –, *(ii)* the self-organisation domain – *SelfOrganising Pattern*, and *SelfOrganising Mechanism* –, and *(iii)* the AOSE methodologies—*Role*.

For the abstractions of the Analysis phases we take inspiration from the main AOSE methodologies [21]. In particular, for the environmental and interaction aspects we adopt the SODA style, since the SODA methodology [25] specifically focuses on the modelling and design of environment and interaction [26]. Environment modelling starts since the Requirements Analysis phase (*Legacy Environment*), then during the Analysis phase we derive the services (*Service*) from both the system requirements (*Requirement*) identified in the previous phase, and from legacy resources. Also, the environment topology is modelled since the Analysis phase (*Virtual Topology*).

Interaction issues are captured in the Requirements Analysis by the *Relation* concept, which represents any kind of relationships among requirements, and between requirement and legacy environment. In the Analysis phase, the *Relation* generates – red arrow in Figure 4 – both *Interaction* and *Constraint*. *Interactions* represent the acts of interaction among *Tasks*, among *Services* and between *Tasks* and *Services*; *Constraints*, instead, enable and bound the entities' behaviour.

Finally, in order to correctly model the requirements, in the Analysis phase we decided to perform first a goal-oriented analysis (*Goal*), then to derive tasks (*Task*) by goals—as done in [27].

**The Phases.** Here we introduce the five SAPERE methodology phases, by shortly discussing the high-level process diagrams.

Figure 5*(left)* presents the process diagram of the Requirements Analysis phase, composed by three main activities, namely: *Requirements Modelling, Legacy Enviroment Modelling, Relations Modelling*. There, requirements, legacy resources and relations, and dependencies among them are analysed. In this phase, traditional techniques coming from the AOSE field are adopted for analysing both the requirements and the legacy environment.

Figure 5*(right)* presents the process diagram of the Analysis phase. The Analysis is composed by five main activities. In particular, *Goals Analysis* and *Task Analysis* lead the engineers to identify firstly the system's goals and then the tasks necessary to accomplish them. *Services Analysis* is devoted to derive and to analyse the system's services coming both from the legacy environment and from the system's requirements, while *Virtual Topology Analysis* analyses the system's environment topology. Finally, *Interactions Analysis* and *Constraints Analysis* respectively accounts for the interactions among system's entities and the possible constraints about entities behaviours, or about the system environment.

Figure 6 presents the process diagram of the Architectural Design phase. This phase is composed by nine main activities, namely: *Topologies Design, SelfOrganisations Design, Roles Design, Context Awareness Design, Models Extraction, Exact Prediction, Approximate Prediction, Simulation*, and *Tuning*. The process

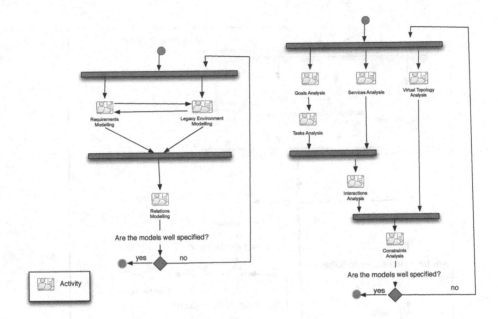

**Fig. 5.** Requirements Analysis *(left)* and Analysis *(right)* activities diagrams

here is more complex since the system, following problem analysis, have to be designed according to the SAPERE approach. In particular, the first four activities – *Topologies Design, SelfOrganisations Design, Roles Design, Context Awareness Design* – define the models for system roles (their behaviours and interactions), the self-organisation mechanisms for the services identified in the analysis, the requisite context or situation recognition in terms of roles and their communications, and the topological structure of the environment. Then, taking inspiration from [22,23], we design five activities (*Models Extraction, Exact Prediction, Approximate Prediction, Simulation,* and *Tuning*) devoted to system prediction and simulation. Thus, the effect of the architectural design on the system behaviour could be verified through the study of emerging properties. Adopting simulation during architectural design makes it possible for engineers the early discovery of problems due to either unsatisfactory architectural choice or inaccurate problem analysis.

Figure 7*(left)* presents the process diagram of the Detailed Design phase. This phase is composed by five main activities, namely: *Eco-Laws Design, Agents Design, Neighbourhood Design, Bonds Design, Validation.* The first four activities are devoted to the detailed design of system according to the SAPERE abstract model, while *Validation* allows engineers to effectively validate the behaviour of the whole system entities before starting the implementation phase.

Finally, Figure 7*(right)* presents the process diagram of the Implementation phase. This phase is composed by six main activities, namely: *Middleware Adaptation, Coding, WhiteBox Testing, BlackBox Testing, SystemTesting,* and *Quantitative Measures. Middleware Adaptation* plays a key role in this phase since in

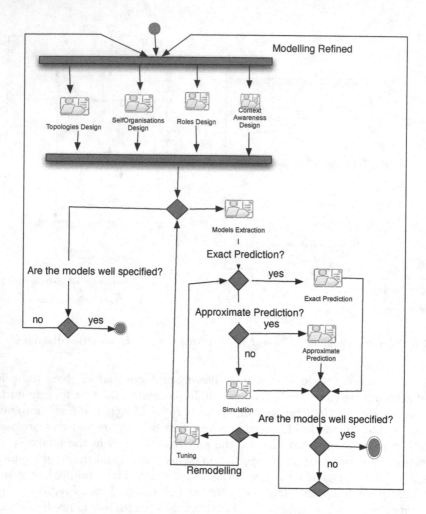

**Fig. 6.** The Architectural Design activities diagram

this activity the detailed design entities have to be mapped onto the middle-ware entities. This activity should be "trivial" – i.e., one-to-one mapping – if the middleware totally supports the detailed design entities, otherwise it could be very complex and require a lot of re-engineering work, such as the ex-novo creation of ad hoc self-organisation mechanisms. Then, *Coding* has to start before *WhiteBox Testing* and *BlackBox Testing*, but after that their executions could be interleaved. *WhiteBox Testing* represents the classical test activity conducted by the system developers during the implementation, while *BlackBox Testing* is conducted by team members not directly involved in the development of the system part under test. *SystemTesting* represents the test of the whole system for evaluating the system requirements satisfaction accuracy. Only when the system developing is concluded it is possible to execute specific Quantitative Measures – *Quantitative Measures* activity – for measuring system performances.

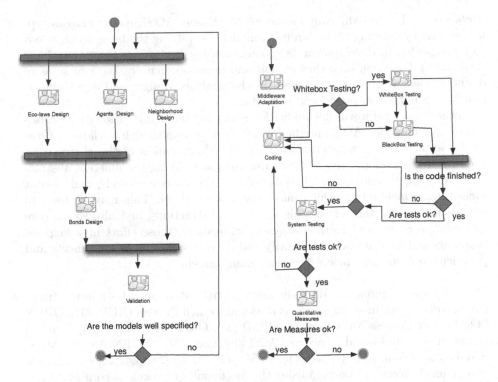

**Fig. 7.** The Detailed Design *(left)* and Implementation *(right)* activities diagram

# 5    Related Works in the AOSE Field

As far as software engineering is concerned, the key implication is that the design and development of software systems according to a (new) paradigm can by no means rely on conceptual tools and methodologies conceived for a totally-different (old) paradigm [28]. Even though it is indeed possible to develop a complex distributed system in terms of objects and client-server interactions, such a choice appears odd and complicated when the system is a Multi-Agent System (MAS), or, it can be assimilated to a MAS. Rather, a brand new set of conceptual and practical tools – specifically suited to the agent-oriented abstractions – is needed to facilitate, promote, and support the development of MASs, and to fulfil the huge potential of agent-based computing as a general-purpose approach to the modelling and engineering of complex systems.

The definition of agent-specific methodologies is definitely one of the most explored topics in Agent-Oriented Software Engineering (AOSE), and a large number of AOSE methodologies – describing how the process of building a MAS should/could be organised – has been proposed in the literature, which should be compared to the SAPERE approach presented in this paper. For a rather exhaustive survey of all the related activities in the AOSE field, we refer the interested reader to [21].

*Meta-model.* In the same way as the SAPERE one, AOSE methodologies typically start by defining their own meta-model, identifying the basic abstractions to be exploited in development (e.g., agents, roles, environment, organisational structures). Based on this, they exploit and organise such abstractions so as to define guidelines on how to proceed in the analysis, design, and development, and on the output to produce at each stage.

Actually, several works [29,30] are focussing on the identification of appropriate meta-models for AOSE methodologies and process models—where a meta-model is intended as a rational analysis and identification of the abstractions used in MAS development. Those efforts aims at unifying the different abstractions adopted in existing methodologies and the process models, and also at identifying which relationships may exist among them. This may be used to better understand the real usefulness of the abstractions, and also to improve or unify processes and methodologies. Furthermore, those effort may help researchers and practitioners to identify and develop conceptual instruments and practical tools for an efficient processes management.

*Process model.* Among the different methodologies developed both in the traditional software engineering – such as Rational Unified Process (RUP) [31], OPEN [32], Object Process Methodology (OPM) [33], OMT [34], Fusion [35] – and in the agent-oriented world – such as PASSI [36], Gaia [37], INGENIAS [38], MESSAGE [39], Adelfe [40], Tropos [41], MaSE [42], SODA [25,43,44,45] etc. –, there is a general agreement on organising the methodology process according to two main phases: Analysis and Design. However, the different methodologies often introduce other phases or sub-phases. In particular, the Analysis phase is typically split into Requirements Analaysis and Analysis, while the Design is typically organised in terms of Architectural Design and Detailed Design [46]. In addition, different methodologies guide the system development until the implementation phase—among them RUP, OPEN, PASSI, INGENIAS, and ADELFE.

As discussed in Subsection 4.2, according to the general agreement on the main phases of a development process, the SAPERE methodology is organised in five main phases: Requirements Analysis, Analysis, Architectural Design, Detailed Design, and Implementation.

*Meta-model vs. process model.* Quite different and heterogeneous abstractions are adopted by the different methodologies for modelling complex MAS: typically, in the AOSE world, each methodology defines its own set of abstractions. This is why AOSE methodologies typically start by providing the so-called *abstractions meta-model* [30,47] that shows all the abstractions adopted by the methodology, along with their mutual relationships.

Names for abstractions are used quite liberally: different names sometimes refer to similar abstractions, whereas identical names may denote quite diverse abstractions—even within one single methodology, when the same name is sometimes used for abstractions holding different meanings, depending on the different process phases they belong to. For instance, the "agent" concept, quite unsurprisingly, is exploited by all AOSE methodologies. However, whereas in some methodologies – such as PASSI, MaSE, and ADELFE – the agent abstraction appears since the Analysis phase, in other methodologies – such as Tropos, Gaia, and SODA – the agent is a concept occurring only in the Design phases. So, the issue is not merely which abstractions meta-model is adopted by a given AOSE methodology: but, more precisely, which abstractions are used in each phase of the methodology, and how the different resulting abstractions meta-models relate to each other.

Even more, also the structure of the abstractions meta-model differs a lot among the methodologies. For example, PASSI and SODA adopt a "transformational" structure – i.e., each phase/domain has its own particular set of abstractions – taking inspiration from the Model-Driven Engineering ideas. Instead, other methodologies such as ADELFE use the same set of abstractions, which are refined by each phase. For a more detailed work about the study, comparison, and fusion of some AOSE methodologies meta-models, we refer the interested reader to [27].

Taking inspiration from the work done in the AOSE field, the SAPERE methodology meta-model was in fact defined according to the transformational structure: this allow each phase to be more clearly specified, and makes it easier to move from one phase to another—see Subsection 2.2.

# 6    Conclusion

The definition of a novel and coherent methodological process for the engineering of SAPERE pervasive service ecosystems was the main motivation behind this work. In order to allow the reader to fully understand the SAPERE process, in this paper we first introduce the SAPERE model, then discuss how a SAPERE system could be programmed, by providing some simple examples, finally we illustrate the SAPERE methodology, by defining the software development process according to the IEEE-FIPA Standard Design Process Documentation Template (DPDT) [24].

The space available for this paper is obviously not enough to provide the reader with all the details of the SAPERE methodology: for a full account of the SAPERE methodology we refer the interested reader to [48]. In this paper we discuss the main issues of the engineering of pervasive service ecosystems according to the SAPERE approach, thus showing how agent-oriented technologies and methodologies can be effective in the design and development of complex software systems.

**Acknowledgements.** This work has been supported by the EU-FP7-FET Proactive project SAPERE – Self-Aware PERvasive service Ecosystems, under contract no. 256873.

# References

1. Krumm, J.: Ubiquitous advertising: The killer application for the 21st century. IEEE Pervasive Computing 10(1), 66–73 (2011)
2. Zambonelli, F.: Toward sociotechnical urban superorganisms. Computer 47(8), 76–78 (2012)
3. Zambonelli, F.: Pervasive urban crowdsourcing: Visions and challenges. In: 2011 IEEE International Conference on Pervasive Computing and Communications Workshops (PERCOM Workshops), pp. 578–583. IEEE CS Press (2011)
4. Zambonelli, F., Viroli, M.: A survey on nature-inspired metaphors for pervasive service ecosystems. International Journal of Pervasive Computing and Communications 7(3), 186–204 (2011)
5. Babaoglu, O., et al.: Design patterns from biology for distributed computing. ACM Transaction on Autonomous Adaptive Systems 1(1), 26–66 (2006)
6. Mamei, M., Menezes, R., Tolksdorf, R., Zambonelli, F.: Case studies for self-organization in computer science. Journal of Systems Architecture 52(8), 443–460 (2006)
7. Kari, L., Rozenberg, G.: The many facets of natural computing. Communications of the ACM 51, 72–83 (2008)
8. Zambonelli, F., Castelli, G., Ferrari, L., Mamei, M., Rosi, A., Di Marzo Serugendo, G., Risoldi, M., Tchao, A.E., Dobson, S., Stevenson, G., Ye, Y., Nardini, E., Omicini, A., Montagna, S., Viroli, M., Ferscha, A., Maschek, S., Wally, B.: Self-aware pervasive service ecosystems. Procedia Computer Science 7, 197–199 (2011), Proceedings of the 2nd European Future Technologies Conference and Exhibition 2011 (FET 2011)
9. Parunak, V.: Go to the ant: Engineering principles from natural multi-agent systems. Annals of Operations Research 75, 69–101 (1997)
10. Omicini, A.: Nature-inspired coordination for complex distributed systems. In: Fortino, G., Badica, C., Malgeri, M., Unland, R. (eds.) Intelligent Distributed Computing VI. SCI, vol. 446, pp. 1–6. Springer, Heidelberg (2012)
11. Gelernter, D.: Generative communication in Linda. ACM Transactions on Programming Languages and Systems 7(1), 80–112 (1985)
12. Mamei, M., Zambonelli, F.: Programming pervasive and mobile computing applications: The TOTA approach. ACM Transactions on Software Engineering and Methodology 18(4) (July 2009)
13. Viroli, M., Casadei, M., Montagna, S., Zambonelli, F.: Spatial coordination of pervasive services through chemical-inspired tuple spaces. ACM Transactions on Autonomous and Adaptive Systems 6(2), 14:1–14:24 (June 2011)
14. Fernandez-Marquez, J.L., Di Marzo Serugendo, G., Montagna, S., Viroli, M., Arcos, J.L.: Description and composition of bio-inspired design patterns: A complete overview. Natural Computing 12(1), 43–67 (2013)
15. Zambonelli, F., Castelli, G., Mamei, M., Rosi, A.: Integrating pervasive middleware with social networks in sapere. In: 2011 International Conference on Selected Topics in Mobile and Wireless Networking, pp. 145–150 (October 2011)
16. Nath, S., Gibbons, P.B., Seshan, S., Anderson, Z.R.: Synopsis diffusion for robust aggregation in sensor networks. In: 2nd International Conference on Embedded Networked Sensor Systems (SenSys 2004), pp. 250–262. ACM, New York (2004)
17. Bicocchi, N., Mamei, M., Zambonelli, F.: Self-organizing virtual macro sensors. ACM Transaction on Autonomous Adaptive Systems 7(1) (2012)

18. Mamei, M., Zambonelli, F.: Field-Based Coordination for Pervasive Multiagent Systems. In: Models, Technologies, and Applications. Springer Series in Agent Technology. Springer (March 2006)
19. Beal, J., Bachrach, J.: Infrastructure for engineered emergence on sensor/actuator networks. IEEE Intelligent Systems 21(2), 10–19 (2006)
20. Osterweil, L.J.: Software processes are software too. In: 9th International Conference on Software Engineering (ICSE 1987), pp. 2–13. IEEE Computer Society Press, Los Alamitos (1987)
21. Molesini, A., Omicini, A.: Early methodology. Technical Report TR.WP1.2012.6, EU-FP7-FET Proactive project SAPERE Self-Aware PERvasive service Ecosystems (2012), http://www.sapere-project.eu/TR.WP1.2012.6.pdf
22. Gardelli, L., Viroli, M., Casadei, M., Omicini, A.: Designing self-organising environments with agents and artefacts: A simulation-driven approach. International Journal of Agent-Oriented Software Engineering 2(2), 171–195 (2008), Special Issue on Multi-Agent Systems and Simulation
23. Molesini, A., Casadei, M., Omicini, A., Viroli, M.: Simulation in agent-oriented software engineering: The SODA case study. Science of Computer Programming (August 2011), Special Issue on Agent-oriented Design methods and Programming Techniques for Distributed Computing in Dynamic and Complex Environments
24. IEEE-FIPA: Design Process Documentation Template (January 2012), http://fipa.org/specs/fipa00097/SC00097B.pdf
25. SODA: Home page, http://soda.apice.unibo.it
26. Molesini, A., Omicini, A., Viroli, M.: Environment in Agent-Oriented Software Engineering methodologies. Multiagent and Grid Systems 5(1), 37–57 (2009), Special Issue "Engineering Environments in Multi-Agent Systems"
27. Dalpiaz, F., Molesini, A., Puviani, M., Seidita, V.: Towards filling the gap between AOSE methodologies and infrastructures: Requirements and meta-model. In: Baldoni, M., Cossentino, M., De Paoli, F., Seidita, V. (eds.) 9th Workshop From Objects to Agents (WOA 2008), Palermo, Italy, Seneca Edizioni, pp. 115–121 (November 2008)
28. Zambonelli, F., Omicini, A.: Challenges and research directions in agent-oriented software engineering. Autonomous Agents and Multi-Agent Systems 9(3), 253–283 (2004), Special Issue: Challenges for Agent-Based Computing
29. Henderson-Sellers, B.: Evaluating the feasibility of method engineering for the creation of agent-oriented methodologies. In: Pěchouček, M., Petta, P., Varga, L.Z. (eds.) CEEMAS 2005. LNCS (LNAI), vol. 3690, pp. 142–152. Springer, Heidelberg (2005)
30. Bernon, C., Cossentino, M., Gleizes, M.P., Turci, P., Zambonelli, F.: A study of some multi-agent meta-models. In: Odell, J.J., Giorgini, P., Müller, J.P. (eds.) AOSE 2004. LNCS, vol. 3382, pp. 62–77. Springer, Heidelberg (2005)
31. Kruchten, P.: The Rational Unified Process: An Introduction, 3rd edn. Addison-Wesley Professional (December 2003)
32. OPEN: Home page, http://www.open.org.au/
33. Dori, D.: Object-Process Methodology: A Holistic System Paradigm. Springer (2002)
34. Rumbaugh, J.E., Blaha, M.R., Premerlani, W.J., Eddy, F., Lorensen, W.E.: Object-Oriented Modeling and Design. Prentice-Hall (1991)
35. Coleman, D., Arnold, P., Bodoff, S., Dollin, C., Gilchrist, H., Hayes, F., Jeremaes, P.: Object-Oriented Development. The Fusion Method. Prentice-Hall (1994)
36. Cossentino, M.: From requirements to code with the PASSI methodology. In: [49], ch. IV, pp. 79–106

37. Zambonelli, F., Jennings, N., Wooldridge, M.: Multiagent systems as computational organizations: the Gaia methodology. In: [49], ch. VI, pp. 136–171
38. Pavòn, J., Gòmez-Sanz, J.J., Fuentes, R.: The INGENIAS methodology and tools. In: [49], ch. IX, pp. 236–276
39. Garijo, F.J., Gòmez-Sanz, J.J., Massonet, P.: The MESSAGE methodology for agent-oriented analysis and design. In: [49], ch. VIII, pp. 203–235
40. Picard, G., Bernon, C., Gleizes, M.P.: Cooperative agent model within ADELFE framework: An application to a timetabling problem. In: Jennings, N.R., Sierra, C., Sonenberg, L., Tambe, M. (eds.) AAMAS,, July 19-23, vol. 3, pp. 1506–1507. ACM Press, New York (2004)
41. Bresciani, P., Giorgini, P., Giunchiglia, F., Mylopoulos, J., Perini, A.: Tropos: An agent-oriented software development methodology. Autonomous Agent and Multi-Agent Systems 8(3), 203–236 (2004)
42. Wood, M.F., DeLoach, S.A.: An overview of the multiagent systems engineering methodology. In: Ciancarini, P., Wooldridge, M.J. (eds.) AOSE 2000. LNCS, vol. 1957, pp. 207–221. Springer, Heidelberg (2001)
43. Omicini, A.: SODA: Societies and infrastructures in the analysis and design of agent-based systems. In: Ciancarini, P., Wooldridge, M.J. (eds.) AOSE 2000. LNCS, vol. 1957, pp. 185–193. Springer, Heidelberg (2001)
44. Molesini, A., Omicini, A., Ricci, A., Denti, E.: Zooming multi-agent systems. In: Müller, J.P., Zambonelli, F. (eds.) AOSE 2005. LNCS, vol. 3950, pp. 81–93. Springer, Heidelberg (2006)
45. Molesini, A., Omicini, A., Denti, E., Ricci, A.: SODA: A roadmap to artefacts. In: Dikenelli, O., Gleizes, M.-P., Ricci, A. (eds.) ESAW 2005. LNCS (LNAI), vol. 3963, pp. 49–62. Springer, Heidelberg (2006)
46. Cernuzzi, L., Cossentino, M., Zambonelli, F.: Process models for agent-based development. Engineering Applications of Artificial Intelligence 18(2), 205–222 (2005)
47. Cossentino, M., Gaglio, S., Galland, S., Gaud, N., Hilaire, V., Koukam, A., Seidita, V.: A MAS metamodel-driven approach to process fragments selection. In: Luck, M., Gomez-Sanz, J.J. (eds.) AOSE 2008. LNCS, vol. 5386, pp. 86–100. Springer, Heidelberg (2009)
48. Molesini, A., Omicini, A., Viroli, M., Pianini, D., Montagna, S.: The complete methodology. Technical Report TR.WP1.2013.1, EU-FP7-FET Proactive project. SAPERE Self-Aware PERvasive service Ecosystems (2013), http://www.sapere-project.eu/TR.WP1.2013.1.pdf
49. Henderson-Sellers, B., Giorgini, P. (eds.): Agent Oriented Methodologies. Idea Group Publishing, Hershey (2005)

# An Infrastructure
# for the Design and Development
# of Open Interaction Systems

Daniel Okouya[1], Nicoletta Fornara[1], and Marco Colombetti[1,2]

[1] Università della Svizzera Italiana,
via G. Buffi 13, 6900 Lugano, Swizterland
{daniel.okouya,nicoletta.fornara,marco.colombetti}@usi.ch
[2] Politecnico di Milano,
Piazza Leonardo da Vinci 32, 20135 Milano, Italy
marco.colombetti@polimi.it

**Abstract.** We propose an infrastructure for the design and development
of Open Interaction Systems (OISs), based on solutions from Service
Oriented Architecture, Semantic Technologies, and Normative Multiagent Systems. OISs are open to diverse types of participants (software
agents), and enable them to interact with each other to achieve their objectives. To do so the participants are allowed to interact in compliance
with previously agreed-upon regulations provided by the system and on
the basis of the semantics of the communicative acts performed, both of
which are enforced by the system. The infrastructure we propose, based
on the OCeAN metamodel of Artificial Institutions, involves four layers:
(i), the Messaging Layer, which enables observable ACL message exchanges between heterogeneous participants while respecting ownership
boundaries; (ii), the Core Service Layer, which enables the participants
to perform observable non-communicative actions relevant to the ongoing
application; (iii), the Bridging Layer, in charge of interpreting the participants' actions in a form suitable for regulation; and (iv), the Regulation
Layer, which holds the regulations and enforces them with respect to the
participants' activities.

**Keywords:** Open Interaction System, Artificial Institution, Ontology,
Normative System, Agent Communication.

# 1 Introduction

Open Interaction Systems (OISs) are distributed systems which diverse types
of participants (i.e., software agents) can freely join with the goal of interacting
with each other to achieve their personal objectives. To do so the participants
are allowed to interact by exchanging messages with rigorously defined syntax
and semantics, in compliance with previously agreed-upon norms provided by
the system; both the norms and the syntax and semantics of the communication
language are enforced by the system.

M. Cossentino et al. (Eds.): EMAS 2013, LNAI 8245, pp. 215–234, 2013.

In our past work we have proposed the OCeAN metamodel [13] for the specification of OISs. In this paper we describe an infrastructure, currently under development, for the actual implementation of such systems. In designing this infrastructure we aim at guaranteeing openness and interoperability, while exploiting as far as possible technologies that are sufficiently mature and stable, and are already adopted by a large industrial community. Among such technologies we include standard Service Oriented Technologies [5] and Semantic Web Technologies [15].

The infrastructure we propose involves four layers: (i), the *Messaging Layer*, which enables heterogeneous participants to interact with each other through communicative actions while respecting ownership boundaries; (ii), the *Core Service Layer*, which allows the participants to exploit the support services offered by the OIS to perform non-communicative actions; (iii), the *Bridging Layer*, in charge of interpreting the participants' actions in a form suitable for regulation; and (iv), the *Regulation Layer*, which holds the norms regulating the interactions and enforces them relative to the participants' actions. More specifically:

- The Messaging Layer provides a Messaging Protocol based on standard technologies (HTTP, SOAP, WSDL) and uses Web Service Technologies for the transfer of messages between participants, by prescribing the use of a specific message transfer service exposed via WSDL; messages realize communicative or institutional acts and comply with OCeAN-ACL [11], an Agent Communication Language based on Semantic Web Technologies, and on OWL 2 DL in particular.
- The Core Service Layer makes certain complementary services available to the participants (e.g., an OIS realizing an e-marketplace may offer services related to payment, product delivery, and so on), and thus allows them to perform observable non-communicative actions relevant to the ongoing interaction.
- The Bridging Layer interprets the participants' communicative and non-communicative actions in a form suitable for regulation; coherently with the OCeAN metamodel, such actions either result into commitments (like in the case of acts of informing, requesting, etc.) or are regarded as attempts to perform institutional actions relying on suitable *count-as* rules.
- Finally, the Regulation Layer realizes a normative context (again according to the OCeAN metamodel), that is, a set of artificial institutions specifying the institutional actions that can be performed and the set of norms that have to be followed.

In this paper we provide a detailed specification of all layers and describe the implementation, currently under development, of an infrastructure oriented to the implementation of an open e-marketplace. A graphical representation of the layered architecture is given in Figure 1; the components, the ontologies, and the relationships among the components shown in the figure will be explained in the sections describing the corresponding layers. The paper is organized as follows. In Section 2 we describe the functionalities pertaining to the Messaging

Layer and how we implement them by exploiting standard Web Service Technology. In Section 3 we briefly sketch how the core services offered by the OIS can be actually realized, considering an e-marketplace as an example. In Section 4 we describe the functionalities pertaining to the Regulation Layer and how we implement them by exploiting Semantic Web Technologies, and OWL ontologies in particular. In Section 5 we explain how relevant events taking place at either the Messaging or the Core Service Layer are made available to the Regulation Layer. In Section 6 we review some related works. Finally in Section 7 we draw some conclusions and briefly describe our plans for future work.

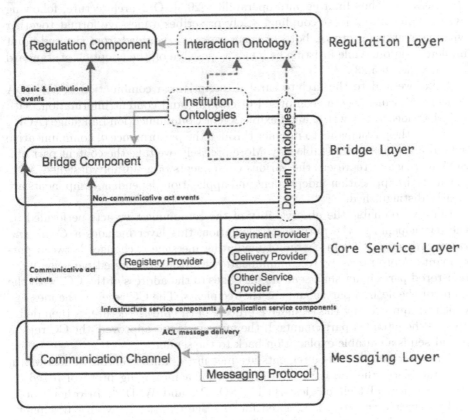

**Fig. 1.** An Architecture for Open Interation Systems

## 2 The Messaging Layer

In an OIS, a large part of the participants' interactions is carried out through the exchange of suitable messages. Therefore the bottom layer of our infrastructure provides the means to enable heterogeneous participants to interact with each other by exchanging messages in a fully interoperable fashion. In addition, it does so in such a way that it ensures the observability of these interactions, to the purpose of regulation.

To this end our infrastructure integrates principles from Service Oriented Architecture (SOA) and from Multiagent Systems (MAS). First, a message transfer approach is prescribed that is neutral to the internals of the participants, and leverages standard technologies to facilitate widespread adoption. This is in contrast with approaches based on some of the most well known ready-to-use messaging technologies like JMS[1], RMI[2], and CORBA [18], which bind either to a particular programing language [14] or to a programing language paradigm [18]. Such approaches do not fully decouple the end-point implementation from the messages, thus limiting interoperability [20,3]. Our architecture, following SOA's principles of loose coupling, solely prescribes a message format together with its transfer protocol, both of them strictly decoupled from the end-point implementation, while insisting as much as possible on the adoption of standard technologies [6,5,23].

Next, we add to the architectural prescriptions a combination of the SOA concept of a message, as comprised of carrying and content information, with the MAS idea of a powerful and flexible Agent Communication Language (ACL), to enable the participants to interact through the performance of communicative acts in a totally interoperable way. More precisely, we take the content part of a SOA message to represent the various components of a suitably designed ACL, in which the application-independent and application-dependent components are clearly distinguished.

Finally, to enable the observability of the communicative acts performed by the participants to the purpose of regulation, this layer includes a *Communication Channel* (CC) in charge of mediating message exchanges between participants. More precisely, to communicate with other registered participants, a registered participant shall send its messages to the address of the CC, with the name of the desired participants as the recipients. The CC receives the message which, if approved by the regulative process of the infrastructure, is then delivered to the intended participants. If the message is not approved, the CC rejects it and sends a suitable explanation back to the sender.

These architectural requirements are met in the infrastructure as follows. In the first place, the infrastructure provides for a messaging protocol based on standard neutral technologies: HTTP, SOAP[3], and WSDL[4]. In other words, Web Service Technology is adopted for message transfer between participants, by specifying a message transfer service, exposed via WSDL, in which HTTP is used for the transport of messages and SOAP for their structure. Our choice is motivated by the fact that this technology represents a standard approach for making available over the network functionalities that are triggered or delivered by exchanging messages.

---

[1] http://docs.oracle.com/javaee/6/tutorial/doc/bncdr.html
[2] http://docs.oracle.com/javase/7/docs/technotes/guides/rmi/index.html
[3] http://www.w3.org/TR/soap
[4] http://www.w3.org/TR/wsdl

In the second place, the infrastructure implements the messages of our ACL[5] as the body of SOAP messages. From the syntactic point of view, the ACL we propose is very close to KQML[6] and FIPA ACL[7], from which however it substantially departs as far as semantics is concerned (see Section 5). As with FIPA standards, our ACL comes with a separate Content Language (CL). Our CL is defined as an OWL Ontology, the *Content Language Ontology* [11], which plays a role similar to FIPA-RDF in FIPA ACL.

Thus, realizing the first two requirements, we define a WSDL file with only one service, which is the delivery of an ACL message, carried in the body of a SOAP message. The WSDL contract represents all message forms that can be exchanged between entities of our OIS, with the requirement that the message contains the address to reply to according to the same contract. Communication between participants is only allowed through the use of this service; consequently, all participants are required to be equipped with a suitable communication module, composed of: (i), a *listening point*, that is, a web-service provider exposing a message delivery service defined according to our WSDL contract; and (ii), a *talking point*, that is, a web-service client that requests the delivery of a message in conformance with that contract [10].

A crucial advantage of this approach is the provision of a messaging protocol in the form of a WSDL contract, which is both human readable and machine processable. Such a contract can be easily handled with the support of runtime frameworks coming along with Web Service Technology, such as Apache CXF [1,16]. We use CXF to automatically generate the core of the communication module of the participating component of our infrastructure; hence anyone can easily generate the necessary facilities to handle the transmission of messages abiding to the exposed messaging protocol and adapt it to their need, in order to participate in the OIS.

Finally, to deal with message transfer the infrastructure provides an implementation of the CC as a Java component, developed with CXF as exposed above.

## 3   The Core Service Layer

As we have already remarked, in an OIS a large part of the participants' interactions is carried out by exchanging suitable messages; as required by the Messaging Layer, in our infrastructure such messages are always ACL messages realizing communicative acts. However, most types of applications will also require the execution of actions that are not strictly speaking communicative. We identify these actions as *non-communicative acts* and classify them into two categories: first, non-communicative acts concerning the interaction between the participants and certain components of the infrastructure, designed to provide support to the participants' activities (as we shall see, these non-communicative acts are typically

---

[5] http://www.people.lu.unisi.ch/okouyad/AclOverSoapHttpMP.wsdl

[6] http://www.csee.umbc.edu/csee/research/kqml/

[7] http://www.fipa.org/repository/aclspecs.html

application independent); second, application-specific non-communicative acts concerning the interaction between participants.

More specifically, on the one hand some of the application-independent non-communicative acts are intended to support the enforcement of ownership boundaries between participants, enabling them to connect with each other without introducing dependencies. For example, the infrastructure provides for a Registry component (see below), through which the participants can register or deregister by performing suitable actions. Although the registration and deregistration processes do require the performance of certain communicative acts (more precisely, of the request to be registered or deregistered), the actions of registering or deregistering a participant are not themselves communicative; rather, they are non-communicative actions made available to the participants by the infrastructure, through the provision of services that may be invoked using communicative acts (requests). On the other hand, some of the application-specific activities (i.e., some of the activities that are carried out between the participants) may require the performance of application-specific non-communicative actions which, as in the case of communicative acts, must be made observable to the infrastructure. In an e-marketplace system, for example, when engaging in a purchasing activity, after settling a contract by performing suitable communicative acts, the buyer may be required to carry out a payment, while the seller may be required to deliver a product. Both of these are non-communicative actions inherent to the purchasing activity, and as such must also be visible to the infrastructure.

To sum up, the objective of this layer is to equip the infrastructure so that: (i), it enables the participants with performing all the infrastructure-specific non-communicative actions belonging to the direct interactions between the participants and the infrastructure itself; and (ii), it can observe the performance of the application-specific non-communicative actions inherent to some of the activities occurring between the participants. In order to achieve these goals our infrastructure requires that the participant register to the IOS; to this end it provides a Registry component, implemented in Java, to serve as a White Pages Service. The Registry provides, among others, for the *registering* and *deregistering* actions; as this component is endowed with ACL-processing capabilities, the participants can request its services using ACL messages.

In unison with the approach used for the communicative acts (i.e., that the actions occurring between the participants are mediated by the infrastructure), the infrastructure can also mediate the non-communicative actions that are application-specific. In this respect, however, the Core Service Layer proceeds differently than the Messaging Layer. Indeed, the different communicative actions that can be performed by the participants are the same across applications; thus, the observation process necessary to handle them is also application-independent, and therefore can be achieved by a generic component (the Communication Channel). In contrast, non-communicative acts occurring between participants are typically application dependent: their presence, what they achieve, and how they achieve it, always depend on the application being realized. Therefore unlike communicative acts that are always available to the participants, the presence of non-communicative actions is application-specific; for instance, the availability of a shipping action could be irrelevant for certain applications, such as an e-market for computational services. Moreover, when present the performance of non-communicative acts can substantially vary depending on the requirements of the applicatios in which they are performed. In the case of a payment, for instance, while one application may require a system like PayPal, another one may require a direct bank-to-bank transfer or a cheque payment, which would need to go through different steps and to supply different information. Another important difference is that, unlike communicative acts, non-communicative actions can also vary in nature, that is, they can be electronic, physical, or involve both aspects.

Hence, to mediate non-communicative actions the infrastructure must take into account their fundamental application-oriented features, as well as the fact that they can involve any combination of physical and electronic aspects. To achieve this, our architecture prescribes that the Core Service Layer provides for the incorporation of observable application-specific components, offering to the participants specific services of mediation for application-specific, non-communicative actions. These components must be such that they seemingly interoperate with the participants for the invocation of the actions that they mediate, whose performances must be observable by the infrastructure.

To this purpose, on the one hand this layer specifies the interfaces of the mediating components, so that the relevant parts of the infrastructure can take into account the performance of the non-communicative actions they are in charge of; on the other hand, it prescribes the characteristics that the components must posses so that their services can be seemingly consumed. In support of that latter point, the layer mandates the use of communicative acts to invoke the mediation services; that is, theses services are invoked using ACL messages, which brings the advantage of providing a unique invocation protocol, independently of the nature and level of complexity of the services. Of course, this implies that the mediating components must be able to process certain ACL messages. This contrasts with the message-transfer mediation service provided by the Communication Channel, which is invoked using a SOAP message (as a typical web-service).

Meanwhile, it is important to remark that our infrastructure does not require that the mediating components directly perform the non-communicative actions they supply: indeed they may do so, or guarantee that they are performed by certain external systems, or simply acknowledge their external realization when so informed by a group of participants who have agreed to exploit an external service. In this regard, the layer classifies theses services into two distinct categories: *internal services* and *external services*. In the former case, the service is internally managed by the component itself; this means that when requested by a participant, the component takes charge of the execution of the activities involved in the service. In the latter case, which represent a very decentralized approach providing more freedom to the participants, the execution is guaranteed by the participants themselves, which then inform the infrastructure of the results. Here mediation plays the role of a neutral authority that acknowledges the realization of services taking place out of its direct control, according to the specific rules governing the application.

## 4    The Regulation Layer

Once heterogeneous participants, possibly belonging to different owners, can interact with each other as exposed above, it is necessary that they get provided with some form of harnessing framework defining norms that regulate their interactions. This is particularly important as it allows the participants to have reasonable expectations with respect to the interactions they engage in order to achieve their objectives. Moreover given that we target systems as e-marketplaces, taking in account the sensitive nature of their activities, the architecture prescribes the realization of a neutral third-party component in charge of analyzing the participants' interactions (by using the information received by the Bridging Layer as described in Section 5), with the aim of monitoring the evolution of the interaction and specifying and enforcing the norms of the regulating context.

To realize all these functionalities we introduce in the proposed architecture the *Regulation Layer*. This is based on the OCeAN metamodel [12], in which regulating contexts are defined as *artificial institutions* that provide a high-level representation of a specific set of institutional actions together with the norms that govern them, and of the institutional objects that need to be observed to monitor the evolution of the state of the interactions. For every specific application, such institutions are operationalized by grounding them in the current domain [13,8].

The Regulation Layer must possess a formal representation of the state of the interaction suitable to carry out automated reasoning. In particular this representation has to include specifications of: (i), the regulating context in force; (ii), the types of events and actions the application is dealing with; (iii), the application-independent and application-dependent knowledge defining the relevant objects and their states during the interaction; and (iv), the instances of the institutional actions and events that actually take place in the system. Reasoning will then allow the system to monitor the evolution of the state of the interaction, detecting in particular norm fulfillments and violations.

Our infrastructure meets these requirements in the following way. We define our regulating context as an OCeAN artificial institution. The first regulating context we have operationalized so far is the *Commitment Institution*, which regulates agent interactions in terms of the commitments they make to each other by performing communicative acts [8,9]. This is an application-independent foundational institution, from which more specific application-dependent institutions (like for example the institutions formalizing different types of auctions) can be defined. The Commitment Institution specifies commitments as institutional objects, together with their life-cycle rules and the institutional actions that allow an agent to create, cancel, or otherwise manipulate them; this enables us to monitor the state of an interaction in term of the evolution of the commitments that the participants make to each other. Application-dependent regulating contexts (like for example those relevant to e-commerce) are also represented as OCeAN institutions.

In our infrastructure, institutions as well as domain entities (e.g., the products that are exchanged in the e-market) are represented by ontologies specified in OWL 2 DL [15], the standard language for defining ontologies in the Semantic Web. Also the state of an interaction is represented in an OWL ontology, that we call the *Interaction Ontology*, which is continually updated while the interaction proceeds (see Section 5). More precisely, the Interaction Ontology contains a representation of the institutional objects defined by the institutions in force, together with the institutional actions that can create and manipulate them. To serve this purpose, the Interaction Ontology imports:

- an *Upper Ontology* specifying common application-independent concepts like *agent*, *action*, *event*, and *object*;
- the *SWRL Temporal Ontology*[8] used for representing and reasoning on instants and intervals of time;
- the OWL ontologies used for representing the relevant artificial institutions, like in particular the *Commitment Institution Ontology*[9];
- the *Domain Ontology* used for representing relevant domain knowledge.

Some of these ontologies are described in details in [11]. The ontology imports are realized according to an architecture [11] that we have crafted specifically to avoid conflicts and duplications of the application-independent concepts (like agent, action, temporal interval, etc.) on which several ontologies overlap.

Using OWL 2 DL reasoning, our representation makes it possible to monitor the state of the interactions according to the rules of the context. Thus, equipped with it, in compliance with the prescriptions of the architecture which require a neutral third-party component to enact this functionality, our infrastructure provides for a regulation component which plays the role of interaction manager, in charge of monitoring regulations and requesting their enforcement when necessary. To this purpose, the regulation component relies on the Pellet OWL 2 reasoner[10], used in conjunction with the OWL-API[11]. When started with the paths to the relevant ontologies as parameters, it loads them and creates the initial Interaction Ontology. Then, a suitable assertion is added to the ABox and the reasoning process is triggered every time a relevant event happens, such as the elapsing of a pertinent instant of time, or the realization of an institutional or non-institutional action or event. As we shall see below (Section 5), suitable representations of relevant actions and events are provided by the Bridging Layer.

Implementing interaction monitoring by OWL 2 DL reasoning is not straightforward. First, as participants interactions have to be represented over time, it is

---

[8] http://protege.cim3.net/cgi-bin/wiki.pl?SWRLTemporalOntology

[9] http://www.people.lu.unisi.ch/okouyad/CommitmentOntology.owl

[10] http://clarkparsia.com/pellet/

[11] http://owlapi.sourceforge.net/

necessary to carry out some kind of temporal reasoning. For instance, if a participant is committed to another agent to realize a given action before a deadline, in order to deduce that after the deadline the commitment is either fulfilled or violated it is necessary to deduce that the deadline has elapsed. This cannot be specified by OWL axioms alone; therefore, SWRL[12] rules containing temporal built-ins have been added to perform suitable temporal inferences. Such rules exploit the SWRL Temporal Ontology developed by the Protege group [17], which provides a time representation format that is suitable for calculation, is aligned with the current XSD standards, and defines a rich set of temporal builts-ins that can be used to extend our OWL ontologies with SWRL rules. However, given that these built-ins are not SWRL standards, they are not natively supported by reasoning engines; as the Protege group has provided an implementation for reasoning with these built-ins only with the Jess rule engine, we have developed our implementation for extending the reasoning capabilities of the Pellet reasoner by using the custom built-ins definition mechanism provided with it.

Representing the evolution of the state of interactions (including for example the new commitments that the participants bring about), by means of a continuous update of the Interaction Ontology at run-time [9], is a delicate task because it may introduce inconsistencies. More specificaly, in our formalization of the Commitment Institution Ontology[9] (presented in [7] with the name *Obligation ontology*), we specify that an *actioncommitment* (i.e., a commitment to perform an action, intuitively equivalent to an obligation), has an associated temporal interval, within which the action must be executed. Determining this interval can involve several steps depending on the properties inherited by the commitment at its creation. In certain situations, such as when the action-commitment is conditional, it only becomes activated if a specific triggering event or action takes place; when this activation occurs, the beginning and the end instants of the interval associated to the action-commitment have to be set. For example, if the exchange of a message commits a participant to deliver a product within two days, on condition that the receiver of the product performs a payment, then the action-commitment will be created as soon as the message is exchanged, but will only be activated when the payment takes place. At activation time the interval will be determined as follows: (i), its beginning is set at the time instant of the activation; and (ii), its end is set at the beginning plus two days. In principle, all this may be expressed by a suitable SWRL rule. However, if several actions belonging to the activation class of the obligation take place, the SWRL rule will be activated several times and the interval of the obligation will be represented incorrectly. It turned out that this problem cannot be solved inside the OWL ontology, even if additional SWRL rules are used; therefore we regulate the activation of the relevant SWRL rule with an external Java program that exploits the OWL-API to check that an interval that is already set is not further changed. In short, some reasoning steps and calculations have to be made outside of the reasoner, in order to properly manage the Interaction Ontology.

---

[12] http://www.w3.org/Submission/SWRL/

# 5  The Bridging Layer

To regulate the interactions it is necessary to capture the participants' actions and other relevant events that take place in the system, and represent them in a form that suits the abstraction level at which regulation operates. This is the purpose of the Bridging Layer (or Bridge, for short). This layer, which shares with the Regulation Layer the definition of the institutions in force, operates as detailed in the sequel.

First, all events (inclusive of the participants' actions) that are relevant for regulation must be observed by the Bridge. These events take place either at the Messaging Layer or at the Core Service Layer. As far as the former is concerned, the relevant events consist in exchanges of ACL messages, which are made available for observation by the CC (Communication Channel) component of the Messaging Layer. To the purpose of regulation, it is crucial that all message exchanges between participants take place through the CC provided by the infrastructure. As we have already remarked, however, message exchanges are not the only events that need regulation. Among these also certain non-communicative events are included, like for example the actions of paying or delivering a product. These events are made observable by the Core Service Layer.

The observed events have to be represented in a form that is suitable for regulation. In particular, given that the Regulation Layer relies on artificial institutions, representing an actual observed event in a form suitable for regulation involves producing a representation that is compatible with the specification of the artificial institution.

In the OCeAN metamodel, artificial institutions deal with two types of events, that we respectively call *basic* and *institutional events*. An institutional event $Y$ is an event that is brought about by the performance of a lower level event $X$, thanks to suitable *counts-as* rules, provided that certain enabling conditions $C$ hold. For example, an artificial institution may specify that a certain type of message sent by a suitably empowered agent $A$ will count as an institutional action of opening an auction. Contrastingly, a basic event is an event that can be directly produced by a participant, without the need of realizing it through the performance of another, lower level event. For example, performing the concrete action of sending a message to another participant is represented in the institution as a basic event of message exchange.

Transforming an observed concrete event in a form suitable for regulation requires producing a representation of either a basic or institutional event. In the Regulation Layer, both artificial institutions and the concrete domains over which they operate are specified as OWL ontologies. Thus the infrastructure transforms the actual observed event into OWL individuals that belong to classes of events pertaining either to the institution ontologies or to the domain ontologies. More accurately, as institutional events are always grounded on basic events, this transformation process consists of: (i), creating an OWL individual representing the basic event; and (ii), creating an OWL individual representing the institutional event, if this is dictated by a count-as rule belonging to the institution in force.

As specified by the OCeAN metamodel, we provide a set of application-independent *counts-as* rules that associate to message exchanges (considered as basic events) the creation of suitable commitments (considered as institutional events): these rules are part of the Commitment Institutions and specify the application-independent component of the semantics of OCeAN-ACL. In general, according to the semantics of OCeAN-ACL the exchange of a message is interpreted as an attempt to perform an institutional action of commitment manipulation, which is precisely specified by a $counts-as$ rule; such an attempt will be successful if, and only if, the enabling conditions $C$ associated to the rules hold. For example, the exchanges of commissive messages (like promises) and of directive messages (like requests) are interpreted in the Commitment Institution as attempts to perform institutional actions that create *action commitments* [22], that is, commitments to perform the action described in the content part of the message. Commitments of this type can be considered as equivalent to *obligations*; for example, if agent $A$ promises to agent $B$ to pay a given sum of money $M$ for a given product $P$, the communicative act will be interpreted as an attempt to create an obligation of agent $A$ to pay $M$ euros to $B$ for product $P^{13}$. When the Bridging Layer delivers this institutional action to the Regulation Layer, the Interaction Ontology will be updated with a new institutional object of type *Obligation*, with $A$ as the debtor, $B$ as the creditor, and the payment of $M$ euros for $P$ as the content. Thereafter, the obligation will be monitored for its fulfillment, violation or cancellation as part of the process of interaction monitoring carried out by the Regulation Layer. Requests are treated in a similar way, except that they involve one more step; more precisely, a request is interpreted as the attempt to create an *action precommitment* (or *preobligation*), which in turn leads to an attempt to create an obligation for the receiver, if the receiver accepts the request (i.e., the preobligation).

Assertive communicative acts (like the acts of informing) are conceptually different from commissives and directives, because they introduce *propositional commitments* [22], which cannot be interpreted as ordinary obligations. For example, if agent $A$ informs agent $B$ that the product delivered is damaged, this commits $A$ to the truth of what is said (i.e., that the product is indeed damaged), but does not immediately obligate $A$ to perform any predefined action (in particular, of course, it does not obligate $A$ to damage the product). We have not yet worked out a representation of propositional commitments for our infrastructure: this issue is therefore deferred to future works.

Finally, there is another type of communicative acts, which following the terminology of Searle's Speech Act Theory [21] we call *declarations*; examples are declaring that an auction is open, or that a specific agent is the winner of an

---

[13] Note that a message exchange, considered as an attempt to perform an institutional action, is successful only if the enabling conditions associated to the relevant $counts-as$ rule hold; for example, as specified by the OCeAN metamodel, a message stating that a commitment is cancelled will be successful if it is sent by the creditor of the commitment to its debtor, while it will fail to achieve the cancellation if it is sent by the debtor to the creditor.

auction run. Declarations are carried out by exchanging suitable ACL messages, with *declaration* as the performative, and a content that represents the institutional action whose performanceis being attempted. Coherently with the OCeAN metamodel, such messages are interpreted within an artificial institution through a *counts-as* rule, which generates the declared institutional action provided that certain enabling conditions hold. Typically, a condition for the successful performance of a declaration is that the actor has the *institutional power* to perform the declared institutional action (e.g., only an auctioneer can possibly open an auction). Such institutional powers are associated at design time to the different roles that can be played by a participant in an institution, and are checked at runtime by the Regulation Layer.

In practice, to achieve this transformation from basic events to institutional events, the OWL specifications of application-independent concepts (such as agent, action, event, object, time instant, time interval, etc.) are shared between the Content Language Ontology (see Section 2), the relevant Institution Ontologies, and the Domain Ontologies over which the ongoing application operates and on which the institutions are grounded. Sharing is achieved thanks to the ontological architecture introduced in the Regulation Layer, which eliminates all the ontological mapping hurdles that would have otherwise been necessary to handle for the full transformation process to take place. Indeed it allows to seemingly go from one representation to another; for instance, going from the communicative action $promise(A, B, pay(book01, 5))$ (which involves the Content Language Ontology and a concrete Domain Ontology) to the institutional action $create - obligation(A, B, pay(A, B, book01, 5), instant01)$ (which involves the Commitment Institution Ontology and the same Domain Ontology) is achieved smoothly thanks to the underlying shared concepts of agent, action, and object. If these concepts were not shared appropriately, mappings would have been necessary between the specifications of these concepts in different ontologies. The same principle applies, for example, when a non-communicative action of payment takes place: the actual action is represented by the OWL individual $pay01$ of class $Pay$, suitably related with individuals $A$ as its actor, $B$ as its recipient, $book01$ of class $Book$ as its object, 5 as its amount in euros, and $instant01$ as its instant of performance; this individual can imply the institutional event $tranfer - ownership(B, A, book01, instant01)$ of a hypothetical Ownership Institution (where the target representation is understood as $B$ transferring the ownership of $book01$ to $A$ at $instant01$).

In sum, to perform this bridging process so as to update the regulation component, the Bridge is launched with the paths to all the relevant ontologies (that it loads using the the OWL-API), and a reference to the regulation component. The process is then triggered each time it receives updates from the the Communication Channel or a Core Service component.

## 6 Related Work

Among the recent multiagent infrastructures focused on OISs, which in particular share the aim of providing the regulation of the participants' interactions in the form of a neutral third-party functionality as part of the overall support that they deliver, the Magentix2 Open multi-agent systems platform[14][4] represents the state of the art on the matter. In particular it is the most advanced operational infrastructure, which includes many of the recent advances in the OIS area. Interestingly, we happen to share strong architectural similarities. We therefore start by exhaustively comparing it with our infrastructure. Then we will provide another comparison with a promising infrastructure currently under development, 2COOM, which exemplifies the rising trend of environment-based MAS infrastructures.

At a very abstract level our infrastructure and Magentix2 share the same architectural approach. More precisely, although their respective layered architecture are slightly differently structured, they present the same abstract organisation: a top part concerned with regulation specification and management, a bottom part concerned with the support of observable interactions between heterogeneous participants, and a middle part concerned with the monitoring of the participants' interactions according to the rules in force and their enforcement when deemed appropriate. Consequently, differences only appear in the way the parts are concretely realized, with the most fundamental of them occurring in the middle part. This reflects a common vision of the role of the infrastructure, but divergences on how its different parts may concretely operate to achieve it.

More specifically, at the top level, Magentix2 adopts the metamodel of virtual organizations, which specifies roles with norms including platform generic roles such as OMS (Organization Management System) and DF (Directory Facilitator), for the specification of a regulation structure. Our infrastructure also defines a regulation structure at this level, but one that is based on the OCeAN metamodel of artificial institutions (see Section 4). While a thorough comparison of the two metamodels is outside the scope of this paper, it can be safely said that both infrastructure intend to provide similar regulating structures, which in particular are centered on non-regimented norms, to harness the participants' activities.

At the bottom level, both infrastructures provide an observable vehicle for the participants to interact with each other. To that end, they use similar approaches, but differ in the general understanding of interactions. Indeed the OCeAN metamodel classifies actions into communicative and non-communicative ones, which Magentix2 does not, in that it only considers communicative actions. Consequently, while we divide the bottom part of the infrastructure into two layers (Messaging and Core Service), with the upper one devoted to non-communicative actions and the lower one devoted to communicative ones, Magentix2 only provides one interaction level which corresponds to our lower layer.

As far as communicative interactions are concerned, the two infrastructures operate in a similar manner (as they both provide an end-point neutral messaging protocol with a broker for interoperable communication between heterogenous participants), but diverge in the choice of the technology. Where we use Web Service Technology (SOAP, HTTP, WSDL) with the SOAP body structure

---

[14] http://www.gti-ia.upv.es/sma/tools/magentix2/

defined as an OCeAN-ACL message for messages exchange, Magentix2 adopts the Advanced Message Queuing Protocol (AMQP)[15], with the message body structure defined as a FIPA-ACL message. The use of Web Service Technology is more widespread and therefore we expect its adoption to be less problematic than that of AMQP.

As previously mentioned, the sharpest differences between the infrastructures occur in the middle part, whose functionalities can be summarized as follows: (i), observing actual events such as message exchanges or core-service events; (ii), representing observed events in a form suitable for regulation; (iii), checking them against the regulations for monitoring purposes; and (iv), enforcing the relevant regulations when deemed appropriate. It is with (ii) and (iii) that the two infrastructures differ substantially.

With our infrastructure, checking against regulations is done by means of reasoning over a representation of the state of the interaction, carried out within an OWL ontology that includes the institutions in force and the norms coming along. While our norms and their instantiations (in terms of obligations and prohibitions) are represented as OWL individuals, their activation, cancellation, fulfillment and violation conditions are represented as event types (i.e., as subclasses of class Event). With this approach we can use the full power of DL reasoning to match the representations of actual events and actions with the conditions and contents of norms. This process is much more powerful than the one adopted by Magentix2, which relies on the matching of a restricted subset of first-order logic formulas.

A further important difference between Magentix2 and our infrastructure is that the latter does not rely on an application-independent semantics of ACL messages. In our infrastructure, based on the OCeAN metamodel, the application-independent part of messages (i.e., all the components of an ACL message with the exception of its content) is given a uniform semantics across applications. Moreover, such semantics allows for a representation of messages (produced by the Bridging Layer) that immediately relates message exchanges to the Regulation Layer. This means that only application-specific non-communicative events will need to receive a special treatment in different applications of the infrastructure. Conversely, Magentix2 does not provide for any application-independent connection between the participants' actions and regulation, thus making the conversion to different application more expensive and error prone.

Another relevant infrastructure for OISs currently under development is 2COMM [2] which, similarly to ours, firmly relies on the principle of artificial institutions to structure interactions. 2COMM is mainly build on top of the CArtAgO framework [19], which is based on the Agents & Artifacts metamodel, and to a lesser extent on the JADE infrastructure. In its essence, 2COMM proposes to use the programmable artifacts of CArtAgO to provide for a mediated communication between participants and to model the institutional framework. More specifically, an *artifact* provides for a set of operations, which in the case of 2COMM are communicative actions, and it also manages the institutional inter-

---

[15] http://www.amqp.org/

pretation and monitoring of those actions in terms of operations on commitments; this is the reason why those artifacts are called *commitment-based communication artifacts*. The set of available actions, together with the roles to which they belong and their institutional interpretation, constitute what 2COMM calls a *commitment protocol*. 2COMM provides for an abstract *BasicCommitmentCommunicationArtifact*, defining agent available operations such as *enacting* or *deacting* a role, as well as the internal operations to manage commitments (*create, realize*, and so on). Then, through an inheritance process, a designer can define every specific commitment-based communication artifact protocol that will be available to the participants, like for example the *Contract Net Protocol communication artifact*; the inheritance process consists in adding specific pairs of public operations-internal commitment operations grouped by roles. 2COMM also provides for the necessary management infrastructure, thus enabling agents to use the protocols in a coherent fashion by means of the *ArtifactManager* Jade Agent, which communicates with the requesting agents via FIPA-ACL messages (as provided by Jade).

Although the infrastructure proposed in this paper and the 2COMM one share similar intents, they are sharply different and they significantly diverge in the way we use institutions to harness the interactions, but also in some specific supports that our infrastructure provides. These differences can be delineated as follows. First, at the lowest level, while we provide *intrinsic interoperability* as a support to openness, 2COMM, due to its dependence on the CArtAgO and the JADE infrastructure, does not. Indeed, on one hand, initiating the CArtAgO services, entering the workspaces where the artifacts are situated, as well as programming or using such artifacts, can only be done through the use of Java code. For instance, artifact operations must be implemented as Java methods, called using introspection through a Java API made available by the CArtAgO framework. Therefore, given that the agents that interact with a CArtAgO Environment should be developed using Java, the resulting infrastructure is not completely interoperable with agents developed using other programming languages. We think that this is an important aspect in the realization of OIS in the domain of electronic marketplace, which in essence tries to reach out to as many participants as possible. Indeed even if our infrastructure is developed in Java, its usage does not prescribe agents developed in Java or somehow using it, nor does its customization to a specific application (i.e., the development of new service providers for the core service layer). For no participating component (i.e., core service provider or OIS participant) we make any assumption on how they should be realized, and simply require that they abide to our interoperable messaging protocol.

At a higher level, the differences could be articulated around the following points: (i), how we represent and monitor institutions; (ii), how we use institutions, in particular in the light of the commitment-based semantics of communicative acts; (iii), the set of mechanisms for mediating the interactions at run-time; and (iv), the type of communication.

A fundamental aspect that differentiates our infrastructure is on the approach used for the representation and monitoring of institutions. As previously discussed also in the comparison with Magentix2, we use OWL 2 DL to represent institutions. For instance, we model commitment as OWL individuals, with their contents and conditions modeled as OWL classes. This makes it possible that actions or events that are not known in details in advance, but are simply described by means of a class, will fulfill certain commitments. More generally, we use OWL 2 DL to reason on the evolution of the state of the interaction. Differently, 2COMM uses Java objects to represent both the commitments and the other facts that are relevant to manage the evolution of the overall state of the institution. In particular, a fact has a string field to represent the name of a predicate it represents, and an argument field that is a list of objects. This representation implies a matching process to check whether the content or the condition of a commitment is satisfied (a combination of syntactic string and java object matching). Moreover our model allows to express and manage commitment deadlines, which allows us to detect violations, an aspect that is not tackled in the 2COMM approach.

A second difference is on how institutions are used for the specification of the semantics of communicative acts. Indeed, we make a clear distinction between the application-independent *Basic Institution* (i.e., our definition of an application-independent commitment semantics for OCeAN-ACL) which specifies no norms, and the special-purpose institutions (e.g., auction, ownership) which are fully fledged normative institutions. 2COMM through the use of commitment protocols (i.e., operationalized institution) seems to mix the semantics of communicative acts with the normative aspect of fully fledged institutions. This may have the negative effect of nullifying the advantages of defining a commitment-based semantic of communicative acts. In fact instead of having agents able to freely choose the communicative acts to perform, the 2COMM approach guides the course of message exchange. For instance, an initiator in a *Contract-Net protocol* can only perform the *call for proposals* act and it cannot perform any other act that is not in its role. We believe that the normative dimension should be reserved to aspects that are exclusive to the special-purpose institutions. For instance, in an auction only the auctioneer has the power to open an auction. However, if in the meantime a participant performs a communicative act (e.g., an inform, request, promise, or call for proposal), its institutional effects should be retained. In other words, we want to let the agents free to explore any course of message exchange that they see fit to reach their objectives.

Thanks to the use of the CArtAgO environment, the 2COMM framework provides an efficient checking of the powers for performing institutional actions and the runtime mechanisms for letting the agents to perceive the state of the interaction. Our infrastructure has yet to provide for it, we plan to realize it as part of the ongoing build-up of the support we are providing for the special-purpose institutions. Another difference is on how communication is conducted in the two infrastructures. On one hand, while we both claim to mediate communicative actions, we actually operate differently. Our infrastructure forward ACL messages between participants. It records the actions if necessary, and most importantly their institutional effects. Differently 2COMM does not transfer messages. Actually, messages are Java method call on the artifact, which modifies its state depending on certain conditions. The possible modification can be: the record of the fact that a method was called, the fact that a communicative act was performed, or its institutional effects. Then, it is that change that will be observed by the participating agents. A final observation is that the proposed infrastructure is more agile, because it firmly separates concerns (messaging, core service, bridge, regulation) whereas the 2COMM infrastructure do not, as it combines everything in an artifact. Moreover, by using method calls 2COMM loses the flexibility gained in separating the various components of an agent communication language (i.e., ACL syntax, Content Language, and Domain Ontologies).

We can conclude that, aside from the interoperability issues discussed above, only empirical studies will reveal whether one of the two approaches, or perhaps a mixture of the two, is better and in which domain.

## 7    Conclusions

In this paper we have presented an infrastructure for Open Interaction Systems, based on the OCeAN meta-model and currently under implementation. Our main concerns in the development of the infrastructure are, on the one hand to guarantee openness and interoperability, and on the other hand to rely as much as possible on technologies that are sufficiently mature and stable, like Service Oriented and Semantic Web Technologies, to facilitate adoption by the industry.

The infrastructure has been divided into components to separate different concerns, which brings several advantages: on the one side, it enables us to distribute the infrastructure and to use techniques of dynamic adaptation (such as cloning and self-deletion) to manage overhead issues; on the other side it enables us to provide targeted upgrades and developments of the infrastructure. So far, for prototyping purposes the infrastructure is being implemented as a monolithic multi-threaded Java application; nevertheless, the different components are present and well separated so that they could be easily extracted to provide a fully distributed infrastructure.

In the near future we intend to complete the implementation and test of the prototype. In particular we plan to complete the formalization in OWL of the semantics of the various type of communicative acts, to separate the various component of the prototype, and to test it with the formalization and execution of an e-marketplace, inclusive of the OWL ontologies representing the relevant institutions and domain knowledge.

# References

1. Balani, N., Hathi, R.: Apache CXF Web Service Development. Packt Publishing (2009)
2. Baldoni, M., Baroglio, C., Capuzzimati, F.: 2COMM: a commitment-based MAS architecture. In: Cossentino, M., El Fallah Seghrouchni, A., Winikoff, M. (eds.) EMAS 2013. LNCS (LNAI), vol. 8245, pp. 38–57. Springer, Heidelberg (2013)
3. Chiarabini, L.: CORBA vs. Web Services (May 2004), http://www.itu.dk/~oladjones/mastersthesis/materialsfromportals/corbaversuswebservices.pdf (accessed March 14, 2013)
4. Criado, N., Argente, E., Noriega, P., Botti, V.: MaNEA: A Distributed Architecture for Enforcing Norms in Open MAS. Engineering Applications of Artificial Intelligence 26(1), 76–95 (2012)
5. Erl, T.: Service-Oriented Architecture (SOA): Concepts, Technology, and Design. Prentice Hall (August 2005)
6. Erl, T.: SOA Principles of Service Design (The Prentice Hall Service-Oriented Computing Series from Thomas Erl). Prentice Hall PTR, Upper Saddle River (2007)
7. Fornara, N.: Specifying and Monitoring Obligations in Open Multiagent Systems Using Semantic Web Technology. In: Elçi, A., Koné, M.T., Orgun, M.A. (eds.) Semantic Agent Systems. SCI, vol. 344, pp. 25–45. Springer, Heidelberg (2011)
8. Fornara, N., Colombetti, M.: Specifying Artificial Institutions in the Event Calculus. In: Dignum, V. (ed.) Handbook of Research on Multi-Agent Systems: Semantics and Dynamics of Organizational Models, ch. XIV. Information Science Reference, pp. 335–366. IGI Global (2009)
9. Fornara, N., Colombetti, M.: Representation and monitoring of commitments and norms using OWL. In: AI Communications - European Workshop on Multi-Agent Systems (EUMAS) 2009, vol. 23(4), pp. 341–356 (2010)
10. Fornara, N., Okouya, D., Colombetti, M.: A Framework of Open Interactions based on Web Services and Semantic Web Technologies. In: Proceedings of the 9th European Workshop on Multi-Agent Systems, EUMAS 2011 (2011)
11. Fornara, N., Okouya, D., Colombetti, M.: Using OWL 2 DL for Expressing ACL Content and Semantics. In: Cossentino, M., Kaisers, M., Tuyls, K., Weiss, G. (eds.) EUMAS 2011. LNCS, vol. 7541, pp. 97–113. Springer, Heidelberg (2012)
12. Fornara, N., Viganò, F., Colombetti, M.: Agent communication and artificial institutions. Autonomous Agents and Multi-Agent Systems 14(2), 121–142 (2007)
13. Fornara, N., Viganò, F., Verdicchio, M., Colombetti, M.: Artificial institutions: a model of institutional reality for open multiagent systems. Artif. Intell. Law 16(1), 89–105 (2008), doi:10.1007/s10506-007-9055-z
14. Hapner, M., Burridge, R., Sharma, R., Fialli, J., Stout, K.: Java Message Service Specification Version 1.1. Sun Microsystems, Inc. (April 2002)
15. Hitzler, P., Krötzsch, M., Rudolph, S.: Foundations of Semantic Web Technologies. Chapman & Hall/CRC (2009)
16. Kent, T.K.: Developing Web Services with Apache CXF and Axis2, 3rd edn. Lulu.com (2010)
17. O'Connor, M.J., Das, A.K.: A Method for Representing and Querying Temporal Information in OWL. In: Fred, A., Filipe, J., Gamboa, H. (eds.) BIOSTEC 2010. CCIS, vol. 127, pp. 97–110. Springer, Heidelberg (2011)

18. OMG. The Common Object Request Broker: Architecture and Specification. The Object Management Group, pp. 1–712 (November 1999)
19. Ricci, A., Piunti, M., Viroli, M.: Environment programming in multi-agent systems: an artifact-based perspective. Autonomous Agents and Multi-Agent Systems 23(2), 158–192 (2011)
20. Scordino, C.: How Web Services relate to the well established CORBA Middleware (April 2004), http://retis.sssup.it/~scordino/documents/corba.pdf (accessed March 14, 2013)
21. Searle, J.R.: Speech Acts: An Essay in the Philosophy of Language. Cambridge University Press, Cambridge (1969)
22. Walton, D.N., Krabbe, E.C.: Commitment in Dialogue: Basic concept of interpersonal reasoning. State University of New York Press, Albany (1995)
23. Weerawarana, S., Curbera, F., Leymann, F., Storey, T., Ferguson, D.F.: Web Services Platform Architecture: SOAP, WSDL, WS-Policy, WS-Addressing, WS-BPEL, WS-Reliable Messaging and More. Prentice Hall PTR, Upper Saddle River (2005)

# GoalSPEC: A Goal Specification Language Supporting Adaptivity and Evolution

Luca Sabatucci, Patrizia Ribino, Carmelo Lodato, Salvatore Lopes,
and Massimo Cossentino

ICAR-CNR, Consiglio Nazionale delle Ricerche, Palermo, Italy
{sabatucci,ribino}@pa.icar.cnr.it,
{c.lodato,s.lopes,cossentino}@pa.icar.cnr.it

**Abstract.** The characteristic of being autonomous and proactive makes the agents able to explore a wide solution space, that dynamically changes or contains uncertainty. We propose a language for describing system goals that may be injected at run-time into the system. The novelty of our approach consists in decoupling the business goals (what is expected) and their implementation (how to address the desired behavior). Indeed relieving the tension between 'what' and 'how' provides more degrees of freedom to the system. On the occurrence, agents of our system may exploit their features (mainly autonomy and proactivity, but also learning and planning) for getting benefits from a wider solution space. The result is that the system behavior may adapt to the current operating conditions. Moreover, the injection mechanism contributes to reduce the effort in evolving the system. This paper focuses on the goal specification language that is the base for enabling both adaptivity and evolution.

## 1 Introduction

The current work arises in the context of the project Innovative Document Sharing (IDS) [1], whose aim is the development of an adaptive and autonomous workflow enactment engine for improving task coordination and document management in small and medium local companies. The project exploits the well-known BPMN standard [1], among its assets, because the system will be used in real business contexts. Indeed the BPMN is mainly targeted to humans, being very flexible and expressive and it includes the notation for describing workflows as orchestration of both automatic services and human tasks. Moreover, the business domain is a highly variable application context. Business rules could change very frequently due to the evolution of business strategies, to the change of company short/middle term goals, or due to the dynamic society with its laws and regulations that must be respected. The BPMN does not support a dynamic context. Every external change must be implemented into the workflow as a set of modifications. In other terms, the workflow must be re-designed for implementing any new requirement, checking inter-dependencies and verifying the validity of the result.

It is a matter of fact that the task of designing and evolving business model is not trivial: a great number of malfunctions in workflow systems depend on business analysis

---

[1] The IDS project is funded by the Autonomous Region of Sicily (POR FESR Sicilia 2007-2013).

M. Cossentino et al. (Eds.): EMAS 2013, LNAI 8245, pp. 235–254, 2013.

errors [2–4]. Adopting a workflow system able to autonomously react to changes of the context may simplify the work [2]. An adaptive workflow is conceived as a normal workflow but it is also able to react to some changes in the environment [2]. The need for self-adaptation is often linked to the need of reacting to exceptions [5]. Whereas BPMN already provides mechanisms to specify how the system will react to expected exceptions [1], it is more interesting to define how to react to unexpected exceptions. Indeed these events can not be handled by traditional workflow engine. For all these reasons, self-adaptation is particularly desirable for a workflow system.

In last years, self-adaptation has been gaining more and more attention specially in agent-oriented software systems [6–8]. It is a fact that multi-agent systems encapsulate an adequate level of abstraction useful to implement software capable to react to changes. Agent autonomy makes the system able to modify its behavior without supervision. The agent ability to perceive its environment helps to monitor parameters of the context that may variate. Finally agent pro-activity and the reasoning ability help to plan the appropriate reaction strategy according to agent's goals.

Generally agent goals are an higher level of abstraction with respect to the programming language (for instance in Belief-Desire-Intention systems), so that they disappears into agents' code. More recently, an interesting feature of agent is the self-awareness, that is the ability of agents to know its capacities and its goals. It is the direction of works like that of Morandini et al. [7], or that of Buhler and Vidal [6], in which the agent selects the most appropriate behavior by reasoning on a goal-model. Goal-models [9–11] have been a great advance in requirement engineering, because they provide the adequate level of abstraction to reason on the domain, its inhabitants and their needs, translating all this in a precise set of requirements. It has been proved that self-adaptive systems may benefits from relaxing the rigid constraints that is typical of traditional requirement engineering [12–14]. Intuitively a system that must overcome an obstacle must have space to change direction. A rigid set of system requirements could not provide enough space to move around a possible obstacle.

The proposed approach consists in relaxing the link between what is expected the system do (system goals) and how the system is expected to do that (system capabilities and plans). By decoupling these two aspects it is up to the system to know how to match a specific capability with the desired result. This responsibility may be satisfied only if 1) the software is aware of its goals and its capabilities, 2) it is able to reason on how to compose its behavior and 3) it is autonomous to operate without any supervision. Multi-agent systems naturally offer all these characteristics. Such architecture requires a specification language that enables this decoupling. To the best of our knowledge, none of the existing languages for goal specification is completely suitable for our scope. This paper focuses on GoalSPEC, the proposed language to express system requirements in a form that supports adaptivity and system evolution.

The remaining of the paper is organized as follows. Section 2 describes the motivation of our work, and Section 3 presents a literature review of a selection of existing goal-oriented languages. Section 4 describes the characteristic of GoalSPEC and its application to the IDS project domain. Some discussions and final conclusions are presented in section 5.

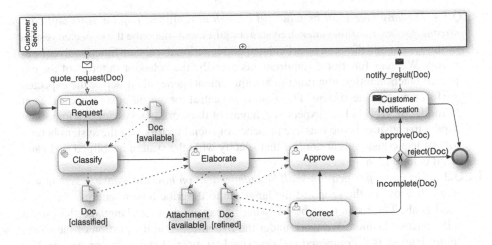

**Fig. 1.** Example of BPMN diagram from the IDS case study

## 2   Motivation

The IDS project aims at developing a workflow enactor system for improving task coordination and document management in small and medium local companies. The project is a benchmark for exploring real motivations since a workflow system shall autonomously configure its behavior. In particular the requirements elicitation phase of the project highlighted that the business domain is a high dynamic context, in which company business goals and rules often vary. In addition the workflow engine runs in a socio-technical context in which human and social factors are relevant. In particular such systems operate in a society whose laws and regulations are frequently revised and modified.

The business process in Fig. 1 models the process for quote request in a generic company. The customer service receives requests from customers via telephone, fax, email or traditional mail. The flow starts when the customer service fills a quote request form. This generates a virtual document to be processed to satisfy the request. The automatic task *Classify* tries to identify the input request type, when possible, by using image processing techniques. Therefore, the classified document is manually elaborated (*Elaborate* task) by the technical responsible who produces the quote as virtual attachment. It is the commercial manager's turn to supervise the attachment and to mark it as approved, incomplete or rejected (*Approve* task). If the document is marked as incomplete, a new revision loop is activated (*Correct* task). Conversely, if the document is approved then the customer notification is responsible to contact the customer and to provide the requested information.

The objective of this paper is to discuss how decoupling business goals and their implementation for self-adaptation purposes. Whereas BPMN is extremely flexible to define the implementation layer, it lacks of an explicit syntax for defining business goals. We look at a goal specification language with the following characteristics.

**REQ.1 -** *The language shall be powerful enough to represent requirements and constraints for information systems.* System requirements describe the expected results of the system and they can be articulated into functional and non-functional requirements. Whereas functional requirements describe the behavior in terms of the expected functionalities, non functional requirements generally describe the expected performances of the system. This feature is central for our purposes since we want to model BPMN goals as expected behavior of the workflow system. An important aspect to consider is the massive presence of social factors into the system behavior: system constraints are norms that specify what the system is obliged to do and what is forbidden.

**REQ.2 -** *The goal specification shall be independent on how the software system will work.* It is out of the scope of the language to describe how to address the specified goals. The focus must be on 'what' is expected, so the language shall be in a declarative fashion. We work under the hypothesis that the portion of the world under interest is decomposed and described by a set of states and properties. For our purposes, describing system goals means to describe the expected result by grounding it on ontological bases.

**REQ.3 -** *The language shall be context-free.* Agents are the main consumers of the goal specifications, because they are responsible to adapt their behavior to the goals. Goals are not statically defined at design-time automatically, but can be modeled or modified after agents' life begins. Therefore, for our purposes, the goal language must be interpreted at-run time by system agents, who must acquire the expected result that is encapsulated in them. Agents that are aware of the expected state of the world (that is desired by humans) can reason on how to adapt their behavior according to perceptions and to desired goals.

**REQ.4 -** *The goal specification shall be compatible with the expressiveness of the BPMN language.* The Business Process Model and Notation is a very expressive graphical language that is able to express almost every process. It includes, among the others, human and software collaborations, conversations and choreography, concurrent task execution, task decomposition, persistent data, handling of error/-compensation/escalation situations. We work under the hypothesis that in a process every task is done because underlying goal exists, and we want to automatically extract these goals every time this is possible. The resulting goal must perfectly synthesize its task, so the specification language must be expressive enough to cover the whole specifications of BPMN.

**REQ.5 -** *The language shall be attractive for a business audience.* Goals will be automatically extracted (when possible) from the BPMN description of the business process. However analysts want to maintain the control of the workflow execution. For this reason they will want to verify and manually refine system goals before these are injected into the system. For our purpose, the language must be simple to learn, to understand and to use by non-technical people. We consider to use a specification language that is closer to the natural language a better choice than a formal language based on mathematics basis.

**REQ.6 -** *The language shall be flexible enough to include points of uncertainty in specifications.* Traditional languages for goals specification generally adopt a strict definition of the functional and non-functional requirements in order to avoid ambiguities or uncertainty. Despite this is perfect for traditional system development, this may represent a limitation for a self-adapting system. Indeed the adaptation mechanism need wider solution space where to move, in which many alternative solutions are possible, each with different trade-offs. For our purpose, we want to increase the degrees of freedom of agents in finding the solution. We want to allow the presence of points of uncertainty in the goal specification to let agents relax some constraints on the necessity.

# 3   Review of Goal Specification Languages

We conducted a systematic literature review, according the principles of Wohlin et al. [15]. The research question is about the expressiveness of *goals* in literature. In particular we check if they match with the characteristics defined in Section 2.

We identified 30 among the most relevant papers in the area, that are distributed according their topic in informal/semi-formal, formal approaches and implementation. The table shown in Fig.1 summarizes the results of this comparison.

Totally informal approaches commonly express goal semantics by using natural language expressions: they are similar (in our classification) to semi-formal representations that mix graphical and text based notation. These are the most frequently used techniques for specifying goals because they facilitate the exchange of knowledge with stakeholders.

*Business Motivation Model* (BMM) [16] is a meta-model and a standard for capturing semantically rich business requirements, useful for analysis, querying, impact analysis, change management and business reasoning. It tries to highlight "why the business wants to do something, what it is aiming to achieve, how it plans to get there and how it assesses the result". Nevertheless, BMM does not come with a standard graphical notation, it has a broader scope than just goal modeling and therefore it has too many concepts (some of which are unclear or overlap with each other), it has no strong formal basis and does not address at all goal analysis and reasoning issues. Finally its goals do not ground on ontological bases and not support reasoning with uncertainty.

The *Goal-Scenario Coupling* [17] is a language that expresses a goal by a structured natural language in which any clause has a main verb and several parameters. For example Display (the error message)$_{Obj}$ (to the customer)$_{Dest}$, where each parameter plays a different role with respect to the verb. We note, among parameters, there are *means* and *manner* that define how to address the goal satisfaction.

The *i*\* [18] framework and *Tropos* [9] are semi-structured language in which goal statement are free-text but relationships are formalized. In particular And/Or Decomposition relations, means/end relationship (setting means to reach a goal), and contribution relationships (expressing positive or negative contribution to goal achievement). The language is perfectly suitable for requirement analysis, but the poor semantics of the natural language goal definition makes it hard to move towards implementation phases.

To overcame this point the *Formal Tropos* [19] extension offers all the primitive concepts of *i*\* [18] but more expressive power, and in particular, temporal specifications. As well as *Tropos* does, *Formal Tropos* describes all the relevant objects of the modeled domains along with their relationships, but it also allows to represent dynamic aspects of the model by a first order linear-time temporal logic with future and past time operators. The language offers existential and universal quantifiers for defining Constraints (which restrict the valid executions of the system), Assertion (which are expected to hold in all valid executions of the system) and Possibility (which are expected to hold in at least one valid execution of the system).

*Tropos* has been also used in the field of self-adaptation [7]. Morandini et al. enriched the goal model by specifying achievement conditions in relationship with the environment, and the possibility to model faults and corresponding recovery activities. They set system goals as invariants, whereas variation points of the global behavior are granted by decomposing the main goals into trees of alternative sub-goals. The system uses advanced decision techniques to select among many alternative strategies to address the main goals. Moreover, the defined goals can be directly mapped to Jadex goals. The technique of designing the expected exceptions was already comprised into the BPMN specification but the main limitation, for our purposes, is that goals and plans are paired at design time.

*GRL* [20] is also based on *i\**. It is a language for supporting goal and agent-oriented modelling and reasoning about requirements, with an emphasis on dealing with non-functional requirements (NFRs). In *GRL*, a goal can be either a business goal or a system goal. A business goal express goals regarding the state of the business affairs the individual or organization wishes to achieve. System goals describe the functional requirements of the information system. *GRL* is a language more suitable for the first phases of analysis. The goal specifications it provides are not suitable for agents. Moreover it not support adaptation and uncertainty factors.

Differently *KAOS* [21] is conceived to produce automated specifications of domain knowledge. The framework grounds on a formal language where goals are defined by means of real-time linear temporal logic (first-order logic with modalities referring to time), that semantically captures maximal sets of desired behaviors. Goals are classified according to some patterns (*Achieve, Avoid, Maintain*, etc...); these verbs in KAOS specify a temporal logic pattern for the goal name appearing as parameter. They implicitly specify that a corresponding target condition should hold some time in the future, always in the future unless some other condition holds, or never in the future. This expressivity makes the language suitable for formal proof of specification correctness.

Winikoff *et al.* [8] present a way to integrate declarative and procedural views of goals in agent systems. They propose a plan notation called CAN (Conceptual Agent Notation) along with a formal semantics expressing both goal aspects. In this paper a goal is represented by means of two logical formulae about the agent's beliefs representing the declarative aspects and a set of plans representing the procedural aspects of goals. This kind of goal representation allows to capture several goal proprieties (such as persistence, consistence, achievement etc ...) but it does not encapsulate uncertainty factors and it is not thought for adaptation and for BPMN mapping. Moreover, it encapsulates procedural aspects that GoalSpec deliberately avoids in order to allow adaptation in our workflow enactor. Subsequently, the GOAL language [22] incorporates declarative aspects of goals in an agent system in order to allow the agent to decide what to do. A declarative goal specifies a state of the world that an agent wants to reach. Thus they do not specify how to achieve such states. A feature of GOAL is that the set of goals is not required to be consistent because not all goals have to be reached simultaneously. Goals can be achieved at some moment in the near or distant future. These features are very close to our needs, anyway whereas the GOAL language grounds on agent mental states, we need a language to define business goals that are, in fact, humans' goals. GoalSPEC should be designed to be attractive for business audience as specified in Section 2. Moreover, our language want to be also a trade off between high-level goal languages and implementation ones.

Finally, there is a lot of work about agent-oriented programming languages (such as JACK [23], AgentSpeak(L) [24], Jason [25], 3APL [26] [27], Jadex [28], etc...) where the goals play a central role. Many of them are associated to sophisticated reasoning engines allowing to develop complex intelligent agents. But in these frameworks goals are strictly linked to plans to reach them. In our system we do not specify a particular representation of the plan. A plan could be as usual a simple sequence of agent actions, a combination of web services, a set of procedures and so on. A strength of our work lies on decoupling the declarative aspect of a goal from its procedural one allowing thus a flexible plan composition in order to satisfy a declared goal.

Table 1 summarizes the results of the review. This table provides a kind of matching between the analyzed goal languages and the requirement we need. At the best of our knowledge, we have not found one approach that fully meets all our requirements. In particular, the attempts to use Goal-based modeling for specifying adaptation do not fully satisfy what we want to realize in our envisioned framework. Therefore, the next section proposes a new language, named *GoalSpec*, that incorporates some features of the reviewed languages but also it introduces new characteristics for our purposes.

**Table 1.** Comparison table among goal languages and features we are interested

| | | KAOS | TROPOS /I* | Formal TROPOS | GRL | Goal Scenario Coupling | TROPOS for adaptivity | BMM | BDI Languages | GOAL | Legend |
|---|---|---|---|---|---|---|---|---|---|---|---|
| | Formal | x | | x | | | | | | | X = complete matching |
| | | | | | | | | | | | V = partial matching |
| | Goal Type | A-I | A-I | A-I | A | A | A-I | A | I | I | A = Analysis |
| | | | | | | | | | | | I = Implementation |
| | Adaptivity | | | x | | | x | | | | |
| **Features** | Requirements/ Constraints Representation | x | x | x | x | V | x | V | V | V | |
| | Oontological Representation | x | | x | | | | | | | |
| | Context-free Grammar | x | | x | | | | | | x | |
| | Uncertainty | | | x | | | | | | | |
| | Human Oriented | | x | | | | x | x | | | |

# 4   GoalSPEC: A Language to Specify System Goals

Here, we define a language for specifying system requirements and constraints. It has to be general enough to cope with several aspects that are key elements in current systems. To do this, we have incorporated some features of existing languages and we have introduced new ones in order to address specific adaptation and business issues. For the sake of clarity we refer to the whole language as an abstract package that contains two sub-languages: *GoalSPEC* that focuses on specifying expected results of the system in terms of functions, and *NormSPEC* that is a norm-based language for specifying non-functional requirements and constraints that generate a boundary where the system is limited to move. This paper focuses on GoalSPEC only, whereas the foundations of NormSPEC are yet published in [29]. The common characteristics of both GoalSPEC and NormSPEC are: (i) their grammar is a subset of the natural language; (ii) they have context-free grammar, thus to be automatically parsed and translated into machine instructions; (iii) some elements of the specifications can be relaxed by using fuzzy modifiers. The concept of system goal is central to our language. Aligned with common definitions we distinguish between business goals and system goals.

*Def.1*: *Business Goals are enterprise strategic interests that motivate the execution of business processes [11]. They are discovered in phase of analysis and they are useful to model a strategic view of domain stakeholders and to elicit system requirements.*

*Def.2*: *System Goals are described as states of the world that the system desires to achieve [9]. System goals are generally the subset of business goals that are delegated to the workflow system in order to implement some kind of automation.*

In the following, an extract of the BNF description of the GoalSPEC language is reported:

```
goal_type : social_goal | system_goal;

social_goal : SOCIAL GOAL goalname ':' trigger_condition actors_list SHALL
              ADDRESS final_state;

system_goal
    : GOAL goalname ':' trigger_condition actor SHALL ADDRESS final_state;

trigger_condition : event
    | trigger_condition AND trigger_condition
    | trigger_condition OR trigger_condition
    | NOT trigger_condition | '(' trigger_condition ')' ;

event : ON date | AFTER delay SINCE trigger_condition
    | WHEN state ;

final_state : state
    | final_state AND final_state
    | final_state OR final_state
    | NOT state | '(' final_state ')';

state : predicate
    | message_sent_state
    | message_received_state ;

message_sent_state : MESSAGE predicate SENT TO actor;

message_received_state : MESSAGE predicate RECEIVED FROM actor;

actors_list : actor AND actors_list | actor;
actor : THE_SYSTEM | THE characters ROLE;
```

***Social goals and agent goals.*** The productions of the language allow to specify system goals. The first production of the BNF describes a goal as composed by an initial triggering *condition*, a list of *actors* that are involved and a desired final *state* of the world. We consider two categories of system goals:

- *agent goals* are atomic goal, related to a specific outcome in the workflow instance; they derive from Tasks in a workflow, and they can not be further decomposed into sub goals. Addressing an agent goal produces an advancement for the achievement of the workflow.
- *social goals* are goals that are decomposable into many sub-goals. These goals derive from Processes or Subprocess in a workflow. A social goal is not necessary satisfied when all its sub-goals are satisfied. It has its own final condition to verify in order to be considered addressed.

For instance, the agent goal, for which the *Elaborate* task in Fig. 1 must be executed, is the following:

```
GOAL doc_management.g2 :
(WHEN classified(Doc) AND WHEN done(classify))
THE worker ROLE SHALL ADDRESS
((refined(Doc) AND available(Attachment)) AND done(elaborate))
```

The *actors* section is strictly related to the concept of BPMN participant. It specifies 'who' is the main responsible to address the given goal. GoalSPEC includes two different categories of participant: human roles and the system. When the actor of a goal is *the system* then the goal may be automatically addressed. On the other hand, when a human role is responsible of a goal, the system can only monitor when the goal is successfully addressed. A social goal, generally contains a list of actors that will collaborate to the workflow enactment.

***Triggering Conditions.*** Each goal specification starts with a set of *conditions* that must hold in order to activate the goal. The BNF specifies that a condition may be a single event or a composition of multiple events. Basic events may be:

- *on < date >*, triggers when a given day arrives. The *date* is a parameter that follows the ISO 8601 specification [30] (International standard date and time notation). Examples are 'on 1995-02-04', or 'on 2013-04-01/23:59:59'.
- *after < delay > since < event >*, triggers after an amount of time since a given event has occurred. The *delay* parameter specifies a duration of delay according to the ISO 8601 standard. For instance '2W' means 2 weeks.
- *when < state >*, triggers when a specified state of the world becomes true: an example is 'when rejected(Doc)'. In the following, in this same section, the specification of state is explained in details.

***States of the World.*** One of the main operative hypothesis of this work is that the portion of the world under interest is described by using states and predicates. Indeed, GoalSPEC adopts an ontological description of the world, and logic predicates play a central role in the specification of elements and their properties. The BNF indicates that each goal specification includes a *final_state* that must be true in order to declare the goal is finally satisfied. A *state* may range from a single logic predicate '*classified(Doc)*', to a composition of multiple predicates by and/or operators '((*refined(Doc)*

*AND available(Attachment)) AND done(elaborate))'*. Also a NOT operator is included to specify the state is true when the predicate is false. Two special occurrences of state are produced by the MESSAGE keyword. These states occur when workflow messages are exchanged (incoming or outgoing). Here two examples of message states:

- *MESSAGE notify_result(Doc) SENT TO THE customer_service ROLE*
- *MESSAGE quote_request(Doc) RECEIVED FROM THE customer_service ROLE*

We used Prolog as the dialect to define GoalSPEC first-order logic predicates in a declarative fashion. This decision has been done also to be compliant with some BDI (belief-desire-intention) frameworks such as the Jason architecture [31]. Prolog predicates use atoms to represent: *(i)* particular individuals or objects (symbols starting with lowercase, or numbers); *(ii)* variables (symbols starting with uppercase) that will assume a value with the mechanism of unification; *(iii)* facts (functors followed by list of arguments), used to represent properties or relationships. Let us consider the example in Fig. 1. After the *Approve* task the document may assume three possible states: *approved(Doc)*, *incomplete(Doc)* or *rejected(Doc)*. The value unified with the variable *Doc* represents the specific instance of the working document. Matching and unification are performed along the same set of goals specification, therefore, considering the following goal:

```
GOAL doc_management.g5 :
(WHEN approved(Doc) AND WHEN done(approve))
THE SYSTEM SHALL ADDRESS
MESSAGE notify_result(Doc) SENT TO THE customer_service ROLE
```

It is worth noting that the variable of the predicate *'approved'* will be unified with the variable of the predicate *'notify_result'*: in other worlds the document that will be sent to the customer service is the same that has been approved and it is the same that has been previously *'refined'* (see goal *doc_management.g2*).

**Human participants.** Business processes describe sequences of operations. The BPMN standard (in contrast with BPEL) allows to declare a human role as responsible of activities. Manual and user tasks are operations that are executed without (or with a limited support) of the machine. In our vision all the activities in a workflow, including the manual ones, exist in order to pursue a business goal, or in technical terms, to take the world in a desired state.

```
GOAL doc_management.g3 :
(((WHEN refined(Doc) AND WHEN available(Attachment)) AND WHEN done(elaborate))
OR ((WHEN refined(Doc) AND WHEN available(Attachment)) AND WHEN done(correct)))
THE manager ROLE SHALL ADDRESS
(done(approve) AND (incomplete(Doc) OR approved(Doc) OR rejected(Doc)))
```

Whereas goals that derive from service tasks are directly delegated to one or more agents of the system, goals of manual/user tasks can not be delegated: they must be addressed by human resources. In these cases system goals differ from business goals, indeed the role of the system is to monitor that the desired state is correctly addressed, or when this is not feasible, to generate user interfaces where human operators may notify their progresses.

**Fuzzy modifiers.** It is very interesting the work by Whittle et al. [13] who defined RELAX, a language for requirement specifications that uses a declarative style for specifying possible sources of uncertainty. Flexibility is obtained by relaxing the rigid 'shall' form typical of requirements and by introducing uncertainty factors. *RELAX* is based on three types of operators (temporal, ordinal and modal) to address uncertainty. The semantics of RELAX expressions (AFTER, AS EARLY AS POSSIBLE, and so on...) is formalized in terms of fuzzy branching temporal logic. The authors suggest that requirements languages for self-adaptive systems should include explicit constructs for specifying and dealing with the uncertainty inherent in self-adaptive systems.

Likewise in *RELAX* [13], the expressiveness of GoalSPEC language is extendable to let the designer relax some constraints. This is possible by using 'fuzzy modifiers' to increase the flexibility of the rigid unification operator. For instance, it is possible to relax time constraints by specifying that a goal shall be addressed AS SOON AS POSSIBLE, or AS LATE AS POSSIBLE. This is particularly useful when the system deals with many parallel goals and must optimize the global behavior by selecting the one with highest priority. It is also possible to relax measures with the following modifiers: AS CLOSE AS POSSIBLE, AS MANY AS POSSIBLE, AS FEW AS POSSIBLE. For instance it is possible specifying the number of items in a list must be as close as possible to a given threshold. A value that is close to the threshold (but not equal) will not raise an exception, as a traditional workflow engine would do, thus allowing the workflow to continue normally. The implementation of these modifiers is a work in progress and is out the scope of this paper.

## 4.1 Translating BPMN into System Goals

Many times in this paper we mentioned BPMN [1] and BPEL [32] as the most common specification languages for workflow. In the IDS project we adopted BPMN because of its capability to describe human tasks whereas BPEL does not support. BPMN and GoalSPEC are not in competition, but rather are complementary. Each of them has a different role in the whole architecture. BPMN is the main interface for business analysts to model their business processes. GoalSPEC is intended to model the business goals that are not explicitly expressed in the BPMN process.

An important requirement gathered in the IDS project is avoiding additional burden to the business analyst. For this reason we elaborated an algorithm that automatically extracts goals from a BPMN specification of a business process. BPMN2GoalSPEC is a Java component that translates the BPMN specification (XML) into a set of goals according to the GoalSPEC grammar. This set of goals could be then manually revised if necessary, however it represents a good starting point for the analyst.

In order to explain what is the idea underlying the extraction of goals, we can observe that a BPMN process can be seen as a graph, where nodes are Tasks, Events or Gateways, and arcs are sequenceFlows. Sub-processes are special kind of Tasks that act as container for other Tasks, Events and Gateways. We already discussed that a process generates a social goal, since it describes a protocol of collaboration among many parts. On the other hand every Task generates an agent goal that encapsulate the business objective to execute it. As a consequence a Sub-process generates both an agent goal and a social goal.

In order to generate a social goal or an agent goal we have to extract both the triggering condition and the final state for the specific goal. The triggering condition is the condition needed for activating a specific goal and the final state is the state of the world the goal indicates to be addressed. Working under the condition that both the triggering condition and the final state could be expresses by considering the states of the world, we want to measure the state at input and output of Task nodes.

We preliminary observed that:

- Gateways do not alter the state of the world. This means the input state of a gateway is equal to the output state;
- Events can be distinguished in catching and throwing. Catching events block the execution waiting that the desired input state triggers. On the contrary, throwing events proactively generate the desired state as output;
- Tasks encapsulate both the waiting/generating behaviors. Indeed a task activates when a given input condition (we call it the waiting condition) is true, whereas it generates a given state as output (we call it the generated condition).

We easily measure the waiting/generated condition by observing at dataObjects, inputSets, outputSets, dataStores and Messages that are consumed as input of a task, or that are produced as output by the task. For instance, the *Classify* task shown in Fig. 1 waits for the *Doc* dataObjects assumes the state 'available' therefore the waiting condition is *WHEN available(Doc)*. Conversely the same task produces a new state for the *Doc* dataObjects ('classified'), so the generated condition is *classified(Doc)*.

Anyway waiting/generated conditions are different from triggering condition and final state because we must also consider that a Task is immersed in a context with predecessor and successor nodes that modify its state at input and output. In general we can say that the triggering condition can be elaborated as the waiting condition plus the backward condition, whereas the final state may be elaborated as the generated condition plus the forward condition.

The backward condition is measured by looking backward at the target node following the incoming sequenceFlow arcs, whereas the forward condition is measured by looking forward at the target node following the outgoing sequenceFlow arcs. In this analysis:

- *Gateways* propagate the state in both backward and forward directions;
- *Throwing Events* block the backward analysis, whereas *Catching Events* block the forward analysis;
- *Tasks* block the propagation in both directions;
- eventual *Conditional sequenceFlows* also provide additional useful information that have to be composed with backward/forward conditions.

Finally, the Algorithm 1 describes the goal generation technique. As an example of goal generation, let us take in consideration the *Approve* task in Fig. 1.

**Inferring the triggering events of a goal.** The waiting condition for the goal is related to the presence of the *refined(Doc)*, where the generated condition is the predicate *done(approve)* (this is generated by default for each task to highlight the correct execution of an activity). To build the backward condition the algorithm selects the two

**Data**: the BPMN workflow graph
**Result**: set of GoalSPEC goals
**forall the** *x, Task and Throwing Event in the workflow* **do**
   let be waiting(x) the waiting event;
   let be generated(x) the generated state;
   generate a new agent goal G;
   add waiting(x) to triggering_condition(G);
   add generated(x) to final_state(G);
   **forall the** *i, incoming SequenceFlow(x)* **do**
      let be cond(i) the sequence flow condition of i (when it exists);
      calculate backward(i,source(i));
      add cond(i) AND backward(i,source(i)) to triggering_condition(G);
   **end**
   **forall the** *j, outgoing SequenceFlow(x)* **do**
      let be cond(j) the sequence flow condition of j (when it exists);
      calculate forward(j,target(j));
      add cond(j) AND forward(j,source(j)) to final_state(G);
   **end**
**end**
**forall the** *p, Process and SubProcess in the workflow* **do**
   generate a new social goal S;
   **forall the** *z, starting event and starting task of the workflow* **do**
      **forall the** *i, outgoing SequenceFlow(z)* **do**
         calculate forward(i,target(i));
         add forward(i,target(i)) to triggering_condition(S);
      **end**
   **end**
   **forall the** *t, ending event and ending task of the workflow* **do**
      **forall the** *j, incoming SequenceFlow(t)* **do**
         calculate backward(j,source(j));
         add backward(j,source(j) to final_state(S);
      **end**
   **end**
**end**

**Algorithm 1.** Extracting Goals from the Workflow

incoming sequenceFlows and, follows them back until reaching the source nodes: 1) *Elaborate* and 2) *Correct*. Because of both are Tasks, the condition is equal to the generated condition. Therefore they are:
*backward(1,Elaborate)=done(elaborate)AND refined(Doc) AND availabe(Attachment)*,
and
*backward(2,Correct)=done(correct) AND refined(Doc) AND availabe(Attachment)*.
The whole triggering condition of the goal is the OR combination of these two results.

*Inferring the resulting state of a goal.* The generated condition of the goal is *done(approve)* by default, since there is no explicitly produced output. For building the forward condition the algorithm follows forward any outgoing sequenceFlow from the task. In this case there is only one outgoing sequenceFlow that arrives to the exclusive gateway. The gateway node does not alter the state, but it propagates in input the state that is in output. Because it is an inclusive gateway the three outgoing sequenceFlows will be in OR. The first flow is conditional (*approved(Doc)*) and arrives to a task that blocks the forward analysis. The second flow is also conditional (*rejected(Doc)*) and terminates to an end event. Finally the third flow is conditional (*incomplete(Doc)*) and arrives to a task that again blocks the forward analysis. As a consequence the forward condition is *incomplete(Doc) OR approved(Doc) OR rejected(Doc)*.

```
GOAL doc_management.g3 :
(((WHEN refined(Doc) AND WHEN available(Attachment)) AND WHEN done(elaborate))
OR ((WHEN refined(Doc) AND WHEN available(Attachment)) AND WHEN done(correct)))
THE manager ROLE SHALL ADDRESS
(done(approve) AND (incomplete(Doc) OR approved(Doc) OR rejected(Doc)))
```

The complete goals set for the book management example (Fig. 1) is the following:

```
SOCIAL GOAL doc_management :
WHEN MESSAGE quote_request(Doc) RECEIVED FROM THE customer_service ROLE
THE worker ROLE AND THE manager ROLE AND THE customer_service ROLE AND THE SYSTEM
SHALLADDRESS((rejected(Doc) AND (done(approve)AND NOT done(costumer_notification)))
OR MESSAGE notify_result(Doc) SENT TO THE customer_service ROLE)

GOAL doc_management.g0 :
WHEN MESSAGE quote_request(Doc) RECEIVED FROM THE customer_service ROLE
THE SYSTEM SHALL ADDRESS
(available(Doc) AND done(quote_request))

GOAL doc_management.g1 :
(WHEN available(Doc) AND WHEN done(quote_request))
THE SYSTEM SHALL ADDRESS
(classified(Doc) AND done(classify))

GOAL doc_management.g2 :
(WHEN classified(Doc) AND WHEN done(classify))
THE worker ROLE SHALL ADDRESS
((refined(Doc) AND available(Attachment)) AND done(elaborate))

GOAL doc_management.g3 :
(((WHEN refined(Doc) AND WHEN available(Attachment)) AND WHEN done(elaborate))
OR ((WHEN refined(Doc) AND WHEN available(Attachment)) AND WHEN done(correct)))
THE manager ROLE SHALL ADDRESS
(done(approve) AND (incomplete(Doc) OR approved(Doc) OR rejected(Doc)))

GOAL doc_management.g4 :
((WHEN refined(Doc) AND WHEN available(Attachment)) AND (WHEN incomplete(Doc)
AND (WHEN done(approve) AND NOT WHEN done(costumer_notification))))
THE worker ROLE SHALL ADDRESS
((refined(Doc) AND available(Attachment)) AND done(correct))

GOAL doc_management.g5 :
(WHEN approved(Doc) AND WHEN done(approve))
THE SYSTEM SHALL ADDRESS
MESSAGE notify_result(Doc) SENT TO THE customer_service ROLE
```

## 4.2 The Proposed Architecture

We have anticipated that social and system goals are injected into the system at runtime. This subsection provides a brief description of the architecture of the workflow

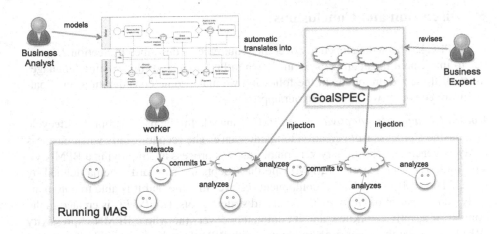

**Fig. 2.** Overview of the proposed system for enacting the workflow

engine. This overview is short because of space concerns, but it helps to provide a justification to the presented language and to answer the challenge introduced in Section 2.
The work assumes that, in a real working environment, BPMN is the main interface for
business analysts. We decided to accept BPMN as it is prescribed by the OMG group
and we avoid to create yet another extension or variation to its metamodel. Indeed, Figure 2 shows that a business analysts uses a BPMN 2.0 tool to edit the workflow. In the
meanwhile, a multi-agent system is already running and its members are greedy to use
their capabilities. Every agent in the system owns some specific capabilities and it is
aware of them. For instance, considering the IDS project, an agent is able to classify
documents, whereas a set of agents are able to communicate with the range of human
roles ('customer', 'worker', 'manager'). When a business process is ready, it is automatically translated into a set of goals in GoalSPEC and then these goals are inserted
into a database. The agents of the system detect when new goals are in the database and
verify whether their capabilities are suitable to commit to one ore more goals. This triggers a social auction for assigning goals to agents. When all the agent goals are assigned
to some agent, the relative social goal is activated and the workflow can be executed.

    This architecture decouples the goals (the 'what') from the capabilities (the 'how')
and it lets the agents to autonomously decide if and how to employ their capabilities to
address them. The advantages are: *(i) Exploration of alternatives* - when more agents
have different implementations of the same ability (for example different classification
algorithms) they are in competition to get a goal assigned. Therefore, if the workflow
fails, for some reason, the commitment is retreated and re-assigned, thus to explore
different alternative tasks to the same objective. *(ii) Learning* - during their execution
agents learn from the result of their actions (by associating the success or failure to the
execution context). In this way, the social auction is won by the most capable agent
according to the current execution context. *(iii) Evolution* - new goals can be injected
into the database or existing goals can be retreated from it. Given that the commitment
is dynamic, it is not a big deal to reorganize the agents thus to make new goals satisfied.

## 5    Discussion and Conclusions

GoalSPEC has been developed to cover the requirements described in Section 2, in order to implement the adaptive system shown in Fig.2. None of the existing languages meet all those requirements. In the following we make some considerations on Goal-SPEC and on other works close to our approach.

*GoalSPEC supports Adaptivity.* GoalSPEC is intended to be used within the lifecycle of a business process from creation to maintenance. The scenario starts when business analysts generate a preliminary version of business process by employing a BPMN visual tool. The tool generates a XML file that adopts the standard schema defined by OMG. The *BPMN2GoalSPEC* component receives this file and it is able to automatically generate a set of *GoalSPEC* social and system goals. *GoalSPEC* is created in the context of adaptive workflow and it completely covers the whole BPMN expressivity (REQ. 6), hence whatever process defined with BPMN, its business goals (functional and non-functional) can be modelled with GoalSPEC (REQ. 1). Before being executed, system goals are proposed to analysts in order to be revised. Since *GoalSPEC* is based on natural language, and it is specifically been conceived to be attractive for a business audience (REQ. 4), analysts can easily understand and modify the results. This is useful since analysts may include other business goals missing in the BPMN specification.

Several time in this paper we have mentioned that social and system goals are injected into the system at run-time. Indeed, the agent system is already running when business analysts work. Agents are specialized workers (each with their specific skills) waiting for something to do. When goals are released, agents perceive them into their environment. They are also able to interpret *GoalSPEC* (REQ. 3) and to absorb goals into their knowledge base. Even if the grammar is context-free, goal specification by *GoalSPEC* is not rigid for two reasons. Firstly a goal does not specify how to operate but it rather defines the expected results in ontological terms (REQ. 2), that is the final state of the world that is desired. In addition, some elements of the behavior specifications may be relaxed by using fuzzy modifiers (REQ. 5). In practice, agents can potentially plan and propose more alternatives for addressing a goal. Social interactions and individual planning capability are out the scope of this paper.

*GoalSPEC supports Evolution.* Agents are allowed to commit to the achievement of injected goals as long as they are perceived into the environment. Certainly current business process will change in the future, maybe as a cause of new business goals, new laws and so on. In a traditional approach, analysts would revision their BPMN models in accordance to changes. Any revision includes to check possible inter-dependencies among related (sub)processes with a consequent hard work to ensure coherence. The *GoalSPEC* approach is that the system intelligence will support this activity. Agents ability to reason on the injected goals may also highlight possible incoherence or conflicts among them. Warning of conflicts are useful for the analysts to improve the process. The workflow system will be always running, but the consequence of a goals revision is that agents will reorganize their behavior to address the new objectives. Probably programmers will also introduce new agents into the system to cover the need for new skills.

*Considerations on the Expressiveness.* *GoalSPEC* adopts an ontological description of the business process. Logic predicates play a central role for the decomposition of the domain in a set of possible states of the world. Comparing *GoalSPEC* to Tropos, it appears that the second proposes a definitively richer semantics for the relationships between goals. *GoalSPEC* does not include operators for and/or decomposition, contributions and means/end. This choice has been deliberately done in order to make agents able to automatically discover these relationships. Any Tropos relationship adds a constraint for the system working. Otherwise, system intelligence must search for alternative solutions that were not designed by analysts. Comparing GoalSPEC to KAOS, it appears that the second uses a temporal logic, definitively more expressive than first order logic. Temporal propositions, in fact, contain some references to time conditions that GoalSPEC does not support. For example, we can't specify that in the time between the event $E1$ and the event $E2$ the action $A$ can be executed at most twice. We accept this limitation because our language needs to be more human oriented and feasible for complex systems. Indeed, systems based on temporal logic are difficultly scalable up and require formal verification. But, in order to further increase the goal expressiveness *GoalSpec* also supports some fuzzy modifiers that may introduce uncertainty with the aim to increase the agent degree of freedom in pursuing their goals.

*Considerations on the Generality.* The proposed language, although developed for a specific project, can also be used in more general information systems. We assert this because, it owns features that make it reusable in the general context in which workflows have to be managed. As it is well known, any information system embeds some kind of workflow even if sometimes that is not explicitly specified.

*Considerations on other related approaches.* Some proposals on the idea to link business processes to goal models exist in literature. To the best of our knowledge, among them those closest to our approach are presented in [33] and in [34].

G.Koliadis and A.Ghose [33] propose an approach, named GoalBPM, to relate BPMN business process to KAOS goal models. In particular, they introduce informal and manual techniques for establishing relations among high-level stakeholder goals and business processes. These relationships are established through two steps that allow to define traceability links between goals and activities and satisfaction links between goals and processes. This method is used to support the evolution of business processes and their consistency respect to the goal models. But the purpose of this approach is quite different from our. In fact, GoalBPM can be used for verify the satisfaction of a process model against a goal model when goal changes occurs. Whilst, our approach based on GoalSpec transforms a BPMN process model into goals that can be easily interpreted by a workflow engine able to satisfy these goals. The evolution of the business processes results on new goals to be managed by the systems.

In [34], the authors propose an approach to business process management based on BDI agent technology to realize agile processes (i.e. flexible and able to proactively adapt themselves). They start with business processes expressed using GO-BPMN [35] modeling language. Differently from BPMN, in GO-BPMN workflows are attached to a goal they fulfill. Thus, this model is directly mapped into BDI agent with goals, plans and beliefs. Similarly to our idea, the authors think that the agent technology can provide an agile process execution. But what we want to realize is a workflow engine, in which agents are aware of *what* they can do, but it is not established in any way *how* to do it. They are able to find out how to complete their business process activities adapting to the available resources. We do not create a static link between the declarative level and the procedural one. By decoupling business goals and their implementation using Goalspec and adopting the workflow engine architecture shown in Fig.2, we are able to create a dynamic binding between goals and plans to reach them which are composed at run-time. Moreover, this allow us to inject new goals in the system without changing the implementation level. In addition, our approach based on a standard notation (i.e. BPMN) to model business processes does not require furthers expertise to be owned by business analysts.

Many other recent works [4, 6, 36, 37] face with self-adaptive workflow engines. The objective of self-adaptive workflows is to make the enactment engine able to recognize anomalous situation that are not included in the specification. A promising approach in literature is to incorporate multiple strategies into the system design and to let the system to select the appropriate one that address the desired goal [7, 38]. Indeed, a goal may be generally addressed in many alternative ways, each with different trade-offs. A representative approach [38] is that of modeling goals in a hierarchy that describes the expected outcome of the system.This goal model is created at design time and then each goal is instructed with the necessary implementing code which execution addresses the target goal.

Surely, these approaches should obtain more precise results but they are less flexible than our. Thus, we accept a small loss of precision in order to achieve greater flexibility and dynamism.

*Final Remarks. GoalSpec* wants to be a step toward the definition of an agent framework able to implement an adaptive workflow enactor in which goals may evolve because the user requirements are changed. Self-awareness is another important issue we are addressing. We are working to realize a kind of agent that is able to decide its own behavior with respect to evolving goals.

**Acknowledgements.** This work has been partially funded by the Innovative Document Sharing (IDS) Project funded by the Autonomous Region of Sicily (PO FESR Sicilia 2007-2013).

# References

1. BPMN, O.: Business process model and notation (bpmn) (2009), www.omg.org/spec/BPMN/2.0/
2. Van der Aalst,, W., Basten, T., Verbeek, H.M.W., Verkoulen, P.A.C., Voorhoeve, M.: Adaptive workflow. In: Enterprise Information Systems. Kluwer Academic Publishers (1999)
3. Casati, F., Ceri, S., Pernici, B., Pozzi, G.: Workflow evolution. Data & Knowledge Engineering 24(3), 211–238 (1998)
4. Kammer, P., Bolcer, G., Taylor, R., Hitomi, A., Bergman, M.: Techniques for supporting dynamic and adaptive workflow. Computer Supported Cooperative Work (CSCW) 9(3), 269–292 (2000)

5. Serral, E., Sabatucci, L., Leonardi, C., Valderas, P., Susi, A., Zancanaro, M., Pelechano, V.: Applying a methodology for developing ami systems: the nursing home case study. In: Proceedings of the 20th International Conference on Information Systems Development Cutting Edge Research on Information Systems (2011)
6. Buhler, P., Vidal, J.: Towards adaptive workflow enactment using multiagent systems. Information Technology and Management 6(1), 61–87 (2005)
7. Morandini, M., Penserini, L., Perini, A.: Towards goal-oriented development of self-adaptive systems. In: Proceedings of the 2008 International Workshop on Software Engineering for Adaptive and Self-managing Systems, pp. 9–16 (2008)
8. Winikoff, M., Padgham, L., Harland, J., Thangarajah, J.: Declarative and procedural goals in intelligent agent systems. In: International Conference on Principles of Knowledge Representation and Reasoning, Morgan Kaufmann (2002)
9. Bresciani, P., Perini, A., Giorgini, P., Giunchiglia, F., Mylopoulos, J.: Tropos: An agent-oriented software development methodology. Autonomous Agents and Multi-Agent Systems 8(3), 203–236 (2004)
10. Van Lamsweerde, A.: Goal-oriented requirements engineering: A guided tour. In: Proceedings of Fifth IEEE International Symposium on Requirements Engineering, pp. 249–262 (2001)
11. Yu, E., Mylopoulos, J.: Why goal-oriented requirements engineering. In: Proceedings of the 4th International Workshop on Requirements Engineering: Foundations of Software Quality, pp. 15–22 (1998)
12. Cheng, B., de Lemos, R., Giese, H., Inverardi, P., Magee, J., Andersson, J., Becker, B., Bencomo, N., Brun, Y., Cukic, B., et al.: Software engineering for self-adaptive systems: A research roadmap. Software Engineering for Self-Adaptive Systems, 1–26 (2009)
13. Whittle, J., Sawyer, P., Bencomo, N., Cheng, B.H.C., Bruel, J.M.: RELAX: a language to address uncertainty in self-adaptive systems requirement. Requirements Engineering 15(2), 177–196 (2010)
14. Van Dyke Parunak, H., Brueckner, S.: Entropy and self-organization in multi-agent systems. In: Proceedings of the Fifth International Conference on Autonomous Agents, pp. 124–130. ACM (2001)
15. Wohlin, C., Runeson, P., Höst, M., Ohlsson, M.C., Regnell, B., Wesslén, A.: Experimentation in software engineering: An introduction. Kluwer Academic Publishers (2000)
16. Team, BMM: Business motivation model (bmm) specification. Technical report, Technical Report dtc/06–08–03, Object Management Group, Needham, Massachusetts, USA (2006)
17. Rolland, C., Souveyet, C., Achour, C.: Guiding goal modeling using scenarios. IEEE Transactions on Software Engineering 24(12), 1055–1071 (1998)
18. Yu, E.: Modelling strategic relationships for process reengineering. Social Modeling for Requirements Engineering 11 (2011)
19. Fuxman, A., Pistore, M., Mylopoulos, J., Traverso, P.: Model checking early requirements specifications in tropos. In: Proceedings of Fifth IEEE International Symposium on Requirements Engineering, pp. 174–181. IEEE (2001)
20. Yu, L.: From requirements to architectural design–using goals and scenarios. University of Toronto (2001),
http://www.cs.toronto.edu/km/GRL/fromr2a/fromr2a/straw01.pdf
21. Dardenne, A., Van Lamsweerde, A., Fickas, S.: Goal-directed requirements acquisition. Science of Computer Programming 20(1), 3–50 (1993)
22. Hindriks, K.V., de Boer, F.S., van der Hoek, W., Meyer, J.-J.C.: Agent programming with declarative goals. In: Castelfranchi, C., Lespérance, Y. (eds.) ATAL 2000. LNCS (LNAI), vol. 1986, pp. 228–243. Springer, Heidelberg (2001)
23. Howden, N., Rönnquist, R., Hodgson, A., Lucas, A.: Jack intelligent agents-summary of an agent infrastructure. In: 5th International Conference on Autonomous Agents (2001)

24. Rao, A.: Agentspeak (l): Bdi agents speak out in a logical computable language. Agents Breaking Away, 42–55 (1996)
25. Bordini, R.H., Hübner, J.F.: A java-based agentspeak interpreter used with saci for multi-agent distribution over the net (2004)
26. Hindriks, K.V., De Boer, F.S., Van der Hoek, W., Meyer, J.J.C.: Agent programming in 3APL. Autonomous Agents and Multi-Agent Systems 2(4), 357–401 (1999)
27. Dastani, M., van Riemsdijk, M.B., Dignum, F.P.M., Meyer, J.-J.C.: A programming language for cognitive agents goal directed 3APL. In: Dastani, M., Dix, J., El Fallah-Seghrouchni, A. (eds.) PROMAS 2003. LNCS (LNAI), vol. 3067, pp. 111–130. Springer, Heidelberg (2004)
28. Braubach, L., Pokahr, A., Moldt, D., Lamersdorf, W.: Goal representation for BDI agent systems. In: Bordini, R.H., Dastani, M., Dix, J., El Fallah Seghrouchni, A. (eds.) PROMAS 2004. LNCS (LNAI), vol. 3346, pp. 44–65. Springer, Heidelberg (2005)
29. Ribino, P., Lodato, C., Lopes, S., Seidita, V., Hilaire, V., Cossentino, M.: A norm-governed holonic multi-agent system metamodel. In: Müller, J.P., Cossentino, M. (eds.) AOSE 2012. LNCS, vol. 7852, pp. 22–39. Springer, Heidelberg (2013)
30. ISO Technical Committee TC 154: Iso 8601 international standard date and time notation (1998), http://www.iso.org/
31. Bordini, R.H., Hübner, J.F., Wooldridge, M.: Programming multi-agent systems in AgentSpeak using Jason, vol. 8. Wiley Interscience (2007)
32. TC OASIS: WS-BPEL - Web Services Business Process Execution Language (2007), http://www.oasis-open.org
33. Ghose, A.K., Koliadis, G.: Relating business process models to goal-oriented requirements models in kaos. Faculty of Informatics-Papers, 573 (2007)
34. Burmeister, B., Arnold, M., Copaciu, F., Rimassa, G.: Bdi-agents for agile goal-oriented business processes. In: Proceedings of the 7th International Joint Conference on Autonomous Agents and Multiagent Systems: Industrial Track, pp. 37–44. International Foundation for Autonomous Agents and Multiagent Systems (2008)
35. Greenwood, D., Ghizzioli, R.: Goal-oriented autonomic business process modelling and execution. Multiagent System (2009)
36. Chen-Burger, Y.H., Stader, J.: Formal support for adaptive workflow systems in a distributed environment. In: Workflow Handbook 2003, p. 93 (2003)
37. Cao, J., Yang, J., Chan, W.: Exception handling in distributed workflow systems using mobile agents. e-Business Engineering (2005)
38. Liaskos, S., Khan, S.M., Litoiu, M., Daoud Jungblut, M., Rogozhkin, V., Mylopoulos, J.: Behavioral adaptation of information systems through goal models. Information Systems (2012)

# Mutation Operators for the GOAL Agent Language

Sharmila Savarimuthu and Michael Winikoff

University of Otago, New Zealand
{sharmila.savarimuthu,michael.winikoff}@otago.ac.nz

**Abstract.** Testing multi-agent systems is a challenge, since by definition such systems are distributed, and are able to exhibit autonomous and flexible behaviour. One specific challenge in testing agent programs is developing a collection of tests (a "test suite") that is *adequate* for testing a given agent program. In order to develop an adequate test suite, it is clearly important to be able to *assess* the adequacy of a given test suite. A well-established technique for assessing this is the use of *mutation testing*, where mutation operators are used to generate variants ("mutants") of a given program, and a test suite is then assessed in terms of its ability to detect ("kill") the mutants. However, work on mutation testing has focussed largely on the mutation of procedural and object-oriented languages. This paper is the first to propose a set of mutation operators for a cognitive agent-oriented programming language, specifically GOAL. Our mutation operators are systematically derived, and are also guided by an exploration of the bugs found in a collection of undergraduate programming assignments written in GOAL. In fact, in exploring these programs we also provide an additional contribution: evidence of the extent to which the two foundational hypotheses of mutation testing hold for GOAL programs.

**Keywords:** Mutation Testing, Agent-Oriented Programming Languages, GOAL.

## 1 Introduction

Testing multi-agent systems (MAS) is a challenge, since by definition such systems are distributed, and are able to exhibit autonomous and flexible behaviour. For example, Munroe et al. note that *"However, the task* [validation] *proved challenging for several reasons. First, agent-based systems explore realms of behaviour outside people's expectations and often yield surprises ..."* [12, Section 3.7.2]. Similarly, Pěchouček and Mařík [16, Page 413] note that[1]: *"Although the agent system performed very well in all the tests, to release the system for production would require testing all the steel recipes with all possible configurations of cooling boxes"*.

There has been work on testing of multi-agent systems, especially in the last 4-5 years. Most of this work has focussed on tool support for executing (manually defined) tests (e.g. [2,3]). However, some work has investigated test generation based on design models [21], ontologies [13], or using evolutionary techniques [14]. Space precludes

---

[1] On the other hand, for another application they note that: *"Even though this negotiation process has not been theoretically proved for cycles' avoidance* [sic], *practical experiments have validated its operation"* [16, Page 407].

M. Cossentino et al. (Eds.): EMAS 2013, LNAI 8245, pp. 255–273, 2013.

a detailed review of testing, and we refer the reader to [20, Section 8.1] for a review of work on testing and debugging MAS. Overall, the conclusion of this review was that *"testing of agent based systems is an area where there is a need for substantial additional work"* [20, Section 8.1].

Given a collection of tests (a "test suite"), a key question when testing an agent system is to what extent is the test suite *adequate*? A test suite is adequate to the extent that it is able to distinguish between a correct and an incorrect program. In developing an adequate test suite, it is obviously useful to be able to *assess* the adequacy of the test suite. This assessment can assist a tester in detecting when a test suite is not sufficient and needs to be refined or extended. It can also guide a tester in knowing when to stop adding test cases.

So far, work on assessing the adequacy of test cases (e.g. [9,11,19]) has only considered the use of various *coverage metrics* to assess test suite adequacy. However, although coverage is necessary, it is not sufficient. Knowing that a test suite covers a certain portion of a program simply indicates that parts of the program were executed by the tests. It doesn't allow us to draw conclusions about whether these parts of the program were tested in a way that allows errors in the program to be detected, i.e. to distinguish between correct and incorrect programs.

An alternative, well-established, technique for assessing test suite adequacy is *mutation testing* [6] (see Section 2.1). Mutation testing directly assesses the ability of a test suite to distinguish between different programs, and is considered a more powerful and discerning metric than coverage. For instance Mathur notes that *"If your tests are adequate with respect to some other adequacy criteria ... then chances are that these are not adequate with respect to most criteria offered by program mutation"* [10, Page 503].

Most work on mutation testing of programs has focussed on programs in procedural and object-oriented languages [6, Figure 5]. There has been a (very) small amount of work on applying mutation to agents [18,1]. However, this work has not considered mutating agent programs written in a cognitive agent-oriented programming language.

In this paper we propose a set of mutation operators for the cognitive agent-oriented programming language GOAL (see Section 2.2 for a brief introduction to the language). Although we derive mutation operators for a specific language, the process by which the operators are derived is generic, and can easily be applied to other agent-oriented programming languages (see Section 6).

In deriving our mutation operators we are guided by an exploration of actual bugs in GOAL programs. We want mutation operators to generate "realistic" bugs, and we assess this by considering a collection of GOAL programs (written by undergraduate students at another university). Section 4 compares the bugs that exist in these programs against the sorts of bugs that our mutation operators generate, and uses the results to guide the selection of mutation operators. In fact, the results of this assessment of bugs also forms an additional contribution, in that it provides evidence of the extent to which the two foundational hypotheses of mutation testing hold for GOAL programs.

The remainder of this paper is structured as follows. We begin by briefly reviewing mutation testing (Section 2.1) and introducing the GOAL programming language (Section 2.2). We then present our mutation operators in Section 3. Section 4 looks at

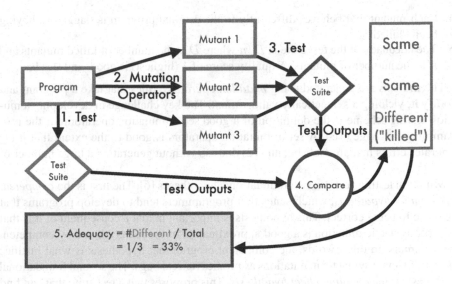

**Fig. 1.** Mutation Testing Process

a collection of GOAL programs and considers what bugs they contain. We then (Section 5) describe an implementation of the mutation operators, and report the number of mutants generated by different operators for a number of example GOAL programs. Finally, we conclude with a discussion, including future work (Section 6).

## 2   Background

### 2.1   Mutation Testing

We now very briefly introduce the key ideas of mutation testing, which is a long established field, going back to the 70s. For a detailed introduction to mutation testing see Chapter 7 of [10], and for a recent review of the field see Jia & Harman [6]. In a nutshell, mutation testing assesses the adequacy of a test suite by generating variants ("mutants") of the program being tested, and assessing to what extent the test suite is able to distinguish the original program from its mutants (termed "killing the mutant"). Given a test suite, a program $P$ written in a programming language, and a set of mutation operators for that programming language, the process of mutation testing is as follows (see Figure 1):

1. Execute the program $P$ against all tests in the test suite, recording the results;
2. Use the mutation operators to generate a set of mutant programs $P_1 \dots P_n$ from $P$ (where each $P_i$ is the result of applying a single mutation);
3. Test each mutant $P_i$ against the tests in the test suite;

4. Each mutant that behaves differently to the original program is flagged as having been "killed"[2];
5. The adequacy of the test suite is $D/n$ where $D$ is the number of killed mutants and $n$ is the number of mutants. A quality score of 1 (highest) is good, and 0 is bad.

The mutants are generated using *mutation operators*: rules that take a program and modify it, yielding a syntactically valid variant. The key challenge in developing a mutation testing scheme is the definition of a good set of mutation operators for the programming language used. A set of mutation operators is good to the extent that it (1) generates errors that are realistic; and (2) does so without generating a huge number of mutants.

Mutation testing rests on two foundational hypotheses [6]. The first is the *competent programmer hypothesis*, which states that programmers tend to develop programs that are close to being correct. This hypothesis is important in that a consequent of it is that a simple syntactic mutation is a good approximation of the faults created by competent programmers. In other words, the competent programmer hypothesis is what justifies the use of simple syntactical mutations as proxies for real bugs. The second foundational hypothesis is the *coupling effect hypothesis*. This proposes that a test suite that can find the simple faults in a program, will also find a high proportion of the program's complex faults [15]. This hypothesis justifies the generation of mutants by the application of a single mutation operator instance, rather than having to consider the application of multiple mutation operators to generate a mutant.

In Section 4 we consider a collection of GOAL programs and assess to what extent these two foundational hypotheses hold. Although there is empirical evidence to support both these hypotheses for procedural programs, this paper is the first to consider evidence for these hypotheses in the context of agent systems.

## 2.2  GOAL

This section briefly introduces GOAL (**G**oal **O**riented **A**gent **L**anguage); for further details we refer the reader to the existing literature [5,4]. A Multiagent System in GOAL is defined using a configuration file that specifies the environment, configuration options, and a number of GOAL agents, each with a GOAL program. A GOAL agent program consists of five components: domain knowledge (e.g. Prolog rules), initial beliefs, initial goals, action definitions, and a program. Note that both the domain knowledge and the beliefs are specified using a knowledge representation language which can be varied (the GOAL implementation uses SWI-Prolog). In this paper we focus on the program component, both because it corresponds most closely to other agent-oriented programming languages (AOPLs), and because that is usually where the complexity of the agent is [17], and where errors are made (see Section 4).

---

[2] Some mutants may be equivalent in behaviour to the original program ("equivalent mutants"), and, since program equivalence is undecidable, identifying and removing these mutants is a manual and partial process. This is a standard problem in the field of mutation testing but there is evidence that most equivalent mutants are actually fairly easy to detect. A related issue is where a mutant may be non-equivalent, but may still be correct. Mutation testing is not concerned with whether a mutant is correct, but with whether it is *different*, and whether this difference can be detected by a test suite.

GOAL programs are built out of actions and mental state conditions. Actions in GOAL are either user-defined (pre and post condition), or are one of the five built-in actions that insert or delete beliefs, adopt or drop goals, or send a message. GOAL also defines an achievement goal $\textbf{a-goal}(\phi) \equiv \textbf{goal}(\phi) \wedge \neg\textbf{bel}(\phi)$ and an achieved goal $\textbf{goal-a}(\phi) \equiv \textbf{goal}(\phi) \wedge \textbf{bel}(\phi)$. A mental state condition (MSC) in GOAL is built out of conditions over the agent's beliefs and its goals. A GOAL program definition then, in essence, consists of a sequence of rules of the form[3] "if MSC then $\text{action}_1 + \ldots + \text{action}_n$" where the actions are performed in order[4], and there can be at most one user-defined action.

These rules are actually placed within modules. However, in this paper we do not consider the mutation of modules, since the module construct is unique to GOAL, and was not used in the programs we considered (see Section 4). The grammar in Figure 2 summarises the subset of the language that we focus on. It thus differs from the original grammar given by Hindriks [5] in that it omits modules. It also differs in a couple of places where it has been changed to match what the implementation supports (specifically for $\textbf{drop}(\phi)$ the $\phi$ must not contain negations; and in fact in mentalatoms belief conditions can actually contain disjunctions).

Semantics: A rule "if condition then action" is *applicable* if the condition holds, and is *enabled* if the actions' preconditions are met. Applicable and enabled rules are *options*. The execution cycle consists of the following steps:

1. Clear previous cycle's percepts.
2. Update percepts by executing *all* options (i.e. enabled rules) in the distinguished event module.
3. Focus on the main module: compute the options, select one (by default rules are evaluated in linear order and the first option is selected), and perform its actions.
4. Update goals by dropping goals that are believed to hold.

Compared with other cognitive agent programming languages, GOAL's most distinctive (relevant) features are: (a) The limitation that an action rule can only result in a sequence of actions, rather than a mixture of actions and subgoals; and (b) The lack of a trigger condition. This makes GOAL action rules more general, in that a rule doesn't require a particular trigger. However, it also means that a rule can be applied repeatedly: in, say, Jason a rule of the form $+!goal : context \leftarrow planBody$ can be applied (if the *context* is true) to deal with the creation of a *goal*. However, the rule will not be applied subsequently unless the goal is re-posted. By contrast, in GOAL a rule of the form "if goal(*goal*) then *actions*" can be applied repeatedly, as long as *goal* remains a goal of the agent.

---

[3] There is also a form "forall MSC do actions" used in the percept processing module.

[4] The GOAL documentation states that "The actions that are part of a composed action may be put in any order in the action part of a rule. However, the order the actions are put in is taken into account when executing the composed action: **The actions are executed in the order they appear**" (emphasis added).

$$
\begin{aligned}
program &::= actionrule^+ \\
actionrule &::= \textbf{if } mentalstatecond \textbf{ then } actioncombo \\
&\mid \textbf{forall } mentalstatecond \textbf{ do } actioncombo \\
\\
mentalstatecond &::= mentalliteral \;\{\; , mentalliteral \;\}^* \\
mentalliteral &::= \textbf{true} \mid mentalatom \mid \textbf{not(} mentalatom \textbf{)} \\
mentalatom &::= \textbf{bel(} litconj \textbf{)} \mid \textbf{goal(} litconj \textbf{)} \\
\\
actioncombo &::= action \;\{\; \textbf{+} \; action \;\}^* \\
action &::= user\text{-}def\text{-}action \mid built\text{-}in\text{-}action \mid communication \\
user\text{-}def\text{-}action &::= id[parameters] \\
built\text{-}in\text{-}action &::= \textbf{insert(} litconj \textbf{)} \mid \textbf{delete(} litconj \textbf{)} \\
&\mid \textbf{adopt(} poslitconj \textbf{)} \mid \textbf{drop(} poslitconj \textbf{)} \\
communication &::= \textbf{send(} id \textbf{ , } poslitconj \textbf{)} \\
\\
poslitconj &::= atom \;\{\; , atom \;\}^* \; . \\
litdisj &::= litconj \;\{\; ; litconj \;\}^* \; . \\
litconj &::= literal \;\{\; , literal \;\}^* \; . \\
literal &::= atom \mid \textbf{not(} atom \textbf{)} \\
\\
atom &::= predicate[parameters] \mid ( litdisj ) \\
parameters &::= ( term \;\{\; , term \;\}^* )
\end{aligned}
$$

**Fig. 2.** GOAL Agent Program syntax (adapted from [5]): *term* is a legal term and *id* is an identifier

## 3  Deriving GOAL Mutation Operators

*"the design of mutation operators is as much of an art as it is science."* [10, Page 530].

In deriving a set of mutation operators for GOAL we follow the approach of Kim *et al.* [8] and derive mutation operators based on HAZOP and the *syntax* of the language. HAZOP (Hazard and Operability Study) is a technique for identifying hazards in systems by considering each element of the system and applying "guide words" such as NONE, MORE, LESS, PART OF, AS WELL AS, or OTHER THAN. For example, in a chemical processing system, engineers might consider what hazard exists if a certain pipe carries MORE chemical than it should, or if there is a contaminant ("AS WELL AS"). Kim *et al.* applied this idea to generating mutation operators by applying these guide words to the *syntax* of Java. For example, when considering a method invocation, the guide word OTHER THAN suggests that the designer consider the possibility that a different method to the intended one is invoked. This then leads directly to the definition of a mutation operator that rewrites a method invocation by changing the method name. Figure 3 shows their interpretation of the HAZOP guide words (note that some of the guide words, such as those to do with scope, or quantitative changes, are not applicable to GOAL, and so have been left out of the figure).

| Guide Words | Interpretation |
|---|---|
| NO/NONE | No part of the intention is achieved. No use of syntactic components. |
| AS WELL AS | Specific design intent is achieved but with additional results |
| PART OF | Only some of the intention is achieved, incomplete |
| REVERSE | Reverse flow - flow of information in wrong direction ... negation of condition |
| OTHER THAN | A result other than the original intention is achieved, complete but incorrect |

**Fig. 3.** HAZOP guide words and their interpretation for software (copied from [8])

In deriving mutation operators for GOAL we actually go through two stages. We firstly apply HAZOP to abstract syntactical classes in order to develop generic mutation schemas (Figure 4). These are generic in that they are applicable to a wide range of programming languages. We then apply these schemas to the GOAL syntax to generate specific mutation rules for GOAL (Figure 5). The advantage of doing the derivation in two stages is that we can then more easily derive mutation operators for other AOPLs by applying the generic schemas.

In deriving our generic schemas we consider three generic syntactical types: a sequence of elements, a (binary) operator that has two sub-elements, and a unary operator. For each of these generic syntactical types we consider what mutations are suggested by the HAZOP guide words, which gives a set of generic mutation schemas for that syntactical type. In addition, there is also a generic schema, suggested by the NO/NONE HAZOP guide word, that can be applied to delete ("drop") *any* syntactical type. Formally we write drop:$x \rightsquigarrow \epsilon$ to capture this: the "drop:" is a label, $x$ is a variable for a syntactical element, the arrow "$\rightsquigarrow$" indicates a mutation, and $\epsilon$ denotes the empty syntactical construct of the appropriate form (e.g. empty sequence, "True" Boolean value).

Consider now a sequence of elements ($x_1 \ldots x_n$). The HAZOP guide word PART OF suggests that we consider removing an element in the sequence ("drop1" in Figure 4). The OTHER THAN guide word suggests changing part of the sequence, specifically, we select an element, and replace it with a variant (derived using other appropriate mutation operators; "mut1"). The REVERSE suggests changing the order of the sequence. However, in general reversing a sequence of syntactic elements doesn't make much sense, and instead we propose a rule to swap two adjacent elements in the sequence ("seqswap"): note that we choose to only swap adjacent elements in order to avoid generating a large number of possible mutants (but see the discussion of program:seqtop and seqbot later in this section). The AS WELL AS guide word suggests that we add an item to the sequence. However, we prefer to avoid adding things because this raises the issue of what to add? If we add, say, a new rule to a GOAL program, what rule should we add? It is possible to define a way of creating a new rule from existing fragments in the program, but this tends to result in a very large number of possible mutations. The NO/NONE guide word has already been handled by a rule that applies to all syntactical types, including sequences.

Consider now a binary operator (notation: $x \oplus y$ or $x \otimes y$, where we assume that $\oplus$ and $\otimes$ are different). Using similar reasoning, we are inspired by PART OF to consider dropping either the left or right element ("dropL", "dropR"); by REVERSE to swap the elements ("swap2"); and by OTHER THAN to change either the operator ("op2") or to mutate one of the elements ("mutL", "mutR").

Finally, consider a unary operator (notation: $\Box x$ or $\Diamond x$, assuming $\Box \neq \Diamond$). Using similar reasoning, we are inspired by the PART OF guide word to delete the operator ("delop"); by OTHER THAN to change the operator ("op1") or mutate the component ("mut"). We also can add an operator ("addop") which can be seen as inspired by the "negation of condition" interpretation of the REVERSE guide word (e.g. $F \rightsquigarrow \neg F$).

Figure 4 shows the resulting generic mutation schemas. Recall that each rule is of the form "keyword : $x \rightsquigarrow y$". We also employ a convention that where we have $p(x) \rightsquigarrow p(x')$, there is an implied "if $x \rightsquigarrow x'$". In other words, the mut1 rule, for instance, is really shorthand for "mut1: $x_1 \ldots x_j \ldots x_n \rightsquigarrow x_1 \ldots x_j' \ldots x_n$ if $x_j \rightsquigarrow x_j'$".

---

drop: $x \rightsquigarrow \epsilon$

seqswap: $x_1 \ldots x_j\, x_{j+1} \ldots x_n \rightsquigarrow x_1 \ldots x_{j+1}\, x_j \ldots x_n$
mut1: $x_1 \ldots x_j \ldots x_n \rightsquigarrow x_1 \ldots x_j' \ldots x_n$
drop1: $x_1 \ldots x_j\, x_{j+1} \ldots x_n \rightsquigarrow x_1 \ldots x_{j+1} \ldots x_n$

dropL: $x \oplus y \rightsquigarrow y$      dropR: $x \oplus y \rightsquigarrow x$      swap2: $x \oplus y \rightsquigarrow y \oplus x$
op2: $x \oplus y \rightsquigarrow x \otimes y$      mutL: $x \oplus y \rightsquigarrow x' \oplus y$   mutR: $x \oplus y \rightsquigarrow x \oplus y'$

addop: $x \rightsquigarrow \Diamond x$      delop: $\Diamond x \rightsquigarrow x$      op1: $\Diamond x \rightsquigarrow \Box x$      mut: $\Diamond x \rightsquigarrow \Diamond x'$

---

**Fig. 4.** Generic Mutation Schemas

The second step is to apply these generic mutation schemas to the GOAL syntax in order to derive a set of mutation operators specific to GOAL. In doing so, we sometimes leave out rules that don't make sense. For example, when a binary operator is commutative, it doesn't make sense to mutate by swapping its arguments ("swap2"). We now proceed to consider in turn each syntactical element type in GOAL and consider how the generic mutation schemas apply to it.

We begin by considering a GOAL program. This is a *sequence* of action rules, and therefore the relevant generic mutation schemas are those for a sequence (seqswap, mut1, drop1), as well as the universal "drop" schema. In this case, it doesn't make sense to drop the whole program, so we have three rules (labelled in Figure 5 "program:seqswap", "program:mut1" and "program:drop1"). For example, given a program that consists of the rules $r_1 r_2 r_3$ we could apply the mutation operator program:seqswap to swap any two rules, for example swapping $r_1$ and $r_2$ to obtain the mutated program $r_2 r_1 r_3$. We could alternatively apply program:drop1 to remove a single rule, for instance dropping $r_1$ yielding the mutated program $r_2 r_3$. A final option is to select a rule, for instance $r_2$, and mutate it using a rule mutation operator, yielding the mutated rule $r_2'$, and the overall mutated program $r_1 r_2' r_3$.

In fact, in our exploration of bugs in example GOAL programs, we also found that the limitation to only swap adjacent rules in a program was too strong: there were a number of cases where bugs corresponded to other sorts of changes to the order of rules in a program. Although we do not want to introduce a mutation operator to allow arbitrary reorderings of the rules in a program, we do propose a compromise that allows many of the bugs seen to be generated by our mutation rules, whilst not increasing the number of possible mutants too much. This compromise is to add mutation operators that allow a single rule in the program to be moved to the start ("program:seqtop") or end ("program:seqbot") of the program. Applying these rules to the program $r_1r_2r_3r_4r_5$ with rule $r_3$ being moved yield respectively the mutated programs $r_3r_1r_2r_4r_5$ and $r_1r_2r_4r_5r_3$.

Next we consider a GOAL action rule (abbreviated AR). An action rule is effectively a binary connective with two sub-components, and hence the generic schemas for binary connectives apply (i.e. dropL, dropR, swap2, op2, mutL, mutR, as well as drop). However, for an AR the components cannot be deleted, since a rule must have both a condition and actions (although an MSC could be replaced with "true"), and they cannot be swapped, so we only have rules for op2, mutL, and mutR. For op2 we consider replacing "if *MSC* then *AC*" with "forall *MSC* do *AC*" (and vice versa), but only in the context of the percept processing module. Note that op2 has two instances, and that it is fairly specific to GOAL: other AOPLs don't deal with percepts in the same way. The universal "drop" rule isn't needed for actionrules, since actionrules only occur within a sequence, and we already have a rule to delete an element in the sequence. Thus, for an action rule in the main module (i.e. not in the percept module), we can only mutate it by selecting either its mental state condition or its action combo, and using an appropriate mutation operator to mutate the selected element.

A mentalstatecond (MSC) is also a sequence. Here it *does* make sense to also consider the overall drop rule, dropping the whole MSC, as well as the usual mut1 and drop1 rules. However, in fact the result of dropping an MSC completely is rarely a valid GOAL program: GOAL requires that variables appearing in the actions of a rule also appear in that rule's condition. Since this requirement only holds for a "true" condition when the action list has no variables, the MSC:drop rule is unlikely to ever be applicable (see Section 5). Note that we only consider mutation by dropping an MSC if it has more than one element (otherwise the same effect is achieved by the ML:drop rule). Finally, we did not initially define mutation operators to change the order of conditions in an MSC, since in many cases the order doesn't matter, for instance where each condition has disjoint variables. However, in other cases the order may matter, and we could consider extending our set of mutation operators with rules to change the order as future work.

A mentalliteral (ML), as defined in the GOAL syntax, is an optional unary operator ("not") that is applied to a mental atom (which itself is either a **bel** or a **goal** operator applied to a litconj). We can mutate a mentalliteral by dropping it completely. We can also add or remove a "not" ("addop", "delop"), or we can mutate the mental atom. Mutating a mental atom (MA) can be done by either changing a **bel** to a **goal** (or vice versa), or by mutating the literal conjunction. Note that we cannot mutate the "not" into another operator, since there is no alternative operator.

An actioncombo (AC) is a sequence of actions. It cannot be entirely deleted. However, we can mutate an individual action or drop one. Note that the swap rule doesn't really make sense: although GOAL specifies that actions in an actioncombo are executed sequentially, it would in fact be non-idiomatic to have a sequence of actions that is order dependent.

An action (A) is either user defined ("id[parameters]") or is one of the five built-in actions: insert, delete, adopt, drop, send. Dropping an action completely is already covered by the rule AC:drop1, so we only consider mutating the parameters of the action, or the action type. In mutating the action type we exclude changing a belief operation to a goal operation and vice versa, since this doesn't make sense, and is unlikely to yield a sensible mutant. When mutating a message, we can mutate the message content, or the recipient. Finally, we can mutate a user-defined action by mutating either the id (by replacing it with a different user defined action or by mutating the parameters. In replacing a user-defined action with a different user-defined action we need to ensure that the two actions have the same number of parameters (which we term being "compatible"). This condition also applies when mutating atoms by changing their predicate.

We did observe that some programs had "typos" (e.g having "at" instead of "at-Block") in predicates. However, we did not introduce a mutation operator to create such typos for the simple reason that this operator would be redundant. Consider, for example, replacing the action "delete(p)" with "delete(typo)". This is actually equivalent to just deleting the action. Similarly, replacing "bel(p)" with "bel(typo)" in an MSC is equivalent to replacing it with "false", i.e. with deleting the rule; and having "adopt(typo)" is equivalent to a null action since the goal won't have rules that handle it, so won't have any effect.

A poslitconj (PLC) and a litconj (LC) are both sequences (respectively of Atoms "At" or Literals "Lit"), so we can remove an element of the sequence or mutate an element of the sequence. As for MSCs, we did not define swapping operations, but these could be considered as future work.

A Literal is an optional unary connective ("not") applied to an Atom, and hence can be mutated by adding or removing a negation, or by mutating the atom. Mutating an atom can be done by mutating the predicate (replacing it with another predicate found in the program), or by mutating the parameters. Parameters are a sequence of terms (we abbreviate $term$ to $t$), but we do not want to change the length of the sequence, hence can only mutate individual terms. However, swapping terms is a reasonable mutation.

Mutating a list (of the form $[t_1|t_2]$) is done similarly to any other binary connective, yielding the following rules (for space reasons, these are not shown in Figure 5):

| | | |
|---|---|---|
| termlist:drop1 | $[A|As] \rightsquigarrow A$ | $[A|As] \rightsquigarrow As$ |
| termlist:seqswap | $[A|As] \rightsquigarrow [As|A]$ | |
| termlist:mut | $[A|As] \rightsquigarrow [A'|As]$ | $[A|As] \rightsquigarrow [A|As']$ |

Finally, we consider the mutation of terms (excluding lists). A term is of the form $f(t_1, \ldots, t_n)$ and, viewed as a sequence of arguments, can be mutated by dropping a sub-term ("term:drop1"), mutating a sub-term, or swapping adjacent sub-terms. There is one special case: equality. For the term $t_1 = t_2$ it does not make sense to drop either sub-term, nor to swap the sub-terms.

Figure 5 shows the collected mutation operators for GOAL. Recall that by convention where we have $p(x) \rightsquigarrow p(x')$, there is an implied "if $x \rightsquigarrow x'$". We also assume that there are implicit checks for syntactic elements being of the correct type. For instance, in the rule ML:addop, the element $MA$ must be a MentalAtom, and hence cannot be "true" or "not($MA$)". There is also a constraint: for those rules that involve an element $j+1$ (i.e. the swap and drop1 rules) we have $1 \leq j$ and $j+1 \leq n$, and hence that $n \geq 2$ (so we don't drop the last element in a list). For other rules we have $1 \leq j \leq n$. Finally, the program:mut rule has an additional condition, discussed above, that all variables appearing in the actions also appear in the rule's condition.

program:seqtop $AR_1 \ldots AR_j \, AR_{j+1} \ldots AR_n \rightsquigarrow AR_j \, AR_1 \ldots AR_{j+1} \ldots AR_n$
program:seqbot $AR_1 \ldots AR_j \, AR_{j+1} \ldots AR_n \rightsquigarrow AR_1 \ldots AR_{j+1} \ldots AR_n \, AR_j$
program:seqswap $AR_1 \ldots AR_j \, AR_{j+1} \ldots AR_n \rightsquigarrow AR_1 \ldots AR_{j+1} \, AR_j \ldots AR_n$
program:mut1 $AR_1 \ldots AR_j \ldots AR_n \rightsquigarrow AR_1 \ldots AR'_j \ldots AR_n$ (see text for condition)
program:drop1 $AR_1 \ldots AR_j \, AR_{j+1} \ldots AR_n \rightsquigarrow AR_1 \ldots AR_{j+1} \ldots AR_n$

AR:op2 **if** *msc* **then** *actioncombo* $\rightsquigarrow$ **forall** *msc* **do** *actioncombo* (only percept rules)
AR:op2 **forall** *msc* **do** *actioncombo* $\rightsquigarrow$ **if** *msc* **then** *actioncombo* (only percept rules)
AR:mutL **if** *msc* **then** *actioncombo* $\rightsquigarrow$ **if** *msc'* **then** *actioncombo*
AR:mutR **if** *msc* **then** *actioncombo* $\rightsquigarrow$ **if** *msc* **then** *actioncombo'*
AR:mutL **forall** *msc* **do** *actioncombo* $\rightsquigarrow$ **forall** *msc'* **do** *actioncombo*
AR:mutR **forall** *msc* **do** *actioncombo* $\rightsquigarrow$ **forall** *msc* **do** *actioncombo'*

MSC:drop $ML_1 \ldots ML_j \, ML_{j+1} \ldots ML_n \rightsquigarrow$ true
MSC:mut1 $ML_1 \ldots ML_j \ldots ML_n \rightsquigarrow ML_1 \ldots ML'_j \ldots ML_n$

ML:drop $ML \rightsquigarrow$ true   (if $ML \neq$ true)
ML:addop $MA \rightsquigarrow$ **not**( $MA$ )                    ML:delop **not**( $MA$ ) $\rightsquigarrow MA$
ML:mut $MA \rightsquigarrow MA'$                              **not**( $MA$ ) $\rightsquigarrow$ **not**( $MA'$ )
MA:op1 **bel**( *litconj* ) $\rightsquigarrow$ **goal**( *litconj* )    **goal**( *litconj* ) $\rightsquigarrow$ **bel**( *litconj* )
MA:mut $\Diamond$( *litconj* ) $\rightsquigarrow \Diamond$( *litconj'* ) where $\Diamond \in \{$**bel**, **goal**$\}$

AC:mut1 $A_1 \ldots A_j \ldots A_n \rightsquigarrow A_1 \ldots A'_j \ldots A_n$
AC:drop1 $A_1 \ldots A_j \, A_{j+1} \ldots A_n \rightsquigarrow A_1 \ldots A_{j+1} \ldots A_n$

A:op1 **insert**( *litconj* ) $\rightsquigarrow$ **delete**( *litconj* )       **delete**( *litconj* ) $\rightsquigarrow$ **insert**( *litconj* )
A:op1 **adopt**( *poslitconj* ) $\rightsquigarrow$ **drop**( *poslitconj* )   **drop**( *poslitconj* ) $\rightsquigarrow$ **adopt**( *poslitconj* )
A:mut $\Diamond$( *litconj* ) $\rightsquigarrow \Diamond$( *litconj'* ) where $\Diamond \in \{$**insert**, **delete**$\}$
A:mut $\Diamond$( *poslitconj* ) $\rightsquigarrow \Diamond$( *poslitconj'* ) where $\Diamond \in \{$**adopt**, **drop**$\}$
A:mut **send**( *id* , *poslitconj* ) $\rightsquigarrow$ **send**( *id* , *poslitconj'* )
A:mut **send**( *id* , *poslitconj* ) $\rightsquigarrow$ **send**( *id'* , *poslitconj* )
A:mut(*) $id[parameters] \rightsquigarrow id'[parameters]$
A:mut $id[parameters] \rightsquigarrow id[parameters']$

PLC:mut1 $At_1 \ldots At_j \ldots At_n \rightsquigarrow At_1 \ldots At'_j \ldots At_n$
PLC:drop1 $At_1 \ldots At_j \, At_{j+1} \ldots At_n \rightsquigarrow At_1 \ldots At_{j+1} \ldots At_n$
LC:mut1 $Lit_1 \ldots Lit_j \ldots Lit_n \rightsquigarrow Lit_1 \ldots Lit'_j \ldots Lit_n$
LC:drop1 $Lit_1 \ldots Lit_j \, Lit_{j+1} \ldots Lit_n \rightsquigarrow Lit_1 \ldots Lit_{j+1} \ldots Lit_n$

Lit:addop $At \rightsquigarrow$ **not**( $At$ )                    Lit:delop **not**( $At$ ) $\rightsquigarrow At$
Lit:mut $At \rightsquigarrow At'$                               **not**( $At$ ) $\rightsquigarrow$ **not**( $At'$ )
At:mut(*) $predicate[parameters] \rightsquigarrow predicate'[parameters]$
At:mut $predicate[parameters] \rightsquigarrow predicate[parameters']$
At:mut $lit_1; \ldots; lit_j; \ldots; lit_n \rightsquigarrow lit_1; \ldots; lit'_j; \ldots; lit_n$
parameters:seqswap $t_1 \ldots t_j \, t_{j+1} \ldots t_n \rightsquigarrow t_1 \ldots t_{j+1} \, t_j \ldots t_n$
parameters:mut $t_1 \ldots t_j \ldots t_n \rightsquigarrow t_1 \ldots t'_j \ldots t_n$
term:drop1    $f(t_1 \ldots t_j, t_{j+1} \ldots t_n) \rightsquigarrow f(t_1 \ldots t_{j+1} \ldots t_n)$
term:mut1     $f(t_1 \ldots t_j, t_{j+1} \ldots t_n) \rightsquigarrow f(t_1 \ldots t_j, t', t_{j+1} \ldots t_n)$
term:seqswap  $f(t_1 \ldots t_j, t_{j+1} \ldots t_n) \rightsquigarrow f(t_1 \ldots t_{j+1}, t_j \ldots t_n)$
term:mut      $X = Y \rightsquigarrow X' = Y$              $X = Y \rightsquigarrow X = Y'$

Constraints: $1 \leq j$ and $j + 1 \leq n$ for constraints that have $j + 1$, otherwise $1 \leq j \leq n$
(*) = compatibility constraint (see text)

**Fig. 5.** Mutation Operators for GOAL

These rules have the property that when applied to a valid GOAL program, they result in another valid program, since they always replace a syntactical element of a certain type (e.g. MSC) with another valid syntactical element of the same type (see also Section 5). Figure 6 shows an example GOAL rule and its mutations (generated by the implementation described in Section 5).

```
Original:   if not(goal(target(A, B))), bel(holding(C)) then adopt(target(C, table)).
ml:drop     if true, bel(holding(A)) then adopt(target(A, table)).
ml:delop    if goal(target(A, B)), bel(holding(C)) then adopt(target(C, table)).
ma:op1      if not(bel(target(A, B))), bel(holding(C)) then adopt(target(C, table)).
ml:addop    if not(goal(target(A, B))), not(bel(holding(C))) then adopt(target(C, table)).
ma:op1      if not(goal(target(A, B))), goal(holding(C)) then adopt(target(C, table)).
lit:addop   if not(goal(target(A, B))), bel(not(holding(C))) then adopt(target(C, table)).
at:mut      if not(goal(target(A, B))), bel(block(C)) then adopt(target(C, table)).
a:op1       if not(goal(target(A, B))), bel(holding(C)) then drop(target(C, table)).
parameters:seqswap
            if not(goal(target(A, B))), bel(holding(C)) then adopt(target(table, C)).
```

**Fig. 6.** GOAL clause and example mutations, with the changes highlighted

## 4   An Empirical Evaluation of Programs

We now turn to an empirical evaluation by examining a collection of GOAL programs. The aim of this examination is primarily to assess how well the mutation operators are able to generate realistic bugs. However, we also briefly consider what our empirical evaluation tells us about the two foundational hypotheses of mutation testing (Section 4.1).

Methodology: We obtained a collection of 55 GOAL programs, written as an assignment by first year undergraduate students at Delft university. These programs each implement a solution to "Blocks World for Teams" (BW4T) [7]: a single[5] agent that moves around an environment with a number of rooms (see Figure 7), collecting blocks of various colours, and delivering them to the "dropzone" in a specified order (e.g. a red block, then a blue block). The environment (which runs in a separate process) provides the agent with percepts (e.g. in(Room), color(BlockID, Color), holding(BlockID)), and four actions (goTo(Location), goToBlock(BlockID), pickUp, and putDown).

We are interested in assessing how well the mutation operators are able to generate realistic bugs. We therefore consider the collection of GOAL programs as being a source of realistic buggy programs, and consider whether each of the buggy programs could have been generated from a correct program by applying our mutation operators. We therefore proceeded by testing each program to locate bugs, and then fixing the bugs. In fixing bugs we were careful to only make changes that were necessary, and to consider what alternative changes might be used to fix the bug. Once a bug was fixed we retested the program to confirm that the fix was correct. When testing the programs we

---

[5] We only considered the initial version of the assignment with one agent.

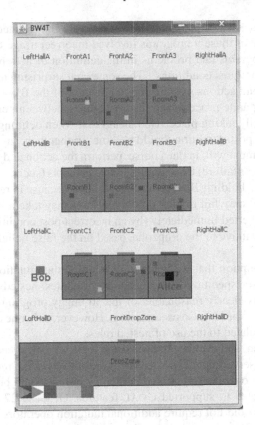

**Fig. 7.** Blocks World for Teams

used a number of test suites: the two example scenarios that were used in the original assignment, a set of ten randomly generated test cases, and a generated enumeration of all possible starting configurations within a limited scope (for scope sizes 1 and 2). Overall, we considered a program to be correct if it managed to deliver the desired blocks in all runs. Note that in some cases programs were successful in delivering all blocks, but had other issues, for example, a program might deliver incorrect blocks along the way, or may require a large number of additional actions. However, as long as it ended up delivering the desired blocks, we considered it to be "correct". Of the 55 programs, 4 were excluded, since they did not run at all (e.g. syntax errors), and 15 further programs were excluded since they did not have any (detected) bugs. This left a total of 36 buggy programs.

Before we consider how well the mutation operators are able to generate realistic bugs (as represented by the 36 buggy programs), we need to consider the assumptions that were made in developing the mutation operators. To what extent do these assumptions hold?

Recall that GOAL programs have a number of components (e.g. domain knowledge, action definitions), and that we have focussed on the program rules, i.e. assumed that errors only occur in the program rules. Is this a valid assumption? Out of the 36 programs with bugs, only 9 programs involved errors that related to non-supported GOAL features. One of these 9 programs involved incorrect usage of nested rules, and the remaining 8 programs had problems in the definition of actions, mostly incorrect definitions of their pre/post conditions[6]. The somewhat surprising number of programs with issues in defining actions may be due to a feature of the BW4T environment: the environment is a separate process, and there is a delay between performing an action, and the action actually taking place. This means that when defining an action, such as pickUp, the action's post-condition should be "true", rather than, say, "holding(Block)", because the environment will, in due course, perform the action and inform the agent of the action's success (or failure) by sending suitable percepts (such as "holding(Block)"). Having pickUp make holding(Block) true is a problem because in reality (i.e. in the environment) the agent may fail to pick up the block, or may take a while to succeed. If holding(Block) is asserted immediately (by an incorrect post condition), then the agent may then proceed to move to the dropzone, based on the false belief that it has already picked up the block.

The second assumption that we made in developing the mutation operators was to ignore certain features specific to GOAL, namely modules, nested rules, and macros. This assumption was clearly reasonable: of the 36 buggy programs, only 6 programs used nested rules (2 of these 6 also used macros). However, only one of these 6 programs had a bug that was related to the use of nested rules.

Having considered, and evaluated, the assumptions, we now consider to what extent the bugs that we observed could be seen as the result of one or more applications of the defined mutation operators. As noted earlier, 27 out of the 36 buggy programs had bugs that solely related to supported GOAL features. Of these 27 programs, 16 programs had errors that did not require additional mutation operators. The remaining 11 programs had errors that corresponded to the application of a number of mutation operator instances, where at least one of the operators was additional to the ones that we had defined. The additional mutation operators were: (i) addition of elements (either actions or literals) [7 programs]; (ii) changes to the order of rules in a program other than the cases defined[7] [3 programs]; (iii) mutating a variable to another (legal) variable name [3 programs]; and (iv) replacing an "insert" with a "drop" [1 program]. As discussed in Section 3, mutation operators that add to the program are problematic; however, the other three types of rules could be easily added.

Finally, we consider *which* of the mutation operators are used to generate the observed bugs. Figure 8 contains a summary of the number of times that each rule was used in deriving buggy programs, summed up over the 36 programs. Note that since some programs had bugs that corresponded to the application of multiple mutation operators, the sum of the number of rule applications (final row) is greater than the number of buggy programs. As can be seen in Figure 8, many of the rules that we defined actually do *not* correspond to the sorts of errors that we found in real buggy programs. Indeed, as often appears to be the case in mutation testing, only a few rules account for most of the bug types. For example, the four most commonly used rules (program:seqswap,

---

[6] Of these 8, one also had an error in the domain knowledge where a ">" should have been "≥", and two had incorrectly defined actions using e.g. pickUp(Block) instead of pickUp.

[7] These could, in principle, be regarded as repeated application of program:seqswap.

| Rule | Observed Bugs |
|------|------|
| a:mut | 0 |
| a:op1 | 0 |
| ac:drop1 | **14** |
| ar:op2 | 6 |
| at:mut | 4 |
| lc:drop1 | **18** |
| lit:addop | 0 |
| lit:delop | 0 |
| ma:op1 | 0 |
| ml:addop | 1 |
| ml:delop | 0 |
| ml:drop | 13 |
| msc:drop | 0 |
| parameters:seqswap | 0 |
| plc:drop1 | 0 |
| program:drop1 | **29** |
| program:seqbot | 9 |
| program:seqswap | **31** |
| program:seqtop | 5 |
| term:drop1 | 0 |
| term:seqswap | 0 |
| TOTAL | 130 |

**Fig. 8.** Summary of observed bugs and the rules involved

program:drop1, LC:drop1, and AC:drop1, which are bolded in Figure 8) correspond to 71% of the mutation operator applications.

Overall, we conclude that: 75% (27 out of 36) of the programs had bugs that did not involve excluded GOAL features, such as modules, action definitions, or nested rules; 59% of these (16 out of 27) had bugs that were able to be generated by the mutation operators that we defined; and many (71%) of the mutation operator applications were instances of only four rules.

One question that might be asked is whether we could derive the mutation operators based on the buggy programs, rather than using the syntax-based approach discussed in Section 3. The advantage of the approach that we used is that it is based on the programming language itself, rather than on a given set of programs. In this case, since we had programs that all solved the same problem, if we had derived the operators based on the programs, there would be a danger that the operators would be biased to this specific problem.

## 4.1 Evidence for the Foundational Hypotheses

Recall that the field of mutation testing rests on two foundational hypotheses. The *competent programmer hypothesis* states that programmers write programs that are "almost correct", i.e. programs that are "a few mutants away from a correct program" [10, Page

| # Mutation Operator Applications | # Programs |
|---|---|
| 1 | 7 |
| 2 | 7 |
| 3 | 2 |
| 4 | 3 |
| 5 | 3 |
| 6 | 5 |
| 7 | 0 |
| 8 | 2 |
| 9 | 1 |
| 10 | 2 |
| >10 | 4 |

**Fig. 9.** Number of programs that are $N$ mutants away from being correct, for different values of $N$ (see also Figure 10)

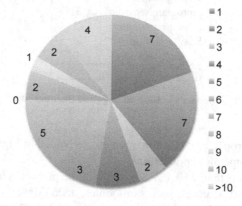

**Fig. 10.** Number of programs that are $N$ mutants away from being correct, for different values of $N$ (see also Figure 9)

531]. Of the 36 buggy programs, we found that 27 programs (75%) were indeed a few mutants away from a correct program (defining "a few" to be "6 or fewer"). Thus we conclude that the there is evidence that the competent programmer hypothesis holds for GOAL programs, even when they are written by first-year students. Figures 9 and 10 show how many programs were $N$ mutation operators away from being correct. For instance, 7 of the 36 buggy programs corresponded to the application of a single mutation operator (first row of Figure 9), and 7 programs had 2 mutations (second row). The last row indicates that there were 4 programs that required more than 10 mutation operator applications: these required 11, 16, 20, and 22 applications respectively.

The *coupling effect hypothesis* states that a test set that is adequate with respect to single mutations is also adequate for multiple mutations. Since it concerns test sets and adequacy, this hypothesis is not easy to assess, and a full assessment is beyond the scope of this paper. However, we can provide some initial evidence: if, in fact, most of the observed bugs are generated by the application of a single mutation, then this would be evidence for the coupling effect hypothesis. Note that the converse is not true: even if the observed bugs mostly involve the application of multiple mutations, this does not mean that the coupling effect hypothesis fails to hold. There could be other mutants that can be used to assess whether the test suite is adequate with respect to the given bug. Considering the programs we found that of the 36 programs, 7 (19%) were generated by a single mutation operator application.

## 5   Implementation

The mutation operators defined in Figure 5 have been implemented. The implementation reads in a GOAL program and generates a collection of mutated programs, each of which is the result of applying a single mutation. The implementation considers mutations in both the main module, and in the percept processing module. It changes a single GOAL program rule, and then reassembles the complete program, including generating a modified mas2g file to run the mutated program.

We have run the implementation on three example GOAL programs (we selected the three longest examples in the GOAL distribution, excluding an example which uses modules extensively). The results were used in two ways. Firstly, we ran the mutants (for the 1st and 3rd programs) to check that each mutant was indeed a syntactically valid GOAL program (we couldn't do this for the 2nd program, because it could not be run from the command line, due to the way the agent's environment was implemented). Secondly, we observed which of the mutation operators were applicable to each program, and how many mutants were generated by the different rules. Figure 11 shows how many mutants were generated by the application of each of the mutation operators. Note that mutation operators that simply select part of a rule and invoke another mutation operator to make the change are not shown, since they do not actually change the program.

## 6   Discussion

We have presented rules for generating mutants of programs in a typical cognitive agent-oriented programming language (namely GOAL). We have also presented initial evidence that the rules are able to generate a significant proportion of the realistic bugs encountered in a simple problem, as well as evidence that supported the competent programmer foundational hypothesis of mutation testing in an agent context.

There are a number of issues (threats to validity) that need to be acknowledged. Firstly, we only considered a single problem, and although we considered 55 different programs, all these programs only involved a single agent, and all were written by relatively inexperienced programmers. Clearly, one area for future work is to revisit the empirical evaluation using a wider range of problems, and a wider range of programmers. Note that these limitations are the reason why we have derived the mutation operators systematically based on the syntactical structure of GOAL, rather than by considering what mutation operators correspond to errors in the GOAL programs.

| Rule | Tower/ towerbuilder | BW4T2/ robot | Elevator/ elevatoragent |
|---|---|---|---|
| a:mut | 0 | 0 | 0 |
| a:op1 | 16 | 8 | 8 |
| ac:drop1 | 2 | 2 | 0 |
| ar:op2 | 6 | 6 | 6 |
| at:mut | 11 | 27 | 40 |
| lc:drop1 | 20 | 8 | 13 |
| lit:addop | 39 | 17 | 20 |
| lit:delop | 8 | 4 | 5 |
| ma:op1 | 26 | 7 | 12 |
| ml:addop | 27 | 8 | 12 |
| ml:delop | 4 | 0 | 2 |
| ml:drop | 19 | 0 | 5 |
| msc:drop | 0 | 0 | 0 |
| parameters:seqswap | 29 | 2 | 9 |
| plc:drop1 | 0 | 0 | 6 |
| program:drop1 | 18 | 8 | 9 |
| program:seqbot | 16 | 6 | 7 |
| program:seqswap | 16 | 6 | 7 |
| program:seqtop | 16 | 6 | 7 |
| term:drop1 | 8 | 0 | 6 |
| term:seqswap | 4 | 0 | 3 |
| TOTAL | 285 | 115 | 177 |

**Fig. 11.** Mutants generated by different operators for three example GOAL programs

Another area for future work is assessing the prevalence of equivalent mutants, and whether equivalent mutants are generated by all mutation operators with roughly equal likelihood, or by certain rules. We also intend to apply this approach to define mutation operators for other AOPLs. Indeed, we have already defined mutation operators for AgentSpeak, but space precludes presenting them here. More broadly, the data that we have collected also tells us information on the sorts of mistakes that (novice) GOAL programmers make. Analysing the data from this perspective would be valuable.

**Acknowledgements.** We would like to thank our colleagues at Delft university for providing access to the student projects, and for answering questions about GOAL, and fixing bugs that we found in the BW4T environment.

# References

1. Adra, S.F., McMinn, P.: Mutation operators for agent-based models. In: Proceedings of 5th International Workshop on Mutation Analysis. IEEE Computer Society (2010)
2. Ekinci, E.E., Tiryaki, A.M., Çetin, Ö., Dikenelli, O.: Goal-oriented agent testing revisited. In: Luck, M., Gomez-Sanz, J.J. (eds.) AOSE 2008. LNCS, vol. 5386, pp. 173–186. Springer, Heidelberg (2009)

3. Gómez-Sanz, J.J., Botía, J., Serrano, E., Pavón, J.: Testing and debugging of MAS interactions with INGENIAS. In: Luck, M., Gomez-Sanz, J.J. (eds.) AOSE 2008. LNCS, vol. 5386, pp. 199–212. Springer, Heidelberg (2009)
4. Hindriks, K.V.: Programming rational agents in GOAL. In: Bordini, R.H., Dastani, M., Dix, J., El Fallah Seghrouchni, A. (eds.) Multi-Agent Programming: Languages, Tools and Applications, ch. 4, pp. 119–157. Springer (2009)
5. Hindriks, K.V.: Programming rational agents in GOAL (May 2011), http://mmi.tudelft.nl/trac/goal
6. Jia, Y., Harman, M.: An analysis and survey of the development of mutation testing. IEEE Transactions on Software Engineering 37(5), 649–678 (2011)
7. Johnson, M., Jonker, C., van Riemsdijk, B., Feltovich, P.J., Bradshaw, J.M.: Joint Activity Testbed: Blocks World for Teams (BW4T). In: Aldewereld, H., Dignum, V., Picard, G. (eds.) ESAW 2009. LNCS, vol. 5881, pp. 254–256. Springer, Heidelberg (2009)
8. Kim, S., Clark, J.A., McDermid, J.A.: The rigorous generation of Java mutation operators using HAZOP. Technical Report 2/8/99, Department of Computer Science, University of York (1999)
9. Low, C.K., Chen, T.Y., Rönnquist, R.: Automated test case generation for BDI agents. Journal of Autonomous Agents and Multi-Agent Systems 2(4), 311–332 (1999)
10. Mathur, A.P.: Foundations of Software Testing. Pearson (2008) ISBN 978-81-317-1660-1
11. Miller, T., Padgham, L., Thangarajah, J.: Test coverage criteria for agent interaction testing. In: Weyns, D., Gleizes, M.P. (eds.) Proceedings of the 11th International Workshop on Agent Oriented Software Engineering, pp. 1–12 (2010)
12. Munroe, S., Miller, T., Belecheanu, R.A., Pěchouček, M., McBurney, P., Luck, M.: Crossing the agent technology chasm: Lessons, experiences and challenges in commercial applications of agents. Knowledge Engineering Review 21(4), 345–392 (2006)
13. Nguyen, C.D., Perini, A., Tonella, P.: Experimental evaluation of ontology-based test generation for multi-agent systems. In: Luck, M., Gomez-Sanz, J.J. (eds.) AOSE 2008. LNCS, vol. 5386, pp. 187–198. Springer, Heidelberg (2009)
14. Nguyen, C.D., Perini, A., Tonella, P.: Goal-Oriented Testing for MASs. International Journal of Agent-Oriented Software Engineering 4(1), 79–109 (2010)
15. Offutt, A.: Investigations of the software testing coupling effect. ACM Transactions on Software Engineering and Methodology 1(1), 5–20 (1992)
16. Pěchouček, M., Mařík, V.: Industrial deployment of multi-agent technologies: review and selected case studies. Journal of Autonomous Agents and Multi-Agent Systems 17, 397–431 (2008)
17. van Riemsdijk, M.B., Hindriks, K.V., Jonker, C.M.: An empirical study of cognitive agent programs. Multiagent and Grid Systems 8(2), 187–222 (2012)
18. Saifan, A.A., Wahsheh, H.A.: Mutation operators for JADE mobile agent systems. In: Proceedings of the 3rd International Conference on Information and Communication Systems, ICICS (2012)
19. Thangarajah, J., Sardiña, S., Padgham, L.: Measuring plan coverage and overlap for agent reasoning. In: van der Hoek, W., Padgham, L., Conitzer, V., Winikoff, M. (eds.) International Conference on Autonomous Agents and Multiagent Systems, AAMAS 2012, 3 Volumes, Valencia, Spain, June 4-8, pp. 1049–1056. IFAAMAS (2012)
20. Winikoff, M., Padgham, L.: Agent oriented software engineering. In: Weiss, G. (ed.) Multi-agent Systems, ch. 5, 2nd edn. MIT Press (2013)
21. Zhang, Z., Thangarajah, J., Padgham, L.: Automated unit testing for agent systems. In: 2nd International Working Conference on Evaluation of Novel Approaches to Software Engineering (ENASE 2007), pp. 10–18 (2007)

# Automatic BDI Plan Recognition from Process Execution Logs and Effect Logs

Hongyun Xu[1,3], Bastin Tony Roy Savarimuthu[2], Aditya Ghose[3],
Evan Morrison[3], Qiying Cao[1], and Youqun Shi[1]

[1] School of Information Science and Technology,
Donghua University, Shanghai, 201620, P.R. China
[2] Department of Information Science,
University of Otago, P.O. Box 56, Dunedin, New Zealand
[3] College of Computer Science and Software Engineering,
University of Wollongong, Wollongong, NSW, 2522, Australia
xjyc2007@gmail.com, tonyr@infoscience.otago.ac.nz,
aditya@uow.edu.au, {caoqiying,yqshi}@dhu.edu.cn

**Abstract.** Agent applications are often viewed as unduly expensive to
develop and maintain in commercial contexts. Organizations often settle for less sophisticated and more traditional software in place of agent
technology because of (often misplaced) fears about the development and
maintenance costs of agent technology, and the often mistaken perception that traditional software offers better returns on investment. This
paper aims to redress this by developing a plan recognition framework
for *agent program learning*, where behavior logs of legacy applications
(or even manually executed processes) are mined to extract a 'draft' version of agent code that could eventually replace these applications or
processes. We develop, implement and evaluate techniques for inferring
agent plans from behavior logs, with both positive and negative examples. After obtaining the plans, we resort to an effect log to identify the
context (i.e. precondition) for each plan. The experimental results show
that our framework generates a first draft of an agent program (i.e. the
code) which can then be modified as required by a developer.

## 1 Introduction

Agent applications are often viewed as unduly expensive to develop and
maintain in commercial contexts. Even in organizations where there is recognition that the agent technology has benefits, people often settle for less sophisticated, and more traditional software in place of agent technology because of
(often misplaced) fears about the development and maintenance costs of agent
technology, and the (often mistaken) perception that traditional software offers
better return on investment [8]. This paper posits that *agent program learning*
offers a solution to this problem. We define the general *agent program learning*
problem as follows:

M. Cossentino et al. (Eds.): EMAS 2013, LNAI 8245, pp. 274–291, 2013.
© Springer-Verlag Berlin Heidelberg 2013

– *Given:* A *behavior log* describing the behavior of a system over a given audit period, and an *effect log*[1] describing the states of the system at some point in time.
– *Determine:* An *agent program* such that if that agent program were executed with the same set of inputs from the environment, the original behavior log would be obtained (with the exception of failure instances, to be discussed below, which would be avoided).

An agent program learning system can lead to significant improvements in programmer productivity. Instead of having to develop an agent program from scratch, which is an expensive and time-consuming proposition, especially in light of the well-known *knowledge acquisition problem* [3,13], an agent programmer would be provided with an initial, 'draft' program, which the programmer could edit with far less effort relative to writing a program from scratch to obtain a complete and correct agent program. Agent technology is often deployed to 'upgrade' legacy applications [8]. The behavior logs required for an agent program learning system could thus be obtained by auditing the behavior of the legacy system.

A typical BDI agent program consists of three components [9]: (1) A set of *beliefs*, which may be dynamically generated by sensor inputs. (2) A set of *plans*, where each plan contains a triggering event, context conditions and plan body (a set of action sequences). (3) A set of *goals* that an agent wants to achieve. Each goal can be achieved by executing plans in the plan library. The goals involved are related to plans recognized and are given a unique label (e.g. goal *g1* can be achieved by executing plan *p1*).

Thus, the *general agent program learning system* which is the overarching direction of our work, should have modules to support the following: (1) plan recognition; (2) goal recognition; (3) preference recognition[2]. In this paper, we only focus on *plan recognition* for learning a BDI agent program, as exemplified by the BDI agent programming language AgentSpeak(L) [9]. In other words, the plans of an agent program that are automatically created by our system will conform to Jason's AgentSpeak specification [1]. The plan recognition activity comprises of two parts: a) plan body recognition and b) context recognition. Our contributions to the field of the automatic plan recognition are two-fold: i) we show how the plans are inferred both from positive and negative examples, i.e. behavior logs containing both successful and failed actions; ii) we identify contexts using effect logs to form the precondition for a plan.

This paper is organized as follows. Section 2 introduces the related work on plan recognition. Section 3 provides an overview of the plan recognition framework. Section 4 describes how the plan body recognition works using an example from the banking domain. Both positive and negative behavior logs of process executions

---

[1] An effect log contains the resultant states of a program as it continues executing different steps. In contrast, the behavior log contains details about actions that succeeded or failed. In other words, the behavior log captures actions that are executed and the effect log captures the state of the system.

[2] Each agent can have a set of preferences and these preferences contribute to the selection of an appropriate plan from a set of available plans [2].

are used as inputs for inferring plans. Section 5 presents the algorithm used for context recognition. The algorithm uses the positive logs, effects logs and the plan body inferred in the previous step as inputs to infer contexts. Section 6 presents the pilot experiment we have conducted and discusses its results. Section 7 draws conclusions from the results and discusses future research directions.

## 2    Preliminaries and the Overview of the Plan Recognition Framework

### 2.1    WF-Nets

Petri nets [7] are a graphical and mathematical modeling notation that allows users to describe business processes. Formally, a Petri net is a tuple $(P, T, F)$, where $P$ is a set of places, $T$ is a set of transitions $(P \cap T = \emptyset)$, and $F \subseteq (P \times T) \cup (T \times P)$ is a set of arcs between the places and transitions. A Petri net which models the control-flow dimension of a workflow, is called a WF-net. Let $N = (P, T, F)$ be a Petri net, $N$ is a WF-net if and only if it satisfies the following three requirements. (1) It has only one input place $i \in P$, such that $\bullet i = \emptyset^3$. (2) It has only one output place $o \in P$, such that $o \bullet = \emptyset^4$. (3) If a new transition $t'$ is added to $N$, $T \cup \{t'\}$, and $t'$ is used for connecting the output place to the input place, $F \cup \{(o, t'), (t', i)\}$, such that the new net is strongly connected, $N' = (P, T \cup t', F \cup \{(o, t'), (t', i)\})$. The WF-net that we use in this work is a structured WF-net (SWF-net) [13]. A sample WF-net is given in Figure 2.

### 2.2    Norms Identification

Norms are the societal rules that govern the prescription and proscription of certain behavior. In multi-agent systems, norms are viewed mostly as constraints on the actions that an agent can perform. We focus here on two types of norms that are obligation norms and prohibition norms. For obligation norms, it means that a certain action must happens after a specified action. For prohibition norms, it means that a certain action or some actions are prohibited to happen before or after a correct action.

Savarimuthu et al. have proposed two algorithms, prohibition norm identification (PNI) [10] and obligation norm identification (ONI) [11] respectively. The starting point for ONI and PNI is sanction recognition. Once sanctions are recognized, the reasons for these sanctions are investigated (i.e. norm violations are reasons for sanctions to occur). PNI algorithm [11] identifies those actions that occur 100% of the time before the sanctions. ONI algorithm [10] identifies those actions that fail to occur whenever a sanction occurs. In order to identify those actions it compares two lists of action sequences, one containing missing actions

---

$^3$ The expression $\bullet i = \emptyset$ denotes that there are no incoming edges to the input place $i$ (the dot here represents a set of transitions).

$^4$ The expression $o \bullet = \emptyset$ denotes that there are no outcoming edges from the output place $o$ (the dot here represents a set of places).

(followed by sanctions) and the other containing the expected actions (without sanctions). On comparing these lists, the algorithm identifies missing actions. These algorithms were originally proposed to be used in artificial agent societies where interacting avatars can automatically learn norms based on observation of actions. For example, an agent that litters a park might be sanctioned by another agent. An observer, based on actions observed can infer that littering is prohibited. Also, an agent that does not tip (a violation of an obligation) might be sanctioned. PNI and ONI algorithms identify two norms, i.e., prohibit(litter) and obliged(tip)) respectively.

The PNI and ONI algorithms can not only identify norms but also preconditions and post conditions of norms. This is useful in our context, because if we view agents as entities being norm aware (e.g. action $x$ is prohibited and action $y$ is obliged), then they need to make plans to adhere to norms. Hence, the precondition and postcondition can be viewed as parts of a plan for achieving a goal (normative goal in this case). Failures in business processes can happen because of many reasons such as equipment malfunction, actions happening out of order or a required action not being performed. In this work, we assume failures happen because of the latter two and the failures are recorded in behavior logs (i.e. negative examples). We use the negative examples to infer plans.

## 2.3  Framework Overview

The goal of this work is to describe how a first draft of an agent's plans can be automatically recognized from actions recorded in the business process execution log (i.e. a behavior log) and the effect log. The process of plan recognition is shown in Figure 1. A plan consists of two main aspects, a plan body and a context (i.e. precondition that results in the execution of a plan body when it evaluates to true). These two aspects of plan recognition are carried out by two modules namely the plan body recognizer and context recognizer.

A typical behavior log contains information about both successful process executions and failures. In our work, from the log containing successful executions, we generate a workflow diagram (i.e., a WF-net) using the process mining tool, ProM [14]. Then, we demonstrate how a plan body recognizer (a set of

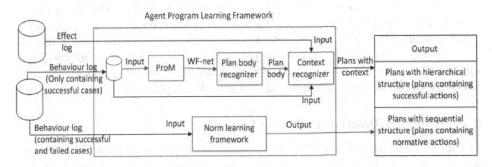

**Fig. 1.** Overview of the plan recognition framework

transformation rules and algorithms) can be used to infer BDI plans (without context) from the WF-net in Section 3. Then, the context recognizer is used to identify the context which takes an effect log, the behavior log, and the plan body that was identified in the previous step (details provided in Section 4). The plans obtained from the positive examples are hierarchical in nature (nested plans with successful actions). Also, based on failure sequences, we demonstrate how a data mining based approach previously used for norm extraction can be used to identify sequential normative actions (obligations and prohibitions).

## 3    Plan Body Recognition

In this section, we first describe a motivating example that is used throughout the paper. Then we present the plan body recognition, first from handling positive behavior logs containing no failure information, and then from negative behavior logs containing failure information.

### 3.1    Motivating Example

A typical banking system contains many business applications. We refer to two of these business applications throughout the paper. They are the processes in a banking system for *loan applications* and *money transfers*, respectively. Assume that a banking system (or an agent) receives loan applications which are handled according to the type of loan (e.g. personal and business loans). If a loan application is for a personal loan, personal information such as credit history and the risk (e.g. high, medium, low), will be evaluated and then a decision will be made. At the end of the process, the applicant will be informed of the acceptance or rejection. If an application involves a business loan, the bank will check whether the information provided is correct and also check other relevant sources in order to assess the credibility of the business entity (e.g. whether it is registered member of the chamber of commerce). The bank will also audit and evaluate the business's assets. Then it will make a decision and also notify the business. If the banking system receives a money transfer application during the handling process for loan applications, the account of the applicant will be checked to see if the money in the account is enough to be transferred. Then it will check whether the target account specified in the application exists. Then, the money will be transferred by the banking system. The examples includes a set of actions as follows: *receive_loan_application*, *check_personal_loan_application*, *check_business_loan_application*, *audit_assets*, *check_credit*, *check_risk*, *evaluate_personal_loan_application*, *inform_loan_applicant*, *receive_money_ transfer_application*, *check_applicant_account*, *check_target_account* and *evaluate_money_transfer_application*.

### 3.2    Handling Positive Behavior Logs

In this sub-section, we describe how a behavior model is constructed from the actions available in a behavior log, and then present the transformation rules and the algorithms that transform a WF-net to BDI plans.

**Behavior Model Construction.** As shown in Table 1, there are five cases in a positive behavior log from a banking system where each action in the behavior log has a timestamp indicating the starting time of that action. For example, the actions associated with case 1 are ⟨receive_loan_application, check_personal_loan_application, check_credit, check_risk, evaluate_personal_loan_application, inform_loan_applicant⟩. The actions appear in the order they were executed. The actions logged for case 2 are ⟨receive_loan_application, check_personal_loan_application, check_risk, check_credit, evaluate_personal_loan_application, inform_loan_applicant⟩, and actions logged for cases 3 and 5 are ⟨receive_loan_application, check_business_loan_application, audit_assets, inform_loan_applicant⟩, and the actions executed as a part of case 4 are ⟨receive_money_transfer_application, check_applicant_account, check_target_account and evaluate_money_transfer_application⟩.

**Table 1.** Sequential Behavior Log

| Case ID | Action ID | TimeStamps(yyyy/mm/dd hh:mm) |
|---|---|---|
| case 1 | receive_loan_application (rla) | 2011/06/19 08:53 ($t_1$) |
| case 1 | check_personal_loan_application (cpla) | 2011/06/19 11:00 ($t_2$) |
| case 2 | receive_loan_application (rla) | 2011/06/19 11:10 ($t_3$) |
| case 1 | check_credit (cc) | 2011/06/19 12:38 ($t_4$) |
| case 3 | receive_loan_application (rla) | 2011/06/19 12:40 ($t_5$) |
| case 2 | check_personal_loan_application (cpla) | 2011/06/19 12:51 ($t_6$) |
| case 4 | receive_money_transfer_application (rmta) | 2011/06/19 13:28 ($t_7$) |
| case 1 | check_risk (cr) | 2011/06/19 13:56 ($t_8$) |
| case 5 | receive_loan_application (rla) | 2011/06/19 14:01 ($t_9$) |
| case 1 | evaluate_personal_loan_application (epla) | 2011/06/19 14:53 ($t_{10}$) |
| case 3 | check_business_loan_application (cbla) | 2011/06/19 15:24 ($t_{11}$) |
| case 4 | check_applicant_account (caa) | 2011/06/19 15:32 ($t_{12}$) |
| case 1 | inform_loan_applicant (ila) | 2011/06/19 15:41 ($t_{13}$) |
| case 3 | audit_assets (aa) | 2011/06/19 15:59 ($t_{14}$) |
| case 5 | check_business_loan_application (cbla) | 2011/06/19 16:04 ($t_{15}$) |
| case 4 | check_target_account (cta) | 2011/06/19 16:13 ($t_{16}$) |
| case 2 | check_risk (cr) | 2011/06/19 16:25 ($t_{17}$) |
| case 5 | audit_assets (aa) | 2011/06/19 16:30 ($t_{18}$) |
| case 2 | check_credit (cc) | 2011/06/19 16:48 ($t_{19}$) |
| case 3 | inform_loan_applicant (ila) | 2011/06/19 16:55 ($t_{20}$) |
| case 4 | evaluate_money_transfer_application (emta) | 2011/06/19 17:08 ($t_{21}$) |
| case 2 | evaluate_personal_loan_application (epla) | 2011/06/19 17:10 ($t_{22}$) |
| case 5 | inform_loan_applicant (ila) | 2011/06/19 17:17 ($t_{23}$) |
| case 2 | inform_loan_applicant (ila) | 2011/06/19 17:34 ($t_{24}$) |

The plan recognition framework uses the ProM tool to construct a behavior model, i.e., a WF-net that describes the behavior of a system based on the actions recorded in the behavior log. ProM enables the extraction of information from event logs, and it supports several process mining techniques in the form of plug-ins, such as the Alpha-algorithm [13]. We exploit the Alpha-algorithm in ProM to automatically generate a WF-net from the log.

The WF-net shown in Figure 2, is constructed from the log given in Table 1 using the Alpha-algorithm in ProM. The start and end transitions as endpoints are added automatically when there is no common start action (or actions) and no common end action (or actions) among cases in the behavior logs. This is required to tie-together distinct set of processes a system can execute (e.g. a business system can run ten different processes at any point of time) and a WF-net is a representation of all these different processes. The other transitions in the diagram are the actions that an agent must perform. The places in the WF-net are labeled $p_1$, $p_2$, ..., $p_{14}$ for easier referencing.

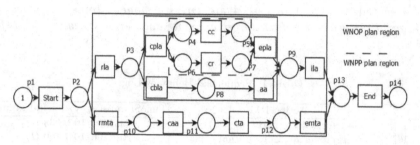

**Fig. 2.** A WF-net generated based on a behavior log

**Transformation Rules and Algorithms.** WF-nets are commonly used to represent a process which is composed of various applications (e.g., different business applications in the context of the banking example). The business process when executed will produce different outputs depending upon the inputs given to the process (e.g., the path taken for evaluating a personal loan will be different from the path taken for evaluating money transfer application). That is, the business process will produce different results (i.e. outputs) depending on the triggering events (i.e., inputs). We argue that the behavior exhibited by the traditional system could be viewed as the behavior exhibited by an agent that follows some plans (i.e., plans for different goals are different). Different triggering events could be handled by distinct plans. In Figure 2, the condition in place $p_2$ could be triggered by different external events such as submission of personal loan application and money transfer application. Hence, we argue that, it is reasonable to view the number of branches emanating $p_2$ as the number of plans for different goals. That is, the paths that originate from $p_2$ can be different, where each path represents a different goal (e.g., the plan involving actions from case 4, represents the goal of transferring money from one account to another). In our work, each inferred plan is a BDI plan, consisting of a sequence of actions and/or subgoals. Before presenting the algorithms for generating plans for a goal, we first present the *types of sub WF-nets* and the related *rules* for inferring plans from WF-nets.

A sub WF-net starts at a node $N$ and ends at node $N'$ where $N, N' \in P \cup T$ (as per usual convention $\bullet N = \emptyset$ and $N' \bullet = \emptyset$). The number of branches deviating at $N$ is greater than 1, i.e. $|N \bullet| > 1$. At $N'$ all of the branches join together, i.e., $|\bullet N'| > 1$. A sub WF-net is called $WNOP$ (WF-net for Optional Plans) iff $N, N' \in P$, highlighted using solid boxes in Figure 2. And, a sub WF-net is called $WNPP$ (WF-net for Parallel Plans) iff $N, N' \in T$, highlighted using the dotted box in Figure 2. The *transformation rules* for inferring plans from WF-nets are as follows.

1. The number of top-level plans for achieving different goals are determined by the number of branches emanating the node (the place), that is located next to the start transition.
2. Each transition is viewed as an action in a plan, in other words, a transition node has the same label as an action.
3. Each sub WF-net is considered as a subgoal in a plan.
4. If a subgoal is of $WNOP$ type, the number of possible plans achieving the subgoal is determined by the number of branches emanating the start node in the sub WF-net, and these obtained plans are alternative plans, of which only one will be chosen for execution at run-time.
5. If a subgoal is $WNPP$ type, the number of possible plans relies on the number of branches emanating the start node in the sub WF-net, and these plans can be executed in parallel.

---

**Algorithm 1.** Recognize plans for one goal

---

**Input:** wf, i.e., a WF-net; currentNode
**Output:** planList, i.e., BDI agent-oriented plans
1: **while** currentNode $\neq$ wf.endNode **do**
2:     **if** currentNode.type is transition AND currentNode.type $\neq$ wf.startNode **then**
3:         put currentNode.name in a plan
4:     **end if**
5:     **if** count(currentNode.outgoingEdges)= 1 **then**
6:         currentNode←currentNode.nextNode
7:     **else if** count(currentNode.outgoingEdges)>1 **then**
8:         generate a new subgoal in a plan
9:         **if** currentNode.type is place **then**
10:             planList← obtain plans for $WNOP$ goal
11:         **else if** currentNode.type is transition **then**
12:             planList← obtain plans for $WNPP$ goal
13:         **end if**
14:     **end if**
15: **end while**
16: planList ← planList ∪ {plan}
17: **return** *planList*

---

Algorithm 1, presents the process of inferring plans for one goal. If there are multiple goals, the algorithm will be used iteratively (which is the case in our work for the WF-net given in Figure 1). Also, note that top-level goals (first iteration goals) are represented as *goal1* and *goal2*. The next level goals are represented as *subgoal1, subgoal2* and so on. The WF-net is encoded as a graph, and the node after start transition in the WF-net is viewed as *currentNode*. Each node has its type, i.e., place and transition, and its name. If the node type is transition, its name will be viewed as an action label, which will be added in a plan, following rule (2). If there exists a sub WF-net, a new subgoal is generated in the plan, following rule (3). If a subgoal is *WNOP* type, the number of plans for the subgoal depends on the number of branches emanating the start node of the sub WF-net, as described in rule (4). Each branch constructs a new plan for the subgoal, recursively using the Algorithm 1. Likewise, for the *WNPP* type of subgoal, the number of plans for this subgoal depends on the number of branches emanating from start node of the sub WF-net, as presented in rule (5). There is no parallel construct in AgentSpeak(L) [1], hence we handle the *WNPP* type of subgoal using the interleaved actions among the paths to obtain all possible plans. In the running example, two actions E and F can be executed in parallel. It means that, there are two possible ways in which these actions could have been executed, E followed by F or F followed by E.

The results of using Algorithm 1 when the WF-net shown in Figure 2 is given as the input (recursively for each goal) are given in Table 2. There are six plans in total ($p0$ to $p5$). We can observe that there are two top-level goals achieved by these plans, i.e., *goal1* and *goal2* (rule 1). The first goal, *goal1* can be achieved directly using plan $p_0$, while the second goal *goal2* can be achieved using $p_1$ that has a subgoal *subgoal1*. There are two alternative ways to achieve this subgoal (either using plan *p2* or using plan *p3*). Note that plans $p_0$ and $p_1$ are of *WNOP* type. So are plans $p_2$ and $p_3$ that are used to achieve *subgoal1*. On the other hand plans $p_4$ and $p_5$ are of *WNPP* type. They are used to achieve *subgoal2*. Note that the preconditions for each of the plans is set to true. Identifying preconditions of these plans is discussed in Section 5.

**Table 2.** Results of Plan Body Recognition

| |
|---|
| @$p_5$  +!subgoal2: true ← *check_credit; check_risk.* |
| @$p_4$  +!subgoal2: true ← *check_risk; check_credit.* |
| @$p_3$  +!subgoal1: true ← *receive_personal_loan_application;*  !subgoal2;  *evaluate_personal_loan_application.* |
| @$p_2$  +!subgoal1: true ← *check_business_loan_application; audit_assets.* |
| @$p_1$  +!goal2: true ← *receive_loan_application;*  !subgoal1;  *inform_loan_applicant.* |
| @$p_0$  +!goal1: true ← *receive_money_transfer_application; check_applicant_account;  check_target_account; evaluate_money_transfer_application.* |

## 3.3  Handling Negative Behavior Logs

In this sub-section, we discuss how plans are extracted from a behavior log that contains failure information. Failures could be caused when obligated actions do not occur or when prohibited actions are performed. We acknowledge that there could be other reasons for failures such as a printer failing because of power failure. We do not model those because those type of failures are explicit failures and the reasons are known to the agent (i.e., power failure is the reason for failed printing job). Obligated and prohibited actions can be identified using ONI and PNI algorithms.

Failures in business process executions are logged in behavior logs (e.g. failure of a task due to a mechanical error or human error). These failures are similar to sanctions. When a sanction happens, a special event ($) gets recorded in the norm identification framework. Similarly, in this work, when a failure happens a special event ($\otimes$) will be recorded. When these failures happen, the reasons for the failures can be investigated. In our work we assume failures happen either because a prohibited action is performed (i.e. the action that does not fit in a sequence, such as sending rejection notification before decision is made) or an obliged action does not happen (e.g. credit check is not performed before a decision can be made). We use slightly modified versions of PNI and ONI to identify the reasons for failures (prohibited and obliged actions respectively). The modifications made are two fold. First, we eliminate the norm verification stage (where an agent asks another agent to verify whether a norm holds) because we only consider an action to be prohibited by setting the threshold for norm identification to be 100% (i.e. only those actions that have the probability of 1 to be causing violations are considered). Second, we create two lists to handle the two types of norms separately (details discussed in Algorithm 2).

Algorithm 2, describes the process for identifying plan sequences from a behavior log with failure using these two norm learning algorithms. First, the correct entries without failure information are stored in a correct list, and are also removed from the behavior log (lines 4-9). Second, the entries with failure information are classified into two lists, prohibition list and obligation list. If a failed sequence (i.e. a case) has a matching super sequence(s) in the correct list, then that sequence will be added to the obligation list. Assume actions $a, b$ and $c$ were supposed to happen in sequence. Let us assume that the observed sequence is $ac$, resulting in a failure. Here action $b$ is the obligated action. By identifying the supersequence of $ac$ (which is $abc$), we are able to identify the obliged action (i.e. $b$). Otherwise, it will be added to a prohibition list (lines 10-17). Third, the ONI and PNI algorithms are invoked (lines 18, 19). Given the correct list and the obligation list as inputs to the ONI algorithm, it produces plan sequences as outputs. Next, the PNI algorithm is invoked. Given the correct list and the prohibition list as inputs, it produces plan sequences as output.

To demonstrate how Algorithm 2 works, a sample log with failure information is given in Table 3. Note that $\otimes$ is used to indicate failures in the behavior log. If there is a failure, then other steps of the process are not executed. The algorithm first creates three empty lists (lines 1-3), the correct list, prohibition list and the obligation list. The correct list is then populated with four entries: (rla, cpla, cc, cr, epla, ila), (rla, cpla, cr, cc, epla, ila), (rla, cbla, aa, ila) and (rmta, caa, cta, emta). Then the algorithm populates the obligation list which contains the following entries: (rla, cpla, cc, cr, ila, $\otimes$), (cpla, cr, cc, ila, $\otimes$), (rla, cbla, ila, $\otimes$) and (rla, cpla, cc, epla, $\otimes$). The prohibition list contains the following entries: (rmta, Z, $\otimes$), (rmta, caa, cta, Y, $\otimes$), (rmta, caa, rmta, $\otimes$) and (rla, cbla, aa,

---

**Algorithm 2.** Identifying plans from negative behavior logs

---

**Input:** bl, i.e., a behavior log containing failures
**Output:** ps, i.e., plan sequences with obligated actions or prohibited actions
1: Let correctList←∅                                    ▷ entries without ⊗
2: Let prohibitionList←∅                      ▷ entries with prohibited actions
3: Let obligationList←∅                         ▷ entries with missing actions
4: **for** each entry E ∈ bl **do**
5:      **if** E contains no ⊗ **then**
6:          Add E to correctList
7:          Remove E from bl
8:      **end if**
9: **end for**
10: **for** each entry E ∈ bl **do**
11:     remove ⊗ in E
12:     **if** E has super sequence(s) in correctList **then**
13:         Add E to obligationList
14:     **else**
15:         Add E to prohibitionList
16:     **end if**
17: **end for**
18: ps←ONI Algorithm(correctList, obligationList)
19: ps←PNI Algorithm(correctList, prohibitionList)
20: **return** ps

---

L, ⊗). Then, the ONI and PNI are executed in sequence to identify plans. The results of using the norm learning mechanisms are shown in the last column of Table 3.

There are two benefits of the outputs obtained from the norm learning mechanisms. First, the outputs are the correct sequences (i.e. corrected failure sequences). For example, (rla, cpla, cc, cr, ila, ⊗) has been corrected to (rla, cpla, cc, cr, epla, ila). So, the first benefit of norm learning mechanisms is their ability to correct erroneous sequences. Second, the output produced by the algorithms can be viewed as a plan which contains a precondition, an obliged/prohibited action (or actions) and a postcondition. For example, the failure corrected version of (rla, cpla, cc, cr, ila, ) is (rla, cpla, cc, cr, Obliged(epla), ila). The precondition of the norm Obliged (epla) is the occurrence of actions rla, cpla, cc, cr, and the the post condition is the occurrence of action ila. A prohibition sequence only contains a precondition and a normative action because there could be many different post conditions depending upon which action should have occurred in the place of the prohibited action.

In the future, agents in our framework can use the results generated to create plans that ensure those already generated plans do not violate the normative action(s) (e.g. none of the existing plans should execute action L after executing actions rla, cbla and aa (entry 12 in Table 3)). This can be particularly valuable when the human programmer modifies the first draft of agent code generated by our framework to suit application needs (i.e. have plans to capture errors accidentally introduced by the humans that could potentially violate the norms). We note that some results obtained are incomplete (e.g. (rla, cpla, cc, epla, $\otimes$)) is corrected to be (rla, cpla, cc, cr, epla, ila) or (rla, cpla, cr, cc, epla, ila). The complete sequence must be (rla, cpla, cc, cr, epla, ila) and (rla, cpla, cr, cc, epla, ila). However, we address this problem by identifying supersequences of the results in the correct list to produce the correct and complete sequence.

Table 3. A Log with Failure Information

| Entry ID | Sequence of Actions | Results from Algorithm 2 |
|---|---|---|
| 1 | (rla, cpla, cc, cr, epla, ila) | |
| 2 | (rla, cpla, cr, cc, epla, ila) | |
| 3 | (rla, cbla, aa, ila) | |
| 4 | (rla, cpla, cc, cr, ila, $\otimes$) | (rla, cpla, cc, cr, Obliged(epla), ila) |
| 5 | (rla, cpla, cr, cc, $\otimes$, ila) | (rla, cpla, cr, cc, Obliged(epla), ila) |
| 6 | (rla, cbla, ila, $\otimes$) | (rla, cbla, Obliged(aa), ila) |
| 7 | (rla, cpla, cc, epla, $\otimes$) | (rla, cpla, Obliged(cr), cc, epla) (rla, cpla, cc, Obliged(cr), epla) |
| 8 | (rmta, caa, cta, emta) | |
| 9 | (rmta, Z, $\otimes$) | (rmta, prohibited(Z)) |
| 10 | (rmta, caa, cta, Y, $\otimes$) | (rmta, caa, cta, prohibited(Y)) |
| 11 | (rmta, caa, rmta, $\otimes$) | (rmta, caa, prohibited(rmta)) |
| 12 | (rla, cbla, aa, L, $\otimes$) | (rla, cbla, aa, prohibited(L)) |

Table 4. Sample effect log

| Time | States | Time | States | Time | States | Time | States |
|---|---|---|---|---|---|---|---|
| $t_1$ | $c3 \wedge c4$ | $t_7$ | $c15$ | $t_{13}$ | $c11$ | $t_{19}$ | $c7 \wedge c8$ |
| $t_2$ | $c5 \wedge c6$ | $t_8$ | $c7 \wedge c8$ | $t_{14}$ | $c13 \wedge c14$ | $t_{20}$ | $c11$ |
| $t_3$ | $c3 \wedge c4$ | $t_9$ | $c3 \wedge \neg c4$ | $t_{15}$ | $c12 \wedge \neg c20$ | $t_{21}$ | $c18$ |
| $t_4$ | $c1 \wedge c7$ | $t_{10}$ | $c9 \wedge c10$ | $t_{16}$ | $c17$ | $t_{22}$ | $c9 \wedge c10$ |
| $t_5$ | $c3 \wedge \neg c4$ | $t_{11}$ | $c12 \wedge c20$ | $t_{17}$ | $c1 \wedge c7$ | $t_{23}$ | $c11$ |
| $t_6$ | $c5 \wedge c6$ | $t_{12}$ | $c16$ | $t_{18}$ | $c13 \wedge c14$ | $t_{24}$ | $c11$ |

## 4  Context Recognition

In Section 4, we described how plans are recognized. However, the preconditions of all the plans were true. Recognizing preconditions is a key part of plan recognition. We note that preconditions cannot be inferred from the behavior log alone. So, we assume, in addition to behavior log we also have the effect log. Behavior log contains actions that were executed and effect log contains the state of the system. For example, the state of the system can contain information such as the loan application of customer 1 was in the *pending allocation* state at time t1 and the state was changed to *assigned to risk analyst* at t2. By using effect log in conjunction with the behavior log and the plan body of the all the recognized plans, we demonstrate how preconditions for the plans can be identified.

We assume that the sample effect log given in Table 4 can be obtained during the execution of a traditional system. We model states using propositional logic (states represented as a conjunction of propositions). We also assume that timestamps of these states are recorded. For example, at timestamp $t_1$, $c_3$ and $c_4$ hold (assume c3 is *application received* and c4 is *data verified for completeness*).

---

**Algorithm 3.** Mining preconditions in plans

---

**Input:** a) sblog - a behavior log; b) elog - an effect log; c) plans resulting from plan body recognition
**Output:** plans with context
 1: **for** each plan $\in$ plans **do**
 2:     planTraces $\leftarrow \emptyset$
 3:     stateArr$\leftarrow \emptyset$
 4:     **if** plan.planbody has subgoal **then**
 5:         planTraces $\leftarrow$ obtain all possible plan traces
 6:     **else**
 7:         planTraces $\leftarrow$ plan.planbody
 8:     **end if**
 9:     **for** each trace $\in$ planTraces **do**
10:         **for** each case $\in$ sblog **do**
11:             **if** case contains the trace **then**
12:                 $T_a \leftarrow$ obtain the timeStamp of first action of the plan
13:                 **if** elog contains $T_a$ **then**
14:                     stateArr $\leftarrow$ states at $T_a$ should be adding to stateArr
15:                 **end if**
16:             **end if**
17:         **end for**
18:     **end for**
19:     **if** stateArr.size $>1$ **then**
20:         plan.context$\leftarrow$compute common proposition
21:     **else**
22:         plan.context$\leftarrow$stateArr
23:     **end if**
24: **end for**
25: **return** plans

---

Algorithm 3 presents how preconditions of plans are recognized. The input to the algorithm are a) the behavior log, b) the effect log and c) plan body of all the recognized plans. The algorithm contains three main stages.

**Stage 1** (lines 4-8) - For each plan, if it has subgoals, all the possible action sequences for subgoals are identified. This is done by unfolding subgoals recursively to the inner most plan with subgoals. The identified set of these action sequences will be stored in an array called *planTrace*. Each entry in the *planTrace* is a possible execution sequence of a plan (i.e. actions that would be executed if a plan were to be invoked). Note that there there could be more than one plan trace for a plan because a subgoal of a plan produce different results. If a plan has no subgoals, the action sequence itself will be stored in *planTrace* as a plan trace. For example, let us consider plan $p_5$ which does not have any subgoal. In this case, the planTrace contains actions *ef*. However, for plan $p_3$ that contains a subgoal in its plan body, there will be two plan traces (*befg* and *bfeg*) since subgoal2 can be realized in two different ways.

**Stage 2** (lines 9-18) - For each plan trace in *planTrace*, if there exists a case in the behavior log, that contains either the same sequence of the plan trace, or the supersequence of the plan trace, the timestamp of the first action in plan trace is stored in $T_a$ (a variable), and the entry corresponding to $T_a$ in the effect log is stored in an array called *stateArr*. Note that there could more than one one result.

For plan $p_5$, the planTrace contains the action sequence *ef* as described above. There exists only case (case 1) containing the supersequence of *ef* which is *abefgi*. Then we consider the first action of *ef*, i.e., action *e*, and obtain its timestamp in case 1, which is $t_4$. So, the context for $p_5$, is the entry corresponding to $t_4$ in the effect log, which is $c_1 \& c_7$ (which gets stored in *stateArr*). For plan $p_3$, there are two plan traces *befg* and *bfeg* as described above. For the plan trace *befg*, case 1 has its supersequence, *abefg*. We obtain the timestamp corresponding to the first action *b* which is $t_2$. The entry corresponding to $t_2$ in the effect log is $c_5 \& c_6$ which is stored in *stateArr*. Similarly, case 2 contains the supersequence of *bfeg* which is *abfeg*. The timestamp corresponding to the first action *b* is identified which is $t_6$. The entry $c_5 \& c_6$ in effect log at $t_6$ is obtained. Note that for plan $p_3$, there are two entries in *stateArr* and both these entries have the same propositions ($c_5$ and $c_6$).

**Stage 3** (lines 19-23) - For a given plan, if the *stateArr* has only one entry, then the entry is the precondition of the plan. If there are more than one entry, then the propositions that are common to these entries will be computed to be the context. For example, for plan $p_3$, there were two entries in the *stateArr*. Common propositions among these two entries are chosen as the preconditions for $p_3$ which are $c_5$ & $c_6$ in this case. For plan $p_5$, there is only one entry in the *stateArr* ($c_1 \& c_7$) which becomes its precondition.

## 5   Experiments and Results

Using the simplified motivating example throughout the paper, the plans resulting from context recognition are shown in Table 5, applying the positive behavior log given in Table 1 and the effect log given in Table 4.

We can see that there are two different top-level goals to achieve for an agent, under different contexts (i.e. *goal1* and *goal2*). The context (i.e. precondition) is the same for the parallel plans, $p_4$ and $p_5$, but is different for the optional plans, $p_2$ and $p_3$. However, only one of the parallel plans should be executed at run-time. Since AgentSpeak(L) does not allow two plans to be executed in parallel, one of these plans is randomly picked for execution with respect to our implementation. Note that the plans $p_2$ and $p_3$ for achieving *subgoal1* have different context conditions which mean that only one of them will be executed at run time.

**Table 5.** Results of Plan Body and Context Recognition

| | |
|---|---|
| @$p_5$ | +!subgoal2: c1&c7 $\leftarrow$ *check_credit; check_risk.* |
| @$p_4$ | +!subgoal2: c1&c7 $\leftarrow$ *check_risk; check_credit.* |
| @$p_3$ | +!subgoal1: c6&c5 $\leftarrow$ *receive_personal_loan_application*; !subgoal2; *evaluate_personal_loan_application.* |
| @$p_2$ | +!subgoal1: c12 $\leftarrow$ *check_business_loan_application; audit_assets.* |
| @$p_1$ | +!goal2: c3 $\leftarrow$ *receive_loan_application*; !subgoal1; *inform_loan_applicant.* |
| @$p_0$ | +!goal1: c15 $\leftarrow$ *receive_money_transfer_application; check_applicant_account; check_target_account; evaluate_money_transfer_application.* |

In order to evaluate the plans generated by our plan recognition framework, we employed human subjects. A pilot study was conducted with eight participants. A small-sized problem specification (including the functional requirements such as the high level goals of the agent program and the expected behavior in terms of output) was provided to the participants, who are students pursuing their postgraduate research work in computer science. They had to handwrite the BDI agent program to achieve these goals. We divided the participants into two groups of four programmers. For one group (group A), we provided just the specification. For the second group (group B) we provided both the specification and the resulting 'draft' agent program code generated by our plan recognition framework. Our results show that the average time for programmers in group B to finish the program is much shorter than that of programmers in group A. On average, programmers in group B finished 12 minutes earlier than group A. The maximum time taken to finish the program in group A was 36 minutes, but in group B it was only 17 minutes. The types of errors made by the groups A and B were different. The errors made by programmers in group A include the wrong ordering of actions, assigning wrong preconditions and assigning wrong actions. Group B on the other hand, made few changes to preconditions (addition and deletion). Some did not make changes to the body of the program since the 'draft' version provided was adequate in most cases. Since, group B did not start a program from the scratch, they did not make many mistakes. So, the average number of errors in group B was less than that of programmers in group A. Thus, the initial results obtained from the pilot study is promising. However, extensive studies with complex requirements with large number of participants are required to firmly establish our initial findings.

# 6    Related Work

Very few work have addressed the problem of automatic recognition of plans in the area of agent-oriented software engineering (e.g. [4]). The work in [4] proposes an incremental plan recognition in an agent programming framework, which is similar to our work. However, our work is distinct from theirs. They focus on the formal model of plan recognition based on situation calculus and the ConGolog agent programming language. In their work, the plans are filtered as more actions are observed based on the existing plan library. In contrast, plans in our work are generated from scratch and they are added to an initially empty plan library. Also, we use a process mining approach to infer BDI plans from both positive and negative examples in behavior logs produced by a traditional system. Our goal is thus to create a framework that generates plans of an agent program which when executed will produce the same behavior as that of a traditional (legacy) system. This new program is the first cut of the 'agentified' version of the traditional program.

A difference of our work when compared to the work of Traverso and Pistore [12] where they convert a OWL-based business process to Hierarchical Task Network (HTN) plans is the ability of our system to derive an agent program just based on observed outputs and effects (i.e. we do not start with a process involving a particular technology, i.e. OWL-S), and our approach is generic (i.e. can involve composition). Meneguzzi and Luck [6] have investigated how context conditions can be derived for plans in AgentSpeak(PL), which is similar to our work. A difference between our work and their work is that the cited work generates new plans using AgentSpeak(PL) when a plan in the plan library fails or if an appropriate plan does not exist. However, in our work we start with an empty plan library and add new plans generated by our plan recognition system. Even though the context conditions derived in our work are also plans in AgentSpeak(L), the process of obtaining the plan is different. Their work uses an action model for context derivation (i.e., the precondition and postcondition of actions are known), while our work requires an effect log for context derivation (i.e., the state of a system is known at different points in time). Also, the work [6] do not consider the identification of the erroneous conditions (i.e. the actions that caused failure) and the possibility of creating plans to handle those failures.

There exist other work where method preconditions are learned using the HTN [5,15]. In [15], a set of constraints are constructed from observed decomposition trees under partial observations, and then solved by a constraint solver. HTN planning systems are related to BDI agent systems when it comes to know-how information used, that is, learning preconditions for a method amounts to learning context condition of a plan in BDI systems. As opposed to the work in [15], our work utilizes a complete behavior log and an effect log for context derivation. Also, we use propositional logic to represent the state of a system at different timestamps, and the actions are without parameters. The work in [5] learns preconditions from plan traces and HTN structures, where the task decomposition is known a priori (i.e. task dependencies are known), while in our work, we derive task composition according to a Workflow net (WF-net, see Section 2.1) transformation rules (discussed in Section 3.2). They use a candidate elimination method to obtain a set of candidate predicates for preconditions (contextual conditions) of plans. However, in our work, we derive context conditions from effect logs obtained (i.e. resultant state of the system). More importantly, our work encompasses a higher level objective of generating a first draft of a plan library.

# 7   Conclusions and Future Work

In this paper, we have proposed a novel plan recognition mechanism where BDI-style plans are generated by our plan recognition framework. This plan recognition is a part of a larger scope project which aims to learn agent programs (i.e. automatically generate a first draft of an agent program) from the behavior log and the effect log produced by a traditional ('legacy') system. The two main aspects of our plan recognition framework are the plan body recognition and the context recognition. In order to generate plans, first, a WF-net is generated from a behavior log using ProM. Second, we have proposed a set of transformation rules and a procedure (Algorithm 1), which transforms the WF-net into a set of plans (without context). Then, we demonstrated how the preconditions for the plans can be identified using an effect log (Algorithm 3). It should be noted that we have demonstrated how both positive and negative examples can be used to obtain plans. We leveraged existing norm learning mechanisms [10, 11] to infer normative plans (with prohibited and obligated actions) in the context of handling negative examples (Algorithm 2).

We have demonstrated that our plan recognition framework creates a 'draft' agent program which can then be extended by a programmer. We have conducted a pilot study with eight participants and the results of the study are encouraging. We believe the work presented here is an important step for BDI-type agent systems development since it shows that agent programs can be developed for existing traditional systems (or at least a draft version of the system can be developed). Especially, these agent programs can be considered as an viable alternative for 'legacy' systems that need to be redeveloped in an appropriate language.

The plan recognition framework has some simplifying assumptions. First, business processes with loops have not been considered in this work. That forms the focus of our future work. Second, the propositional logic is used to demonstrate the feasibility of the system. Other more expressive logics could be investigated in the future. Also, parameterized actions and states can be included in the behavior log and effect log respectively. In the future, we plan to evaluate our plan recognition framework with complex applications (complex WF-nets). We believe it is in those complex systems, our framework will offer significant advantages (i.e. reduction of programming time and effort). We will also conduct extensive testing involving substantial number of developers.

# References

1. Bordini, R.H., Hübner, J.F., Wooldridge, M.J.: Programming Multi-Agent Systems in AgentSpeak using Jason. John Wiley & Sons, Ltd. (2007)
2. Dasgupta, A., Ghose, A.K.: BDI agents with objectives and preferences. In: Omicini, A., Sardina, S., Vasconcelos, W. (eds.) DALT 2010. LNCS, vol. 6619, pp. 22–39. Springer, Heidelberg (2011)

3. Gómez-Pérez, J.M., Erdmann, M., Greaves, M., Corcho, O., Benjamins, R.: A framework and computer system for knowledge-level acquisition, representation, and reasoning with process knowledge. International Journal of Human-Computer Studies 68(10), 641–668 (2010)
4. Goultiaeva, A., Lespérance, Y.: Incremental plan recognition in an agent programming framework. In: Working notes of the American Association for Artificial Intelligence (AAAI) Workshop on Plan, Activity, and Intention Recognition, PAIR (2007)
5. Ilghami, O., Nau, D.S., Aha, D.W.: Learning preconditions for planning from plan traces and HTN structure. Computational Intelligence 21, 413 (2005)
6. Meneguzzi, F., Luck, M.: Leveraging new plans in agentSpeak(PL). In: Baldoni, M., Son, T.C., van Riemsdijk, M.B., Winikoff, M. (eds.) DALT 2008. LNCS (LNAI), vol. 5397, pp. 111–127. Springer, Heidelberg (2009)
7. Murata, T.: Petri nets: Properties, analysis and applications. In: Proceedings of the Institute of Electrical and Electronics Engineers (IEEE), vol. 77, pp. 541–580 (1989)
8. Pechoucek, M., Marík, V.: Industrial deployment of multi-agent technologies: review and selected case studies. Autonomous Agents and Multi-Agent Systems 17(3), 397–431 (2008)
9. Rao, A.S., Georgeff, M.P.: BDI agents: From theory to practice. In: Proc. of the First International Conference on Multiagent Systems (ICMAS), pp. 312–319 (1995)
10. Savarimuthu, B.T.R., Cranefield, S., Purvis, M.A., Purvis, M.K.: Obligation norm identification in agent societies. Journal of Artificial Societies and Social Simulation 13(4) (2010)
11. Savarimuthu, B.T.R., Cranefield, S., Purvis, M.A., Purvis, M.K.: Identifying prohibition norms in agent societies. Artificial Intelligence and Law 21, 1–46 (2012)
12. Traverso, P., Pistore, M.: Automated composition of semantic web services into executable processes. In: International Semantic Web Conference, pp. 380–394 (2004)
13. van der Aalst, W.M.P., Weijters, T., Maruster, L.: Workflow mining: Discovering process models from event logs. IEEE Transactions on Knowledge and Data Engineering 16(9), 1128–1142 (2004)
14. van Dongen, B.F., de Medeiros, A.K.A., Verbeek, H.M.W(E.), Weijters, A.J.M.M.T., van der Aalst, W.M.P.: The proM framework: A new era in process mining tool support. In: Ciardo, G., Darondeau, P. (eds.) ICATPN 2005. LNCS, vol. 3536, pp. 444–454. Springer, Heidelberg (2005)
15. Zhuo, H.H., Hu, D.H., Hogg, C., Yang, Q., Muñoz-Avila, H.: Learning HTN method preconditions and action models from partial observations. In: Proc. of the Twenty-First International Joint Conference on Artificial Intelligence (IJCAI), pp. 1804–1810 (2009)

# Multi-Agent Programming Contest 2013

Tobias Ahlbrecht, Jürgen Dix, Michael Köster, and Federico Schlesinger

Department of Informatics, Clausthal University of Technology,
Julius-Albert-Str. 4, 38678 Clausthal-Zellerfeld, Germany
{dix,tobias.ahlbrecht,michael.koester,
federico.schlesinger}@tu-clausthal.de

**Abstract.** This is about the ninth edition of the Multi-Agent Programming Contest[1], an annual, community-serving competition that attracts groups from all over the world. Our contest enables head-to-head comparison of multi-agent systems and supports educational efforts in the design and implementation of such systems. This year we have generated a multitude of statistical data for each match and give a detailed interpretation of them.

## 1 Introduction

In this paper we (1) briefly introduce the Contest, (2) elaborate on the 2013 scenario and its differences with the 2012 edition, (3) introduce the five teams that took part in the tournament, and (4) present many statistical data to interpret the matches and the performance of the teams.

The Multi-Agent Programming Contest [1] (MAPC) is an annual international event that has started in 2005 as an attempt to stimulate research in the field of programming multi-agent system by 1) identifying key problems, 2) collecting suitable benchmarks, and 3) gathering test cases which require and enforce coordinated action that can serve as milestones for testing multi-agent programming languages, platforms and tools. In 2013 the competition was organized and held for the ninth time.

More detailed information about the strategies of the teams are to be found in the subsequent five papers in this volume. In addition, we compiled a companion paper [1] that contains short answers from each team to more than 50 questions that allows the reader to easily compare the teams.

### 1.1 Related Work

For a detailed account on the history of the contest as well as the underlying simulation platform, we refer to [2,7,5,6,10]. A quick non-technical overview appeared in [3].

---

[1] http://multiagentcontest.org

M. Cossentino et al. (Eds.): EMAS 2013, LNAI 8245, pp. 292–318, 2013.

Similar contests, competitions and challenges have taken place in the past few years. Among them we mention *Google's AI challenge*[2], the *AI-MAS Winter Olympics*[3], the *Starcraft AI Competition*[4], the *Mario AI Championship*[5], the *ORTS competition*[6], the *Planning Competition*[7], and the *General Game Playing*[8]. Every such competition rests in its own research niche. Originally, our Contest has been designed for problem solving approaches that are based on formal approaches and computational logics. But this is not a requirement to enter the competition.

## 1.2   The Contest from 2005–2013

Through the history of the Contest, changes to the scenarios were introduced with every new edition, with three major redesigns.

From 2005 to 2007, a classical *gold miners* scenario was used [8]. We introduced the *MASSim* platform: A platform for executing the Contest tournaments.

From 2008 to 2010 we developed the *cows and cowboys* scenario, which was designed to enforce cooperative behavior among agents [4]. The topology of the environment was represented by a grid that contained, besides various obstacles, a population of simulated cows. The goal was to arrange agents in a manner that scared cows into special areas, called corrals, in order to get points. While still maintaining the core tasks of environment exploration and path planning, the use of cooperative strategies was a requirement of this scenario.

In 2011, the *agents on Mars* scenario [5] was newly introduced. In short, the environment topology was generalized to a weighted graph. Agents were expected to cooperatively establish a graph covering while standing their ground in an adversarial setting and reaching certain achievements. The basics of the *agents on Mars* scenario remained until the 2013 edition discussed in this paper, although several modifications were introduced to keep the Contest challenging.

## 2   MAPC 2013: Agents on Mars, Third Edition

For the 2013 edition of the Contest, a few significant modifications were made to the agents on Mars scenario used in 2012, in order to keep the challenge up to date. This section focuses on these modification; a more detailed description of the scenario can be found in Appendix A.

The number of agents in each team was increased again this year, to a total of 28 agents: 6 Explorers, 6 Repairers, 6 Sentinels, 6 Inspectors and only 4 Saboteurs. The 2012 edition comprised instead 4 agents of each role per team,

---

[2] http://aichallenge.org/
[3] http://www.aiolympics.ro/
[4] http://eis.ucsc.edu/StarCraftAICompetition
[5] http://www.marioai.org/
[6] http://skatgame.net/mburo/orts/
[7] http://ipc.icaps-conference.org/
[8] http://games.stanford.edu/

whereas in the 2011 edition there were only 2 vehicles for each role, totaling 10 vehicles per team.

A big addition to the 2013 edition was the introduction of *ranged actions*. Agents could now act at a distance, i.e., having a target node that is different than the one where the agent stands (`probe`), or having a target agent that stands on a different node (`inspect`, `attack` and `repair`); these, as long as the target is within the visibility range. The successful execution of ranged actions depends on a probability factor that is based on both the distance to the target and the visibility range of the executor.

A slightly more subtle change was made to the map-generating algorithm, to get different (parametrized) levels of connectivity between the nodes that the teams should adapt to.

On a more general level, not concerning directly with the playability of the scenario, a lot of effort was invested in easing the development process to the participants, by means of improving the visualization tools, as well as the feedback sent to the agents. The new visualization lets the viewer distinguish at glance the roles of the agents, the last actions executed by each agent and their success/failure, the executor and target of ranged actions, and the nodes that were already probed by each team, all directly from the map.

## 3   The Tournament

Following the mode implemented in 2012, a *qualification round* was held prior to the tournament, in which teams were required to show that they were able to maintain good stability (i.e. timeout-rates below 5%) during a round of test matches. Only then were they allowed to take part in the tournament.

### 3.1   Participants and Results

Five teams from around the world registered for the Contest and were able to pass the qualification round, thus taking part in the tournament (see Table 1).

Table 1. Participants of the 2013 Edition

| Team | Affiliation | Platform/Language |
|---|---|---|
| AiWXX | Sun Yat-Sen University, China | C++ |
| GOAL-DTU | Technical University of Denmark | GOAL |
| LTI-USP | University of Sao Paulo, Brazil | Jason, CArtAgO, Moise |
| SMADAS-UFSC | Federal University of Santa Catarina, Brazil | Jason, CArtAgO, Moise |
| TUB | TU Berlin, Germany | JIAC |

**AiWXX:** The team AiWXX [11] from Sun Yat-Sen University, China, took part in the contest for the second time, slightly changing its name (formerly AiWYX), and incorporating a second developer. The agents were developed in C++, using no agent-specific technologies. The approach used is centralized, where one agent gets all the percepts from the other agents and makes the decisions for the whole team.

**LTI-USP:** The team LTI-USP [9] from University of São Paulo, Brazil, also competed for the second time; this time with two developers, one less than in 2012. Agents were implemented using Jason, CArtAgO and Moise. There is one agent that determines the best strategy, but each agent has its own thread, with its own beliefs, desires and intentions. Agents broadcast new percepts, but communication load decreases over time.

**SMADAS-UFSC:** The team SMADAS-UFSC [14] from Federal University of Santa Catarina, Brazil, was the winner of the 2012 edition. It had 7 team members (one more than in 2012). The language of choice for agent development was Jason combined with CArtAgO and Moise. Besides normal agent-communication provided by Jason, agents shared a common data-structure (blackboard) for storing the graph topology.

**GOAL-DTU:** The team GOAL-DTU [12] from the Technical University of Denmark is a regular contender of the Multi-Agent Programming Contest. This incarnation counted with 7 team members. The language of choice (as well as the team name) changed to GOAL for this edition, after having used a Python-based system for the previous two editions. The agents follow a decentralized approach, where coordination is achieved through distributed algorithms, e.g. for auction-based agreement.

**TUB:** The team TUB [13], Technical University Berlin, Germany, is another regular contender of the Multi-Agent Programming Contest, presenting this time a team with 12 members (originally working as two separate groups). The agents are developed in the JIAC V platform (which won the contest several times in previous years).

The tournament took place on the 9th and 10th of September, 2013. Each day each team played against two other teams so that in the end all teams played against all others. We started the tournament each morning at 12 pm and finished at around 6 pm. A match between two teams consisted of 3 simulations differing in the size and connectivity level of the graph: the first simulation was always 550 nodes with a *thinning factor*[9] of 10%, the second one 580 nodes with a thinning factor of 20%, and the third one 600 nodes with a thinning factor of 30%. Teams got 3 points for winning a simulation and 1 point in case of a draw. The results of this year's Contest are shown in Table 2.

All the participating teams of the 2013 edition had also participated in the 2012 edition (with a few different members in some cases), and the final results remained very similar, in spite of the modifications to the scenario and the new strategies implemented. SMADAS-UFSC was crowned champion for the second

---

[9] The *thinning factor* is a configuration parameter that is inversely proportional to the connectivity level of the graph.

**Table 2.** Results

| Pos. | Team | Score | Difference | Points |
|------|------|-------|-----------|--------|
| 1 | SMADAS-UFSC | 2702948 : 1455163 | 1247785 | 36 |
| 2 | GOAL-DTU | 2284575 : 1614711 | 669864 | 27 |
| 3 | LTI-USP | 2117299 : 2083105 | 34194 | 15 |
| 4 | TUB | 1412702 : 2238820 | -826118 | 6 |
| 5 | AiWXX | 1516760 : 2642485 | -1125725 | 6 |

consecutive time, improving their previous year's performance and winning in every single simulation they took part in. GOAL-DTU was again a clear second, after winning every simulation except when they faced the Contest winners. LTI-USP obtained a respectable third place surpassing TUB and this was the only modification in the ranking of the five teams with respect to the 2012 edition. Both TUB and AiWXX got six points, so no team ended the Contest empty handed, but the difference in the simulation scores favoured the former to secure the fourth place.

### 3.2 Overview of the Teams' Strategies

In this section we collect a few facts about the participating teams. For more detailed information we refer to the team description articles[11,12,9,14,13] and to the joint paper[1] in these proceedings.

**SMADAS-UFSC:** The strategy can be divided into two phases: In the first phase the agents explore the map to obtain achievement points and to find good zones as early as possible. In this phase the agents try to build one big zone. If occupying such a zone is not possible in the first 130 steps the second phase is activated: The agents conquer the best nodes and try to protect several small zones. Additionally, the developers specified some special algorithms for building zones when the map has only a few connections.

While implementing the team the developers defined five different strategies and tested them with different maps against their team from last year and decided for the particular one right before the contest.

They claim that occupying several small zones was one of the main reasons why the performance was so good.

**GOAL-DTU:** The overall strategy was as follows: After around 70 steps one Explorer computed the best positions for the Sentinels and Inspectors to build a zone. After 150 steps the Explorer agents joined them. Saboteurs and Repairers were responsible for destroying the opponent's zones.

The team claims that their agents had two strong points: the ability to control a zone and the preemptive repairing, i.e., the Repairers anticipate an attack on a teammate and start repairing the agent right in that moment. One of the weak points was that the Saboteurs had an unresolved bug.

**LTI-USP:** The main strategy was basically the same as last year, namely, to divide the agents into three subgroups: two for occupying zones and one for sabotaging the enemy. However, the team organization was implemented in a different way. Instead of using the roles (like Explorer, Sentinel, etc.) from the scenario, additional roles with different strategies were defined. An agent then could adopt a particular role and execute the associated strategies to fulfill her mission.

The team believes that a strong point of their implementation was a defensive strategy, resulting in more stable zones. The weak point was the size of the zones.

**TUB:** The strategy was twofold: Each agent followed its own strategy for collecting achievement points. Second, the team had a coordinator agent for computing and building zones. The agents had various roles they can take on, thus they could decide to help building a zone or to disturb the zone building of the opponent.

The authors claim that a strong point of their implementation was that the agents' strategies could be easily replaced due to the modular implementation. One of the main weak points was the zone building strategy.

**AiWXX:** The main strategy of the team was to probe the whole map first and then occupy several stable and valuable zones.

The team claims that one of the strong points was the computational speed of their pure C++ implementation. However, a weak point was that they did not take the actions of the opponent into account while developing the agents and therefore did not specify a defense or counter-strategy.

# 4    Overview of Teams' Performance

We collected a lot of data throughout the matches concerning the score and the zones (discussed in Section 4.1), the achievements (cf. Section 4.2) and the overall stability and reliability of the teams (see Section 4.3). Additionally, in Section 4.4 we analyse the behaviour of the agents regarding their roles. The underlying data can be downloaded from our web page[10].

## 4.1    Score, Zone Values, and Zone Stability

In this section we analyse for each team the overall performance (summed scores), the development of the achievement points and the zone stability.

All these values somehow depend on each other. The curves for the achievement points are usually quite flat but monotonically increasing: They could also, due to buying actions, decrease, but this does not really show in our curves. The reason is that this effect of buying is too small (i.e. the teams did not use it extensively) to have a visible effect.

To interpret the curves for zone stability, one has to take into account that *monotonically increasing* parts show that the zones are stable: the steeper it is, the more stable it is. Dually, if parts of the curve are *monotonically decreasing*

---

[10] http://multiagentcontest.org/downloads/
Multi-Agent-Programming-Contest-2013

this means that zones are attacked by the opponent and are unstable. So the derivative of these curves gives a better picture.

This behaviour follows from the computation of the the values in the chart: each node gets a counter that is initialised to 0 once the node belongs to a zone. In each step, the counter is incremented if it still belongs to the zone. The counter is set to 0 if the zone does not exist anymore. The values depicted in the chart are the sum over all counters of all nodes.

**SMADAS-UFSC.** The winner of our contest, won all matches and scored perfectly. GOAL-DTU came closest and the following figure shows the first simulation which was almost a draw.

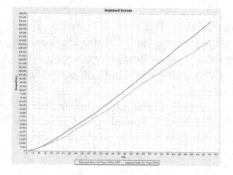

**Fig. 1.** UFSC-SMADAS vs. GOAL-DTU Simulation 1: Summed scores

**Fig. 2.** UFSC-SMADAS vs. GOAL-DTU Simulation 1: Step-scores and Achievement points

Fig. 3 shows that both teams were good in defending their zones and building up more (in the last third, SMADAS-UFSC was better in achieving this). The step scores were also narrow and oscillating between the two teams. The achievement points from SMADAS-UFSC were consistently better from early on in the match.

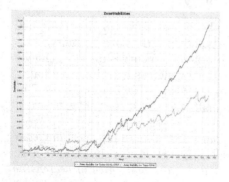

**Fig. 3.** UFSC-SMADAS vs. GOAL-DTU Simulation 1: Stability

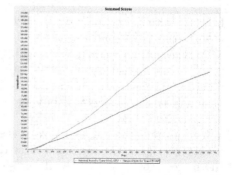

**Fig. 4.** GOAL-DTU vs. LTI-USP Simulation 2: Summed scores

**GOAL-DTU.** The runner up (for the third consecutive time) played very well and this also shows in the charts. As a typical example we chose the second simulation against LTI-USP. Fig 5 shows that green (GOAL-DTU) performed consistently better than LTI-USP, both in the achievements as well as in the step scores. This is even more immediate in the zone stability.

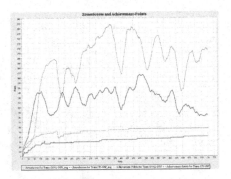

**Fig. 5.** GOAL-DTU vs. LTI-USP Simulation 2: Step-scores and Achievement points

**Fig. 6.** GOAL-DTU vs. LTI-USP Simulation 2: Stability

In the paragraph above about SMADAS-UFSC, we discussed the first simulation with GOAL-DTU which was a close match. Interestingly, GOAL-DTU did not as well in the other two simulations. There, its zone stability was not on par with its competitor.

**LTI-USP.** The team came third but showed some strong playing.

**Fig. 7.** LTI-USP vs. SMADAS-UFSC Simulation 3: Step-scores and Achievement points

**Fig. 8.** LTI-USP vs. SMADAS-UFSC Simulation 3: Stability

Figure 8 shows that zone stability worked well from the middle of the game to almost the end (LTI-USP is blue). Also the scores are well over the achievement points. A good result, only the opponent was a bit better in this match.

**TUB.** The german team did usually quite poor on zone stability. The following figures show the first simulation of TUB against LTI-USP.

**Fig. 9.** TUB vs. LTI-USP Simulation 1: Step-scores and Achievement points

**Fig. 10.** TUB vs. LTI-USP Simulation 1: Stability

In Fig. 9 one notices that the score of the green team (TUB), consists mainly of achievement points (the green curve is oscillating around or even under the achievements line). The poor performance on zone stability is of course clearly shown in Fig. 10.

However, TUB was doing much better in the third simulation against LTI-USP, where it almost drawed: So it did much better on the bigger scenario (which is usually more difficult to handle).

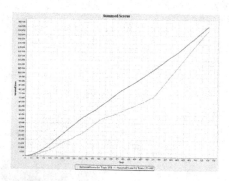

**Fig. 11.** TUB vs. LTI-USP Simulation 3: Summed scores

**Fig. 12.** TUB vs. LTI-USP Simulation 3: Step-scores and Achievement points

**AiWXX.** Although AiWXX came last, a few games were very close. The next figures show such a close match. The step scores in Fig. 13 show clearly that AiWXX was performing on par until the middle of the game, when the scores went quite dramatically down, and then up and down without stabilizing. The same is showing in Fig. 14: the team was not able to defend their zones.

**Fig. 13.** AiWXX vs. LTI-USP Simulation 2: Step-scores and Achievement points

**Fig. 14.** AiWXX vs. LTI-USP Simulation 2: Stability

**Conclusion.** This year we saw some very interesting matches. Some of them were close to a draw. For some teams the building of zones did not work well when the opponent was too agressive. It worked better against other teams.

### 4.2 Achievements

In general, all teams gave more priority to achievement points *as part of the score* than as a resource to improve agents' attributes. In fact, only two of the five teams made use of the buy action at all, and they did it in a planned, limited, and consistent manner: GOAL-DTU spent 14 achievement points per simulation, and LTI-USP spent 20 points per simulation.

The average number of achievement points earned by each team, without taking the buys into consideration, is consistent with the final ranking of the contest: 71 points for SMADAS-UFSC, 70,5 for GOAL-DTU (56,5 after buys), 67,5 for LTI-USP (47,5 after buys), 64,5 for TUB and finally 56 for AiWXX. Interestingly, these numbers varied only a little for each team in the different simulations: they were not in any relation to the map sizes.

Figure 15 corresponds to Simulation 1 of the match between GOAL-DTU and LTI-USP, and reflects how the different buying strategies of these two teams affect the evolution of the achievement points. GOAL-DTU realizes all buys in a single phase that starts at around step 140, whereas 4 peaks[11] can be seen in the graph for LTI-USP, the first one at the very beginning of the simulation and

---

[11] The number of achievement point can only decrease through the buying action.

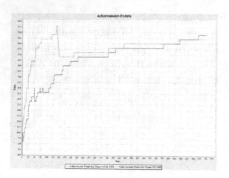
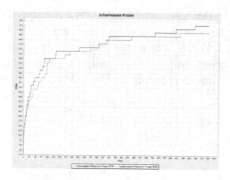

**Fig. 15.** GOAL-DTU vs. LTI-USP Simulation 1: Achievement Points

**Fig. 16.** UFSC vs. TUB Simulation 3: Achievement Points

the last one prior to step 90. Even though at the end of this simulation LTI-USP manages to earn more achievement points than GOAL-DTU, it is clear that the achievement points of GOAL-DTU had more effect on the final score.

Figure 16 on the other hand, shows the typical evolution of the achievement points for teams that did not use the buying action. In these case, SMADAS-UFSC and TUB are almost on par, with a slight margin in favor of the former.

Regarding the composition of the achievements, it is worth noting the following:

- The survey action was the fastest to pay-off in terms of achievements, providing up to 10 achievement points in the very first step (up to surveyed160).
- The area achievements varied from simulation to simulation, but as expected, the best-performing teams were the ones who earned these achievements earlier.
- LTI-USP was markedly slower than the rest of the teams in probing more than 320 nodes (probed320 achievement). The rest of the teams reached this number in general at around step 140, almost always before step 200. LTI-USP, on the other hand, never obtained this achievement before step 300, and often after step 400.
- The attack-related achievements were a major source of differences in the final count of achievement points earned. Aggressive teams, for example SMADAS-UFSC, performed better in this respect.
- Attack-related achievements were also the main source of achievement points in the end of each simulation.
- AiWXX's agents never used the parry action, and therefore never got any parry achievements.

**Conclusion.** Differently from the previous edition, this year there were no simulations in which the achievement points played a significant role in the final score. Although some teams performed better than others, the differences were much smaller than the differences in zone-score.

Whether it really pays off to implement a buying strategy, is not clear. This year's winners proved that a team can do very well without one. At the same time, the second and third ranked teams spent some of their achievement points in improvements, and clearly outperformed the fourth and fifth, even though the average achievement points remaining at the end of the simulations was better for the latter. For the two teams that did use the buying action, however, the strategy was rather conservative, and they kept most of the achievement points for scoring.

## 4.3   Agents' Reliability and Stability

In this section we analyse the success and failure of executing actions by the agents. The set of failure codes can be divided into three classes: a random failure, a technical failure, and a failure with rerspect to the semantics of the simulation.

While the first failure is introduced by the scenario[12] to ensure a certain degree of stability of the agents' perceive-think-act cycle (i.e. the agents are able to detect a failure and act accordingly), the second one is directly connected to the stability of the platform respectively to the agent program. If an agent is not able to send her action in a reasonable time slot then it can be only because of two reasons: the network communication was too slow or the agent had some problems due to a crash or some computational issues. Indeed, in this year's competition the participants did not have any network problems but some agents crashed during a run and had to be restarted and/or were using too much time for their computations[13].

The last class of failures is directly related to the game logic of the scenario. An attack-action can fail when the attacked agent executes the parry-action. A ranged action or goto-action can fail because the node or opponent is out of range. Even if the agent is in range, it can fail with a certain probability (determined by the visibility). Additionally, it fails in case of lack of resources, when the agent got successfully attacked or the status or role does not allow to execute a particular action. For the complete description of all actions and failure codes we refer to the scenario description in Appendix A.

For the reliability and stability of the agent we will focus on the following failure codes: We will look at all technical failures because they allow us to directly deduce some stability properties. On the semantical level we will consider the *out of range failures*, the *unreachable failures*, the *status* and *role failures* as well as the *resources failures*. These failures show that the agent did not respect her internal status or made some wrong conclusions regarding the environment and allow us therefore to speak about the reliability of the agent.

Finally, we will mention the other failures only if their occurrence is much higher than the average.

---

[12] For this year we let 1% of the actions fail randomly.
[13] The time limit was set to almost 4 seconds.

**SMADAS-UFSC.** Concerning the stability we can conclude from the data that the SMADAS-UFSC agents were very stable. In total, only 12 actions were not sent in time. Interestingly, it was one action per simulation. More precisely, it was always the very same Inspector that did not send an action in the last step.

When it comes to reliability there are only very few failures because of lack of resources. Thus, we can say the agents were very reliable. However, one reason might be that the UFSC team did not use the ranged actions—a potential source of error—a lot.

Typical results for SMADAS-UFSC are shown in Figure 17 and Figure 19.

| Reason | SMADAS-UFSC | % | LTI-USP | % |
|---|---|---|---|---|
| parried | 812 | 3,87 | 514 | 2,45 |
| out of range | | | 69 | 0,33 |
| random | 206 | 0,98 | 226 | 1,08 |
| resources | 1 | 0 | 13 | 0,06 |
| attacked | 285 | 1,36 | 191 | 0,91 |
| no action received | 1 | 0 | | |
| status | | | 1 | 0 |
| in range | | | 1187 | 5,65 |

**Fig. 17.** LTI-USP vs. SMADAS-UFSC Simulation 1: Failed Actions

**GOAL-DTU.** The GOAL-DTU agents were also very stable. Around 0.5 percent of the actions got lost due to computational issues and the agents did not crash at all. From the scenario perspective the GOAL-DTU team made more mistakes than the SMADAS-UFSC team. One reason for this was caused by the use of ranged actions. Nevertheless the team was robust and did not try to execute an action forbidden by the role or the current status. Figure 18 contains some exemplary data of one simulation.

| Reason | TUB | % | GOAL-DTU | % |
|---|---|---|---|---|
| parried | 286 | 1,36 | 3 | 0,01 |
| out of range | 8 | 0,04 | 4 | 0,02 |
| random | 203 | 0,97 | 231 | 1,1 |
| resources | 4 | 0,02 | | |
| unreachable | 573 | 2,73 | | |
| attacked | 138 | 0,66 | 259 | 1,23 |
| no action received | | | 19 | 0,09 |
| status | 17 | 0,08 | | |
| in range | 52 | 0,25 | 118 | 0,56 |

**Fig. 18.** TUB vs. GOAL-DTU Simulation 2: Failed Actions

**LTI-USP.** The stability of LTI-USP was in between the first two teams. While SMADAS-UFSC was the most stable team in the field the LTI-USP was following closely afterwards. In only two simulations (Simulation 3 against AiWXX and Simulation 3 against GOAL-DTU) LTI-USP had some stability issues. Less than 0.1% and 0.8% respectively of actions failed due to that.

Regarding the failures depending on the scenario we can say that the number of failures due to the lack of resources and the out of range actions was comparable with the ones from GOAL-DTU, however the number of actions that failed in range was significantly higher (around 5 Percent). Buying more visibility range for the agents would have decreased that value.

Figure 17 shows an example.

**TUB.** The TUB team's stability was similar to that from GOAL-DTU. In some simulations the agents did not loose one action in others they lost some (but always not more than 1%). Thus the agents were stable and answering normally in time.

When it comes to the reliability of the agents' code we noticed some differences to the first three teams. The agents often tried to go to a node that was not reachable from their position. This was especially the case in Simulation 1 against GOAL-DTU. More than 6% of the actions returned that failure. Also, some actions failed due to the status. Concerning the ranged actions and the resources the results are comparable with GOAL-DTU.

Figure 18 depicts a typical result for TUB.

**AiWXX.** Finally, the stability of AiWXX (Example shown in Figure 19) was the worst in the contest although (except for one simulation against LTI-USP where the computer or the agents crashed) it was still in the range of 2 to 5 percent and therefore quite good.

The reliability was as for the other teams. One thing we noticed was that quite some actions failed due to an attack of the opponent. So it might be that a better strategy for parrying or avoiding attacks would have helped to get a better position in the final ranking.

| Reason | AiWXX | % | SMADAS-UFSC | % |
|---|---|---|---|---|
| parried | 52 | 0,25 | | |
| random | 237 | 1,13 | 201 | 0,96 |
| unreachable | 3 | 0,01 | | |
| attacked | 261 | 1,24 | 39 | 0,19 |
| no action received | 1120 | 5,33 | 1 | 0 |
| status | 4 | 0,02 | | |
| in range | 7 | 0,03 | | |

**Fig. 19.** AiWXX vs. SMADAS-UFSC Simulation 1: Failed Actions

**Conclusion.** In summary, we can say that this year all teams were stable and reasonable reliable. This was expectable since we only slightly changed the scenario in the last two years and all teams from this year were participating last year as well.

### 4.4    Actions Per Role

In this section we take a look at the frequency at which actions are executed per agent role and team. For a description of the agents' roles and their respective available actions we refer to Appendix A. Sometimes, we shall mention the percentage of failed actions on a *per role* and a *per team* basis. For a more general perspective of failed actions per team only, we refer to Section 4.3.

**Explorer.** The Explorer role's inherent task is to scout the map and `probe` nodes to get information about their value.

Comparing all teams, the actions `goto` and `recharge` are dominant over all others. Most of the teams (all except AiWXX) execute a similar number of `probe` actions in all simulations. Although maps of different sizes are played (550, 580 and 600 nodes each), the number of executed `probe` actions does not increase proportionally and at times even decreases for those teams. Also, no Explorer used the `buy` action and thus nobody was able to execute a ranged probing.

SMADAS-UFSC: This teams' Explorers did not use the `survey` action at all. Apart from this, the amount of probing was in line with most of the other teams and settling down around 13% in each simulation. Most actions were `goto` and `recharge`, however, neither one dominates the other in all simulations.

GOAL-DTU: This team's Explorers used the least `probe` actions (directly followed by LTI-USP), peaking below 10%. The amount of `survey` actions is negligible and the most used action was `recharge` at 75% to 80%. From this we can deduce that these Explorers seemingly always explored an equally sized portion of the map. Since only a small percentage is left for the `goto` action, we can further assume -also based on the overall outcome- that suitable zones were found swiftly and could be held for a long time. A characteristic performance of these Explorers is given in Figure 20. Each bar represents one action that is available to the role. They allow for analyzing how often the respective actions were used by the agents of the current role and team. The green colored part indicates how many actions were successful while the red part represents the failed actions. Above each bar are a couple of numbers. The blue ones describe the total amount (in absolute and relative numbers) of usages of the action. Accordingly, the green numbers below describe the successful actions.

LTI-USP: Everything said in the previous paragraph also applies for these Explorers. The only difference to GOAL-DTU is the amount of `goto` actions which ranges from 17% to 31% for LTI-USP. The behaviour of this team was also very uniform over all simulations.

TUB: The TUB Explorers were the only ones to use an observable amount of `skip` actions (which also holds for every other role of TUB). Usage of the

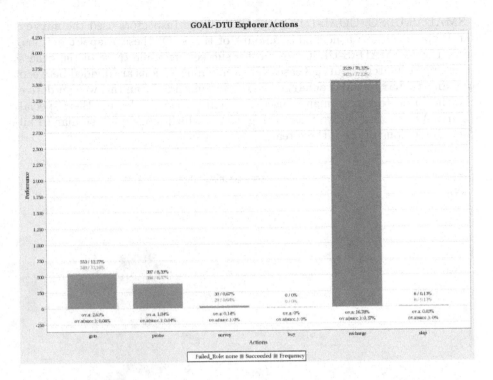

**Fig. 20.** AiWXX vs. GOAL-DTU Simulation 1: GOAL-DTU Explorer Actions

**recharge** action might have proven to be a better alternative, however, there was no case of unexceptionally many 'failed resources' failures for TUB. The relative number of **probe** and **survey** actions was uniform for all simulations. However, one simulation showed a large number of failed **survey** actions. Nevertheless, the number of successful **survey** actions in this simulation is comparable to that of the other simulations.

AiWXX: Their Explorers used the **probe** action to a varying degree ranging from 6% to as much as 30% which is the peak percentage of all teams. Besides some simulations, in which they used the **survey** action more than every other team, the majority of actions falls upon **goto** and **recharge**. However, there is no clear favorite between these two actions regarding all simulations. This points to a varied degree of mobility that is neither dependent on the opponent nor the size of the map.

**Inspector.** The Inspector is the only role that is able to inspect, that is to gain information about agents of the other team aside from their observable properties.

The teams used the **inspect** action to a varying degree. However, SMADAS-UFSC, GOAL-DTU and LTI-USP show a similar performance (of actions) over all simulations.

SMADAS-UFSC, GOAL-DTU, LTI-USP:.These Inspectors used the survey and inspect actions a negligible amount of times. Of these inspect actions, only those of SMADAS-UFSC are mostly succeeding while those of the others fail in approximately 2 out of 3 cases. The remaining actions are divided between goto and recharge with recharge clearly dominating. From this we can derive that the Inspectors were mainly used to occupy zones neglecting their special feature. As an example, we refer to Figure 21, which looks quite similar to all other simulations of these three teams.

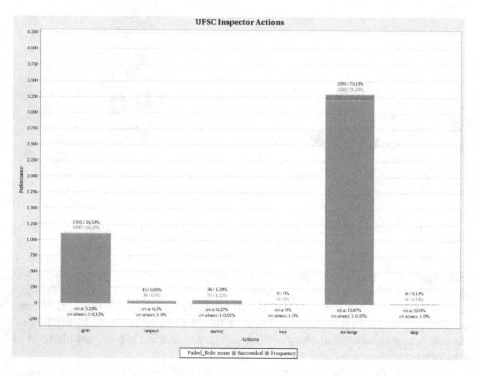

**Fig. 21.** LTI-USP vs. SMADAS-UFSC Simulation 2: SMADAS-UFSC Inspector Actions

TUB: The TUB Inspectors used the inspect action a lot more, ranging from 15% to 55%. In addition, these were mostly successful (i.e. more than 75% in the worst case). Another distinction is the amount of goto actions dwarfing the number of recharge actions. However, only these agents had a tendency to fail at using this goto action making up for the increased usage.

AiWXX: These Inspectors used the inspect action only at 1-3% of times, thus falling in line with every other team but TUB. The survey action was used in 1-15% of steps and the remaining numbers of goto and recharge actions were alternating over simulations, which differs from all other teams.

**Repairer.** The Repairer is able to enable agents which have been disabled by attacks from other teams. As this strongly depends on the performance of the competitor, there is no uniform behavior over all simulations.

SMADAS-UFSC: This team was the one to use the repair action the least. Aside from this, the survey and parry actions were used a few times leaving the goto and recharge actions again with the greatest number of executions. The latter actions were mostly used equally with no action dwarfing the other. These Repairers showed a uniform performance over all simulations.

GOAL-DTU: The Repairers used the survey action more than the average. The agents also parried the most. However, most of the parry actions failed. The repairing ranged from 5% to 30% and most repair actions were successful.

LTI-USP: Their Repairers used 6 buy actions per simulation on average. The recharge action was used at varying amounts, in one simulation even peaking at 85%. The repair action was mostly used a lot, however, less than 50% of these uses were successful. If the agents repaired more, the recharge action was used less (probably only being the default action).

TUB: These Repairers did not parry at all. The repair action was used in 5% up to 40% of steps and mostly succeeded. The repair and recharge actions were alternating similar to LTI-USP.

AiWXX: The AiWXX Repairers used the repair action the most. At times it was used in more than 60% of steps and mostly successful. These agents also did not parry at all (so, of course requiring more repairs). An example can be seen in Figure 22.

**Saboteur.** The Saboteur is opposite to the Repairer, being able to disable other agents if they do not parry.

Three of the teams did not make use of the buy action. However, those who did were not affected by a higher percentage of failures in general.

SMADAS-UFSC: This team did not buy anything for the Saboteurs. The attack action was used 25% to 50% and the success percentage depended on the respective opponent. It was used more often than the recharge action.

GOAL-DTU: These agents used the buy action 7 times on average. An effect of this is not reflected in the charts. The attack action was used in 20% to 50% of steps and again failed according to the respective competitor. The survey and parry actions were ignored.

LTI-USP: These Saboteurs used 4 to 5 buy actions per simulation. The attack action was used in 15% to 55% of steps and failed quite often, except in one single simulation. The independence of the opponent is possibly due to ranged attacks that were not used by many other teams. Buying more visibility range would have increased the number of successful attacks.

TUB: The TUB team did not use the buy action. The attack action was used in 5% to 50% of steps. Slightly distinctive, the percentage of failures did not vary per opponent but per simulation. An example can be seen in Figure 23.

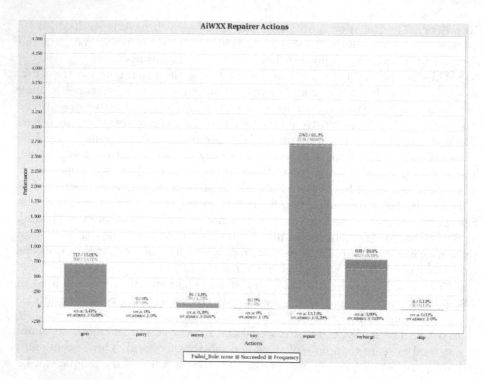

**Fig. 22.** AiWXX vs. GOAL-DTU Simulation 3: AiWXX Explorer Actions

AiWXX: The `attack` action was used in 5% to 40% of steps without using a bought upgrade. Similar to TUB, the failure percentage differed per simulation and not per opponent.

**Sentinel.** The Sentinel role is best suited to defend a zone, since it can use the `parry` action and has no other distinctive characteristic.

SMADAS-UFSC: This team parried in 12% of steps while succeeding at around 75% of these actions. The dominant actions here were `goto` and `recharge` with the latter occurring more often.

GOAL-DTU: This team parried more often, ranging from 3% to 30% of possible executions. However, the Sentinels were mostly succeeding in less than 50% of these actions. This might be a sign of increased pre-emptive parrying. The most used action again was `recharge` at 60-80%. This again underlines the tendency of GOAL-DTU to use the fewest `goto` actions.

LTI-USP: These Sentinels used the `parry` action in 1 to 17% of steps. A relation to the map size is not in evidence, however, exceptionally many `parry` actions were used in the match against SMADAS-UFSC. An example of such a match is given in Figure 24. This might be due to their Saboteurs being the most aggressive ones in using the `attack` action against LTI-USP and shows a certain degree of flexibility in adapting to the amount of incoming attacks.

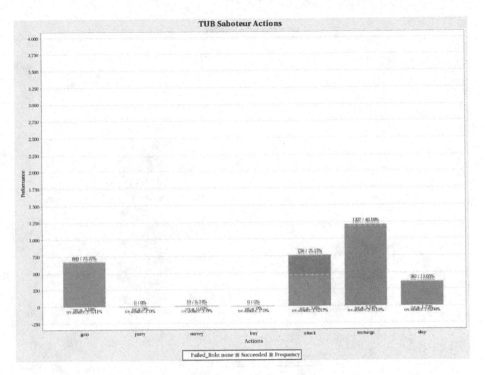

**Fig. 23.** TUB vs. GOAL-DTU Simulation 2: TUB Explorer Actions

TUB: The TUB agents were again the only ones to use the `skip` action. The `parry` action was only used in 1-6% of steps and mostly failed. Also, the agents used the `survey` action in 1% of steps. In two occasions, the percentage was 5% and 15% respectively, however, the successful `survey` actions still made up only 1% of the total actions.

AiWXX: The `parry` action was not used at all. The agents performed a small amount of `survey` actions and otherwise used the `recharge` and `goto` actions in varying proportions.

**Conclusion.** We have seen that the teams did not use the actions as diverse as one could have expected. For some teams and roles, the proportions of actions were very similar. However, some teams (mostly the ones coming 4th and 5th) showed completely different behavior. Also, some teams showed to behave similar over all simulations while others varied more with respect to using the available actions.

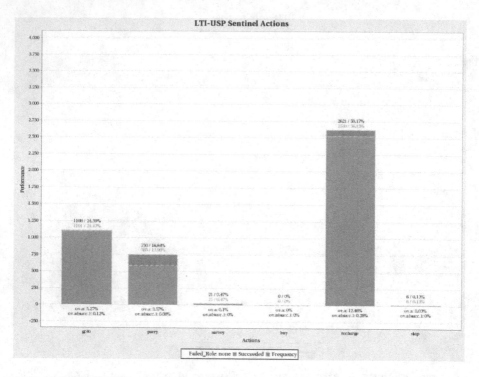

**Fig. 24.** LTI-USP vs. SMADAS-UFSC Simulation 1: LTI-USP Explorer Actions

## 5    Summary, Conclusion and Future of the Contest

This paper provides an overview of the most recent edition (2013) of the Multi-Agent Programming Contest. We introduced the Contest in general, and we elaborated on the current scenario, with an emphasis on the changes to the last edition in 2012.

In this year, we had a plethora of statistical data available that we carefully analysed in the sections above. In a companion paper, [1], we collected the answers to 50 questions posed to the teams. They are arranged in a way to facilitate the comparison of the teams.

Here are a few observations, not just for this edition, but for the last three (where we introduced the Mars scenario).

- In all three editions a dedicated Multi-Agent Programming language or platform won.
- The runner-up in all three editions was the team headed by Jørgen Villadsen (DTU). For the first two editions they used Python, for the third one GOAL (a dedicated agent programming language which also won the first edition).
- We believe it is fair to say (taking all the results into account) that ad hoc implementations seem to perform worse than MAS inspired systems.
- The introduction of a qualification round increased the stability of the teams and therefore the whole contest a lot. We shall keep this feature.

- Teams performing for the second time usually perform better. But all teams performed in previous editions (sometimes only the team leader remained and started with a new crew).
- The overall performance of the teams is improving with each new contest, although we increased the complexity considerably (size of the map, number of agents, difficulty of the task).
- Some teams were playing well when the opponent was not too agressive, but they played very bad when the opponent attacked them.
- Only two teams (placed second and third) used the buy-actions and invested money to improve agents. All others used achievements solely to improve the overall score. The part of the score related to achievements did not play a major role.
- Only one team, placed last, showed slight problems with the stability of the agents. Otherwise this did not play any role.
- Only the team placed last did not use any *parry* action (to defend a zone).
- Compared with the *cows and cowboys* scenario, we see much more cooperation among the agents, more dynamic behaviour, and a lot more interaction with the opposing team. In addition, the data to be handled (observing the environment, messages between the agents) has also increased a lot. While we have not yet excluded centralized approaches, the sheer amount of data makes it difficult for the systems to provide each agent with the central memory for the whole system.
  Also, in the current scenario, the computational costs of shortest path finding is high so that it is not feasible for all agents to execute it at the same time.

How can we make the contest even more exciting?

**Agents:** Why not using a massive number of agents: many agents with different roles and thus different capabilities. Not just 10-30, but hundreds of them. This would allow us to take into account the *scalability* of agent-oriented programming platforms.

**Uncertainty:** Up to now our environments were pretty observable, the amount of failing actions or wrong sensors was small. This could be changed to more indeterministic environments, where agents have to find out the effects of their actions.

**Communication:** It might also be worthwhile to focus on agent communication and to evaluate that aspect of the tournament by routing agent-messages through the *MASSim* server for proper evaluation.

Last but not least, the most important part of the contest are the contestants: This year, three teams started as student projects.

We hope to attract more teams and students in the future: the contest is an excellent opportunity to learn about multi-agent systems.

**Acknowledgements.** We would like to thank Alfred Hofmann from Springer for his support right from the beginning and for endowing the price of 500 Euro in Springer books.

# References

1. Ahlbrecht, T., et al.: Multi-Agent Programming Contest 2013: The Teams and the Design of their System. In: Cossentino, M., El Fallah Seghrouchni, A., Winikoff, M. (eds.) EMAS 2013. LNCS (LNAI), vol. 8245, pp. 366–390. Springer, Heidelberg (2013)
2. Behrens, T., Dastani, M., Dix, J., Köster, M., Novák, P.: Special Issue about Multi-Agent-Contest. Annals of Mathematics and Artificial Intelligence, vol. 59. Springer, Netherlands (2010)
3. Behrens, T., Dastani, M., Dix, J., Hübner, J., Köster, M., Novák, P., Schlesinger, F.: The multi-agent programming contest. AI Magazine 33(4), 111–113 (2012)
4. Behrens, T., Dastani, M., Dix, J., Novák, P.: Agent contest competition: 4th edition. In: Hindriks, K.V., Pokahr, A., Sardina, S. (eds.) ProMAS 2008. LNCS, vol. 5442, pp. 211–222. Springer, Heidelberg (2009)
5. Behrens, T., Dix, J., Hübner, J., Köster, M., Schlesinger, F.: MAPC 2011 Documentation. Technical Report IfI-12-01, Clausthal University of Technology (December 2012)
6. Behrens, T., Dix, J., Hübner, J., Köster, M., Schlesinger, F.: MAPC 2011 Evaluation and Team Descriptions. Technical Report IfI-12-02, Clausthal University of Technology (December 2012)
7. Behrens, T., Köster, M., Schlesinger, F., Dix, J., Hübner, J.F.: The Multi-agent Programming Contest 2011: A Résumé. In: Dennis, L., Boissier, O., Bordini, R.H. (eds.) ProMAS 2011. LNCS, vol. 7217, pp. 155–172. Springer, Heidelberg (2012)
8. Dastani, M., Dix, J., Novák, P.: The second contest on multi-agent systems based on computational logic. In: Inoue, K., Satoh, K., Toni, F. (eds.) CLIMA 2006. LNCS (LNAI), vol. 4371, pp. 266–283. Springer, Heidelberg (2007)
9. Franco, M.R., Sichman, J.S.: Improving the LTI-USP Team: A New JaCaMo Based MAS for the MAPC 2013. In: Cossentino, M., El Fallah Seghrouchni, A., Winikoff, M. (eds.) EMAS 2013. LNCS, vol. 8245, pp. 339–348. Springer, Heidelberg (2013)
10. Köster, M., Schlesinger, F., Dix, J.: The multi-agent programming contest 2012. In: Dastani, M., Hübner, J.F., Logan, B. (eds.) ProMAS 2012. LNCS, vol. 7837, pp. 174–195. Springer, Heidelberg (2013)
11. Li, C., Liu, L.: Prior State Reasoning in Multi-agent systems and Graph-Theoretical Algorithms. In: Cossentino, M., El Fallah Seghrouchni, A., Winikoff, M. (eds.) EMAS 2013. LNCS (LNAI), vol. 8245, pp. 356–365. Springer, Heidelberg (2013)
12. Villadsen, J., Jensen, A.S., Christensen, N.C., Hess, A.V., Johnsen, J.B., Woller, Ø.G., Ørum, P.B.: Engineering a Multi-Agent System in GOAL. In: Cossentino, M., El Fallah Seghrouchni, A., Winikoff, M. (eds.) EMAS 2013. LNCS (LNAI), vol. 8245, pp. 329–338. Springer, Heidelberg (2013)
13. Werner, S., Bender-Saebelkampf, C., Heller, H., Heßler, A.: Multi-Agent Programming Contest 2013: TUB Team Description. In: Cossentino, M., El Fallah Seghrouchni, A., Winikoff, M. (eds.) EMAS 2013. LNCS (LNAI), vol. 8245, pp. 349–355. Springer, Heidelberg (2013)
14. Zatelli, M.R., de Brito, M., Schmitz, T.L., Morato, M.M., de Souza, K.S., Uez, D.M., Hübner, J.F.: SMADAS: A Team for MAPC Considering the Organization and the Environment as First-class Abstractions. In: Cossentino, M., El Fallah Seghrouchni, A., Winikoff, M. (eds.) EMAS 2013. LNCS (LNAI), vol. 8245, pp. 319–328. Springer, Heidelberg (2013)

# A   Scenario Description

It is now a tradition to accompany the technical description of each scenario with a motivating little story:

> In the year 2033 mankind finally populates Mars. While in the beginning the settlers received food and water from transport ships sent from earth shortly afterwards – because of the outer space pirates – sending these ships became too dangerous and expensive. Also, there were rumors going around that somebody actually found water on Mars below the surface. Soon the settlers started to develop autonomous intelligent agents, so-called All Terrain Planetary Vehicles (ATPV), to search for water wells. The World Emperor – enervated by the pirates – decided to strengthen the search for water wells by paying money for certain achievements. Sadly, this resulted in sabotage among the different groups of settlers.
>
> Now, the task of your agents is to find the best water wells and occupy the best zones of Mars. Sometimes they have to sabotage their rivals to achieve their goal (while the opponents will most probably do the same) or to defend themselves. Of course the agents' vehicle pool contains specific vehicles. Some of them have special sensors, some are faster and some have sabotage devices on board.
>
> Last but not least, your team also contains special experts, e.g. the repairer agents, that are capable of fixing agents that are disabled. In general, each agent has special expert knowledge and is thus the only one being able to perform a certain action. So your agents have to find ways to cooperate and coordinate among them.

## A.1   The Map

The environment's topology is constituted by a weighted graph. Each edge has a weight, which is a number that represents the costs of moving from one of its vertices to the other. Each vertex has a unique identifier and a value indicated by a number from 1 to 10. The vertices' values are crucial for calculating the values of zones. A zone is a subgraph that is covered by a team of agents according to a coloring algorithm that is based on a domination principle.

Several agents can stand on a single vertex. If a set of agents dominates such a vertex, the vertex gets the color of the dominating team. A previously uncolored vertex that has a majority of neighbors (at least 2) with a specific color, inherits this color as well. Finally, if the overall graph contains a colored subgraph that constitutes a frontier or border, such that there are no rival agents inside of it, all the nodes that are inside the border are colored as well. This means that agents can color or cover a subgraph that has more vertices than the overall number of agents. Figure 25 shows a screenshot of a relatively small map, depicting, amongst other things, the graph coloring.

## A.2   The Agents

Before elaborating on the agent roles we have to specify the effectoric capabilities of the agents. Each agent, or vehicle, has a state that is defined by its position on the map, its current energy available for executing actions and its current health, plus a visibility

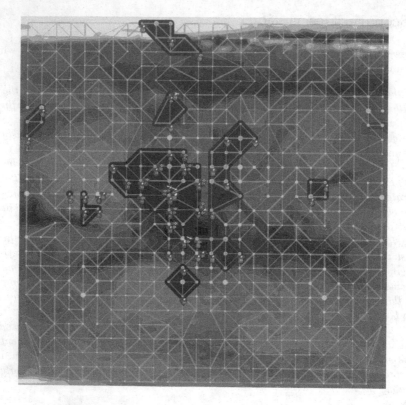

**Fig. 25.** A screenshot of the agents on Mars scenario

range and a strength level. On top of that, each team has a budget for equipping the vehicles during the simulation.

Of course, all the actions that cost energy will fail if the vehicle under consideration does not have enough energy. When the health level drops to 0 (due to opponent attacks), the vehicle becomes *disabled* until repaired: it can then only perform a subset of the actions, and it does not count for node domination nor for zones calculation.

**Actions.** These actions are defined by the scenario:

- skip is the noop-action, which does not change the state of the environment,
- recharge increases the current energy of a vehicle by a fixed factor and can be performed at any time without costs,
- attack decreases the health of an opponent that stands within the visibility range from the attacker, if successfully executed, and decreases the current energy of the attacker,
- parry parries an attack and decreases the energy of the defending agent,
- goto moves the vehicle to a neighboring vertex while decreasing its energy by the weight of the traversed edge,

- **probe** yields the exact value of a given vertex within the visibility range,[14] and decreases the vehicle's energy,
- **survey** yields the exact weights of visible edges while decreasing the energy,
- **inspect** costs energy and yields the internals of all opponents standing on the same node, or a given opponent within the visibility range,
- **buy** equips the vehicle with new components, which increase its performance, and cost money, and
- **repair** repairs a given teammate in the visibility range, which, again, costs energy.

The actions that can act at a distance (**probe**, **inspect**, **attack** and **repair**) are regarded as *ranged actions*. When the target of such actions is not the same node where the agent stands nor is an agent standing on the same node, the action can fail randomly following a probability factor, that is calculated based on the visibility range and the distance to the target.

**Roles.** We have defined five different roles. Each role defines the vehicle's internals and its capabilities. The roles differ with respect to energy, health, strength and visibility range. The effectoric capabilities are as follows:

- **explorer** can skip, move to a vertex, probe a vertex, survey visible edges, buy equipment and recharge its energy,
- **repairer** can skip, move to a vertex, parry an attack, survey visible edges, buy equipment, repair a teammate and recharge its energy,
- **saboteur** can skip, move to a vertex, parry an attack, survey visible edges, buy equipment, attack an opponent and recharge its energy,
- **sentinel** can skip, move to a vertex, parry an attack, survey visible edges, buy equipment and recharge its energy,
- **inspector** can skip, move to a vertex, inspect visible opponents, survey visible edges, buy equipment and recharge its energy.

Each team consists of 28 agents: 6 Explorers, 6 Repairers, 6 Sentinels, 6 Inspectors and only 4 Saboteurs.

## A.3    The Scoring

A *step-score* is calculated for each team in every step, and the final score of a simulation is the sum of all step-scores. The step-score is the sum of all area values plus the achievement points that the team retains at the given step.

**Achievements.** Achievements are tasks that, when fulfilled, contribute to the teams' budgets. We have defined a set of achievements that includes having zones with fixed values, inspecting a specific number of vehicles, probing a number of vertices, surveying a fixed number of edges and successfully performing and parrying a number of attacks. The numbers needed to reach an achievement of a certain type increase exponentially, making them harder to get as the game advances.

For every achievement, a team gets 2 achievement points. These can act as money, that the team may opt to spend in improvements for the agents at any time of the simulation. If not spent, these points contribute to the step-score.

---

[14] It is required to probe a node in order to get its full value summed to score when the node belongs to a zone. Otherwise, it only sums as 1 point.

## A.4  The Execution Cycle

In each step, each vehicle is provided with its currently available percepts:

- the state of the simulation, i.e. the current step,
- the state of the team, i.e. the current scores and money,
- the state of itself, i.e. its internals,
- all visible vertices, i.e. identifier and team,
- all visible edges, i.e. their vertices' identifiers,
- all visible vehicles, i.e. their identifier, vertices and team,
- probed vertices, i.e. their identifier and values,
- surveyed edges, i.e. their vertices' identifiers and weights, and
- inspected vehicles, i.e. their identifiers, vertices, teams and internals.

After sending percepts, the server grants some time for deliberation. After that the new state is computed. The simulation state transition is as follows:

1. collect all actions from the agents,
2. let each action fail with a specific probability,
3. execute all remaining **attack** and **parry** actions,
4. determine disabled agents,
5. execute all remaining actions,
6. calculate zones and step-score
7. prepare percepts,
8. deliver the percepts.

# SMADAS: A Team for MAPC Considering the Organization and the Environment as First-Class Abstractions*

Maicon Rafael Zatelli, Maiquel de Brito, Tiago Luiz Schmitz,
Marcelo Menezes Morato, Kaio Siqueira de Souza, Daniela Maria Uez,
and Jomi Fred Hübner

Department of Automation and Systems Engineering
Federal University of Santa Catarina
CP 476, 88040-900 Florianópolis - SC - Brasil
{xsplyter,tiagolschmitz,marcelomenezes73,dani.uez}@gmail.com,
maiquel.b@posgrad.ufsc.br, kaiossouza@hotmail.com,
jomi.hubner@ufsc.br

**Abstract.** This paper describes the SMADAS team for the Multi-Agent Programming Contest 2013. Throughout this paper we highlight the design, main strategies, tools, and results of our team. For this year we used the JaCaMo platform to develop the team, which is composed of Jason (to program the agents), CArtAgO (to program the environment), and Moise (to program the organization). We also improved the last year team with new strategies focused on the updated "Agents on Mars" scenario.

## 1 Introduction

The Multi-Agent Programming Contest (MAPC) [6][1] is an important event to stimulate research in the multi-agent systems programming field. The MAPC 2013 used the "Agents on Mars" scenario, which was improved from the last year scenario, therefore the efforts must continue concentrated in cooperation, coordination, and decentralization. Our agent team, called SMADAS, acronym for our research group, named Multi-Agent Systems from Systems and Automation Department (in Portuguese, **S**istemas **M**ulti**a**gentes do **D**epartamento de **A**utomação e **S**istemas) was developed by a group formed by one PhD, four PhD students, and two undergraduate students from the Federal University of Santa Catarina (UFSC). This is our second participation in the contest and we have two main aims this year: improve our MAS developing skills and evaluate some proposals developed in our thesis.

## 2 System Analysis and Design

For this year's contest, we opted for developing a new team using the JaCaMo [2] platform instead of just improving the last year team. The programming model of JaCaMo

---

* We are grateful for the support given by CAPES and CNPq (grant numbers 140261/2013-3, 306301/2012-1).

[1] http://multiagentcontest.org

M. Cossentino et al. (Eds.): EMAS 2013, LNAI 8245, pp. 319–328, 2013.

provides high-level support for developing MAS considering agents, environment, and organization as *first-class* entities. The development of these three dimensions is based on three different technologies: Jason [3], for programming the agents; CArtAgO [7], for programming the environment; and $\mathcal{M}$oise [5] for programming the organization. Thus, this year the organization and environment, which were previously implemented as part of the agent code, have now been programmed with proper organizational and environmental elements according to the aforementioned models and technologies.

## 2.1 Organizational Dimension

As JaCaMo supports organizational programming, part of the coordination of team agents is modeled in the organizational dimension instead of being modeled as skills of the agents. The organization provides guidelines for the achievement of the overall system goals, but the agents remain autonomous to decide how to achieve them. For example, the organization informs that an agent is obligated to probe the vertices, but the agent is autonomous about "how" to do it, based on its local knowledge about the world. However, the autonomy can be constrained by means of organizational norms.

Fig. 1(a) shows the structural specification (SS) of the team using the $\mathcal{M}$oise notation. Notice that the SS is designed based on the roles of the contest scenario. The team is divided into two *sub-teams*. Besides, the team has three minor subgroups: *special operations*, *special exploration*, and *pivots*. An agent can play more than one role at the same time. For example, an *explorer* can also play *explorer leader* and *special explorer* roles. One agent plays the role *leader* and is responsible to manage the overall organization (e.g. designating the roles of the other agents). The functional specification (FS) (Fig. 1(b))) specifies the goals (i.e. specific states of affairs) that the agents must achieve and distributes these goals to the agents (by means of missions). The overall goal (*domain mars*) consists in a decomposition tree where the leaves are the goals that can be achieved by the agents. The goals are grouped in four *missions* ($m1$, $m2$, $m3$, and $m4$). Finally, the normative specification (NS) (Fig. 1(c)) relates roles to missions. For example, as the *explorer leader* is obligated to commit to mission $m4$, it is obligated to achieve the goals *define initial hill*, *conclude first phase*, and *dismiss agent*.

Along the development of the team, we performed some experiments introducing *count-as rules* [4]. Count-as rules changes in the organization as the result of facts occurring in the environment. For example, without count-as rules, a specific agent has to set up the organizational infrastructure and explicitly adopt the role of *leader*. With count-as rules, it is possible to state that such setup *counts-as* the adoption of the *leader* role. In another example, without count-as rules, the agents have to reason about the organizational structure, checking their roles, and committing to missions according to that roles. With count-as rules, it is possible to model that playing of a specific role *counts-as* the commitment to a specific mission. The use of count-as rules simplifies the reasoning and action of the agents, as they do not need to perform some actions on the organization (e.g. they do not need to reason and to act to commit to missions). Besides, count-as rules contribute to keep the organization in a consistent state as some organizational actions do not depend on the agents actions. Due to time constraints, the count-as rules were not added to the tournament team. However, the experiments indicate that the rules seem a suitable approach for further versions of the team.

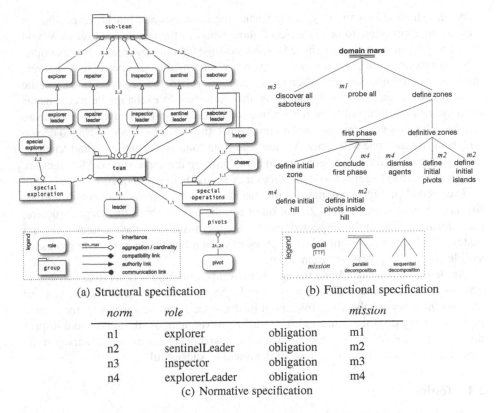

(a) Structural specification        (b) Functional specification

| norm | role | | mission |
|------|------|--|---------|
| n1 | explorer | obligation | m1 |
| n2 | sentinelLeader | obligation | m2 |
| n3 | inspector | obligation | m3 |
| n4 | explorerLeader | obligation | m4 |

(c) Normative specification

**Fig. 1.** Organizational Specification

## 2.2 Environment Dimension

The environment for our agents has two parts. The first part provides integration with the contest simulation by means of EISMASSim framework [1] and is well defined in the contest documentation. The second part is provided by JaCaMo artifacts that agents perceive and use to achieve their goals. In our team, the information about the inspected enemies is managed by an artifact. We also conceived an artifact responsible to manage all the graph structure. However, since we used the same graph structure and algorithms of the last year, which were based on Java shared memory, we decided to not move this previous implementation into a specific CArtAgO artifact because it would require more time. Therefore, part of the environment is developed in CArtAgO and another part was kept in "pure Java", accessed by means of Jason internal actions, as we did last year. It is a future work to unify all perceptions and actions under the CArtAgO approach.

## 2.3 Agent Dimension

The agents may behave proactively or reactively, in accordance with the needs. For example, a damaged agent will proactively call a repairer and all agents promptly react to the environment events, like the start of a new simulation step.

Agents share information by two mechanisms: messages and blackboards. Since it was not so appropriate to broadcast everything between the agents because we would have $28 \times 27$ messages[2], we chose to send messages about few things. For example, when agents are disabled, they call a repairer; when enemies invade some team area, the saboteurs are notified; and when some vertex is probed, the explorers broadcast the value of the vertex. Some information is also important to exchange between agents of the same kind to avoid them performing the same action. For example, when there are two saboteurs with enemies in the same vertex, they need to communicate to decide which enemy each one will attack. We used the same solution for explorers and repairers to avoid repairing the same agent and to avoid probing the same vertex. Messages are also used to inform agents about the zones they should help to conquer.

The second (indirect) communication mechanism is the use of blackboards and artifacts as commented on Sec. 2.2. In this case, the agents share the graph structure, the information about the inspected agents, and the position of the enemies and team mates. Finally, the remaining data, such as their own health, energy, zone scores, or visible vertices, is private for each agent.

We defined a priority among the agents to avoid conflicting actions (like two agents probing the same vertice). The agent with the highest priority chooses its action first and informs the others of the same role about its decision. Then the agent with the second highest priority does the same and so forth.[3] However, actions like survey and inspect do not follow this priority approach. That means two agents can inspect or survey at the same target to try to guarantee some of them will be successful.

## 2.4  Testing

To develop the team we used a particular incremental process. We performed weekly meetings to define the team strategies. These strategies were implemented and tested during the week and, in the next meeting, these results were considered to define new improvements. To evaluate the team strategies and ensure the competitiveness, we tested our team by simulating a great amount (more than 1000) of matches against our 2012 team [8], the 2012 Python-DTU team, and previous versions of our current team. The aim of the tests was to evaluate the overall performance of the team in different maps, adopting different strategies and facing different strategies from the opponent. In addition, we participated in all test matches during the testing phase to evaluate the connection and a couple of strategies.

## 3  Software Architecture

As we done in the edition of 2012 [8], in the current edition of MAPC we used the EIS-MASSim [1] to communicate with the contest server. However, while in the previous edition the team was developed essentially using Jason, in the current edition, our team

---

[2] The team is composed of 28 agents.

[3] Notice that sharing the information about the chosen action is not enough to solve the problem. Some coordination is required to efficiently solve it. Although this coordination is an organizational issue, this priority solution was coded in the agent dimension and it remains as a future work to model it in the organizational dimension.

has been developed with JaCaMo platform. This was the main change in the software architecture for this year. Furthermore, even with the increase number of agents, from 20 to 28, we were still able to run the agents in a single machine, therefore we decided to avoid distributing the agents between several machines. We also made several contributions for the tools that we used in this year. In Jason, we added features to handle goals with deadlines, new mechanisms for the .wait internal action, and we fixed some bugs. In $\mathcal{M}$oise, we added a new feature to reset organizational goals to avoid creating new schemes at runtime and we added an organizational monitor accessed via HTTP, so that we were able to watch our team organization remotely.

The source code of the team has 3794 lines of Jason code, 135 for $\mathcal{M}$oise, 96 for CArtAgO, and 4434 for Java, totaling 8459 lines. Although the implemented strategies of these year are more complex, we can notice that the number of lines coded in Jason has decreased from 5504 in last year's team to 3794 this year. It is an expected consequence of the organization and the environment programming available in JaCaMo. Coordination strategies that previously required several lines of Jason code, could now be coded in a few lines of $\mathcal{M}$oise, since $\mathcal{M}$oise is a proper language for that. Not only have we reduced the size of the programs, but the new approach has allowed us to debug and change the organization of the team quite easily. Instead of monitoring the agents internal state, we can now monitor the state of the organization, which is a more general view of the state of the team. Since the organizational program is the same as the specification, to change the team sometimes is simply reduced to update the organization. For instance, to change the order of organizational goals, we simply need to change the scheme of Fig. 1(b).

# 4    Strategies, Details and Statistics

In this section, we describe the main strategies of our team (Sec. 4.1) and we highlight the main results that we got (Sec. 4.2).

## 4.1    Team Strategies

The strategy of the team has two moments. In the former, the agents explore the map to obtain achievement points and to define good zones as soon as possible. Thus, it is possible to get a good score in the first steps. In the latter, the agents start to conquer and protect several small zones. During the whole match, the saboteurs disturb the enemy and the repairers help disabled agents.

The good zones are defined in terms of *hills*, *pivots*, and *islands*. A hill (the big zone in Fig. 2(a)) is a zone formed by several vertices that have a good value and are in the same region of the map. As in the 2012 team, the agents try to discover two hills. The hills are defined as follows: for each vertex $v$ of the graph, the algorithm sums the values of all vertices up to two hops away from $v$, including $v$. The two vertices with the highest sums are defined as the center of the hills, and then the agents try to stay on the neighborhoods. The agents control the hills simply moving to the border of the hills in order to expand them. If they break the zone, they come back to the previous places and try to expand again. We also defined that the sentinels need to conquer the

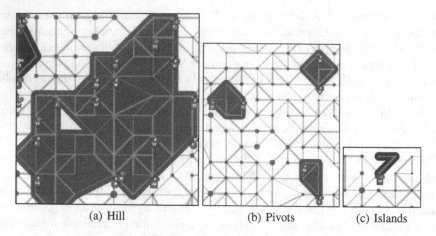

(a) Hill                    (b) Pivots                    (c) Islands

**Fig. 2.** Hills, pivots, and islands

best vertices in the hills and stay over them all the time until the strategy changes. Sometimes, it induces the opponents to avoid those places and we guarantee a fixed gain of scores of the hills, even if the enemy is disturbing. Moreover, the explorers of the group *special exploration* prefer to probe first the vertices in the hills, because it increases the gain of points in the first steps.

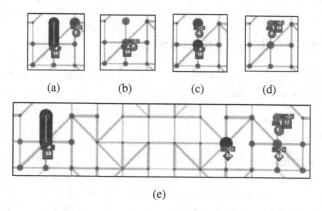

(a)         (b)         (c)         (d)

(e)

**Fig. 3.** Protecting islands

Islands (Fig. 2(c)) are regions of the map that can be conquered by a single agent. An island is a zone that has only one vertex (a *cut vertex*) in common with the remaining graph. They are found by disconnecting the edges of each cut vertex of the graph. It produces two disconnected subgraphs, and the smallest one, plus the cut vertex, are an island. If there are enemies on the island, the controller agent will go to the same vertex of the enemy. Thus, both teams do not get the points of that island. The figures 3(a), 3(b), 3(c), and 3(d) illustrate this situation. In addition, the controller agent notifies the saboteur leader about the invader. If the saboteur leader is already busy protecting another island, the saboteur leader calls the saboteur helper of the group *special operations*. If both are busy the saboteur leader keeps a list of islands with enemies for a further attack. Fig. 3(e) illustrates a probable call of the saboteur leader (the diamond not at the cut vertex) that is going to fight against an explorer (the circle) and a saboteur (the diamond at the cut vertex).

Pivots (Fig. 2(b)) are regions of the map that can be conquered by just two agents. For each pair of vertices $(u,v)$ we search all vertices $w$ connected to $u$ and $v$. For all vertices $w$ (including $u$ and $v$) we also search all vertices only connected to these vertices. For example, if there is a vertex $k$ connected only to the vertice $w$, then $k$ also belongs to the pivot. Furthermore, if there is an island connected to some of these vertices we consider all the vertices of the island. The best pivots are chosen considering the sum of all vertices. The agents that control pivots do not move away from their places, since most of the time the enemy does not stay fixed in those places. However, if the enemy stays in the same vertex both teams do not get the points, and so our team also cancels the enemy strategy. This is another reason to not leave the vertices. Otherwise the opponent will get the points.

The hills are defined in the first phase of our strategy, until around step 130. We chose to use hills instead of islands and pivots in the beginning of the match because most of the vertices are still unprobed and so we would not get so many points. The use of hills can keep all agents together and getting higher points because the zones are bigger. After a while the agents start conquering pivots and islands. The agents also need to decide if it is better to conquer two islands or one pivot. The decision is taken by simply summing the value of two islands and comparing with the pivots. If the two islands provide the same gain of the pivot or if they are more valuable, the agents will prefer to conquer two islands instead of conquering one pivot. The pivots and islands are very stable and so our agents are not disturbed by the enemy while our agents can disturb their zones since it is harder to protect a big zone than several small zones.

**Table 1.** Implemented strategies by agent type

| Action | Repairer | Saboteur | Explorer | Sentinel | Inspector |
|---|---|---|---|---|---|
| attack | | x | | | |
| repair | x | | | | |
| parry | x | | | x | |
| probe | | | x | | |
| inspect | | | | | x |
| recharge | x | x | x | x | x |
| goto | x | x | x | x | x |
| survey | x | x | x | x | x |

The achievements continue to be as important as in the last year. We decided do not waste money buying items and get as much achievements as possible and as soon as possible, since accumulate in each step. We made this decision since in our tests we did not see any advantage in buying items. Finally, the specific strategies of each kind of agent are explained below while Table 1 summarizes the strategies implemented for each kind of agent.

**Explorer:** the explorers have an important role in the beginning of the match. They need to probe all vertices as soon as possible. To do so, the explorers avoid performing the survey action and conquering zones until they have probed all vertices. Furthermore, the *explorer leader* defines the initial two hills.

**Saboteur:** the main aims of the saboteurs are to protect the islands and disturb the enemy. The saboteur with the role *saboteur chaser* has the aim to attack mainly explorers, inspectors, sentinels, and repairers to avoid staying in the same vertex fighting against saboteurs all the time. The saboteurs with the roles *saboteur leader* and *saboteur helper* have the main aim to protect islands against enemies. The *saboteur leader* is also the main contact of the other agents to ask for help. In other cases, the saboteurs simply search and destroy enemies. In addition, the saboteurs attack following a priority. First of all they prefer to attack saboteurs, followed by explorers, inspectors, repairers, and sentinels. The saboteurs prefer to attack explorers and inspectors because they can not parry.

**Repairer:** the main aim of the repairers is to keep the agents enabled. All agents that are disabled inform the *repairer leader*. The *repairer leader* asks all the other repairers if they can help the disabled agents. If a repairer is not committed to an agent and it is not getting high points and it is enabled, then it is apt to help the other agent. All apt repairers inform the path size until the disabled agent and the *repairer leader* chooses the closest repairer to help the disabled agent. To make the repair operation faster, both the repairer agent and the disabled agent follow the same path to meet each other. If there is some repairer next to the disabled agent, that repairer will repair the agent and the agent will cancel the appointment with its repairer. Finally, when the repairers are not helping the disabled agents, they also go to the pivots or islands that they belong to.

**Sentinel:** the sentinels always protect the best zones, since they are harder to get disabled and they can parry. They are usually avoided by the enemy because they do not have an important role like repairers, explorers, and saboteurs. Therefore, the sentinels are not disturbed so often. The sentinels also try to survey if they find some vertex with edges with unknown value. Finally, the *sentinel leader* has the aim to define the islands and pivots and inform the agents about it.

**Inspector:** the inspectors protect the next best zones, since they are also not so disturbed by the enemies. Their aim is to inspect all the enemy agents and they do it just once, since we do not care about what the enemy is buying. Doing so, the inspectors can stay in the same vertices until the end of the match, getting more points than by inspecting enemies.

## 4.2 Comparison to Other Teams

In order to highlight the main results of our strategy we chose to use some statistics of the second match against the GOAL-DTU team [4], which got the second place. Due our strategy of small zones, we can verify in the Fig. 4(b) that after step 325 our team (blue) kept almost the same zones until the end of the match. This behavior is usual in all matches against the other teams. The reason is that no matter what the opponent does, our agents will rarely leave their positions.

---

[4] http://multiagentcontest.org/downloads/func-startdown/1716/

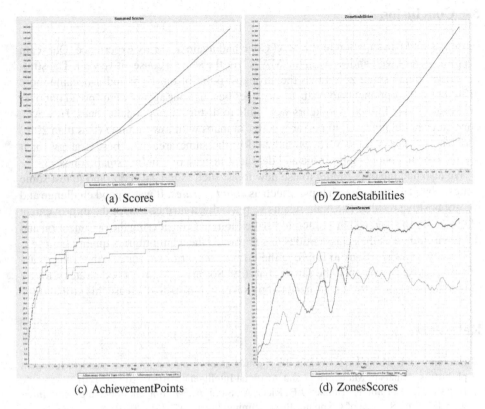

(a) Scores

(b) ZoneStabilities

(c) AchievementPoints

(d) ZonesScores

**Fig. 4.** Statistics

Another interesting result can be drawn from the zones scores plot (Fig. 4(d)). We can see that our team (blue) kept getting almost the same zone scores after step 350 and always more than the opponent. The phase of hills can also be noticed in the beginning of the match, between step 25 until around step 130, where the team is getting high scores because of the big zones. After step 130 our team started to conquer small zones (pivots and islands) and, therefore, spreading the agents out over the whole map. It is also possible to see that, sometimes, our zone scores were lower than the enemies. This was an expected behavior when the agents were still changing their positions because the explorers were still probing new vertices. We can see it after step 250 and after around step 315, where our team decreased the gain of zone scores. After probing all vertices (around step 325), the agents started to get higher scores because they defined the fixed zones and all agents were participating.

We can see the same behavior in Fig. 4(a), where the opponent score gets closer and then the difference of scores increases again. Notice that after step 325 the difference of scores increased continuously because all vertices were probed. On the other hand, in the Fig. 4(c) we can see that our team always has more achievement points than the opponent after step 125. It means we are getting more points because the opponent was buying items while our team was saving money.

## 5    Conclusion

In our second participation in the MAPC we had again a worthy experience. Our team performed very well and we won the MAPC for the second consecutive year. The strategy to get many small zones was the strongest point of our team and it became more difficult for the opponents to disturb our zones because our agents were spread out over the whole map while our saboteurs were able to disturb the opponent zones. However, our team can be improved to perform better in maps with low thinning (less than 20%) and with too many good vertices gathered in the same area. The best strategy for it seems to be to conquer a big zone and defend it instead of building small zones.

We also had the opportunity to use new tools, such as the JaCaMo and to test some issues related to our research topics, such as *count-as rules*. It was a good challenge and we got positive results. The main results were ($i$) the contributions for the improvement of the used tools and ($ii$) the concrete verification that considering the organization and the environment as first-class entities has improved the team program quality.

Finally, as suggestions to improve the current scenario, we suggest that ranged actions be revised to balance the fail probability. So far, it is not a good strategy to use ranged actions, since the agents need to buy several sensors to decrease this probability.

## References

1. Behrens, T.M., Hindriks, K.V., Dix, J.: Towards an environment interface standard for agent platforms. Annals of Mathematics and Artificial Intelligence 61(4), 261–295 (2011)
2. Boissier, O., Bordini, R., Hübner, J.F., Ricci, A., Santi, A.: Multi-agent oriented programming with JaCaMo. Science of Computer Programming 78(6), 747–761 (2013)
3. Bordini, R.H., Wooldridge, M., Hübner, J.F.: Programming Multi-Agent Systems in AgentSpeak using Jason. John Wiley & Sons (2007)
4. de Brito, M., Hübner, J.F., Bordini, R.H.: Programming institutional facts in multi-agent systems. In: Aldewereld, H., Sichman, J.S. (eds.) COIN@AAMAS 2012, pp. 31–25 (2012)
5. Hübner, J.F., Sichman, J.S., Boissier, O.: Developing organised multi-agent systems using the MOISE+ model: Programming issues at the system and agent levels. International Journal of Agent-Oriented Software Engineering 1(3/4), 370–395 (2007)
6. Köster, M., Schlesinger, F., Dix, J.: The multi-agent programming contest 2012. In: Dastani, M., Hübner, J.F., Logan, B. (eds.) ProMAS 2012. LNCS, vol. 7837, pp. 174–195. Springer, Heidelberg (2013)
7. Ricci, A., Piunti, M., Viroli, M.: Environment programming in multi-agent systems: an artifact-based perspective. AAMAS 23, 158–192 (2011)
8. Zatelli, M.R., Uez, D.M., Neri, J.R., Schmitz, T.L., de Castro Bonson, J.P., Hübner, J.F.: SMADAS: A cooperative team for the multi-agent programming contest using jason. In: Dastani, M., Hübner, J.F., Logan, B. (eds.) ProMAS 2012. LNCS, vol. 7837, pp. 196–204. Springer, Heidelberg (2013)

# Engineering a Multi-Agent System in GOAL

Jørgen Villadsen*, Andreas Schmidt Jensen, Nicolai Christian Christensen,
Andreas Viktor Hess, Jannick Boese Johnsen, Øyvind Grønland Woller,
and Philip Bratt Ørum

Algorithms, Logic and Graphs Section
Department of Applied Mathematics and Computer Science
Technical University of Denmark
Matematiktorvet, Building 303B, DK-2800 Kongens Lyngby, Denmark
jovi@dtu.dk

**Abstract.** We provide a brief description of the GOAL-DTU system,
including the overall design, the tools and the algorithms that we used in
the Multi-Agent Programming Contest 2013. We focus on a description
of the strategies and on an analysis of the matches. We also evaluate our
experiences with the GOAL agent programming language. Our strategies
worked well in general and we earned a second place in the contest only
losing to the winning team. Finally we provide some suggestions for
future contests.

## 1 Introduction

This paper documents our work with the GOAL-DTU system, which participated in the Multi-Agent Programming Contest 2013.[1] We also participated in
the contest in 2009 and 2010 as the Jason-DTU team [1,2], where we used the
Jason platform [5] and in 2011 and 2012 as Python-DTU where we used the
programming language Python [3,4].[2] Our focus for the 2013 version of the contest was on developing even more specialized behavior for our agents as well as
gaining further experience with the GOAL agent programming language [6].[3]
We took the HactarV2 system [7] that won the contest in 2011 as a starting
point for our system.

The 2013 scenario is based on the scenario from 2012 and has only been
changed in a few ways. The most interesting changes are the increase in number
of agents from 20 to 28 agents per team and the introduction of ranged actions.

The paper is organized as follows. In section 2, we discuss some of the ideas
we have pursued. In section 3, we describe some of the facilities we have added
to improve the system. Section 4 describes in detail our strategies and analyses
our matches. Finally, we conclude our work by discussing possible improvements
of our system and the contest in section 5.

---

* Corresponding author.
[1] http://multiagentcontest.org/2013 (the source code can be downloaded)
[2] http://www2.compute.dtu.dk/~jovi/MAS/
[3] http://ii.tudelft.nl/trac/goal

M. Cossentino et al. (Eds.): EMAS 2013, LNAI 8245, pp. 329–338, 2013.
© Springer-Verlag Berlin Heidelberg 2013

## 2    System Analysis and Design

GOAL-DTU is written in the GOAL agent programming language. It is based on the 2011 HactarV2 system that won the MAPC 2011. It was reworked first for the 2012 scenario, before being reworked again for the 2013 scenario. However, our algorithms have changed substantially from HactarV2. The code for each agent role has been rewritten, but the basic knowledge and the design of the flow is still the same. Ideas from Python-DTU which took second place in the contest in 2012 have also been incorporated into the code. The ideas behind Python-DTU were discussed with the Python-DTU team. The most notable idea which was incorporated into GOAL-DTU was the zone control algorithm. GOAL-DTU was also tested against a slightly updated version of Python-DTU which was compatible with the 2013 scenario.

The GOAL-DTU agents are separate entities that only communicate through the GOAL messaging system. Messages are used to communicate new information about the map as well as the status and position of all visible agents. The only centralized information is each agent's zone control position, which is known by a single agent. This also means that no data structures are shared among the agents.

The agents are able to autonomously decide which action to perform in any given situation, based on their individual beliefs and knowledge, and by communication. The GOAL-DTU agents are mostly reactive, for example, when attempting to disrupt zones controlled by the enemy as they are noticed. The *Repairers* attempt to be proactive in certain cases, for example, by assuming that allied *Saboteurs* will be prioritized targets for the opponent. In cases where a *Repairer* believes that a *Saboteur* will be attacked, and the *Repairer* has no better repairing options, it will attempt to repair the *Saboteur* at the same time as it believes it will be attacked. This works because of the way the server handles actions. Attack actions and handling disabled agents happens before repairs are handled. This effectively allows the *Saboteurs* to be attacked without taking damage giving our agents an advantage in battles.

We have invested approximately 500 man hours and we wrote 1288 lines of code (not counting comments and blank lines).

## 3    Software Architecture

We briefly discuss some of the more interesting aspects of our system, as well as our solutions to some of the issues we encountered during development.

**Pathfinding.** In order to improve the performance of our system, we worked on developing an efficient pathfinding algorithm. Our initial idea was to use an implementation of the A* algorithm. A* repeatedly compares the cost of each edge to how close it is to the goal and selects the best alternative. The algorithm requires a suitable heuristic function, $h(n)$, which returns a value describing how close the node $n$ is to the goal. If the coordinates of each node are known, the obvious choice for a heuristic function is the straight-line distance between $n$ and the goal node.

However, we are only provided with an identifier for each node in the scenario, so an alternative heuristic is required. We considered various methods such as triangulation using fixed nodes as reference points, but this proved to be too inefficient. In the end, we decided that it was more efficient to not use any heuristics. This effectively makes our algorithm equivalent to Dijkstra's Algorithm, but since the maps are relatively small, it is sufficient.

**Unresolved Bugs.** During the contest GOAL-DTU still had some unresolved bugs. One severe bug was that our agents would sometimes recharge for several consecutive steps despite being at full energy. By debugging we found that this happens at several different places in the code, even though the agents should be able to take other actions. This weakened some of our agents a great deal; especially *Saboteurs*, who should almost always be attacking, were limited in their potential.

Another bug was discovered in a part of the specialized code for our *Saboteurs*. One *Saboteur* is able to adopt a goal, which makes it harass the enemy in order to disrupt their zones. When the goal has been achieved, the agent should return to its normal behavior. However, when a *Saboteur* decided to harass the enemy, which then left the area, our agent would wander back and forth between nodes aimlessly, instead of returning to normal behavior. We made one fix in order to get rid of this bug, but it was not enough.

**Implementing a Debugging Library.** We implemented a separate debugging library in GOAL which enabled us to log any data from the multi-agent system to a file while running, along with a timestamp and the current step number. For instance, it is possible to log the entire contents of a mail received by an agent along with any relevant comments. After we implemented this, we were able to find and remove bugs that were preventing our agents from performing their actions in time, which in turn allowed us to qualify for and participate in the contest.

## 4   Strategies, Details and Statistics

We describe our most important strategies, and discuss a number of interesting situations from the simulations in the competition.

### 4.1   Team Strategies

Most of the strategies used by GOAL-DTU are able to be performed without communication between the agents of the team, apart from, as stated above, general information about the map and the agents, which is synchronized between agents.

This communication consists of sending new information about new nodes, probed nodes, or surveyed edges, and is sent to all agents of the team, such that everyone has the same knowledge about the map. The communication also includes sending information about the status (role, health, and position) of all agents, both allies and enemies (especially when an enemy is inspected).

The algorithms that are used to decide which target to repair or attack therefore avoid having multiple agents choosing the same target, without communication between the agents. This prevents, for example, that the same agent being repaired multiple times unnecessarily in a single step.

Because of time constraints, we were unable to implement and test ranged actions, apart from the inspect action.

**Zone Control.** After about 70 steps of the simulation have elapsed, one *Explorer* will calculate the best positions for *Sentinels* and *Inspectors* to stand on for controlling high-valued zones. Each position is then sent to the respective agent which in turn adopts a goal making it move towards and stand on this position. This ensures that the zones are stable.

After about 150 steps the *Explorers* will also join the controlled zones, but first calculate new zones to control based on updated map information.

The *Saboteurs* and *Repairers* do not contribute to controlling zones as they should be occupied with attacking and repairing agents respectively.

The best positions are calculated by first placing an agent on a high valued node with the highest valued surrounding area, then successively placing one agent on another node which contributes most to the zone score. However, only the first two phases of the coloring algorithm are utilized. The calculation also considers the number of connections to other agents when placing an agent, most of the time sacrificing a higher zone score for a more resilient zone.

**Buying Upgrades.** After 140 steps of the simulation have elapsed, our *Saboteurs* will consider buying health and strength depending on the health and strength of the opposing team's *Saboteurs*. They will buy these upgrades such that our *Saboteurs* are able to disable enemy *Saboteurs* in one step while surviving at least one attack, assuming that the *Saboteurs* are attacking each other on the same node. To prevent overspending, the *Saboteurs* determine if they should buy upgrades by observing the values of the second highest strength and health among the opposing team's *Saboteurs*.

**Probing.** Our *Explorers* undergo three stages when probing the map:

1. **Finding a highest valued node.** At the beginning of the simulation each *Explorer* moves towards a node with a higher value until it has probed a node of value 10. It accomplishes this by successively moving towards a higher valued neighboring node, probing if the node it stands on is unprobed, and also backtracking to the previous node it were at if the current node has a lower value than the previous.

2. **Probing the area around the found highest valued node.** When an *Explorer* has found a node of value 10 it will calculate a list of neighbors around this high value node that have not been probed yet. It will then

probe those nodes. This ensures that the valuable nodes around a node of value 10 are also probed, which is useful when deciding on zones to control.

3. **Probing the rest of the map.** The *Explorers* will find any nodes left on the map that are not probed and then probe them, unless it is supposed to aid in controlling zones.

After the three stages have been completed, or a sufficient amount of steps have elapsed, the *Explorers* will join in controlling zones.

**Attacking.** To prevent the *Saboteurs* from attacking the same targets, the targets are delegated amongst the enabled *Saboteurs* by rank. This rank is determined by each agent's position in a simple lexicographical ordering of the agents' names. Since all enemies on a node are visible to all the *Saboteurs* there, it is possible to sort the enemies and choose a target in the resulting list by order. This ensures that the *Saboteurs* do not choose the same targets. Furthermore, the targets are sorted by their role as not all roles are equal. The ordering is as follows, in descending order of importance: *Saboteurs, Repairers, Explorers* and *Inspectors, Sentinels*. In particular *Sentinels* have lower priority than *Explorers* and *Inspectors* because they are able to parry.

If an enemy *Saboteur* has been seen near an allied agent in a zone, then one of the *Saboteurs* will hunt the enemy *Saboteur* until it is disabled. This should prevent our controlled zones from being destroyed.

Also, at least one *Saboteur* will consider moving towards and attacking an enemy *Sentinel, Explorer,* or *Inspector,* if it has any previous knowledge about their positions. By doing so, our agents are able to purposefully disrupt the opponents controlled zones.

**Repairing.** *Repairers* will rank themselves among the *Repairers* on the same node, such that they will choose different targets. This rank is calculated using the same method that is used for ranking *Saboteurs* as explained above. They prioritize repairing *Saboteurs* and *Repairers* as these are important to keep functioning for winning battles.

To prevent neglecting disabled agents that are located far away, the *Repairer* with the lowest rank, determined using the method described previously, will adopt a goal to repair such agents and will prioritize this goal above every other goal until the agent in question has been repaired.

An important part of the repairing strategy is that a *Repairer* will repair an uninjured *Saboteur* if it anticipates that the *Saboteur* will be attacked in the same step. This prevents the *Saboteur* from becoming disabled, because the contest server processes attacks and determines disabled agents before it processes repairs.

**Other Strategies.** The *Inspectors* attempt to inspect any uninspected opponent agent that is nearby, such that GOAL-DTU knows the role of each agent. This information is then sent to all the other agents of the team. They also inspect *Saboteurs* multiple times so that our *Saboteurs* can determine if they need to buy upgrades or not. If there are no agents nearby to inspect, they will survey unsurveyed nodes or aid in controlling zones if necessary.

The *Sentinels* will primarily survey and aid in controlling zones.

## 4.2  Comparison to Other Teams

We describe some interesting cases from the matches, which show both the strengths and weaknesses of our team.

**Performance Issues against AiWXX.** In our match against AiWXX, they unfortunately had connection problems. This became the main deciding factor in those simulations, as our agents would score many points during the periods where AiWXX was disconnected. During their periods of inactivity, our *Saboteurs* were also able to disable a lot of AiWXX's agents. However, AiWXX's connection issues also caused problems for some of our agents.

One problem was that a lot of the AiWXX agents would occasionally gather on the same node. When our *Saboteurs* and *Repairers* moved to that node to attack, the number of agents on the node caused some algorithms to run for a long time. This delay caused some of our agents to occasionally miss the deadline, which resulted in 285 missed actions over the course of the 3 simulations with 28 agents and 750 steps (the number of missed actions is from the statistics files available for each simulation). This is a substantial increase compared to the other simulations. Against USP we had only 2 missed actions, 3 against UFSC and 20 against TUB. This indicates that some refinement and refactoring of the code for *Saboteurs* and *Repairers* may be necessary to ensure that our agents do not miss the deadline.

**Agent Mobility in the Match against USP.** Even after establishing our zones, we continue to search the map for better locations. If we discover a better place to establish our zone, we are often willing to adapt to the new information and reposition ourselves even though this results in a temporary drop in zone score; we know that having the better zone will benefit us more in the long run. An excellent example of this behavior can be seen in the first simulation against USP.

At the beginning of the simulation, we have a well-established zone in the lower left corner, while USP has the mirrored zone in the lower right corner, as can be seen in fig. 1. Eventually, our *Explorers* have probed enough of the map to determine that the area at the top of the map contains a zone that is larger and more valuable than our current zone.

This prompts our entire team of agents to uproot and migrate across the map, leaving the previous area behind. This can be seen in fig. 2.

We quickly reach the valuable area at the top where we establish a new and better zone (see fig. 3). As an added benefit, USP still seems to think we are in the lower left for a while after we move. The increased zone score eventually carries us to victory in the simulation.

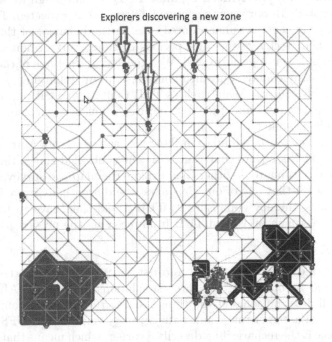

**Fig. 1.** The arrows indicate *Explorers* discovering a better zone (step 115)

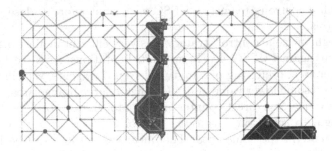

**Fig. 2.** The swarm is moving towards a better location (step 165)

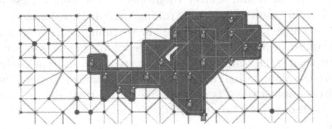

**Fig. 3.** The agents have taken full control of a high value zone (step 195)

**Observations from the Match against TUB.** Even though we won all simulations against TUB, our team performed different than expected. There seems to be a bug, or at least an unaccounted case, in the behavior of the *Saboteurs* that makes them recharge for long periods of time. Furthermore, the harass strategy did not seem to perform well. We expected at least one of the *Saboteurs* to find and destroy enemy controlled zones instead of recharging. This is especially important against a team such as TUB that tries to cut off, and control, a large part of the map and therefore receives a much larger zone score than GOAL-DTU is capable of.

In the first and second simulation, however, as our agents were able to disable many of TUB's agents that were near our controlled zones, the *Repairers* sometimes had nothing to do other than explore the map and survey unsurveyed edges. This meant that one of our *Repairers* would eventually move into TUB's controlled zones, thereby collapsing it. TUB would then have to find another zone to control, which prevented TUB from receiving the needed zone score to win.

**Shortcomings of Our Strategies against UFSC.** UFSC was the only team we lost to, and by analyzing the three simulations between GOAL-DTU and UFSC we will describe some of the things that did not work for our team and why they played a bigger role against the strategy employed by UFSC.

A huge issue is the recharge bug described earlier, which means that our agents stand around doing nothing. When this happens our agents are not participating in the overall strategy and are not contributing to the step score in an efficient manner. Against a strong team like UFSC we cannot afford to lose points due to bugs like this.

Even though our zone control strategy was very efficient against other teams, the simulations against UFSC clearly reveal its limitations. As we seek to control a single, larger area, preferring proximity between the agents, we will almost inevitably control some lower value nodes (see fig. 4, large orange area, simulation 2). UFSC's strategy is a direct counter strategy to this approach on two fronts.

As we begin to settle on a zone to control it seems as if they are doing the same, usually in the same area. This means that there will be fighting in the area we want to control, which leads to a less stable zone score for us. At some point UFSC will recall many of its agents except for *Repairers* and *Saboteurs* from this area and scatter them around the map. These agents will place themselves in small groups controlling extremely valuable clusters (see fig. 4, smaller red areas). All the while they are earning points from several small high value locations we are fighting them in the middle of our own (inferior) zone (see fig. 4, purple area), leading to a lower step score for us. The reason all their small zones are left alone is due to the other bug mentioned earlier. The *Saboteur* responsible for harassing them is not reliable and so they are left to do as they please. That said, one *Saboteur* might not be enough to prevent their strategy from working.

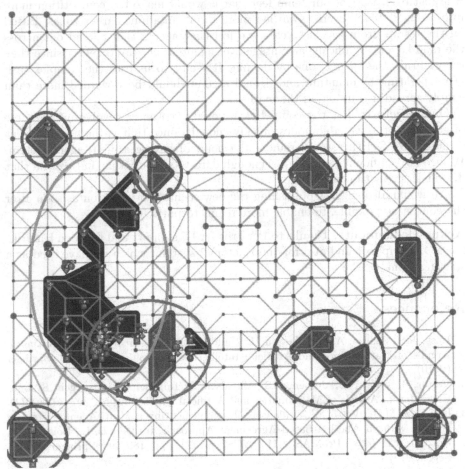

**Fig. 4.** GOAL-DTU zone strategy versus UFSC zone strategy (step 740)

## 5    Conclusion

By participating in this year's contest we have gained further experience with the GOAL agent programming language. In light of problems we encountered in the GOAL system during development of our agent program, we are satisfied with how it performed during the contest and with our team taking second place.

We attribute our good performance to the strong zone control strategy of our system, which was robust and reliable in finding good zones. An additional strength is our preemptive repairing, where our *Repairers* anticipate attacks on our *Saboteurs*.

Unfortunately there was an unresolved bug in our *Saboteurs* that prevented them from performing optimally. This meant that an important strategy for harassing the enemy was not available to us.

**Suggestions.** Part of our team feel that it would make the competition more interesting if teams were rewarded more for maintaining larger zones. Based on the results from the last years, we feel that agents that spread out across the map have a significant advantage over agents that stay together since they tend to ruin the enemy zone by default. It seems to us that the complex task of cooperating to maintain and defend a zone should be rewarded more than simply spreading out across the map.

Our concern is that the competition would eventually devolve into a game of getting to the valuable nodes quickly enough, since that is the most efficient strategy. We feel this would remove the point of having a multi-agent system. We are not confident that there is enough data to support this, but we feel that it is at least worth considering.

We would also suggest publishing the new scenario description as soon after the contest as possible, to enable more teams to participate.

**Acknowledgements.** Thanks to Per Friis for IT support and to Koen Hindriks for GOAL support and also for the HactarV2 system, which we have used as a starting point.

# References

1. Boss, N.S., Jensen, A.S., Villadsen, J.: Building Multi-Agent Systems Using Jason. Annals of Mathematics and Artificial Intelligence, vol. 59, pp. 373–388. Springer (2010)
2. Vester, S., Boss, N.S., Jensen, A.S., Villadsen, J.: Improving Multi-Agent Systems Using Jason. Annals of Mathematics and Artificial Intelligence 61, 297–307 (2011)
3. Ettienne, M.B., Vester, S., Villadsen, J.: Implementing a Multi-Agent System in Python with an Auction-Based Agreement Approach. In: Dennis, L., Boissier, O., Bordini, R.H. (eds.) ProMAS 2011. LNCS, vol. 7217, pp. 185–196. Springer, Heidelberg (2012)
4. Villadsen, J., Jensen, A.S., Ettienne, M.B., Vester, S., Andersen, K.B., Frøsig, A.: Reimplementing a Multi-Agent System in Python. In: Dastani, M., Hübner, J.F., Logan, B. (eds.) ProMAS 2012. LNCS, vol. 7837, pp. 205–216. Springer, Heidelberg (2013)
5. Bordini, R.H., Hübner, J.F., Wooldridge, M.: Programming Multi-Agent Systems in AgentSpeak Using Jason. John Wiley & Sons (2007)
6. Hindriks, K.V.: Programming Rational Agents in GOAL. In: Bordini, R.H., Dastani, M., Dix, J., El Fallah Seghrouchni, A. (eds.) Multi-Agent Programming: Languages, Tools and Applications, pp. 119–157. Springer (2009)
7. Dekker, M., Hameete, P., Hegemans, M., Leysen, S., van den Oever, J., Smits, J., Hindriks, K.V.: HactarV2: An Agent Team Strategy Based on Implicit Coordination. In: Dennis, L., Boissier, O., Bordini, R.H. (eds.) ProMAS 2011. LNCS, vol. 7217, pp. 173–184. Springer, Heidelberg (2012)

# Improving the LTI-USP Team: A New JaCaMo Based MAS for the MAPC 2013

Mariana Ramos Franco and Jaime Simão Sichman

Laboratório de Técnicas Inteligentes (LTI)
Escola Politécnica (EP)
Universidade de São Paulo (USP)
mafranko@usp.br, jaime.sichman@poli.usp.br

**Abstract.** This paper describes the architecture and core ideas of the multi-agent system created by the LTI-USP team which participated in the 2013 edition of the "Multi-Agent Programming Contest" (MAPC). This is the third year of the "Agents on Mars" scenario, in which the competitors must design a team of agents to find and occupy the best zones of a weighted graph. The team was developed using the *JaCaMo* multi-agent framework and it is an improvement of the system used in the last year contest.

## 1 Introduction

The "Multi-Agent Programming Contest" (MAPC) is held every year in an attempt to stimulate research in the field of programming Multi-Agent System (MAS) [1] [1]. In the MAPC, two teams of agents are located in the same environment and compete directly in a scenario set by the organizers. By being a direct competition, it is an interesting scenario to evaluate and compare different systems, allowing to identify strengths and weaknesses, promoting the development of all participants.

The LTI-USP, located at the University of São Paulo is one of the most relevant research groups in multi-agent systems in Brazil. The group participated in the 2009 [2], 2010 [3] and 2012 [4] MAPC editions. Since our first participation, the MAPC has been used to evaluate platforms and tools, and to improve our knowledge in developing MAS.

For this year's contest the LTI-USP team was formed by only one M.Sc. student (Mariana Ramos Franco), supervised by Prof. Jaime Simão Sichman; and like last year our main motivation to participate in the Contest was to test and evaluate the *JaCaMo* [5] framework.

*JaCaMo*[2] is a platform for multi-agent programming which supports all levels of abstractions – agent, environment, and organisation – that are required for developing sophisticated multi-agent systems, by combining three separate

---

[1] http://multiagentcontest.org

[2] Available at http://jacamo.sourceforge.net/

M. Cossentino et al. (Eds.): EMAS 2013, LNAI 8245, pp. 339–348, 2013.

technologies: $Jason^3$ [6], for programming autonomous agents; $CArtAgO^4$ [7], for programming environment artifacts; and $Moise^5$ [8], for programming multi-agent organisations.

## 2    System Analysis and Design

The team was developed using the *JaCaMo* multi-agent framework and it is an improvement of the system used in the last year.

In order to cope with the new rules, we changed the team, that is now composed of 28 agents. Moreover, in contrast with our team that participated last year, this new team is more decentralized. One agent, the `coordinator`, is still responsible for determining which are the best zones in the map; however, each agent decides by itself which empty vertex it will occupy in order either to create a zone or to expand it.

In our team, each agent has its own view of the world, and communicates with others for the following purposes: (i) informing the other agents about the structure of the map; (ii) informing about the agent's or the opponent's position, role and status; and (iii) asking for a repair.

The agents' communication occurs via the speech acts provided by *Jason* and, to reduce the communication overhead, agents broadcast to all others only the new percepts, i.e., only percepts received from the contest server which produces an update on the agent's world model are broadcasted. For this reason, there is a strong exchange of information between the agents in the beginning of the match due to the broadcast of new percepts, specially those related to the map, such as vertices and edges. However, the communication overhead decreases as the agents' world model starts to be more complete.

The agent architecture is based on the BDI model [9]. Each agent has its own beliefs, desires, intentions and control thread. The agents are autonomous to decide by themselves the next action to be performed, but in cooperation with each other. The agents have a proactive behaviour, for example, to find the better vertices in the map, and to move to the closest repairer when they are damaged.

At each step, the agent decides which new plan will be executed to achieve a determined goal given only the state of the environment and the results of previous steps. There are no plans that last for more than one step and the plan's priority is determined by the order in which the plans were declared, i.e., the executed plan will be the first one to have its conditions satisfied. Some high priority plans can be considered reactive, such as the one which tells the agent to perform a recharge when running low on energy.

For the development of this project, we choose to not use any multi-agent methodology, because we already had the 2012 team from where we start to work, and mainly because we decided that it was better to spend our time to improve the system performance.

---

³ Available at http://jason.sourceforge.net/
⁴ Available at http://cartago.sourceforge.net/
⁵ Available at http://moise.sourceforge.net/

To achieve this goal, first we changed the team to 28 agents and the coordination mechanism to form the zones. Next, we added to the agents the possibility to perform some actions from a distance. Then, many strategies were tested, such as: to divide or not the agents in groups to occupy more zones in the map, to buy or not upgrades to the agents, and to use more or less agents to attack the opponents. Finally, based on the results of our tests, we selected the best team to use in the Contest.

Approximately 150 person hours were invested in the team development and before the tournament we participated in some test matches set by the organizers to ensure the stability of our team. Only during the competition we discussed the design and strategies with the other teams, without performing any change to our team from a match to another.

# 3    Software Architecture

The architecture of the LTI-USP team, showed in Figure 1, is the same used in 2012 [4]. In this architecture, the agents are developed using the *Jason* MAS platform, which is a *Java*-based interpreter for an extended version of the *AgentSpeak* programming language for BDI agents. Each agent is composed of plans, a belief base and its own world model. The plans are specified in *AgentSpeak* and the agent decides which plan will be executed according to its beliefs and the local view of the world.

The world model consists of a graph developed in *Java*, using simple data structures and classes. It captures every detail received from the MASSim contest server, such as: explored vertices and edges, opponents' position, disabled teammates, etc. At each step, the agent's world model is updated with the percepts received from the MASSim server, and with the information received from the other agents.

Some of the percepts received from the MASSim server are also stored in the agent's belief base, such as the agent's role, energy, position and team's money, thus allowing the agent to have a direct access to these information without have to access its world model. Percepts about vertices, edges and other agents were not stored in the belief base so as to not compromise the agent's performance, as it could be very expensive to update and to access the belief base with so much information. Moreover, since we wanted to update a belief when a new instance was inserted (instead of adding a second one), we decided to use an indexed belief base in which some beliefs are unique and indexed for faster access.

Agents communicate with the MASSim server through the EISMASSim environment-interface included in the contest software-package. EISMASSim is based on EIS[6] [10], which is a proposed standard for agent-environment interaction. It automatically establishes and maintains authenticated connections to the server and abstracts the communication between the MASSim server and the agents to simple Java-method-calls and call-backs. In order to use this interface,

---

[6] Available at http://sourceforge.net/projects/apleis/

we extended the *JaCaMo* default agent architecture to perceive and to act not only on the *CArtAgO* artifacts, but also on the EIS environment as well.

*CArtAgO* is a framework for environment programming based on the A&A meta-model [11]. In *CArtAgO*, the environment can be designed as a dynamic set of computational entities called artifacts, organized into workspaces, possibly distributed among various nodes of a network [5]. Each artifact represents a resource or a tool that agents can instantiate, share, use, and perceive at runtime. For this project, we did not create any new artifact; we only made use of the organisational artifacts provided in *Moise*.

*Moise* [8,12] is an organisational model for MAS based on three complementary dimensions: *structural*, *functional* and *normative*. The model enables a MAS designer to explicitly specify its organisational constraints, and it can be also used by the agents to reason about their organisation. We used the *Moise* model to define the agent's roles, groups and missions.

The code of our team can be found in the MAPC website [7], and consists of approximately 2000 lines of code in Java and 1800 lines in *AgentSpeak*, and the development was all carried on using the Eclipse IDE with the *Jason* plugin. The main developer was already familiar with both the development and the runtime platforms, i.e. the Eclipse IDE and the *JaCaMo* framework.

The agents were not distributed across several machines due to time constraints, but is our intention to work in the future on a distributed team, since this is supported by *JaCaMo*.

## 4    Strategies, Details and Statistics

### 4.1    Team Strategies

For this year's contest, we changed substantially the team organisation by adding different roles to the agents, as shown in Figure 2.

We kept the strategy of distributing the agents in three subgroups (`best_zone`, `second_best_zone` and `attack`), two of them in charge of occupying the best zones in the map, and the other one in charge of attacking the opponents. However, regarding the agents' roles, we decided not to map the five types specified in the scenario (explorer, inspector, repairer, saboteur and sentinel) directly to the roles in our team. Instead, we defined additional different roles in our system according to the adopted strategy. Each of these roles has a mission associated to it, and can be played by one or more type of agents. For example, the `map_explorer` role can be played only by the explorer type, while the `soldier` role can be played by all types of agents. Below we describe the missions related to each role:

---

[7] Available at http://multiagentcontest.org/downloads/
   Multi-Agent-Programming-Contest-2013/Sources/LTI-USP/

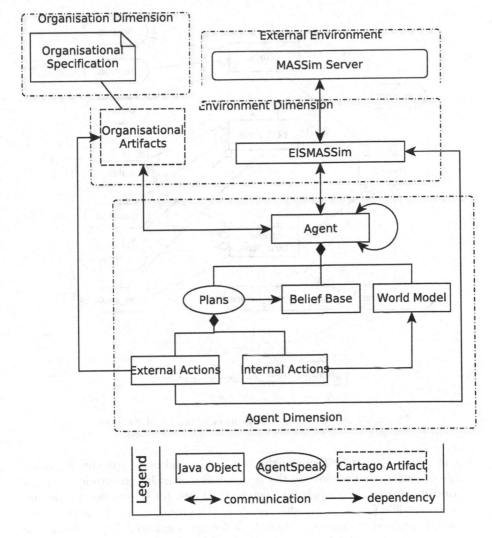

**Fig. 1.** LTI-USP Team Architecture [4]

- **map_explorer** (explorer): Explores the whole graph by probing every vertex and surveying all edges on its path;
- **map_explorer_helper** (explorer): Helps the **map_explorer** to explore the graph, but only in the first 250 steps. After that, the agent leaves this role to adopt the **soldier** role in the **best_zone** subgroup;
- **soldier** (all types): Tries to occupy the best (or second best) zone in the graph indicated by the **coordinator** agent. When all the vertices of the best zone are occupied the **soldier** starts to look to the neighbour vertices of the team's zone in which he can move to increase its size;

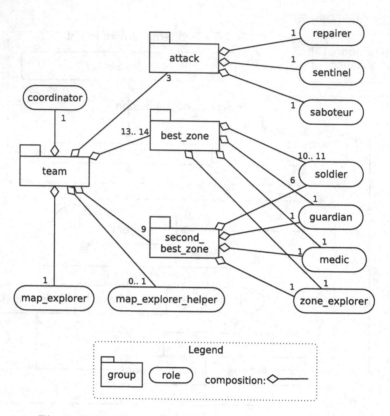

**Fig. 2.** *Moise structural specification* of the LTI-USP team

- **guardian** (saboteur): Defends the best (or second best) zone by attacking any opponent that is close to the team's zone, or trying to invade it;
- **medic** (repairer): Occupies the center of the best (or second best) zone and is responsible for repairing the agents in the group, or other agents which eventually need to be repaired, such as the `map_explorer`. In our team, the damaged agents move to the repairers to be repaired;
- **zone_explorer** (explorer): Explores the team's zone by probing the vertices which value is unknown. When all vertices are probed, the `zone_explorer` helps the `soldiers` to increase the zone size;
- **saboteur** (saboteur): Attacks any close opponent, or the opponent who occupies a good vertex;
- **sentinel** (sentinel): Tries to sabotage the opponent by moving inside its zone;
- **repairer** (repairer): Follows the `saboteur`, but always staying two vertices away from it, in order to be prepared to repair the `saboteur` when necessary, but without taking too much risk;
- **coordinator** (none): Agent internal to our system which does not communicate with the MASSim server. It builds its local view of the world through

the percepts broadcasted by the other agents. Whenever the world model is updated, it computes which are the two best zones in the graph and send this information to the other agents. The `coordinator` is also responsible for creating the organisational artifacts, in the beginning of the simulation, and for distributing the groups, roles and missions among the other agents, in order to eliminate the performance issues caused by two or more agents trying to adopt the same role in a group, or trying to commit to the same mission.

The best zone in the map is obtained by calculating for each vertex the sum of its value with the value of all its direct and second degree neighbours. The vertex with the greatest sum of values is the center of the best zone. Zones with the sum of values below 10 are not considered in the calculation. The same computation is performed again to determine if there is a second best zone, but this time removing the vertices belonging to the first best zone from the analysis.

If two best zones are found, the `coordinator` agent will designate the first best zone for the `best_zone` subgroup, and the other for the `second_best_zone` subgroup. Otherwise, the same zone will be assigned for the two groups.

At each step, the team's score is computed by summing up the values of the zones and the current money. Thus the money obtained by the team through the achievement points has a big impact on its score. For this reason, we decided to limit the buy action, allowing only the agents of type saboteur and repairer to purchase an unique extension pack of `sensors`, in order to enable them to attack or repair agents in neighbour vertices.

Figure 3, taken from the beginning of the first match against the TUB team, shows the described strategies in action. It is possible to notice that the LTI-USP team (in blue) occupies two different zones in the map, while in the right bottom the `saboteur` (followed by the `repairer`) is going to attack the opponent. The `map_explorer` and `sentinel` are in the center of the map, and in the right top the `soldier` attacks an opponent in the neighbour vertex.

## 4.2   Comparison to Other Teams

All other teams (AiWXX, GOAL-DTU, TUB and UFSC) participated in the previous Contest as well, and their improvement was noteworthy. The LTI-USP team finished the competition in the third place, behind UFSC and GOAL-DTU, which had very strong teams.

The UFSC team won all matches against all teams thanks to their strategy of creating many small zones distributed in the map, instead of only one or two big zones. We also lost all matches against GOAL-DTU which had a very aggressive team, in which all saboteurs and repairers attacked the opponent, while the other agents were creating good scoring zones.

In the first day of the Contest, we won all the three matches against the TUB team. During these matches, our team was able to defend itself very well from the attacks of the other team, keeping a stable zone score, while the `sentinel` agent sabotages the opponent's zone, as shown in Figure 4.

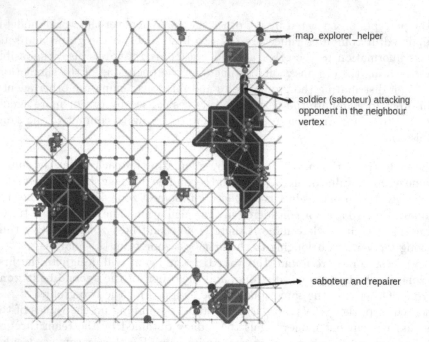

**Fig. 3.** LTI-USP vs TUB (first match, step 69)[8]: Strategies in action

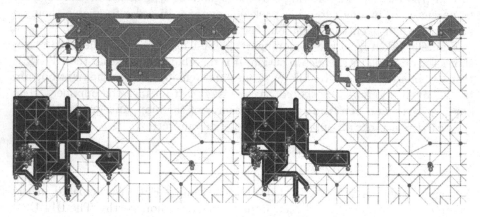

**Fig. 4.** LTI-USP vs TUB (third match, step 736)[9]: **Sentinel** invading the TUB's zone

The AiWXX team came to the last day of the tournament with a very good strategy of finding the map corners to create big zones. Despite this, even with smaller zones, our team won the second match against them (ensuring the third place), thanks to the stability of our team's zone, and because we started to score early (cf. Figure 5).

---

[8] Available at http://multiagentcontest.org/downloads/func-startdown/1696/
[9] Available at http://multiagentcontest.org/downloads/func-startdown/1704/

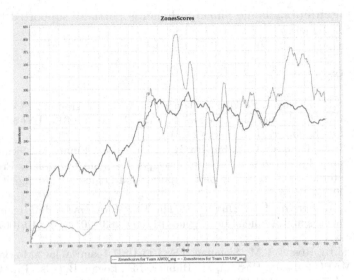

**Fig. 5.** LTI-USP vs AiWXX (second match)[10]: Zone score by step

## 5    Conclusions

Participating in the MAPC was a great opportunity to improve our knowledge on developing MAS, and on the *JaCaMo* framework.

Due to the modularity of the *JaCaMo* framework it was not complicated to change our team for this year Contest. We could reuse all the architecture built to communicate with the MASSim server, and to capture the agent's local view of the world. The main changes were in the team's organisation, through the *Moise* specifications, and in creating the plans for the new roles. We believe that *JaCaMo* proved to be a flexible platform, allowing us to easily change our strategy and to test some of its variations.

In summary, given the effort put to the development of the team, we were pleased with the final result. Comparing with last year, we reached a better zone stability by (i) moving to a more decentralized approach, with the agents deciding by their own were to move to create or expand the team's zone, and by (ii) adopting a defensive strategy, with the `guardian` ready to attack any close opponent, and the `medic` in the center of the zone focused on repairing the agents.

Regarding possible improvements for the current scenario, we would propose to increase the probability of success for the ranged actions, since we noticed during the competition that these actions have a huge chance to fail, not being worth to use them. Another idea is to change the score computation to consider only the zones values. In this way, the buying strategy will not impact directly the team score and it will be interesting to see how each team would invest their achievement points.

---

[10] Available at http://multiagentcontest.org/downloads/func-startdown/1671/

**Acknowledgements.** Jaime Simão Sichman is partially supported by CNPq and FAPESP/Brazil.

# References

1. Köster, M., Schlesinger, F., Dix, J.: The Multi-Agent Programming Contest 2012. In: Dastani, M., Hübner, J.F., Logan, B. (eds.) ProMAS 2012. LNCS, vol. 7837, pp. 174–195. Springer, Heidelberg (2013)
2. Bordini, R.H., Gouveia, G.P., Pereira, R.H., Picard, G., Piunti, M., Sichman, J.S.: Using Jason, Moise, and CArtAgO to Develop a Team of Cowboys. In: Proceedings of 10th International Workshop on Computational Logic in Multi-Agent Systems, pp. 203–207 (2009)
3. Gouveia, G., Pereira, R., Sichman, J.: The USP Farmers herding team. Annals of Mathematics and Artificial Intelligence 61, 369–383 (2011), doi:10.1007/s10472-011-9238-x
4. Franco, M.R., Rosset, L.M., Sichman, J.S.: LTI-USP Team: A JaCaMo Based MAS for the MAPC 2012. In: Dastani, M., Hübner, J.F., Logan, B. (eds.) ProMAS 2012. LNCS, vol. 7837, pp. 224–233. Springer, Heidelberg (2013)
5. Boissier, O., Bordini, R.H., Hübner, J.F., Ricci, A., Santi, A.: Multi-agent oriented programming with JaCaMo. In: Science of Computer Programming (2011)
6. Bordini, R., Hübner, J., Wooldridge, M.: Programming multi-agent systems in AgentSpeak using Jason (2007)
7. Ricci, A., Piunti, M., Viroli, M.: Environment programming in multi-agent systems: an artifact-based perspective. Autonomous Agents and Multi-Agent Systems 23(2), 158–192 (2010)
8. Hübner, J.F., Boissier, O., Kitio, R., Ricci, A.: Instrumenting multi-agent organisations with organisational artifacts and agents. Autonomous Agents and Multi-Agent Systems 20(3), 369–400 (2009)
9. Rao, A.S.: AgentSpeak(L): BDI agents speak out in a logical computable language. In: Perram, J., Van de Velde, W. (eds.) MAAMAW 1996. LNCS, vol. 1038, pp. 42–55. Springer, Heidelberg (1996)
10. Behrens, T.M., Dix, J., Hindriks, K.V.: The Environment Interface Standard for Agent-Oriented Programming - Platform Integration Guide and Interface Implementation Guide. Department of Informatics, Clausthal University of Technology, Technical Report IfI-09-10 (2009)
11. Omicini, A., Ricci, A., Viroli, M.: Artifacts in the A&A meta-model for multi-agent systems. Autonomous Agents and Multi-Agent Systems 17(3), 432–456 (2008)
12. Hübner, J., Sichman, J., Boissier, O.: Developing organised multiagent systems using the MOISE+ model: programming issues at the system and agent levels. International Journal of Agent-Oriented Software Engineering, 1–27 (2007)

# Multi-Agent Programming Contest 2013: TUB Team Description

Sebastian Werner, Christian Bender-Saebelkampf, Hendrik Heller, and Axel Heßler

Technische Universität Berlin, Germany

**Abstract.** We describe our contribution to the Multi-Agent Programming Contest 2013, which has been developed by students and researchers of the DAI-Labor at TU Berlin, Germany, using the JIAC V agent framework and the agile JIAC methodology.

## 1 Introduction

Our team is called "TUB" and has participated consistently in the Multi-Agent Programming Contest (MAPC)[1] since 2007. Since our first participation, we consider the contest a very good opportunity to evaluate our platform and tools. The current team has been developed in the course "Multi Agent Contest"[2] by the following students: Christian Bender-Saebelkampf, Hendrik Heller and Sebastian Werner supervised by the following agent researchers: Axel Heßler (main contact). The students did not hear about agent programming nor the contest before and started from scratch (only reusing the server communication code from last year).

The DAI-Labor and the chair "Agent technologies in business applications and telecommunication (AOT)" at the Technische Universität Berlin, headed by Prof. Dr. Sahin Albayrak, perform research and development in the multi-agent technologies field and its application to many real-world domains (see e.g. [1]). Dr. Axel Heßler is part of the "Agent Core Technologies" research team and is mainly interested in software engineering using agents in the design and development of complex, distributed applications.

We have invested 840 man hours and wrote about 8000 lines of code approximately to create the contest version of our system and we have seen that our version is competitive but is still not winning.

## 2 System Analysis and Design

The methodology, which we have used during the course, borrows from the JIAC methodology, and can be described as bottom-up and agile methodology:

---

[1] http://multiagentcontest.org
[2] Project 0435 L 774 at TU Berlin, Germany

M. Cossentino et al. (Eds.): EMAS 2013, LNAI 8245, pp. 349–355, 2013.

we start with domain analysis, which is to build a first ontology: find the concepts of the domain, their structure and relationships with each other: agents, own team, opponents, nodes, edges, visited, probed, surveyed, weight. As a second step the methodology says: make a role model and a user interface (UI) prototype. A role is specified by a number of capabilities or behaviors and the relationships with other roles. Identifying the roles was an easy task because they are easily collected from the scenario document. We then assigned simple and basic capabilities to the roles. As many of them were identical in each role, we created the generalized role of a Mars Agent, which is a collection of the capabilities that all roles share, such as surveying, charging and moving. All other roles inherit from the generalized role and add special capabilities such as probing, inspecting, and so on.

The system is designed with the JIAC agent framework in mind. Both, methodology and framework, share the same agent meta-model, so concepts such as agent, role component or service is the basic vocabulary of the agent developer (see also [2]).

In principle, every contest agent in this role model could take every role, but during this contest the roles are static properties given by the contest server to every agent in the team at the beginning of each simulation. Based on the role given to an Agent, JIAC would instantiate a DecisionAgentBean for this Agent and a Strategy. A total of twelve strategy Classes were implemented, more than one per role. Depending on the evaluation of the simulation at a given point a strategy could be switched to alter the behavior of an agent. For instance after the map was fully probed the ExplorerStategy would switch to a ZoneStrategy. Special capabilities (probe, inspect, attack, repair) are implemented in the corresponding role specific component. Every agent instance has a specialization of the ServerCommunicationBean component with the credentials for authentication.

The system can be distributed over several machines if available, without changing any line of code, even at runtime. This is one of the features of the JIAC agent framework that is usually used for MAS administration and self-administration. However, we could not use this feature during the contest due to a lack of available hardware.

The agent system that runs our bots is mostly decentralized. As we use a component framework to build our agents, the functionalities for the roles are implemented within a dedicated component for each role. However, in order to simplify configuration, we decided to equip all of our agents with all components. The agents then decide based on the first message from the server, which role they take and keep that role for the remainder of the match. During the match, the basic cycle of our agents was triggered by the perceptions from the server. Whenever an agent receives a new perception, it starts the decision making cycle. In this cycle, the current state is evaluated and the agent decides what to do, based on its strategy it is using. This decision is then forwarded to all other team members.

Regarding the communication strategy of our team, we followed our 2007 – 2009 successful approach [3,4] to distribute all perceptions and intentions among all other agents, where we could reach an appreciable enhancement of the team performance.

We have implemented general agent attributes such as autonomy, proactiveness and reactiveness as follows: JIAC V agents have their own thread of control and decide and act autonomously. We see the agents with low health level proactively seeking the repairers' help using a simple request, whereas probing, repairing or surveying has been implemented as a simple reactive behaviour: if the node is unprobed then goto it an probe. Finally, our team was tested during the training matches that were organized before the tournament. During the test matches we played against other competitors in order to ensure that the agents run stable and can send their actions to the server within the allocated time.

## 3  Software Architecture

We have used the JIAC V agent framework to implement the contest MAS of our TUB team. For our agent researchers the contest is always an excellent reliability benchmarking of the framework, and also a test case for teaching principles of agent programming. We used a set of dedicated JIAC V plugins for the Eclipse IDE to create basic project structures and configurations. Then we added a number of components that were already available form last years contest, such as server communication. Finally, the biggest part of the work was invested in implementing and tuning the algorithms that control the actual actions of the agents. This was mostly done in Java, because the decisions and calculations are time critical, and we wanted to avoid the overhead from interpreting our declarative agent language.

As far as algorithms are concerned we used a modified Dijkstra path finding algorithm where edges and nodes could be filtered from the Graph (e.g. to avoid the opponents agents or costly edges). We used other algorithms such as breadth first search to find agents or other targets in a limited range of a given node (for example to determine if a repairer should move towards a team member to do repairs).

## 4  Strategies, Details and Statistics

Every agent maintains its own world model. Once the perception arrives, unknown vertices are added to the graph, which represents the physical world where the agents act in. Already known vertices are updated with the values from the perception. The perception is also shared with all other agents so that they can update their world model with information that is not visible to them. The world model also contains a number of agent lists, i.e. team bots and enemy bots. As well as a list of zones, an ordered list which tells the ZoneStrategy where the best zone is and a few more information that is important for some but not all agents.

Furthermore, the world model is updated by a number of zones that support the decision process. As mentioned before, an agent's decision is defined by the strategy Class it is using. The main strategy of our team is twofold: First, individual agents follow a simple, straightforward achievement collection strategy based on their roles. And, second, there is an additional agent that calculates the best zone that is free of enemies.

The single agent behavior is as follows:

**Explorer.** Find unprobed nodes and probe them, recharge when necessary, go to the closest unprobed node first. Avoid other Explorers from our team to avoid duplicate behavior. Seek repair if health is zero. Switch strategy if the graph has been probed completely.

**Repairer.** There are two strategies for the repairer.

> **Simple Repairer.** Search for hurt team members and go to the closest one to heal. If no team member is hurt survey and participate in zone building.

> **Craven Repairer.** Same as the Simple Repairer but avoid enemy attackers at all cost. Using a breath first search and a range, this repairer searches for an enemy saboteur and avoid it.

**Sentinel.** used for Zoning, see Zoner.

**AggressiveSaboteur.** As the name suggests the Saboteur tries to attack as many agents as possible.

**ZoneDefender.** This Agent is part of the zone and upon a detected intrusion into the Zone, this agent tries to disable the intruder.

**AnnoyInspector.** This strategy tries to find enemy zones and plans paths through those zones to destroy them while inspecting the enemy.

**ZoneInspector.** The inspector is part of the zone and if an intruder is detected it tries to inspect the intruder.

**Zoner.** The Zone is a strategy which will build a Zone using the zoning algorithm to identify a good Zone and coordinates all Zoner to build that zone.

The agents did not use the buying mechanism yet, so they did not improve their skills or attributes. They were also not aware of the achievements they collect.

### 4.1   Team Strategies

The only centralized or hierarchical part of the team organization is the zoning calculation. While this calculation can be performed by every agent, we have instead decided to create a new agent which receives all messages from its team members and does the calculation of the best zone taking into account all free agents (agents that switched to zoning strategy). Since this Agent is not bound by the two second simulation cycle a more expensive calculation can be made in parallel to the simulation. The result of this calculation is then shared with all other agents.

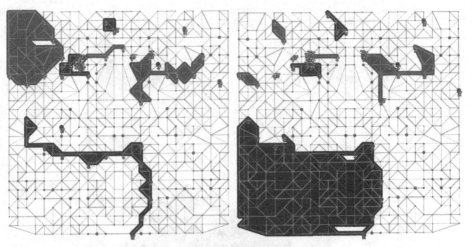

**Fig. 1.** Illustration of the TUB Zoning algorithm (simulation 1 against AiWXX, step 468f.)

Our zoning algorithm samples a chosen length and count (i.e. 50 – 100) of paths per step. A path is randomly generated and its zone and zone value is calculated. The best path is the path of the samples with the best zone value. To make the zone calculation independent from the agents, we use several other threads: one for getting the best found zone (best zone thread) and several others to calculate samples (sample threads). A sample thread is started every step to calculate paths on the most recent informations about the graph. To avoid enemy agents, the best zone thread can get their positions and give a zone back, in which no enemy agent is.

In Figure 1 you can see how it works. The images are taken from the match against AiWXX[3] On the left image the agents position themselves along the path that marks the zone border. When all agents have placed on the their node the zone appears (right image).

## 4.2  Comparison to Other Teams

Comparing our zoning approach to the winner of the contest, UFSC, there is a clear advantage of the UFSC zoning strategy (see Figure 2). The UFSC stategy uses small teams of two agents to create small zones on many high-weighted nodes. In contrast, our team creates on big zone with all available agents, which is harder to create and maintain in the long run. Even if we destroyed one UFSC zone, all others hold and bring a high zone score, whereas only one UFSC agent is needed to destroy our big zone.

---

[3] http://multiagentcontest.org/downloads/Multi-Agent-Programming-Contest-2013/XMLs-for-MarsFileViewer/

**Fig. 2.** Comparison of two different strategies to build a zone: UFSC team prefers many small zones, whereas TUB team creates one big zone (sim 1, step 563)

## 5   Conclusion

The main experience in the 2013 MAPC was that we should have built fallback systems for every important part of the MAS program. After the first simulation during the contest our ZoneFinder stopped working due to a bug in our code. If we had build a backup system for the ZoneFinding all agents that depended on the ZoneFinder would have worked instead of doing random moves. Secondly, we have learned that we should have made smaller zones as for example UFSC or AiWXX did. That would have significantly increased our chance of Zone points.

We think the strongest point of our implementation was its flexibility. We could switch relatively fast between agent implementations and test different ideas out without changing much code. That led to our good Explorer and Inspector behaviors. As mentioned above, our biggest weak point was the fact that we were not able to recover from a system failure easily. The one best zone strategy did not pay off: our implementation tried to build one zone with all availabe agents instead of two or more zones.

The framework and the language were ideal for making fast iterations on the code, sadly we did not had the time to improve the software to the maximum.

We definitely should improve zoning and recovery. A nice addition to the current contest would be the ability to buy a role switch were you would give the id of two agents and they would switch roles dynamically. Another interesting feature in the contest setting would be to block edges. As long as an agent blocks a node no other agent can enter or pass that edge. This could be especially interesting for smaller maps.

# References

1. Lützenberger, M., Küster, T., Konnerth, T., Thiele, A., Masuch, N., Heßler, A., Keiser, J., Burkhardt, M., Kaiser, S., Albayrak, S.: Jiac v — a mas framework for industrial applications (extended abstract). In: Ito, T., Jonker, C., Gini, M., Shehory, O. (eds.) Proceedings of the 12th International Conference on Autonomous Agents and Multiagent Systems (AAMAS 2013), Saint Paul, MN, United States of America (2013)
2. Hirsch, B., Konnerth, T., Heßler, A.: Merging Agents and Services — the JIAC Agent Platform. In: Bordini, R.H., Dastani, M., Dix, J., Seghrouchni, A.E.F. (eds.) Multi-Agent Programming: Languages, Tools and Applications, pp. 159–185. Springer (2009)
3. Hessler, A., Keiser, J., Küster, T., Patzlaff, M., Thiele, A., Tuguldur, E.-O.: Herding agents - JIAC TNG in multi-agent programming contest 2008. In: Hindriks, K.V., Pokahr, A., Sardina, S. (eds.) ProMAS 2008. LNCS, vol. 5442, pp. 228–232. Springer, Heidelberg (2009)
4. Heßler, A., Küster, T., Niemann, O., Sljivar, A., Matallaoui, A.: Cows and Fences: JIAC V - AC'09 Team Description. In: Dix, J., Fisher, M., Novák, P., eds.: Proceedings of the 10th International Workshop on Computational Logic in Multi-Agent Systems 2009. Volume IfI-09-08 of IfI Technical Report Series., Clausthal University of Technology (2009)

# Prior State Reasoning in Multi-agent Systems and Graph-Theoretical Algorithms

Chengqian Li and Lu Liu

Dept. of Computer Science,
Sun Yat-sen University
Guangzhou 510006, China
{lichengq,liul63}@mail2.sysu.edu.cn

**Abstract.** The Multi-Agent Programming Contest is held every year to stimulate research in the area of multi-agent systems. Our system mainly exploits four strategies: prior state reasoning, task allocation optimization, dijkstra with recharge and surrounding several stable and valuable zones with shorter boundaries. With these strategies, our team is able to conquer several large zones as early as possible, optimize collaboration, and ensure efficiency. The system was implemented in C++, and in this paper, we will introduce the design and architecture of AiWXX, and discuss the algorithms and implementations for these strategies.

**Keywords:** multi-agent systems, prior state reasoning, graph algorithms.

## 1 Introduction

The Multi-Agent Programming Contest (MAPC)[1] is held annually, in order for researchers to deepen the understanding about the cooperation and competition among rational agents and also develop some powerful strategies in such environments. This year, a team, called AiWXX, reached the fifth place. It consists of two members, Chengqian Li and Lu Liu. They both are second-year postgraduate students, whose research interests are random boolean satisfiability solver (SAT solver), data structures and algorithms. Our motivation in participating in this contest was to gain experiences in designing multi-agent systems to facilitate our future research in this area. Last year Chengqian Li participated in MAPC 2012 and won the 5th place. This year we enhanced the strategy we used last year, and the performance was even better than that for the strategy last year.

## 2 System Analysis and Design

We took part in the contest using the language C++, without using any multi-agent programming languages, because we are proficient in this language which is well-known for its efficiency. We started to use functional programming this year

---

[1] http://multiagentcontest.org/2013

M. Cossentino et al. (Eds.): EMAS 2013, LNAI 8245, pp. 356–365, 2013.

because it is more efficient than object-oriented programming. We changed many parts of the source codes we used last year into those of functional programming, and it proved to be several times faster than before. Our implementation is a decentralized solution, however, the current implementation is restricted because we only deal with common knowledge base. When any agent's knowledge state is updated, other agents' knowledge states will be updated synchronously. As to how to implement such strategies on a computer, we apply for a piece of main memory from the operating system, which stores the common knowledge. Hence, each agent has the same authority to access this memory space in order to communicate with other agents. Then agents communicate with each other by this shared memory space because this is almost the most efficient way. Hence, each agent has the same authority to access the knowledge base (KB) they shared in order to communicate with other agents.

All agents decide their actions according to their knowledge state. If the environment is changed, then their knowledge state will also be changed when they realize the changes. This means that agents will response to the changes actively. While such a team of agents is running in the competition, each agent has the goal that her team should reach a score higher than that of their rival, and we made strategies to ensure that agents tried to achieve this goal actively. Given a task, when there is only one agent intending to accomplish it, she will act by herself. Otherwise, if there are more than one agent intending to accomplish the same type of tasks, all of them will collaborate to accomplish their tasks, that is, the task will be allocated to the agents in an optimal way. Moreover, the agents here are aggressive, that is, they keep exploring new areas of the world, never passively waiting for changes of the environment. Finally, in any state of the world, any agent will recognize her state, and she is able to perform some action to approach her goal, which was ensured by our strategies.

To design and implement our system, we spent about 250 hours based on the work last year[7]. During this period, we did not discuss the design and strategies of our agents with others, because we focused on the cooperation of agents this year rather than the competition with different strategies. Each agent has only one private data structure, which stored the perceptions received from the server. This is to avoid the data inconsistency in multiple threads.

## 3    Software Architecture

We used C++ as the programming language, because various mature data structures are easy to code in C++. Each of the agents runs a separate program which is designed at four different levels. Level 1 is the *coordination level*, which generates proposals for agents to accomplish team work, and thus to prevent multiple agents from achieving the same subgoal. Such a group of agents are to accomplish a task which cannot be handled by a single agent.

Level 2 is the *prior state reasoning level*, at which agents will accept their respective proposal, or generate an action according to the current state. Level 2 is the most significant level. There is always a potential problem when the

---

**Algorithm 1.** Framework of Prior State Reasoning

---

 **input** : $KB$
 **output**: *action*

1 // if role=saboteur and Energy_too_low()
2 **if** $KB \models state1$ **then return** *action1* // recharge
3 // if role=saboteur and health=0 and Repairer_near_me()
4 **if** $KB \models state2$ **then return** *action2* // recharge
5 // if role=saboteur and Find_enemy_near_me()
6 **if** $KB \models state3$ **then return** *action3* // Attack_enemy_near_me()
7 // if role=saboteur and Have_destination()
8 **if** $KB \models state4$ **then return** *action4* // Go_to_next_node_to_destination()
9 ...
10 **return** *recharge*

---

agents are executing a plan: we may abort the plan being executed, and go to do another plan instead. Too many unpredictable events may happen during a plan execution. For example, suppose an agent wants to go to a node, and she generates a plan to do so. However, on her way she suddenly finds out that her energy is too low. After that she is attacked by an enemy, so she may become dead or injured. Later she may find an enemy, and she wants to attack the enemy. There are four strategies of different priorities in this long story. The most prior strategy is recharging when the agent's energy is too low since we value this as the most emergent situation. The second most prior strategy, is finding a repairer to repair herself if she is injured. The third most prior one, is attacking the enemies she found. The least prior one, is moving to the destination if she has one. In every step, she will scan her prior state table which maps every state to an action, as shown in Algorithm 1. The comments in Algorithm 1 show an example to merge these strategies. Now the agent can perform reasoning in her KB, figure out what is her state and map the state to the respective action. The key idea is that we will classify all possible states according to a given strategy. The priority of the state should be valued as well, because it has an influence on which action will be decided. After that we can decide an action according to the strategy.

Level 3 is responsible for updating and reasoning upon the KB. When a perception is received by an agent, Level 3 will automatically update the knowledge base. On the other hand when being asked about the current state, it will retrieve specific information from the KB, so we call it *reasoning level*. Level 4 *(physical level)* contains various physical implementations, including KB, network communication (TCP/IP), and special algorithms such as string processing, a Dijkstra algorithm [2], a breadth-first search algorithm [1], a minimum cost flow algorithm [8], a Hungarian algorithm [3,6] and graph-theoretical algorithms [7].

We invested little time in learning development platforms and tools, because we used Gedit Text Editor in the Linux system, together with the g++ compiler. With the flexible C++ programming language, we were able to implement all the features of our system quite efficiently, so no features were lost in our implementation. We had to rent a virtual private server (VPS) since the network performance between Germany and China is not satisfactory. Furthermore, sharing memory in one computer is almost the most efficient way for communications between agents. We could still run all our agents on a single computer, because the size of the problem and the number of agents both were not so large to require more. Therefore we did not distribute the agents on different machines.

We use multiple threads to receive perceptions from the server, and our strategy ensures that the knowledge bases of different agents are always synchronized. In the receive-percept period, no agents will perform reasoning until all agents receive the new perception. The most difficult part of the whole development process was the optimization of team strategies against different strategies. That is, how to figure out the possible strategy of the other teams and find an optimal strategy with respect to rivals. In total, we wrote 11,000 lines of C++ code for our system.

## 4    Strategies, Details and Statistics

The main strategy of our agent system is that the whole team will try to probe the whole map first, then occupy several stable and valuable zones, as was described in Fig1[2]. Our team occupied three corners of the map, and won this match ultimately. There were two reasons for our success: (1) our system explored the map quite fast, so we were also able to obtain the achievements fast, and our agents were more likely to discover and occupy those stable and valuable zones; (2) the three zones we occupied were stable, so they were not easy to be discovered and disturbed by our rival. According to our experiments, we found that large zones, covering a great proportion of the nodes of the map, were often discovered and disturbed by the enemies, so they were not stable, thus in this year, we view zones not too large as stable ones. In implementations, we set an argument $\gamma$, and we treat all zones covering a proportion not greater than $\gamma$ as stable ones. Fig2[3] shows the stabilities of both teams in one match involving our system, indicating that our occupied zones were often more stable than those of this rival. At the beginning of this match, the rival immediately started to occupy zones nearby, while our system simply explored the map, so their zones proved to be more stable. However, as we started to occupy the desirable zones (at around Time Step 138), the stability of our zones quickly increased and surpassed theirs significantly. Later, at Time Step 600, our stability decreased abnormally, because network problems occurred and we restarted our program. Next our agents would be allocated new tasks and failed to keep their already

---

[2] http://multiagentcontest.org/downloads/Multi-Agent-Programming-Contest-2013/SVG-Videos/Mars2013-AiWXXLTI-USP-contest-sim1-2013-09-10-14-49.tar/

[3] http://multiagentcontest.org/downloads/Multi-Agent-Programming-Contest-2013/Statistics/statistics-Mars2013-AiWXXLTI-USP-contest-sim1-2013-09-10-14-49.tar/

occupied zones, but they remembered those parts of the map having been explored. Agents will survey the edges and probe the nodes of the whole map to search for available areas. If some agents find an enemy, a saboteur will go to her node to attack her. If a certain agent gets injured, the agent will abort her task and find a repairer to repair herself. To avoid redundant work and accomplish tasks with the lowest cost, the agents will cooperate in an optimal manner to explore a map or try to occupy some area.

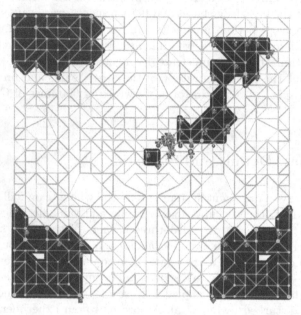

**Fig. 1.** Step 308 of Mars2013_AiWXXLTI-USP_contest-sim1

Because the visible range is limited, we may not know all the edges connected to a visible node. To survey all the edges, agents will go to every node to perform a survey action. It is worth noting that if a node is visited or inside the visible range, then we know all the edges connected to this node. If all the edges of a node are surveyed at its neighbor nodes, then we do not need to perform Survey actions again at this node. This will reduce many steps to survey all the edges, because many redundant Survey and Recharge actions have been avoided.

Because the agents can recharge energy at any time, and an agent can only move to a neighbor node in any single time step, a path containing too many nodes can be an undesirable option. So apart from the length between two nodes, we also have to consider the number of edges in the path. In this sense given a source and a destination, we are to compute a path through which an agent spends the least time steps, breaking ties by preferring the one which costs the least energy. To do this, we propose an adaption of the classic dijkstra algorithm in order to compute a certain kind of costs from a root node to all other nodes, which should be minimized to achieve our optimization goal. Given a map, the

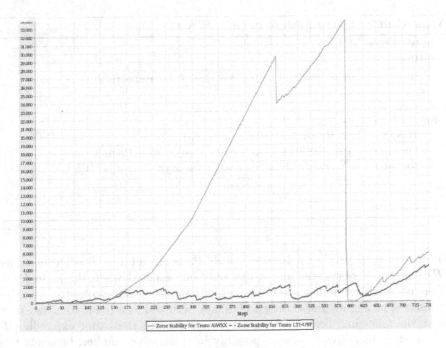

**Fig. 2.** Zone Stabilities of Mars2013_AiWXXLTI-USP_contest-sim1

set $V$ of nodes, the set $E$ of edges, the weight $W_{(a,b)}$ of each edge $(a, b) \in E$, the root node *root*, the points $r$ of energy recharged by an agent each time, our adapted algorithm will return the minimum costs from *root* to every other node (see Algorithm 2). It is worthwhile to note that the notion of cost here loses its original meaning, the length between two particular nodes. It does not have an intuitive meaning on the map, but is used technically to compute the optimal paths. Although we only change a single line of the original dijkstra algorithm, the result of this adaption is interesting, and our algorithm here has the same time complexity as the Dijkstra Algorithm. Dijkstra algorithm [2] runs in $O(n^2)$ time, where $n$ is the number of vertices in a graph. This algorithm can enhanced with a priority queue, and if the Fibonacci heap [4] is used to implement the priority queue then the time complexity becomes $O(m + n \log n)$ where $m$ is the number of edges in the graph.

### 4.1   Expanding Zones

When a group of agents wants to occupy a zone, they need to find a promising one. We improved the expand algorithm used last year[7] so that the agents can occupy more than one zone and such zones will be more stable. Given a map, the set $V$ of nodes, the set $E$ of edges, and the weight $W_x$ of any node $x \in V$, the set of nodes $O$ is the set of the nodes occupied by enemies or some of our agents. We set an argument $\gamma$, and we think a zone as unstable if its coverage percentage is

---

**Algorithm 2.** dijkstra_with_recharge(V,E,W,r)

---

**input** : root, V, E, W, r
**output**: cost

1  Initialize elements of $cost$ and $in$ to be $\infty$ and $false$ respectively
2  $cost_{root} \leftarrow 0$; $in_{root} \leftarrow true$
3  $N_x \leftarrow \{y \in V | (x,y) \in E\}$
4  **for** $i = 1$ **to** $|V| - 1$ **do**
5  $\quad$ $Bound \leftarrow \{a \in V | in(a) = false \text{ and } cost(a) \neq \infty\}$
6  $\quad$ find a node $a \in Bound$ such that $cost_a \leq cost_b, \forall b \in Bound$
7  $\quad$ **foreach** $b \in N_a$ **do** // Origin: $cost_b \leftarrow \max(cost_b, cost_a + W_{(a,b)})$
8  $\quad\quad$ $cost_b \leftarrow \max(cost_b, cost_a + W_{(a,b)} + r)$

9  **return** $cost$

---

greater than $\gamma$. *Expanding a boundary node $P$*, means adding all adjacent nodes of $P$ into the current zone, and it can only be executed when the node $P$, as well as its neighbor nodes, are not occupied by any agents, no matter enemies or friends. The agents first choose a node not occupied as a point zone and then repeat the following: find the boundary node $P$ such that after expanding $P$ the boundary increases the least (possibly by a negative number, breaking ties by preferring to the one which increases the value most), and then, expand it. During the expanding process, we maintain the most valuable zones found for different boundary lengths. In details, we have the following Algorithm 2. The complexity of this algorithm is $O(\gamma N^2 M)$, where $N$ is the number of nodes and $M$ is the number of edges in the graph. Note that Algorithm 3 can be made distributed, in that the expanding procedure can simultaneously begin at any number of nodes on the map. In particular, if we have as many machines as the nodes, we allocate each machine a unique node and instruct it to run a separate expanding procedure with that respective node.

### 4.2 Strategy Details

Given a set of all the nodes $V$ and a threshold $\gamma$ denoting the stability requirement of a zone. It is set to 0.15 in the contest. Formally below is the evaluation function for computing the value of a zone:

$$value_{Zone} = \begin{cases} \sum_{i \in Zone} value_i & \text{if } \frac{|Zone|}{|V|} \leq \gamma, \\ 0 & \text{otherwise.} \end{cases}$$

Our system will find out several promising zones with Algorithm 3, and then instruct the agents to move to the boundary of those zones and conquer them. Among them, a saboteur will always attack an enemy who has not been targeted by any friend saboteurs. If they are attacked by the enemies, they will recompute a new area not occupied by the enemies, move there, and stand on the boundary such that there is at least an agent at any two adjacent boundary nodes. During the procedure of path finding, we exploited Algorithm 2 and Breadth-First

**Algorithm 3.** Surround(V, E, W, O, $\gamma$)

> **input** : V, E, W, O, $\gamma$
> **output**: Best
>
> 1   $N_x \leftarrow \{y|(x,y) \in E\}$ for each $x \in V$
> 2   $NE \leftarrow \{x|x \in O$ or $O \cap N_x \neq \emptyset \}$
> 3   Initialise(Hash)
> 4   **foreach** $v \in V$ **do**
> 5     $Zone \leftarrow B \leftarrow \{v\}$
> 6     **while** *exists* $x$ *s.t.* $x \in B$ *and* $(N_x - Zone - O \neq \emptyset)$ **do**
> 7       **if** $B \subseteq NE$ **then** // no point can be Expanded
> 8        $S \leftarrow \{x \in B|\forall y \in B, |N_x - Zone - O| \leq |N_y - Zone - O|\}$
> 9       **else**
> 10        $S \leftarrow \{x \in B - NE|\forall y \in B - NE, |N_x - Zone| \leq |N_y - Zone|\}$
> 11      find $x \in S$ s.t. $\forall y \in S, \sum_{a \in N_x - Zone - O} W_a \geq \sum_{b \in N_y - Zone - O} W_b$
> 12      $Zone \leftarrow Zone \cup (N_x - Zone - O)$
> 13      $h \leftarrow Hash\_encode(Zone)$
> 14      **if** $|Zone| \leq |V| \times \gamma$ or $Zone \in Hash_h$ **then** break
> 15      $Hash_h \leftarrow Hash_h \cup Zone$
> 16      $B \leftarrow \{x \in Zone|N_x \not\subseteq Zone\}$
> 17      **if** $\sum_{x \in Best_{|Zone|}} W_x < \sum_{x \in Zone} W_x$ **then** $Best_{|Zone|} \leftarrow Zone$
>
> 18 **return** *Best*

Search Algorithm, and we also used arrangement algorithm last year[7] to prevent any two agents from exploring the same location. During the contest, no agent will buy any facilities because our system prefers to save money. According to empirical results, it is best not to buy any facilities. In the contest, we value achievements, from which we are able to obtain some scores at each step, so we try to acquire achievements swiftly, never spending them.

As mentioned earlier, all agents in our team are rational and perfect team players, that is, each will always try to complete the mission of the group. Moreover, recall that all communications are perfect and no agents will perform any actions when a certain perception is being used to update the knowledge base. When a list of agents are applying for the same type of missions, one of them will become a temporary project manager, which is responsible for allocating the mission in an optimal way. Later this project manager will become an ordinary agent and each agent will accomplish her allocated mission separately. Hence we organize our agents explicitly and no hierarchy is exploited. When an agent encounters something emergent, she immediately interrupts her allocated mission and tell all others in the group. The group will possibly relax the team mission so that they are able to accomplish it without this agent. Our agents do not perform any planning because we think the current planning technology is not efficient enough to deal with on-line problem.

# 5    Conclusion

The participation of this contest has greatly improved our knowledge of multi-agent systems and stimulated our interests in conducting research in this area. One strong point of our team is efficiency, in that it only cost about 0.2 second to make all decisions, on the 500-node map, in a perfect network. Our framework is compatible enough to develop more complex strategies in future contests. The weaknesses of our team are that we do not observe the enemy and we are not familiar with the other teams. Because there is a great number of agents and the map is complex, our programs have to run with great efficiency. Hence we chose C++, which is known for its efficiency and flexibility, supporting various data structures and algorithms. Next year we will stick to this choice even after the experience of this contest, because we have established the framework and many multi-agent system (MAS) concepts have been encoded, so any improvements will easily be implemented in C++. So far we do not think that there are big problems in the overall design of our MAS, but we do lack of intelligent strategies in our current system, so next year we are to develop some smarter strategies. Next year we are going to observe the enemy and analyze the strategies of them. And we will refer to the strategies of other teams rather than blind research. The performance this year is not so satisfactory and there are many reasons. Our VPS broke down during the final contest, so we lost 357,931 points in one match. This was the second time for us to participate, and we did not have enough time to implement all our ideas.

For the next year, we think some changes should be made to improve the current scenario. Firstly, the perception should be compressed so as to relieve the pressure of network communication. The XML style is unnecessary. And the name in perception should be as short as possible. For example, an edge, "< *visibleEdge node*1="vertex0" *node*2="vertex11"/>", in the competition, can simply be replaced by "*e* 0 11", meaning that there is an edge between node 0 and node 11. When we read the letter "e" in the message, we will know that there are two integer to read next. Secondly, the server should add an option that allows a team to simply use one TCP connection to receive perception, since almost every team chose not to distribute their agents on different machines. This may reduce the difficulties of network programming, and encourage more people to participate in this contest. Compression algorithms like Haffman Coding algorithm[5] should be used to reduce the size of the messages. And we think the organizers should offer automatic test servers for us, so any two teams can join in a test match whenever they want. The network performance is very poor between Germany and some countries, so we need to rent a VPS to participate in the contest. However, some team in some year may fail to afford the rents. And as said before, our VPS broke down during the final contest. To encourage more people from such countries, we strongly recommend that the organizers should offer computers to these people like us. After all, these optimizations cost the organizers very little.

**Acknowledgements.** We are deeply grateful to Yi Fan supported by NICTA for his generous and valuable help with the writing of this paper. NICTA is funded through the Australian Government's *Backing Australia's Ability* initiative, in part through the Australian National Research Council.

# References

1. Cormen, T.H., Leiserson, C.E., Rivest, R.L., Stein, C.: Section 22.2: Breadth-first search. In: Introduction to Algorithms, pp. 531–539. MIT Press and McGraw-Hill (2001)
2. Dijkstra, E.W.: A note on two problems in connexion with graphs. In: Numerische Mathematik, vol. 1, pp. 260–271. Springer (1959)
3. Edmonds, J.: Maximum matching and a polyhedron with 0,1 vertices. J. of Res. the Nat. Bureau of Standards 69 B, 125–130 (1965)
4. Fredman, M.L., Tarjan, R.E.: Fibonacci heaps and their uses in improved network optimization algorithms. Journal of the ACM (JACM) 34(3), 596–615 (1987)
5. Huffman, D.A.: A method for the construction of minimum-redundancy codes. Proceedings of the IRE 40(9), 1098–1101 (1952)
6. Kuhn, H.W., Yaw, B.: The Hungarian method for the assignment problem. Naval Res. Logist. Quart., 83–97 (1955)
7. Li, C.: Conquering large zones by exploiting task allocation and graph-theoretical algorithms. In: Dastani, M., Hübner, J.F., Logan, B. (eds.) ProMAS 2012. LNCS, vol. 7837, pp. 234–244. Springer, Heidelberg (2013)
8. Orlin, J.B.: A faster strongly polynomial minimum cost flow algorithm. Operations Research 41(2), 338–350 (1993)

# Multi-Agent Programming Contest 2013: The Teams and the Design of Their Systems

Tobias Ahlbrecht[1], Christian Bender-Saebelkampf[5], Maiquel de Brito[6],
Nicolai Christian Christensen[3], Jürgen Dix[1], Mariana Ramos Franco[4],
Hendrik Heller[5], Andreas Viktor Hess[3], Axel Heßler[5], Jomi Fred Hübner[6],
Andreas Schmidt Jensen[3], Jannick Boese Johnsen[3], Michael Köster[1],
Chengqian Li[2], Lu Liu[2], Marcelo Menezes Morato[6], Philip Bratt Ørum[3],
Federico Schlesinger[1], Tiago Luiz Schmitz[6], Jaime Simão Sichman[4],
Kaio Siqueira de Souza[6], Daniela Maria Uez[6], Jørgen Villadsen[3],
Sebastian Werner[5], Øyvind Grønland Woller[3], and Maicon Rafael Zatelli[6]

[1] Department of Informatics, Clausthal University of Technology,
Julius-Albert-Str. 4, 38678 Clausthal-Zellerfeld, Germany
[2] Dept. of Computer Science,
Sun Yat-sen University
Guangzhou 510006, China
[3] Algorithms, Logic and Graphs Section
Department of Applied Mathematics and Computer Science
Technical University of Denmark
Matematiktorvet, Building 303B, DK-2800 Kongens Lyngby, Denmark
[4] Laboratório de Técnicas Inteligentes (LTI), Escola Politécnica (EP)
Universidade de São Paulo (USP)
[5] Distributed Artificial Intelligence Laboratory
Technische Universität Berlin, Germany
[6] Department of Automation and Systems Engineering
Federal University of Santa Catarina
CP 476, 88040-900 Florianópolis - SC - Brasil

**Abstract.** Five teams participated in the Multi-Agent Programming Contest in 2013: All of them gained experience in 2012 already. In order to better understand which paradigms they used, which techniques they considered important and how much work they invested, the organisers of the contest compiled together a detailed list of questions (circa 50). This paper collects all answers to these questions as given by the teams.

## 1 Introduction

One of the main aims of the Multi-Agent Programming Contest [1,2] is to test and evaluate multi-agent systems: Are they better suited for decentralized scenarios than more traditional approaches? Do they offer tools that can be easily used and are still sufficiently scalable? Compared to pure Java based approaches, what do we gain?

In the past, we have seen several teams not using multi-agent platforms. Some of them have been chosen by students who wanted to participate in the contest,

M. Cossentino et al. (Eds.): EMAS 2013, LNAI 8245, pp. 366–390, 2013.
© Springer-Verlag Berlin Heidelberg 2013

but who did not have a deep background in multi-agent programming. This year, only one team decided not to use any dedicated multi-agent programming language and to stick to C++ (as they did last year). It is interesting to note that the runner-up in 2011 and 2012, Python-DTU, did not use an agent programming language, but many concepts and techniques from multi-agent reasoning (programmed in Python).

An important point in the contest is the choice of the scenario. We do *not* want to evaluate a particular smart strategy to solve the task, we would like to evaluate the agent platform or software system that is used for the solution. Therefore the scenario has to be sufficiently complex, otherwise we risk that a smart team comes up with a clever solution that has noting to do with the tools provided by the underlying programming language.

It is also obvious that we can test only some features of agent platforms and languages. To evaluate the whole software development life-cycle, from requirements phase to deployment, we would have to evaluate all these phases, from the design to the final software code. This is not possible and therefore we decided only to test the final system. We hope that the questions and the answers that we have collected here shed some light on these phases as well.

## 2   The Contest in 2013

All five contestants in 2013 (see Table 1) also participated in the contest in 2012. However, for TUB the team members changed completely. Only one of the teams (AiWXX) did not use a multi-agent programming platform or language. The winner in 2013 already won in 2012: SMADAS-UFSC. TUB, who came fourth in 2013, won several times in the past (for different scenarios).

**Table 1.** Participants of the 2013 Edition

| Team | Affiliation | Platform/Language |
|------|-------------|-------------------|
| AiWXX[5] | Sun Yat-Sen University, China | C++ |
| GOAL-DTU[6] | Technical University of Denmark | GOAL |
| LTI-USP[3] | University of Sao Paulo, Brazil | Jason, CArtAgO, Moise |
| SMADAS-UFSC[8] | Federal University of Santa Catarina, Brazil | Jason, CArtAgO, Moise |
| TUB[7] | TU Berlin, Germany | JIAC |

The person-hours invested to implement the teams range from 150 (LTI-USP), 250 (AiWXX), 400 (SMADAS-UFSC), 500 (GOAL-DTU) to 840 (TUB). The lines of code written for the teams range from 1300 (GOAL-DTU), 4000 (LTI-USP), 7996 (TUB), 8500 (SMADAS-UFSC), to 11000 (AiWXX).

LTI-USP and AiWXX used a centralized approach, TUB decided for a hybrid method, i.e., centralized regarding zone building, decentralized otherwise.

The remaining two teams, winner SMADAS-UFSC and runner-up GOAL-DTU implemented a purely decentralized approach.

Table 2 shows the results. SMADAS-UFSC won again (after 2012) and GOAL-DTU was again runner-up (but using this time a different agent programming language).

**Table 2.** Results

| Pos. | Team | Score | Difference | Points |
|------|------|-------|------------|--------|
| 1 | SMADAS-UFSC | 2702948 : 1455163 | 1247785 | 36 |
| 2 | GOAL-DTU | 2284575 : 1614711 | 669864 | 27 |
| 3 | LTI-USP | 2117299 : 2083105 | 34194 | 15 |
| 4 | TUB | 1412702 : 2238820 | -826118 | 6 |
| 5 | AiWXX | 1516760 : 2642485 | -1125725 | 6 |

When we introduced our Mars-scenario for the first time in 2011, a team from the Netherlands (headed by Koen Hindriks) won using the agent language GOAL. A detailed description of the team and the architecture of the system recently appeared in [4].

When we introduced the Mars scenario in 2011, three teams used a multi-agent platform (among them the winner and the third place) and six did not. In 2012, again three teams used a multi-agent platform, the remaining four did not. As the year before, the winner and third place in 2012 used a multi-agent platform. Interestingly, the runner-up in both years (DTU) used Python and not a dedicated agent programming language. In 2013, DTU used GOAL (the language of the winning team in 2011) but again came second.

## 3   Questions and Answers

We have collected over 50 questions, arranged into five different groups: (1) information about the team (motivation, number of members and time invested, background of team members), (2) system analysis and design (centralized or not, multi-agent language or not, communication, mental states), (3) software architecture (programming language, development/runtime tools, algorithms used, reasoning of the agents, lines of code), (4) strategies and some details related to the MARS scenario (strategy, information sharing, exploring the topology, communication with the server, building zones, assigning roles to agents, changing behaviour at runtime, achievements, mental state of agents), and, finally, (5) lessons learned (reasons for the performance of the team, weak and strong points when compared with other teams, how to improve the contest in the future).

### 3.1   Teams and Their Background

This group of questions collects information about the motivation of the teams, their size and their background.

**What was the motivation to participate in the contest?**

*SMADAS-UFSC:* Testing the JaCaMo platform in the contest scenario and evaluate some other technologies developed in our master and PhD thesis.

*GOAL-DTU:* We participated in the contest because we find the contest very interesting for both research and teaching.

*LTI-USP:* The main motivation to participate in the contest was to test and evaluate the JaCaMo framework.

*TUB:* The main motivation was and is to test, benchmark and improve our JIAC V agent framework; the contest was the first application of the framework; we still need to improve a lot of things and the contest then says whether it is with good performance or works reliably; the benefit of a solid agent framework can be seen in many applications of the JIAC framework in projects whenever a distributed architecture makes sense.

*AiWXX:* Our motivation was to gain a deeper understanding about Multi-agent Systems.

**What is the history of the team? (course project, thesis, ...)**

*SMADAS-UFSC:* Our team was formed by members from the Multi-Agent Systems research group (called SMADAS) at Federal University of Santa Catarina (UFSC).

*GOAL-DTU:* The team consists of both researchers/students from previous years and students taking a special course.

*LTI-USP:* The LTI-USP participated in the 2012 edition of the MAPC and also in previous years. Since our first participation, the MAPC has been used to evaluate platforms and tools, and to improve our knowledge in developing MAS. The previous Cows and Cowboys scenario was used in the last two years of the Multi-Agent course held at the Department of Computer Engineering and Digital Systems of the University of São Paulo.

*TUB:* We started participation in 2007 with the JIAC IV agent framework, which was heavily loaded with AI concepts such as own ontology language, trinary propositional calculus, first-order logic, situation calculus, reaction rules, an own agent programming language (JADL), an own component system. At this time, it was already clear that such a framework is not maintainable, too difficult to learn and to use. We then started a bottom-up approach where we used a third-party component framework and added those components that we really needed to make the agents and a programming language people really use. One year later the contest was the first touchstone where we tested if our concept holds in reality, and what nobody could envision we won. In 2008 the contest helped us to get the teething troubles out of the way and to develop really useful features that make the life of the programmer easier. We then started to offer a course on multi-agent programming where we use the JIAC framework and the contest scenarios to teach agent programming principles, usually to students that do not have experience neither in software engineering nor in agent programming. The schedule of this course is to develop a solution for the Multi-Agent-Contest and participate in the contest at the end of the semester, implicitly testing and improving our agent framework.

*AiWXX:* Our team consists of two members, Chengqian Li and Lu Liu. Last year Chengqian Li participated in MAPC 2012. And a Multi-Agent scenario was used in his thesis.

**How many developers and designers did you have? At what level of education are your team members?**

*SMADAS-UFSC:* Our team has seven developers and everyone was involved with the system design. We have one PhD, four PhD students, and two undergraduate students.

*GOAL-DTU:* We are 7 computer scientists: associate professor Jørgen Villadsen (PhD), Andreas Schmidt Jensen (PhD student), Nicolai Christian Christensen (MSc student), Andreas Viktor Hess (BSc student), Jannick Boese Johnsen (MSc student), Øyvind Grønland Woller (BSc student) and Philip Bratt Ørum (MSc student).

*LTI-USP:* The LTI-USP team was formed by Mariana Ramos Franco (M.Sc. Student) and Jaime Simão Sichman (Professor).

*TUB:* During the course we had twelve students split into two teams. During preparation to the contest our team consisted of three computer science students: Hendrik Heller, Christian Bender-Seaelkampf and Sebastian Werner. As well as the course supervisor Axel Heßler. The students start their fourth Bachelor semester when they joined the course.

*AiWXX:* Our team consists of two second-year postgraduate students.

**What is your field of research? Which work therein is related?**

*SMADAS-UFSC:* All team members work with Multi-Agent Systems and Artificial Intelligence.

*GOAL-DTU:* Our field of research is AI with an emphasis on algorithms and logic.

*LTI-USP:* The LTI-USP, located at the University of São Paulo, is one of the most relevant research groups in multi-agent systems in Brazil. In cooperation with other research groups in DAS/UFSC (Brazil) and ISCOD / LSTI / ENSMSE (France), our group is one of the responsibles for the development and maintenance of the *Moise* organisational model.

*TUB:* Main field is agent-oriented software engineering, distributed and complex systems, we usually do more projects that apply agent principles and methods than basic research.

*AiWXX:* Data structures, algorithms and the Boolean Satisfiability (SAT) problem.

## 3.2    System Analysis and Design

Moreover, we wanted to know why (if at all) an agent approach has been chosen and whether the approach was centralised or not. Did agents share some information with others? How did the agents communicate and how were autonomy and proactiveness implemented.

## Did you use multi-agent programming languages? Why?

*SMADAS-UFSC:* We used the JaCaMo framework. Thus, we used Jason for implementing the agents, CArtAgO for the environment and the $\mathcal{M}$oise organizational model to specify the organization.

*GOAL-DTU:* We use GOAL, which is a dedicated multi-agent programming language.

*LTI-USP:* We developed our team using the JaCaMo framework. JaCaMo is a platform for multi-agent programming which supports all levels of abstractions - agent, environment, and organisation - that are required for developing sophisticated multi-agent systems, by combining three separate technologies: Jason, for programming autonomous agents; CArtAgO for programming environment artifacts; and $\mathcal{M}$oise for programming multi-agent organisations.

*TUB:* No. The choice of language is up to the students. In fact, we use Java intentionally, for several reasons: platform independence (usually students and developer use an evil mix of operating systems, versions and distributions), the JIAC framework is written in Java although we have several language ports (e.g. JADL, Python, Scala, BPMN), most multi-agent programming languages are logic-based and most students at that point in their studies are not familiar with logic programming.

*AiWXX:* No, we did not because we are proficient in the C++ language which is well-known for its efficiency.

## If some multi-agent system methodology such as Prometheus, O-MaSE, or Tropos was used, how did you use it? If you did not, why?

*SMADAS-UFSC:* We did not use any existing AOSE method. The problem seemed too easy and there was no need to use a complete methodology.

*GOAL-DTU:* We have not used a multi-agent system methodology as we based our system analysis on the earlier Python-DTU system (2012) and our overall design on the HactarV2 system (2011).

*LTI-USP:* For the development of this project, we chose to not use any multi-agent methodology, because we already had the 2012 team from where to start to work, and mainly because we decided that it was better to spend our time improving the system than learning a methodology.

*TUB:* We use the JIAC development methodology (MIAC). MIAC focusses on efficient and fast development and is closely related to the concepts and architecture of the JIAC framework. Although most methodologies state to be general, but implicitly they are build on an concrete (multi-)agent models and thus they are often not applicable in another context. Many agent methodologies focus on design and thus often leave out important software engineering disciplines such as requirement elicitation, implementation and testing, deployment, management and maintenance. MIAC is still not complete in that sense but gives developers useful guidelines for intuitive understanding of what to do based on what they already know about programming and development and then they can focus on solving the problem.

*AiWXX:* No, we did not use any of them because we thought our framework was good enough for almost every strategy. And we are proficient in C++ language which is well-known for its efficiency.

**Is the solution based on the centralisation of coordination/information on a specific agent? Conversely if you plan a decentralised solution, which strategy do you plan to use?**

*SMADAS-UFSC:* The coordination is mostly based on the *Moise* organizational structure. However, we use an agent - called coach, which adopts the role of *leader* - that manages the organization and performs the setup of organizational structure.

*GOAL-DTU:* Our solution is generally a decentralized system, though some features are centralized. Our implementation uses the new multi-threading feature of GOAL.

*LTI-USP:* Our team is decentralised. Each agent decides by itself which empty vertex it will occupy in order to create the zone or expand it. There is no centralisation of information. Each agent has its own view of the world.

*TUB:* The behaviour of the agents (i.e. the roles) is completely decentralised. Each agent has its own world model and decides on its own what to do next. The agent communicate their perception and their decision with each other, so the world model is more complete. There is one exception, the calculation of promising zones to be captured is done by an extra agent, which assigns positions to agents that are free to build a zone.

*AiWXX:* Our framework is a decentralised solution. However, the current implementation is restricted because we only deal with common knowledge.

**What is the communication strategy and how complex is it?**

*SMADAS-UFSC:* The agents use message exchange to call repairers, saboteurs or inform others about good vertices and map regions. Other information is shared through a blackboard.

*GOAL-DTU:* We aim to send as few messages between the agents as possible. Our agents communicate the status of themselves and enemy agents as well as map information.

*LTI-USP:* In our team, each agent has its own view of the world and they communicate with each other for the following purposes: (i) informing the other agents about the structure of the map; (ii) informing about the agent's or the opponent's position, role and status; (iii) asking for repair.

The agents' communication occurs via the speech acts provided by Jason and, to reduce the communication overhead, an agent broadcasts to all the other agents only the new percepts, i.e., only percepts received from the contest server which produce an update of the agent's world model are broadcasted. For this reason, there is a strong exchange of information between the agents in the beginning of the match due to the broadcast of new percepts, specially those related to the map, such as vertices and edges. However, the communication overhead decreases as the agents' world model starts to be more complete.

*TUB:* Each agent communicates its perception and decision with each other agent. Thus, the complexity is $2n \cdot (n-1)$ where n is the number of agents in the setting and we are using multicast messaging to solve this. Additionally, there is a communication for zoning: each free agent communicates its availability to the zoning agent and is informed about the best position for zoning as a reply, so complexity is $2n$ in the worst case.

*AiWXX:* When any agent's knowledge state is updated, the other agents' knowledge states will be updated in precisely the same way because of the assumption of common knowledge.

### How are the following agent features considered/implemented: *autonomy, proactiveness, reactiveness*?

*SMADAS-UFSC:* Our agents are autonomous to decide how to achieve their specific goals, but all of them have to attend to the organizational norms. Similarly, the agents may behave proactively or reactively in accordance with the needs. For instance, a damaged agent will call a repairer and all agents react to the environment events like the start of a step.

*GOAL-DTU:* Agents do not cooperate in making choices. One proactive feature is that *Repairers* repair agents that are likely to be attacked. Otherwise we are mostly reactive.

*LTI-USP:* The agents are autonomous to decide by themselves the next action to be performed, but in cooperation with each other, particularly with the coordinator agent. The agents have a proactive behaviour, for example, to find the better vertices in the map, and to move to the closest repairer when they are damaged.

At each step, the agent decides which plan will be executed given only the state of the environment and the results of previous steps. The plan's priority is determined by the order in which the plans were declared, and the executed plan will be the first one to have its conditions satisfied. Some high priority plans can be considered reactive, such as the one which tells the agent to perform a recharge when running low on energy.

*TUB:* JIAC V agents have their own thread of control and decide and act autonomously. We see the agents with low health level pro-actively seeking the repairer's help using a simple request, whereas probing or surveying has been implemented as a simple reactive behaviour: if the node is unprobed then probe.

*AiWXX:* Every agent chooses her action according to her state and no agent can control other agents. If the environment is changed, their knowledge state will also be changed as soon as they realize the changes. The agents are aggressive, that is, they keep exploring new areas of the world, never passively waiting for changes of the environment.

### Is the team a truly multi-agent system or rather a centralised system in disguise?

*SMADAS-UFSC:* Our team was developed as a true MAS composed by three dimensions: agents, organization and environment.

*GOAL-DTU:* It is truly a multi-agent system.

*LTI-USP:* Our system is a true multi-agent system. Each agent has its own beliefs, desires, intentions and control thread. Each agent decides by itself its next action.

*TUB:* We consider it a true multi-agent system as the agents run independently of each other in their own threads for life-cycle, sense-decide-act cycle, and can be distributed over CPUs, CPU-cores and the network without change to architecture, protocols and agent implementation.

*AiWXX:* We have exploited a decentralization framework in implementing various strategies, however, the implementation now is so restricted because we only deal with common knowledge.

## How much time (person hours) have you invested (approximately) for implementing your team?

*SMADAS-UFSC:* Together, we used around 400 person hours divided between tests and programming.

*GOAL-DTU:* We have invested approximately 500 person hours.

*LTI-USP:* Approximately 150 person hours were invested in the team development.

*TUB:* Approximately 840 person hours.

*AiWXX:* About 250 person hours.

## Did you discuss the design and strategies of you agent team with other developers? To which extent did you test your agents playing with other teams.

*SMADAS-UFSC:* We did not share our strategy in advance. However, we participated in all test matches provided by the contest's organization.

*GOAL-DTU:* We discussed our strategies with the creators of the Python-DTU system and also tested against that system.

*LTI-USP:* Only during the competition did we discuss the designs and strategies with the other participants, and before the tournament, we participated in some test matches set by the organizers to ensure the stability of our team.

*TUB:* During the course we split the students into two teams that compared their solutions every week, both in discussion and in simulation. We also used the test games provided by the organizers of the contest, where we mainly tested for reliability and conformance.

*AiWXX:* During this period, we did not discuss the design and strategies of our agents with others because this year, we were focusing on the cooperation of agents and not on the competition with different strategies.

## What data structures are shared among the agents, and which are private?

*SMADAS-UFSC:* Our agents share information about the graph structure, the enemy position and inspected agents. Information about health, energy, zones and others is private for each agent.

*GOAL-DTU:* No data structures are shared among the agents.

*LTI-USP:* Only the organisational artifacts are shared among the agents. Each agent has its own world model.

*TUB:* Each agent maintains its own world model, i.e., it updates the world model with perceptions and action results, then calculates the next step and remembers the decision. Perceptions and decisions are shared among all other agents and each agent also maintains the state of each other agent in its own world model. The exception is again the agent that calculates the best zone. It also knows the perceptions and decisions of all other agents but it is the only agent that knows the best zone. All other agents only know their position in the best zone.

*AiWXX:* Each agent has only one private data structure, which stores the perceptions received from the server.

## 3.3  Software Architecture

Here we are interested in the specific approach. Which agent platform or programming language was used? How were agent-related concepts implemented? Which tools, which algorithms were used? How is the reasoning of an agent realized? What were the hardest problems and how many lines of code were written?

**Which programming language did you use to implement the multi-agent system?**

*SMADAS-UFSC:* Our Multi-Agent System is developed in JaCaMo platform, using Jason, CArtAgO and Moise.

*GOAL-DTU:* We used the GOAL agent programming language to implement the multi-agent system. As a knowledge representation language we used SWI-Prolog.

*LTI-USP:* Java and AgentSpeak.

*TUB:* Java.

*AiWXX:* The C++ language.

**How have you mapped the designed architecture (both multi-agent and individual agent architectures) to programming codes, i.e., how did you implement specific agent-oriented concepts and designed artifacts using the programming language?**

*SMADAS-UFSC:* We used an environment and organizational multi-agent framework, which provides abstractions to develop specific agent-oriented concepts, environmental artifacts and organizational rules.

*GOAL-DTU:* We used the inherent architecture in the GOAL language since it is a dedicated agent programming language.

*LTI-USP:* The agents are developed using the Jason MAS platform, which is a Java-based interpreter for an extended version of the AgentSpeak programming language for BDI agents. Each agent is composed of plans, a belief base and its own world model. The plans are specified in AgentSpeak and the agent decides which plan will be executed according to its beliefs and the local view of the world. The world model consists of a graph developed in Java, using simple data structures and classes.

*TUB:* Functionality in JIAC is implemented in components (AgentBeans), so each function is an AgentBean: e.g. the communication with the contest server (ServerCommunicationBean), each role is implemented as a different Strategy managed by the DecisionAgentBean, the game concepts are reflected by the ontology where we mapped them to Java classes.

*AiWXX:* Each of the agents runs a separate program which is designed at four different levels, from the coordination level to the physical level.

**Which development platforms and tools are used? How much time did you invest in learning those?**

*SMADAS-UFSC:* We used Eclipse platform with Jason 1.3.8 plug-in. These tools were known by all team members. So we spent just a few hours learning new features.

*GOAL-DTU:* We use the GOAL IDE as a development platform as well as Eclipse as a code editor/IDE. We were already familiar with the platforms from earlier projects.

*LTI-USP:* All our code was written using the Eclipse IDE with the Jason plugin. All members were familiar with Eclipse.

*TUB:* We used the JIAC V framework. The frame implementation was given by the course organizer, the rest was implemented by the students starting from a message parser. We additionally used a Swarming approach for the visual reconstruction of the graph, developed by our colleague Tobias Küster, as the MarsViewer maps the graph to a grid, but this information is not available to the agents.

*AiWXX:* Just Gedit Text Editor. We invested little time in learning it.

**Which runtime platforms and tools (e.g. Jade, AgentScape, simply Java, ...) are used? How much time did you invest in learning those?**

*SMADAS-UFSC:* We used EISMASSim framework to communicate with the environment, Jason centralized infrastructure for communication among the agents and ORA4MAS, a CArtAgO and Moise based platform.

*GOAL-DTU:* We used Linux running the newest version of GOAL from the GOAL SVN repository as the runtime platform for the competition.

*LTI-USP:* We have used the JaCaMo platform to run our team. The main developer was already familiar with JaCaMo.

*TUB:* We used the JIAC runtime platform, which usage is fairly easy and straight forward. The platform manages the life cycle of the agents and the communication infrastructure. With the ASGARD agent management tool we can remotely control the life cycle and state of each agent.

*AiWXX:* Just the GCC compiler. We invested little time in learning it.

**What features were missing in your language choice that would have facilitated your development task?**

*SMADAS-UFSC:* The JaCaMo framework provided most of the features needed. To build graph algorithms we used Java because it is a powerful language and it is quite simple to integrate with JaCaMo.

*GOAL-DTU:* Even though GOAL has debugging features these were not fully functional at the time of the contest. For this reason we developed our own debugging tools.

*LTI-USP:* The JaCaMo framework provided all the necessary features that we needed to develop our team.

*TUB:* We still miss an easy agent language at all, our approach to JADL++ was to combine powerful features of a logic language with C-like surface syntax, which is not finished yet. A second point is the BDI decision cycle which is implemented in the framework but is not been used and tested, although we see every year that the decision component's implementation always produces similar solutions, so a generalizing concept is overdue.

*AiWXX:* We have implemented all proposed features efficiently due to the flexibility of the C++ language.

**Which algorithms are used/implemented?**

*SMADAS-UFSC:* We implemented some graph algorithms like Dijkstra, breadth-first search and identification of cut vertices.

*GOAL-DTU:* We use our own implementation of the A* algorithm for pathfinding, but since there is no usable heuristic this is basically Dijkstra's algorithm.

*LTI-USP:* We used the breadth-first search algorithm to find the minimum path between two vertices in the graph.

*TUB:* Path finding is based on Dijkstra, breadth-first search for finding agents and other targets from a given node.

*AiWXX:* The breadth-first search, the dijkstra algorithm, the minimum cost flow algorithm and the hungarian algorithm.

**How did you distribute the agents on several machines? If not why?**

*SMADAS-UFSC:* We did not distribute the agents on several machines. Our agents run fast enough on a single machine for the contest.

*GOAL-DTU:* We did not distribute our agents on several machines since this feature was not fully functional in GOAL.

*LTI-USP:* We did not distribute the agents over several machines due to time constraints, but it is our intention to work after the tournament on a distributed team, since the JaCaMo framework facilitates this.

*TUB:* No, we didn't. There was no need to. During the contest we used a multi-core machine with huge RAM connected to a GigaBit switch.

*AiWXX:* We did not distribute the agents on several machines because sharing memory in one computer is almost the most efficient way for communication between agents.

**Do your agents perform any reasoning tasks while waiting for responses from the server, or is the reasoning synchronized with the receive-percepts/send-action cycle?**

*SMADAS-UFSC:* While waiting for the server, our agents reason about some information which is not used to perform an action, like the good zones definition, graph synchronization, repairer allocation, etc.

*GOAL-DTU:* Our agents do not perform any reasoning while waiting for the server since they are synchronized with the receive-percepts/send-action cycle.

*LTI-USP:* At each step, the agent decides which action will be executed given only the state of the environment and the results of previous steps. So the reasoning agent is completely synchronized with the receive-percepts/send-action cycle.

*TUB:* Almost all agent are synchronized to the server cycle, only the agent that calculates the best zone is doing this all the time.

*AiWXX:* If an agent receives a new percept, any other agent will perform no actions until this percept is updated to the knowledge base.

**What part of the development was most difficult/complex? What kind of problems have you found and how are they solved?**

*SMADAS-UFSC:* The most difficult part was to decide which strategy to use for the contest. We implemented several strategies and tested each one a lot. As we used Moise and CArtAgO technologies, we also found issues to improve on this technologies.

*GOAL-DTU:* The most difficult/time consuming part of development was fixing bugs in both the GOAL system and our own code.

*LTI-USP:* Due to the modularity of the JaCaMo framework, it was not complicated to change our team for this year's contest. The most difficult part was to remove the centralized coordination and define the rules that the agents must obey to create the zone or expand it.

*TUB:* the most challenging part is to predict the behaviour of the enemy team and then to derive the best strategy against it, e.g. in last years discussion many participants believed holding a huge area was key to success, when analysing the winners matches we realized that they maintained many small zones only held by two agents on high-weighted nodes.

*AiWXX:* The most difficult part of the whole development process was the optimization of team strategies against different strategies.

**How many lines of code did you write for your software?**

*SMADAS-UFSC:* We used 8459 lines to implement our team: 3794 for Jason agents; 135 for Moise organization; 96 for CArtAgO environment and 4434 lines in Java.

*GOAL-DTU:* We wrote 1288 lines of code (not counting comments and blank lines).

*LTI-USP:* Approximately 2000 lines in Java and 1800 lines in AgentSpeak.

*TUB:* About 7996 lines.

*AiWXX:* About 11,000 lines.

### 3.4   Strategies, Details and Statistics

The questions in this part are related to the particular approach used by each team. How are the roles of the agents implemented, which strategies do they follow? How are zones computed or conquered and defended? Is the buying-mechanism considered important? Are achievements? Does the agent behaviour emerge on an individual or the team level?

## What is the main strategy of your team?

*SMADAS-UFSC:* Our main strategy is to acquire achievement points and define good zones as soon as possible. After that, we spread the agents in the map and keep the agents in their places until the end of the game. We also use the saboteurs to disturb the enemy and the repairers to help disabled agents.

*GOAL-DTU:* The main strategy is as follows. In the first part of a simulation the agents explore the map to find the most valuable nodes. In the second part our agents establish a zone of control on the most valuable clusters of nodes. Meanwhile, our *Saboteurs* defend our zone as well as harass the enemy to disrupt their zones.

*LTI-USP:* The main strategy was to divide the agents into three subgroups: two in charge of occupying the best zones in the map, and the other one in charge of sabotaging the opponents.

*TUB:* The main strategy of our team is twofold: First, individual agents follow a simple, straightforward achievement collection strategy based on their roles. And, second, there is an additional agent that calculates the best zone that is free of enemies.

*AiWXX:* The whole team explores the entire map for available areas and then tries to occupy several stable zones with higher values.

## How does the overall team work together (coordination, information sharing, ...)?

*SMADAS-UFSC:* We use an explicit organizational structure to coordinate the agents. It defines the role for each agent and the goals they have to achieve. In addition, we use an artifact where the information about the graph structure is shared.

*GOAL-DTU:* Our agents work together by coordinating their behavior when they have to establish a zone of control. They also communicate the status of themselves and enemy agents as well as map information.

*LTI-USP:* One agent is responsible for determining which are the best zones in the map. Then, each agent decides by itself what to do to create a zone in the specified location. Each agent has its own world model, and only percepts received from the contest server which produce an update of the agent's world model are broadcasted.

*TUB:* The basis of the team work is information sharing: perceptions and decisions are communicated among all agents. There are simple conventions on how a broken agent finds the repairer. The calculation of the best zone is done by an extra agent on behalf of all interested agents (that are free to zone).

*AiWXX:* We allocate to each agent a unique task. When any agent receives a new percept, any other agent will not perform any actions until this percept is passed to all of them. This ensures that all agents share a synchronized knowledge base.

**How do your agents analyze the topology of the map? And how do they exploit their findings?**

*SMADAS-UFSC:* We do not try to find a map topology. However, we identify the cut vertices, which usually represent good zones that can be conquered by a single agent.

*GOAL-DTU:* Our agents share information about probed and surveyed nodes with each other. This way they know the structure of the whole map and can find their way around more easily.

*LTI-USP:* The explorers probe all unknown vertices and the results of the map analysis are exploited to find the best zones to be occupied.

*TUB:* Our first approach was to use a heat map to calculate the best zones. The current implementation calculates about 50 to 100 paths, where the best one is selected that separates the biggest enemy free zone from the rest of the map depending of the number of free agents.

*AiWXX:* Each time an agent arrives at an unexplored location, it collects all information about edges and nodes. Her strategy then is to move to those nodes on the boundary, survey them and repeat this process again and again.

**How do your agents communicate with the server?**

*SMADAS-UFSC:* We used the EISMASSim libraries to communicate with the server.

*GOAL-DTU:* Our agents communicate with the server using the provided EIS-MASSim library (version 2.1).

*LTI-USP:* Using the EISMASSim interface.

*TUB:* Via IP sockets.

*AiWXX:* The agents generate multiple threads and use the TCP/IP protocol to communicate with the server.

**How do you implement the roles of the agents? Which strategies do the different roles implement?**

*SMADAS-UFSC:* Explorers are responsible to probe all vertices and they define which is a good place to conquer. Saboteurs are responsible to protect the zones and to attack enemies. Repairers are responsible to help damaged agents. Inspectors are responsible to protect the best places and inspect the enemies. Sentinels are responsible to protect the best places and the whole team is responsible to survey the map.

*GOAL-DTU:* All agents share the same basic behavior. Depending on the role given to them by the server, they access a part of the code that is specific to their role. The agents implement strategies relevant to their role.

*LTI-USP:* We decided to not map the five types specified in the scenario (explorer, inspector, repairer, saboteur and sentinel) directly to the roles in our team. Instead, we defined different roles in our system according to the adopted strategy. Each role has a mission associated to it, and each role can be played by one or more types of agents. For example, the `map_explorer` role can be played only by the explorer type, while the `soldier` role can be played by all types of agents.

*TUB:* A role has at least one strategy, if it has more then one strategy role switching is possible dynamically.

**Explorer** Find unprobed nodes and probe them, recharge when necessary go to the closed unprobed node first. Avoid other Explorers from our team to avoid duplicated behaviour. Seek repair if health is zero. Switch Strategy if the graph has been probed completely.

**Repairer** There are two strategies for the repairer.

>**Simple Repairer** Search for hurt team members and go to the closest one to heal. If no team member is hurt survey and zone.

>**Craven Repairer** Same as the Simple Repairer but avoid enemy attackers at all cost. Using a breath first search and a range that repairer would search for a enemy attacker and if it would find one it would create a path to avoid that agent.

**Sentinel** used for Zoning see Zoner

**AggressiveSaboteur** As the name suggests the Saboteur tries to attack as many agents as possible.

**ZoneDefender** This Agent is part of the Zone and upon a detected intrusion into the Zone, this agent tries to disable the intruder.

**AnnoyInspector** This strategy tries to find enemy zones and plans paths trough those zones to destroy them while inspecting the enemy.

**ZoneInspector** The inspector is part of the zone and if an intruder is detected it tries to inspect the intruder.

**Zoner** The Zone is a strategy which will build a Zone using the zoning algorithm to identify a good Zone and coordinates all Zoner to build that zone.

*AiWXX:* The agent considers her role as a state. We have designed a particular strategy for each of the five roles in the game. When an agent realizes that it is acting in a certain role, say, repairer, it will follow the respective strategy. Only explorers accept the mission of exploring the map and probe the value of the newly encountered node. Only sentinels, inspectors and explorers will occupy the zones. Repairers will run to the injured and repair their teammates while saboteurs will go to the front line and fight with enemies.

**How do you find good zones? How do you estimate the value of zones?**

*SMADAS-UFSC:* The good zones are defined in terms of *hills*, *pivots* and *islands*. A hill is a zone formed by several vertices that have a good value and are in the same region of the map. As in the 2012 team, the agents try to discover two hills. The hills are defined as follows: for each vertex $v$ of the graph, the algorithm sums the values of all vertices up to two hops away from $v$, including $v$. The two vertices with the highest sums are defined as the center of the hills. Then, the agents try to stay on their neighborhoods. Islands are regions of the map that can be conquered by a single agent. An island is a zone that has only one vertex (a *cut vertex*) in common with the remaining graph. They are found by disconnecting the edges of each cut vertex of the graph. It produces two disconnected subgraphs, and the smallest one, plus the cut vertex, is an island. Pivots are regions of the map that can be conquered by just two agents. For each pair of vertices $(u,v)$ we search all vertices $w$ connected to $u$ and $v$. For all vertices $w$ (including $u$ and $v$) we also search for all vertices only connected to these vertices. For example, if there is a vertice $k$ connected only to the vertice $w$, then $k$ also belongs to the pivot. Furthermore, if there is an island connected to some of these vertices, we consider all the vertices of the island. The best pivots are chosen considering the sum of all vertices.

*GOAL-DTU:* Our agents find several of the most valuable nodes on the map, and they calculate the total value of the area around each of those nodes.

*LTI-USP:* The best zone is obtained by calculating for each vertex the sum of its value with the value of all of its direct and second degree neighbors. The vertex with the greatest sum of values is the center of the best zone. Zones with the sum of values below 10 are not considered in the calculation.

*TUB:* see above.

*AiWXX:* First, we will choose each node as a point zone with no enemies standing at and then repeat the following: find the boundary node $P$ such that after expanding $P$ the boundary increases the least (possibly by a negative number), and then, expand it. During the expanding process, we maintain the optimal zone ever found.

**How do you conquer zones? How do you defend zones if attacked? Do you attack zones?**

*SMADAS-UFSC:* The agents which control islands do the following: if there are enemies in the island, they go to the same vertex as the enemy, so both teams do not get scores from that island. In addition, they call the saboteur leader to fight against the enemy agent. If the saboteur leader is already busy protecting another island, the saboteur leader calls the saboteur helper of the group special operations. If both are busy, the saboteur leader keeps a list of islands with enemies. The agents that control pivots do not move away from their places, since most of the times, the enemy would not stay in the same place. Therefore, we defined that these agents do not need to move. If the enemy also continues in the same vertex, both teams do not get scores, so our team also cancels the enemy strategy. The agents which control the hills are simply moving to the border of the big zone in order to expand it. If they break the zone, they come back to the previous places in order to try to expand it again. We also defined the sentinels to stay in the same places all the time in the big zones (hills) because it can make the enemies avoid those places and we can get some fixed scores of the hills. Finally, our saboteurs disturb the enemy all the time.

*GOAL-DTU:* The agents will move towards the most valuable zones regardless of any enemy presence. Our *Saboteurs* engage enemy *Saboteurs* that get near our zones. We try to find enemy zones and attack them with one dedicated *Saboteur*.

*LTI-USP:* Given that the coordinator has assigned a zone for a group, all agents of the group move to the specified location and then each agent decides by itself which empty vertex it will occupy in order to create the zone or expand it.

We have implemented a defense strategy, with the `guardian` agent ready to attack any close opponent, and the `medic` in the center of the zone focusing on repairing other agents.

We also developed a group to attack the opponent's zone.

*TUB:* the main strategy here is to avoid enemy agents while zoning, only the AnnoyInspector is trying to destroy enemy zones, the only approach to defence at the moment is inspecting the intruding agent.

*AiWXX:* Our agents will compute several promising zones and then move to the boundary and conquer it. Among them, the saboteurs will attack enemies they found because this may attack the area occupied by the rival.

**Can your agents change their behavior during runtime? If so, what triggers the changes?**

*SMADAS-UFSC:* The agents change their behavior in some pre-defined steps. For instance, in step 7 the agents start to search for a good zone in order to get as much achievement points as possible. In the step 130 they look for the smallest ones. When all vertices are probed, all the agents start to participate in conquering pivots and islands.

*GOAL-DTU:* Several of our agents change behavior by adopting new goals during runtime. These changes can be triggered by reaching a specific step, enemy behavior, disabled agents etc.

*LTI-USP:* Yes. In the beginning, one `map_explorer_helper` has the mission of helping the `map_explorer` to explore the graph. After the step 250, the agent leaves this role to adopt the `soldier` role in the `best_zone` subgroup.

*TUB:* Yes, role changing is possible, among all agents that have a server identity. They are configured as such that they can play all roles. But as the setting is static according to the assigned role by the server it is not yet necessary. Where we already use it is when switching between different role implementations.

*AiWXX:* Yes. We set some random target to change their behaviors with a relatively small probability at each step.

**What algorithm(s) do you use for agent path planning?**

*SMADAS-UFSC:* We used the Dijkstra algorithm to find the shortest path between two vertices.

*GOAL-DTU:* We use an A* algorithm without heuristic for agent path planning.

*LTI-USP:* Breadth-first search algorithm.

*TUB:* Dijkstra.

*AiWXX:* Breadth-First Search Algorithm and our own algorithm mentioned in the paper.

**How do you make use of the buying-mechanism?**

*SMADAS-UFSC:* We did not use the buying-mechanism.

*GOAL-DTU:* We buy strength and health for our *Saboteurs* when necessary.

*LTI-USP:* We decided to limit the buy action, allowing only the agents of type saboteur and repairer to purchase a unique extension pack of `sensors`, in order to be able to attack or repair agents in neighbouring vertices.

*TUB:* Not at all (this aspect was given a lower priority during development).
*AiWXX:* Our agents will not buy anything.

**How important are achievements for your overall strategy?**

*SMADAS-UFSC:* The achievements are important. We try to get most achievements as soon as possible, since they accumulate in each step. However, we guess the achievements did not make the difference for our team in this year.

*GOAL-DTU:* Achievements are fairly important for our strategy, since we need achievement points for our *Saboteur* buying strategy.

*LTI-USP:* The achievements were very important in the team score, which is why we limited the buy action.

*TUB:* Not at all at the moment.

*AiWXX:* In the contest, we use achievements only for the score. So we save them and do not buy anything.

**Do your agents have an explicit mental state?**

*SMADAS-UFSC:* Yes, our agents use a BDI architecture and use their beliefs to decide on their actions.

*GOAL-DTU:* Our agents have explicit mental states.

*LTI-USP:* The agents' mental states consist of internal beliefs, desires, intentions, and plans.

*TUB:* In a sense, yes. The agents maintain their own world model on the basis what they perceive and what they are told by other agents. The model consists of the own status, the environment, and the own intention. To a small extend they can predict what other agents are going to do based on the role and their possibilities.

*AiWXX:* No.

**How do your agents communicate? And what do they communicate?**

*SMADAS-UFSC:* The agents communicate by message exchange and a blackboard. They use message exchange to call a repairer or a saboteur, to inform about the good zones and vertices, to exchange information about probed vertices and to communicate their current action (which prevents two agents from performing the same action). The blackboard is used to share information about the graph structure and the agents' positions.

*GOAL-DTU:* Our agents communicate using the built-in messaging system in GOAL. They communicate agent status and map information.

*LTI-USP:* The agents' communication occurs via the speech acts provided by Jason. They communicate with each other for the following purposes: (i) informing the others agents about the structure of the map; (ii) informing about the agent's or the opponent's position, role and status; (iii) asking for a repair.

*TUB:* Agents share their perception and the next action using multicast communication.

*AiWXX:* The agents communicate by sharing memory. They communicate about the map, enemies, status of teammates and proposals of team work missions.

**How do you organize your agents? Do you use e.g. hierarchies? Is your organization implicit or explicit?**

*SMADAS-UFSC:* To organize our agents we use a *Moise* organization model. Also, the agents follow a hierarchy, since we defined a leader for each agent kind and an overall leader.

*GOAL-DTU:* We do not organize our agents. We sometimes perform actions based on a ranking system in order to prevent that several agents perform the same action with the same target.

*LTI-USP:* We used the *Moise* model to explicitly specify the organizational constraints of our team. We organized our agents in three groups: two in charge of occupying the best zones in the map, and the other one in charge of attacking the opponents.

*TUB:* Organization is implicit as there is no explicit organisational concept except for roles. A role is the function that the agent plays in the MAS.

*AiWXX:* They share the same knowledge base at any time and act by themselves. They are all at the same status. Hence, we organize our agents explicitly and no hierarchy is exploited.

**Is most of your agents' behavior emergent on an individual or team level?**

*SMADAS-UFSC:* A team behavior is important for our agents' strategy. Thus, our agents' behavior is mostly on the team level.

*GOAL-DTU:* The behavior of the *Saboteurs* and *Repairers* is mostly emergent on an individual level. For the rest of the team it is on a team level.

*LTI-USP:* Each agent acts individually and they are autonomous to decide by themselves the next action to be performed, but in cooperation with each other.

*TUB:* No, mainly. We saw clotting as negative effect of the repairers' and saboteurs' behaviour.

*AiWXX:* The behavior of our agents is mostly emergent on an individual level because we think autonomy is the key idea of MAS.

**If your agents perform some planning, how many steps do they plan ahead.**

*SMADAS-UFSC:* The agents do not plan in advance. Since the environment is dynamic, the agents choose their action in each step.

*GOAL-DTU:* Our agents do not plan ahead.

*LTI-USP:* Our agents do not plan ahead.

*TUB:* A planned path holds path length steps unless something went wrong, e.g. action fails or health status is down.

*AiWXX:* The agents do not perform any planning because we think that the current planning technology is not efficient enough.

**If you have a perceive-think-act cycle, how is it synchronized with the server?**

*SMADAS-UFSC:* We used EISMASSim to communicate with the server. After getting the percepts, the agents reason about it and decide what action to do. Both percepts and actions are performed by EISMASSim.

*GOAL-DTU:* Our perceive-think-act cycle is synchronized with the server by preventing agents from performing more than one action each step.

*LTI-USP:* After sending an action, the agent waits until it receives new percepts from the server and then starts a new perceive-think-act cycle.

*TUB:* The cycle must complete within the server cycle.

*AiWXX:* To synchronize with the server, agents listen to the message from the server and the respective agent will decide which action to perform. Furthermore, they will send the action to the server. Our program is so efficient that any agent is always able to send its action to the server before the next percept arrives.

## 3.5   And the Moral of It Is ...

Finally, it is important to find out lessons learned. What are positive and negative experiences of the particular approach? Given the performance in this contest, critically evaluate your team. What was good, what was bad in the current scenario? How can it be improved.

### What have you learned from the participation in the contest?

*SMADAS-UFSC:* We learned more from MAS development and about the technologies we used, like Moise and CArtAgO. Also, the contest allowed us to evaluate and improve these technologies.

*GOAL-DTU:* From the participation in the contest we gained further experience with the GOAL agent-programming language.

*LTI-USP:* Participating in the MAPC was a great opportunity to improve our knowledge on developing MAS, and on the JaCaMo framework.

*TUB:* First, to have a simple implementation of each relevant aspect in the contest that works reliable, then improve it. Second, to make more and smaller zones: they are easier to form and to maintain.

*AiWXX:* The participation in this contest has greatly improved our knowledge of multi-agent systems and stimulated our interest in conducting research in this area.

### Which are the strong and weak points of the team?

*SMADAS-UFSC:* The strategy to get many small zones was the strongest point of our team and it turned out to be hard for the opponents to disturb our zones since our agents were spread over the whole map while our saboteurs were able to disturb the opponent zones. However, our team can be improved to perform better in maps where there are too many good vertices gathered in the same place. In that case, the best strategy seems to be to build a big zone and defend it instead of building just small zones.

*GOAL-DTU:* One of the strong points of the team is our ability to control a zone. Another is our preemptive repairing; our *Repairers* anticipate attacks on our *Saboteurs*. One of the weak points is the harass strategy for our *Saboteurs* because of unresolved bugs.

*LTI-USP:* We believe that the strong point of our team was the defensive strategy, since it resulted in more stable zones. The weak point was the size of our zones.

*TUB:* The strong point is the easy exchange between strategies that makes an easier and faster development cycle, the weakest point was the one best zone strategy.

*AiWXX:* One strong point of our team is that it only costs about 0.2 seconds to make all decisions, on a 500-node map, in a perfect network. Our framework is compatible enough to develop more complex strategies in future contests. The weaknesses of our team are that we do not observe the enemy and we are not familiar with the strategies of the other teams.

## How suitable was the chosen programming language, methodology, tools, and algorithms?

*SMADAS-UFSC:* All the technologies we used are suitable to MAS development. However, during tests we created some new features to improve these technologies.

*GOAL-DTU:* The GOAL system performed excellent during the contest and we only lost to USFC who used better algorithms. However, we encountered a number of bugs and other issues in GOAL during the development of our system.

*LTI-USP:* The JaCaMo framework proved to be a very complete platform for the development of sophisticated multi-agent systems by providing all the necessary features that we needed to developed our team.

*TUB:* The easy thing is that the student do not need to know about agent theory, framework implementation details to solve the contest problem. The agent metaphor is intuitive as such and the framework delivers the implementation so the student developers can concentrate on the domain specific parts.

*AiWXX:* Our framework can support almost every strategy we can imagine. The C++ language we used is suitable to MAPC, because we are proficient in this language which is well-known for its efficiency and flexibility, supporting various data structures and algorithms.

## What can be improved in the contest for next year?

*SMADAS-UFSC:* The contest scenario should be released earlier and new features should not be made after the release. In this contest, the scenario changed (the thinning was added) after the first releases and it made us change our strategies before the contest.

*GOAL-DTU:* The contest could be improved by presenting the description of the specific scenario and the requirements for the contest as early in the year as possible. Furthermore, test-matches should not be 750 steps but rather 300-400 steps.

*LTI-USP:* Besides the test matches, the organization could leave a server running set up with a dummy team, so that the participants could test the connection and communication with the server at any time. We believe also that the early release of the software package, given more time for the development of the teams, can bring more participants for the contest.

*TUB:* Dynamic role assignment and role switching to a certain extend, in principle, nearly every human can do nearly every job, and one can use a pencil as a weapon, too.

*AiWXX:* Next year, we are going to observe the enemy and analyze the strategy of the other teams.

## Why did your team perform as it did? Why did the other teams perform better/worse than you did.

*SMADAS-UFSC:* Our team performed very well, except in maps with low thinning (below 20%) with most of the good vertices located in the same regions. The other teams performed worse most of times because they tried to conquer big zones, which are harder to protect.

*GOAL-DTU:* We believe that our team had strong strategies for zone control, *Saboteurs*, and *Repairers*. Some of the other teams did not have as stable zone control strategies as we did, and performed worse. UFSC, who won, had a very strong zone control strategy.

*LTI-USP:* Given the effort put to develop the team (only 150 hours and one developer), we were pleased with final result. The two teams that performed better had much more human resources to test different strategies.

*TUB:* We build the team from scratch, although there was an contest implementation of last year. Time is always a limiting factor, i.e. the overall time to the contest and also the time that is then used for the implementation and testing. We did not know where we are standing. And we also had an avoidable bug in the first match, we should have won this.

*AiWXX:* The performance this year was not so satisfactory and there are many reasons. Our VPS was down during the final contest and we did not have enough time to implement all the ideas.

## Which other research fields might be interested in the Multi-Agent Programming Contest?

*SMADAS-UFSC:* Machine learning is one interesting field to improve our next team.

*GOAL-DTU:* Other research fields such as algorithms, logic, game theory and AI might be interested in the contest.

*LTI-USP:* Algorithms, Game development, Game theory, AI, Robotics.

*TUB:* Even within our institution people always produce central server solutions in the following fields: information retrieval, HCI, home control.

*AiWXX:* Distributed algorithms, Game Theory.

## How can the current scenario be optimized? How would those optimizations pay off?

*SMADAS-UFSC:* The ranged actions should be revised in order to balance the fail probability.

*GOAL-DTU:* The current scenario could be optimized by making upgrades more viable. Furthermore, ranged actions should have fewer drawbacks.

*LTI-USP:* Regarding possible improvements for the current scenario, we would propose to increase the probability of success for the ranged actions, since we noticed during the competition that these actions have a huge chance to fail and it is not worth it to use them. Another idea is to change the score computation to consider only the zones' values. This way, the buying strategy will not directly impact the team score and it will be interesting to see how each team will invest their achievement points.

*TUB:* The very interesting part could be how can agents from different teams work *together*? Could be interesting for the interoperability part of different frameworks, toolkits, languages and libraries.

*AiWXX:* The perception should be compressed so as to relieve the pressure of network communication. And the organizers should offer VPS for the participants.

## 4   Conclusion

In this paper we have tried to put together detailed information about how the participants of this years agent contest approached the Mars scenario. We did this through a series of concrete questions and requested brief answers. By listing for each question the answers of all teams one after another, we get a good comparison of the similarities and distinctions of the individual systems. We believe this information is helpful not only for future participants of the contest, but also for other people who are interested to apply multi-agent technology to similar problems.

## References

1. Ahlbrecht, T., Köster, M., Schlesinger, F., Dix, J.: Multi-Agent Programming Contest 2013. In: Cossentino, M., El Fallah Seghrouchni, A., Winikoff, M. (eds.) EMAS 2013. LNCS (LNAI), vol. 8245, pp. 292–318. Springer, Heidelberg (2013)
2. Behrens, T., Dastani, M., Dix, J., Hübner, J., Köster, M., Novák, P., Schlesinger, F.: The multi-agent programming contest. AI Magazine 33(4), 111–113 (2012)
3. Franco, M.R., Sichman, J.S.: Improving the LTI-USP Team: A New JaCaMo based MAS for the MAPC 2013. In: Cossentino, M., El Fallah Seghrouchni, A., Winikoff, M. (eds.) EMAS 2013. LNCS (LNAI), vol. 8245, pp. 339–348. Springer, Heidelberg (2013)
4. Hindriks, K., Dix, J.: Goal: A multi-agent programming language applied to an exploration game. In: Shehory, O., Sturm, A. (eds.) Research Directions Agent-Oriented Software Engineering, pp. 112–137. Springer, Heidelberg (2013)
5. Li, C., Liu, L.: Prior State Reasoning in Multi-agent Systems and Graph-Theoretical Algorithms. In: Cossentino, M., El Fallah Seghrouchni, A., Winikoff, M. (eds.) EMAS 2013. LNCS (LNAI), vol. 8245, pp. 358–367. Springer, Heidelberg (2013)
6. Villadsen, J., Jensen, A.S., Christensen, N.C., Hess, A.V., Johnsen, J.B., Woller, Ø.G., Ørum, P.B.: Engineering a Multi-agent System in GOAL. In: Cossentino, M., El Fallah Seghrouchni, A., Winikoff, M. (eds.) EMAS 2013. LNCS (LNAI), vol. 8245, pp. 329–338. Springer, Heidelberg (2013)

7. Werner, S., Bender-Saebelkampf, C., Heller, H., Heßler, A.: Multi-Agent Programming Contest 2013: TUB Team Description. In: Cossentino, M., El Fallah Seghrouchni, A., Winikoff, M. (eds.) EMAS 2013. LNCS (LNAI), vol. 8245, pp. 349–355. Springer, Heidelberg (2013)
8. Zatelli, M.R., de Brito, M., Schmitz, T.L., Morato, M.M., de Souza, K.S., Uez, D.M., Hübner, J.F.: SMADAS: A Team for MAPC Considering the Organization and the Environment as First-Class Abstractions. In: Cossentino, M., El Fallah Seghrouchni, A., Winikoff, M. (eds.) EMAS 2013. LNCS (LNAI), vol. 8245, pp. 319–328. Springer, Heidelberg (2013)

# Author Index